CW01186759

SCOTTISH HISTORY SOCIETY

SIXTH SERIES

VOLUME 20

Scottish Witchcraft Trials

Scottish Witchcraft Trials

Edited by

Julian Goodare and Liv Helene Willumsen

SCOTTISH HISTORY SOCIETY
2025
THE BOYDELL PRESS

First published 2025
ISBN 978-0-906245-50-7

A Scottish History Society publication in association with The Boydell Press.
The Boydell Press is an imprint of Boydell & Brewer Ltd
PO Box 9, Woodbridge, Suffolk IP12 3DF, UK
and of Boydell & Brewer Inc.
668 Mt Hope Avenue, Rochester, NY 14620–2731, USA
website: www.boydellandbrewer.com

A CIP catalogue record of this publication is available
from the British Library

Printed and bound in Great Britain by
TJ Books Limited, Padstow, Cornwall

CONTENTS

THE EDITORS

Julian Goodare is Emeritus Professor of History, University of Edinburgh. His books include *The European Witch-Hunt* (London, 2016). His edited book *The Supernatural in Early Modern Scotland* (Manchester, 2020; co-edited with Martha McGill) was runner-up for the Katharine Briggs Prize of the Folklore Society. He is Director of the online Survey of Scottish Witchcraft.

Liv Helene Willumsen is Professor Emerita of History, University of Tromsø – The Arctic University of Norway. Her books include *Witches of the North: Scotland and Finnmark* (Leiden, 2013) and *The Voices of Women in Witchcraft Trials: Northern Europe* (London, 2022). She has written the texts for the 91 memorial plaques at Steilneset Memorial, Vardø, commemorating the victims of the Finnmark witchcraft trials in northern Norway.

ACKNOWLEDGEMENTS

Our greatest debt is to the professional researcher Diane Baptie. She carried out about two-thirds of the transcriptions. Not only did she execute this task to a high standard of palaeographical accuracy, but she also used her knowledge of the language of historical documents to provide glosses for a number of unfamiliar words. She transcribed the following cases (in the order in which they appear in the book): Sir William Stewart, Barbara Napier, Earl of Bothwell, Margaret Crawford, Alexander Drummond, Michael Erskine, Barbara Bowndie, Helen Clark, Jean Craig, Inverkeithing Witches, Janet Sawyer, Margaret Beveridge and John Corse, Three Lists of Witches (document 3), parts of Alloa Witches, parts of Dalkeith Witches, Magnus Laurenson (document 2), Paisley Witches, Haddingtonshire Witches, Bargarran Witches, Ratter Family and Margaret Watson. Diane Baptie and Liv Helene Willumsen have enjoyed a fruitful working relationship over several years, and have also published scholarly research together.

Several other scholars and archivists have generously contributed draft transcriptions to this edition: John H. Ballantyne (Janet Irvine, Marion Pardoun and Magnus Laurenson document 1); Tom Barclay (Janet Sawyer document 1); Julie Elliot (her transcription of the lengthy case of Elizabeth Bathgate deserves special mention); Iain Flett (Dundee Witch); Ciaran Jones (Isobel Watson); Pam McNicol (Stirling Witches and Jean Brown); and Allan Ronald (Anna Wood and Janet Drysdale). Transcriptions not mentioned above were made by Julian Goodare. We as editors have revised all the transcriptions and brought them into a standard format.

Various scholars and archivists have kindly contributed to this edition in further ways, for instance by drawing our attention to particular cases, offering advice on the sources, or providing us with photographs of manuscripts. Here we wish to thank Taylor Aucoin (Alexander Drummond); Laurna Cron (Janet Sawyer); Richard Cullen (Dundee Witch); Jane Dawson (Sir William Stewart); Leslie Dodd (Barbara Napier); Mark Godfrey (Forfarshire Witches); Kevin Hall (Leith Witches, William Murray and Christian Watson); Charlotte Holmes (Alexander Drummond and Magnus Laurenson); Alan R. MacDonald (Janet Drysdale); Alasdair A. MacDonald (Sir William Stewart); Ross MacFarlane (Three Lists of Witches); Hector MacQueen (Barbara Napier); Sarah Maycock (Sir William Stewart and Janet Boyman); Jean Petrie

(Jean Brown); Alasdair Raffe (Janet Drysdale); Jamie Reid-Baxter (Barbara Napier); Scott Richardson-Read (Alexander Drummond); Jane Ridder-Patrick (Sir William Stewart); Andrew Simpson (his identifications, translations and explanations of the juristic citations in the cases of Barbara Napier and the Earl of Bothwell deserve special mention); Brian Smith (Janet Irvine, Marion Pardoun, Magnus Laurenson and Ratter Family); and Louise Yeoman (Isobel Watson, Barbara Napier and John Kincaid).

This edition is a joint project, and both editors have worked together on all the documents. It may nevertheless be helpful to note which editor was responsible for taking the lead in editing which document. Julian Goodare was responsible for Forfarshire Witches, Sir William Stewart, Janet Boyman, Leith Witches, Isobel Watson, Marion McNab, Dundee Witch, Barbara Napier, Earl of Bothwell, William Murray, Janet Irvine, Christian Watson, Peebles Witches, Stirling Witches, Elizabeth Bathgate, Three Lists of Witches, Alloa and Related Witches, John Kincaid, Anna Wood, Janet Drysdale, Bargarran Witches and Jean Brown. Liv Helene Willumsen was responsible for Margaret Crawford, Alexander Drummond, Michael Erskine, Barbara Bowndie, Helen Clark, Marion Pardoun, Jean Craig, Inverkeithing Witches, Janet Sawyer, Margaret Beveridge and John Corse, Dalkeith Witches, Magnus Laurenson, Paisley Witches, Haddingtonshire Witches, Ratter Family and Margaret Watson.

We are grateful to the National Records of Scotland for permission to publish material from the B, JC, PA, PC and SC series of public records that they hold, and to the National Records of Scotland and the Church of Scotland for permission to publish material from the CH2 series of ecclesiastical records, owned by the Church and held by the NRS. This permission also applies to those CH2 records that are held in local archives under the charge and superintendence of the Keeper of the Records of Scotland. We have drawn such CH2 material from Falkirk Archives and Stirling Council Archives. We are grateful to these institutions, and to Glasgow City Archives, for providing access and offering advice on the records that they hold.

We are also grateful to the following for permission to publish editions of documents in their custody or ownership: the Earl of Airlie; Ayrshire Archives; the British Library, London; Dundee City Archives; Edinburgh City Archives; the National Library of Scotland, Edinburgh; Orkney Library and Archive; Pollok & Corrour Ltd.; Sir John and Wendy Scott, Gardie House Archive, Bressay, Shetland; Shetland Museum and Archives; the Wellcome Library, London; and the Provost and Fellows of Worcester College, Oxford.

Finally, we are grateful to Kelsey Jackson Williams, General Editor of the Scottish History Society, for his guidance throughout the preparation of this edition.

ABBREVIATIONS

NRS	National Records of Scotland, Edinburgh.
ODNB	*Oxford Dictionary of National Biography* (2004).
RMS	*Registrum Magni Sigilli Regum Scotorum (Register of the Great Seal of Scotland)*, 11 vols., eds. J. M. Thomson *et al.* (Edinburgh, 1882–).
RPC	*Register of the Privy Council of Scotland*, 38 vols., eds. J. H. Burton *et al.* (Edinburgh, 1877–).
RPS	Records of the Parliaments of Scotland, eds. Keith M. Brown *et al.* (www.rps.ac.uk, 2007).
SHS	Scottish History Society.
SSW	Julian Goodare, Lauren Martin, Joyce Miller and Louise Yeoman, 'The Survey of Scottish Witchcraft, 1563–1736' (https://witches.hca.ed.ac.uk/, 2003).

INTRODUCTION

Witchcraft was a statutory offence in Scotland between 1563 and 1736, and the authorities held many trials and executions for witchcraft in this period. This book presents a selection of the records of these trials.

Witch-hunting was intense in Scotland, but every European country executed witches, and witch beliefs shared broad similarities all over Europe. Peasants believed that witches could harm them, their families and their livelihoods. Witchcraft accusations often originated in quarrels between women, and women's curses seem to have been feared more than men's. About 85 per cent of Scottish witches were women. One typical pattern of accusation was that someone would suffer a misfortune which they would then link back to a quarrel that they had had with someone else; they would conclude that the other person was getting their revenge through witchcraft. However, people usually sought to end such quarrels through reconciliation; peasants rarely seem to have taken the initiative in demanding the execution of their local witches. Numerous reconciliations, successful at the time, are recorded in the documents below.

Educated people shared some of the beliefs of the common folk, but they also developed a set of distinctive views about witchcraft, which can be collectively described as demonology. In this, witches were held to make personal pacts with the Devil, entering his service and gaining from him the power to do harm. One particular power they received was the power to fly, and they could also inflict illness and death. Witches met collectively to worship the Devil. Thus, the beliefs of the peasants and the elite were compatible with each other, but still distinct. For the peasants, the crime was practising witchcraft, while for the elite, it was a thought crime: the crime of being a witch. For the peasants, there was usually only one witch at a time; for the elite, once they started to panic about the threat of witches, it was a conspiracy.

Prosecutions for witchcraft in Scotland were part of a broader pattern of enforcement of godliness after the Reformation of 1560. The authorities embarked on a campaign to inculcate correct Protestant Christianity, and to eradicate sin and superstition. The intensity of Scottish witch-hunting may well reflect the successful establishment of local religious institutions: kirk sessions in each Lowland parish, and presbyteries to back up the kirk sessions. These church courts gathered evidence of witchcraft, either from neighbours (usually evidence of quarrels and bewitchments) or from the confessions of accused witches themselves (often evidence of dealings with the Devil). They then had to turn accused witches over to the secular criminal courts. It was secular criminal courts that held the formal trials in which accused witches were convicted, strangled and burned at the stake. Most of the documents edited in this book come either from church courts or from secular criminal courts.[1]

THIS EDITION OF SCOTTISH WITCHCRAFT TRIAL DOCUMENTS

Study of witchcraft prosecutions requires close engagement with the texts of the trial records. Repeated close reading of the court records and other related documents helps to open the texts and enable interpretations to be made at various textual levels. To attain this aim, accurate transcriptions of the recorded documents are fundamental requirements. This volume contains a large selection of such documents, with editorial commentary.

Witchcraft trial records are not just about 'witchcraft'; they also contain material on many other topics concerning everyday life in early modern Scotland. Suspicions of witchcraft led the authorities to investigate people's doings in sometimes minute detail. In confessions and witnesses' statements we find many details of agriculture, housing, clothing, childcare, health and illness, brewing of ale, cloth manufacture, marriage negotiations, seasonal festivities, and many other topics.

The documents in this volume are a selection from a wide range of possibilities. Scottish witchcraft trial records survive only patchily, but the quantity of surviving records is nevertheless considerable. The aim in the present selection has been to illustrate, as far as possible, the range of Scottish witch-hunting. There are cases from early in the period, and also very late ones. There are cases from most Lowland regions of mainland Scotland, and from Orkney and Shetland. Although there are no cases from the Highlands (such cases are very rare), individual Highlanders are mentioned in various Lowland cases. Most of those prosecuted were women; the proportion of women in the volume is about the same as that in the Scottish witch-hunt as a whole, in which 85 per cent were women and 15 per cent men.

Various different themes are also present. Some cases focus on neighbourhood quarrels, misfortune and maleficent witchcraft; others have more

1 For a more detailed introduction to witch-hunting in Scotland see Julian Goodare, 'Witchcraft in Scotland', in Brian P. Levack (ed.), *The Oxford Handbook of Witchcraft in Early Modern Europe and Colonial America* (Oxford, 2013), 300–17. A classic study, though now a little dated, has still not been superseded: Christina Larner, *Enemies of God: The Witch-Hunt in Scotland* (London, 1981). For a research resource see Julian Goodare, Lauren Martin, Joyce Miller and Louise Yeoman, 'The Survey of Scottish Witchcraft, 1563–1736', online at <https://witches.hca.ed.ac.uk/home/>.

about alleged dealings with the Devil. There are visionary experiences and accounts of relationships with fairies. There are instances of folk healing, some of which involved unwitching (curing or counteracting the effects of alleged witchcraft). There is political conspiracy involving witchcraft and divination. There are cases from kirk sessions and presbyteries, cases involving local secular jurisdictions, and cases heard in the central justiciary court. There are letters and accounts describing the burning of witches.

In order to understand executions, we also need to understand why some cases went all the way to execution while others did not. Some of the cases edited here ended in acquittals, and some cases were dropped at an early stage before the case came formally to trial. Sometimes we do not know the outcome.

In making our selection, we have given preference to cases that are recorded in detail, while bearing in mind that the lengthiest cases are not necessarily typical. Some very short documents with notable details have also been included. Indeed, it could be argued that there is no such thing as a 'typical' witchcraft case that can be studied as such in isolation. Rather, there is a *range* of cases, each of which is 'typical' of some aspects. Each individual case also has its own uniqueness; these are all individual human stories, often tragic ones. Publishing each record as fully as possible may enable us to recognise that humanity and its uniqueness. And the range of cases needs to be grasped as a whole, in order to understand each individual case in its context. This volume attempts to show that range.

Most of the manuscripts are held in the National Records of Scotland, mostly in the records of local church courts or in the records of the central justiciary court. Thirteen other archives have also been drawn on. A few documents are in private hands. Locations of all manuscripts are noted in the introductions to individual texts. Most of the church court manuscripts with archival reference numbers beginning 'CH2' have been digitised, and digital images are available online in the 'Virtual Volumes' section of the ScotlandsPeople website.[2] These images can be used to compare our edited texts with the appearance of the original manuscript.

Many of the trials in the present edition are individual ones. However, Scottish witches were sometimes prosecuted in groups or linked chains, and the edition includes several such prosecutions, often signalled in titles like 'Forfarshire Witches' or 'Paisley Witches'. Some cases are edited individually but can be seen to be part of a group, such as Barbara Napier and the Earl of Bothwell, both of whom were caught up in the notorious North Berwick panic of 1590–2.

2 <https://www.scotlandspeople.gov.uk/virtual-volumes/>.

OTHER EDITIONS OF SCOTTISH WITCHCRAFT TRIAL DOCUMENTS

From the nineteenth century onwards, various scholars have recognised the importance of witchcraft documents, and have published editions of individual trials or of various groups. The present edition seeks to complement their work rather than to replace it, so it may help to indicate where other such documents may be found in print.

Scholarly editions that focus specifically on witchcraft trial records are listed in a 2013 bibliography, to which readers are referred for details.[3] In addition, there are editions of primary sources that contain witchcraft material interspersed among other documents, and these are discussed here. Such scholarly editions begin with Robert Pitcairn's pioneering edition of *Criminal Trials in Scotland* (1833); this contains several much-cited witchcraft cases, as does its successor, *Selected Justiciary Cases*, published by the Stair Society.[4] The multi-volume *Register of the Privy Council of Scotland* contains a very large number of commissions of justiciary (orders to hold trials); these mostly give only brief details of the individuals concerned, and are thus more useful for quantitative surveys than for detailed qualitative research. One volume of the register, unusually, does contain numerous detailed trial records.[5] These editions have been important in facilitating scholarly research to date.

One edition that should be particularly mentioned is that of the records of the so-called North Berwick trials of 1590–2, published by the literary scholars Lawrence Normand and Gareth Roberts in 2000.[6] Normand and Roberts gathered as many pre-trial and trial documents as they could find, producing a fuller collection than ever before. Their volume also included the contemporary pamphlet about the trials, *Newes from Scotland* (*c.*1591), and James VI's treatise *Daemonologie* (1597), a first draft of which had been written in response to the trials of 1590–2. Some of these records had previously been published by Pitcairn. Normand and Roberts' edition modernised the text, producing a more accessible text that nevertheless retained its links with the original through a

3 Julian Goodare, 'Bibliography of Scottish Witchcraft', in Julian Goodare (ed.), *Scottish Witches and Witch-Hunters* (Basingstoke, 2013), 234–45. See particularly the section 'Published primary sources', pp. 235–6. Since 2013, one further publication has appeared: Allan Kennedy (ed.), 'The Trial of Isobel Duff for Witchcraft, Inverness, 1662', *Scottish Historical Review*, 101 (2022), 109–112.

4 Robert Pitcairn (ed.), *Criminal Trials in Scotland, 1488–1624*, 3 vols. (Edinburgh: Bannatyne Club, 1833). Pitcairn's project, to publish material from the records of the court of justiciary, was continued under a different title by S. I. Gillon and J. I. Smith (eds.), *Selected Justiciary Cases, 1624–1650*, 3 vols. (Edinburgh: Stair Society, 1954–74). These publications include detailed records of a number of witchcraft trials.

5 *Register of the Privy Council of Scotland*, 2nd ser., viii, ed. P. Hume Brown (Edinburgh, 1908). This volume contains 'supplementary papers', not part of the regular series of minutes, covering the period 1544–1660. Its numerous witchcraft cases are listed in the index.

6 Lawrence Normand and Gareth Roberts (eds.), *Witchcraft in Early Modern Scotland: James VI's 'Demonology' and the North Berwick Witches* (Exeter, 2000).

full apparatus of explanatory footnotes and editorial endnotes.[7] The present edition, following conventional historical practice, does not modernise its texts, but does provide a full editorial apparatus. Two documents omitted by Normand and Roberts are printed below, and may be read in conjunction with their edition (Barbara Napier, 1591, and Earl of Bothwell, 1593).

The documents selected for inclusion in the present edition are mostly being published for the first time. A few of the documents have been partially published in earlier editions, as noted individually below, but none have been published in full. The range of unpublished manuscript material is so wide that it has proved possible to make a selection from that material that both complements existing publications and, in itself, illustrates the full range of Scottish witch-hunting.

PRESENTATION OF THE DOCUMENTS

The documents are printed in this book in largely chronological order. Each case has a title, usually in the format 'Name, Place, Date'. Cases involving groups usually have titles like 'Haddingtonshire Witches, 1678'. A few cases depart from this format, but all titles have dates.

Each case has an 'Introduction' of its own, which is followed by the 'Text' itself. A heading to the text states the 'Source', that is, the location of the manuscript and the archival reference. Many of the cases are editions of just one document, but sometimes we bring together several documents from different sources, indicated by further headings within the text.

LEGAL PROCEDURE AND TERMINOLOGY

The following outline of criminal trial procedure in witchcraft cases is intended to assist comprehension of the records printed below. The main stages of the procedure are laid out, with attention to the vocabulary of the documents. Key technical terms are mentioned, in *italics*, and briefly explained.

Most documents recording Scottish witchcraft trials can be divided into two types: pre-trial documents and trial documents. Pre-trial documents record the evidence that was gathered in advance of the trial, while trial documents were those connected with proceedings in the courtroom itself. We will take these two types in turn.

[7] For a discussion of the editorial principles involved see Lawrence Normand, 'Modernising Scottish Witchcraft Texts', *EnterText*, 3 (2003), 227–37. Pitcairn's material on the North Berwick panic was printed in his *Criminal Trials in Scotland*, i, part II, 209–57. This edition, in old spelling and using special characters to represent obsolete letters, also included the text of *Newes from Scotland*, and extracts from other related documents.

Pre-trial investigations of alleged witches were carried out in two main ways: either by interrogating the suspected witch herself or himself to obtain a confession, or else by gathering statements about alleged witchcraft from the suspect's neighbours. As we shall see, the local church courts – kirk sessions and presbyteries – often took a leading role in organising this process.

Confession evidence tends to contain information about a suspect's alleged dealings with the Devil, and often about their alleged meetings with other witches. In witchcraft panics, interrogations and confessions could be used to gather information about further suspects, who could then be arrested and interrogated in their turn. The details in such confessions are often implausible, and they were probably extracted under torture. A church court could order a suspect to be imprisoned during investigation; imprisonment was often called '*warding*'. This would facilitate the torture of the suspect in order to obtain a confession.

Records of individual cases are usually reticent about torture, but the most common form of torture, sleep deprivation, is occasionally mentioned as '*watching*' or '*waking*'. Sleep deprivation may not have been regarded as 'torture', however. A statement in the records that a suspect made their confession 'without torture' may mean that the suspect was subjected to sleep deprivation but not to physical torture; or it may mean that the suspect assented to their confession after the torture had ceased. Various contemporaries commented that torture was common, and it is intuitively unlikely that suspects would have confessed to incriminating, humiliating and impossible demonic activities without being coerced into doing so.

Confessions reveal much about elite views of witchcraft as demonic conspiracy. Occasionally they also reveal a suspect's experience of visionary encounters with spirits; the interrogators usually assumed that these spirits were really the Devil or demons, but we, today, can recognise a diverse range of visionary encounters with spirits such as fairies. Sometimes it is apparent from a confession that torture has not been applied. For instance, there are 'confessions' in which the suspect actually denies witchcraft and offers alternative explanations.

Statements gathered from a witch's neighbours often read very differently from confessions. They usually say little or nothing about the Devil, and tend to concentrate on individual instances of malefice: quarrels, curses and misfortune. These documents reveal much about popular views of witchcraft as individual magical harm, motivated by anger and a desire for revenge. Neighbours testifying were sometimes called '*deponents*' or '*declarants*' in the documents; the term '*delator*' (accuser) could also be used.

A third type of evidence is sometimes mentioned: evidence of the Devil's mark. The Devil was thought to imprint a physical mark on witches at the time when they made the demonic pact. This mark was sometimes discovered by pricking the witch's body with a pin; if the pin could be inserted in an insensitive spot without drawing blood, this was evidence of the Devil's mark. The word 'pricking' was often used, but '*trying*' or '*brodding*' are occasionally found instead. Pricking had a different formal purpose from torture. Torture inflicted pain in order to force a confession, whereas pricking aimed to inflict *no* pain in order to discover physical evidence. In practice, pricking was a coercive and humiliating procedure that probably had the secondary effect of inducing some suspects to confess. Some confessions also mentioned receiving the Devil's mark as part of the narrative of making the demonic pact.

Pre-trial documents were usually compiled by local authorities, partly for their own use and partly because (as we shall see) they would need to present evidence to the central government in Edinburgh. The local courts of the Protestant church were particularly important: the kirk session of each parish, and the presbytery, a co-ordinating body covering groups of parishes. Many of the documents printed below come from these local church records. A kirk session consisted of the parish minister plus up to about a dozen lay elders. Kirk sessions often kept detailed records, and witchcraft investigations that they undertook would lead to them recording either confessions or neighbours' statements or both. The seriousness of witchcraft sometimes led kirk sessions to pass cases on to the presbytery, which would conduct and record its investigations in a similar way. Occasionally the synod, the regional court above the presbytery, was also consulted. The minutes of a kirk session or presbytery often began with a list of those present, using the Latin word '*sederunt*' ('sat'). The members could be referred to as the '*brethren*'. A particular meeting of a regular body like a church court was known as a '*diet*' of the court. To be summoned before such a body was to be '*warned*'; to present oneself formally in response to a summons was to '*compear*'. Some urban suspects were investigated by burgh magistrates instead of church courts. Witchcraft information may be recorded in the regular minutes of these bodies, or the investigators may have compiled separate dossiers of evidence. A written record of evidence or court proceedings could be called a '*process*' (the word '*process*' could also mean 'trial').

Actual trial records were produced by, or for the use of, the secular criminal courts that executed Scottish witches. Witchcraft was a serious crime; local courts could gather evidence, but usually had no power to conduct trials for this crime. It is thus necessary to outline the criminal courts and their procedure, and the evidence that this procedure generated. Perhaps about one-tenth of witchcraft trials were held in the court of justiciary, the central criminal court in Edinburgh. However, most witches were tried by temporary, local criminal courts, constituted by local propertied laymen who had obtained a '*commission of justiciary*' from central government. The usual central body to grant commissions of justiciary was the privy council (sometimes called the '*secret council*'). The commission of justiciary converted these local laymen into temporary judges with authority to constitute a court.

The most common type of Scottish witchcraft trial was thus held in the accused person's locality. The court was known as a '*justice court*', and the venue was often the '*tolbooth*' of the nearest town. A tolbooth was a multi-purpose administrative building, functioning as prison, council house and court house. The court personnel would be as follows. A judge would preside, usually a local propertied layman holding a commission of justiciary. Commissions were often issued to groups of three or five; usually just one of these would preside in court, sometimes known as a '*preses*'. There would be a '*prosecutor*', sometimes known as a '*pursuer*' or a '*procurator fiscal*', to present the prosecution's case, an '*officer*' to run errands and to be responsible for the accused person's custody, and a '*clerk*' to keep records. The accused person would be given the opportunity to defend herself or himself. There would be a jury, usually called an '*assize*' or occasionally an '*inquest*', usually consisting of fifteen propertied laymen from the locality, who would listen to the evidence and return a verdict. The assize's verdict could be reached unanimously ('*all in ane voice*') or by majority vote ('*by pluralitie of voices*').

If the verdict was guilty, then the judge would pass sentence – usually death by strangulation followed by burning. The '*dempster*', a minor ceremonial official who announced the sentence (but did not decide it), is mentioned in some records. Finally, there would be an executioner, sometimes called a '*lockman*' or '*hangman*', to take charge of the practicalities of judicial killing. The terms 'lockman' and 'hangman' should not be misunderstood. A 'lockman' was not a jailer (the term derived from the executioner's traditional right to collect a 'lock', or handful, of oatmeal from each meal-seller in the market), and Scottish witches were burned at the stake rather than being hanged from a gibbet. Death sentences sometimes specified that the person was to be '*wirried*', strangled, at the stake before being burned, and indeed this seems to have been normal practice.

Procedure in the central court of justiciary was largely similar to this, but with elaborations. The judge would be a '*justice depute*' – a legally-trained official employed by the court. He was sometimes referred to as '*the justice*'. He might have one or more '*assessors*', advisers who sat with him. The prosecutor would be a member of the lord advocate's legal staff, or sometimes the '*lord advocate*' himself, the crown's chief law officer (sometimes called the '*king's* or *queen's advocate*', or just the '*advocate*'). The accused person would probably have their own legal representation; even a poor person would usually have a defence advocate assigned to them. The involvement of trained lawyers sometimes generated additional documentation, as we shall see. Other central court personnel could include a '*macer*' or '*serjeant*', who was a messenger and security guard, equivalent to the 'officer' of a local court.

The way in which a typical trial unfolded on the day can be seen in many of the records printed below. The court would be constituted by a formal announcement from the clerk, commanding all those present to obey the judge and not to speak without his permission. This would be reflected in the opening paragraph of the court minutes, usually in Latin, usually giving the place, the date, the name of the judge or judges, and the statement that the court had been '*legally fenced*' (the technical term for the constituting procedure). All Latin text has been translated in footnotes in the present edition.

The accused person would be named in the record at this point, often described as the '*panel*' or sometimes the '*defender*'. The fact that they were 'entering' upon their trial sometimes led to the word '*intrant*' being recorded at this point. The word '*delated*' (accused) was often used about them, and the phrases '*to underlie the law*' or '*to underlie trial*' (to undergo prosecution) could be used. The accused person could be said to be '*art and part*' of the crime – to be guilty by direct participation or by aiding the commission of the crime. They might have a '*procurator*' or '*prolocutor*' to speak in their defence, either a lawyer or a relative, sometimes more than one. To speak on behalf of the accused person was to '*procure*' for them. The prosecutor might be named at this point along with the defence team. Once proceedings began, both the prosecution and the defence could be referred to as '*parties*'.

The substantive trial would begin with the prosecutor reading out the indictment, usually called the '*dittay*', or occasionally the '*libel*'. This was a list, often a detailed list, of the specific acts that the accused person was alleged to have committed, and a claim that these acts constituted the crime of witchcraft. Some of the most valuable historical evidence for witchcraft prosecutions is found in these dittays.

Dittays were often framed in the logical form known as a syllogism: two linked propositions from which a third proposition could logically be drawn. Addressed directly to the accused person, witchcraft dittays tended to take the following form: '1. Witchcraft is a crime; 2. You have carried out acts of witchcraft (listed here); therefore 3. You have committed the crime of witchcraft.' Thus, many dittays began by quoting from the 1563 statute against witchcraft, sometimes cited as '*the 73rd act of the 9th parliament of Queen Mary*';[8] occasionally the Bible was also quoted. Historical interest falls particularly on the details of witchcraft that were then listed. Dittays often incorporated text derived from documents that had been gathered at the pre-trial stage; the two versions can be compared with each other if both the dittay and the pre-trial documents survive. A pre-trial confession would usually be written in the third person ('She confessed that she did such-and-such'), which would then be rewritten for the dittay in the second person ('You did such-and-such'). Pre-trial documents themselves could be produced before the court, and copies of such documents were occasionally written into the minutes or preserved by the court.

[8] For a modern edition of the 1563 act see RPS, A1563/6/9. For a discussion of the text of the act and how the courts used it in practice see Julian Goodare, 'The Scottish Witchcraft Act', *Church History*, 74 (2005), 39–67.

The debate that followed the reading of the dittay was almost always conducted orally, and few details were usually recorded of the accused person's statements in their own defence, known as their '*pleadings*'. Occasionally brief annotations were made in the margin of the dittay, indicating whether the accused person had admitted or denied guilt on specific items. If neighbours' testimony was being used, these neighbours were sometimes brought into court to testify, or else their written statements could be read out.

There were supposed to be two stages to the debate. In the first stage, the defence could argue against the '*relevancy*' of individual charges in the dittay, hoping to persuade the judge to rule them irrelevant. The prosecution would reply with its own arguments as to why the charges were relevant. Only the 'relevant' charges were supposed to be presented to the assize; the judge would decide which these were. The assize would then be sworn in, and a second stage of argument would ensue in which the prosecution and defence argued for and against each charge, with the aim of persuading the assize directly. These two stages are not always visible in the records, and whether a local court even observed the distinction is an open question, but the central court's records do sometimes reveal this aspect of the procedure. Various documents below show the judge making rulings on the relevancy of specific charges.

If the trial was in the central court, '*written pleadings*' could be used. The defence advocate would submit a written statement on the accused person's behalf, arguing point by point against the dittay. A further written 'reply' could then be made by the prosecution, and the argument could continue with a '*duply*' by the defence and even a '*triply*' by the prosecution. Such written arguments by professional lawyers rarely survive, but there are revealing examples below in the cases of Barbara Napier (1591), the Earl of Bothwell (1593), Elizabeth Bathgate (1633–4) and the Bargarran Witches (1697).

In these debates, evidence was sometimes described as '*probation*' (proof), and it could be said to be '*led*' or '*adduced*' (presented) by the prosecution. It might involve '*bruit*' (rumour) or '*fame*' (reputation). Particular points might be said to be '*qualified*' (supported by evidence) or '*condescended upon*' (specified in detail). Legal debate might focus on the '*relevancy*' of specific allegations by the prosecution, or on '*practick*' (or '*practique*'), recognised legal customs of procedure or interpretation.

The court minutes sometimes record other procedural details, such as an '*interloquitur*' – an interim order by the judge. A judge or other official could '*decern*', making an order, or could '*interpone*' his authority, taking responsibility for coercive actions. Either the judge or the assize could be said to '*cognosce*', to deliberate judicially and authoritatively. Summonses and other formal orders could be made '*on pain of horning*', meaning that a person who did not comply would be '*put to the horn*' (outlawed). Monetary penalties, sometimes called '*amercements*' or '*unlaws*', could be mentioned. The defence arguments could include a '*protest for remeid of law*', a formal (but usually ineffective) objection to a procedural decision by the judge. The prosecution could '*protest for wilful error*' – a threat to prosecute the members of the assize for the crime of 'wilful error' if they should acquit an obviously-guilty accused person. (This threat was in fact carried out in the case of Barbara Napier.) A procedural initiative by the defence could take the form of a '*petition*', formally addressed either to the judge or to some other authority like the privy council; such petitions sometimes survive as separate documents among the court papers. Accused persons or other participants could be expected to '*find caution*', to name a person (a '*cautioner*') who would vouch for them. The phrases '*to ask instruments*' or '*to take instruments*', meaning to request or obtain a written copy of a formally recorded legal statement, are sometimes found. Most local trials were completed within one day, but the central court's more elaborate procedures sometimes took several days, minuted separately. A postponement of a court's proceedings to a later date could be called a '*continuation*'.

Once both sides had presented and debated their respective cases, the members of the assize would retire to deliberate in private (there is usually no record of what they discussed), and would then return to the courtroom to deliver a verdict of guilty or not guilty. These phrases were sometimes used, or else the accused was said to be '*fylit*' (guilty) or '*clengit*' or '*assoilyit*' (not guilty). Occasionally the dittay was annotated, or other notes were made, on whether the person had been found guilty or not guilty on specific charges. A '*chancellor*' of the assize, a spokesman who announced the verdict, is sometimes mentioned. Assizes' decisions were reached by majority voting (they did not have to be unanimous), and very occasionally there are notes of how individual members of the assize voted. A verdict of guilty would be followed by a sentence, sometimes called a '*doom*', decided by the judge and formally announced by the dempster. A death sentence could be accompanied by an order to '*escheat*' (confiscate) the person's movable goods, sometimes specifying that this was '*for his majesty's use*'. Most witches were too poor to have goods worth confiscating, but confiscations did occasionally happen, with the royal exchequer usually reallocating the goods locally. Sentences were final; there was no appeal procedure, and a convicted person was sometimes executed on the day of their trial. Since it took some time to assemble the materials for a pyre, an execution on the same day implies that the authorities had had the pyre constructed in advance. Some execution dates were set a few days into the future, presumably to allow time for the construction of the pyre, and also for the condemned person to be visited by a minister who could prepare them spiritually for their death.

The surviving records are often incomplete. There will originally have been thousands of pre-trial and trial records for Scotland's many witches; only a minority of these now survive. Moreover, even for a given case, not all the documents necessarily survive. For instance, there may be trial documents but no pre-trial ones, or vice versa. When we have only pre-trial documents, we sometimes need to consider whether the trial records have been lost, or whether the case was dropped and no trial was ever held. The introductions to the individual documents, below, comment on such questions where possible.

Two of the documents edited below are financial accounts (Dundee Witch, *c.*1591; Peebles Witches, 1629). These provide an unusual view of the trials. They do not name the witches involved, and they are unconcerned with evidence, but they do reveal aspects of the process not recorded elsewhere. The Peebles document tells us about the burgh authorities' negotiations with the central authorities to obtain authorisation for the trial, while both documents reveal much about the practicalities of the witches' executions. Finally, one document concerns not an individual witch, but a witch-pricker and his practices in gathering evidence about the Devil's mark (John Kincaid, 1662).

ORALITY IN THE DOCUMENTS

In the court records of witchcraft trials, it is possible to perceive different voices that come to the fore: the voice of the accused person, the voices of the witnesses, the voice of the interrogator, the voice of the law and the voice of the scribe. Each of these voices has an impact during the trial, and influences interpretation of the trial by giving access to different aspects of trial development, courtroom practice and judicial conditions.

Of particular interest is the voice of the accused person, coming to the fore in the confession. This voice, taken down in a formal setting by a scribe, is heard in a confession formed as a narrative about how to learn and perform witchcraft. It gives via narrative competence access to the imagination and belief of the accused person, most often ordinary people. The contents of the confessions are valuable contributions to the history of mentality in early modern Scotland.

While all text-critical considerations must be taken into account when interpreting witchcraft trials, including the role of the scribe, orality features in the confessions strengthen the understanding that the voice of the accused person is reliable. Most people accused of witchcraft lived in predominantly oral societies and learned stories about witchcraft by oral transmission. In the court records we see that words and expressions rooted in orality surface in the confessions, thus emphasising that the scribe took down what was actually said in the courtroom. The occurrence of orality features in witchcraft confessions adds an extra dimension to the multilayered documents that witchcraft court records are.

An example can be given from the interrogation of Anna Wood (1694), showing how the voice of the accused woman can be perceived. The introductory verb 'answered' signals her voice. Orality features in her speech come to the fore by the use of expanded repetition of 'noe envy', thus: 'The said Anna Wood cited and compearing was interrogate what envy she had at Robert Nimmo that she should have offered to kill him: answered she had noe envy at him, indeed she had noe envy at the young man.' Early modern documents rarely enable us to hear the voices of the common people, but these voices can be heard in some of the documents printed below. Unfortunately, these documents also illustrate the grim realities of the prosecution and execution of witches.

EDITORIAL CONVENTIONS

The manuscripts have been transcribed letter by letter, with the following provisos. The obsolete letters thorn and yogh have been transcribed as 'th' and 'y' respectively; ampersand has been transcribed as 'and'. The letters i/j and u/v, where scribal practice often depended on placement within the word, have normally been modernised. Scribal abbreviations have been expanded silently; superscript letters in abbreviations have been transcribed as normal letters. Letters in square brackets have occasionally been added to aid comprehension, e.g. 'to[o]', 'the[e]'. Capitalisation is given as in the original, except that personal names (including 'the Devil') and place-names, and opening words in sentences, have always been capitalised. Punctuation is given as in the original, except that occasional full stops or commas have been added if this was desirable for clarity. Latin words have been italicised, and translations have been given in footnotes. For repetitive Latin phrases, footnote translations have usually been given only on their first occurrence in a given case; the same applies to footnote explanations of difficult passages. Underlined text has been italicised, with an explanatory footnote. Scribal additions to the text (words inserted above the line or in the margin) are shown \thus/. Important scribal self-corrections or deletions have been noted. This is sometimes done in the text, e.g. '[*word crossed out*]', but more complicated matters are dealt with in footnotes. Deleted text has been transcribed if it can still be read, with a footnote stating the deletion; thus '[*word crossed out*]' on its own indicates that the word is illegible. Marginal rubrics or other such comments have been placed in footnotes. Some short, loose documents have endorsements on the back, which are sometimes comparable to titles. We have printed such endorsements at the head of the text of the document, preceded by '[*Endorsed:*]'. Signatures in documents are preceded by '[*Signed:*]'. Signatures appear in various formats, which we have not altered, nor have we extended abbreviated forms like 'AColvill'. We have printed signatures roughly in order, but have not attempted to reproduce their exact positioning on the page. Although many signatures are evidently holographs, some scribes may have copied signatures. When a document is written or annotated in more than one hand, we have sometimes noted this in footnotes, but we have not analysed multiple hands comprehensively. When a manuscript is damaged or illegible, or if blanks are left, the nature and extent of the problem has been indicated as far as possible, either in the text, e.g. '[*1 word blank*]', or in a footnote. When the transcript consists of extracts from a longer record (often because a kirk session or presbytery dealt with a witchcraft case in instalments among other items of business), discontinuities in the text have been indicated by three dots, or four at the end of a sentence, thus.... Folio or page numbers of the original documents have been added in curly brackets, thus {*fo. 1r.*} {*p. 2*}. Personal names and place-names in editorial text, and in the index, are given in standard modern form as far as possible. For most surnames these are the forms given by George F. Black, *The Surnames of Scotland* (New York, 1946), and for most place-names the Ordnance Survey forms are followed. The introductions to some of the individual documents below give additional guidance on how problems specific to those documents have been dealt with.

1. FORFARSHIRE WITCHES, 1568

INTRODUCTION

This document is a commission of justiciary – an order empowering a group of men in Forfarshire to hold criminal trials for witchcraft in Arbroath. It was issued in the name of Scotland's justice general, Archibald Campbell, fifth earl of Argyll, in April 1568. The justice general was the nominal superintendent of the criminal justice system; he rarely acted in person, but this seems to have been an instance of his doing so. The system was usually operated by the justice clerk using the name of the crown directly; the justice clerk (John Bellenden of Auchnoull) was involved in this commission too, being mentioned near the end of the text. Seven local commissioners were appointed to hold the trials; there was a quorum of three, two of whom had to be James, fifth Lord Ogilvy, and John Erskine of Dun. The commission was to endure for six months. It empowered the commissioners to try forty named suspects, and any other witches who might be accused. It is clear evidence of a regional witchcraft panic.

The document is neatly written on a single large sheet, complete with a seal. It has been slightly damaged in places, and a few of the names present challenges of interpretation, but it is otherwise clear. The details of legal phraseology in its wording reveal much about the mechanics of a sixteenth-century criminal court.

Michael Wasser has recently analysed this commission, setting it in context of the broader prosecution of witches and other criminals during the regency of the earl of Moray (1567–70).[1] He argues that the Forfarshire document was issued during a broader panic in eastern Scotland in 1568 and 1569. In the latter year in particular, Moray himself instigated a number of witchcraft trials, and several executions are known. Moray's efforts, however, lost focus through being directed against various crimes, not just witchcraft; he also had

[1] This paragraph is based on Michael Wasser, 'Scotland's First Witch-Hunt: The Eastern Witch-Hunt of 1568–1569', in Julian Goodare (ed.), *Scottish Witches and Witch-Hunters* (Basingstoke, 2013), 17–33.

inadequate local support in gathering evidence. The 1568 commission, which was focused more specifically on witchcraft, may well have been instigated by John Erskine of Dun, one of the two members of the commission's quorum. Erskine held the important religious office of superintendent of Angus, and was also a secular laird who had previously acted as a justice depute to hold numerous criminal trials. However, this commission too probably failed. Only weeks after it was issued, Mary Queen of Scots escaped from the prison to which Moray had confined her. Her bid to recover power was defeated, but it caused upheaval and split the political nation, with the named commissioners taking opposite sides (Lord Ogilvy supported the queen, Erskine of Dun the regent). No surviving source mentions trials being held, and it is quite likely that none of the witchcraft suspects named in the commission were brought to trial.

The commission is nevertheless full of interest. In particular, the names of the individual witches, and the variety of formats in which these names are presented, call for careful study. Most of the witches are given a place of residence, and from these it may be possible to perceive patterns that reveal something about how the document was compiled – how the witch-hunt was conducted, in fact.

The following list presents an interpretation of the names and other designations of all the accused witches, in the order that they appear in the document. Personal names and place-names have been modernised so far as this is possible, and instances of uncertainty and incompleteness have been noted:

Agnes Whitelaw, spouse of Andrew Brown, younger of Candy[2]
Elizabeth Hunter, spouse of John Lyne, burgess of Arbroath
Agnes Paramour,[3] in Arbroath
Geillis Feriar, spouse of John Carmichael, in Arbroath
Janet Barrowman, in Arbroath
Agnes Gordon, in Arbroath
Bessie Ramsay, spouse of William Christie, in Arbroath
Janet Lamb, in Arbroath
Geillis Durie[4]
Bessie Brodie, in Arbroath
Maud Sturrock, in Arbroath[5]
Isobel Robertson, alias 'Yules-wife', in Arbroath
Janet Garden, in Arbroath

2 'Canny' in the text is probably Candy, to the east of Glenbervie in Kincardineshire.

3 This is a rare surname, but in George F. Black, *The Surnames of Scotland* (New York, 1946), the only fifteenth-century example is from Arbroath.

4 This woman has no place of dwelling recorded, but she is grouped with others from Arbroath.

5 'Maldye' has been taken to mean Maud. It may be a diminutive, so perhaps it should be understood as 'Maudie'.

Dame Logie,[6] in Arbroath
John Steven, in Auchmull
Henry Steven, in Auchmull
The goodwife of the Muirhouse,[7] spouse of John Durward
Janet Herbertson, in 'Got' beside Kelly[8]
Janet Newton, alias 'Tapster',[9] in Carmyllie
Carmyllie's Murie[10]
'Lang' Lowrie[11]
Christian Tough
Betty Webster, beside Coupar Angus, wife of Hobart[12]
Janet Duncan, at the barns of the mains under Fintry[13]
Katherine Cousin, at 'Eliott' under Clova[14]
Isobel Suttie, in Balgavies
[*blank*] Law, servant to John Angus, in Panbride
The daughter of the fisherman of Lundie, under John Campbell of Lundie[15]
James Auchterlonie, called 'the Lang Nurse', under the laird of Kelly[16]
Margaret Mowbray, at the large mill of Brechin
[*blank*] Douglas, in Kirriemuir, under the earl of Angus
Christian Incheoth,[17] in Tealing

6 An incomplete name, apparently of a gentlewoman.

7 An incomplete name. 'Muirhouse' or 'Muirhouses' is a common place-name, with four instances in Forfarshire alone.

8 Kelly is just to the west of Arbroath. 'Got' was evidently a small settlement in that vicinity.

9 A tapster was an alehouse keeper, but here this seems to be a nickname rather than an occupational designation.

10 An incomplete name, apparently a nickname. Carmyllie is a local place-name that this person seems to have adopted as an appellation. The name itself, fairly clearly written 'Murier', is best interpreted as the surname Murie. The small possibility that the phrase 'Carmylis Murier Lang Lowrye' may designate a single person cannot be ruled out.

11 Evidently a nickname. 'Lowrye' may be a surname, or it may be a diminutive of the personal name Lawrence. At this point the scribe seems to have been forced temporarily to abandon the practice of recording each person's place of dwelling.

12 'Hobbert' is probably the surname Hobart, but it might be the related personal name Hubert. The small possibility that 'Betie Wobster' and 'Hobbertis wyfe' are two separate people cannot be ruled out.

13 A 'mains' farm was a farm managed directly by the landlord, rather than being rented to a tenant. The place is Fintry near Dundee rather than other places of that name. Sir David Graham of Fintry was one of the commissioners.

14 'Eliott' was evidently near Clova, in Glen Clova.

15 A woman identified only by her relationship to her father, who in turn is identified only by his occupational connection to a laird. Hitherto in the document, 'under' has meant 'near', but here and in some later instances it means 'servant of' or 'tenant of'. The place is Lundie near Dundee, not Lundie near Edzell (cf. *RMS*, iv, no. 1195). Although this was inland, there were lochs nearby in which fishing could have taken place.

16 The nickname 'Lang [i.e. tall] Nurse' evidently related to some episode in this man's life. The laird of Kelly was William Auchterlonie of Kelly.

17 This puzzling surname is written 'Incheo^t'.

'Lifelike', at the church of Kinloch[18]
James Kilgour
Effie Rodger, in Stormont[19]
Christian Johnstone, in Perth
Janet Turcan, in Perth
James Chalmers, in Perth
Katherine Campbell, in Fowlis, under Lord Gray
Christian Jack, in Fowlis, under Lord Gray

It is beyond the scope of this introduction to analyse this list exhaustively, but some comments may be made. There were thirty women, five men, and five suspects whose gender was not indicated. The place-names display several clusters, notably twelve or thirteen suspects in Arbroath, but there were also a number of isolated individuals, such as one in remote Glen Clova. A few suspects, notably three in Perth, lived outside Forfarshire, the county to which the commission in most respects was limited. Most of the suspects were from the common folk, but there were two gentlewomen, Agnes Whitelaw and Dame Logie, and a burgess's wife, Elizabeth Hunter.

Some clues as to how the document was compiled may be gleaned from its limitations. Four suspects were listed with no place of dwelling. Eight, including some of those with no place, were listed with incomplete names, and occasionally with only vague means of identification. Even the name of one of the commissioners, 'Haliburtoun of Petcur', was incomplete and ambiguous. The document is neatly written, but it reads in places like a work in progress: the organisers of the hunt have not yet gathered all the information that they will need.

It may be suggested, therefore, that these names were gathered by means of an initial trawl through the region, conducted either by John Erskine of Dun himself or by parish ministers under his supervision. At this early date in the Reformation, fewer than half of the parishes in the region had ministers; most of the rest had 'readers' who were not qualified to preach and who were probably unable to establish kirk sessions.[20] Perhaps a few names were supplied by the lairds who were mentioned in connection with some suspects' names. Further study of the witchcraft suspects' places of residence might identify local patterns. At any rate, the names we have, and the incomplete form in which the commission presents several of them, would make sense if ministers had asked their congregations for names of witchcraft suspects, but had not

18 A person with no name beyond a nickname. There are various places called Kinloch; the most likely one is located to the north of Coupar Angus.

19 Stormont was in Perthshire. This name is followed by three names from Perth ('Sanctjohnnestoun') itself.

20 Frank D. Bardgett, *Scotland Reformed: The Reformation in Angus and the Mearns* (Edinburgh, 1989), 87–118.

pursued the detailed local enquiries that would have enabled them to gather the evidence that would have had to be presented in court. As of April 1568, the commissioners may have known very little indeed about 'Lang Lowrye' or 'The fischearis dochter of Lundye undir John Campbell of Lundye'.

The twelve or thirteen names from Arbroath are noteworthy; this is a lot of names to gather from a small town simply on the basis of local suspicions. It is just possible that the authorities have already arrested an initial suspect in Arbroath, and interrogated that person coercively in order to generate further names. That is how Scotland's later witchcraft panics would spread. But there is vagueness in the Arbroath names, as in the others; only three of the thirteen women have husbands named, and the name of 'Dame Logye' is incomplete even though she seems to be a gentlewoman. This survey of the text of the Forfarshire commission thus supports Michael Wasser's conclusion that Scotland's central and local authorities in 1568 were not yet familiar with the most effective ways of generating the detailed and specific evidence of witchcraft that would enable witches to be convicted in large numbers.

TEXT

Source: NRS, Papers of the Earls of Airlie, GD16/25/4.

[*Endorsed:*] Ane commissioun of mi lord of Ergyle for witchis 1568.

Archibald erle of Ergyle lord Campbell and Lorne justice generale to our soverane lord over all his realme Till all and sindry quhome it efferis[21] Quhais knawlege thir present lettres sall to cum greting: wit ye we to have maid depute constitute and ordanit and be the tennor heirof makis constitutis and ordanis the nobill and mychtie lord James Lord Ogilvye Johnne Erskyn of Dwn David Graham of Fintrey knycht [*1 word blank*] Haliburtoun of Petcur[22] Jhone Ogilvy of Innerquharityie knycht David Persoun and Johnne Hailis baillies of Abirbrothok Or ony thre of thame conjunctlie the saidis James Lord Ogilvye and Johnne Erskyn of Dwn being twa of that nowmer Our verray lauchfull undowtit and irrevocabill justice deputtis and lieutennentis in our said office of justiciarie in that parte to the effect undirwrittin Gevand grantand and committand to thame or ony thre of thame conjunctlie in maner foirsaid Oure verray full fre plane power speciale mandment[23] expres bidding and charge Court or courtis of justiciarye within the toun of Abirbrothok

21 'efferis': pertains to.

22 This was either the young laird, George Haliburton of Pitcur, or else his more prominent uncle, James Haliburton, tutor of Pitcur, provost of Dundee. The blank shows that the scribe had not been fully informed, and may also indicate that the organisers themselves were unsure which man to involve.

23 'mandment': mandate.

at quhatsumevir dayis neidfull to sett begin afferme hald and continew as oft as neid beis sectis[24] to mak be callit absentis to amerchiat unlawis and amerchiamentis[25] of the saidis courtis to ask lift and raiss And to this effect Agnis Quhytelaw spous to Andro Broun younger of Canny Elizabeth Hunter spous to Johnne Lyn burges of Abirbrothok Agnes Peramouris thair Geilis Feirour spous to Johnne Carmichaell thair Jonet Barroman thair Agnes Gordoun thair Bessie Ramsay spous to Williame Cryistie thair Jonet Lamb thair Gelis Durye Bessye Brodye thair Maldye Sturrok thair Issobell Robertsoun alias Yulisswyfe thair Jonet Gardyn thair Dame Logye thair Johnne Stevin in Auchmwlye Henrye Stevin thair The gudewyfe of the Muirhous spous to Johnne Durwart Jonet Harbertsoun in Got besyde Kellye Jonet Newtoun alias Topstair in Carmylie Carmylis Murier Lang Lowrye Cristiane Twych Betie Wobster besyde Cowper in Angus Hobbertis wyfe Jonet Duncane at the bernis of the manys undir Fintrey Katherine Cusing at Eliott undir Cloway Issobell Sutye in Balgawye [*1 word blank*] Law servand to Johnne Angus in Panbryde The fischearis dochter of Lundye undir John Campbell of Lundye James Ochterlonyes callit the lang nwreise undir the lard of Kellie Margret Mowbray at the mekle mylne of Brechin [*1 word blank*] Dowglass in Kerymuir undir the erle of Anguss Cristeane Incheo[t] in Teling Lyvelyke at the kirk of Kinloch James Kilgour Effe Roger in Stormond Cristeane Johnnestoun Jonet Turchan and James Chalmer in Sanctjohnnestoun Catherine Campbell and Cristeane Jak in Fowlis undir the Lord Gray and all utheris persones duelland within the boundis of the sherefdome of Forfar delatit or suspect of certane abhominable crymes of sorcerye and wychecraft laitlie committit be thame upoun diverss our soverane lordis liegis To serche seik tak and apprehend quhairevir thai may be fundin within the boundis of the scherefdome of Forfar and putt thame in sure firmance captivitie and presoun And thane severalie in greit or small nowmer in the samin court or courtis To call and be dittay to accuis and to the knawlege of ane assyiss or assissis to putt And as thai be fundin innocent or culpable of the saidis crymes of sorcerye or wychecraft To minister or caus be ministrat justice upoun thame Conforme to the lawis and consuetude[26] of this realme assyiss or assisis neidfull thairto of the scherefdome of Forfar and foure halfis about[27] leist suspect an[d quha][28] best knawis the veritie in the said mater[29] to sufficient nowmer to compeir

24 'sectis': suits. The 'suitors' of a feudal court were men from whom an assize could be drawn. A regular court like a sheriff court had permanent suitors whose duties of attendance were attached to their hereditary landholding, but how suitors could be identified for an *ad hoc* court like the present justice court is unclear. Perhaps the intention was to use the suitors of the sheriff court of Forfar.

25 'unlawis and amerchiamentis': monetary penalties.

26 'consuetude': custom.

27 'and foure halfis about': this is probably a stock phrase indicating localities within the sheriffdom, thus underlining the requirement for assizers to be resident within the sheriffdom.

28 This is the first of nine lines damaged at the end, each with about one word missing. Here and later, conjectural restoration has been made in square brackets where the sense is clear.

29 This idea that the assizers should 'know the verity' expresses the older role of the assize as in some sense witnesses to the crime, rather than simply as decision-makers on the basis of

befoir our saidis jus[tices] and lieutenentis the saidis day and place Ilk persoun undir the pane of xl pundis To summound cy[te and] caus be sworne actis instrumentis and documentis thairupoun neidfull To ask lift rais and [...] And generalie all and sindry uthir things to do use and exerce that to the office of justice deputrye a[nd lieu]tennandrye in sic causis of law or consuetude of this realme necessar ar knawin to pertene Or [that we] mycht do our self and[30] we wer present in propir persoun Firme and stabill haldand[31] and for to hauld all [and] quhatsumevir thingis our saidis justice deputtis and lieutenentis in our name in the premissis laufulie leidis [...] done And attour[32] Becaus our saidis justice deputis and lieutenentis wer nocht heir present befoir ws and our [...] to accept the said office and this our commissioun in and upoun thame and to gif thair aithis for trew administratioun of justice thairintill as use is We have maid constitut and ordanit and be thir present lettris makis constitutis and ordanis our welebelovittis The sheref of Forfar[33] and his deputtis and the prowestis and baillies of the burrowis of Forfar and Dunde[34] conjunctlie and severalie our commissionaris in that part for ressaving of the aithis of our saidis justice deputtis and lieutenentis for administratioun of justice in thair officis Eftir the forme and tenour of this our commissioun and for accepting of the samin in and upoun thame as use is Committand to thaim conjunctlie and severalie our full power to that effect And ordanis this our commissioun for the space of sex monethis efter the day of the dait heirof allanerly to indure and that all process usit in the premissis within the samin space Togidder with the samin commissioun be brocht agane to the justice clerk and his deputtis In witnes of the quhilk thing to thir presentis The sele of the office of justiciarie of our said soveran lord is affixt At Glasgw the [*1 word blank*] day of Apryle the yeir of God i^{m} v^{c} lxviii yeiris.

[*Fragment of seal, red wax, about 1 13/16" across, attached to the centre of the paper just below the last line of writing.*[35]]

evidence presented in court. See Ian Douglas Willock, *The Origins and Development of the Jury in Scotland* (Edinburgh: Stair Society, 1966), 149, 197. The court may have been intended to have a single assize to try all the suspects, but the wording of the commission ('assyiss or assisis neidfull') leaves open the possibility that more than one assize could be used.

30 'and': if.

31 This phrase indicates that the justice general will accept and support the decisions of the subordinates whom he appoints by means of this commission.

32 'attour': also.

33 The sheriff of Forfar was Patrick, fourth Lord Gray.

34 The involvement of the burgh magistrates of Forfar and Dundee is intriguing, given that the court was to be held in Arbroath. Forfar was the head burgh of the sheriffdom of Forfar, while Dundee was by far the largest town in the sheriffdom. The provost of Dundee was James Haliburton, tutor of Pitcur, who may have been intended to be one of the commissioners (see footnote 22 above).

35 This is probably an impression of the seal of the justice general. It is, however, larger than the 1 1/16" seal of the office of justice general, of which two impressions (1577 and 1596) are known: J. H. Stevenson and M. Wood, *Scottish Heraldic Seals*, vol. i: *Public Seals* (Glasgow, 1940), 43.

2. SIR WILLIAM STEWART, EDINBURGH, 1569

INTRODUCTION

This case is about much more than 'witchcraft'. It is one of the most spectacular instances of necromancy and elite magic ever to have occurred in Scotland. It involved political conspiracy at high levels of government, the ritual summoning of spirits using a book of learned magic, and prophecies by witches in Scotland and Norway. The central figure in the conspiracy was Sir William Stewart.

William Stewart was a herald, one of the ceremonial messengers of the crown. This did not give him great political power, but he moved in elite circles and was involved in international diplomacy. He was probably the son of Alexander Stewart of Dalswinton, in Dumfriesshire, and may have been born around 1540. He married a Norwegian woman, Dorothea Christoffersdatter Thronsden (or Tronds).[1] His father, knighted in 1565, was a kinsman and ally of the earl of Lennox, and Stewart himself may have owed his initial advancement to this Lennox connection during the personal reign of Mary Queen of Scots.[2] He first appears as Ross herald in 1566.[3] He had connections with the Protestant church, contributing a prefatory 'Table for the shyneing of the Mone', and a sonnet, to Scotland's new Protestant prayer book in 1565.[4] The table shows him to have had an interest in astronomy and numbers which must have fed into the astrological activities revealed at his trial. Also in 1565, he published a Scots translation of a French Calvinist tract, displaying a learned acquaintance with theology and etymology.[5]

1 Alex Maxwell Findlater, *The Armorial of Sir David Lyndsay of the Mount*, 2 vols. (Edinburgh: Heraldry Society of Scotland, 2018), ii, 323.

2 Julian Goodare, 'Queen Mary's Catholic Interlude', in Michael Lynch (ed.), *Mary Stewart: Queen in Three Kingdoms* (Oxford, 1988), 154–70, at p. 158.

3 Queen Elizabeth to Mary, 9 Jan. 1566, *Calendar of State Papers relating to Scotland and Mary, Queen of Scots, 1547–1603*, vol. ii, *1563–1569*, ed. Joseph Bain (Edinburgh, 1900), 250.

4 *The Forme of Prayers and Ministration of the Sacraments … Approued & Receiued by the Churche of Scotland* (Edinburgh: Robert Lekprevik, 1565), unpaginated preface. The sonnet is the earliest known sonnet published by a Scottish person. We are grateful to Alasdair A. MacDonald for this information.

5 *Ane Breif Gathering of the Halie Signes, Sacrifices and Sacramentis* (Edinburgh: Robert Lekprevik, 1565). For discussions of this work see Stephen Mark Holmes, *Sacred Signs in Reformation*

Stewart was also connected with the queen's illegitimate half-brother, James Stewart, earl of Moray, who became regent of Scotland in August 1567 after Mary's deposition. We are told that William Stewart had been 'brocht up witht the regent'.[6] One of Moray's early acts as regent was to send Stewart as ambassador to Norway, Denmark and Flanders in September 1567.[7] Moray promoted him to be Lyon King of Arms, the head of the Scottish heralds, on 20 February 1568. He also knighted him and granted him rents from the estate of Luthrie in Fife, formally making him Sir William Stewart of Luthrie.[8] Stewart made another diplomatic visit to Denmark in the spring of 1568, for which he was paid expenses on 9 June – the last date at which he is known to have retained the regent's favour.[9]

For Stewart had turned against the regent and was plotting to restore Queen Mary, who had been imprisoned in Lochleven Castle after her deposition. This might well have been a popular or at least widely supported move. The queen's deposition had split the political nation, and Moray as regent faced widespread resentment that would soon explode into revolt. However, Stewart's route into Marian politics was a devious and idiosyncratic one. He did not simply attach himself to the main existing networks of pro-Mary aristocrats; he wanted to marry the queen himself. And he resorted to magic and prophecy in order to advance his cause.

Stewart recruited a few heavyweight political allies. Indeed, perhaps they recruited him; further study of the conspiracy would be necessary in order to elucidate the role of the other participants. One important ally was Sir Archibald Napier of Merchiston, a wealthy and well-connected laird. Some of the necromantic rituals were carried out at Merchiston. Another conspirator was Gilbert Balfour, an Orkney laird whose brother, Sir James Balfour of Pittendreich, had recently been an officer of state. Patrick Bellenden of Stenness, also an Orkney laird, would later be arrested for his involvement. Patrick Hepburn, bishop of Moray, and his son, also Patrick Hepburn, parson of Kinnoir, were also mentioned.[10]

Scotland: Interpreting Worship, 1488–1590 (Oxford, 2015), 195–9; Alasdair A. MacDonald, 'Reformation Controversy and the Practice of Historical Lexicography', *Scottish Language*, 39 (2020), 87–100.

6 Robert Lindesay of Pitscottie, *The Historie and Cronicles of Scotland*, 3 vols., ed. Æ. J. G. Mackay (Edinburgh: Scottish Text Society, 1899–1911), ii, 206. Stewart seems to have been about eight years younger than the regent, so perhaps he served, as a child, as a page in the future regent's household.

7 *Accounts of the Treasurer of Scotland*, vol. xii, *1566–1574*, ed. Charles T. McInnes (Edinburgh, 1970), 75. He was then Albany herald.

8 *RSS*, vi, no. 158.

9 *Accounts of the Treasurer of Scotland*, xii, 128–9.

10 For Bellenden see Sir William Drury to Sir William Cecil, 8 Aug. 1568, *Calendar of State Papers, Foreign Series, of the Reign of Elizabeth, 1566–8*, ed. Allan J. Crosby (London, 1871), 515. He was the brother of Sir John Bellenden of Auchnoull, the justice clerk. The other conspirators are named in Stewart's dittay, below.

The conspiracy against Moray, based in Edinburgh, seems to have taken shape in the summer or autumn of 1567. The document edited below, the dittay used at Stewart's eventual trial, mentions a prophecy of the regent's death that was to occur on 17 November 1567. Earlier prophecies are also mentioned, including one allegedly made in January 1567. The conspirators seem to have devoted most of their efforts to divining the future, predicting various outcomes that they thought were relevant to their ambitions. Several of these prophecies reveal the conspirators' thinking about their potential opponents and allies. One apparently crucial prophecy was that Stewart himself should marry the queen and have children with her. How these outcomes were to be achieved was less clear, but in the minds of contemporaries there was overlap between magically predicting events and magically causing them to occur – as Stewart's dittay itself makes clear.[11]

The government discovered the conspiracy in July 1568. Stewart fled to Dumbarton Castle on 27 July (a date given in the dittay), which was held by Lord Fleming for the queen's party, and he was deprived of office.[12] He wrote from Dumbarton, claiming to be innocent of plotting, on 19 August.[13] He was formally outlawed on 20 August.[14] He was still taking refuge in the castle in October.[15] At some point after this, however, he ventured into the town of Dumbarton and was captured. He was imprisoned in Edinburgh Castle to await trial.[16]

We next hear of Stewart on 5 August 1569, when he wrote to the Regent Moray from prison, asserting his innocence. His version of events was that he had received information about a possible conspiracy against Moray on 21 July 1568, but had kept quiet about it, thinking it indefinite or unlikely. He assured Moray that his informant (whom he did not name) had power to foretell the future, listing various recent events that this person had correctly foretold.[17]

However, on that same day, 5 August 1569, Stewart was taken from Edinburgh Castle to St Andrews for trial (the venue apparently being dictated by the regent's presence in the town) and, on the 15th, 'being convicted for witcherie, wes brunt'.[18] His dittay specified that he had confessed, so this

11 For more on political prophecy see Julian Goodare, 'Witchcraft and Prophecy in Scotland', *Journal of the Northern Renaissance*, 12 (2021), online.

12 Lindesay of Pitscottie, *Historie*, ii, 206; *RSS*, vi, no. 489.

13 British Library, London, William Stewart to the secretary (William Maitland of Lethington), Dumbarton, 19 Aug 1568, Cotton MS Caligula B IX, fo. 326r.

14 *RPC*, i, 638.

15 Offences by the Queen's Party, 4 Oct. 1568, *Calendar of State Papers relating to Scotland*, ii, 516.

16 Lindesay of Pitscottie, *Historie*, ii, 217.

17 Stewart to Moray, 5 Aug. 1569, *Calendar of State Papers relating to Scotland*, ii, 665–6.

18 *A Diurnal of Remarkable Occurrents that have Passed within the Country of Scotland since the Death of King James the Fourth till the Year 1575*, ed. Thomas Thomson (Edinburgh: Bannatyne Club, 1833), 146. The trial judge was a local laird, Patrick Learmonth of Dairsie, to whom a commission of justiciary was issued on the day of the trial, 15 Aug. 1569: NRS, JC26/1/51. No minutes of the trial itself are extant. The trial may be seen in context of a broader if

confession was presumably obtained in the short period between those two dates. What pressure was placed upon him to confess must remain a matter of speculation, but he gave many details of magical rituals, and named several other conspirators. A few additional points in the dittay seem to derive from other informants. On conviction, Stewart was pardoned for conspiring against the regent, but was burned for what was reported as 'conjuration' and witchcraft.[19] An official document listed his offences as 'certain crymes of witchecraft, negromancie and uthiris crymes'.[20]

The other conspirators were not prosecuted. Perhaps the regent and his councillors hesitated to unravel the full extent of the conspiracy, and decided tactically that an isolated prosecution would be enough to keep other disaffected persons in line. One small indication of leniency is that Stewart's widow was allowed to keep his movable goods.[21]

The dittay below provides many details of Stewart's magical activities, and a brief introduction to them can be given here.[22] Although the actual word 'magic' is rarely found in contemporary sources concerning witchcraft, it does occur in this document. The summoning of Obirion is described as 'art magic', and the conspirators use a 'magical figure' (diagram) in their book of magic. The dittay uses other unusual terms, like 'enchantment' and 'mystery'. Prophecies are described as 'oracles', and Stewart himself is called a 'soothsayer'.

Five of the charges involved divination using a sieve and shears (the sieve is called a 'riddle'). This was folk divination rather than learned magic. The sieve would be balanced upside down on the upturned points of the shears, and a question would be put to it, using a formal verbal charm. The sieve would 'turn' or tremble at the significant moment, for instance when a guilty person was named; this also enabled yes/no questions to be asked.[23] Stewart seems to have been regarded as an expert in the technique.

sometimes ineffectual panic about witchcraft in 1568–9: Michael Wasser, 'Scotland's First Witch-Hunt: The Eastern Witch-Hunt of 1568–1569', in Julian Goodare (ed.), *Scottish Witches and Witch-Hunters* (Basingstoke, 2013), 17–33, at pp. 18–19. Another aspect of this panic is discussed in the edition of 'Forfarshire Witches, 1568', above in the present volume.

19 Lord Hunsdon to Cecil, Berwick, 30 Aug. 1569, *Calendar of State Papers, Foreign Series, of the Reign of Elizabeth, 1569–71*, ed. Allan J. Crosby (London, 1874), 119. Hunsdon, an English diplomat, may have used the term 'conjuration' because it was familiar in English witchcraft discourse, occurring for instance in the title of the English witchcraft act of 1563.

20 *RSS*, vi, no. 744. The term 'necromancy' occurred in the Scottish witchcraft act, but was not otherwise common in Scottish witchcraft trial records.

21 *RSS*, vi, no. 744.

22 There is a valuable discussion of this topic in P. G. Maxwell-Stuart, *Satan's Conspiracy: Magic and Witchcraft in Sixteenth-Century Scotland* (East Linton, 2001), 57–60.

23 George L. Kittredge, *Witchcraft in Old and New England* (New York, 1929), 198–200; Edward Bever, *The Realities of Witchcraft and Popular Magic in Early Modern Europe: Culture, Cognition and Everyday Life* (Basingstoke, 2008), 224–8.

The ritual invocation of the spirit 'Obirion', with which the dittay seems to have begun, was a long way from folk magic. The name 'Obirion' was a variant of the German name 'Alberich', which had been used as a name for spirits since the middle ages.[24] William Shakespeare would later make his 'Oberon' the king of the fairies;[25] however, there is no direct allusion to fairies in Stewart's case. Instead, Stewart called Obirion a 'lunall' (lunar) spirit, a concept that seems to have come from astrologically influenced elite magic. There may be influence here from Neoplatonism; the lunar table that Stewart had published in 1565, mentioned above, may also be relevant. The ritual involved a 'picture' (a tablet or statuette) made of lead; perhaps this was a planetary amulet, made during an auspicious planetary conjunction.

The interest in control and mastery of Obirion is noteworthy. Necromancers who summoned demons or other dangerous spirits were particularly concerned to retain control over them. The conspirators were accused of having 'worshipped' Obirion, a word that perhaps imposed a demonological understanding on the process. As well as Obirion, the dittay displays an unusual interest in plural demons – 'devillis and wickit spiritis' – in contrast to most Scottish witchcraft cases, which emphasise the singular Devil.

Stewart had magical assistants: Edmond Willock, Thomas MacCartney and their unnamed 'complices'. It was they whom Stewart sent to perform an elaborate magical ceremony in Holyrood Park, with hot coals, doves, and a magical diagram from a book. Perhaps Willock and MacCartney had also made the lead 'picture'. The doves were probably to be sacrificed. As for the unnamed 'complices', one wonders whether they included a young boy, whom some magicians used for scrying – perceiving images in a reflective surface or crystal. The magical ceremony in Holyrood Park was the only one where magical purposes other than foretelling the future were mentioned. The conspirators also wanted to find buried treasure (treasure was often thought to be guarded by demons), and to find the gold lost by an Edinburgh merchant, John Uddart, who may or may not have been one of the conspirators. This was evidently the episode about which the English agent was reporting when he sent 'some peace off the woorke that the conjurors that dyd use theyre divelysche skylle did devyse above Edenborogh, the platte whereoff I sente you before paynted'. He added: 'Some monye they founde', and mentioned Stewart's name.[26]

[24] Johannes Dillinger, *Magical Treasure Hunting in Europe and North America: A History* (Basingstoke, 2012), 156. For the use of the name in Yorkshire, England, in 1510, see p. 110.

[25] For Oberon among Shakespeare and his contemporaries see Ronald Hutton, *Queens of the Wild: Pagan Goddesses in Christian Europe* (New Haven, 2022), 96–107.

[26] The National Archives, London, Drury to Cecil, 20 July 1568, SP59/15, fo. 153v.; cf. *Calendar of Foreign Papers, 1566–8*, 504. Unfortunately, neither the 'peace off the woorke', nor the painted 'platte', are now extant.

The conspirators' use of at least one book is a key point, taking their rituals beyond the world of everyday witchcraft and folk magic. Further research is required on this, but the dittay calls it a 'buke of Agrippa' containing a 'magicall figour' (diagram). This book was probably the *Liber Quartus De Occulta Philosophia* (Fourth Book of Occult Philosophy), a necromantic work first printed in the 1560s, and attributed – spuriously, as is now known – to the Renaissance magus Heinrich Cornelius Agrippa von Nettesheim (1486–1535).[27]

The incantation summoning Obirion was said to have been in Italian – though the scribe added this point as an afterthought, and he also crossed out the statement that the words were 'uncouth and insensible'. (Prosecutors thought that unknown words were dangerous because they could turn out to be the names of demons.) A Latin phrase was also quoted. The use of Italian may indicate the influence of Italian magical writers like Marsilio Ficino or Giambattista della Porta (though their major works were published in Latin), or perhaps contact with Italy through travel.

Stewart pursued his enquiries into the future in one further way: he consulted at least three 'witches' who made prophecies for him. At least, the dittay calls them 'witches' – but that could have been based on conventional demonological assumptions. Whether Stewart himself used the word 'witches' about them, or whether the prophetic women called *themselves* 'witches', are open questions.

The name of the first witch is a remarkable one: Marion Nicneven. 'Nicneven' has been recognised in previous scholarship as a name or sobriquet that was apparently used by several witches or magical practitioners from the 1560s onwards.[28] The word is a Gaelic phrase meaning 'little daughter of the holy one', and its users seem to have adopted it in order to signal a claim to magical powers. A contemporary narrative relates that 'a notabill soceres callit Nicniven was condemnit to the death and brunt' together with Stewart.[29] Stewart's dittay calls her 'umquhyle' (late), so her execution evidently preceded

27 Agrippa's genuine work was published as *De Occulta Philosophia Libri Tres* (Three Books of Occult Philosophy) in 1533. For the spurious attribution to him of the 'Fourth Book' see Lynn Thorndike, *The History of Magic and Experimental Science*, 8 vols. (New York, 1923–58), vi, 360. One edition of the 'Fourth Book' that Stewart could have used was Henricus Cornelius Agrippa, *Liber Quartus De Occulta Philosophia, seu de Cerimonijs Magicis* ([Basel,] 1565). For an English version see Henry Cornelius Agrippa, *Fourth Book of Occult Philosophy*, trans. Robert Turner (London, 1665). This book contained several diagrams, and instructions for summoning spirits. It listed the shapes likely to be assumed by spirits of the different planets; for the 'Formæ familiares spiritibus Lune' ('forms familiar to the spirits of the moon') see pp. 34–5 (Latin edition), 44–5 (English edition).

28 Alison Hanham, '"The Scottish Hecate": A Wild Witch Chase', *Scottish Studies*, 13 (1969), 59–65; Julian Goodare, 'Nicneven (fl. 1560s)', in Elizabeth Ewan, Rose Pipes, Jane Rendall and Siân Reynolds (eds.), *The New Biographical Dictionary of Scottish Women* (Edinburgh, 2018), 340. The case of Isobel Watson (1590), edited below, also mentions Nicneven.

29 *The Historie and Life of King James the Sext*, ed. Thomas Thomson (Edinburgh: Bannatyne Club, 1825), 66.

his. But it is only from the dittay that we learn that he had actually consulted her. The dittay shows him travelling to do so ('passing to the presence'), unlike with the second witch whom he summoned to his chamber. Other sources associate Nicneven with southern Perthshire, so perhaps this is where he went. The name 'Marion' Nicneven has not been identified from previous sources, and may add significantly to our knowledge.

The second witch named in the dittay was 'Dame Steill' in Edinburgh. This was evidently a nickname for Janet Boyman, who lived in Edinburgh and whose husband was William Steill. We know a lot about her because her dittay survives, and is edited below in the present volume. It says that Stewart named her 'at the hour of his death' (perhaps the nickname 'Dame Steill' had been an earlier attempt to shield her), and that she fled from arrest at that time. She was eventually arrested and tried in 1572. Boyman's dittay sheds valuable additional light on the conspiracy, revealing further prophecies that she had made for Stewart. She also revealed a third witch whom Stewart had consulted, and with whose prophecies Boyman herself disagreed: 'the wich of Norraway wes ane leyard quhilk had foirspookin thai thingis to him.' Presumably Stewart had consulted this Norwegian witch during one of his diplomatic visits. She does not appear in Stewart's own dittay.

The document is a long sheet made of three sheets stitched together. The top of the first sheet, written in two columns, has been torn away, and there is further intermittent damage to the right-hand margin of all three sheets. The second and third sheets do not have columns, and are written with a wide left-hand margin, used for annotations in the same hand. The text is neatly written, but with numerous corrections, emendations and marginal additions. Some of the marginal additions represent Stewart's responses to the accusations, perhaps in the courtroom itself, admitting to some accusations while qualifying others. There are also notes of the verdicts given on each point. This thus seems to have been the actual document used in court. The use of a much-amended document in court may indicate that the trial was carried out in a hurry, with no time to produce a fair copy.

TEXT

Source: NRS, Dittay of Sir William Stewart, 1569, JC40/1/2.[30]

[…][31] and[32] practizing of w… [*2-3 words damaged*] art magik In cumpany[33] with Archibald Naper of Merchanstoun in the loft or upper chalmer of the tour of Merchanstoun Makand invocatioun and worshipping of the spirite Obirioun quhilk ye terme a lunall[34] spirite having his picture drawin in leid[35] cryand thir wordis *servitus pulcherorum*[36] Obirion desirand his presence to gif yow revelation of thingis to cum for quhais comperance ye [*2-3 words damaged*] the forme of a king or fair yong may[37] as ye your self hes confessit Thairthrow riectand[38] the cair and providence of God and wickitlie and abhominablie committand witchecraft socery [*sic*] and Inchantment \and ydolatirie/ prohibit baith be the lawes of God and man as is notourlie kend quhilk ye can nocht deny.[39]

[…] and [*4-5 words damaged*] of your hand [*3-4 words damaged*] makand Invocatioun[40] usand [*1 word damaged*] your Invocatioun \in Italian/ words and sentences[41] \dessirand the sperite to answer upoun vii puntis/ quhilk Invocatioun ye purposlie maid to haif the comperance of devillis and wickit spirits To gif yow revelatioun and knawlege of thingis to cum concerning the estait of this realm and utheris and this ye did in the said yard of Merchanstoun quhilk ye can[42] nocht deny.[43]

30 This untitled document is part of a bundle, JC40, entitled 'Witchcraft Papers', which has evidently been assembled at a later date from unsorted papers of the justiciary court. The name of the accused person, which would have been given at the beginning of the document, is now missing. However, comparison of the document with Janet Boyman's dittay below, which does name Stewart, leaves no doubt that this document pertains to him.

31 The top of the page has been torn away, taking an unknown amount of text with it.

32 In margin: 'confessit filit'.

33 MS damaged: 'cump…'.

34 This word does not appear in dictionaries, but the meaning seems to be 'lunar'.

35 Either a lead tablet with an image drawn on it, or a lead statuette.

36 Maxwell-Stuart, *Satan's Conspiracy*, 58, reads '*servitus pulcher*', meaning, he argues, 'handsome slave'. He points out that '*servitus*' is strictly an abstract noun meaning 'servitude', but argues plausibly that the meaning is intended as '*servus*', slave. Or perhaps '*servitus*' is a variant of '*servitor*', servant. If the reading preferred here, '*servitus pulcherorum* Obirion', is correct, the meaning seems to be 'Obirion, slave of the handsome ones'.

37 'may': maiden.

38 *Sic*. The meaning is 'rejectand', i.e. rejecting.

39 The first of two columns of text ends here. The tearing away of the top of the page has removed an unknown amount of text from the beginning of the second column.

40 MS damaged: 'Invoca…'. At this point the following words are crossed out: 'upoun the name of the s… [*word damaged; probably 'spirit'*] Obirioun quhilk ye call a lunall spreite'.

41 At this point the words 'uncouth and insensible' are crossed out.

42 MS damaged: 'quhi… can'.

43 In margin: 'confessit fillit [*sic*]'. The first sheet ends here.

Item[44] ye ar Indyt for the unlefull and diabolicall using and practizing to turne the scheir and the riddle for getting of response and knawlege of divers thingis exegitat[45] be your self and Inquirit of yow be utheris, as in speciall be the same mistery art and meanys ye schew spak and affirmit that my lord Regentis grace suld dee a violent deith befoir the xvii day of November 1567. Item[46] ye said and affirmit upoun the same assurance that the quene suld \wyn/[47] the feild at Langside,[48] and thairwithall tressonablie dissuadit Williame Pennycuke persoun of Pennycuke and divers otheris that thay suld na wyis pas to the Regent nor assist him in the defence and mantenance[49] of the king our soverane Lordis actioun and auctorite, doand thairthrow that wes in [*1-2 words damaged*] to put his hienes self his estait and auctorite in extreme perell and dangeir of [*1-2 words damaged*] throw the default of the support of his Loving and gude subjectis \quhilk/[50] willinglie [*1 word damaged*] haif spendit thair blude in his defence and querrell, gif ye had not tressonabillie persuadit thame that he and his party suld tyne the said feild quhilk ye can nocht deny.

Item[51] ye said and affirmit being be word and write (quhilk ye haif confessit to knaw be turnyng of the said scheir and riddle), That ye knew of befoir of the death and murthur of \umquhill/ the king fader to our soverane Lord, and sua in conceling [*sic*] thairof committit plane and [*1 word damaged*] tressoun quhilk ye can nocht deny.

Item[52] ye practizit and tryit be the said sheir and riddle and be your unlefull comm… [*word damaged*] usit thairon, that the kipe[53] moneth and day of your nativitie wes just and richtlie [*1-2 words damaged*] be yow and this ye did in the upper chalmer within the bishop of Morayis ludgeing[54] In Edinburgh quhilk ye can nocht deny.

Item ye calculat tryit and practizit be the said sheir and riddle and reportit the samyn to utheris as ane infallible trewth and undoubtit oracle in your

44 In margin: 'he spak this bot of the calculatioun of his Janitour'. Here, 'janitour' is probably the scribe's attempt to spell the rare word 'geniture', meaning nativity or horoscope.

45 'exegitat': not in dictionaries, but evidently a verb from 'exegesis', thus meaning 'explained or interpreted from a text'.

46 In margin: 'confessit filit'.

47 The word 'tyne' (lose) has been crossed out here, and 'wyn' inserted above the line.

48 The Regent Moray's army defeated the forces of the recently escaped Queen Mary at the battle of Langside, near Glasgow, on 13 May 1568.

49 MS damaged: 'man…'.

50 The word 'and' has been crossed out here, and 'quhilk' inserted above the line.

51 In margin: 'grantis the samin Bot denys the conceling tressoun; filit'.

52 In margin: 'confessit filit'.

53 *Sic.* The word that one would expect here is 'time' (or perhaps 'hour'), since Stewart's 'nativitie' (horoscope) would have required knowledge of the time and date of his birth. Perhaps the non-word 'kipe' arises from the scribe's puzzled or careless attempt to read the badly written word 'time' in the rough notes from which he was copying.

54 The bishop of Moray, Patrick Hepburn, was an associate of James Hepburn, fourth earl of Bothwell, and was generally aligned with the queen's party. 'Ludgeing': lodging.

maist tressonabill and dissaitfull maner that[55] \the quene suld be maryt on ane man besowth Forth[56] and that Gilbert Balfour said that it wes ye suld be that man/ with hir quhilk ye can nocht deny.

Item[57] ye ar Indyt for the unlauchtfull ungodlie and diabolicall practizing of the said sheir and[58] riddl[e], upoun thir questionis following and for geving of answers [*1-2 words damaged*] responsis thairupoun as a soyt[h] sear, first howsone the king suld die, ye answerit befoir the xxvi of Merche 1567 Secundlie quhat kynd of deid ye answerit he suld be slane, this ye usit and practizit in the ludgeing of Gilbert Balfour within Edinburgh In the month of Januar or thairby 1566[59] quhilk ye can nocht deny.

Item[60] ye said and affirmit upoun the response and oracle ressavit throw turning of the said riddle and sheir, that the erll of Argile and Sir William Murray of Tulibardin [*1 word damaged*] comptrollair suld not agrie togidder, Bot suld fecht within the burgh of Edinburgh [*1-2 words damaged*] October then nixt following, quhair thai suld bayth be \hurt/[61] and thairfoir wes a \wikkit/[62] meane and instrewment to hald thame in continewall disordor to the hurt of the commoun weill and hindrance of the kings service quhilk ye can nocht deny.

Item[63] ye said[64] affirmit and gaif responsis upoun the deathis destanys and accidentis that suld happin in the lyffis of the said comptrollair[65] the Maister of Grahame[66] avowand the same as undoutit oracles and trew foir speking quhilk ye can not deny.

55 The words 'ye suld marie the quene moder to our soverane lord and procreat children' have been crossed out here, and a caret inserted to indicate that the 23 words that follow, added in the margin, should be taken into the text. The words 'with hir' that come after this addition no longer make sense, and should presumably have been crossed out also.

56 'besowth Forth': on the south side of the Firth of Forth.

57 In margin: 'confessit filit'.

58 MS damaged: 'sa... and'.

59 That is, January 1567 by modern reckoning. The king, Henry Stewart, Lord Darnley, was murdered on 9 February 1567. Nicolas Hubert alias 'French Paris', one of the alleged murderers, was tried and executed along with William Stewart: *Historie and Life of King James the Sext*, 66.

60 In margin: 'confessit filit'.

61 The word 'slane' has been crossed out here, and 'hurt' inserted above the line. The earl of Argyll was Archibald Campbell, fifth earl.

62 A word now illegible has been crossed out here, and 'wikkit' inserted above the line.

63 In margin: 'confessit filit'.

64 The word 'and' has been crossed out here.

65 The words 'the Erll of Mortoun' have been crossed out here. This was James Douglas, fourth earl of Morton.

66 The words 'the secretare and Sir James Balfour of Pettindrycht knycht' have been crossed out here. The master of Graham was John Graham, future third earl of Montrose. The secretary was William Maitland of Lethington. Sir James Balfour was the elder brother of Gilbert Balfour, named earlier in the document as one of the conspirators.

Item[67] ye ar Indyt for the unlawchtfull wickit and ungodle passing to the presence of umquhyle Marioun Nikniving ane Notorious knawin witche at quhome ye socht response and assurance of divers thingis to cum and specialie anent the libertie \of the quene/ quha wes then in Lochlevin as is notourlie kend quhilk ye can nocht deny in[68] Merche or Aprile 1568.[69]

Item[70] ye ar Indyt For art and part of the divers Invention causing and geving [*1 word damaged*] the exemplar of the magicall figour Maid and socery Incantation and Invocation following thairupoun maid within the park of Halirudhous beside Arthour Satt be Edmond Willok Thomas McCartnay and thair complices be your instruction and leryng, usand beside utheris ciremonyis[71] haitt colis of fire twa dowis,[72] Solicitand[73] the presens of devillis and wickit spiritis to get revelatioun and knawlege[74] of Jhone Udartis[75] gold latelie stollin, To get knawlege of sum tresour or hurd hid in the earth, and in fyne to get knawlege quhat suld[76] becum of the quene and how the estait of Scotland suld be, quhilk last pryer ye gaif[77] thame speciall grund to Inqure [*sic*] and gaif unto the said Edmond Willok the buke of Agrippa quhairupoun he found be your advyce the said magicall figour as ye your self hes confessit quhilk ye can nocht deny.

Item[78] ye ar indyt and accusit for seking of responsis and answer in wnlachtfull and diabolicall maner at ane Notorious and knawin witche Namyt Dame Steill[79] in Edinburgh For quhome ye send Thomas Afflek your boy[80] and brothir to your awin chalmer in Edinburgh quhair upoun your spering[81] and inquisition of hir ye ressavit thir answeris that is to say the quene suld

67 In margin: 'confessit filit'.

68 The words 'Merche or Aprile or May 1568' have been crossed out here.

69 The second sheet ends here.

70 In margin: 'confessit he Lent Lent [*sic*] the buke and baid thaim gif thai gat comperance sper the estait of the affares; filit'. The meaning of 'gif thai gat comperance sper the estait of the affares' (the reading of which is not entirely certain) seems to be 'if they got the spirits to appear, ask about the political situation'.

71 MS damaged: 'ciremony…'.

72 'dowis': doves, pigeons.

73 Conjectural expansion of what seems to be an unusual abbreviation.

74 MS damaged: 'knawl…'.

75 John Uddart was a merchant of Edinburgh who occasionally served on the town council: Michael Lynch, *Edinburgh and the Reformation* (Edinburgh, 1981), 173, 234, 242.

76 MS damaged: 's…'.

77 MS damaged: 'ga…'.

78 In margin: 'confessit filit'.

79 Probably Janet Boyman. See the introduction to this document, above.

80 'boy': servant.

81 'spering': asking.

be furth of Lochlevin[82] the first Sunday[83] of Maii[84] 1567[85] That ye suld be in grit credit with the quene, *that the quene suld be maistres of Scotland and suld mary yow and haif bairnis to yow*,[86] This ye ressavit as a trew oracle and seditiousle tressonabillie shew the samen to utheris as ye haif your self confessit quhilk ye can nocht deny.

Item[87] ye are Indyt for the heich tressoun efter specifyt done be yow aganis our soverane lord[88] and his royall auctorite untrewlie aganis your fayth and allegeance, Insafar as beand[89] constitute and solemnptlie creat Lyon king of armes, gevand your bodily aith to be trew to his hienes, ye nevertheles about the xxvii day of July the yeir of God i^m^ v^c^ Lxviii yeiris, without respect to God or your promissit fayth and allegeance, to underly trall[90] of the thingis ye wer suspectit, and voluntary and obstinatle takand upoun yow the schame and ignominy of all thir detestable and tressonabill crymes past to the castell of Dumbertane being than and as yit hald agains his hienes and his auctoritie be certane personis delait[91] rebellis to his majestie assistand[92] thame with your body counsell and laubouris in all things, alsweill be your accesory[93] art of socery divinatioun as utherwys that mycht move thame to continew in thair rebellioun, castand of[f] and renunceand be word and write \and your haill actioun/ your promissit fayth and allegeance to our soverane Lord, and travelland and procurand all means that mycht owerthraw and distroy his maist noble persoun, the estait and government of this realm establishit be parliament during his hienes minorite quhilk ye can nocht deny.

Item[94] for a common using and exercising of the art and craft of socery [*sic*] and divination gevand your self as ane that culd revell the misteris and secretis of thingis to cum To the slander of God and illusion of the peple[95] quhilk ye can nocht deny.

82 The word 'befoir' is crossed out here.
83 The scribe first wrote 'day', then amended it to 'Sunday'.
84 MS damaged: 'Ma…', plus part of a descender that may represent 'j'.
85 *Sic*. This seems to be an error for 1568. Mary was imprisoned in Lochleven Castle on 16 June 1567, and remained there until she escaped on Sunday 2 May 1568. Janet Boyman's dittay, edited below, displays a parallel interest in the first Sunday in May. If '1567' is correct, the damaged month that precedes it could be 'Marche', making the date 1567/68 by modern reckoning, but this seems less likely.
86 The words italicised here are underlined in the MS.
87 In margin: 'assiss filit'.
88 MS damaged: 'lo…'.
89 MS damaged: 'be…'.
90 *Sic*. Read 'triall'.
91 'delait' (delated): accused.
92 MS damaged: 'assista…'.
93 MS damaged; reading uncertain.
94 In margin: 'assiss filit'.
95 'illusion': deceit. This phrase was an imprecise echo of the phrase 'abusand the pepill' in the witchcraft act. For the act's terminology see Julian Goodare, 'The Scottish Witchcraft Act', *Church History*, 74 (2005), 39–67, at pp. 61–4.

3. JANET BOYMAN, EDINBURGH, 1572

INTRODUCTION

Janet Boyman was a visionary, healer and prophet who practised in Edinburgh for twenty-four years. Her dittay, edited below, is full of remarkable detail about encounters with fairies and other spirits. She provides important evidence for the cult of the 'seely wights' – fairy-like nature spirits. She was also involved in the political conspiracy of Sir William Stewart, whose case is edited above in the present volume.

The main dittay edited below calls Boyman's crime 'diabolicall', but there is otherwise nothing in these documents about the Devil. Her spirits are not equated with the Devil or demons, and there is no sign of the demonic pact that would later attain such importance in Scottish witchcraft. Instead, the authorities recognised Boyman principally as a *practitioner*. They initially thought of her as having a 'trade', a word used in the draft dittay; the main dittay changed this to 'craft'. Unlike most healers, she specialised in 'supernaturall seiknessis', which presented particular challenges to the practitioner. She found her clients among the local gentry and craftspeople.

Boyman was a practitioner of charisma and power. She possessed the power to *summon* and *command* spirits, unlike most visionaries who waited passively for their spirit-guides to appear to them.[1] She could also induce visionary experiences in her clients, warning them that strange experiences were ahead and instructing them how to cope.[2] In the detailed case that opens the accusations against her below, Alan Anderson and his wife reported experiencing frightening nocturnal noises after they had carried out a ritual that she prescribed. Most of the information in the dittay comes from Boyman's

1 For a survey of Scottish visionaries' experience, setting Boyman in comparative context, see Julian Goodare, 'Visionaries and Nature Spirits in Scotland', in Bela Mosia (ed.), *Book of Scientific Works of the Conference of Belief Narrative Network of ISFNR, 1–4 October 2014, Zugdidi* (Zugdidi: Shota Meshkia State Teaching University of Zugdidi, Georgia, 2015), 102–16.

2 Further study of this is required, but see Edward Bever, *The Realities of Witchcraft and Popular Magic in Early Modern Europe: Culture, Cognition and Everyday Life* (Basingstoke, 2008), 163–7, 236–8 and *passim*.

confession, but some material in this initial case seems to derive from statements by Anderson's unnamed wife, Boyman's client over several years.

The dittay begins, then, with a detailed account of Boyman's healing of the smith Alan Anderson. She used the sick man's sark (shirt) for divination, and performed the kind of renunciation ritual on it that many other healers would have used: she washed it, and commanded that it should be dried without using the sun. She also ordered her clients to perform a ritual without speaking. These rituals are all interesting enough, and washing a sark recurs several times in the dittay. However, this was just a prelude to one of Boyman's remarkable performances in summoning spirits.

Her characteristic procedure was to go to an 'elrich' well – a spooky or otherworldly well – on Arthur's Seat, the rugged and craggy hill near Edinburgh, where she summoned a spirit which she ordered to do her bidding. This spirit in the 'shape of a man' was, it later emerged, 'a man of our guid nychtbouris' – something like a fairy. Boyman's repeated encounters with him give him the character of a spirit-guide.[3] He appeared solid from the front, but when he turned away his back was hollow.[4] This was a vivid way of imagining a spirit that was simultaneously *like* a person and also *unlike* a person.

One important aspect of Boyman's testimony is the evidence that she provides about the cult of the seely wights.[5] The phrase 'seely wights' means 'blessed beings' or 'magical beings'. The seely wights were nature spirits rather like fairies, who could provide important information or healing power, but who could also be dangerous. Human associates of the seely wights, like Boyman, warned their clients about illnesses induced by the spirits, and tried to protect them against such illnesses. Quite possibly the 'man of our guid nychtbouris' was a seely wight, but this remains obscure, as does the precise relationship between the fairies and the seely wights. We can at least be certain that they were all nature spirits of some kind.

One of the episodes related by Boyman seems to have been her own initiation into her practices by a mentor, Maggie Denholm. Denholm healed her of an illness using a ritual with herbs and a bath, and then took her to Arthur's Seat where they performed a further ritual that led to Boyman's first encounter with her spirit-guide. There was roaring and rumbling in the sky, and Salisbury Crags heaved and made a noise. Multi-sensory, hallucinatory

3 Cf. Julian Goodare, 'Emotional Relationships with Spirit-Guides in Early Modern Scotland', in Julian Goodare and Martha McGill (eds.), *The Supernatural in Early Modern Scotland* (Manchester, 2020), 39–54.

4 For another instance of fairies with hollow backs see Emma Wilby, *The Visions of Isobel Gowdie: Magic, Witchcraft and Dark Shamanism in Seventeenth-Century Scotland* (Brighton, 2010), 43.

5 Julian Goodare, 'The Cult of the Seely Wights in Scotland', *Folklore*, 123 (2012), 198–219 (Boyman is discussed in detail at pp. 204–6); Julian Goodare, 'Seely Wights, Fairies and Nature Spirits in Scotland', in Éva Pócs (ed.), *Body, Soul, Spirits and Supernatural Communication* (Newcastle, 2019), 218–37.

experiences like this, which Denholm and Boyman did not control precisely but seem to have brought on deliberately, are examples of dissociative trances, which have been studied by Georgie Blears.[6]

There is much more in Boyman's confessions about fairies and related spirits – and about how those spirits related to the beings of orthodox Christianity. Her commands to the spirit that she summoned were made in the name of the Father, the Son, King Arthur and Queen Elspeth, thus combining two persons of the Holy Trinity with a legendary hero (a type of ghost) and a woman who was probably the queen of the fairies. In another version of the command, the Son was replaced by the Holy Ghost. She used the term 'good neighbours', a recognised euphemism for fairies, and claimed acquaintance with them when they rode at Hallowe'en. She also used the actual word 'fairies' several times. She mentioned children being taken by the fairies. She warned that a child would die because it had no heart – its heart having been taken away as the result of a blast of wind that the seely wights had brought. She was interested in fairy whirlwinds or 'evil blasts', which proved to be terrifying phenomena.

Boyman's clients were well aware of her contact with spirits. Not only did she speak openly about her dealings with the 'guid nychtbouris', but on at least one occasion she took several clients with her to Arthur's Seat when she performed her ritual. This ended in a traumatic disaster. The members of her company were scattered by a fairy whirlwind; one of them soon died as a result, and Boyman herself was taken ill. This account of being caught in a 'blast' sounds like an account of flying.[7] Her client Alan Anderson had his own nightmare vision of Boyman 'riding', presumably with fairies or other spirits. Boyman related the suicide of a woman, very possibly a client, who had experienced one of the whirlwinds that featured in her dealings with spirits. Further indications of past trauma come in Boyman's tale of having herself been subject to the fairies for seven years. One result of this 'subjection' was that during it she did not feel the pains of childbirth. She may have experienced this as a loss of a human attribute, rather than as a practical medical benefit. The overall experience seems to have been a negative one for her.[8]

Boyman was particularly interested in the future. When healing, she emphasised prognosis. She began her treatment of Anderson's illness by

[6] Georgie Blears, 'Experiencing the Invisible Polity: Trance in Early Modern Scotland', in Goodare and McGill (eds.), *The Supernatural in Early Modern Scotland*, 55–71. Boyman is discussed at pp. 60, 63–4 and 66.

[7] Julian Goodare, 'Flying Witches in Scotland', in Julian Goodare (ed.), *Scottish Witches and Witch-Hunters* (Basingstoke, 2013), 159–76; whirlwinds are discussed at pp. 164–5. For the related concept of 'blasting', considered as magical harm wrought by fairies, see Liv Helene Willumsen, *Witches of the North: Scotland and Finnmark* (Leiden, 2013), 137.

[8] For Boyman's possible traumas in the context of other comparable visionaries see Julian Goodare, 'Away With the Fairies: The Psychopathology of Visionary Encounters in Early Modern Scotland', *History of Psychiatry*, 31 (2020), 37–54.

considering 'gyf he wald mend thairof or nocht'. On two other occasions she refused to treat someone who, she predicted, would not recover. Further study of her characteristically two-part, conditional prophecies would be desirable. One form of these prophecies was 'X will happen, but, if it does not, Y will happen later'; other forms were 'if X happens, then Y will follow later', or 'X will happen by a given date, or else it will never happen'. Her cures, too, were often accompanied by two-part kill-or-cure prognoses. She seems to have seen the future as an ominous place.

Sir William Stewart, the subject of the previous case in the present volume, initiated Boyman's troubles in 1568 when he recruited her into his political conspiracy. Stewart and Boyman form an intriguing contrast: he was interested in learned magic and astrological planetary spirits, while she was in contact with folkloric nature spirits. But they shared an interest in prophecy. Boyman's confessions show that she was willing to answer Stewart's questions about future political events, and that she gave him at least some of the encouraging answers for which he had been hoping.

Boyman's prophetic language as she advises Stewart is vivid and concrete, conveying a sense of the charisma that her clients experienced in her presence. Not only will Stewart be king: he will bear the sword of honour. Not only will the queen be restored: she will tread her enemies under her feet. But she warns Stewart with equal vigour that his downfall will follow. Perhaps this warning is unsurprising, since his downfall had already occurred by the time she came to tell her story. More remarkably, she tells of a Norwegian witch who had also made prophecies to Stewart – prophecies with which she herself had disagreed. In this passage, where she asserts her identity as a prophetic practitioner of comparable status to 'the wich of Norraway', she makes an implicit admission that she herself is also a 'wich' – an admission that perhaps carries more weight as a piece of genuine self-identification than many hundreds of other coerced confessions to witchcraft.

When Stewart was at the point of execution on 15 September 1569, he named Boyman as one of the witches who had assisted him. We learn this from Boyman's own dittay, since in Stewart's own recorded confession he had identified her only by a nickname, 'Dame Steill', evidently derived from the surname of her husband, William Steill. When the authorities heard Boyman's real name, the magistrates of Edinburgh moved to arrest her, but she fled; it later emerged that she had gone to Irvine. However, she eventually returned to Edinburgh and resumed her magical practice. Her downfall seems to have been initiated by Janet Cunningham, wife of William Bothwell of Whelpside, a minor laird near Edinburgh. Cunningham had been Boyman's client, but she testified against her concerning ominous predictions that Boyman had made about the fate of the current regent, the earl of Morton. Morton became regent on 24 November 1572, so Boyman's predictions about him must have been made after that date – but not long after, because Boyman's own trial took place on 29 December 1572. Presumably Cunningham reported Boyman to the authorities, whereupon her arrest, interrogation, confession, trial and execution followed in rapid succession.

The edition below consists of three documents. The first, Boyman's main dittay, is the most important. This is a clearly written fair copy, on a single sheet of paper, well over a metre long, assembled from several smaller sheets. A few words have been worn away. The scribe writes neatly but copies carelessly. It may well have been the document used in the courtroom, since there are marginal annotations about her conviction or acquittal on specific accusations. The main dittay can be compared with a briefer draft dittay, edited as the second source below. This is less than half the length of the later, complete version. Presumably it was written after Boyman made an initial confession, but before a subsequent interrogation obtained more information from her. It has nothing about Sir William Stewart, for instance. The fact that it omits the information from Janet Cunningham, which the authorities presumably knew about even before Boyman's arrest, indicates that it is an interim document that is not seeking completeness. Its phrasing drifts between the second person ('You ...'), characteristic of a dittay, and the third person ('She ...'), characteristic of a confession. Both the main dittay and the draft dittay have occasional oddities of wording that may indicate their scribes' imperfect understanding of the notes from which they were working. Finally, the third source edited below is the brief, formal court book entry for Boyman's trial, simply recording the names of the judge and assize, and the fact that she was convicted and burned.

TEXTS

Source 1: NRS, Dittay of Janet Boyman, 1572, JC26/1/67.

Jonet Boyman spous to Williame Styill in the Cowgait Ye are Indytit and accusit For arte and part of the sorcerie witchcraft and diabolicall incantatioun usit and practesit be yow upoun umquhill Allane Andersoun smyth in the Cannongait beand seik for the tyme Ye said that ye culd nocht help him without he sand[9] yow his sark first, Be the sycht quhairof ye wald knaw quhat seiknes he had and gyf he wald mend thairof or nocht, and the sark being brocht to yow ye past thairwith to ane well[10] under Arthours Saitt thatt rynnis southwert, quhilk ye call ane elrich well, and thair maid incantatioun and invocatioun of the evill spreitis quhome ye callit upoun for to come to yow and declair

[9] 'sand': send.

[10] This word is obscured by a blot, but from the context it must be 'well'. This is corroborated by the draft dittay below.

quhat wald becum of that man, and thair come thaireftir first ane grit blast lyke a quhirll wind and thaireftir thair come the schaip of ane man and stuid on the uther syde of the well foiranent yow, To quhome ye said thir wordes or siclike, I charge the[e] in the name of the fader and the sone king Arthour and quene Elspith That the unerthlie ghing[11] schaw to the erthlie ghying [*sic*] wit and witterance[12] to the help of this seik man and that ye owther gif him his health or ellis tak him to yow and releif him of his pane, And thairefter ye weschet his sark and send it to the said umquhill Allane and bad streik it abone him the left arme of the sark abone his left arme and the rycht arme abone his rycht arme and the bodye of the sark abone his bodye, and this ye did becaus the said Alane wald not thoill[13] the sark to be put on him, he was swa wod.[14] Forder ye gaif command to his wyf That sche suld caus this be done and to keip his clois that nyght and that sche quhat evir sche hard[15] or quhat evir sche saw suld nocht speik ane word out of hir mouth, And it is of veritie alswa that quhen the said Alaneis wyfe, Takand litill heid to your commandement, kaist up the sark to dry upoun ane dure and nocht upoun the bed as ye bad, thairefter sche sitting in the hous hir allane[16] walking[17] hir husband, about midnyght thair come lyke grit wind about the hous and ane verrye gritt dyn quhilk maid hir verrie effrayit, and als thair being ane quantitie of hors schone[18] lyand in the chalmer besyde the seik man, thair wes ane grit noyce as thai had bene telland the hors schone[19] ratland throw uther,[20] And the bed, almerye[21] and all that was within the hous trimblit and the hammaris war hard knokand on the studye[22] in the buith verrye fast, Na mortale creatour being thairin for the tyme. And upoun the morne befoir ye war spokin to be onye of that hous ye come and reprovit the wyfe Becaus sche had nocht usit your directioun as ye ordainyit hir, and said to hir That giff sche wald do as ye bad hir ye suld be content to giff your lyfe giff hir husband mendit nocht of that seiknes, and giff sche wald nocht do your bidding he wald be ane crippill all his dayes, And the said Allanes wyfe for love sche bure to hir husband Causit hir servand woman do with the sark as

11 This word has first been written 'gyng', then crossed out and 'ghing' written. The draft dittay, below, also struggles with these unusual words, which may originate in a scribal error by the original note-taker. The meaning of the passage is evidently 'unearthly thing ... earthly thing', as in the phrase 'witles thing' below.

12 'witterance': utterance.

13 'thoill': tolerate.

14 'swa wod': so mad.

15 'hard': heard.

16 'hir allane': by herself.

17 'walking': waking, i.e. keeping him company while he was awake.

18 'hors schone': horseshoes.

19 'telland the hors schone': counting out the horseshoes.

20 'uther': each other.

21 'almerye' (aumbry): chest or cupboard.

22 'studye': anvil.

ye had biddin, and that nixt nycht thair was als grit dyn in the hous and the smiddie as was the uther nycht precedand, And sone thairefter he convalescit, To the mair takin quhen ye come first in to the said Allanes hous, thair being ane grit companye of wemen thairin, the said Allane spyit yow ower all thair heidis and bad sayne him fra yow[23] for he saw yow rydand yistrene.[24]

Item the said Alane within thre yeiris thairefter fell in the samin seiknes and send for yow to cum to mend him as ye did of before, ye ansuerit and sayit ye culd nocht do him na guid at that tyme, Becaus it was past Halow evin, for had thay cumit to yow befoir Halow evin Ye culd have helpit, And ye being inquirit quhairfoir on Halow evin nor ane uther day Ye ansurit Becaus the guid nychtbouris rysis[25] that day and ye had mair acquentance with thame that day nor anie uther.[26]

Item quhen the said Allanes wyfe efter his departing[27] had borne ane sone to ane uther husband and gevand the barne sowke[28] in hir armes, ye said to hir, quhairto tak ye pane to foster that barne for it hes nocht ane hart and can nocht life,[29] and it come to pas that it deit sone thaireftir, and ye being inquirit quhow ye knew that the barne wald de, ye ansuerit That it had gottin ane blast of evill wind for the moder had nocht sainit[30] it wele aneuch and gane furth of the hous and the sillye wychtis had fund it unsanit and had gevin it the blast and swa it was ane tane away schitte, And ye being inquirit quhat was the remeid to saif barnis fra that perell, ye said that giff thair had bene ane disch quhommillit[31] on the feit of the barne It had beine[32] saif.[33]

And ye being inquirit quhow ye lernit this craft, efter monye sundrye ansueris gevin be yow, sayit That ane umquhile Meggie Dennowme dwelland in the Potter raw helpit yow being seik in this maner, First sche hett walter [*sic*] in ane kettill with leves of wodbind and pot yow in it saying thir wordis, Blist Benedicite in the name of the fader and \the/ holye gost king Arthour and dame Elspeth send this witles thing hir witt agane Or ellis tak hir to yow of this warld, and this was done in the said \Meggie/[34] Dennowmes hous in the Potterraw.[35]

23 'bad sayne him fra yow': bade (that those around should) bless him to keep him away from you.
24 In margin: 'fylis in respect of this hir confession'. Also 'Confest' (in different ink).
25 *Sic*. Probably an error for 'rydis', as below.
26 In margin: 'filis'. Also 'Confest' (in different ink).
27 'departing': death.
28 'gevand … sowke' (suck): breastfeeding.
29 'leve' written first, then crossed out and 'life' written. Evidently the meaning is 'live'.
30 'sainit': blessed.
31 'quhommillit': turned over. For a comparable instance of the ritual turning over of a dish see A. E. Truckell (ed.), 'Unpublished Witchcraft Trials, Part 2', *Transactions of the Dumfriesshire and Galloway Natural History and Antiquarian Society*, 3rd ser., 52 (1976), 95–108, at p. 107.
32 'had beine': would have been.
33 In margin: 'confest' (in different ink).
34 'Bessie' written, then crossed out and 'Meggie' inserted above the line.
35 In margin: 'filis'. Also 'confest' (in different ink).

And as ye say that the said Meggie Dennowme lerit yow to wesch the sarkis and that ye within xxiiii houris eftir that ye wer weschin The said Meggie Dennowme past to the park and gait ower the wall at Sanct Leonardis to the said elrich wall[36] evin at the none tyde in the day and thair maid your prayaris, ye haldand evir the thowme of your rycht hand lukkin in your neith,[37] and as ye war cumand away and had weschin your handis at the well thair come to yow a man of our guid nychtbouris wele anewch cled to your sycht wele faceit with ane baird a blew pictowrit[38] he on the ane syde of the well and ye with the said umquhile Meggie Dennowme on the uther syde of the well, and quhen he departit he was waist behind lyke ane stok,[39] and ye hard wele the wordis that he spak bot at his departing ye say thair was rowting and rumbling in the lift[40] and the craiggis schewit[41] and dynnit, and thaireftir ye come hame togidder and the said Meggie said to yow that ye suld gett your health.[42]

Item ye haif confessit that ye haif sene twentie tymes the evill blast that is to say the wind with a thing lyke ane hatt in it quhirland about the stray[43] and ay at sic tyme thair is ane evill spreit or ane war[44] thing neir hand by, For the same yeir in the west houssis besyde Newbottill ane honest woman that dwelt in the hous with hir sone at the syght of the said quhwrll wind hangit hir self, and this say ye was the last quhirill wind that ye hard of, And ye say that thai wald nocht suffer this woman to be bureit within the parroche kirk yaird Bot bureit hir in ane litill chapell, and forder ye say that hir dochter and hir guideris tald yow the samin and that thai saw the said quhirll wind betuix the hall and the chalmer.[45]

Item ye grant that Jonet Cwninghame spous to William Boithwele of Quhelpsyde send to yow twa sarkis to weisch, The ane was ane gentill womannis quhome ye call Ladye Giltownes quhais seiknes ye culd nocht mend and thairfoir ye wald nocht weische hir sark.[46]

36 *Sic*. Evidently read 'well'.

37 *Sic*. This last word should evidently be 'neive', with the phrase 'lukkin in your neive' meaning 'clenched in your fist'. Keeping one's thumb inside one's hand was noted as a protection against bewitchment in Naarden, Netherlands, in the modern period: Willem de Blécourt, 'Boiling Chickens and Burning Cats: Witchcraft in the Western Netherlands, 1850–1925', in Willem de Blécourt and Owen Davies (eds.), *Witchcraft Continued: Popular Magic in Modern Europe* (Manchester, 2004), 89–106, at p. 99.

38 *Sic*. This passage apparently sets out to describe the spirit's dress, but the scribe has garbled something, possibly omitting a line of text.

39 'waist behind lyke ane stok': wasted (away) behind like a stick.

40 'rowting and rumbling in the lift': roaring and rumbling in the sky.

41 *Sic*. The meaning appears to be 'heaved', with the phrase 'schewit and dynnit' meaning 'heaved and made a noise'.

42 In margin: 'filis'. Also 'confest' (in different ink).

43 'stray': straw.

44 'war': worse.

45 In margin: 'filis'. Also 'confest' (in different ink).

46 In margin: 'filis'. Also 'confest' (in different ink).

Item quhen ye war desyrit to help ane woman in Grantoun callit Jonett Scott quha hes lyne seik and kepit bed sen Mertymes was twa yeir,[47] and ye said to the said Jonet Cwninghame that giff ye had hir sark ye suld tell giff ye culd do hir guid, Quhilk sark being brocht to yow ye did thairwith as ye thoucht guid and send it agane to Grantoun and bad put it upoun the woman, And gif sche war ony thing bettir within nyne dayes thaireftir Sche wald nocht faill to convales of that seiknes, And thaireftir ye past doun your self to Grantoun and layit ane plaister to hir heid quhilk ye say was maid onlie of barme[48] and Ry breid, and als maid ane bath of certane herbis sic as wodbein [*about 2 words worn away*] feggis and okstaris[49] thairwith and did use sic sorcerye as ye thocht convenient upoun hir, To the takin Jeane Murray servand to the said Jonet Cwninghame and at hir command past with yow to Grantoun, As ye your self and sche baith confessit, And forder ye haif said that the said guid wyfe in Grantoun sall nocht faill to amend of this seiknes, For that hes bene Revelit to yow at the wesching of the sark.[50]

Item ye haif usit the said sorcerie and witchcraft upoun William Craig broder to Jo… [*1 word blank*] Craig the spous to Henrye Nevin the blind taburnare[51] quhais sark ye causit wesch of your maner, and bad wesch it after the doun ganging of the sone and dry it in the nycht and that without owther the sycht of the sone or onye fyre, and putt it on the seik man befoir the sone rysing And he suld owther mend of the seiknes within nyne dayes or incontinent depart,[52] And swa was done to the said William Craig.[53]

Item ye war art and part with umquhile Williame Stewart als lyone herauld in his abhominable magik, wichcraft and sorcerie as ye haif confest,[54] and namelie quhen the said umquhile William requirit of yow responce of certane thingis tocum, and namelie quhen the quene suld escaip furth of Lochlevin, Sayand will nocht the quene be furth befoir the first Soneday of Maii,[55] your ansure was The quene suld cum furth the first Soneday of Maii or ellis never, lyke as sche did, And als quhen he inquirit at yow giff he suld marye the quene and beir the swerd of honour and be king, ye sayit to him agane That he that maid him ane king suld mak him ane dirtin dring,[56] And quhen he inquirit at

47 'sen Mertymes was twa yeir': since Martinmas (11 November) two years ago, i.e. 1570.

48 'barme': yeast.

49 This passage is difficult. The most likely reading is 'feggis', figs, but the text is worn, and it could be 'seggis', sedges, or even (if the first letter has been crossed out) 'eggis'. As for 'okstaris', the reading is clear; if it is correct, the word means 'armpits'. However, the meaning is hard to interpret. Just conceivably the scribe has omitted a line of text in which it was said that Janet Scott was to be put in the bath up to her armpits. A more likely error is that the scribe has written 'okstaris' in error for 'oystaris', oysters.

50 In margin: 'filis'. Also 'confest' (in different ink).

51 'taburnare' (taverner): innkeeper.

52 'incontinent depart': immediately die.

53 In margin: 'filis'. Also 'confest' (in different ink).

54 In margin: 'filis of arte and part with him in wichecraft and sorcerie'.

55 Mary Queen of Scots escaped from Lochleven Castle on Sunday 2 May 1568.

56 'dirtin dring': filthy wretch.

yow quhat deid he suld,[57] ye ansurit he suld de in his[58] fais handis[59] and that the wich of Norraway wes ane leyard[60] quhilk had foirspookin thai thingis to him, Thir thingis haif ye confessit.[61]

And to the mair takyn The said umquhile William at the hour of his death planelie confest That ye had revelit to him That the quene wald be furth of Lochlevin the first Soneday of Maii, That sche wad be maister ower Scotland, That sche wald tred with hir feit uppone all hir ennemies, That the said umquhile William wald be verrie grit with hir and that he suld be mareit upoun hir and that sche suld beir bairnis to the said William quhilkis suld regnne ower this realme.[62]

Item ye according to your accustumat maner[63] abusand Christeane peple hes confessit That the fareis rydis ay on Halow evin, and that the last tyme ye war in the park upoun Arthours Saitt ye saw thame and that thair war with yow umquhile Jonet Henderson the moder to George Purrok and Bessie Purrok hir dochter and thair servand, quha past all thair to seik auntowris and antouris thai gatt,[64] For with ane blast thai war all sched sundrye[65] and come nocht hame togidder, And the said umquhile Jonet tuik sic fray[66] thairat That eftir hir hamecuming within few dayes sche departit, and ye your self lay four or fyve dayes and was nocht wele, And this ye haif confest And swa ye are art and part of the slauchter of the said umquhile Jonet Hendersoun.[67]

Item ye haif Be way of prophecye schawin to the said Jonet Cwninghame That the Regent quhome God preserwe sall not leif quhill Newermes[68] and gif he past Newermes he suld nocht pas Candilmes be na way, To ye The said Jonet Cwninghame and Jehane Murray hir servand hes planelie awowit[69] this in your face and sworne the samin to be trew, And als ye your self haif confessit That ye said at that tyme in the said Jone Cwninghames hous befoir maister Robert Young That thair wald be ane change at Newyeirmes and it wald be fochtin within the toun of Edinburgh And that the castel wald be randrit to the king befoir Candilmes,[70] And this ye haif confessit upone your examinatioun.[71]

57 A word seems to have been omitted here. The phrase is evidently 'what death he should die'.

58 Written 'his^r', but this appears to be an error.

59 'de in his fais handis': die in his foes' hands.

60 'leyard': liar.

61 In margin: 'assisa' (in different ink); 'acquit'.

62 In margin: 'assisa' (in different ink).

63 'hes confessit That' has been crossed out here.

64 'to seik auntowris and antouris thai gatt': to seek answers, and answers they got.

65 'sched sundrye': driven apart.

66 'fray': fear.

67 In margin: 'confest' (in different ink).

68 'quhill Newermes' (New-year's-mas): until New Year, apparently the future 1 January 1573. The current regent was James Douglas, fourth earl of Morton.

69 'awowit' (avowed): asserted.

70 At the time of Boyman's trial, during the Marian civil wars, Edinburgh Castle was held by the queen's party.

71 In margin: 'confest'.

Item ye haif confessit That ye war sewin yeir subiectt to the farye and that during all that tyme ye culd do na thing quhill that courss war rin out, and that within thai sevin yeiris ye bure fyve bairnis quhairof ye nevir felt paine in your bering, Bot sen the sevin yeir was run out ye haif borne sundrye bairnis sensyne quhairof ye haif sufferit payne as uther wemen do.[72]

Item ye haif continewalie be the space of xxiiii yeiris bypast or thairbye gevin your self furth for ane wyiss woman That culd mend diverss seiknessis and namelie bairnis that ar tane away with the farye,[73] men and wemen That war gane lycht[74] and sic uther supernaturall seiknessis, Takand proffeit thairfoir And swa drawand the hertis of the peple frome thair God.

And swa for haifing conversatioun, familiaritie and speche with spreittis and swa for ane commoun and notorious wich, sorcerare, nigromanceir and abusare of the peple of God[75] Be geving to thame responsis upoun difficulteis and hid materis of thingis tocum and of tint[76] and stollin geir, and als for ane commoun and notorious charmer and using of invocatioun, crossingis and conjuratiounis upoun dum creatouris, pekillis and coirnis of quheit, stanes, herbes, salvis, dissavand and deludand the peple under cullour and pretence of medecine and geving of drinkis to thame biddand thame beleve yow, and of observand dayes, tymes and seasownis of the yeir in geving of your ansueres and making of your inchantmentis, To the contempt of God and aganis the tennour of the lawis and actis of parliament of this realme, Incurrand the paine of deid contenit in the saidis actis, Quhilk ye can nocht deny.[77]

The same Takin The tyme[78] of the said Williams convictioun Thair being ane chairge directit be umquhile James erle of Murray than[79] Regent To the provost and baillies of Edinburgh For taking and apprehending of yow, ye being adverteist thairof fled of the toun to Irwing quhair ye Remanit during all the tyme of the said umquhile Regentis lifetyme and nevir Returnit to his departing,[80] Fering to be puneist as is notour be your awin confessioun quhilk ye can nocht denye.[81]

72 In margin: 'confest' (in different ink).

73 A reference to the belief in changelings. For more details of this, see the case of Isobel Watson, edited below in the present volume.

74 'gane lycht': become deranged in their minds.

75 An echo of the phraseology of the witchcraft act, which mentioned 'witchcraftis, sorsarie or necromancie' and 'abusand the pepill'.

76 'tint': lost.

77 In margin: 'filis'.

78 Text worn; reading uncertain.

79 'than': then. This passage refers back to the trial of Sir William Stewart on 15 September 1569, when the earl of Moray was regent.

80 'to his departing': until his death. The Regent Moray was assassinated on 21 January 1570.

81 In margin: 'confest' (in different ink). Endorsed: 'Witches Dittaye'.

Source 2: NRS, Draft Dittay of Janet Boyman, 1572, JC40/1/1.

Jonet Boyman witch said schee could not cure or help[82] Allan Andersone smyth in the Cannogait without he send to hir his sark be the sight quhairof[83] schee could knaw quhat seiknes he had and gif schoe could mend him thairof or nocht, quha eftir hir ressait of the sark schoe past thairwith to an well under the arthor sut[84] that runs southward quhilk shoe callit an elrich well and thair mad[85] incantatione and Invocatione[86] of the evill spreit to come to hir and declair quhat wald come of the man, And thair cam thaireftir first an grit blast lyke a quhirlewind and thaireftir \thair cam/[87] the schap of an man and stud one the uthir syd of the well *foiranent hir to quhom shee said thir words or siclyk I chairge Yow in the nam of the father and the sone king Arthour and quene Elspeth that ye unerthelie ghing [sic] shaw to the earthlie*[88] *ghying wit and wtterance to the help of this seik man and that ye owther giff him his healthe*[89] or ells tak him to yow and releive him of his pan[e], And thaireftir shoe wish hir[90] sark and send it to umquhyle Allan and bad streik it abone him, the left arme of the sark above his left arme and the rycht arme thairof above his rycht arme and the body of the sak [*sic*] above his body, And this shoe did becaus the said Alan wald nocht[91] tholl the sark to be put one him, he was soe wod. Farder shoe gave command to his wyfe that shoe sould caus this be done and to keip him clos that nycht and that quhat evir shoe hard or saw sould not speik an word out of hir mouth, bot Allanes wyf not fallowing hir directione in hinging the sark to dry upone ane dur and not upone the bed as shoe bad, schoe sitting walking hir husband that nycht about midnycht Thair cam lyk an grit [*sic*] round about the hous and an very grit dyn quhilk mad hir very affrayed, And thair being \some/ hors schone in the chalmer besyd the seik man Allan thair was an grit noys as thai had bene telland the schone ratland throw uther, and the bed almery and all that was in the hous trimbled and the hamers war hard knokand on the studie in the buith very fast, na creatour being thairin for the tyme, And upone the morne ye reprovet the wyfe that shoe uset nocht your directione, for ye ssad[92] gif shoe wald follow the samyn ye sould gif your lyf gif hir husband mendit not of his seiknes bot gif nocht he wald be an cryple all his days, And hir woman using the sark the nixt nycht as ye directed hir husband mendit.

82 'William B' has been crossed out here.
83 'be the syght quhairof' (repeated) has been crossed out here.
84 *Sic*. The scribe has run several words together (as he often does): 'underthearthor'. The meaning is evidently 'under Arthur's Seat'.
85 Probable reading. An insertion at this point has been crossed out.
86 'and Invocatione' (repeated) has been crossed out here.
87 'lyke' has been crossed out and 'thair cam' inserted above the line.
88 'ghing' has been crossed out here.
89 The words italicised here are underlined in the MS.
90 *Sic*. Read 'washed his'.
91 'sp...' has been crossed out here.
92 *Sic*. Read 'said'.

Item within thrie yeiris eftir he falling in the same seiknes send for yow to help mend him as befoir, Ye ansuered ye could not that tyme becaus it was past Hallowevin for[93] had thai cum to yow befoir Hallow evin ye could have helpit, And ye being inquyret quhairfoir on Hallowevin nor any uther day, ye answeret because the good nychtbours resp[94] that day And ye had mair acquentance with tham that day nor any uther.

Item the said Allanes wyfe being thaireftir geving souk to hir bairne ye said to hir, quhairfoir tak ye paynes to foster that barne for it hes not an heart and cannot live, and it followit that it deiet sone eftir, ye being inquyret how ye[95] knew it wald die, answerit it had gottin an blast of evill wind and the mother had not sand it weill anneughe and the sillie witches[96] finding it out of the hous unsaind had gevin it the blast and sua it was an tane away schit, Ye being ynquyret quhat was the remeid to saiff bairnes fra that perell Said, gif an dish had bene quhomlet one the feit of the bairne it had bene saiff.

Ye being inquyret how ye leirnit the said tred[97] answerit Megie Denholme in the Potterraw helpit yow being seik in this maner, First shoe het water in an kettill with leaves of woodbind and put yow in it, saying In the name of the fader and the holy gest king Arthour and dame Elspet send this witles thing hir wit agan or els tak hir to yow aff this worald, and this was done in the said Megis hous in Pot…[98]

Item ye have sene tuentie tymes the evill blast that is to say the wind with an thing lyk an hat in it quhirland about the stray And ay at sic tyme thair is an evill spreit or ane war thing neir hand by, confessit be yow.

Item William Crag being seik ye[99] caused wesh his sark in the maner, That it be wishin [*sic*] eftir the doun going of the sone and dryit in the nyght without the sight of the sone or the fyre, And put it one the seik man befoir the sone ryseing and he sould ather mend of his seiknes within nyne dayes or incontinent depairt and sua was done.

Item ye confessit that the fareis rydis apon Hallow evin, And the last tyme ye was in the park on Arthour Seat ye saw thame, thair being with yow umquhile Janet Hendersone, Bessie Purok and thair servand quha past to yow thair to seik antouris and antouris ye gat, for in an blast of wind ye war all shed sindrie and come nocht hame togidder,[100] the said Jonet Hendersone for feir deit within 8 dayis eftir and ye lay 4 or 5 dayis seik.

93 'befoir' has been crossed out here.

94 *Sic.* Read 'ride'.

95 'being in' has been crossed out here.

96 *Sic.* Read 'wychtis', as in the final dittay above.

97 'tred': trade. The final dittay, above, switches to the word 'craft'.

98 *Sic.* Read 'in Potterrow'. The scribe has reached the end of a line and forgotten to complete the word on the next line.

99 'wyth' has been crossed out here.

100 1 or 2 illegible words inserted above the line.

Source 3: NRS, Justiciary Court Book, 1566–1573, JC1/13.

{fo. 219r.-v.} Curia tenta xxixo die mensis Decembris anno &c lxxiio per Magistrum Thomam Craig[101]

Intran

Jonet[102] Boyman spous to William Steill delatit of diverss crymis of witchecraft.[103]

Assisa

Johne Dunbar burges of Edinburgh
Alexander Thomesoun thair
David Levingstoun thair
Edward Galbrayt thair
John Arthurmill[104] thair
James Foirman thair
John Watsoun
Charles Geddes
James Aikman
Robert Gourlaw
John Harwod thair
David Kinloch thair
Archibald Senyeor thair
William Broun thair
James Neisbet thair
William Patersoun thair
Andro Lummisden thair

[101] 'Court held 29 December 1572 by Master Thomas Craig'. The venue is not given, but when a venue is given for other trials around this time it is always the tolbooth of Edinburgh. The trial judge, Thomas Craig, was an advocate who later became a celebrated jurist: John W. Cairns, 'Thomas Craig (1538?–1608)', *ODNB*. He had also published Latin poems celebrating the Stewart royal family: Steven J. Reid and David McOmish (eds.), *Corona Borealis: Scottish Neo-Latin Poets on King James VI and his Reign, 1566–1603* (Glasgow: Association for Scottish Literary Studies, 2020), 39–65.

[102] The word 'Steill' has been crossed out here.

[103] In margin: 'convict and brunt'.

[104] Reading unclear.

4. LEITH WITCHES, 1579

INTRODUCTION

Three witches were tried in a session of the regality court of Broughton on 18 July 1579: Christian Douglas, Janet Fulton and Janet Carswell. Douglas and Fulton were both from Leith, and Carswell was probably from there too (since she was tried by the same assize). Douglas and Fulton were both convicted and executed; Carswell was acquitted. Here we have the minutes of the court, but not the full dittays.

We have some suggestive and even vivid fragments of information about Christian Douglas's case, but the details are obscure because the scribe, in writing up the minutes, seems to have confused her with one of the other two accused persons. The central part of the record of her case makes 'Cristiane' the victim of the witchcraft of 'Jonet', with an apparent instance of sleep paralysis in which the victim and her husband spend the night of Easter Saturday and Easter Sunday being tormented.[1] Perhaps this whole episode really belongs in the trial of Janet Fulton (the 'Jonet' who was convicted). Yet the episode is described as 'conversance with the Devill' on Christian Douglas's part. Whoever was being accused at this point, this case is thus a remarkably early instance of overtly demonic witchcraft.

Janet Fulton, alias 'Fitlowne', seems to have been a classic neighbourhood witch, being described as responsible for the deaths of several people over several years and as having had a neighbourhood reputation for witchcraft. She had previously lived in Prestonpans. While she was there, she had been summoned for witchcraft before a justice ayre at Haddington, but had fled rather than face trial – which the Broughton court treated as firm evidence of guilt.

Finally, Janet Carswell was clearly a magical practitioner. Several of her cures were described in detail, with unusual vocabulary. She was said to have cast sickness on an ox that she had sold, and to have been called a witch, but in general was seen as doing good rather than harm. A laird was named among her clients. She was acquitted.

[1] For sleep paralysis see Margaret Dudley and Julian Goodare, 'Outside In or Inside Out: Sleep Paralysis and Scottish Witchcraft', in Julian Goodare (ed.), *Scottish Witches and Witch-Hunters* (Basingstoke, 2013), 121–39.

The regality court of Broughton operated in tandem with the Canongate burgh court. The trial took place in the Canongate tolbooth, and the regality court's minutes were recorded in the Canongate burgh court book. The regality court showed no hesitation in imposing the death penalty for witchcraft. The mention of the justice ayre of Haddington is also interesting. Both these types of court – regality courts and justice ayres – would cease to try witchcraft once witch-hunting became more common.[2]

TEXT

Source: Edinburgh City Archives, Burgh Court Book of Canongate, 1577–1580, SL150/1/3.

{p. 370} Curia Justiciarie Regalitatis et baronie de Brochtoun tenta in pretorio burgi Vicican[on]orum Coram Johanne Grahame et Johanne Watsoun ballivis deputatis eiusdem xviiio Julii 1579.[3] *{p. 371}*

Williame Hume in Leyth
Williame Downy thair
James Gourlaw thair
George Bennet smyth thair
Henry Verno smyth thair
Henry Jamesoun thair
Johnne Quhippo thair
Johnne Downy thair

\William/[4] Drumo thair
Niniane Hammiltoun
Robert Greissum
Richart Henrysoun
Mr James Sandelands[5]
Johnne Wetherspune
Andro Lowrie
Adame Weddell

Johnne Henrysoun
Johnne Bains in Leyth
Johnne Quhytehynde in Wauchtoun
Nicole Biehynde in Clekgorne
William Keir in Markill
Johnne Johnestoun in Myrrielawis
Hary Lermount
George Williamesoun
James Robesoun in Myrrilawis

2 Julian Goodare, 'Witch-Hunting and the Scottish State', in Julian Goodare (ed.), *The Scottish Witch-Hunt in Context* (Manchester, 2002), 122–45, at pp. 126–30.

3 'Court of justiciary of the regality and barony of Broughton, held in the tolbooth of the Canongate before John Graham and John Watson, bailies depute of the same, 18 July 1579'.

4 This word is written above 'Johnne', which has been crossed out.

5 This name has been bracketed by two symbols '¢', apparently added later, probably to indicate that he acted as chancellor of the assize.

The quhilk day the said Cristiane Dowglas the spous of Johnne Thomsoun indueller in Leyth on the north syde of the brig thairof wes convict be the forsaid assyiss of the poynt of wichcraft and socerie [*sic*] And speciallie of haiffing conversance with the Devill upoun Pasche[6] evin lastwes,[7] Be the quhilk socerie the said Cristiane and hir said spous wes vexit and tormentit with grit seiknes fra ten hours that same nycht to twelf hours on Pasche day quhairby thair bed continuallie schuke and trimblit during the said space and this of the said Jonetis[8] awin confessioun,[9] as alsua be hir inchantmentis, socerie and plaine wichecraft of Laying of grit seiknes, Infirmiteis and trubles upoun diverss and sindrie personis notourlie knawin and practisit be hir at sindrie tymes of before, dwynning thame[10] thairby continuallie to thair Lyves end and deceiss, And siclik the said Jonet wes convict as ane commoun Rank wiche, ane usar and practisar of plaine socerie and wichcraft thir diverss and sindrie yeiris Lastbipast notourlie knawin be the forsaid assyiss expres agains the law of God, as ass[11] be diverss utheris persouns quhome be complaintis wes gevin in agains the said Jonet for using of the samin by ony thame schawand to hir speciall signes and taknis thairof, Quhilk cryme and poynt of wichcraft in having conversatioun with the Devill quhairby the said Johnne Thomsoun and his said spous[12] wes trublit with grit seiknes and thair bed schuik during the space foirsaid in maner abovementioneit the said Cristiane {*p. 372*} Dowglas plainlie confessit the samin and being convict thairof as said is wes adjugit to be tane to the north syde of the brig of Leyth And thair to be bund to ane staik and worreit[13] thairat quhill scho be deid And thairefter hir haill body to be brint in ase,[14] And this wes gevin for dome and pronunceit be the mowth of Peter Alexander dempster of the said court for the tyme.

The quhilk day Jonet Fultoun the spous of Alexander Dormount feirar[15] als callit Fitlowne[16] indueller in Leyth on the north syde thairof wes convict be the foirsaid assyiss of the poyntis of plaine wichcraft and socerie usit and practisit be the said Jonet upoun diverss and sindrie personis thir diverss

6 'Pasche': Easter, which in 1579 fell on 19 April.

7 'lastwes' (last was): the most recent.

8 Here the scribe starts to become confused about names. Two other persons called 'Jonet' were tried in this session of the court, but the present trial is that of Christian Douglas.

9 In margin: 'Dowglas usta'. '*Usta*' (Latin): burned.

10 'dwynning thame': causing them to dwindle or waste away.

11 *Sic*. Read 'als' (also).

12 After the word 'spous', the scribe has written 'bod…' and then crossed it out. This 'spous' is Christian Douglas, the person being tried. At this point the text seems to suggest that she and her husband John Thomson were *victims* of the witchcraft of 'Jonet', but a few words later the text reverts to treating Christian Douglas as the person who is being tried.

13 'worreit': strangled.

14 'ase': ash, ashes.

15 *Sic*. Possibly 'feriar', i.e. ferryman, is meant. Or this may be a nickname.

16 This nickname, presumably originating from wordplay on Fulton's surname, seems to mean 'foot-loon' ('loon': rascal).

yeiris bipast be Laying of grit infirmiteis, vexatiouns and tormentis upoun thame Quhairby and be hir socerie and wichcraft hes vigousit and duynit[17] sindrie personis to thair deid and deces onlie throw hir occasioun,[18] To the mair takin quhairof[19] the said Jonet is convict for being fugitive fra the airis of Hadingtoun[20] efter that scho wes indytit thairto as ane commoun Rank wiche and usar of socerie notourlie kend,[21] Knawand hir thairby to be ane usar and practisar of the same filthie and wickeit cryme Lik as scho wes bruitit for the samyn during the haill space that duelt[22] in Prestoun Pannis[23] for utherwaiss gif the said Jonet had beine saikles[24] and Innocent of the said cryme had nocht bene fugitive nor fled away out the said Prestoun Pannis quhairin scho wes duelland for the tyme bot had Remanit and compeirit before the Justice of the saidis airis of Hadyngtoun and tane hir to the censament[25] of God and ane guid assyiss quhidder scho had bene Innocent or filthie of the foirsaid cryme, And siclik the said Jonet is convict as said is as ane commoun wiche, usar of socerie and Layar of diseassis and infirmiteis upoun sindrie persouns thir diverss yeris bipast etc, As in hir dittay and accusatioun gevin in thairanent at mair Lenth is contenit etc, Quhilk Cryme and poynt of the said Jonets being fugitive fra the said airis of Hadingtoun is Knawand hir self to be giltie of the cryme foirsaid Scho planlie confessit, And being convict thairof and of utheris poynts above specifiet as said is wes adjudgit tobe tane to the said north syde of the brig of Leyth and thair tobe bund to ane staik and worait thairat quhill scho be deid and thairefter hir haill body tobe brint in ass And this wes gevin for dome and pronuncit be the mowth of Peter Alexander dempster of the said court for the tyme.

The quhilk day the said Jonet[26] Carswell als[27] Caldueil being indytit and accusit of the airt and pairt of socerie and commoun wichcraft and thairby Laying of diseassis, infirmiteis and {*p. 373*} seiknes upoun diverss persouns and speciallie of curing and mending of Patrik Hepburne of Fortoun be the space of fowr yeiris syne or thairby be Laying of plaisteris and bathis of Luvis[28] and blak snailles upoun ane pece blak mantillene[29] thairunto, And als of Laying of grit seiknes and tormentis upoun ane ox sauld be hir and Williame Bissat hir

17 'vigousit and duynit': both words mean 'declined', here used transitively.

18 'throw hir occasioun': through her action.

19 'To the mair takin [i.e. token] quhairof': to the further proof of which.

20 'airis of Hadingtoun': justice ayres (criminal courts) of Haddington.

21 In margin: 'Fultowne usta'. '*Usta*' (Latin): burned.

22 *Sic*. The meaning is 'the period in which she dwelt'.

23 Prestonpans, in Haddingtonshire, was where Fulton had lived when she had been accused in Haddington.

24 'saikles': guiltless.

25 'censament': judgement.

26 'Cald…' crossed out here.

27 'als': alias.

28 'love': a kind of crape or mourning-cloth.

29 'mantillene': possibly from French '*manteline*', a short cloak.

spous to Eufame Lamb, Lik as also be the said Jonetis socerie and wichcraft of curing and mending of Patrik Lethamis leg cuik to Robert Hwme in the Hewch be Laying of the bluid, creiss[30] and fell[31] of ane ganer[32] upoun ane pece blak clayth thairunto,[33] And sa be hir socerie be[34] thairof mending of the samin and als brutit as ane commoun wiche and usar of socerie etc, As at mair Lenth is contenit in the said Jonets dittay gevin in aganis hir tharanent etc, Quhilks crymes of wichcraft and socerie the said Jonet Carswell alluterlie denyit and tuik hir to the censament of God and the assyis abovewrittin, Quhilk assiss past furth of court And efter Lang consultatioun and avisement had and tane be thame upoun the said Jonets dittay and accusatioun And being weill and ryiplie[35] avisit thairwith and haill contentis thairof, Inenterit againe haiffand God and guid conscience afoir ee[36] fand and deliverit the said Jonet Carswell Innocent and clene of the saidis crymes of wichcraft and socerie and of all airt and pairt thairof and of utheris poyntis contenit in hir dittay allegit committit and done be hir, And thairfore the baillie deputes foirsaids decernit the said Jonet acquite of the samyn in all tyme heirefter.

30 'creiss' (grease): tallow.
31 'fell': skin.
32 'ganer': gander, male goose.
33 In margin: 'Carswell als Caldwell acquit'.
34 *Sic.* After this second 'be', a further word has been crossed out.
35 'ryiplie' (ripely): thoughtfully, carefully.
36 'ee': eye.

5. ISOBEL WATSON, PERTHSHIRE, 1590

INTRODUCTION

This case came to the attention of the authorities in April 1590 when James Kinnaird and his wife Janet Henderson, in Auchlinsky in the parish of Glendevon, southern Perthshire, were discovered to have some magical objects: nine grains of wheat, a piece of rowan tree, and the joint of a man's finger. This information may have emerged during a commissioner's visitation of the presbytery or diocese. The presbytery of Stirling summoned Kinnaird, who testified that the objects belonged to Isobel Watson. Possibly she had provided them to help Kinnaird's wife in childbirth. Kinnaird brought Watson with him to the presbytery, whose attention was immediately focused on her.[1]

Watson said that she was aged about sixty. She seems to have grown up in Muthill and spent her young adulthood in Perth. Her husband, a fisherman, had died three years after the Reformation, thus in about 1563, and since then she had begged for a living, mainly in the Glendevon area.[2] She was a magical practitioner and apparently a midwife, healing people and finding lost and stolen goods. What particularly attracted the presbytery's attention, however, was Watson's account of her visions of fairies and visits to fairyland – visions that, she said, she had experienced since the age of eighteen.

These visions included some extraordinary folkloric detail, making this case one of Scotland's most valuable sources of material for fairy belief. Perceptive discussions of it have been published by Michael F. Graham and P. G. Maxwell-Stuart.[3] Just a few points may be picked out here. Watson mentioned 'Nicneven', known from other sources as a name or sobriquet for

[1] For an overview of Isobel Watson's case see Ciaran Jones, 'Isobel Watson: Fairies and Witchcraft in 16th-Century Perthshire', *History Scotland*, 20, no. 2 (March-April 2020), 13–15.

[2] She may be the same as the Isobel Watson who was received into the hospital (poorhouse) of Perth in 1580 and was noted as receiving weekly alms in 1585: *Perth Kirk Session Books, 1577–1590*, ed. Margo Todd (Woodbridge: SHS, 2012), 156, 318.

[3] Michael F. Graham, *The Uses of Reform: 'Godly Discipline' and Popular Behavior in Scotland and Beyond, 1560–1610* (Leiden, 1996), 299–301; P. G. Maxwell-Stuart, *Satan's Conspiracy: Magic and Witchcraft in Sixteenth-Century Scotland* (East Linton, 2001), 115–21.

more than one witch, and associated particularly with southern Perthshire. This may offer an opportunity to take that subject further than has been done by previous scholars.[4] Watson's case predates the North Berwick panic by some months, but she provides an additional piece of information on it by mentioning that during four visits to the fairy court she had seen Richard Graham, the necromancer who would later play a central role in that panic. Not all of Watson's visions were of fairies, since she also testified to having received a vision of Jesus in the form of an angel, who had informed her about goods stolen from one of her clients.[5]

On fairies themselves, Watson mentioned the famous 'teind to hell' that they were said to pay, and gave a detailed account of a changeling – a child taken by the fairies. She discussed the 'meikill stanes' of Gleneagles, a megalithic stone circle, attributed to the fairies; the fairies gaining things from humans; visiting the fairy court at each change of the moon; and acting herself as a midwife to the elf queen in that court. It turned out that the magical objects that had provoked the investigation had distinct powers: to keep a sleeping man from danger, to protect a man from whirlwinds, to cure toothache, and to protect Watson herself from being beaten by the fairies as she had been in the past. Watson had seen various people, both alive and dead, at the fairy court, including her own former lover, Thomas McRae. She thought that the world had been better in the past, when the fairies rode more often.

During her imprisonment, Watson had a conversion experience of some kind, giving herself to God and refusing to renew the temporary promise that she said she had made to the Devil. As a result, she said, the Devil beat her severely. Some of her ideas about the Devil seem to have been supplied to her by the interrogators (they persuaded her that her vision of Jesus had actually been the Devil), and perhaps it was really the interrogators who had beaten her. However, Watson also described being beaten by the fairies. Her ideas about an agreement with the Devil may also have been influenced by the anointing ritual which, she said, she had experienced at the hands of the king of the fairies. The interrogators failed to probe what she said about her temporary promise to the Devil. This was an early case, and the demonic pact was not yet as well known in Scotland as it would later become.[6] The presbytery summed Watson up as a 'Consultar with the Devill and the ded', recognising the Devil's role but also, unusually, specifying her encounters with ghosts separately.

4 Alison Hanham, '"The Scottish Hecate": A Wild Witch Chase', *Scottish Studies*, 13 (1969), 59–65; Julian Goodare, 'Nicneven (fl. 1560s)', in Elizabeth Ewan, Rose Pipes, Jane Rendall and Siân Reynolds (eds.), *The New Biographical Dictionary of Scottish Women* (2nd edn., Edinburgh, 2018), 340.

5 On folkloric angels, see Martha McGill, 'Angels in Early Modern Scotland', in Julian Goodare and Martha McGill (eds.), *The Supernatural in Early Modern Scotland* (Manchester, 2020), 86–106, at pp. 94–7.

6 For a review of the debate on the origins of the demonic pact in Scotland see Julian Goodare, 'Witchcraft in Scotland', in Brian P. Levack (ed.), *The Oxford Handbook of Witchcraft in Early Modern Europe and Colonial America* (Oxford, 2013), 300–17, at pp. 303–4.

Watson was interrogated at least twice – firstly before the presbytery of Stirling, and secondly in the tolbooth, evidently having been sent there as a prisoner. On the second occasion she changed her story at several points, possibly under pressure. The clerk wrote up the minutes of both interrogations together, but made some attempts to distinguish between them. Two points from the second interrogation have been added in the margin, while others are in the main text. The two interrogations require careful disaggregation.

Although Watson may have been interrogated coercively and even tortured, the text indicates that she retained some initiative in accounting for herself. She had travelled voluntarily to Stirling, about twenty miles from Glendevon, in order to tell her story to the presbytery. On one occasion she refused to give names that she was asked for, and then said that 'scho wald tell na mair now', which the interrogators accepted. She urged her interrogators to speak of the fairies with respect. Historians may be grateful to her for her outspokenness, but she probably did not realise that it would get her executed.

Isobel Watson's case had an aftermath in June, when William Wilson alias Culross and Elizabeth Stalker alias Huggotour were summoned for allegedly slandering each other as witches. Both lived in the parish of Dollar, which was in Clackmannanshire but adjacent to Watson's home parish of Glendevon. Wilson had visited Watson in prison in Stirling – surely a foolhardy act – and obtained advice from her about how to restore his cows' milk. Watson apparently advised him to seek Stalker's assistance. The parish minister's enquiries about this may well have given rise to the initial slander accusations.

Did Watson give this advice because she knew that Stalker was a magical practitioner who might be able to help, or because Wilson informed her that he suspected Stalker of having bewitched his cows herself? Stalker's reaction suggests that the second possibility is more likely. Wilson knew that another man, David Brown, had also sought the restoration of his cows' milk from Stalker. When the presbytery put this to Stalker, she replied that Brown had made this request 'without ony occasione done be hir'; in other words, she denied that she had previously bewitched Brown. This suggests that others around her did think, or suspect, that she bewitched people.

However, if the presbytery initially suspected witchcraft, they soon changed their minds. And, because neither Wilson nor Stalker persisted in accusing the other of witchcraft, the slander case fizzled out too. Eventually Wilson was ordered to perform repentance – not for slander, and certainly not for witchcraft, but for having asked Stalker to restore his cows' milk (evidently this was thought to have been a superstitious request), and for having consulted the witch Watson. Stalker's case was referred back to the parish minister for a further report as to whether she practised witchcraft, but nothing more is heard of this, so the case against her seems to have been dropped. The record ends by reminding us of Isobel Watson, who by then 'hes sufferit for witchcraft'. No trial records are known to survive for her, but the presbytery's initiative had evidently led to her trial and execution.

TEXT

Source: Stirling Council Archives, Minutes of Presbytery of Stirling, 1589–1596, CH2/722/2.

{*p. 20*} At Sterlyng the xxi day of April 1590
Mr William Cowper moderator, Johnn Duncansone, Alexander Fargy, Masters Henrie Levingstone, William Sterling, Johnne Davidsone, Gawin Donaldsone, Richard Wryght and Andro Murdo Ministers of the presbyteriis of Sterling and Dunblane and Andro Forester.[7] … {*p. 21*}

The[8] quhilk day ane summonds beand prodwcit dewlie execute and indorsit upone James Kynnaird and Jonet Hendirsone his spous in Awchlensky in the parochin of Glendoven chairgeing thame to compeir the said day To answer for wsein of Wichcraft and charmis wsit be thame etc Compeirit the said James and grants he recevit fra ane pwre woman callit Issobell Watsone certane pickills of quhyt quhairof he wndirstude thair wes ix ane peice of Rawne trie and ane peice of ane ded personis finger quhilk scho gaif him for to haill him of the worme quhilk hes bein tryit at lenth befoir the commissionar in his visitatione Quhilk Issobell Watsone the said James producit personallie befoir this assemblie And siclyk he declairit that the said Jonet Hendirsone his spous myght nocht compeir this day berassone[9] scho is neir the tyme of delyverance of hir birthe And thairfor desyrit the brethrein to accept this his excuse for hir in gude pairt. The brethrein continewis further proceiding with the said James and his spous literallie.[10]

The[11] said Issobell Watsone beand producit confessis hir self to be dochtir to wmquhill Johne Watsone at the kirk of Mwthill, hir mother callit x[12] Margaret Drummond sistir to wmquhill Andro Drummond in Middil Drummaqwhaus and that scho is iii^xx^ yeirs of aige or thairby, and that scho dwelt in Perthe xvi yeris and come furth of it the tyme of the pest,[13] and that scho dwelt in Mwthill befoir that scho dwelt in Perthe. And that scho was mareit in Perthe on Johnne Rogie ane fischer quha deit thre yeirs aftir the reformatione {*p. 22*} of Religione, and sence scho come furth of Perthe sayis scho beggit in Tullibairdin, Mwthill, Glendoven etc.

7 In margin: 'Presentes'.
8 In margin: 'James Kynnaird and his wyff'.
9 'berassone' (by reason): because.
10 'Literally': by letters, in writing. The point is that they will summon James Kinnaird and Janet Henderson in writing if they want them to appear again (which they never did).
11 In margin: 'Ane Wiche'.
12 This 'x' is added above the line. In margin: 'x in the tolbuth confessit hir name to be Cristane Moyll'.
13 There was a plague epidemic in Perth in 1584–5.

And[14] beand Inquyrit how scho gat the mark in hir hed confessit that quhen scho was xviii yeirs of aige beand keipand scheip in the mwre of Tullibairdin, scho sleipit in ane fauld yet[15] at quhat tyme scho was takin away be the fair folk and hauldin with thame xxiiii hours In the quhilk tyme scho said scho past in ane craig wndir the erd[16] in ane fair hous quhair thair was folk meikill and litill And that ane woman offirit hir bred lyk ane peice of ait caik quhilk scho refusit Inrespect hir mother sistir callit Issobell Drummond forbad hir to tak the samin, bidding hir gif thair meat[17] to the gress and grein eard,[18] And affermis that scho gat na meat the speace of thre dayis and thre nyghts eftir hir said taking At the quhilk tyme of hir taking scho sayis scho gat the mark in hir hed with ane h[19] knyf quhilk James Watsone hir brother haillit within the speace of thre oulkis.[20]

Eftir farder examinatioun scho confessit that scho gaif ane Laid[21] of hirs of twa yeir auld wnto the farie furth of the creddill to Lett hir self allane and to succor hir husband quha fell a sleip on the waltir bray[22] and was lang seik thaireftir At the quhilk tyme the fair folk laid in the creddill ane stock in liknes of hir bairne to the quhilk she gaif na meat, And that hir gude mane caist it in the fyr quhilk almaist brunt the houss. And thaireftir to the end scho myght recovir hir bairne agane scho made promeis to serve thame In taikin quherof scho recevit thair mark upone hir head be ane Thomas M^c^ray quha is with thame quha hade ains carnall deall with hir.[23]

Farder scho confessis that scho gangs ains everie mone with the fair folk And that scho was with thame at the last chainge.[24] And that thair is anew[25] of folks with thame fra quhome scho hes gottin meat and drink To wit wmquhill James Hog, Issobell Leiche at the loch of Glennageis, James Broun, Margaret Bill, James Tod, quha is thair fidlar Scho knew that Nicnevein was meid wyff to the elff quein. In the tolbuth scho confessit that scho was midwyf to the elff quein.

14 In margin: 'Ane Wiche Confessione'.

15 'fauld yet': sheepfold with a gate (yett).

16 'in ane craig wndir the erd': in a hill or crag, under the earth.

17 'meat': food.

18 'gress and grein eard': grass and green earth.

19 Single letter, probably 'h', possibly deleted. The scribe may have begun to write a word and abandoned it.

20 'oulkis': weeks. In margin: 'confessis in the tolbuth scho was heallit with Kippilgerss or banwart be Johne Frensche in Muthill'. 'Kippilgerss' (presumably 'couple-grass') has not been identified; 'banwart' (bone-wort) is a daisy or other plant considered to have bone-healing properties (*Oxford English Dictionary*).

21 'Laid': lad, son.

22 A 'water brae' was a sloping bank beside a river or loch.

23 For changeling beliefs see Lizanne Henderson and Edward J. Cowan, *Scottish Fairy Belief: A History* (East Linton, 2001), 94–100.

24 'chainge': new moon.

25 'anew': enough; 'anew of folks': quite a lot of people.

Siclyk confessis that upone James Kynnairds wyff praying for Gods saik in hir husbands name scho gaif him {*p. 23*}[26] ix pickills of qwhyt ane peice Rauntrie with ane baine or Junt for the tuthe yaik[27] quilk scho receavit fra Sir Johne Row Minister of Perthe.[28] This saying of hirs being refutit for that the quheit was fresche, The piece Roun trie grein and the Junt having sennous at it lyk luit strings.[29] Then scho allegit that scho gat the samin in the court fra hir mother sister to keip hir fra all straiks of the fair folk (quha wsit to straik hir sair) in the chainge of the mone. In the tolbuth scho confessis scho gat the premissis[30] fra the qwein of faires dochtir.

And beand Inquyrit quhat vairtew the said ix pickills of quhyt Rountrie and Joint hade, ansrit the ix pikkills will keip ane mane fra all dainger gif he war slepand. The Rountrie will keip ane mane fra the whorl wind[31] The Jount was to keip hir fra the straikis as said is. Farder scho confessit scho was befoir the kingis wand in Perthe.[32] Mairattour scho confessis the elff quein baid hir refuis God and byd with thame becaus scho wald fair bettir and that scho yid[33] in at sindrie tymis at the dragone holl of Kynnowll.[34] And that scho dancit sum tymis with thame about the loch of Glennageiss at xii hours of the day.

Item that scho hes sein with thame William Fintone and his wyff And that our gude nychburs liftit the meikill stanes in Glenageis[35] And war nocht that sum of the fair folk was that nyght with James Hogs wyf travaling[36] thair hade ma of tha stanis bein liftit, In the tolbuth scho confessit that scho was thair.

Scho grants that scho saw all the court at the last chainge and that scho wald be with thame the nixt Tyisday lykas scho is with thame ilk chainge, And that the fair folk gaitts all things we curss, And that scho hes sein sundrie of the court by maill in the commone mercat with uthers quhome na uthir folk will ken bot sic as hes bein in the court.

26 In margin: 'Ane Wiche Confessione'.

27 'tuthe yaik': toothache.

28 John Row, minister of Perth, was a prominent Reformer, whom Watson had evidently encountered during her time in the town: Richard L. Greaves, 'Row, John (*c.*1526–1580)', *ODNB*; *Perth Kirk Session Books, 1577–1590*, 23–4. Watson gives Row the pre-Reformation title for a priest, 'Sir'.

29 'sennous ... luit strings': sinews, lute strings.

30 'premissis': aforesaid things.

31 This protection was probably against a *fairy* whirlwind. For a later case discussing cures for people having been 'blasted' by fairy whirlwinds, see Liv Helene Willumsen, *Witches of the North: Scotland and Finnmark* (Leiden, 2013), 137.

32 To be 'under a wand' was to be subject to correction by authority, so perhaps Watson was describing an appearance before a court. If so, this was probably the fairy court; Watson had only just mentioned this court and its queen, and went on to mention them further.

33 'yid': went.

34 The Dragon's Hole of Kinnoull is a cave in Kinnoull Hill, east of Perth. For the kirk session's attempts to prevent May festivities there in 1580 and 1581 see *Perth Kirk Session Books, 1577–1590*, 151, 182.

35 This evidently refers to the Gleneagles Stone Circle. See the entry for it in the Canmore database (Historic Environment Scotland), at <http://canmore.org.uk/site/25929>.

36 'travaling' (travailing): in childbirth.

Item scho sayis thay gang to the Devill and seiks thair Leving, And thai that is with thame vii yeir is gevin to the Devill in teind.[37] And that ane lytill ane of thame bait[38] hir in the mid finger of hir left hand the last chainge, quhilk scho shew to the presbyterii. And said it was ane gude warld quhen thai yid ofter nor thai do now, and said quhen evir we spak of thame, we sauld say God send thame rowme gaitts[39] and fair feilds. {*p. 24*}

Confessit[40] the fair folks Ryds on ony bwnwalds[41] thay gait And that James Watsone bowmane[42] in Glennageis bot thre yeir syne was takin away be thame And that it is bot God that haulds Petir Lambert on his feit And that [*1 word blank*] Cowpper his brother in Law hes wrakkit that houss this xx yeir, And being askit quhat was the remed thairof, Sche baid chaing[e] the dwrs of his houss efter mair, And that sche causit ane dosone do that, bot refusit to tell thair nams, and declairit scho wald tell na mair now, bot schew ane uthir Mark on hir arme quhilk thai gaif hir.

In Maii 1590 in the tolbuithe

Confessit[43] that the king of the court gaif hir oyll lyk the yok of ane egg at baithe the tymis scho was markit, on the hed first and nixt on the arme with the quhilk he rubbit hir hed, craig and breist,[44] and said sa lang as ony of that oyll was on hir na mane sould haif powar to do hir skayth,[45] and sayis the same is now all aff hir, And that the king twik fra hir, hir hair, and that the kings dochtir gaif hir the pikills of quhyt the Rountrie and Junt of the fingar and said thai wald keip hir fra all perrells.

Confessit the Devill come to hir lyk ane aingell on Thurisday last befoir bed tyme and said gif scho wald serve him out he sould keip hir fra this dainger. Scho answerit that the tyme promesit be hir to serve him was run out. And that now scho hade gevin hir self to God, And Immediatlie thaireftir scho said that scho was swa strukin that all hir body was abost,[46] And gif scho hade

37 Cf. Emily Lyle, 'The Teind to Hell in "Tam Lin"', in her *Fairies and Folk: Approaches to the Scottish Ballad Tradition* (Trier, 2007), 128–31. Lyle links this belief to belief in changelings, discussed above.

38 'bait': bit.

39 'rowme gaitts': wide roads.

40 In margin: 'Ane Wiche Confessione'.

41 Probably this word should be understood as 'bunwand', meaning a hollow stalk.

42 'bowmane': probably a cattle-keeper rather than an archer.

43 In margin: 'In the tolbuth confessit the elff quein held doun hir hed quhill sum thing lyk oyll was put on hir hed'.

44 Anointing with oil on the head, 'craig' (neck) and breast may resemble a part of a royal coronation ritual. On 17 May 1590, when the investigation of Watson was in progress, Queen Anna was crowned and anointed (on the shoulder and right arm) at Holyrood: Maureen M. Meikle, 'Anna of Denmark's Coronation and Entry into Edinburgh, 1590: Cultural, Religious and Diplomatic Perspectives', in Julian Goodare and Alasdair A. MacDonald (eds.), *Sixteenth-Century Scotland: Essays in Honour of Michael Lynch* (Leiden, 2008), 277–94, at p. 285.

45 'skayth': harm.

46 'abost': abused.

bein out of the houss scho wald have gaine wod.[47] Farder confessis that thair is ane womane in this toun with thame bad uesit[48] with quhome scho saw the king have carnall deall bot knew nane of thair naims.

Being Inqwyrit how scho hade knawledge of thame quha staw[49] Thomas Boyds gair[50] Answerit that Jesus Christ come to hir in the liknes of ane aingell and schew the same to hir, And eftir farder examinatione confessit that it was the Devill quha schew hir the samin. {*p. 25*}

Confessis[51] scho hes sein in cumpanie with the fair folk Issobell Murray spous to David [*1 word blank*] chapman[52] in Mountsyming in Rossie Hill bewest the waltir of [*1 word blank*] besyd Pervie and Jonet Murray in the toun of Pervie wsis with thame.

xii° Maii 1590

Confessis scho saw with the fair folk Richie Grahame four severall tymis. First betuix the miln and the park of [*1 word blank*] Secund tyme upone the hill above Kincardin The thrid tyme, betuix Machanie and Tullibairdin, The last tyme at the galluss[53] of Kincardin. And that scho saw in the court Jonet Litiljohnne and hir sister and thair mother quha is ane wyf in Ochtirardir callit Saul to God.

At Sterling the x of Junii 1590

The brethrein of the Synodall Assemblie of the presbyteriis of Sterling, Dunblane, Perthe and Dunkeld having hard the confessione above writtin of Issobell Watsone, Judgs hir ane abusar of the pepill Consultar with the Devill and the ded And thairfor worthie to die according to Gods Law And Requyris the civill magistrat to put hir to the knawledge of ane assyss *Sic subscribitur*[54] AYoung moderator.... {*p. 36*}

At Sterling the secund day of Junii 1590[55]

47 'gaine wod': gone mad.

48 The reading is fairly clear, and the word is thus probably 'visit', but the meaning of this sentence is obscure. Watson may be saying that a woman in this town (Stirling) is 'with' the fairies (in the sense that, like Watson herself, she visits them from time to time) and 'bade' other people to visit them also. However, the word 'visit' could also mean 'afflict' (with illness).

49 'staw': stole.

50 'gair' (gear): possessions.

51 In margin: 'Ane Wiche Confessione'.

52 'chapman': pedlar.

53 'galluss': gallows.

54 'Thus it is subscribed'.

55 This entry is dated 2 June, while the previous entry about Isobel Watson, eleven pages earlier in the minute book, is dated 10 June. That 10 June entry is immediately followed by an entry dated 21 April (not about Watson and thus not included in the present edition), following which there are several more pages of entries dated at various dates in May. Evidently the clerk wrote up the fair copy of the minutes in this minute book some while

Mr William Cowper moderator, Andro Forester, Alexander Fargy, Masters Henrie Levingstone, Andro Ywng, Williame Sterling, Gawin Donaldsone, Alexander Wallace, James Duncansone, Richard Wryght, ministers of the presbyteriis of the presbyteriis [*sic*] of Sterling and Dunblane and Mr Alexander Iull ane brother of exerceis.[56] …

The quhilk day It was Reported to the Brethrein be Mr Gawin Donaldsone \minister/ that William Wilsone als Culross in his parochin of Dolur and Elizabeth Stalkar als Huggotour thair[57] hes mwtuallie sclandirit everie ane of thame ane uthir of wichcraft and consultein with wichis. The Brethrein ordanis bayth the saidis personis to be summoned to the secund day of the nixt synodall to answer for the said offence, with certificatione gif thai compeir nocht thai salbe reput for wichis and apprehendit for the same…. {*p. 40*}

At Sterling the xxiii day of Junii 1590

Mr William Cowper, Henrie Levingstone, Henrie Layng, William Sterling, James Duncansone, Gawin Donaldsone, Richard Wryght and Alexander Fargy Ministers and Mr Alexander Iull ane brother of exerceis.[58] … {*p. 42*}

In the terme assignit to the last synodall assemblie to William Wilsone als Culross in the parochin of Dolur and Elizabeth Stalkar thair, to compeir and wndirly tryell anent the mater wndir writtin. Compeirit the said William personallie,[59] and confessis he come to Issobell Watsone ane wiche beand deteinit in presone thairfoir in the Tolbuth of Sterling, to quhome he schew that his cow gaive na milk, upone quhais informatione he past to the said Elizabeth, and mait[60] with hir on the hie feilds quhair he upone his kneis askit fra hir \the proffeit of/ his cowis milk quhilk was tane fra him. And confessis that his cow gaif milk within twa dayis thairefter, and that his brother Johne Wilsone informit him that David Broun in Fairnihest [*sic*] within the parochin of Crumbie[61] confessit to the said Johne that he come to the said Elizabeth Stalkar befoir, and cravit his cowis milk quhilk was tane fra him quhilk he gat.

---

afterwards. Thus, writing no earlier than June, he has taken the opportunity to gather together various proceedings relating to Watson, dated at various dates from 21 April to 10 June, before resuming his regular series of minutes. Watson now reappears in this regular series, because this 2 June entry and those that follow are principally about William Wilson and Elizabeth Stalker.

56 In margin: 'Presentes'.

57 In margin: 'William Culross, Elizabeth Stalkar'.

58 In margin: 'Presentes'.

59 In margin: 'William Wilsone als Culross'.

60 'mait': met.

61 Crombie, a parish in south-western Fife, later amalgamated with Torryburn. 'Fairnihest' has not been identified; possibly Cairneyhill (near Crombie) was intended, with a copying error influenced by the better-known Ferniehirst in Roxburghshire.

Compeirit the said Elizabeth Stalkar[62] and beand accusit of the premissis and everie point thairof, Scho confessit that the said William come to hir, bot scho hard nocht quhat he said and denyis simpliciter that scho can give ony cow thair milk that wantis it, and that scho hes na knawledge of witche craft, Bot grantis that David Broun foir said come to hir and socht his kowis milk of befoir Quhilk scho affermis was done maist Iniwstlie[63] to hir without ony occasione done be hir, quhairof scho was maist innocent.

The Brethrein continewis the said Elizabeth[64] to farther tryell And ordanis hir minister to serce diligentlie in his parochin gif scho hes ony wiche craft and give scho wsis the samin, and mak report quhat he findis to the brethrein of this presbyterii.

The Brethrein Ordanis the said William Wilsone[65] to mak publict repentence in the first forme as ane adulterar[66] quhill the nixt synodall assemblie, for asking of his cowis milk fra the said Elizabeth beand ane creatur,[67] and for consultein with the said Isobell Watsone thairanent quha is convict and hes sufferit for witchcraft.

62 In margin: 'Elizabeth Stalkar alledgit ane witche'.

63 'Iniwstlie': unjustly.

64 In margin: 'Elizabeth Stalkar'.

65 In margin: 'William Wilsone als Culross'.

66 The point here is not that Wilson is an adulterer, but that he should perform the same standard repentance as an adulterer.

67 The point here is that this is a request that should be made only to God in prayer, not to a human 'creatur'.

6. MARION McNAB, PERTHSHIRE, 1590

INTRODUCTION

This case arose in Lecropt, a parish south of Dunblane, and was pursued by the presbytery of Stirling between July and September 1590. In the record it begins almost immediately after the case of Isobel Watson, edited above, but seems not to have been connected with it.[1]

The accusation of witchcraft came from Janet Mitchell, wife of William Mayne. Mitchell complained that Marion McNab was a witch, and told a story of how McNab had bewitched her husband's malt. This initially prompted Mitchell to seek reparation and reconciliation – she told of having given McNab malt and honey in order to restore the quality of the malt. There was also mention of William Mayne's own sickness. Evidently the reconciliation attempt failed, and Mitchell then complained to the presbytery. The earliest record shows that she had already been induced to put the complaint in writing – she 'producit in wret certane hedds of wiche craft practesit be the said Marione and of hir abwsione of the said Jonet'. This document does not survive, but the presbytery's procedurally inquisitorial response has its own interest.

McNab was then summoned. She denied most of what Mitchell had said, but her own story also told of a reconciliation attempt. She related setting out with Mitchell to seek the aid of 'ane womane callit NcGilerss' – probably a Highlander, whose name seems to have been a patronymic, 'daughter of Gillies'. This woman was evidently a magical practitioner. But, McNab explained defensively, on the way she became uneasy about the mission and turned back.

The presbytery arranged for McNab to be imprisoned by the magistrates of Stirling, where she remained for two months, but they do not seem to have attempted to interrogate her there. By imprisoning her, the presbytery showed that they took the case seriously, but they seem to have assumed that evidence against her was obtainable only from her accuser, Janet Mitchell. A presbytery more determined to obtain evidence for the prosecution, or

[1] For a discussion of McNab's case see Michael F. Graham, *The Uses of Reform: 'Godly Discipline' and Popular Behavior in Scotland and Beyond, 1560–1610* (Leiden, 1996), 304–5.

more experienced in how to do so, would have carried out interrogations, and perhaps torture, in the prison itself. The members of the presbytery had recently interrogated Isobel Watson, the previous case edited above, in prison, but this was evidently not a routine practice. The practices of determined and coercive witch-hunting would grow up only gradually.

So the presbytery expected Janet Mitchell to produce further evidence – which she did, in the form of a large number of other witnesses. These all received written summonses, sometimes more than one; someone, probably the clerk to the presbytery, seems to have been kept busy writing these summonses and arranging for them to be delivered. The witnesses appeared piecemeal at several meetings between late July and early September. They made written statements that were unfortunately not entered into the presbytery minutes, and so do not survive. However, these statements evidently did not encourage the presbytery to believe in McNab's guilt.

Eventually the presbytery brought McNab back from prison and got her to make another statement. This time she told how she dealt with a cow whose calf had died – either to get it to continue to give milk or to persuade it to suckle another calf not its own. Her practice mainly involved presenting the cow with the skin of the dead calf, but she also spoke a verbal formula that the presbytery may have thought was superstitious. However, they evidently did not think that it was witchcraft. They ordered her freed, with the magistrates of Stirling being requested to find a cautioner for her who would present her again should the presbytery find further evidence against her. Thus, the presbytery's inquisitorial practice was maintained: they were not declaring McNab innocent, merely failing to find evidence of guilt.

Overall, this case is notable for the persistence of a private accuser, for the fluidity of the concepts that were raised – what exactly was McNab suspected of, was she a witch, or was she an abuser of the people, or what? – and for the rigid narrowness of the presbytery's procedural approach. This narrowness may have saved McNab in the end.

TEXT[2]

Source: Stirling Council Archives, Minutes of Presbytery of Stirling, 1589–1596, CH2/722/2.

{p. 47} At Sterling the xxi day of Julii 1590
Mr Williame Cowper Moderator, Johne Duncansone, Masters Richard Wryght, Henrie Layng, Andro Murdo, Alexander Fargy, Andro Ywng, Johne Davidsone, Alexander Chisholme, Ministeris of the presbyteriis of Sterling and Dunblane, and Mr Alexander Iull ane brother of exerceis.[3] … *{p. 48}*

[2] A previous transcript of most of the text below has been printed in R. Menzies Fergusson, *Alexander Hume, An Early Poet-Pastor of Logie, and his Intimates* (Paisley, 1899), 256–60.

[3] In margin: 'Presentes'.

The said day[4] comperit Jonet Mitchell the spous of Williame Mayne in Lawhed in Knokhill and producit ane Summondis dewlie execute and indorsit upone Marione McNab in the parochin of Lecrop chairgeing hir to compeir the said day To answer and be examined for abwsing the pepill wndir the paine of disobedience And lykwyss producit in wret certane hedds[5] of wiche craft practesit be the said Marione and of hir abwsione of the said Jonet as thay bear in thame \selffis/ And desyrit the said Marione to be examinat thairupone and of sic uther particularis as \scho/ sall informe the brethren[6] And this to be done at hir instance quha offiris hir self reddie to persew {*p. 49*} hir for the samin. Compeirit the said Marione McNab and confessis hir mareit on Donald Scharar in Knokhill and that scho was borne at the burn of Camp[7] dochtir to wmquhill Patrik McNab thair ane husband mane and Jonet Parcar hir mother And that scho come to Knokhill xii yeir syne, And beand accusit on the accusationis gevin againis hir Scho denyis thame all simpliciter, and denyis that scho recevit fra the persewar ane peck of malt, quhilk scho alledgis scho gave hir to mak hir husbandis malt gude quhilk was befoir wichit be hir, bot grantis the receat of ane exampill of malt, denyis the receat of any huning,[8] denyis the Curis alledgit gevin be hir to cwre the persewaris husbandis seiknes, Confessis scho past with the persewar in gait ward to ane womane callit NcGilerss in Kilmaling xiiii dayis eftir S[aint] Lowrence day last[9] to gait hir remade[10] to hir malt Becaus scho hard say that, that woman could do it, Bot alledgis be the way scho Rewit and returnit againe and past nocht with the persewar to the said NcGilerss hous. The brethrein finds the accusationis gevin in againis the said Marione McNab to be odius,[11] and the persewar offris to prove be diverss famwss witnes[12] that scho is ane wiche or ane consultar with wichis at the least ane abusar of the pepill.[13] Inrespect quhairof and of diverss utheris considerationis moving the brethrein, thay have thought gude that the said Marione be deteinit in closs frimance[14] quhill farther tryall be tane in the said mater And to that effect hes delyverit hir in the

4 In margin: 'Jonet Michell contra Marione McNab alledgit ane wiche'.

5 'hedds': itemised points.

6 'thame' crossed out here, and these two words inserted above the line.

7 Fergusson, *Alexander Hume*, 256, reads 'Cams'.

8 'huning': honey. Fergusson, *Alexander Hume*, 256, reads 'linning' (linen).

9 St Lawrence's Day was 10 August.

10 'gait hir remade': get her remedy.

11 To call the accusations 'odius' indicated that the offences alleged were serious.

12 'diverss famwss witnes': several reputable witnesses.

13 This phraseology echoes the 1563 witchcraft act, which forbade people 'to use ony maner of Witchcraftis, Sorsarie or Necromancie, nor gif thame selfis furth to have ony sic craft or knawlege thairof, thairthrow abusand the pepill: Nor that na persoun seik ony help, response or consultatioun at ony sic usaris or abusaris foirsaidis of Witchcraftis, Sorsareis or Necromancie, under the pane of deid'. However, the presbytery seems to have thought that 'ane abusar of the pepill' was committing a lesser offence. For the text of the act, and a discussion of its confusing terminology, see Julian Goodare, 'The Scottish Witchcraft Act', *Church History*, 74 (2005), 39–67.

14 *Sic*. 'Firmance' (imprisonment) is meant.

handis of David Forester and of the bailleis of Sterling, And admittis the persewaris accusationis to hir probatione and answeris thairto the xxviii of Julii instant.... {*p. 50*}

At Sterling the xxviii day of Julii 1590
Mr Williame Cowper, Henrie Levingstone, Henrie Layng, Richard Wryght, Andro Murdo, Alexander Chisholme, Andro Ywng, and Johne Davidsone, Ministeris of the presbyteriis of Sterling and Dunblane.[15] ...

The quhilk day compeirit Jonet Michell spous to William Mayne in Lawhed and producit ane summondis dewlie execute and indorsit upone the witnes wndirwrittin for preving of the accusatione gevin in be hir againis Marione McNab the spous of Donald Scharar in Knokhill, Thay ar to say Johne Baxter at the miln of Innerallane, Thomas Cwnynghame in Law, James Kemp ywnger millar in Acheray, Moreis Finlay in Lecrop, Sir Johne Kemp[16] thair, Alexander Michell thair, Johne Grahame in Acheray, Margaret Duncansone in Pathfut, Thomas Arthur alias Skinner browster in Keir, Williame Krowne his mane, Ewffame Gilleis in Ovir Keir, James Wrycht in Innerallane, James Wilsone thair, Johne Wilsone thair, Hellein Ady, Patrik Haigy in Keir, Jonet Forfair, Margaret Meikiljohne hir dochtir, Donald Wrycht in Innerallane, Johne Gentilmane in Acheray, and Ewffame {*p. 51*} Mayne in Sterling, chargeing thame to compeir the said day to bear lell and suthfast[17] witnessing in the actione foirsaid. Compeirit the said defender personallie and lykwyss of the witnessis foirsaid compeirit the personis wndirwrittin viz. Johnne Baxter, Thomas Cwnynghame, Thomas Arthur alias Skinner, William Browne, James Wrycht, James Wilsone, Johne Wilsone, Donald Wrycht, and Johne Gentilman in Acheray Quhilkis witnessis comperand now in presens of the said defender recevit sworne and admittit, and the xviii day of August nixtocum assignit to the \persewar/[18] to wse farther diligence on the saidis witnessis disobedient and the defender ordeinit to be deteinit in captivitie in the mentyme.... {*p. 53*}

At Sterling the xviii day of Awgust 1590
Mr Williame Cowper Moderator, Andro Forester, Alexander Fargy, Masters Gawin Donaldsone, Henrie Levingstone, Henrie Layng, James Duncansone, Alexander Wallace, Andro Murdo, Andro Ywng, Malcolme Hendirsone, and Johne Davidsone, Ministeris of the presbyteriis of Sterling and Dunblane.[19] ... {*p. 54*}

15 In margin: 'Presentes'.

16 Sir John Kemp, a pre-Reformation priest rather than a knight, was vicar at Lecropt in 1562 and reader there in 1574: Charles H. Haws, *Scottish Parish Clergy at the Reformation, 1540–1574* (Edinburgh: Scottish Record Society, 1972), 157.

17 'lell and suthfast': faithful and truthful.

18 'defender' crossed out here, and this word inserted above the line.

19 In margin: 'Presentes'.

The quhilk day[20] compeirit Jonet Mitchell spous to William Mayne in Lawhed and producit ane summondis dewlie execute and indorsit upone the witnes wndirwrittin for preving of the accusatione gevin in be hir agains Marione McNab the spous of Donald Scharar in Knokhill Thay ar to say James Kemp ywnger millar in Acheray, Jonet Anguss his spous, Moreis Finlay in Lecrop, Sir Johne Kemp thair, Alexander Mitchell thair, Johne Grahame in Acheray, Margaret Duncansone in Pathfutt, Euffame Gilleis in Ovir Keir, Patrik Haigie in Keir, Hellein Adie at the {*p. 55*} Miln of Achray, Jonet Forfar in Knokhill, Margaret Mukiljohne thair hir dochter, Ewffame Mayne in Sterling, Thomas Forester in Brighan[t],[21] Finlay Millar in Inverallone, Cathrein Candw his spous, Robert Cwnynghame sone to Hellein Blakwod in Acheray, Henrie Gentilmane thair, and Alexander Fargy minister, chairgeing thame to compeir the said day to bear leall and suthfast witnessing in the actione foirsaid. Compeirit the said defendar personallie And lykewys of the witnessis foirsaid compeirit the personis wndirwrittin, viz. James Kemp ywnger millar, Jonet Anguss his spous, Sir Johne Kemp in Lecrop, Alexander Michell thair, Johnne Graham in Acheray, Euffame Gilleis in Ovir Keir, Patrik Haigy in Keir, Jonet Forfar in Knokhill, Margaret Mukiljohne thair hir dochter, Euffame Mayne, Finlay Millar, Cathrein Candw his spous, Henrie Gentilmane, and Alexander Fargy, Quhilkis witnessis comperand now in presens of the said defendar recevit sworne and admittit and the xxv day of this instant assignit to the persewar to wse farther diligence on the saidis witnessis disobedient And the defender ordeinit to be deteinit in captivitie in the mentyme.... {*p. 56*}

At Sterling the xxv day of August 1590
Masters Alexander Iull, Neill Campbell visitur of Argyll, Henrie Layng, Gawin Donaldsone, James Duncansone, Alexander Wallace, and Alexander Fargy ministeris.[22] ...

The quhilk day[23] compeirit Jonet Michell spous to William Mayne in Lawhed and producit ane summondis dewlie execute and indorsit upone the witnes wndirwrittin for preving of the accusatione gevin in be hir agains Marione McNab the spous of Donald Scharar in Knokhill Thay ar to say Moreis Finlay in Lecrop, Margaret Duncansone in Pathefutt, Hellein Adie at the miln of Achray, Thomas Forester in Brig Han[t], Robert Cwnynghame sone to Hellein Blakwod in Acheray, James Duncansone in Fossowy, Hellein McCalpie his spous, Marione Patersone, Elisabeth Watsone, chairgeing thame to compeir the said day to bear lell and suthfast witnessing in the actioun foirsaid. Compeirit the said defendar personallie And lykwyss all the witnessis foirsaid (Except

20 In margin: 'Michell contra McNab'.
21 Fergusson, *Alexander Hume*, 259, reads 'Brighau[t]'. This place has not been identified, but it may have related to a bridge over the Allan Water.
22 In margin: 'Presentes'.
23 In margin: 'Michell contra McNab'.

the saidis Marione Patersone and Elisabeth Watsone) quha war in presens of the said defender recevit sworne and admitted, and the viii day of September is assignit to the persewar to wse farther diligence on hir witnessis And the defender ordeinit to be deteinit in captivitie in the mentyme.... *{p. 58}*

At Sterling the viii day of September 1590
Masters Richard Wryght, Henrie Levingstone, Andro Murdo, James Duncansone, Andro Ywng, Johne Davidsone, ministers of the presbyteriis of Sterling and Dunblane, and Mr Johnne Millar.[24] ... *{p. 59}*

The quhilk day[25] compeirit Jonet Michell spous to William Mayne in Lawhed and producit ane summondis dewlie execute and indorsit upone Robert Hendirsone in Acheray and Marione Patirsone at the brig of Inverallone chairgeing thame to compeir the said day to bear lell and suthfast witnessing anent the accusatione gevin in be the said Jonet upone Marione McNab the spous of Donald Scharar in Knokhill Quhilkis witnessis compeirit personallie and in presens of the defendar was recevit sworne and admittit And the brethrein twke to advyss with the depositionis literallie.[26] ... *{p. 61}*

At Sterling on Thurisday the xvii day of September 1590
Mr Robert Rollok, Johnne Duncansone, Masters Patrik Simsone, Henrie Levingstone, Richard Wryght, James Duncansone, William Sterling, Andro Ywng, ministers, and Mr Alexander Iull ane brother of exerceis.[27]

The said day Marione McNab[28] the spous of Donald Scharar confessit that scho can gar ane cow tak with ane uther calf,[29] Be laying the skin of the ded calf befoir the cow with ane loik[30] salt on it, and saying thryss in the name of the father the sone and the holy gost. And siclyk to gar ane cow tak with ane qwick[31] calf Be putting the ded calffis skin on ane quick calf and saying the saidis wordis, in the name of the father, the sone and the holy gost, thryss ovir, And siclyk confessit that scho hes practesit and done thir thingis.

The Brethrein being willing that the accusatione off wichcraft and abwsein of the pepill gewin in agains Marione McNab[32] the spous of Donald Scharar in Knokhill be mair cleirlie provin and farther tryit Desyris the provest and

24 In margin: 'Presentes'.
25 In margin: 'Michell contra McNab'.
26 'Literally', i.e. by letters, in writing. (The scribe may have in mind the Latin word '*litteratorie*', which has the same meaning.) The point is that the members of the presbytery will take the written 'depositionis' away, read them, and 'advyss with' them (i.e. consider and discuss them).
27 In margin: 'Presentes'.
28 In margin: 'Marione McNab'.
29 'scho can gar ane cow tak with ane uther calf': she can induce a cow to suckle a calf that is not its own (after its own calf has died).
30 'loik': small quantity.
31 'qwick': living.
32 377 In margin: 'Marione McNab'.

bailleis of Sterling quha presentlie hes hir in custodie to tak responsall cawtione within this burgh actit in thair bwkis that the said Marione salbe presentit befoir this presbyterii upone fourtie awcht houris Warning to be made to the cawtionar And that quhow oft soevir the cawtionar salbe warnit ay and quhill[33] the said Marione be clengit or fyllit[34] be ane assyss wndir the paine of fyve hundreth pwndis to be payit be the cawtionar to the saidis bailleis To be convertit *ad pios usus*[35] be the advyss and sicht of the said presbyterii Quhilk beand done Requiris the saidis provesst and bailleis to put the said Marione McNab to libertie.[36]

33 'ay and quhill': until.

34 'clengit or fyllit': acquitted or convicted.

35 'to pious purposes' (such as poor relief).

36 The case appears to have been dropped after this. From this point until at least October 1591, there is nothing more in the presbytery records about McNab or indeed about any other case of witchcraft, despite the panic that would break out elsewhere concerning the North Berwick witches.

7. DUNDEE WITCH, *c*.1591

INTRODUCTION

This rare financial document itemises the payments made by the burgh of Dundee for executing a witch in about 1591. From it we can learn about the practicalities of executions. The context of the document may also shed light on the notorious North Berwick witchcraft panic of 1590–2.

There are many things that this document does not tell us. It does not tell us the witch's name or even gender. And it does not give the exact date of the execution. The financial accounts cover the terms of Martinmas 1590 and Whitsun 1591 – the financial year 16 May 1590 to 15 May 1591 – and the text gives no more precise date. As we shall see, a date towards the end of this period seems likely. Another significant point that the document omits is the nature of the court that tried and convicted the witch.

It may, however, be possible to reconstruct some of this contextual information. Here we may begin with a consideration of four hypothetically possible types of court that might have tried the witch.[1] Hypothetically, it could have been the burgh court, or the sheriff court, or a justice court held under royal authority (a commission of justiciary), either in Dundee or in Edinburgh. These options might overlap if (for instance) the magistrates of the burgh were granted a commission of justiciary. Unfortunately, the keeping of the records of a court held under a commission of justiciary did not form part of the responsibilities of any local officials, and the survival rate for such courts' records is very low. Before 1608, there is no surviving central record of the granting of commissions of justiciary either. So it would not be surprising if gaps in the record evidence were to limit what could be said. Nevertheless, some probable conclusions can be drawn.

Let us return at this point to the four hypothetically possible types of court. The burgh court itself almost certainly did not try the witch. Its records survive for the years 1590 and 1591, and there is no record of the witch in

[1] For more details of the jurisdictions that tried witches see Julian Goodare, 'Witch-Hunting and the Scottish State', in Julian Goodare (ed.), *The Scottish Witch-Hunt in Context* (Manchester, 2002), 122–45, at pp. 124–30.

them.[2] The sheriff court for Dundee usually sat in Forfar; its records do not survive for this period, but it seems unlikely that a witch tried in Forfar would have been executed in Dundee. Burgh and sheriff courts indeed rarely tried witches. We are more likely to be looking for a court held under the authority of a commission of justiciary. And we might hypothesise that this witch, since she or he (as we know from this document) was executed by those involved in the government of the burgh, would also have been *tried* by those involved in its government. This makes a justice court trial in Edinburgh unlikely. If we eliminate these three options, the fourth option – a justice court trial in Dundee, with some of the Dundee authorities having been granted a commission of justiciary by the royal government – becomes much more likely. In which case we would be looking for traces of negotiations, between the Dundee authorities and the royal government in Edinburgh, about the grant of a commission.

Traces of such negotiations can indeed be found in the council minutes, the record of policy-making decisions by the burgh authorities. On 4 May 1591, the council nominated James Carmichael and Patrick Lyon to attend a convention of estates on 6 May, 'anent order to be tane With sorcereris and certane practiseris aganis his Majesties persoun'.[3] This entry is the only mention of witchcraft in the council minutes for this period.[4] The king had summoned this convention of estates on or shortly before 27 April, in order to discuss what should be done with the earl of Bothwell, who had recently been imprisoned on suspicion of witchcraft.[5] The panic had grown in intensity during the first few months of 1591, but, up until that point, most of the known witches had come from East Lothian.[6]

In the event, many noblemen and others absented themselves from May's convention of estates, and the king had to abandon his plan of using it to launch a trial of Bothwell.[7] But Carmichael and Lyon, when they visited Edinburgh to discuss witchcraft early in May 1591, could have used the

2 We owe this information to the kindness of Iain Flett, who has examined these records.

3 Dundee City Archives, council minutes, vol. ii (1587–1603), fo. 57r. The record continues: 'ordanis ane Commissioun to be maid to thame conjunctlie and severallie under the privie seall'. This was the *burgh's* privy seal empowering Carmichael and Lyon to represent the burgh at the convention of estates, not a *royal* seal that might have been affixed to a commission of justiciary. The clerk used similar phraseology in the next entry, when two burgesses were commissioned on 8 June to attend a convention of royal burghs in Montrose: ibid., fo. 57v.

4 Alexander Maxwell, *The History of Old Dundee* (Edinburgh, 1884), 294.

5 Robert Bowes to Lord Burghley, 27 April 1591, *Calendar of the State Papers Relating to Scotland and Mary, Queen of Scots*, vol. x (1589–93), ed. William K. Boyd and Henry W. Meikle (Edinburgh, 1936), 506. For more about Bothwell see the document concerning his 1593 trial, edited below in the present volume.

6 For the main events of the North Berwick panic see Lawrence Normand and Gareth Roberts (eds.), *Witchcraft in Early Modern Scotland: James VI's 'Demonology' and the North Berwick Witches* (Exeter, 2000). The known witchcraft cases for this period were included in SSW. The present case, however, is not in SSW.

7 Bowes to Burghley, 5 & 8 May 1591, *Calendar*, x, 511, 513.

opportunity to obtain a commission of justiciary for Dundee's own local witch. Alternatively, they could have been the ones to be sent to Edinburgh on that date because they already had recent experience of trying Dundee's own local witch; however, this would have entailed a separate journey to Edinburgh, for which the expenses might have been itemised in the present document. The burgh's provost (Sir James Scrymgeour of Dudhope), who is mentioned in the document, would probably also have been a commissioner. Thus, although it seems impossible to be definite on present evidence, we do have a strong suggestion that the North Berwick panic spread to Dundee in some form, and that the trial of this Dundee witch was held in May 1591.

So much for the context of this document. Let us now turn to the question of what specific information it contains. Perhaps the earliest part of the story is the glimpse that we catch of the witch in prison, where the council 'vos at' her or him, and candles were bought. This may indicate that sleep deprivation was used, with a rota of people to keep the suspect awake round the clock for several days. An alternative explanation for the candles might be that the witch's trial, or at least her or his preliminary investigation, took place in the winter when more of the council's business was carried out beyond the short hours of daylight.

Dundee seems to have had no executioner, or at least none who was willing or able to manage an execution by burning, so an executioner had to be brought from St Andrews. Like the witch herself or himself, the executioner is unnamed. We learn about the involvement of two of the burgh's named executive officers. James Wilkie summoned the assize (incurring the largest single item of costs), and David Jardine made practical arrangements to recruit the executioner. Three tradespeople who supplied materials are also named: Esmée Goldman, Elspeth Duncan and James Guild, who supplied rope, a timber stake (a 'garroun'), and candles respectively.

The site chosen for the execution was the Play Field ('plafild'). This was just outside the town, to the west of the West Port.[8] We learn about the materials from which the pyre itself was constructed: coal and tar. A lot of rope was needed, and also an iron chain, which may well have been used to tie the witch to the stake. Two 'deills' (planks) may have been used as crowd barriers.[9] They clearly did not form part of the pyre, since they were brought back from the execution site afterwards – being carried 'hame and afild'. The iron chain was also retrieved. The other items, including the stake itself, had only to be carried in one direction.

8 Sylvia J. Stevenson and Elizabeth P. D. Torrie, *Historic Dundee: The Archaeological Implications of Development* (Edinburgh: Scottish Burgh Survey, 1988), 37 (map), 47.

9 For the use of such barriers in Aberdeen see Julian Goodare, 'The Aberdeenshire Witchcraft Panic of 1597', *Northern Scotland*, 21 (2001), 17–37, at p. 33.

TEXT

Source: Dundee City Archives, Burgh Treasurer's Accounts of Dundee, 1586–1606, accounts for 1590–1.[10]

The compt of mony debursit upoun the burning off the Wiche

Item in the first delywerit to James Wilky to summond ane assyis	xl s.
Item gevin Ismie Gauldman for four fadem off towis[11]	ii s.
Item to Elspit Duncan for ane aikin garroun[12] to knet[13] the viche to	v s.
Item for the bering hame and afild off tua deills fra the plafild[14]	xxx d.
Item for the bering off the garroun to the plafild	viii d.
Item for thre creill full off collis	xv s.
Item for the bering off them	iiii s.
Item gewin for tua tar barrellis	vii s.
Item for the bering off them to the plafild	xvi d.
Item for the bering off the yroun chanye hame and affild	viii d.
Item gavin [*sic*] at the provest command to the Wiche hanger	x s.
Item gevin to David Gardin offisar at the provest command to gaiff the hang man quhan he vos Jangin[15] ovir the vatir[16]	vi s. viii d.
Item gevin James Guild for candill quhan the counsall vos at the vich	xvi d.
Item gevin Lamb to Jang [*sic*] to Sanct Andrus about the hang man	xx s.

Summa is 5 lib. 16s. 2d.

[10] This volume has no page or folio numbers.

[11] 'four fadem off towis': four fathoms of rope. A fathom was 6 feet. Four fathoms may have been a standard amount, since in the next section of the accounts Goldman was paid for another four fathoms of rope for the town's bells.

[12] 'aiken garroun': oak beam.

[13] 'knet': fasten.

[14] 'plafild': play field. See the introduction, above, for a discussion of this.

[15] *Sic*. Evidently 'ganging' (going) is meant. The scribe often uses this spelling elsewhere in the accounts.

[16] The executioner's journey from St Andrews to Dundee required him to cross the Tay estuary.

8. BARBARA NAPIER, EDINBURGH, 1591

INTRODUCTION

Barbara Napier was one of the high-profile witches accused during the so-called 'North Berwick' witchcraft panic of 1590–2. She was married to an Edinburgh burgess, Archibald Douglas. Both Napier and Douglas were related to aristocratic families. Napier had been a lady in waiting to Jean Lyon, countess of Angus, whose name came up from time to time during the proceedings. Her prosecution arose from the confessions of Agnes Sampson and Richard Graham, two accused witches with whom Napier had had various dealings. The text below consists of the minutes of her trial, held on 8 May 1591.

Napier's trial caused a legal sensation when the assize acquitted her of witchcraft, but convicted her of consulting with witches.[1] The badly-drafted witchcraft act of 1563 declared that both witchcraft and consulting witches were capital offences, but the clause on consulting witches had not been implemented in any trials before this date.[2] The judge, Humphrey Blindseil, hesitated to pass sentence on Napier – quite possibly he intended to free her – and the pyre that had been built for her in advance was dismantled.[3] However, King James intervened on 10 May, ordering the judge to sentence Napier to death for the crime of consulting with witches; clearly he did not share the legal consensus that this should not be a capital crime. Blindseil duly pronounced the sentence, only for Napier to claim that she was pregnant and to demand a delay.

James may have begun to realise at this point that he was not going to get Napier executed. He took another unusual initiative, ordering twelve of the fifteen members of her assize to be prosecuted for 'wilful error' – the crime of wrongfully acquitting an obviously guilty person. The assizers carefully pleaded guilty to the lesser (and indeed symbolic) crime of 'ignorant error';

[1] Lawrence Normand and Gareth Roberts (eds.), *Witchcraft in Early Modern Scotland: James VI's 'Demonology' and the North Berwick Witches* (Exeter, 2000), 247–52.

[2] Julian Goodare, 'The Scottish Witchcraft Act', *Church History*, 74 (2005), 39–67, at p. 65.

[3] *Extracts from the Records of the Burgh of Edinburgh, 1589–1603*, ed. Marguerite Wood (Edinburgh, 1927), 334.

the king accepted this on 7 June, evidently feeling that he had proved his point.[4] He pardoned the assizers, first making a speech in which he justified his intervention in the legal process, and claimed credit for having discovered the witches during his earlier involvement in the interrogations.[5] The text below shows that James's interventions did not begin with the prosecution of the assizers; he had also been consulted by some of those involved in Napier's trial on the day.

Napier herself remained in prison until the panic had largely died down; perhaps she was giving birth. Then, on 23 February 1592, she was freed by royal warrant, with her brother William Napier of Wrightshouses acting as her cautioner.[6] She was neither innocent nor guilty, but she faced no further prosecution. The Register of Deeds shows her to have been still alive and making contracts ten years later.[7]

The document edited below records each stage in Napier's trial, up to the point when the assize retired to consider their verdict. In it are found early details of the appointment of defence lawyers for her, showing their reluctance to act. Her lawyers' allegations against the relevance of some items of her dittay are recorded, as are their objections to some allegedly partisan members of the assize, and to some 'assessors' – politically-influential assistants to the judge who might be expected to have agendas beyond the impartial exercise of justice. The prosecution was led by the king's advocate. His replies to the defence objections are noted, as are the judge's rulings on each of the debated points.

One of the assizers against whom the defence objected was David Seton in Foulstruther, as he is called here. He was a highly significant person in the North Berwick panic, mentioned in many other accounts as the bailie of Tranent. Late in 1590, his torturing of his servant Geillis Duncan in his own house had obtained a crucial early confession from which subsequent accusations had snowballed. Seton was one of the three assizers who were omitted from the king's prosecution of the assizers; clearly, he had voted for conviction. Another assizer who had done so was John Seton; we learn below that he was David's brother. Napier's lawyers' objections against David Seton's obvious partiality were cogent, but the judge overruled them.

The defence made detailed objections to the idea that it might be a crime to consult a witch – objections that may help to explain why the Scottish legal establishment set aside the consulting clause of the 1563 act. How could it be

4 Normand and Roberts (eds.), *Witchcraft*, 253–60.

5 King James VI and I, *Minor Prose Works*, ed. James Craigie (Edinburgh: Scottish Text Society, 1982), 190–2.

6 *Extracts from Edinburgh Records, 1589–1603*, 334. What seems to have been the last execution in the panic, that of Richard Graham, would take place on 29 February.

7 NRS, register of deeds, RD1/82 (2), fo. 266v. (11 December 1601); RD1/89, fo. 13v. (2 July 1602). We are grateful to Jamie Reid-Baxter for these references.

a crime, they asked, to have consulted someone who was not known to be a witch, or who was only later convicted of witchcraft? Napier admitted that she had consulted both Agnes Sampson and Richard Graham, two of the other high-profile witches of North Berwick, but she insisted that she had sought healing from them (healing for her mistress and her son respectively), and that she had not known that they were witches. Indeed, although Sampson had been executed for witchcraft in January 1591, Graham had probably not even been convicted at the time of Napier's trial.

One of the defence's arguments attempted to rule out certain categories of witnesses against Napier – principally women and criminals. These witnesses, said the lawyers melodramatically but with legal correctness, 'wald nocht mak fayth in a civile caus in ane mater of fourtie schillingis'. But the king's advocate replied, also correctly, that such witnesses, although not allowed in ordinary cases, *were* allowed in cases of witchcraft and treason.[8]

The document only occasionally mentions the detailed crimes of which Napier was accused, but when it does we get some information not available elsewhere. The summary of 'the fyrst sevin poyntis of the dittay' is particularly noteworthy, since Napier's dittay itself does not survive. The later trial of her assizers gives details of a number of accusations against her, but bears little resemblance to the points made below. Further analysis of these accusations would be desirable.

The document edited below comes from the minute books of the justiciary court. The minute books partially overlap with the books of adjournal (JC2/2), the more formal documents written up later, from which Lawrence Normand and Gareth Roberts printed important material concerning Barbara Napier's trial. The minute books give a much fuller record of the proceedings on 8 May. The document edited below should thus be read alongside the documents printed by Normand and Roberts.

The text is neatly written by an accomplished scribe, presumably the clerk of the court. However, it carries an air of informality not found in the books of adjournal. Several decisions of the judge are given in abbreviated form, occasionally even as a single word. There are more crossings-out and insertions than one would expect in a neat final copy (noted editorially below except for a few minor crossings-out). Occasional passages are cryptic, ungrammatical or even confused. The text thus seems to have been written during the proceedings themselves.

The arguments in court were mainly conducted orally. However, defence and prosecution may from time to time have written down part of their argument and handed it to the judge, who could then make the paper available

8 For a detailed discussion of this issue see Michael B. Wasser and Louise A. Yeoman (eds.), 'The trial of Geillis Johnstone for witchcraft, 1614', *SHS Miscellany*, vol. xiii (Edinburgh: SHS, 2004), 82–145, at pp. 97–9.

to the clerk for inclusion in the minutes. This would be particularly likely when a Latin legal maxim or quotation was introduced – though it should be remembered that all these lawyers were fluent in Latin, and the quotations may have been given from memory. Some of the grammar of the original arguments has survived in the minutes, for instance first-person or present-tense phrases like 'I insist', which would later have been rewritten as 'he insisted'.

There were two phases to the proceedings recorded here. The initial phase consisted of preliminary, procedural discussion; no assize had yet been sworn in, and so the formal trial had not yet begun. Two defence lawyers were appointed, John Russell and John Moscrop; Russell seems to have taken the lead, and is sometimes mentioned individually.[9] In a typical episode, the defence would raise an objection, the prosecution would reply, and then the judge would make a ruling. The defence tried to persuade the king's advocate to show them the dittay in advance, but the advocate refused, knowing that this would give them more time to work out defences and to find opportunities for objections. The text shows that the defence had some idea of what the prosecution's charges were going to be, and tried to head the charges off in advance or persuade the judge to rule them irrelevant. However, the judge, who generally ruled in favour of the prosecution, 'findis the dittay relevant to be put to ane assys'.

At this point, about one-third of the way through the text, the second phase of proceedings began. The assize (which the clerk usually called the 'inqueist') was sworn in – not without defence objections to several individuals – and the formal trial commenced. Presumably the dittay was read out at this point, though the clerk does not specify this. The defence continued to pour out objections, many of them procedural. It was now that they played their best or at least most eloquent card, the objection to women and criminals as witnesses, only to see it overruled. Some of the arguments on both sides now seem to be addressed to the assize, and the judge does not intervene. The text concludes with prosecution and defence addressing themselves to the assize in a way that might indicate a summing-up – but, if so, it is surprising that little or no discussion has been recorded about specific points of the dittay, which one would expect to be discussed point by point. The absence of the dittay, both from the minute book edited here and from the books of adjournal edited by Normand and Roberts, is regrettable. Perhaps the clerk had a copy of the dittay on a separate sheet of paper, and made further notes in its margins. Nevertheless, the material edited below adds considerably to our knowledge of Barbara Napier's trial.

9 For Russell's career see Michael Wasser, 'Russell, John (*c.*1550–1612)', *ODNB*. Three Napiers, evidently Barbara's relatives, were also named as defending her, but they remain in the background of the text as we have it.

The text contains numerous quotations from Latin juristic sources. These passages are translated in footnotes, and citations to modern editions of these sources are given. For an explanation of these sources, please see the introduction to the case of the Earl of Bothwell, edited below in this volume.

TEXT

Source: NRS, Court of Justiciary Minute Books, 1586–1591, JC6/3.

{*p. 445*} *Curia Justiciarie Supremi Domini Nostri regis Tentum in pretorio de Edinburgh octavo Maii anno 1591 per Magistrum Umphride Blindseil justiciarum deputatum et per Davidem Carnegie de Colluthie et dominum Jacobum Melvile.*[10]

Intran
Barbara Napier spous to Archebald Douglas burges of Edinburgh, giltie of certane crymes of wichcraft and consultatioun with witchis comittit as is contenit in dittayis underwrittin at lenth lyand thairupoun.[11]

Proloquintor for the pannell
Mr John Russell
Mr John Moscrope[12]
William Naipar burges of Edinburgh[13]
Alexander Naipar his brother
Andro Naipar

Persewar
Mr David McGill advocate

Barbara Naipar produceit ane letter \and protestatioun/ subscryvit with her hand and desyrit the samin to be red in[14] Judgement and thairupoun askit

10 'Court of justiciary of our sovereign lord the king, held in the tolbooth of Edinburgh, 8 May 1591, by Mr Humphrey Blindseil, justice depute, and by David Carnegie of Colluthie and Sir James Melville'. The text later makes clear that Carnegie and Melville were assessors (advisers or assistants) to Blindseil as judge. There were also arguments about further proposed assessors.

11 In margin (in two paragraphs): 'convict' / 'convict of the consulting with Annye Sampsoun \ane witche/ seking help of her \at thrie severale/ tymes and convict of the consulting and seking help of Ritche Grahame nigromanceir in John Ramsayis hous at the West Port for the help of her sone.'

12 The beginning of what may be a third lawyer's name, 'Mr L...' (this letter uncertain), is crossed out here.

13 This may well have been William Napier of Wrightshouses, Barbara's brother.

14 'presence of' crossed out here.

instruments quhilk wes red and desyrit the said bill to be insert in register quhairof the tennour followis.[15]

The advocat protestit in the contrar Foralsmekle as scho hes declarit or deponit during hir waird howbeit \hir declaratioun/ be mekle les nor hir knawledge had and the treuth could haif testifeit, yit be ressoun the samin is done frelie be hir and without tortor that all hir confessiounis may mak full fayth aganis hir, and speciallie Becaus the samin is deponit in the gritest libertie in presens of the kings majestie and his counsall quha ar the superior Judges of this realme, to quhome and his counsall this Judgement is far inferioure and swa can nocht be callit ane place of gritar libertie to hir, Bot man be estemit inferiour to the place quhairin scho wes quhen scho deponit in presens of his majestie and counsall as said is.

Barbara produceit ane act of parliament granting Libertie to \ane/ procurator to compeir[16] and procure for hir conform to the tennor of the act and may be compellit to that effect.[17]

The said day the Justice desyrit Andro Naipar, William Naipar and Alexander Naipar To compeir in defence of Barbara Naipar quhairupon they askit instruments and desyrit hir to name [*1 word damaged*] procurators that schoe requirit quha namit Maisteris John Russell and John [*about 2 words damaged*] wer send for be the justice be the awyis of my lord chancellor[18] [*about 2 words damaged*] utheris his majesties secrete counsall assessoris to the justice. {*p. 446*}

Comperit Mr John Russell and declarit that he wald nawayis compeir in this mater without[19] the kingis majestie wald command him be his mouth, and immediatlie the justice with awyiss of his assessoris ordanit him to be commandit.

Robert Fraser commandit and chairgeit Mr John Russell and John Moscrop advocattis under the paine of hoirning to compeir and procure for Barbara Naipar, Quhairupoune he askit instruments and protestit that this compearance \was/ for thair obedience and that they wer compellit to compeir.

Mr John Russell thaireftir comperand desyrit that he may haif the inspectioun of the dittay and that he may delay the samin to Mounday[20] utherwyis he refusit to compeir and wald put him selff in the kingis will of hoirning[21] and offerit

[15] This 'letter and protestatioun' does not seem to survive. The clerk may have intended to copy it into the books of adjournal when the formal record was written up from the present less formal minutes.

[16] 'quhairupoune sche askit instruments' crossed out here.

[17] An act of parliament containing this provision had been passed in 1587: *Acts of the Parliaments of Scotland*, iv, 460–1, c. 57, para. 10; RPS, 1587/7/67.

[18] This is a rare mention of the chancellor, Sir John Maitland of Thirlestane, who usually kept a low profile during the North Berwick trials.

[19] 'without': unless.

[20] This was Monday 10 May. The present proceedings took place on 8 May, a Saturday.

[21] That is, he would accept the likely penalty for his disobedience: horning (outlawry). However, he soon changed his mind, as the minutes go on to state.

to compeir on Mounday nixt to cum at quhat hour as they plesit to assigne swa that[22] he may be answerit with[23] the dittay and knaw the kings mynd.

The advocat protestit that na dittay be gevin in to him to be answerit with unto the tyme that the inqueist be chosin and that he will applaud[24] to the kingis will.

The Justice findis proces[25] nochtwithstanding the said Mr Johnis desyre.

The Justice ordainis ane officer to pas to the mercat croce and denunce Mr John Russell for his disobedience incais he procure not instanntlie.

Thairefter Maisteris John Russell and John Moscrop comperit and procurit according to the fyrst chairge.

Mr John Russell protestis for Barbara Naipar that quhatsumevir scho hes spokin \extra/[26] oute of Judgement and out of the presens of the king and counsall sall nawayis prejudge hir and revoikis the samin.

The Justice findis that this protestatoun nedis na answer.

It is alledgeit for Barbara Naipar that no proces can be had upoun the dittay or any part thairof Insafar as the samin is foundit upoun hir confessioun[27] out of Judgement scho being in captivitie \maid/ be hir to Richard Grahame, Agnes Sampsoun[28] or ony uther particular persoun *extra judicum*[29] out of the presens of the king and counsall. The advocat acceptis the allegance *in quantum*[30] and speciallie of all confest in presens of the king and counsall. {*p. 447*}

Repells the allegance [*1 word damaged*] the speciall [*1 word torn away*] salbe considderit.

The Justice findis that the dittay sould be put to ane assys.

The said Barbara askis instruments that na uther persoun apperis to insist \in hir persoun/ in this Judgement \in hir persut/ except the advocat.

Thaireftir[31] the defendar desyrit the advocat to condiscend upoun[32] his informer, be the nocht condiscending quhairof the partie is prejudgeit, seing Incais the samin wes declarit It mycht furneis ane sufficient defence, To wit that nather the kynnismen, freinds nor servandis of the informer sould ather be Judgeis, assessoris or persounes of inqueist.

22 'swa that': so long as.
23 'answerit with': provided with a copy of.
24 'applaud': appeal.
25 'findis proces': orders that trial proceedings should continue.
26 'lait Judgement' crossed out here, and 'extra' inserted above the line. Possibly 'extra' should have been crossed out too.
27 'out of his majesteis presens and' crossed out here.
28 These were two accused witches whom Napier was being accused of having consulted. Agnes Sampson had been convicted and executed in January, while Richard Graham was still under investigation.
29 'out of judgment' or 'out of court'.
30 'to an extent'.
31 'Allegeit' crossed out at the beginning of this paragraph.
32 'condiscend upoun': specify, give the name of.

Answeris the advocat that he aucht to declair na informer in this cais, nather it is[33] neidfull be ressoun of his chairge and office quhilk is publict and generall, Being also ane cryme of tressoun aganis the kingis majestie, his estait and countrey and als ane cryme of wytchcraft aganis the majestie of God and libertie of his ewangell quhairin ony privat person of his awin motioun may persew but[34] ony Informer, and thairfore may do the samin haifing his majesties command and directioun for my warrand.

To the quhilk It is answerit that the argument foirsaid is nocht proponit for ony part of the dittay concerning the kingis majestie in his awin persoun, Bot insafar as this accusatioun is institute aganis the defendar for witchcraft or consultatioun with wichis, In the quhilk caisis of necessitie he man[35] condiscend upoun ane informer, and forsamekle as concernis his majestie In that cais he desyris him nocht to condiscend upoun ane informer.

The advocat repetis his answer.

The said Barbara yit as of before Justice find that the earle of Mortoun, the thhesaurer [*sic*] and Carmichell and the Lord Lyndsay sall nocht be assessoris safar as concernis the erle of Angus.[36]

It is alledgeit of the law that ane partie declynit for suspicioun in ony part of the caus can nocht be Judges in the rest and trew [*1-2 words torn away*] that the persounes abone writtin ar fund [*1-2 words torn away*] they can nocht be assessoris in an part concerning the erle of Angus. {*p. 448*}

The Justice repellis the allegeance.

The partie protestis for remeid.

33 *Sic*. Read 'is it'.

34 'but': without.

35 'man': must.

36 This paragraph is confusing. The words 'said Barbara yit as', 'earle of Mortoun' and 'the Lord Lyndsay' seem to have been crossed out, which would leave the following text remaining: 'The … of before Justice find that the … the thhesaurer and Carmichell and … sall nocht be assessoris safar as concernis the erle of Angus.' In addition, after the words 'nocht be', the scribe seems to have written 'u' (perhaps intending to write 'upon') and then crossed it out. The four disputed assessors were important politicians: William Douglas, sixth earl of Morton; Thomas Lyon, master of Glamis, treasurer ('thesaurer'); Sir John Carmichael of that Ilk, captain of the royal guard; and James, seventh Lord Lindsay of the Byres. All four had connections with the Douglas family of which Archibald Douglas, eighth earl of Angus, had been the nominal head until his death in 1588. Morton was a leading member of the family; Lyon was the uncle of Angus's widow Jean Lyon (who incurred her own suspicion of witchcraft); Carmichael and Lindsay were politically associated with the Douglases, and Lindsay's mother had been a Douglas. All four were active privy councillors, attending the meeting of the council held on 12 May: *RPC*, iv, 615. The role of the Douglases in the panic, seeking explanations for Angus's death, is noteworthy. For their moves towards a possible prosecution of Jean Lyon, countess of Angus, see Victoria Carr, 'The Countess of Angus's Escape from the North Berwick Witch-Hunt', in Julian Goodare (ed.), *Scottish Witches and Witch-Hunters* (Basingstoke, 2013), 34–48.

The said Barbara allegeis that for ony part of the dittay concerning the kingis majestie scho offeris hir selff *sine mora*[37] to the knawledge of assys, as to the rest of the dittay allegeis that the samin is nocht relevant except safar concerning the kingis majestie, Becaus the act of parliament concernis only twa memberis viz. committeris of wichcraft and consultaris; as to the fyrst thair is na thing qualifeit, as to the secund anent counsall It is nevir affermit that I consultit with the saidis persounis as wichis upoun ane mater of wichcraft *ad finem mali*,[38] Nather yit is it affermit that the saidis persounis the tyme of the consultatioun or att ony tyme before wer convict or declarit wichis or sa commounlie haldin and repute, and a cryme can nocht be committit without speciall knawledge *absque dolo et in delictis non punitur affectus nisi sequatur effectus crimine lese maiestatis*[39] and this is proponit *unico contextuo*[40] aganis the haill dittay except before exceptit.

To the quhilk It is answerit be the advocat that for answer to this alledgance scho is accusit speciallie of wichcraft, and ferder repetis the act of parliament quhilk nocht only makis the using of wichcraft to be criminall Bot also the consultaris with thame, seikaris help [*sic*] att thame or respons or answer, Lyke as in the haill dittay and divers pairtis thairof It is exprest that the said Barbara had consultitt with Richard Grahame and Annie Sampsoun as notorious wichis sa repute and haldin, and speciallie the said Ritche Grahame[41] quha hes bene sa repute the xx yeiris bygaine, and as for convictioun thair is na sic thing contenit in the act of parliament, and repetis the said act of parliament.

Answeris Barbra the alledgance foresaid is nocht provit for ony part of the dittay concerning ony fact or deid, Bot only forsamekle thairof as consistis concerning the consultatioun, for as to the rests scho is content the samin pas to ane assys. And attending to the act of parliament It is certane that thair is na ma persounis contenit thairin Bot usaris of wichcraft, abusaris of the people, persounis geving thame furth for wichis, and persounis[42] seikaris of responsis or consultatioun, quhilk can nocht be without ather convictioun, procedinge and declarator {*p. 449*} or ellis that thay sa be commounlie repute.

The advocat repetis his answer.

Then thaireftir It is allegeit that the fyrst sevin poyntis of the dittay ar alluterlie Irrelevant, viz. anent the doublet of sating, anent the discord betwix hir and hir husband George Ker,[43] and anent hir mishavir [*sic*] towardis him to be in love with him eftir hir husbandis deceis,[44] the lyke accusation anent

37 'without delay'.
38 'for a wicked purpose'.
39 'without intention and in delicts (crimes), states of mind are not punished except in the crime of lese majesty (treason)'.
40 'in each instance'.
41 In margin: 'scho socht responsis att him'.
42 'allege thame' crossed out here.
43 George Ker had been Napier's first husband.
44 The identity of the 'him' in this clause is obscure. It does not seem to be either of Napier's husbands.

Archibald Dowglas hir present husband, the uther poynt anent Cauldwall, the nixt poynt anent hir dochter for the forbidding of hir dochter to use the Lord Bothwellis cumpany, with all the haill remanent poyntis, and speciallie anent the gaist of Carschogill[45] quhikis ar altogidder irrelevant and contenit nather *factum neque animum*.[46]

The advocat for answer repetis the act of parliament and the dittay produceit.[47]

Repellis the allegance and findis the dittay relevant to be put to ane assys.

Assisa

Johnne Boig maister portar to his majestie	Patrik Sandelandis tailyeor in Edinburgh
George Boig maister of the ailsellar	Mr Archibald Wilkie burges of the Cannogait
Walter Bell att mylne of Deane[48] \chancellor/[49]	Andro Cuthbertsoun burges thair[50]
Hector Clavie burges of the Cannogait	Robert Cuninghame burges thair
James Galbraith averieman	William Harper burges thair

David Seytoun in Foulstruther
William Justice merchand burges of Edinburgh
Johnne Seytoun coilman burges thair
Johnne Mowbray merchand burges of Edinburgh
David Fairlie merchand burges of Edinburgh

Absentes

Alexander Oistean tailyeor burges of Edinburgh, William Hutcheson cordiner thair,[51] Patrik Cochran merchand thair, William Geichan merchand thair, Mungo Scot merchand thair,[52] Thomas Fowlis goldsmith thair, Alexander Myllar tailyeor thair, Patrik Eleis merchand, Thomas Somervaill maltman, Johne Edzer[53] merchand thair.

45 Robert Douglas of Coshogle was the elder brother of Napier's husband Archibald Douglas. Coshogle Castle was in Nithsdale. The 'gaist' (ghost or spirit) of Coshogle is not otherwise known.

46 'neither the (criminal) deed nor the intention'.

47 The defence team seem to have been given a copy of the dittay by this point at least.

48 Below the name of Walter Bell, 'Henry Quhyte burgess of Edinburgh' has been crossed out.

49 It is not clear to whom the word 'chancellor' should be attached; it is adjacent not only to Walter Bell but also to Robert Cunningham and the crossed-out Henry White.

50 Andrew Cuthbertson, Robert Cunningham and William Harper were burgesses of Edinburgh, not Canongate as implied here: Normand and Roberts (eds.), *Witchcraft*, 248, 253–4.

51 Four words crossed out, the first illegible and the other three 'Cunninghame merchand there'; illegible amendments have also been added.

52 'John Porterfeild merchand thair' crossed out here.

53 'maltman' crossed out here.

Allegeis that David Seytoun can nocht be put upoun hir assys Becaus he is nocht ane burges, scho[54] being ane burges wyfe.

The advocat he [*sic*] being ane gentilman is equall with ane burges.

Repellis the allegance. {*p. 450*}

Allegeis aganis David Becaus he is tennent to my lord Seytoun ane quhom thair is[55] ane pairt of this dittay consavit.

The advocat answers that in the mater concerning the lord Seytoun he sall nocht voit.

Allegeis aganis John Boig maister portar, Becaus the maist part of this dittay concerns the kingis majestie he can nocht be put to an assys becaus he is domestik.[56]

Allegeis that John Seytoun in the Cannogait can nocht pas on the assys becaus he is brother to David Seytoun in Tranent quha hes gevin up dittay aganis hir, at the leist aganis Effie Makcalzan, and that he hes instructit thame quha ar to be usit as witnesis, and als Is man and servand to the lord Seytoun.

Confest John Seytoun that he is ane man and tennent to my lord Seytoun.

Allegeis aganis Joseph Dowglas of Pumpherstoun becaus he hes gevin up dittay aganis the said Barbara and att leist aganis Effie McCalzan quha ar *socii criminis*.[57]

Repellis.

The advocat comperand passis upoun that pairt of the dittay concerning the lord Seytoun or the baptesing of the catt.

The said Barbara allegeis that the passing fra the the [*sic*] lord Seytoun can nocht prejudge him[58] anent the defensis.

The Justice repellis the allegance.

Allegeis that he[59] can nocht pas upoun this assys Becaus he is the principall informer of the wichis, inventar of this pursuit,[60] bringar in of the wichis, subornar, luikar for ane rewaird.

Mr John requyrit the advocat to sweir the dittay quhairto the advocat answerit that he[61] aucht nocht to sweir.[62]

It is allegeit to the persounes of inqueist that seing the mater is now absolutlie put in thair handis that thairfore sic verificatiounis and probatiounis as my lord advocat hes for verifeing of the dittay and everie poynt thairof aucht to be presentlie produceit and the pairtie hard[63] and object thair aganis. As

54 'scho': i.e. Barbara Napier.

55 'nocht' crossed out here.

56 'domestik': a (domestic) servant of the king.

57 'partners in crime'. One of the accusations against Euphemia MacCalzean was that she had attempted to bewitch Joseph Douglas of Pumpherston into marrying her daughter.

58 *Sic*. Probably 'hir' is meant.

59 The clerk has omitted this person's name, but probably David Seton in Foulstruther is meant.

60 'luikar' crossed out here.

61 'could nocht' crossed out here.

62 This may allude to the reading out of the dittay before the assize.

63 'hard': heard.

to Rytchard Grahame and remanent persounis quhais depositionis hes bene ressavit, nather aucht thay to mak fayth nor can be respectit in ony sort, Becaus of[64] the commoun law and of the law of all nationis, probationis in materis criminall, speciallie in sic a tressoun allegeit attemptit aganis his majestie, aucht to be sa evident and manifest as be confessioun of {*p. 451*} pairtie accusit or utherwyis be sic [*about 1 word torn away*] documentis as may induce ane manifest and concludand probatioun and as the commoun law says *debeant esse Luce meridiana clariores*,[65] For the quhilk caus the commoun law hes reprovit and damnit mony sindrie persounis that thair assertioun, depositioun and confessioun, accusatioun or declaratioun sal nevir be respectit, haif fayth or credite, namelie the depositiounis of wemen, the depositiounis of wichis, of persounis insaine, of persounis dilaitit for crymes, of persounis that ar giltie of the samin cryme, and last of persounis ather dilatit, accusit, convictit or to be accusit, makand manifest and plane professioun and confessioun of the cryme, and trew It is that the depositiounis of the saidis haill persounis tane att onye tyme heirbefore ather in presens of his majestie or counsall or in presens of sic persounis quha wer appointit to the effect ar the depositiounis and assertiounis of wemen, notour and confest wichis, persounis insaine, confessand thame selffis alreddie giltie of the cryme of witchcraft, being puir, miserable and corrupt, quhais depositiounis wald nocht mak fayth in a civile caus in ane mater of fourtie schillingis, farder in the lyfe of man or woman {*p. 452*} in Landis and guidis, namelie In respect of the manifest contradictioun maid be thame selffis in thair depositiounis being fra tyme to tyme subornit and instructit thairto and for verifeing of the propositioun of the argument, seing the samin consistis altogidder in the law and daylie practik of all natiounis, the said Barbara produceit certane allegatiounis in writt quhilk scho desyrit to be red to the assys, as to the probatioun of the assumptioun scho remittis the samin to the tryall of the inqueist and to the verificatioun usit be the advocat, protesting heirfore that nather the despositiounis alreddie tane or ony utheris to be maid heirefter salbe respectit to mak fayth, and this argument is proponit conjunctlie aganis the verificatioun and probatioun of the haill dittay, desyring the assys to remember the tryell quhilk wes usit aganis the lady Foullis, quha althocht divers depositiounis of wichis wer usit and confrontit in hir presens, yit no respect wes had thairto bot the pairtie clangeit.[66] In lyke maner the uther quha wes defendit be Mr William

[64] 'of': by, according to.

[65] 'they must be clearer than the light at midday'.

[66] Katherine Ross, Lady Foulis, had been acquitted of witchcraft in July 1590, shortly before the outbreak of the North Berwick panic: Alex Sutherland, *The Brahan Seer: The Making of a Legend* (Bern, 2009), 34–57.

\Leslye/[67] callit Bessie Roy,[68] and lykewyis recentlie sen the lait brute[69] of the alledgeit wichcraft the twa sister [*sic*] callit Luikwp[70] in Leyth[71] quha haifing offerit thame selffis to the tryall of ane inqueist and the persewer finding that they war libberit be the Mersall[72] upoun cautioun {*p. 453*}, protesting In cais the assys do in the contrar to wilfull error.

\advocat/ for assys[73] the advocat disassents that ony uther wreatt or allegatioun be ressavit to be shewin to the assys nor is presentlie[74] contenit in this his allegance, and as to his allegance of the nocht admitting of hir companyounis in cryme to be brocht heir to heir the dittay red, I am altogidder contrar thairto and sayis the samin aucht to be grantit that thair declaratiounis constantlie maid in the consultatioun with the said Barbara may be confermit and maid knawin to the Inqueist and that the inqueist may decerne upoun certan knawledge, and forder that thair depositiounis and assertionis man[75] be belevit in this cais, It is bayth of the law expreslie and of ressoun quhilk is the moder of all law, speciallie in this accusatioun Quhairin ar contenit twa crymes principallie, the one of witchcraft aganis the majestie of God, the uther of tressoun aganis our soveranes persoun and estait of the realm, In the quhilk twa causis sa detestable gif the companyounis and partakers of the crymes and aither of thame were nocht ressavit to testifie the samin how miserable persounes that evir thay wer utherewyis defamit persounes nor be the cryme it selff, sic crymes could nocht be detectit nor discoverit and that be ressoun na honest man is maid of counsall or knawledge of so vyle, haynous and detestable crymes, Swa that gif the consequens of the former allegance wer allowable It sould follow that sic tressounes aganis God as witchcraft is, and tressoun aganis the king and prince, for laik of probatione sould remane unpwneist, and that wemen of[76] the law may be ressavit witnessis It is universallie trew,

67 'R...' and 'Bessie' crossed out here, and 'Leslye' added above the line.

68 In August 1590, in two related witchcraft cases from Aberdeenshire, Bessie Roy had been acquitted, and William Leslie of Crechie and his wife Violet Auchinleck had been remitted for trial in their locality: P. G. Maxwell-Stuart, *Satan's Conspiracy: Magic and Witchcraft in Sixteenth-Century Scotland* (East Linton, 2001), 132–4.

69 'lait brute': recent rumour. This evidently refers to the beginning of the North Berwick panic itself.

70 Marion 'Linkup' in Leith, and 'the two Linkups', had been named as fellow-witches in Agnes Sampson's dittay in January 1591: Normand and Roberts (eds.), *Witchcraft*, 239–40. There is no record of them being prosecuted. The name has been read here as 'Luikwp' (Lookup), as this is a recognised surname, while 'Linkup' is not. The three minims in the manuscript could in principle be either 'ui' or 'in'.

71 At this point, much of the page has been torn away, but it seems to have been already torn before the scribe wrote on it; the text continues round the edge of the tear.

72 'Mersall': marshal.

73 *Sic.* Possibly these three words should have been written as a marginal rubric, with the main text of the paragraph beginning 'The advocat disassents ...'.

74 'schawin' crossed out here.

75 'man': must.

76 'of': by. Two illegible words added above the line here.

Lex § De testibus;[77] *L. In testamento & mulier de testamentis*[78] and that infamous persounis may be ressavit in tryell of tressoun of sex that evir *{p. 454}* [*1 word damaged*] of man or woman,[79] It is certane of the law *in questionibus et L. famosi F. ad L. Juliam maiestatis*[80] Forder It is the commoun opinoun of all Law and observit universallie in all natiounis quhair utherwyis the veritie can nocht be tryit that the maist vyle persoun, yea evin notour and commoun huiris,[81] ar ressavit for witnes and tryell of the veritie, *Capitulo cauta labet \Ac/ Decemonia L. finali F. ad Legem Juliam de anona,*[82] In respect quhairof my desyre aucht to be grantit nochtwithstanding the allegance abonewrittin.

It is answerit that the commoun law[83] *L. Sciant cuncti de probationibus Co.*[84] *et per legem qui sententiam Co. de poenis*[85] *Et L. legem ad dictos F. de appellationibus*[86]

77 This is probably a reference to Justinian, *Digest*, 22.5.18. *De testibus*, relating to witnesses, is *Digest*, 22.5, and while no pinpoint reference is given to *Digest*, 22.5.18, it supports the proposition being made here. It is a statement attributed to the jurist Paul to the effect that '[t]he fact that the *lex Julia* on adultery forbids a woman found guilty to give evidence shows that women have the right to give evidence at a trial' (Watson translation). In other words, there would have been no need to prohibit adulterous women from giving evidence had there not been a rule allowing women to act as witnesses in general. For an explanation of the 'Justinian' sources cited here and in later footnotes, please see the introduction to the case of the Earl of Bothwell, edited below in this volume.

78 This is probably a reference to Justinian, *Digest*, 28.1.20.6, on the assumption that the writer meant to refer to the title *Qui testamenta*, which discusses which individuals have the power to make wills (there is no title *De testamentis* in the *Digest*, but the writer seems to have had a *Digest* reference in mind). Within *Qui testamenta* (*Digest*, 28.1) there is a section beginning *Lex qui testamenta* (*Digest*, 28.1.20) and a sub-section (*Digest*, 28.1.20.6) beginning '*mulier*', which is to the point. Here a statement attributed to Ulpian reads 'It is true that a woman will not be able to act as a witness in relation to a will, but as an argument that otherwise a woman can be a witness, there is the *lex Julia de adulteriis*, which specifically forbids a woman condemned for adultery to be produced as a witness or to give testimony' (Watson translation).

79 The sense of this is: 'infamous persons (i.e. those of bad reputation) may be admitted (as witnesses) in treason trials, whatever sex they are, men or women'.

80 Justinian, *Digest*, 48.4.7–8, which states that women may bring accusations of treason.

81 'huiris' (whores): prostitutes.

82 The ancient Roman law 'Lex Julia de annona', on the regulation of grain markets, contained a clause allowing women's testimony to be accepted: Justinian, *Digest*, 48.12.3.1 (Papirius 1 *de const.*).

83 'It is allegeit' crossed out here.

84 Justinian, *Code*, 4.19.25, which deals with matters of proof. It states that accusers should report matters for judicial consideration where there are 'suitable witnesses' or 'most transparent documents' or where there is 'evidence indisputable for proof and clearer than the light of day' (Frier translation).

85 Justinian, *Code*, 9.47.16, which deals with punishments, and states that magistrates are not to hand down capital or severe sentences for murder, adultery or sorcery (*maleficium*) without conviction on the basis of 'his or her own confession or at any rate on the evidence of all those who have been examined judicially under torture or (mere) questioning (leading) to one and the same well-aligned conclusion…' (Frier translation).

86 '*De appellationibus*' (on appeals) almost certainly indicates Justinian, *Digest*, 49.1. There is no pinpoint reference, but the writer may have had in mind *Digest*, 49.1.6, which states that an appeal against capital punishment might be brought either by the condemned individual or by anyone else. The passage, attributed to Ulpian, continues by noting that both relatives

ad penalem sententiam nunquam pervenitur nisi vel reus confessus sit vel clarissimum probationibus convictur aut omnium qui tormentis et interrogationibus dediti fuerant in unum conspirantibus quia tutius est impunitum relinqui facinus nocentis[87] *quam Innocentem condemnare.*[88] This matter is mair cleirlie decydit *In L. i § diune*[89] *et l. si quis ultro F. de questionibus*[90] *Nam ipsa confessio confitentis crimen in causa corporali et criminali non Ligat confitentem nisi in ea perseverat constanter nisi aliis adminiculis religio cognoscentis instruatur.*[91] Quhair he gevis the ressoun in this mater in thair confessounis oftymis \maid/[92] *Cum metu tum in carcere tum in puntia tormentorum et per impatientiam*[93] Be the quhilk oftymis the Innocentis ar prejudgeit, Bot to mak this mater mair cleir thair is ane speciall decisioun in *cap 10 Puncta glossa extra de accusationibus*[94] quhair It is expreslie decydit *quia femina pupilla dilatus infamia crimine tentus sortilegus corruptus socius criminis pauper Inimicus et criminosus neque admittuntur ad testimonium ad probationem ad*

---

and non-relatives of the condemned might appeal, 'for I believe that for humanity's sake anyone who appeals should be heard'. Ulpian adds that any such appeal should result in a stay of execution, even if the condemned had 'acquiesced in his sentence' and effectively asked for punishment to be carried out (Watson translation). The point of citing this passage may have been to underline the high threshold that had to be met prior to the execution of a penal sentence.

87 '*aut*' ('or') crossed out here.

88 'It never comes to a penal sentence unless the accused confesses or is convicted by most clear proofs or by the common admission of all those who have been given over to torments and interrogations. For it is better that one who does harm be left unpunished than that the innocent be condemned'.

89 This is probably a reference to Justinian, *Digest*, 48.18.1.pr., the title *De quaestionibus* (on investigations), and to a section beginning with the words '*divus Augustus*', which reads 'The deified Augustus laid down that one should not begin with the application of pain, and that reliance should not be placed entirely on torture, as is contained also in the deified Hadrian's letter to Sennius Sabinus' (Watson translation). It only makes sense in light of the context when read together with the next reference in the text, to *Digest*, 48.18.1.27.

90 Justinian, *Digest*, 48.18.1.27: 'If a person should confess to wrongdoing of his own accord, he should not always be believed; for sometimes people confess out of fear or for some other reason' (Watson translation). There follows a discussion of the matter which is to the point, and which supports the argument which follows.

91 'For the confession itself of the one admitting the charge, in a corporal and criminal case, does not bind the one confessing unless he perseveres in it constantly, (or) unless the scruples of conscience of those acquainted (with the matter) may be furnished with other supporting evidence'.

92 'admittit' crossed out here.

93 'through fear, through imprisonment, through the pains of torture, and through want of endurance'. Here the reference is probably to Justinian, *Digest*, 48.18.1.23 (in addition to Justinian, *Digest*, 48.18.1.27, just cited), where Ulpian states that torture should be used with care. He explains that 'there are a number of people who, by their endurance or their toughness under torture, are so contemptuous of it that the truth can in no way be squeezed out of them'. On the other hand, he continues, others 'have so little endurance that they would rather tell any kind of lie than suffer torture; so it happens that they confess in various ways, incriminating not only themselves but others also' (Watson translation). No mention is made of the fear of imprisonment in the original text of these passages in the *Digest*.

94 Ordinary gloss to *Liber Extra*, 5.1.1, *De accusationibus*, on the word *Legitimus*; this text is paraphrased in the next few lines.

fidem faciendum ad delationem ad inquisitionem aut ad accusationem[95] and as to the haill lawis allegeit in the contrar this haill solutioun is usit in generall in the contrar that the prince be way of inquisitioun *et qui sunt ad Latus imperatoris*[96] may in ane mater of tressoun or ony uther cryme use all minacles[97] quhairby the veritie may be tryit and to ressave the depositiounis of quhatsumevir persounis of quhatsumevir qualitie yit It can nocht be fund be ony law that full fact sould be gevin to the persounes of the qualitie my lord advocat cravis the wichis to be confrontit {*p. 455*} with the said Barbara presentlie It is [*2–3 words torn away*] that seing the mater is now in the handis [*2–3 words torn away*] inqueist the place is nocht propper nather [*2–3 words torn away*] examinatioun[98] or confrontatioun, Bot he man[99] cum heir instructit with manifest and cleir probatiounis, And gif It sall pleis the assys to heir the saidis persounis assertiounis or depositiounis, the said Barbara protestis that the[100] assys sall gif na faith unto thame.

It is answerit be the advocat acceptand the allegance Insafar as it makis for him *et non alias*[101] and that the solutioun of the argument proponit Is easie to be solvit and man be solvit be the variatioun of the proceding of our Law in criminall caussis fra the forme and ordour of proceding in the commoun law, For thir ar the wordis and forme of the propositioun that na sentence can be gevin in a criminall caus Bot ather upoun the confessioun of ane pairtie frelie maid or ellis cleir probatioun of the cryme deduceit to the Judge gevar of the sentence, quhilk ar safar distant fra our forme that nane of thame hes place thairin. For the first a man or woman sall nocht die upoun thair confessioun how trew that evir it be, nather may the Judge criminall pronunce sentence thairupoun, except ane inqueist be cognitioun upoun thair conscience and knawledge had convict the pairtie confessand the cryme and find those giltie thairof, Quhilk convictioun is sufficient probatioun to the Juge[102] criminal of our Law and ordour of Scotland, and upoun that convictioun his sentence is pronunceit as upoun full and sufficient probatioiun, Swa that the Lawis allegeit be the said Mr John ar improperlie allegeit In respect of our forme and ordour abone writtin, alwayis yit as of before I insist that thir persounes may be presentit before or the mater be committit to the inqueist, quhilk I allege

95 'because a woman, a pupil, a person reputed to be a criminal, a sorcerer, a corrupt partner in crime, a poor person, enemies and criminals, are not admitted to testify, to prove, to make faith, to denounce, to investigate or to accuse'.

96 'and who are on the side of the prince'.

97 *Sic* (or possibly 'ninacles'). The meaning is probably 'adminicles'. An adminicle is something that contributes to proving a point without being itself a complete proof.

98 Tentative reconstruction of damaged word: '…minatioun'.

99 'man': must.

100 'said' crossed out here.

101 'and not otherwise'.

102 'of' crossed out here.

is na soner fullie committit to the inqueist nor that all allegances be furnischit tryall for thair informatioun usit thay removit out of court and inclusit.[103]

The said Barbara Naiper takis instrumentis that thair is na kynd of verificatioun of the assertioun of the dittay bot the depositiounes of thir thr[104] persounes and thair[105] assertionis att the [*1 word damaged*] with the depositioun of Agnes Sampsoun. {*p. 456*}

The advocat repetis the assertioun and depositioun of the persounis togidder with the constant assertioun and depositioun of Annie Sampsoun to the end, and protestis for error In cais thay acquit according to ane protestatioun produceit in writt.[106]

In Lyke maner Barbara desyrit the persounis of inqueist to be rememberit[107] hir constant denyall of the haill dittay except the speiking of[108] Annie Sampsoun for the help of the lady Angus mestres Jeane Lyoun, and the speking with Rytchard Grahame for the health of hir sone, and desyrit the inqueist to tak tryall of[109] the provest of Edinburgh[110] and Mr James Balfour and sum of the counsall gif \Jonet Strayton/ confest expreslie in thair presens[111] that thay knew nather Barbara Naipar nor Effie McCalzan mair nor uther persounis, and repetit the argumentis maid of before anent the depositioun of[112] wichis.[113]

103 'inclusit': enclosed. The assize would be 'enclosed' when they retired to deliberate on their verdict.

104 *Sic.* Possibly read 'thrie'.

105 'ditt...' crossed out here.

106 Such a 'protest for error' was usually an empty threat, but Napier's assizers really were prosecuted for 'wilful error'; see the introduction above.

107 'to be rememberit': to be reminded of.

108 'speiking of': speaking to.

109 'tak tryall of': seek evidence from.

110 John Arnott of Birswick was provost of Edinburgh at this time.

111 Janet Stratton, one of the accused North Berwick witches, made several depositions, but this seems to refer to one that is not recorded elsewhere. Her most recent recorded deposition at this point had been on 4 May 1591: Normand and Roberts (eds.), *Witchcraft*, 170–3.

112 'witnessis' crossed out here.

113 The minute book continues at this point (pp. 456–8 of the MS) with a version of the text of 10 May 1591 printed by Normand and Roberts as 'Barbara Napier's Trial Continued'. The latter version, from the books of adjournal, is substantially identical to the minute book and was presumably copied from it: Normand and Roberts (eds.), *Witchcraft*, 250–2. The clerk may have kept a separate record, no longer extant, of further proceedings of 8 May, since Normand and Roberts' text from that date (their pp. 247–50) contains material that is not in the extant minute books.

9. EARL OF BOTHWELL, EDINBURGH, 1593

INTRODUCTION

Francis Stewart (1562–1612), fifth earl of Bothwell, was the highest-status person ever to be formally accused of witchcraft in Scotland. The so-called North Berwick witchcraft panic, beginning in 1590, rapidly developed into a perceived conspiracy against the king. In early 1591, Bothwell, the king's cousin, began to be suspected as the ringleader of the conspiracy. However, he was not brought to trial until 1593, by which time the panic had abated, and he was acquitted. The document edited below relates to this acquittal.

The circumstances and even the date on which Bothwell's name was first brought into the North Berwick panic remain obscure, but the main accused witch to name him was Richard Graham. Graham was a magical practitioner and alleged necromancer with an aristocratic clientele, and his testimony was crucial in incriminating Bothwell. Bothwell admitted that he knew Graham, but denied involvement in witchcraft.[1]

Bothwell was arrested on 15 April 1591 and imprisoned in Edinburgh Castle. Rather than face trial at the height of the panic, he escaped in June. He remained on the run for most of the next two years, carrying out various colourful exploits. In July 1593 he engineered a reconciliation with the king, though it would turn out to be only temporary. As part of this process, he agreed to undergo a trial on the charge of witchcraft, evidently hoping for an acquittal that would aid his rehabilitation.

Lawrence Normand and Gareth Roberts identified and printed three important documents relating to Bothwell's trial. There is a narrative of Richard Graham's evidence against Bothwell; a list of assizers at the trial; and the minutes of the trial itself, on 10 August 1593, with a dittay that

[1] The fullest account of Bothwell's role in the panic is Edward J. Cowan, 'The Darker Vision of the Scottish Renaissance: The Devil and Francis Stewart', in Ian B. Cowan and Duncan Shaw (eds.), *The Renaissance and Reformation in Scotland* (Edinburgh, 1983), 125–40. For Bothwell's wider career see Robin G. Macpherson, 'Francis Stewart, Fifth Earl Bothwell, *c.*1563–1612: Lordship and Politics in Jacobean Scotland' (University of Edinburgh PhD thesis, 1998), and Rob Macpherson, 'Stewart, Francis, first earl of Bothwell (1562–1612)', *ODNB*.

closely follows the previous record of Graham's evidence, underlining its importance for the prosecution.[2]

The brief document edited below is a memorandum by one of Bothwell's defence lawyers, arguing against Richard Graham's testimony. It is undated and anonymous; we do not know who Bothwell's advocates were. He would have been sure to engage professional lawyers, though, and the memorandum is clearly the work of such a person.

The memorandum is carefully thought out and organised, but hurriedly written and informally expressed. It may have been written as an aide-memoire for a lawyer's speech in court, or perhaps it was handed to the judge at an early stage in the trial, or both. It presents its main text on the right-hand side of the page, with a wide left-hand margin for citations to juristic sources. The main text is written in a mixture of Scots and Latin, while the citations are entirely in Latin. In the edition below, the Latin text has been italicised (as is usual in this volume), but translations are not given in footnotes because the text is instead explained in the table below (to be discussed in a moment). Because there are occasional uncertainties in transcription of the Latin, scribal abbreviations have been expanded in square brackets. There are letters written at the end of eleven of the twelve main-text paragraphs, referring across to the citations on the left; here these letters have been printed editorially in ***bold italics*** for clarity. Thus, each right-hand paragraph needs to be read before the corresponding left-hand citations.

The citations, to texts of Roman law and canon law, are so important to the lawyers' argument that we have expanded the citations at the end of the edition.[3] After the text itself we have provided a table, 'The juristic citations explained', listing each of the citations, explaining where the citation can be found in modern sources, quoting the Latin text of the original texts of Roman law and canon law that Bothwell's lawyers were citing, and summarising those texts with comments. Each item in the table begins with one of the italicised letters given in the memorandum itself, '***a***', '***b***' and so on. Several of these letters include more than one citation, so these are broken down in the table as '**a** *(i)*', '**a** *(ii)*', and so on. We are indebted to Professor Andrew Simpson for this table.

The Roman law citations are all taken from the *Digest* or the *Codex* of Justinian.[4] In some cases, the lawyers who referred to these texts evidently

2 Lawrence Normand and Gareth Roberts (eds.), *Witchcraft in Early Modern Scotland: James VI's 'Demonology' and the North Berwick Witches* (Exeter, 2000), 275–87.

3 The citations are unscrambled below. For an introduction to legal citations in this period see James A. Brundage, *Medieval Canon Law* (London, 1995), 190–205.

4 Reference has been made to Alan Watson (ed.), *The Digest of Justinian*, 4 vols. (Philadelphia, 1985); Bruce W. Frier *et al.* (eds.), *The Codex of Justinian*, 3 vols. (Cambridge, 2016); Yves Lassard and Alexandr Koptev (eds.), *The Roman Law Library*, n.d., online at <https://droitromain.univ-grenoble-alpes.fr/>; Paul Krueger and Theodore Mommsen (eds.),

meant their readers to consider the ordinary gloss which accompanied manuscript and printed editions (see e.g. the commentary on citation ***f(i)*** below). The canon law citations are taken from the *Decretum Gratiani* or the *Liber Extra* (the *Decretales* of Gregory IX).[5] Once again, the lawyers occasionally expected the court to consider the ordinary glosses to these texts as well.

The use of these sources is unsurprising, given the extensive reliance on Roman law and canon law in legal practice at this time.[6] These were the two laws taught in university law faculties – sometimes referred to as 'both the laws' or the *utrumque ius*. At a time when lawyers could envisage law 'as a body of learning fashioned through expert debate', this university learning was used in disputations within the College of Justice to refine the judges' understanding of the law.[7] Similar assumptions were presumably at work here, albeit in a criminal court. It is curious that Bothwell's lawyers frequently cited a text from canon law – *Decretum Gratiani* C. 4 q. 2-3 c. 3 – which was in essence lifted from two texts of Roman law – *Digest* 22.5 and *Codex* 4.20. The lawyers also cited those Roman law texts separately, making one wonder why they bothered to cite the text from the canon law too. The point may have been to show that the learning of *both* the laws supported Bothwell's position.

The audience for the memorandum is the court as a whole, but more particularly it is probably addressed to the judge, hoping that he will rule that Richard Graham's testimony is unacceptable and should not even be presented to the assize. It does not engage with anything specific that Graham had said about Bothwell or about witchcraft. Instead, it pursues a more fundamental line of counter-attack: Graham is an untrustworthy person, so that *any* testimony by him should be disregarded. In effect it argues that, because Graham really is a witch, his statements that Bothwell is a witch cannot be believed.

The argument is simple enough in conception, but broken down into twelve smaller numbered parts. These small parts can be reassembled into three main groups, relating to Graham himself, to the law on witnesses, and to technical points. Further study of all of these would be desirable, but here they can be outlined.

Four of the twelve points relate to Graham as a person. As a witch he has renounced his baptism and thus the truth of Christ (point 5); he has been known to lie under oath (point 6); he has contradicted himself (point 9); and he has led a disreputable life (point 10).

Corpus Iuris Civilis, 3 vols. (Berlin, 1922); *Digestum Vetus* (Lyons, 1560); *Informatium* (Lyons, 1560); *Digestum Novum* (Lyons, 1560).

5 Reference has been made to *Decretum Gratiani* (Venice, 1584) and *Decretales Gregorii IX* (Venice, 1584), and to Emil Friedberg (ed.), *Corpus Iuris Canonici*, 2 vols. (Leipzig, 1879–81).

6 For the ways in which lawyers justified the use of the learned laws in practice, see J. D. Ford, *Law and Opinion in Scotland during the Seventeenth Century* (Oxford, 2007), 181–246.

7 Ford, *Law and Opinion*, 4–5.

Six points relate to the law on the kind of person who may or may not be accepted as a witness, and on what kind of witness evidence can be conclusive. The first of these is not about Graham's position at all, but about the absence of *other* witnesses: a crime cannot be proven by a single witness (point 1). But his position also invalidates his testimony in various ways. He has given his testimony in return for a promised reward (point 3); as a criminal he is by definition an infamous person (point 4); he is an accomplice in the very crime of which Bothwell is accused (point 7); he has been incited by someone else to give his testimony (point 8); and he should be regarded as an 'accuser', and as such cannot be trusted to give impartial and true evidence (point 11).

Finally, there are two arguments on technicalities. Graham's testimony was not given under oath (point 2), and the documents recording it are not signed by him (point 12). These points mattered because Graham himself could no longer testify in person; he had been executed on 29 February 1592.

Overall, then, this document is more about the criminal law in general than about the specific crime of witchcraft. Nevertheless, there are interesting details about witchcraft. In particular, there is an unusually explicit account of the demonic pact. Not only has Graham renounced his baptism, but he has been 'baptysit of new be the Devill'.

Bothwell was acquitted. The influence of this memorandum on the court cannot be known, but it expounds high-level legal argument in an articulate way. It shows that his lawyers tried hard, and did not regard his acquittal as a foregone conclusion. They succeeded – but only in this one case. If the Scottish legal establishment had accepted these defence arguments in full, then the testimony of confessing witches against other alleged witches would have been ruled unacceptable, and the great Scottish witch-hunt would have claimed far fewer lives.

TEXT

Source: NRS, Court of Justiciary Process Papers, 1586–1593, JC26/2, bundle 8, no. 9.[8]

Certane infallible reasons quhairfor of law nor practik Richart Grahames depositiones can nocht make fayth aganis my lord Bothuell.

8 P. G. Maxwell-Stuart, *Satan's Conspiracy: Magic and Witchcraft in Sixteenth-Century Scotland* (East Linton, 2001), 156, gives a précis of this document.

a. *cau[sa] si testes § unius 4 quest[iones] 2 et 3 l[ex] Iurisiura[n]di C. de testib[us].*	1. First he is singular and only witnes without concurrent adminicle of ony uther witness or apperance and thairfor albeit he wer the maist excellent persoun of the warld he can nocht prove. ***a***
b. *d[ictus] l[ex] Iurisiura[n]di.*	2. He wes nocht sworne in Judgement to declair the treuth. ***b***
c. *l[ex] 3 § lege Iulii ff. de testib[us], l. i i[n] pri[ma]. de falsariis.*	3. He wes corruptit for gud ded [*'quhilk' crossed out*] viz. for his lyff and sauftie thairof to depone. ***c***
d. *l[ex] 3 § lege Iulii de testibus, c. forus § testes de verborum significatione ex[tr]a.*	4. He is *i[n]fam tam i[n]famia Iuris qu[am] facti*. ***d***
e. *cap. alieni cap. non potest cum seq[uentibus]. 2 q. 7.*	5. He is ane sorcerar and prevaricat in his fayth renunciand his baptesme in Christ quha is the veritie and baptysit of new be the Devill quha is ane lyar and murtharar from the begining. **e**
f. *l[ex] lucius ff. de i[n]famib[us] l. qui cu[m] uno de re militarii.*	6. Mensworne. ***f***
g. *l[ex] quonia[m] C. de testib[us], c. veni[en]s ex[tr]a De testibus c. p[er] sonas ibid[em] gl[ossa] i[n] cap. 2 ibide[m] cau[sa] quod Iudex 4 c. 3 q. 7.*	7. *Socius et particeps crimini*. ***g***
h. *d[icta] cau[sa] si testes c. liberis de testib[us].*	8. *Socius pene et cui i[m]pertiri*[9] *potuit*.[10] ***h***
i. *d. cau[sa] si testes 8 qui falso.*	9. *Vacillans et sibi contrarius*. ***i***
k. *cau[sa] suspectos causa 3 q. 5.*	10. His lyf haillely accusable led in mischief and nocht haldand the rycht fayth. ***k***
l. *cau[sa] accusatorib[us] 3 q. 5.*	11. He is the accusar to quhom na creditt aucht to be gevin. ***l***
	12. The said depositionis ar neither subscryvit be him self nor na autentik persone.

9 Reading uncertain, as some letters are not fully formed.

10 This passage is difficult to interpret. It may have meant that even if the accuser was only virtually or almost (*pene*) one who had shared (*socius*) in the crime, then the arguments advanced in section **g** would still follow. The phrase '*et cui impertiri potuit*' literally means 'and for which he was able to be made a partaker', presumably developing this idea.

THE JURISTIC CITATIONS EXPLAINED

Manuscript citation: **a** *(i). cau[sa] si testes § unius 4 quest[iones] 2 et 3.*

Modern citation: Decretum Gratiani, C. 4. q. 2-3 c. 3. '*Causa*' indicates a reference to the second major part of Gratian's *Decretum*, the *Causae* or cases. Cases were divided into *quaestiones*, and so this is a reference to *Causa* 4 *quaestiones* 2 & 3. The third heading (c. 3) within *quaestiones* 2 & 3 begins '*Si testes*' and a sentence within '*Si testes*' begins '*Unius*'. The reference is to that sentence. One should note that C. 4 q. 2-3 is largely based on two titles in the Justinianic corpus, these being *Digest* 22.5 and *Codex* 4.20.

Latin text of citation: 'Unius vero testimonium nemo iudicum in quacumque causa facile patiatur admitti: immo unius testis responsio omnino non audiatur: etiam si praeclarae curiae honore praefulgeat.'

Summary and comments: This states that no judge should rely on the evidence of a single witness alone, however distinguished that witness might be. It is lifted from a passage in the *Codex* of Justinian, cited below.

Manuscript citation: **a** *(ii). l[ex] Iurisiura[n]di C. de testib[us].*

Modern citation: The *Codex* ('C.') of Justinian, IV.20.9 (*De Testibus*, 'on witnesses', is IV.20; its section 9 opens with the word '*Iurisiurandi*').

Latin text of citation: 'Iurisiurandi religione testes, priusquam perhibeant testimonium, iam dudum artari praecepimus et ut honestioribus potius fides testibus habeatur, simili more sanximus, ut unius testimonium nemo iudicum in quacumque causa facile patiatur admitti. et nunc manifeste sancimus, ut unius omnino testis responsio non audiatur, etiamsi praeclarae curiae honore praefulgeat.'

Summary and comments: This states that witnesses must testify on oath, and that the testimony of a single witness must not be accepted. The text of the *Decretum Gratiani* cited above evidently quotes directly from that in the *Codex*.

Manuscript citation: ***b****. d[ictus] l[ex] Iurisiura[n]di.*

Modern citation: 'dictus lex Iurisiurandi': 'the said law "Iurisurandi"', i.e. the section of the *Codex* of Justinian cited above.

Latin text of citation: See above.

Summary and comments: This states that witnesses must testify on oath.

Manuscript citation: **c** *(i). l[ex] 3 § lege Iulii ff. de testib[us].*

Modern citation: The *Digest* ('ff.') of Justinian, 22.5.3.5 (*De Testibus* is *Digest* 22.5, and the third section (*lex* 3) of *Digest* 22.5 has a passage which opens with the words '*Lege Iulia*').

Latin text of citation: 'Lege Iulia de vi cavetur, ne hac lege in reum testimonium dicere liceret, qui se ab eo parenteve eius liberaverit, quive impuberes erunt, quique iudicio publico damnatus erit qui eorum in integrum restitutus non erit, quive in vinculis custodiave publica erit, quive ad bestias ut depugnaret se locaverit, quaeve palam quaestum faciet feceritve, quive ob testimonium dicendum vel non dicendum pecuniam accepisse iudicatus vel convictus erit. nam quidam propter reverentiam personarum, quidam propter lubricum consilii sui, alii vero propter notam et infamiam vitae suae admittendi non sunt ad testimonii fidem.'

Summary and comments: This text explains that certain types of persons should be excluded from giving evidence, including those found guilty of criminal offences, unless reinstated, and those who are in custody.

Manuscript citation: **c** *(ii). l. i i[n] pri[ma]. de falsariis.*

Modern citation: This is possibly a reference to *Liber Extra* 5.20.1. In editions from the late-sixteenth century onwards, *Liber Extra* 5.20 is entitled *De crimine falsi*; but in some older versions it was headed *De falsariis*. The phrase *l. i in prima* may refer to the first chapter, i.e. to *Liber Extra* 5.20.1.

Latin text of citation: 'Falsidicus testis tribus personis est obnoxius; primus Deo, cuius praesentiam contemnit: deinde iudici, quem mentiendo fallit: postremo innocenti, quem falso testimonio laedit. Uterque reus est, & qui veritatem occultat, & qui mendacium dicit: quia et ille prodesse non vult, & iste nocere desiderat.'

Summary and comments: It is not wholly clear that this is the text mentioned in this reference. The text discusses in general terms how the lying witness is an affront or harmful to God, the judge and the innocent party. The gloss to the text also introduced the idea that such a person was a perjurer, an argument which would be developed subsequently in these proceedings.

Manuscript citation: **d** *(i). l[ex] 3 § lege Iulii de testibus.*

Modern citation: Digest 22.5.3.5.

Latin text of citation: See **c** *(i)* above.

Summary and comments: This text also excludes infamous persons from giving evidence.

Manuscript citation: **d** *(ii). c. forus § testes de verborum significatione ex[tr]a.*

Modern citation: Liber Extra 5.40.10. 'Ex[tr]a' is a reference to the *Liber Extra*, the *Decretales* of canon law. The title *de verborum significatione* is *Liber Extra* 5.40, and within the title is a chapter beginning with the word '*Forus*' (*Liber Extra* 5.40.10). Within *Liber Extra* 5.40.10 there are two sentences beginning with the word '*Testes*'; the relevant passage from one of them is quoted here.

Latin text of citation: 'Testes autem considerantur conditione, natura, & vita... Vita, si innocens et integer actu; nam si vita bona defuerit, fide carebit: non enim potest iustitia cum sclerato homine habere commercium.'

Summary and comments: This text says that the lives of witnesses must be taken into account when considering their evidence. Where virtuous life is lacking in a witness, his evidence will receive little or no credit.

Manuscript citation: **e** *(i). cap. alieni 2 q. 7.*

Modern citation: Decretum Gratiani C. 2 q. 7 c. 23. While the abbreviation for *causa* is absent, this is also a reference to the second section of the *Decretum*; the full reference would have been C. 2 q. 7, and indeed in C. 2 q. 7 one finds a chapter – c. 23 – which begins with the word '*Alieni*'. This is to the point.

Latin text of citation: 'Alieni erroris socium, vel a sui voluntarie propositi tramite recedentem, aut sacris Patrum regulis, & constitutionibus non obedientem suscipere non possumus, nec debemus; nec impetere recte credentes, vel sanctorum Patrum sanctionibus obtemperantes permittimus: quai infames omnes esse censemus, qui suam aut Christianam praevaricantur legem, aut Apostolicam, vel regularem libenter postpoununt auctoritatem'.

Summary and comments: As the ordinary gloss to C. 2. q. 7 c. 23 notes, this text provides that heretics and schismatics are not admitted to accuse those who hold the correct beliefs.

Manuscript citation: **e** *(ii). cap. non potest cum seq[uentibus]. 2 q. 7.*

Modern citation: Decretum Gratiani C. 2 q. 7 c. 24. *Decretum Gratiani* C. 2 q. 7 c. 23. While the abbreviation for *causa* is absent, this is also a reference to the second section of the *Decretum*; the full reference would have been C. 2 q. 7, and indeed in C. 2 q. 7 one finds a chapter – c. 24 – which begins with the words '*Non potest*'. These are to the point.

Latin text of citation: 'Non potest erga homines esse fidelis, qui Deo extiterit infidus. Iudaei ergo, qui dudum Christiani effecti sunt, & et nunc Christi fidem praevaricati sunt, ad testimonium dicendum admitti non debent, quamvis esse se Christianos annuntient: quia sicut in fide Christi suspecti sunt, ita & in testimonio humano dubij habentur. Infirmari ergo oportet eorum tesimonium, qui in fide fasli docentur; nec eis est credendum, qui veritatis a se fidem abiecerunt.'

Summary and comments: C. 2 q. 7 c. 24 outlined a rule that Jews who had converted to Christianity were not to be admitted to give testimony against Catholics because they remained suspect in their faith, and those who were deemed lacking in faith in God were not to be given credit amongst good men.

Manuscript citation: **f** *(i). l[ex] lucius ff. de i[n]famib[us].*

Modern citation: The *Digest* ('ff') of Justinian, 3.2.21. *Digest* 3.2 is the title *De his qui notantur infamia*, which the writer seems to have contracted to '*de infamibus*'. *Digest* 3.2.21 begins with the word '*Lucius*'.

Latin text of citation: 'Lucius Titius crimen intendit Gaio Seio quasi iniuriam passus atque in eam rem testationem apud praefectum praetorio recitavit: praefectus fide non habita testationis nullam iniuriam Lucium Titium passum esse a Gaio Seio pronuntiavit. quaero, an testes, quorum testimonium reprobatum est, quasi ex falso testimonio inter infames habentur. Paulus respondit nihil proponi, cur hi, de quibus quaeritur, infamium loco haberi debeant, cum non oportet ex sententia sive iusta sive iniusta pro alio habita alium praegravari.'

Summary and comments: This text dealt with a case where one party alleged that he had suffered an insult at the hands of another. The praetorian prefect rejected the claim, and the question was whether those witnesses the pursuer might have brought were thereby held to have incurred infamy. They did not. The reasoning was that one person ought not to suffer for a judgement given against another. The text itself does not seem particularly relevant until one appreciates that the gloss to the text in e.g. the Lyons edition of the *Digest* (1560) dealt with the situations in which witnesses who committed perjury would be regarded as *infames*. The relevant gloss is on the word '*debeant*'.

Manuscript citation: **f** *(ii). l. qui cu[m] uno de re militarii.*

Modern citation: This is a reference to the *Digest* of Justinian 49.16.4. *Digest* 49.16 is the title *De re militarii* and D.49.16.4 begins with the words '*Qui cum uno*'.

Latin text of citation: '... periurus poenitentiam accipiens vel infamis non testificatur.'

Summary and comments: The passage quoted is in fact taken from the gloss to *Digest* 49.16.4 in the Lyons edition of 1560, and it provides that a perjurer who is *infamis* may not testify. The relevant gloss is on the word '*Absolutus*' in the text, which was really concerned with situations in which individuals might be permitted to give military service.

Manuscript citation: **g** *(i). l[ex] quonia[m] C. de testib[us].*

Modern citation: '*lex quoniam C. de testibus*': the *Codex* of Justinian, C.4.20.11.

Latin text of citation: 'Quoniam liberi testes ad causas postulantur alienas, si socii et participes criminis non dicantur, sed fides ab his notitiae postuletur, in exhibitione necessarium personarum, hoc est testium, talis debet esse cautio iudicantis, ut his venturis ad iudicium per accusatorem aut ab his, per quos fuerint postulati, sumptus competentes dari praecipiat. Idem iuris est et si in pecuniaria causa testes ab alterutra parte producendi sunt.'

Summary and comments: This text deals with the proposition that witnesses' expenses should generally be paid by those on whose behalf they appear, and that judges should ensure this happens. However, the text caveats this, saying that it does not apply in cases where witnesses are alleged to be participants in the crime.

Manuscript citation: **g** *(ii). c. veni[en]s ex[tr]a De testibus.*

Modern citation: Liber Extra 2.20.10. 'Ex[tr]a' is a reference to the *Liber Extra*, the *Decretales* of canon law. The title *De testibus* (on witnesses) is *Liber Extra* 2.20, and *Liber Extra* 2.20.10 begins with the word '*Veniens*'.

Latin text of citation: 'Veniens ad nos L. presbyter sua relatione montravit, quod ei obiectum fuit, quod in ecclesia de Oven. canonicum non habuisset ingressum: quia promisisset unicuique parochianorum quinque barillos vini remittere, qui sacredoti ibi pro tempore servienti, consueruerant pro beneficio dari. Verum cum duo apparuissent, qui iurati deposuerunt praedictum presbyterum talem fecisse promissiovem, & cum altero illorum pactum illud factum fuisse, tu de presbytero prout ordo rationis exigit iudicasti. Et nos tuam sententiam commendamus, eo quod ille qui eodem erat infectus crimine, inde contra eum testificari non posset: nullique de se confesso, adversus alium in eodem crimine sit credendum, nec unius testimonium ad condemantionem sufficiat alicuius.'

Summary and comments: The text said that a partner in crime (in this case, simony) should not be allowed to testify against another.

Manuscript citation: **g** *(iii). c. p[er]sonas ibid[em].*

Modern citation: Liber Extra 2.20.20. 'Ex[tr]a' is a reference to the *Liber Extra*, the *Decretales* of canon law. The title *De testibus* (on witnesses) is *Liber Extra* 2.20, and *Liber Extra* 2.20.20 begins with the word '*Personas*'.

Latin text of citation: 'Personas ecclesiarum: & infra. Verum si coram te, vel alio quolibet negotia ventilenter: nolumus ut aliqui morbo consimili laborantes, si certum sit, aut legitime super hoc possint convici: si ab alterutra parte testes adducti fuerint, in testimonium admittantur.'

Summary and comments: The gloss to this text confirms that it was understood to extend the proposition that no-one who had fallen into a crime could accuse or condemn another of the same.

Manuscript citation: **g** *(iv). gl[ossa] i[n] cap. 2 ibide[m].*

Modern citation: Gloss to *Liber Extra* 2.20.2.

Latin text of citation: 'Vilissimi, quibus non est credendum. 2 q. 1 in primis. quidam considerantur in testibus, quae his versibus notantur. Conditio, sexus, aetas, discretio, fama. Et fortuna, fides, in testibus ista requires.'

Summary and comments: The reference to the gloss was probably to a comment on the sort of witness who should not be admitted – the *vilissimi*, the most base or vile. There then followed a statement concerning the sorts of characteristics one should consider when thinking about the extent to which a witness might be reliable – status, sex, age, discernment, reputation, wealth and trustworthiness.

Manuscript citation: **g** *(v). cau[sa] quod Iudex 4 c. 3 q. 7.*

Modern citation: This is probably a reference to *Decretum Gratiani* C. 3 q. 7 [probably] c. 4. However, c. 4 does not begin with the words '*quod Iudex*' (as one would expect from the citation) but with the words '*Iudicet ille…*'.

Latin text of citation: The relevant section of the text is as follows: *'Iudicet ille de alterius errore, qui non habet quod in seipso condemnet. Iudicet ille, qui non agit eadem, quae in alio putaverit punienda: ne cum de alio iudicat, in se ferat ipse sententiam.'*

Summary and comments: The text identified discusses the fact that judges should not be infected with the same evil or criminal behaviour which they punish in others. The argument was presumably that, by extension, a partner in crime could not accuse another.

Manuscript citation: ***h*** *(i). d[icta] cau[sa] si testes c. liberis.*

Modern citation: '*Dicta causa si testes*' must mean *Decretum Gratiani* C. 4 q. 2-3 c. 3, as cited above. While there is no passage within C. 4 q. 2-3 c. 3 beginning with the word '*liberis*' there is one beginning with the word '*liberi*', and it is assumed that that was what was meant here. Therefore, the reference is to a section in *Decretum Gratiani* C. 4. q. 2-3 c. 3 which begins with the words: '*Liberi testes ad causas postulantur...*'

Latin text of citation: 'Liberi testes ad causas postulantur alienas; si socij, & participes criminis non dicantur, sed fides ab ijs notitiae postuletur.'

Summary and comments: The point here may have been to emphasise again that those who participate in crimes are not in general eligible to act as witnesses. The ordinary gloss and additions to the gloss in some editions note that there were caveats to that principle, but the writer may not have chosen to emphasise them given his argument. Here *liberi* means freemen, not children; see the *Codex* of Justinian, 4.20.11 (Frier translation).

Manuscript citation: ***h*** *(ii). d[icta] cau[sa] si testes c. de testib[us].*

Modern citation: '*Dicta causa si testes*' must mean *Decretum Gratiani* C. 4 q. 2-3 c. 3, as cited above. It seems likely that the words '*de testibus*' are meant to constitute a separate reference from that mentioned in ***h*** *(i)* above. There are two short passages within C. 4. q. 2-3 c. 3 beginning with the words '*de testibus*', and of the two it is likely that the first was meant here.

Latin text of citation: 'In testibus fides, dignitas, mores, gravitas examinanda est: & ideo testes, qui adversus fidem testationis suae vacillant, audiendi non sunt.'

Summary and comments: The text considered a range of qualities to be considered when examining individual witnesses (faith, dignity, morals and gravitas) and noted that those who departed from their own past testimony were not to be heard. It is possible that this text was meant to support the arguments advanced in section ***i*** below, rather than those presented in section ***h***, given the reference to the verb *vacillare* in both section ***i*** and in this text.

Manuscript citation: ***i***. *d[icta] cau[sa] si testes 8 qui falso.*

Modern citation: Again, this is *Decretum Gratiani* C. 4 q. 2-3 c. 3, and the section beginning with the words '*Qui falso*'.

Latin text of citation: 'Qui falso vel varie testimonia dixerunt, vel utrique parti prodiderunt, a iudicibus conpetentur puniantur'.

Summary and comments: This text underlines that those who give false or contradictory testimony may be punished.

Manuscript citation: ***k***. *cau[sa] suspectos causa 3 q. 5.*

Modern citation: This is a reference to the second section of the *Decretum Gratiani*, *causa* 3 *quaestio* 5 – i.e. C. 3 q. 5. c. 4, which begins with the word '*Suspectos*'.

Latin text of citation: 'Suspectos, aut inimicos, aut facile litigantes, et eos, qui non sunt bonae conversationis, aut quorum vita est accusabilis, et qui rectam non tenent et docent fidem, accusatores esse, et testes, et antecessores nostri Apostoli prohibuerunt...'

Summary and comments: This text listed a range of individuals who were not to be given credit as witnesses, including those of blameworthy life and who failed to hold and teach the faith.

Manuscript citation: ***l.*** *cau[sa] accusatorib[us] 3 q. 5.*

Modern citation: This is a reference to the second section of the *Decretum Gratiani*, causa 3 *quaestio* 5 – i.e. C. 3 q. 5 c. 3, which begins with the words '*Accusatoribus*'.

Latin text of citation: 'Accusatoribus vero inimicis, vel de inimici domo prodeunitibus, vel qui cum inimicis immorantur, aut suspecti sunt, non credatur; ne irati nocere cupiant, ne laesi ulcisci velint.'

Summary and comments: The text indicated that hostile accusers should be given no credit.

10. MARGARET CRAWFORD, STIRLINGSHIRE, 1596

INTRODUCTION

Margaret Crawford lived in the parish of Denny,[1] where she was a midwife. She was an older woman, the widow of George Horne. She was imprisoned on 14 January 1596 and brought before the presbytery of Stirling, accused of being a witch and an abuser of the people. She confessed that she had never received the sacrament of the Lord's Supper since before the Reformation. She denied all accusations.

The presbytery then questioned witnesses. On 19 January, several neighbours were summoned to testify against her. Out of fifteen witnesses, four did not want to testify. The same date, Crawford was interrogated, but she denied all charges and did not confess to witchcraft.

On 20 January, a female witness testified against her. On 28 January, nine witnesses were called to testify, but two of these persons did not come. On 4 February, new witnesses were summoned, one man and three women. Of these, one man and one woman testified against her.

On 25 February, the brethren of the presbytery wrote to the sheriff of Stirling and requested him to raise a commission to have Crawford tried for 'witchcraft or abusing of the pepill' (a phrase, echoing the 1563 witchcraft act, that later became 'wichcraft and abusing of the pepill'). Thus, the case was moved from the presbytery to secular authority. This is the last information we get in her case.

Crawford was interrogated on an individual basis. No other persons suspected of witchcraft were mentioned, and no description of her alleged witchcraft was given. At the beginning of her confession, the sacraments of the church are mentioned. Witchcraft was not brought to the fore during the interrogation.

The brief entries are interesting because they show the relations between the presbytery and the sheriff. The brethren in the presbytery had to provide many testimonies against Crawford before they made contact with the sheriff. It is clear that the authority of the presbytery was limited, and it was important for the continuation of the case that the secular authorities took command.

1 The entry is in Stirling presbytery records as Denny was in Stirling presbytery until 1601. Later, Denny became part of Falkirk presbytery.

The presbytery did not expect the trial to take place in the sheriff court itself. Witchcraft was only very rarely tried in sheriff courts. They asked the sheriff to 'rais ane commissione to him self and his deputis', that is, to obtain a commission of justiciary from central government. A commission of justiciary to the sheriff would in effect have converted the sheriff court into a *justiciary* court with the requisite authority from the centre. The presbytery may well have thought that the sheriff would approach the privy council with his request for a commission. The sheriff of Stirling was John Erskine, second earl of Mar, who was not only a privy councillor but also one of the king's leading advisers, so he was in an ideal position to obtain a commission should he wish to do so. But we do not know whether he did.

TEXT

Source: Stirling Council Archives, Minutes of Presbytery of Stirling, 1589–1596, CH2/722/2.

{p. 544} At Stirling the xiiii day of Januar 1595[2]
Mr Richard Wryght Moderator, Masters Patrik Simsone, Adame Bellenden, Henrie Levingstone, James Duncansone, Henrie Layng, Malcolme Henriesone, Andro Ywng, Gawin Donaldsone, William Stirling, Andro Forester, ministars, Masters Niniane Drummond and Alexander Yull brethrein of exerceis.... *{p. 545}*

The quhilk day thair is producit befoir the brethrein Margaret Crawfurd[3] midwyf relict[4] of umquhill Georg Horne sone to George Horne in Grein in Denny at Browster Burne apprehendit as ane wiche or ane abusar of the pepill (as is alledgit) to be tryed thairanent And first confessis she nevir receavit the sacrament of the lordis Supper sen she receavit the samyn in the papisticall[5] maner And denyis all the accusationis layit against hir and thairfor the brethrein ordanis certane of hir nychtburis to be summond to the xix day of this instant to bear lell and suthfast[6] witnessing anent *{p. 546}* sic accusationis as ar and salbe layit to hir chairge insafar as thay knaw or salbe speirit at[7] thame And gevis commissione to Maisteris Henrie Levingstone, Adame Bellenden, William Stirling, Andro Ywng and Niniane Drummond to receave the saidis witnessis, sweir and examin thame, and desyris the provest and bailleis of this brugh to keip the said Margaret in suir firmance[8] quhill she be fullie tryed.

2 This is 1596 by modern dating.
3 In margin: 'Crawfurd'.
4 'relict': widow.
5 'papisticall': Catholic.
6 'lell and suthfast': honest and truthful.
7 'speirit at': asked of.
8 'suir firmance': secure prison.

At Stirling the xix day of Januar 1595
The brethring following conveinit the said day to the effect undirwritin be vertew of the commissione abonewritin gevin to thame be the presbytrie Thay ar to say Maisteris Henrie Levingstone, Adame Bellenden, William Stirling, Andro Yung and Niniane Drummond.

The quhilk day ane summondis beand producit dewlie execut and indorsit upone Marcus Bennie in Denny, Johne Cuthill in Litill Denny, Richard Stark in [*1 word blank*], Johne Murheid in Drum, Alesone Robertsone in Bullhill, Nicoll Baird in Denny, William Chalmeris in West Boirland, Andro Johnesone in Hoillhous, Hellein Benny in Bellis Butis, Thomas Baird in Cuthiltoun, George Murheid in West Boirland, Robert Oswald cordenar[9] in Denny, Johne Baird in Castell Rankin, Robert Ywng in Cuthilltoun Greinis and Johne Herrun in Chapeltoun, chairgeing thame to compeir the said day to bear lell and suthfast witnessing anent the accusationis layit to the chairge of Margaret Crawfurd in Denny for wichcraft and abusing of the pepill insafar as thay knaw or salbe speirit at thame as at mair lenth is conteinit in the said summondis Compeirit all the saidis witnessis Except the saidis Robert Oswald, Johne Baird, Robert Ywng and Johne Herrun quha being oft tymes callit compeirit nocht, The saidis witnessis comperand ar in presens of the said Margaret Crawfurd receavit, sworn and admited And farther diligence ordeined to be done against the saidis witnessis disobedient and sic utheris as best knawis the veritie.

At Stirling the xx day of Januar 1595
The quhilk day compeirit Jane Stewart relict of umquhill Richard Grahame as lawfulie summond to bear lell and suthfast witnessing anent the accusationis layit to the chairge off Margaret Crawfurd in Denny for wichcraft and abusing of the pepill insafar as she knawis or salbe speirit {*p. 547*} at hir, quha in presens of the said Margaret Crawfurd is receavit, sworne and admited be Mr Richard Wrycht and Mr James Duncansone havand powar of the presbytrie to that effect.... {*p. 548*}

At Stirling the xxviii day of Januar 1595
Mr Richard Wryght Moderator, Masters Patrik Simsone, Andro Ywng, Henrie Levingstone, Henrie Layng, Johne Millar, Malcolme Henresone, Edward Brys, Duncan Nevein and Andro Forester ministers, and Mr Johne Aissone ane brother of exerceis....[10] {*p. 549*}

The quhilk day[11] ane summondis beand producit dewlie execut and indorsit upone Robert Oswald cordenar in Denny, Johne Baird in Castell Rankin, Robert Ywng in Cuthiltoun Greingis, Johne Herrun in Chapeltoun, Robert

[9] 'cordenar' (cordwainer): shoemaker.
[10] In margin: 'Presentes'.
[11] In margin: 'Crawfurd'.

Fleming in Denny, Robert Bawhok thair, Robert Donoven in Donoven, Duncan Tailyur in Castelcarie and Johne Blair in Donoven, chairgeing thame to compeir the said day to beir lell and suthfast witnessing anent the accusationis layit to the chairg of Margaret Crawfurd in Denny for wichcraft and abusing of the pepill insafar as thay knaw or salbe speirit at thame as at mair lenth is conteinit in the summondis, Compeirit the saidis witnessis Except Duncan Tailyur and Johne Blair quha being oft tymes callit compeirit nocht The saidis witnessis comperand ar in presens of the said Margaret Crawfurd receavit sworn and admited And farther diligence ordeined to be done against the saidis witnessis disobedient and sic utheris as best knawis the veritie.... {*p. 550*}

At Stirling the iiii day of Februar 1595 {*p. 551*}
Mr Richard Wryght Moderator, Masters Adame Bellenden, William Stirling, James Duncansone, Johne Millar, Alexander Simsone, Andro Ywng, Malcolme Henresone, Patrik Simsone, Neill Campbell, ministers, Mr Alexander Yull and Mr Johnne Aissone brethrein of exerceis....[12]

The quhilk day[13] ane summondis beand producit dewlie execut and indorsit upone Duncan Tailyur in Castelcarie, Barbara Cuthill doghtir to [*1 word blank*] Cuthill in Denny, [*2 words blank*] spous to Nicoll Baird in Denny and Margaret Baird doghtir to the said Nicoll, chairgeing thame to compeir the said day to bear lell and suthfast witnessing anent the accusationis layit to the chairge of Margaret Crawfurd in Denny for wichcraft and abusing of the pepill insafar as thay knaw or salbe speirit at thame as at mair lenth is conteinit in the said summondis, Compeirit the said Duncan Tailyur and Barbara Cuthill quha in presens of the said Margaret Crawfurd is receavit sworne and admitted.... {*p. 556*}

At Stirling the xxv day of Februar 1595
Mr Richard Wryght Moderator, Masters Patrik Simsone, Henrie Levingstone, Malcolme Henresone, William Stirling, Gawin Donaldsone, Johne Millar, Henrie Layng, James Duncansone, Duncan Nevein, Andro Forester, Adame Bellenden, ministars, and Mr Alexander Yull ane brother of exerceis....[14]

The brethrein[15] ordanis ane letter to be direct in thair name to My lord Erlle of Mar Shiref of Stirling shyr desyrand his Lordship to rais ane commissione to him self and his deputis to put Margaret Crawfurd to the knawlege of ane assys for wichcraft or abusing of the pepill.

12 In margin: 'Presentes'.
13 In margin: 'Crawfurd'.
14 In margin: 'Presentes'.
15 In margin: 'Crawfurd'.

11. WILLIAM MURRAY, LEITH, 1599

INTRODUCTION

This case is from the regality court of Broughton, like that of the 'Leith Witches' of 1579 edited above. As with that case, here we have the minutes of the court, summarising the accused's offence and the court's deliberations, but no full dittay.[1]

The case illustrates the overlap found occasionally between witchcraft and beneficial magic. William Murray's crime is categorically stated to have been 'witchecraft and sorcerie', but he was treated basically as a magical practitioner. His first offence was the use of magic to heal John Hutson's child, and there was also mention of the healing of the son of the goodwife of Wariston (Jean Livingston, a member of the elite who later became notorious). Murray was not said to have committed malefice, nor was there any mention of a demonic pact. Nevertheless, this was a criminal court, not a kirk session, and he received a criminal sentence rather than being made to do penance.

The interrogators were John Brand, minister of the Canongate, and Robert Pont, minister of St Cuthbert's, both veteran ministers who had taken leading roles in the church. Pont was also a noted intellectual with an interest in quasi-magical topics.[2] Brand's role is natural, as the court was attached to the burgh of the Canongate, but the reason for Pont's involvement does not appear. It would be interesting to know whether it was Brand and Pont who employed the words 'witchecraft and sorcerie' to describe Murray's offence, but this cannot be ascertained for certain from the record as we have it.

Murray's healing rituals, involving the blood of a cat, a bannock with special ingredients, and a Gaelic incantation, are of interest. The fact that

1 This case has been briefly discussed by Andrew H. Anderson, 'The Regality and Barony of Broughton: Some of its Characters and Personalities, 1592–1600', *Book of the Old Edinburgh Club*, 34 (1974–83), 1–22, at p. 6.

2 Duncan Shaw, 'John Brand (d. 1600)', and James Kirk, 'Robert Pont (1524–1606)', both *ODNB*. In 1599, the year of Murray's case, Pont published *A Newe Treatise of the Right Reckoning of Yeares*, combining biblical chronology, prophecy, astrology and numerology. See Arthur H. Williamson, *Scottish National Consciousness in the Age of James VI* (Edinburgh, 1979), 30–1.

he was a Highlander seems to have been important to the prosecutors. He was noted to have been born in Strathearn, his alias 'Erss Williame' (Gaelic William) was recorded, and he recited 'pater nosteris in Ersche' (the Lord's Prayer in Gaelic). The woman who had taught him his skills (and whom he had wanted to marry), Anny (Agnes) Nicarochie, also had a Highland name.

Murray told Hutson that his child was bewitched. However, there is no mention of official interest in whoever might have committed the bewitchment. The woman who baked the bannock for him, Margaret Pate, might have been regarded as his accomplice, but there is no mention of a prosecution of her either.

In the end, Murray was made to stand in the jougs (an iron collar) for an hour before being whipped and banished from the burgh. No suggestion was recorded that he might have been punished more severely.

TEXT

Source: Edinburgh City Archives, Burgh Court Book of Canongate, 1590–1600, SL150/1/7.

{*p. 485*} *Curia Justiciarie Regalitate et baronie de Brochtoun tenta in pretorio ville de Leith de parte boreali aque eiusdem Coram magistro Archibaldo Wilkie ballivo deputato dicti Regalitatis et baronie decimo quarto die mensis augusti anno domini millesimo quadragesimo nonagesimo Curia affirmata.*[3] {*p. 486*}

Intran upoun pannall
Williame Murray als Erss Williame borne in Stratherne

Assisa dicti Willelmi[4]

Johne Dunlope wobstar	Johne Hendersoun wobster
/Ch/[5] Williame Baine	Andro Archibald baxter
Eduard Mairtene	Williame Gray baxter
Robert Falconar	Thomas Ormistoun baxter
Johne Huchesoun	Robert Kirkpatrik

Robert Auldcorne
Alexander Finlay
James Gavillok
Andro Adamsoun
Adame Kay

[3] 'Court of justiciary of the regality and barony of Broughton, held in the tolbooth of the burgh of Leith on the north side of the water of the same. Held before Mr Archibald Wilkie, bailie depute of the said regality and barony, 4 August 1599. Court fenced.'

[4] 'Assize of the said William'.

[5] An abbreviation for 'chancellor', the spokesman of the assize.

The quhilk day the said William being Indytit and accusit for abhominable and detestable abusing of Gods people in exerceing and using of witchecraft and sorcerie and be geweing of his counsale to Johne Hutson to the helth of his bairne quha wes bewitcheit as the said Williame[6] schew to the said Johne and thairfoir desyrit the said Johne efter that he haid veseit the said bairne to haif ane catt in reddines againe Mononday[7] and he wald bluid the Lwg[8] of hir and rub the bairne with the bluid, And for the causing of Margaret Paitt to mak aine bannok to the guid wyfe of Wairreistonis[9] sone of meill salt and ane eg to haif bene eittin be him quha eitit the samin, and that the said William at the eitin thairof maid thrie pater nosteris in Ersche to the taikin the said William efter he wes examinat upon the particular heidis foirsaidis upon the said day of Junii last[10] in presens of Mr Robert Pont and John Brand ministeris affirmit the samin to be of veretie, and that he learnit the samin of Anny Nicarochie quhilk he wald haif mareit and that the kirk wauld nocht marie thame, As in the dittay gewin in tharin ponis[11] at mair *{p. 487}* lenth is contenit quhilk crymes and offences the said William Murray confest and grantit the samin And the said assyss passand furth of court efter tryell and cognitioun taine be thaime in the said mater In enterand agane all in ane voice but discrepance or variance convictit and fylit the said Williame be vertew of his confessioun be the mouth of the said Williame Baine chancellour of the said assyss, And thairfoir the baillie depuit foirsaid ordanit him to be tane to the[12] Jogis thair to remane and stand for the space of ane hour And thairefter to be tane and skwrgeit throw the friedome of the noirthsyde of the brige of Leith and baneist the samin Nevir to be fund thair againe under the pane of deid, And this wes gewin in dome and pronunceit be the mouth of [*1 word blank*] dempistar of the said court.

6 In margin: 'Murray convict'.

7 'againe Mononday': against Monday, i.e. for next Monday.

8 'Lwg': ear.

9 The 'guid wyfe of Wairreiston' was Jean Livingston, wife of John Kincaid of Wariston (whom she had married in 1594) and daughter of the courtier John Livingston of Dunipace. Her subsequent murder of her husband on 1 July 1600 became a *cause célèbre*. Her son's nurse, Janet Murdo, was one of her accomplices. See Keith M. Brown, 'The Laird, his Daughter, her Husband and the Minister: Unravelling a Popular Ballad', in Roger Mason and Norman Macdougall (eds.), *People and Power in Scotland: Essays in Honour of T. C. Smout* (Edinburgh, 1992), 104–25.

10 No such date has been mentioned here, so this may be the scribe's error in summarising from a more detailed dittay which did give a previous date. The earlier phrase 'to the taikin' is grammatically anomalous, perhaps for the same reason.

11 'ponis': deposits, records.

12 'gowkis' crossed out here. The scribe may have been thinking of 'gowffis', a pillory.

12. JANET IRVINE, ORKNEY, 1616

INTRODUCTION

Janet Irvine was one of over a dozen people to be tried for witchcraft in Orkney and Shetland in 1615 and 1616. These trials were evidently connected with the new regime being established in the islands in this period. The royal government had imprisoned the last autonomous earl of Orkney, Patrick Stewart, in Edinburgh in 1609. Royal authority was tightened after the defeat in 1614 of a rebellion led by the earl's illegitimate son Robert Stewart; father and son were executed early in 1615.[1] These political events were important, not just for the prosecutors, but for Irvine herself.

Irvine seems to have lived in the town of Kirkwall, latterly at least, but when we see her working for a living it is in rural occupations: being employed to herd and milk cattle, carrying a load of corn, stacking her own peat, and gathering shellfish on the shore. She was clearly an older woman. There is no mention of a husband or children.

Most of the evidence against Irvine came from her own confession, but several instances of harm to named individuals were mentioned, and these people may have given information against her. She was twice evicted or threatened with eviction, so she had difficulties with neighbours, and she was stated to have a reputation as a witch. She herself related that the Devil had taught her a ritual to obtain 'hir heartis desyre' (vengeance) upon people with whom she had quarrelled. Usually, she was said to have inflicted illness. She was also alleged to have sunk a boat coming from Westray, drowning several people, but she denied this. The assize acquitted her of this charge, but they convicted her of the other charges, and she was executed.

Irvine confessed to a relationship with the Devil that contained a mixture of stereotypical and idiosyncratic elements. For instance, the Devil appearing as an animal was stereotypical; the Devil, as a bull, sniffing at the witch's cows, was idiosyncratic. Some of the material came from dreams or visions,

[1] These events are detailed in Peter D. Anderson, *Black Patie: The Life and Times of Patrick Stewart, Earl of Orkney, Lord of Shetland* (Edinburgh, 1992).

some of which she experienced as periodic, even regular, occurrences. In one dream, she experienced a premonition of illness, and learned a ritual by which she could cause the illness to fall instead on the first person she saw. The interrogators recorded the material without shaping it into a credible connected narrative; the demonic episodes extended back thirty-two years, but Irvine's making of the demonic pact was dated only two years ago.

Her confession described a curious episode from April 1615, when the authorities were establishing their new regime after the suppression of the rebellion in the previous September. One evening, she was 'angrie with the alteratioun of the estait of the countrey', so she summoned the Devil, and climbed with him to the top of Kirkwall Castle – one of the rebels' former strongholds, which at this point the authorities were planning to demolish. There, she related, she made a formal proclamation and called upon the Devil to 'put thir new reularis away, that the kyndly countrey people [the native-born local people] micht rewle'. The Devil, however, replied that the new rulers would remain for as long as God wished them to do so.

Had Irvine really made such a proclamation? No witnesses were mentioned, and the whole episode may have been a dream or vision like some of her other experiences. She also related, for instance, that the Devil had appeared to her when the rebellion broke out, predicting its initial success and ultimate defeat. Still, many ordinary people in Orkney seem to have sympathised with the rebellion, so the idea of a woman staging a public protest against the new regime is not inconceivable. The interrogators would have been interested in the idea that Irvine, and indeed the Devil, were on the rebels' side. Irvine herself may well have regarded the Devil's message as a discouraging one: she would have to put up with the new regime for the time being. Her confession gives us an unusual glimpse of how ordinary people thought about the providential nature of political upheavals.

In Orkney and Shetland, witchcraft cases were usually tried in the sheriff court. Local courts elsewhere in Scotland were not allowed to try witchcraft on their own authority, and had to seek central authorisation in the form of a commission of justiciary. Here, however, such authorisation was rarely sought, nor do the central authorities seem to have questioned the sheriff court's actions. Perhaps the remoteness of the islands meant that a degree of autonomy was tacitly recognised.

The document edited below is the formal minutes of the court, written up after the event. The clerk has not transcribed the dittay as such, but he has written out the charges in some detail, and may have copied the dittay word for word. He has visibly converted the phrasing from the second person of the dittay ('you …') into the third person ('she …'). Much of the dittay itself will previously have been written by converting the third person of Irvine's original confession into the second person.

TEXT

Source: NRS, Court Book of Orkney and Shetland, 1612–1613, 1615–1630, SC10/1/3.

{*60v.*} *Curia justiciarie vicecomitatus de Orkney et Yetland tenta apud urbem de Kirkwall in nova domo prope palatium de Yeardis ibidem per honorabilem virum Henricum Stewart de Carlongie, vicecomitatem deputatio dicti vicecomitatus, die quinto mensis Martii anno 1616. Curia tenta et legitime affirmata.*[2]

The quhilk day[3] anent the dittayis criminall producit and persewit be Robert Coltart, procurator fiscall of the said sherefdome, againes Jonet Irwing in Kirkwall, For certane poyntis of dittayis for witchcraft underwritten, That is to say, In the first the said Jonet wes indyttit and accusit for art, part, using, conducting and practising of the divilish and supersticious cryme of witchcraft, and in hanting and conversing with the Divell in maner following, viz., in that she confest that she being seiking hir mistris xxxii yeiris syne or thairby, that ane husband man abone the kirk of Harray pat you[4] to keip his kyne[5] quhair the Divell come to the kyne in lyknes of ane bull and efter he haid snokkit[6] upoun thame came to \hir/[7] and changeing him selfe in a man bade \hir/[8] call home the kyne, and he sould cum to \hir/[9] and speik with \hir/[10] the morne, quha come and tuik \hir/[11] under ane grein bra[12] into a hous quhair he gave \hir/[13] fleshe to eat, and as aperit he lay with hir. Item, in that she confest that tua year thairefter she being cuming to Kirkwall with corne on hir bak the Devell came to hir betuix Harray and Rendall upon the hyllis, quhair he lay with hir and gart[14] hir milk the kyne quhilk he suppit als fast as she milkit, at quhilk tyme he promeisit gif she wald serve him that he wald let hir want nothing, quhilk she promeisit, quhairupon the Devell learneit hir that gif she buire ill \will/ to ony bodie that she sould luik upoun thame with opin eyis, and pray evill for thame in his name, that she sould get hir heartis desyre.

2 'Court of justiciary of the sheriffdom of Orkney and Shetland, held in the town of Kirkwall in the new house near the palace of Yards in that place by the honourable man Henry Stewart of Carlongie, sheriff depute of the said sheriffdom, 5 March 1616. Court held and legally fenced.'
3 In margin: 'Jonet Irwing'.
4 *Sic.* Evidently this is the second-person wording of the dittay, which the clerk has failed to convert to the third person of the minutes.
5 'kyne': cattle.
6 'snokkit': sniffed.
7 The word 'yow' has been crossed out here, and 'hir' inserted.
8 The word 'hir' has been written over the original word 'yow'.
9 The word 'hir' has been written over the original word 'yow'.
10 The word 'yow' has been crossed out here, and 'hir' inserted.
11 The word 'hir' has been written over the original word 'yow'.
12 'grein bra' (brae): green hill.
13 The word 'hir' has been written over the original word 'yow'.
14 'gart': caused.

Item, that she confest that the Devell came to hir upoun the nes of Quinines[15] with the lyknes of ane blak doge quhen she wes going to the ebb, att quhilk tyme he bade hir goe, and that she wald get fishe anew,[16] as she gat in deid, and thairefter he come to hir quhen she wes going to put up hir peattis abone grind,[17] quhair he tauld {*61r.*} hir that Robert Stewart haid gottin Birsay,[18] and wald get the castle and countrey, but wald not keip it long, and that he came to hir at everie Alhallow ewin[19] fra the secound tyme he aperit to hir quhairever she wes and lay with hir, as aperit hir. Item, for that she confest that she dreameit a dreame fyve yeiris syne or thairby about midsomer, that she waiding in a watter, and that thair came a voice to hir and said, that that meaneit seiknes, and except she gaid[20] to a watter, and cust ane lwifefull[21] over ilk shoulder and over hir head schoe wald be seik, and in sadoin[22] the seiknes wald fall on thame that shoe saw first, and sua haveing sein David Brow, tailyeour, the seiknes fell upoun him, and his wyfe and bairnes have continwit seik sen syne. Item, that she being dwelling in George Grahames cloiss, and he removeing hir and calling hir witche carling[23] quhair he met hir, that she prayed evell for him as the Devell haid taught hir, quhairthrow he hes bein ever seik sensyne, quhilk she confest. Item, for that she confest that in the moneth of Aprile last, she being angrie with the alteratioun of the estait of the countrey, schoe callit on the Devell quha come to hir, and tuik hir up to the head of the castle quhair sho cryit thrie oyessis[24] about the glomeing of the nycht, and desyrit him to put thir new reularis away, that the kyndly countrey people[25] micht rewle, and the Devell answerit hir (that they wald byde sa lang as God wald).[26] Item, for that William Scottie in Kirkwall haveing avowit to gar hir flitt hir kist,[27] that she be hir develrie and witchcraft causit him and uther fyve men and a woman that wes cuming out of Westray in Robert Sinclairis boit to perishe in Westray firth. Item, in that she confest ane yeir syne or thairby

15 This place is now Quina, on the north side of the Bay of Firth near Kirkwall. The 'ness' (headland) was evidently one of the headlands projecting into the bay, perhaps the nearby Skerries of Coubister.

16 'fishe anew': enough fish. These seem to have been shellfish that she gathered at the 'ebb', on the shore between the low and high tide.

17 'grind': gate. If this is the intended meaning, then Irvine may have been taking her peats through a gate in a dyke above her settlement. However, this word may be a scribal error for 'grund' (ground), indicating that she was stacking her peats in a higher part of the settlement's land.

18 This refers to Robert Stewart's rebellion, which broke out when he and his followers seized the Earl's Palace at Birsay in May 1614.

19 'Alhallow ewin': Hallowe'en (31 October).

20 'except she gaid': unless she went.

21 'lwifefull': handful.

22 Reading uncertain; text cramped at edge of page. Probably read 'in so doing', or possibly 'suddenly'.

23 'witche carling': old woman witch.

24 'sho cryit thrie oyessis': she formally cried 'Oyez' (hear and attend) three times.

25 'kyndly countrey people': native-born local people. 'Kindly' means 'natural' or 'related by kinship'.

26 These brackets should be read as quotation marks.

27 'gar hir flitt hir kist' (chest): cause her to leave her dwelling.

Magnus Hanmie[28] haveing sommondit hir to compeir before the kirk, and haveing challengeit hir for putting fyre in hir wall,[29] that she gave him a drink with a peice bannock into it, the meall quhairof sche gat fra the Devell, quha bad hir quhen she wald do ill to ony bodie gife it thame in a drink, quhairby the said Magnus wes seik be the space of aucht oulkis.[30] And generallie shoe wes indyttit and accusit for airt, part, useing, committing and practizeing of witchcraft, conversing with the Devell at all tymes and occasiounes, and sen she wes wairdit, quhilk she confest, and in casting of seiknes upoun divers and sindrie utheris persones, and speciallie upon James Jackis wyfe,[31] and using and practisyeng of all uther sortis of sorcerie, superstitioun and witchcraft, and sa reput and haldin as ane comoun rank witch, as at mair lenth is contenit in the saidis dittayis,[32] the said procurator fiscall being personalie present, and the said defendar being lykwayis personalie present, quha enterit on pannall haveing no lawfull caus quhy she sould nocht pass to the knawlege of ane assyse wes content {*61v.*} to abyd tryell, quhairupoun the said procurator fiscall askit actis of court, desyring the dittayis to be put to the knawledge of ane assyse, and the pannall to be accusit thairupon. Efter accusatioun the said Jonet confeast the haill poyntis of dittay abonewritten, exceptand the perishing of Robert Sinclairis boit and people that wer thairin, and thairfor the judge remittit the dittayis to the knawledge of ane assyse quhom he ordanet to be callit.

Assysa

David Kincaid of Yinsta
Thomas Knychtsone of Aith
David Moncreif in Kirkwall
James Irwing in Veslabanks
William Irwing of Brekis
Patrick Vaus, merchand
George Traill of Westnes
Magnus Craigie, merchand
Harie Spence in Scapa
David Kirknes, cordiner
Johne Hendersone of Weyland
James Deldall, merchand
Jerome Chalmeris, skipper
Patrick Gardiner, cordiner
Thomas Louttit of Hatstane

28 'Hanmie' is a very unlikely name, and this word may well be a scribal error. The name is clearly written as 'Ha[n]mie', with a suspension mark followed by four minims, one of which (probably the last one) has a dot over it. With one minim fewer, the name could be 'Ha[n]nie' (Hannay was a common surname in Orkney) or 'Ha[r]vie'.

29 This episode is hard to explain. Was this an alleged attempt at fire-raising – a capital crime in its own right? Irvine was a tenant, so 'hir' wall would belong to her landlord.

30 'aucht oulkis': eight weeks.

31 James Jack, notary, is mentioned in 1612: *Court Book of Orkney and Shetland, 1612–1613*, ed. Robert S. Barclay (Kirkwall, 1962), 42.

32 This phrase about 'mair lenth' seems to indicate that the original dittay had more details, and that these minutes are a briefer summary. However, the phrase is a conventional one, and does not necessarily prove that the original dittay was longer. The clerk has provided a good deal of information, and he may often have been transcribing the dittay word for word.

Quhilkis persones of assyse being sworne, admittit but[33] lawfull objectioun of the pannell, and removeit out of judgement, nominat and ellectit Jerome Chalmer to be chancler, and efter dew deliberatioun haid anent the dittayis produceit aganes the said Jonet, and poyntis thairof, and enterand in judgement againe the haill assyse be the mouth of thair said chanceler fyllit the said Jonet of the haill particular poyntis of dittay abonewrittin, except anent the perisheing of Robert Sinclairs boit, and people thairin contenit, and fyllit hir of the generall poynt of dittay, that she hes bein reput and for thir mony yeiris bygane ane rank witch, and remitting sentence to the judge and dome to the dempster, quhilk determinatioun the judge than present acceptit, and decernit and ordanit the said Jonet to be taine to the place of executioun be the lokmane betuix and thrie efternune thair to be weyrryet at ane staik quhill[34] she be dead, and thairefter to be brunt in ashis, quhairupoun dome wes given be the dempster.

[33] 'but': without.
[34] 'quhill': until.

13. CHRISTIAN WATSON, FALKIRK, 1622–1623

INTRODUCTION

This case began in October 1622 when Margaret Davidson started to believe that Christian Watson had harmed her health through magic. Davidson does not seem to have used the word 'witch', but she was thinking about bewitchment. She had fallen ill after a quarrel of some kind, during which Watson had threatened her. Davidson's chosen solution was to make a ritually secret approach to Watson in order to recover her health. She took advice from her mother and others, and recruited a male friend to aid her on the day. Whether Watson genuinely remained in ignorance when Davidson crept up behind her on Falkirk high street on a market day, or whether the 'secrecy' was an open secret understood by both parties, is not entirely clear, but the ritual succeeded and Davidson recovered her health. One remarkable aspect of this case is its detailed account of how a person could negotiate to recover their health once it was alleged that a witch had bewitched them.

However, someone – perhaps an eyewitness on the day – reported the incident to the kirk session. The session immediately described Davidson's ritual approach to Watson as 'consulting hir as ane witche', an intriguing phrase for such a reconciliation ritual. This phrase then recurred at intervals throughout the recording of the case. Summoned before the session, Davidson testified that she had been persuaded to undertake her ritual by Janet Buchanan. Buchanan had previously had her own disputes with Watson about ale-brewing and petty debt, and had also had a successful reconciliation with Watson.

The kirk session spent the month of November interrogating various people who had been involved in Davidson's market-day ritual. It looked as though Margaret Davidson and Janet Buchanan were the ones in trouble. However, Buchanan's stories about her dealings with Watson began to sound like stories of bewitchment. In January 1623, therefore, Christian Watson raised the stakes by counter-attacking. She submitted a written accusation of slander against both Davidson and Buchanan for wrongfully calling her a witch. She added for good measure that Davidson had committed fornication, and that Buchanan 'had bein brought up and hauntit among witches'.[1]

This counter-attack led the kirk session to refer the case up to the presbytery, which heard testimony from several of those involved. The presbytery then sent the case back to the kirk session, instructing them to question Watson about what proof she had of her allegations. The kirk session ordered her to appear at its next meeting for this purpose. One might have expected Watson at this point to produce witnesses to confirm that Davidson and Buchanan had indeed made the slanderous statements that had been alleged. But the real question was not whether they had made these statements; it was whether the statements were true. Thus, Watson now had to produce witnesses to prove that she herself was *not* a witch.

So, at the next meeting of the session (23 January), fourteen witnesses appeared and were asked to declare, on oath, whether they knew of any evidence that Watson was a witch. These witnesses were presumably chosen by Watson herself, though she may have been restricted in her choice by a need to include people who were known to have information about specific episodes. Thirteen of the fourteen testified that they 'knew nothing to hir bot honnestie'. But the fourteenth, Alexander Oswald, told of a sinister if vague life-or-death prediction by Watson, after which he had fallen and broken his leg.

Was Buchanan's and Oswald's evidence sufficient for a witchcraft prosecution? Falkirk's well-connected kirk session, whose members included an earl and several lairds, seem to have thought not. But they did not come down conclusively on Watson's side either. Instead, the session ordered Buchanan to prosecute Watson privately for witchcraft, and threatened her that if she did not do so then they themselves would proceed against her (Buchanan) 'as ane sclanderer and consulter of witches'.

This proposal to bring a private prosecution was remarkable. Private prosecutions were competent in Scottish criminal courts, but witchcraft was invariably prosecuted publicly. Equally remarkable was the court that the kirk session proposed: not a royal justice court, but 'my Lords court' – the local regality court of Falkirk. It would in fact have been irregular for a regality court to try a witchcraft case, as royal justice courts held a monopoly on this

[1] Margo Todd notes that Watson had previously brought a successful slander prosecution against John Dun, the evidently irresponsible church officer: Margo Todd, *The Culture of Protestantism in Early Modern Scotland* (New Haven, 2002), 244–7. Todd argues that Watson 'already had a local reputation for being a witch' when she brought this prosecution (p. 244), but her only cited evidence for this is the *subsequent* witchcraft investigation edited below. The record of Watson's prosecution of Dun, dated 3 October 1622, is at NRS, Minutes of Kirk Session of Falkirk, 1617–1640, CH2/400/1, p. 105. (Todd uses an older pagination of the MSS, so 2 needs to be added to her citations, e.g. her 'p. 103' should be read as 105.) Watson's prosecution of Dun has no obvious connection to witchcraft.

crime.[2] No witchcraft cases have been found in the extant regality court books of Falkirk, so far as these have been published.[3] At any rate, Buchanan failed to prosecute Watson, whereupon the session closed the case, nine months later, by ordering Buchanan to do penance, both for slander and for having consulted Watson 'as ane witche'. The implication in the end seems to have been that, although Watson was not a witch, Buchanan was still somehow a 'consulter of witches'.

TEXTS

Source 1: NRS, Minutes of Kirk Session of Falkirk, 1617–1640, CH2/400/1.[4]

{*p. 107*} Last of October 1622
Convenit the Minister,[5] William Levingstoun, William Burne, David Kers, George Mungell, Patrick Grindlay.

The quhilk day comperit Margaret Davisoune servitrix to Marioun Suord in Falkirk and being accusit for going to Cristiane Watsoune spous to James Packok thair[6] and consulting hir as ane witche by hir cumminge seicretlie behind the said Cristiane upone ane mercatt day on the hie streit and tuitching hir claithis and seiking of hir helth of hir seicretlie for Gods caus, The said Margaret confessis To have done the samyn and that sche was the better in hir helth thairefter. Scho being accusit quhy scho did the samyn depounit that the said Cristiane Watsoune promeist hir ane sark full of sore bainis[7] and that scho sould nocht \wit/ who sould do it, quhilk or[8] the morne thairefter came to pas Sua that scho conceavit sic ane great seiknes imediatlie thairefter that scho suait[9] Licklie to have Lost hir Lyfe quhilk scho is able to qualifie.[10] Scho lykwayes deponis that hir passage to the said Cristiane Watsoune vas at the persuasioun of Jonnet Buchanan spous to David Levingstoun. Ordained the said Margaret To compeir againe the nixt dyat and the said Jonnet Buchanan to summond [*sic*] thairto.... {*p. 108*}

2 Julian Goodare, 'Witch-Hunting and the Scottish State', in Julian Goodare (ed.), *The Scottish Witch-Hunt in Context* (Manchester, 2002), 122–45, at pp. 124–30.

3 The records are extant from 1638 onwards: *Court Book of the Barony and Regality of Falkirk and Callendar*, vol. i: *1638–1656*, ed. Doreen M. Hunter (Edinburgh: Stair Society, 1991). Several people mentioned in the present case (though not Watson herself) can be found in these records.

4 A summary of the text edited below, with lengthy if occasionally inaccurate quotations, is given in *Records of Falkirk Parish*, 2 vols., ed. George I. Murray (Falkirk, 1887–8), i, 31–9.

5 The minister of Falkirk was William Annand.

6 Watson's husband, James Peacock, seems to have had little involvement with the case. He was a 'dagmaker' (maker of pistols) in Falkirk: NRS, Minutes of Kirk Session of Falkirk, 1617–1640, CH2/400/1, p. 105.

7 'sark full of sore bainis': shirt full of sore bones, i.e. physical pain.

8 'or' (ere): before.

9 'suait': sweated.

10 'qualifie': prove.

7 of November 1622
Convenit my Lord Erle of Linlythqw[11] and the minister, Ponitasken,[12] Ballintone,[13] William Levingston, Collen Campbell, David Kers, George Mungell, John Auld, Thomas Fleiming....

The said day comperit Jonnet Buchannan spous to David Levingstoun in Falkirk, and being accusit anent hir going To Cristiane Watsoune spous to James Packok and consulting with hir as ane witche by seiking hir helth of hir for Gods caus, The said Jonnet depones and confessis that scho was adebtit to the said Cristiane Watsoune for fourtein pyntis aill, at the quhilk tyme the said Cristiane Watsoune sent sundrie tymes for hir to cum to hir hous quhilk scho refuissit to do, quhairupone the said Christiane sent hir ane Thrie schilling peice[14] with [*1 word blank*] Packok hir dochter[15] quhilk the said Jonnet resavit and put up in hir purs, and thairefter scho schawing to hir husband that the said Cristiane had sent hir ane Thrie schilling peice nochtwithstanding that scho was adebtit to hir, quhair of scho mervellit, The said David Levingstoun hir husband imediatlie thairefter tuik hir purs and schuik the money out of it and brunt hir said purss and caussit hir send bak the said Thrie schilling peice Togider with the pryce of the said fourteyn pyntis aill quhilk scho was adebtit to the said Cristiane. Efter the quhilk tyme the said Jonnet depones that scho conceavit suche ane great extraordiner seiknes quhairby scho wes movit to ane great heit sueit sua that scho could get no eas nor rest bot Luikit to have Lost hir Lyfe thairby. Quhairupone scho requyrit hir said husband to go and desyre the said Cristiane to cum to hir, quhilk he did bot scho refussit to cum. Efter the quhilk tyme the said Jonnet declaris that scho past to the said Cristianes hous hir selfe accumpaniet with [*1 word blank*] Buchanan ane freind quhilk was ane {*p. 109*} strainger[16] being in hir hous for the tyme, and past in at the said Cristianes bak dore, quhen the said Cristiane persaifit scho speirit at hir[17] rediculouslie geve[18] scho had pairtit with the bairne scho was with[19] quho ansuerit scho was with no bairnes bot had sum uther seiknes, at the quhilk tyme the said Jonnet besocht the said Cristiane for Gods caus to give hir hir helth and that the said Cristianes answer was God send hir it,

11 Alexander Livingstone, second earl of Linlithgow.

12 Alexander Livingstone of Pantaskin. This place is now known as Bantaskin.

13 Probably William Livingstone of Ballinton (also known as Banton).

14 This must be a misunderstanding of some kind, since the Scottish coinage had never included a three-shilling piece. The current coinage, first issued in 1605, included coins of one, two and six shillings.

15 It becomes apparent later that Watson had two daughters, Geillis Peacock ('Jeily') and Margaret Peacock.

16 'ane freind quhilk was ane strainger': a 'freind' means a relative (the person had the same surname as Janet Buchanan herself). By 'strainger', Janet Buchanan seems to have meant that the person was an occasional visitor from another locality.

17 'speirit at hir': asked her.

18 'geve': if.

19 This is an intriguing enquiry. Todd, *Culture of Protestantism*, 246, treats it as an accusation of 'procuring an abortion', but Watson's story, as she later clarified for the presbytery, was that Buchanan had had a miscarriage as a result of a natural disease.

and desyrit hir to go to Allexander Oswald and tak ane drink of hett vyne and spyce, quhilk scho declaryth scho did not, bot passit hame to hir awin hous and tuk ane drink of hett aill and thairefter grew better. The said Jonnet lykvayes deponit that efter the quhilk tyme scho had chapit[20] at hir dore, Jeily Packok hir dochter ansuerit quhat devill is at the dore and that quhen scho come in to the said Cristianes hous, James Packok hir husband gudman of the hous was standing wpone the floir and Imediatlie efter hir incuming departit out of the hous.

The said day comperit John Das [*sic*] in Westkers and being accusit anent his being with Margaret Davidsoune the tyme scho socht hir helth at Cristiane Watsoune he confessis that the said Margaret come slyding up to the Toune that day behind him and tauld him of hir diseas and how scho was of Intentioun to go seik hir helth at the said Cristiane and desyrit him to wait upone hir upone the streit at that tyme quhen scho was to do it and that he wald stand betuix the said Cristiane and hir and at the said tyme quhill scho socht hir helth of hir The said John depones he did the samyn accordinglie scho desyrit him.

The said day the said Cristiane Watsoune being askit give[21] scho promeist to give the said Margaret Davidsoune ane sark full of sore bainis and that scho sould nocht wit quho sould do it, deponis scho said so, and declares albeit scho said so scho was nocht of intentioun to do it hir selfe, bot that scho meanit to caus ane sister sonne of hirs whom the said Margaret knew nocht do it.... {*p. 110*}

28 of November 1622

Convenit the Minister, Pantasken, Ballantine, Mr James Menteath, Collein Campbell, George Mungell....

Compeirit Margaret Davidsoune and confest that Jannet Baird[22] spous to William Davidsoune in Westkirs hir mother counsellit hir to go to Cristiane Watsoune to seik hir helth.

The said day compeirit the said Jonnet Baird[23] and being accusit for counselling the said Margaret hir dochter to go to the said Cristiane Watsoune to seik hir helth confessis the same and that scho informit hir to pas seccretlie behind the said Cristiane Watsoune and caus ane stand betuix the said Cristiane and hir quhill scho Tuichit hir claithis and socht hir helth at hir Thrice secreitlie for Gods caus.... {*p. 112*}

20 'chapit': knocked.

21 'give': if.

22 The MS is damaged here, but from the context the word must be 'Baird'.

23 In margin: 'Jonet Bairds confessioun'.

9 of January 1623
Convenit My Lord Erle of Linlithgow, the Minister, Pantasken, Ballintone, Mr James Menteath, William Levingstoun, Patrik Grandlay, Hew Hall....

The said day compeirit Jonnet Buchannan spous to Davad [*sic*] Levingstoun in Falkirk and deponis that upon ane tyme about half ane yeir efter hir cumminge to the toune to duell, scho borowit ane quickening[24] from Cristiane Watsoune spous to James Paikok, quhilk quickening the said Jonnet sent hame againe with [*sic*] to the said Cristiane with Margaret Packok hir dochter and within ane hour thairefter or thairby the said Cristiane sent it bak againe with the said Margaret and set it doun on hir hous[25] and thairefter past hir way and wald not tarie to speik ane word to hir. Efter the quhilk tyme the said Jonnet depones that thair remanit no barme[26] upone hir haill brewing of aill sua that scho gat never guid of it bot lost it. To the quhilk the said Cristiane replyed and {*p. 113*} said the occasion of hir sending bak of the said quikening to hir was becaus Kathrein Hugein spous to Robert Callander wald nocht tak it from hir to put among hir virt,[27] aledging it nocht to be sufficient. Wpone the quhilk the said Kaithrein Hugein being accussit deponis scho never refussit no quickning that avere come to hir hous, no never sent anie bak againe scho aver resavit, as the said Cristiane alledges scho did.

The said day compeirit Cristiane Lathangie relict of umquhill James Robesoune lorimer[28] in Falkirk and deponis that about the spaice of halfe ane yeir sensyne or thairby scho past to the said Janet Buchananis hous To crave the said Jonnet for sum thing scho vas addebtit to hir. At the quhilk tyme the said Jonnet sould have said scho vad nocht content with hir, and imediatlie thairefter that the said Jonnet Buchanan sould have thrie severall tymes for Godis caus askit the saill of hir aill[29] from hir.

The said day compeirit Cristiane Watsoune spous to James Packok and give in ane bill of sclander against the said Jonnet Buchanan and Margaret Davisoune dochter to William Davisoune in Westkers[30] Compleaning upone them for sclandering her as ane witche and saying scho trubillit them of thair helth. Referid the samin to the presbyterie and ordained the foirsaids persounes Compleande and defenderis thair for that effect the nixt Wedinsday.[31]

24 'quickening': yeast or other leavening agent.
25 Word uncertain, possibly damaged at the end of a line.
26 'barme': froth upon the ale as it fermented. ('Barme' can also mean yeast, but that is not the meaning here.)
27 'virt' (wort): liquid to be fermented.
28 'lorimer': maker of metal parts for horse harnesses.
29 'the saill of hir aill': the opportunity or ability to sell her ale.
30 In margin (MS damaged): 'Cristi ... Buchanan ... referit to ...'.
31 9 January 1623 was a Thursday. The 'nixt Wedinsday' was 15 January.

Source 2: NRS, Minutes of Presbytery of Linlithgow, 1618–1632, CH2/242/2.

{*p. 87*} January 15 1623 …
This day the minister of Falkirk producit a proces of his session anent a slainder of witchcraft imputed to Christin Watsoun spows to James Peacok gunmaker in Falkirk, Be Jonet Buchanan spous to David Levingstoun thair, and Margaret Davieson servitrix to Marion Swerd thair, and Jonet Baird in Westkers.[32]

Jonet Baird thair personalie compeirand, confessit that sche causit the said Margaret Davieson hir dochter, being heavily diseasit, to pass to the toun of Falkirk and put ane persone betuix hir and the said Christin Watsoun, and tak hir be hir coat and secretly within hir self ask hir health of hir thrie severall tymes, quhilk circumstances, quhen the Brethrein Inquyrit of hir quha advysit hir to use, answerit none but hir self. Sche is referrit bak to hir sessioun.

Comperit Jonet Buchannan quha constantly affirmit all that sche had befoir {*p. 88*} deponit befoir the session. The said Christen Watsoun compeirit also, and gave in a bill of complaint agains the said Jonet Buchannan and Margaret Davidsoun. And in this bill alledgit agains Jonet Buchannan that sche wes malitious agains hir, and Infamous, and thairfoir aucht not to be hard in sic a wechtie mater, nor belevit, as also allegit agains Margaret Davidson, that sche had a natural diseas and partit with bairne and so not bewitched. The Brethrein referris thame bak to thair session and ordains the said Christen to qualifie hir bill.

Source 3: NRS, Minutes of Kirk Session of Falkirk, 1617–1640, CH2/400/1.

{*p. 114*} 16 of January 1623
Convenit the Minister, Pantasken, Ballinten, Mr James Menteath, William Levingstoun, William Burne elder, David Kers, George Mungell, Patrik Hassingtoune, Thomas Fleyming, John Auld….

The said day the Minister reportit that Cristiane Watsoune spous to James Packok Comperit in the presbyterie of Linlithgow upone the xv° January instant and gave in ane bill quhairin scho maid exceptioune agaienes Jonet Buchannan and Margaret Davisoune Annent the dellatioune gevin in be them aganes hir to the sessioun heir, in the quhilk bill the said Cristiane alleges the said Jonnet to be ane infamous prophane and wngodlie persoune quho had bein brought up and hauntit among witches as aperid,[33] As also that the said Margaret Davisoune vas infamous and godles {*p. 115*} and that scho had commitit fornicatioun and past to hir motheris hous and pairtit with bairne, quhilk exceptioune foirsaid the said Cristiane tuik her to qualifie.[34] Ordanes

[32] In margin: 'Proces of witchcraft from the session of Falkirk'.
[33] 'aperid': appeared.
[34] 'tuik her to qualifie': said that she would prove.

the said Cristiane Lyk as scho vas ordained and reffered heir be the presbyterie To prove the said exceptiounes aganes the foirsaids persones befor ws and that scho compeir heir this day aucht dayes for probatioun thairof as saids....

23 of January 1623
Convenit My Lord Erle of Linlythgw, Mr Wiliam Annand Minister, Alexander Levingstoun of Pantaskyn, Westquarter,[35] Mr James Menteath, William Levingstoun, William Birnie, George Mungell, David Kers, Patrick Hassingtoun.

The quhilk day Alexander Oswald being askit give[36] he knew onie presumptiounes or appeirances of witchcraft to Cristiane Watsoune spous to James Packoke \declared/ That about the spaice of seven or aucht yeiris sensyne he being upone ane mercatt day upone the hie streit bying ane mowttoun bowk from the fleschours[37] quhair the said Cristiane vas present at that tyme, And that efter the said Cristiane past hame to hir awin hous that it vas reportit to his vyfe be Jonnet Dick that the said Cristane sould have said to the said Jonnet that the said Allexander sould not cum to the grave thairefter for fourtie dayes, and the said Allexander the same day thairefter being in his awin barne floore lifting ane boll beir[38] brak his leg.

The said [*sic*] compeirit James Sympsoune in Falkirk, Cristiane Mitchell his spous, David Kirk thair, Gavin Murray thair, James Book thair, Arthour Hunter thair, John Baird thair, Thomas Quhyt thair, Elspeth Murray spous to George Grahame thair, Marioun Leishman spous to Hendrie Aiking thair, Jonnet Flemyng spous to James Book thair, Thomas Ambrose and the said Hendrie Aiking, and being ewerie ane severallie suorne to depone and declair upone thair conscience give[39] they knew onie presumptiounes or appeirances of witchcraft to the said Cristiane Watsoune, deponed all in ane voice that they knew nothing to hir bot honnestie.

The said day compeirit Jonnet Buchannan spous to Davad Levingstoun quha of befoir be hir awin confessioun had past To the said Cristiane Watsoune and consultit hir as ane witche by seiking hir helth at the said Cristiane. Ordanes the said Jonnet Buchannan Betuixt and this day sex weiks[40] to persew the said Cristiane criminallie in my Lords court as ane witche Sua that scho may be ather condemnit or absolvit, with certificatioun to the said Jonnet give[41] scho failyie We vill proceid aganes hir with the censures of the kirk as ane sclanderer and consulter of witches.... {*p. 125*}

35 Alexander Livingstone of Westquarter.
36 'give': if.
37 'ane mowttoun bowk from the fleschours': a carcass of mutton from the butchers.
38 'ane boll beir': a sack of bere (barley) containing a measure of one boll.
39 'give': if.
40 'Betuixt and this day sex weiks': within the next six weeks.
41 'give': if.

18 of September 1623
Convenit the Minister, Pantasken, Mr James Menteath, Collen Campbell, William Levingstoun, William Burne, Patrick Hassingtoun, David Kers, Georg Mungell, Thomas Fleyming, William Burne younger.

The quhilk day comperit Jonnet Buchannan spous to Davad Levingstoun in Falkirk consulter of Cirstiane Watsoune spous to James Packock thair as ane witche, Quha vas ordanit of befoir be act of the sessioun To have persewit the said Cirstiane befor the ordinar judge criminalie as ane witche quhilk scho hes failyeit to do. Thairfoir decernes and ordanes hir to mak hir publict repentance sex severall sabathes in seckclaith and to stand in the said habite at the churche to [*sic*] \ilk/ day of the said sex sabathes from the ringing of the first bell to the sermoun till the last be rung out, and thairefter ilk day to cum with the said habit in to the churche and remaine thair the tyme of the sermoun and upone the last of the said sabathes in presence of the haill congregatioun quhill scho salbe requyrit be the minister To humblie confes and acknowledge hir filthie and abominable fact to the glorie of God and exempill of wtheris to commit the lyk and thair to protest and mak promeis of amendment of lyfe. Ordaines the bailyies authorities to be interponit for wairding of hir quhill scho find cautioun for obediance and performance of this present act.

14. ALEXANDER DRUMMOND, AUCHTERARDER, 1628–1629

INTRODUCTION

Alexander Drummond was an elderly man, aged eighty-one, living in the parish of Auchterarder in Perthshire. He was a healer with a large number of clients, including gentlemen and even ministers, and had a reputation for having practised healing for about fifty years. He charged money for healing, and was respected for his knowledge. He was transported to Edinburgh for investigation and trial. Numerous clients, in various localities throughout east-central Scotland, were questioned about his practices; the dossier edited here includes some correspondence about how ministers organised this investigation. The full minutes of Drummond's trial do not survive, but there is a list of assize members, and a summons to the assize. He was evidently tried and executed in 1629.

Most of the documents preserved in the dossier are records of this process of pre-trial interrogation. From 28 September 1628 until 8 July 1629, Drummond was questioned about his performance of healing and about his clients. He cured both physical and mental illness, and adults as well as children. He recited two charms that he used for healing, and the scribe carefully wrote down the words, placing the records in a middle position between written and oral. He also knew some words that he would not repeat during interrogation.

Otherwise, the clerk departed from Drummond's own way of describing his practice. The written record stated that he had long been suspected of witchcraft; he was suspected and challenged for sorcery and witchcraft; suspected of unlawful and supernatural healing, and devilish practice, and abusing his majesty's lieges; 'ane witch and sorcerer'; 'crymis of sorcerie witchcraft and divilish chearmingis'; 'curing be diabolical and unlawful meanis'. The depositions are marked 'Alexander Drummond Warlock'. The word 'witchcraft' was frequently used by the interrogators to describe how an unexpected illness came to afflict a person. The Devil was mentioned in the context of casting sickness upon people, sickness that may be cured by Drummond's charm. However, 'Devil' was also used by Drummond himself, to describe sickness caused by evil powers. In the act of curing a man, he said,

'You terrible Devil, come out of the man', and then the sickness was transferred into a mare. However, central demonological ideas like the demonic pact and witches' gatherings are not mentioned in these pre-trial documents. Nor is there any clear mention of quarrels or malefice. There is no indication in the documents that he was tortured.

In contrast to this hostile discourse, Drummond himself used the words 'cure' and 'curing' about his practice. He said that he was a common curer of many incurable diseases, that he was able to steer the direction of life and death by using his charms. He told some clients that they were 'bewitched' or had 'gotten a blast of evill wind', and that he could cure them. He dropped hints to his clients as to who might have caused their bewitchment, but seems to have stopped short of naming names. His interrogators did not pursue the question of who these other witches might have been, even though the period of the interrogations was one of developing panic over multiple witches in other Scottish localities.

Alexander's son John Drummond, and the latter's wife Elizabeth Burgh, helped him in his practice in various ways (there is also a vignette of the three of them harvesting together in the fields). The investigators interrogated John and tried unsuccessfully to interrogate Elizabeth. Both caused annoyance with their loyal and obstructive support of Alexander, but they themselves seem not to have been under suspicion – another indication that the prosecutors saw this as an individual case, even during this period of panic.

The documents give a glimpse into a comprehensive art of healing, counter-magic, love magic, and finding lost and stolen goods. Drummond claimed to heal those possessed with spirits, and even dealt with complications of childbirth. He knew a number of charms and words that he used for healing, where the Devil was mentioned alongside the Trinity and the Lord's Prayer. In one such charm, the Devil cast sickness upon St John and took his tongue from him. Drummond often used the shirt belonging to a sick person in order to cure him or her. He also used such items as a ring, a mutch (hood or nightcap), powder, three stones, and water – particularly south-running water that a Christian king had ridden over. He had a reputation for transferring disease and for removing bewitchment. Quarter days were suitable for practising healing. He also claimed that Sundays were the best days for performing charms, which attracted the authorities' particular disapproval.

Drummond, unusually, owned several books, and used them in his practice. These included *The Regiment of Life*, a sixteenth-century English medical manual, and an unnamed Latin book. He also had a manuscript of extracts from books. He himself could not read, but a local notary and other literate people read to him and wrote letters for him.

The main co-ordinator of the investigation seems to have been Alexander Colville of Blair, a justice depute who may have presided over the trials of more Scottish witches than any other judge, though his personal motives and input usually remain opaque.[1] In these documents we see him, not as a judge in the trial itself (he did act in this capacity, but the minutes of the trial itself do not survive), but as an active participant in pre-trial investigation. Alongside Colville, the role of Adam Bellenden, bishop of Dunblane, seems to have been significant. He interrogated Drummond repeatedly, both in Dunblane itself and later in Edinburgh. An active and ambitious privy councillor, Bellenden was the most politically prominent person among the investigators.[2]

Colville and Bellenden also had local agents. The letter below from John Freebairn, minister of Madderty, presents Freebairn himself and his local ally, George Hay of Keillour, as godly activists: 'The Lord knowes I am bussie for no respect bot for his glory.' They determinedly investigate witchcraft and arrange prosecutions, even in the face of local opposition. Freebairn also mentions John Graham, minister of Auchterarder and Aberuthven (Drummond's own parish minister), as one of his supporters. The letter, written to Alexander Colville, treats the latter as an ally in the struggle against witchcraft.

What exactly led people to see Alexander Drummond as a witch? The question cannot be answered conclusively in the absence of the dittay, which would have presented the formal charges against him in court. These pre-trial documents show him almost entirely as a healer. Sometimes his cures are successful, while at other times they fail, but no overt conclusions are drawn from either outcome. There is no explicit mention of the demonic pact, and no explicit mention of malefice. Nor is there any explicit statement of a view that healing itself constitutes witchcraft – a view that indeed is rarely if ever taken in other Scottish witchcraft trial records.

Drummond's clients never accuse him overtly of witchcraft. They sometimes sound embarrassed about having consulted him, and explain defensively that in doing so they had given in to the persuasions of others; this is understandable, since by the time that they give their testimony they know that Drummond has been accused of witchcraft. Sometimes, too, they sound mildly dissatisfied at his actions – a repeated theme being his failure to return personal items used in diagnosis (Drummond himself explains this by describing such items as being needed for curative rituals). But the clients never mention quarrels, nor do they even suggest that Drummond might have been angry or vengeful. They are sometimes awed at the charismatic power of his ritual performances, but they do not perceive anything directly demonic about these.

Drummond's own statements never constitute a confession to witchcraft; in his own self-presentation he is always a godly healer. The possibility that he caved in to pressure shortly before his trial and confessed to witchcraft cannot

1 Colville's involvement in many other cases from 1629 to 1661 can be traced through the 'People involved' search function in the online Survey of Scottish Witchcraft.

2 Sally Tuckett, 'The Scottish Bishops in Government, 1625–1638', in Sharon Adams and Julian Goodare (eds.), *Scotland in the Age of Two Revolutions* (Woodbridge, 2014), 59–78, at pp. 66–8.

be ruled out in the absence of the dittay, but there is no positive evidence that he did so. However, he himself, and some other deponents, stated that he sometimes advised relatives to dedicate a sick person to the Devil if they wished the person to live, and to God if they wished the person to die. Drummond may have had in mind the biblical idea of the Devil as the prince of this world (e.g. John 12:31), but this advice was certainly unorthodox. A hostile interpretation could have regarded it as evidence of a demonic pact; the surviving documents do not make this connection explicit, but perhaps the dittay did do so.

Because Drummond was so well known among the local gentry, suspicions of him could arise in these circles, and could draw on demonological reasoning. Duncan Eason, the notary who read Drummond's books to him, came to suspect him at the time, though he admitted that his suspicions were slow to arouse:

> I was ane indwellar in Ochterardour ane yeir and moir befor I suspectit the forsaid Alexander of unlawfull and supernaturall healing, and being advertisit be Mr Hary Rollok than my pastour in Abruthven that he was not ane lawfull man, I abstenit from his companye and he from me from thencefurthe.

The naming of the former minister strengthens the impression that Eason's suspicions were not entirely constructed with the aid of hindsight. His phrase 'unlawfull and supernaturall healing' hints at a line of demonological reasoning: if this cure has not been achieved through recognisably natural remedies, and if it used rituals that orthodox religion does not recognise, then by process of elimination it can be concluded that the only agent that can have made the cure effective must have been the Devil. Perhaps the dittay developed such hints into something more explicit.

The final documents edited below show that the case had an unusual aftermath in 1646. Somebody representing Drummond succeeded in obtaining access to King Charles, and persuaded him that Drummond had been a good physician and not a witch. Allegedly, his majesty would not be satisfied until he had seen the details of the case, having been informed that Drummond had performed all his 'wondrous cures' by lawful means. Alexander Colville, the judge who had interrogated and tried Drummond, was with Charles at this time, and bore the brunt of the king's suspicions of miscarriage of justice. Colville wrote three letters to John Bannatyne, justice clerk depute in Edinburgh, asking for a copy of the trial documents in order to persuade the king that the trial had been justified. The outcome of this campaign to exonerate Drummond is not known. The case attracted broad attention and was remembered for even longer. The tale of James Ramsay of Corston's return from Italy and his encounter with Drummond at the bridge of Earn (item 26 below) was still being told in 1678.

The documents are preserved in a bundle of thirty-four loose items. Each item has an archival reference number written in pencil, thus: JC26/9/3/1-34. These numbers are given as subheadings below. The items are printed here in chronological order, not numerical order. Most of the documents are single sheets, written on one or both sides. A few sheets are folded, so that the text is written on four pages. Two documents continue over two sheets, as noted in subheadings and footnotes below. Endorsements on the backs of documents are printed here at the beginning of the texts to which they relate. The documents are easy to read, with ink well preserved, except for item 26, where the ink is bled-through and faded. For some of the documents, the edge of the sheet is damaged, so that it is impossible to read the last word or the last letters of the line.

Many of the documents have contemporary numbers written on them, plus a few letters, apparently by a clerk trying to organise the material. There seem to be two main series of numbers: one series for the documents, and another series for the names of individual deponents. There also seems to be an effort to keep track of the names of alleged victims of witchcraft. One document, item 27, consists of two lists: 'The names of the assyseris' and 'The names of the witnessis'. These witnesses' names are largely separate from those of the deponents recorded elsewhere in the dossier, though there is some overlap. Probably the witnesses were expected to testify personally in court, whereas the other deponents' written statements would have been read to the court without them necessarily being present. The list of assizers has its own pattern of letters and numbers; they may represent a system used by the clerk of the court to keep track of who had been summoned and who had responded to the summons.

TEXT

Source: NRS, Court of Justiciary Process Papers, 1628–1629, JC26/9.

JC26/9/3/10

[*Endorsed:*] 21 John Condeit
{*p. 1*} 14
At Cowdoun Lawis the tuentie aucht day of September 1628 yeiris In presence of Mr Jhon Tullis Minister at Wemyss, Adam Blakwod Reader thair, *Patrik*

Grant[3] webster, Patrik Broune colyour,[4] Jhone Cundeit deponit that he was twys in Ochterardour at \Alexander/[5] Drummond Quha hes beine Lang suspeck of wichcraft, and that the first tyme was at Lammes[6] Last, and he askit help of his Grait seiknes at the said \Alexander/[7] quha first Grippit the pairtis of his bodie thairefter straikit his breist thrys with his naikit hand and spak soume wordis[8] *quhilk he rememberis not, and last straikit his hand thrys upon the Arme, saying I have takin frome yow and Layit upon the earth*[9] and they that hes done the same to yow, ye sei them dayly bot I will not tell yow thair names for that wold breid pley[10] betuixt yow and them, bot ye will sei your herts desyr upon them. He Gave to him at that tyme ten pundis.

Item the said Jhone Cundeit deponit that the last tyme that he was at the said Archbald[11] Drummond, his seiknes cuming to him againe, that the said Alexander did to him as befor and Gave unto him ane litell peice in cullour lykent Roustie ayrone[12] desyring him to keip it upon him,[13] in keiping quhairof he should be releifit of his diseas, notwithstanding quhairof the said persone is vexit with maist noysume[14] seiknes Thretning as apearit the very death, and that Jhone Cundeit gave unto the said Archbald[15] Drummond the secund tyme that he was at him at Lames last uther ten pundis. In witnes Quherof we have subscrivit thir presents with our hands as followis.

[*Signed:*] Mr Jon Tullis Minister at Wemyss, Adam Blakwod Reader their.

JC26/9/3/33

[*Endorsed:*] Depositions Alexander Drummont
xvi October 1629 [*sic*]
[*in another hand:*]
16 Octobris 1628
2 Abrahame Thomesone, 3 the laird of McNab, 4 James Afflect merchand, 5 Robert Prymrois

{*p. 1*} At Dunblaine saxten day of October 1628 In presens of Sir Johne Stirling of Garden knycht and Mr Alexander Colvile of Blair Justice deput

3 'Patrik Grant' is underlined in the MS.
4 'colyour': collier (coal-miner).
5 'Archbald' crossed out and 'Alexander' written above.
6 'Lammes' (Lammas): 1 August.
7 'Archbald' crossed out and 'Alexander' written above.
8 In margin: 'anent the taking af of seiknes and laying it on the earthe be speking of words'.
9 The text in italics is underlined in the MS.
10 'that wold breid pley': that would lead to disputes.
11 *Sic.* 'Alexander' is meant.
12 'in cullour lykent Roustie ayrone': the colour of rusty iron.
13 In margin: 'anent the ammulet gevin of rustie Irne'.
14 'noysume' (noisome): harmful or unpleasant.
15 *Sic.* 'Alexander' is meant.

of this realme, Archibald Stirling of McCoranstoun, William Stirling of Bankell, Coline Campbell sumtyme of Ardbeiche, Mr John Grahame Minister of Aberruthven[16] and Walter Cheisholme bailyie of Dunblane.

The quhilk day[17] Alexander Drummond in Kirktoun of Ochterardor aigit Fourscoir ane yeiris efter lang examinatioun frielie confessit that he was *ane comoun cuirrer of many Incurable diseassis, sic as the cancer, Sanct Banbains fyr and noli me tangerie; mad and furious*[18] and franetik people, and subject to frenecies and widnes, falling evill, runing, worms and glengor.[19]

Item[20] he confessit that he cuirit Abrahame Thomsone indweller in Kirkcady sone to Margaret Eweing of madness, being bund in bandis, and that the deponer past to Kirkcady to do that cuir, and quhen he has cuirit him he gatt ane band for ane thousand pund and four crounis[21] in and quhilk band is yit in his custodie, at the leist knawis quhair it is, And yit onlie as yit hes receavit twenty pund fra the said Margret.

Item[22] confessit that thrie or foire yeiris sine or thairby he went to[23] Kinnellie in Braidalbein to the laird of McNab quhair he wes so mad that he was bund betwixt foir greit stuipis[24] with cors bunded round about quhilkis war mad[e][25] to pas throw the stuipis by hoilis and so ane great geist[26] als great as ane piller at his feit, And[27] that he cuirit him of the said madnes and receavit fra his wyff thairfor fyve merkis, And that he cuirit this diseas be ane puder cassin in grein broth, and that James Stewart sone to Alester or one Patrik McNab brother to the Laird of McNab com for him to this effect.

Item[28] he confessit he cuirit James Auchinlek merchand in Dundie within the toun of Dundie of so great madnes that he wes bound up with Iron Lockis, and recevint[29] thairfoir Twenty pund and mair and that[30] he cuirit this madnes be ane puder cassin in grein broth and drink quhilk he caussit the patient drink. {*p. 2*}

16 John Graham was minister of the united parishes of Auchterarder and Aberuthven. He was thus Alexander Drummond's own parish minister.

17 In margin: 'names of the disseissis curet be him'.

18 The text in italics is underlined in the MS.

19 'noli me tangerie': a skin condition with symptoms of ulceration; 'Sanct Banbains fyr': not found in dictionaries, but possibly related to St Anthony's fire (erysipelas); 'widnes': madness; 'falling evill': epilepsy; 'runing': a disease with symptoms of emission of liquid; 'glengor': syphilis.

20 In margin: 'madnes'.

21 Reading uncertain. Probably the French crown of the sun.

22 In margin: 'mad'.

23 'with' crossed out.

24 'stuipis': posts, pillars.

25 'kirk' crossed out.

26 'geist': joist.

27 In margin: 'curet be poulderis'.

28 In margin: 'mad'.

29 'recevint': received.

30 In margin: 'curet be poulder'.

Item[31] he deponed that he was brocht to Futies mylne four or fyve yeiris syne, and[32] thair cuirit Robert Prymross sone of umquhile James Prymross of madnes *ut supra*,[33] and that Mr Robert Colvile and Mr Robert Roghe ministers wer thair and that they and the deponer dynit togidder at Futies Mylne, And that the ministeris did sie the puder and inquyrit giff he did that cuir be ane guid meinis, And that he receavit fra the said umquhile James ten merk for his painis.

Item[34] deponis that he was accustomit to cum to noble and womenis hameis that wer tormentit in thair birth quhen the bairne turnit in thair billie[35] by saying the wordis in the richt ear.

Marie buir Chryst, Elizabeth buir Sanct John
Marie buir the savior of the warld
And Elizabeth buir the great pastor
I chairg the infant to cum furth – and sie
the host of heavin and earth, quither thow be
deid or quick For Chryst callis the[e] to his
baptisme In the naim of the father, sone
and holie gaist and said then, the Lordis prayer
thrys ower.

Item confessis that he had yit ane uther way to cuir women tormentit in thair chyld birth, viz. be the earne fairne[36] quhilk quhen he tuitched befoir he pullit up he pronuncis thir wordis, In name of the father, sone and hioly gaist I tak the[e] up for sik ane use to help travelling[37] women and thairefter sayis the lordis prayer thrys over – to the herb and than applyis it be the ruit of the womanis left thie – or to hir prime member, and schortlie thairefter – the bairne and efter birth will baith cum away, And giff the herb be nocht cum away Immediatelie efter the birth cum away, The patient wold work continuallie in hir pain to daith, And confessit that he hes cuirit baith \to/ noble and mein women in thair birth be thir meinis formirlie sett doun, And he hes send it to sundrie women Bot refuissis to tak thair names. {*p. 3*}

Item confessis that the people war accustomit to send him mutchis and sarkis thairby to try diseissis, and that he send them bak agane.

Item confessis \that the people war accustomit to send him/ four soirt of madnes, viz. madnes, wodnes, frenecie and possessit with spreitis, and that he hes cuirit persons tormentit with thir diseasis be gifing to tham puder in thair drinkis.

31 In margin: 'mad'.
32 In margin: 'curet be poulder'.
33 'as above'.
34 In margin: 'anent the remeid of the pane in the birth and rymes uset be him thairin'.
35 'billie' (belly): womb.
36 'earne fairne' (eagle fern): bracken.
37 'travelling' (travailing): giving birth.

Item being redemandit that giff he cuirit thais quha said they wer possest with spreitis with the former puderis, confessit he did.

Item being demandit quhairof thais pouderis war composit, deponit that they war composit of the halk berry trie and mugwart brunt in asses and put in the patients drink *ut supra* with the rowne trie.

[*Signed:*] Archibald Sterling, AColville, William Sterling, ASterling, JGrahame Minister at Aberuthven, WCheisholme.

At Edinburgh xii Januarii 1629 In presens of my lord bishope of Dunblane, my lord advocat, my lord Justice depute commissioneris appointit for examination of Alexander Drummond be the lordis of secreit counsall.

The depositiones befoir writtin maid be Alexander Drummond upoune the 16 of October 1628 Being red over to him L [*sic*] he ratifeit the said depositiones everie woird and confessit the samyn to be of veritie being sworne.

[*Signed:*] Ad: B: of Dunblane, Thomas Hop, AColville.

JC26/9/3/26

[*Endorsed:*] 8 anent Corsoun
K
Robert dwelland about Dunkeld
Deposition Alexander Drummont 17 October 1628

{*p. 1*} At Dumblane the seventein day of October i^{m} vi^{c} Tuentie and aught yeiris In presens of Sir James Chisholme of Cromicks knycht, Sir Johne Stirling of Carden knycht, Mr Alexander Colvill of Blair Justice depute of this realme, Mr James Drummond minister of Foulis, Mr Johne Grahame minister of Auchterardour, Mr James Row minister at Muithill, Williame Stirling of Bankell and Walter Chisholme bailyie of Dumblane.

The[38] Quhilk day Alexander Drummond being reexamined freilie and of his awin accord confessit that the laird of Corstoun[39] being travelling in uther countries[40] and being heavielie diseassit with ane troubile of mynd quhilk the deponer callit disperatioun the said laird of Corstoun Inquyrit for phisienis and suche as could cuir his infirmitie, And finding one to quhom he relaittit the maner of his diseas, Receavit helpis and remaidis quhilk easit him of his forsaid disease for the present tyme, And morover the deponer affirmit that Corstoun informit him that the foirsaid phisien gaff him ane preservitive

38 In margin: 'J'.

39 James Ramsay of Corston. Corston Tower is to the west of Strathmiglo in Fife. The story of Ramsay's visit to Italy, and the Italian physician's prediction of his future encounter with Drummond, was still being told in 1678, when it was recorded by Sir John Lauder of Fountainhall, *Historical Notices of Scotish Affairs*, 2 vols., ed. David Laing (Edinburgh: Bannatyne Club, 1868), i, 199–200. Lauder's version has lost all the names except for the bridge of Earn, but the story is the same.

40 In margin: 'anent the laird of Corstounes time in Italie'.

to preserve him from that disease in all tyme cuming, viz. he tuik ane ring with ane certane pulder and inclosit the samyn within the band of his breikis, assureing him that sa lang as he keipit the preservitive saiflie within the place foirsaid that he sould not be supprysit with the former diseas and that it sould not returne againe to him.

Morover deponit that quhen Corstun sould cum hoom throw Ingland he sould sie king James at [*word illegible*] ane place in his prayres quhilk \come to pas/. Moreover he schaw to Corstoun the wyff that he was to marie in Scotland altho than scho was mareit to ane uther husband \quhilk husband thairefter died and Corstoun was thairefter mareit to that sam wyf/. And farder he admonishit the said Corstoun that in cais he sould happen to Loos the foirsaid preservitive at ony tyme that his diseas sould not faill to returne to him againe, Quhilk gif it did he fortald fortoun that thar wes none Living could cuir him except ane of his awin countrie men in Scotland quhom he sould meit betwixt the brig of Earn and Muirmonth ryding on ane grey naig, quhos name, viz. Alexander Drummond was written in Corstouns stane buik.

Yet trew it is that according to the foirsaid informatioun the said Corstoun being in Ingland and haveing [*some words illegible*] therin the physiene has fixit [*end of page curled up*] {*p. 2*} the[41] ring and pulder was Loist and the diseas returnit to Corstoun, Quhairthrew he tuik occasioun to cum to Scoteland and heaveing occasioun to \be/ going to the toune off Perth he mett the deponer,[42] Corstoun being accumpeynit with foure or five horsis, and Luiking narowlie to the said deponer callit to his memorie the descriptioun of the deponers body, statour, Apparell and cullour of his hors, Quhairupon he tuik occasioun to confer with the deponer and tuik him bak againe with him to the brig of Earne that he micht haiff ane mair ampill and particular conference with the deponer, And to that effect that he micht not appeir to the cumpany and behalderis that Corstoun his earand was not directly to confer with the deponer and haveing bissiness with him, Corstoun pretended to inquyre for ane smyth and gave ane remove to tua horsis schone that neidit not in the mein tyme of the conference, And so told the deponer all the forsaid informatioun and estait of his diseas and the fortald meiting, and cravit of the deponer to be cuirit accordinglie quhilk he did, And receivit thairfoir Ten merk and an auld ryding cloik.

Morover[43] the said deponer confessed that he never ressavit harme by cureing any patient but only from one callit Robert wha came from beyond Dunkell to Auchterardour to be cured by him, and being very heavelie diseased and troubled and possessed with a spirit, and being asked how he knew the said possession, he answerit because the said Robert was troubled

41 In margin: 'K'.
42 In margin: 'at the place fortold be the phisiene'.
43 In margin: 'anent the cure of Robert quha dwelt above Dunkell of his madnes'.

in his mynd and thinges followed on him whilk feared him[44] and suffered not his mynd to rest. And being demandit of the maner of the cure, he confessit that he cured him at his first comeing to him giving him ane pouder in ane paper whilk he ordained him to keep upon him, assuring him that so long as he keepit the samyne upon him he should be weell, but if he lossed it he wold be als evill as he was before, and withall deponit that at the using of the cure he himself contracted ane heavie disease by the fear, so that he went in his awin house immediatlie and fand himselff to be unweell being fant in his heart, and continued seek for sundrie weeks wherof he was three dayes that he never spak nor saw, and his kist was made for his buriall as is notoriouslie knawn to all the contrey about, and that sensyne he hes never had his heart nor his tongue as before.

Morover deponit that the said accident fell out on the Tysday befor {*p. 3*} Yoole[45] and that in the tyme when he spak not he was transported and saw[46] strange visiones.[47]

Item he confesses that the pouder *wherwith he cured madnes was compossed of the root of mugwart, the hayberrie trie*[48] and the rantree all brunt in the fyre till they be dissolvit in asches, whilk he did bind in a litle paper or a cleane cloth and send the samyne to the patient to cure madnes, woodnes, frenesie and possession of spiritis by saying of thir wordes, In the name of the father, the sonne and the holy ghost, and repeating the Lords prayer thryse.[49]

Item deponed anent the cure of the falling evill that the *maner how he cured it was as after followes, he took three pickles of rosepionie seed and the stane that is gotten within the heart of a swallow it being the first buird of her dame, together with a litle parchment of paper in the whilk was written the name of the patient in Latine, and put in the said thrie pickles and the forsaid stone in this*[50] parchment or paper and hanged all in a cord of silk about the[51] neck of the patient, saying these words, I put this about thy neck in the name of the father, the sonne and the holy ghost to cure the[e] of the falling seeknes for Christes sake, and so long as they keep of the samyne they salbe frie and weell, but if they loss the samyne thair disease schall *returne to them againe, confesses that he used this cure*[52] to John Grahame sonne to Robert Grahame bailyie of Auchterardour who lossed the said recipe wherupon his diseas returned to him againe.

44 'feared him': frightened him.
45 'Yoole': Christmas.
46 'knowine' crossed out.
47 In margin: 'anent the cure with the mugwart, the hayberie and rowne trie'.
48 The text in italics is underlined in the MS.
49 In margin: 'anent the cure usit for the falling evil'.
50 The text in italics is underlined in the MS.
51 Letter crossed out.
52 The text in italics is underlined in the MS.

Item confessed that a certane young gentleman in the north haveing gotten wrong sa that he became impotent[53] contracted ane heavie disease that wasted his body, A certane Lady in the north did wryt a letter to the deponer with a man that culd read wrett, and when the deponer ressavit the letter and had opened it he gave it againe to the bearer to read, schawing him that he himselff culd not read, and haveing understand by reading of the letter which was the gentlemanes disease he sent with the bearer[54] to the patient about tua unce weight of a powder, whilk cured the patient for the tyme so that he was able to travell as of before, who immediatlie therafter went to the place where he had ressavit his wrong to shaw unto them that he had recoverit his health, but howsoone soever[55] he came to the place he fell in his former disease againe, Wherupon the forsaid Lady who was mother of the patient sent another letter againe to the deponer in the whilk sche secreetlie confessit and acknowledgeit[56] the weaknes and frailtie of her sex and that the gentleman patient was not the sonne of her maryed husband[57] but was begotten of another, and therfore in this second letter sche gave him the surname of the unlawful father wheras in the former letter sche had callit him by the surname of her lawfull husband, wherupon the deponer took occasion to change the nature of the cure conforme to the change of the surname, and by his second cure the patient was perfytlie cured, at the delyverie of {*p. 4*} whilk second cure the said deponer said these words to him who caried the letter, That he sent his cure to the gentleman and not to a bastard schawing that if they had sent him the right surname in the first letter the cure wold have prevailed at the first tyme.

Item deponit that he cured Mr David Burrel[58] in Lindores of madnes, and lykwayes Robert Cunninghame in Litle Fordell of the samyne diseas.

Item deponit that he went to the burgh of Lanerick and cured a barne that had a gangrene in his fingers and toes who had before ane of his fingers cut of[f], but he cured him and made the rest of his members that remained sound and wholl.

Item he gave a powder Latelie to [*1 word blank*] Bruce sonne of Andro Bruce indwellar in Yetland to cure him of madnes.

Item deponed that the laird of Stainlie \Maxwell/ being diseased in such sort that he culd not love his awine wyff nor dwell at home but had a preposterous desyre to any other woman, who haveing come to Auchterardour seeking to be cured by the said deponer he gave him some of the forsaid powders.

53 'having' crossed out.
54 'with' crossed out.
55 'howsoone soever': as soon as ever.
56 MS damaged: 'acknowledge…'.
57 MS damaged: 'husban…'.
58 'of' crossed out.

Item[59] *deponit that he cured a certane noble man of a consuming seiknes with a litle blak*[60] woll whilk he put round about his heid under his mutch.

[*Signed:*] JoCheisholme, AColville, JSterling, JDrummond minister of Foulis, William Sterling, JGrahame minister at Augterardour, WCheisholme, MJRowe minister at Muithill.

At Edinburgh the xii Januare 1629 In presens of my lord Bishop of Dumblane, [*words crossed out*] My lord advocat, My lord Justice clerk, My lord Justice depute, Commissioners appointit be the Lordis of Secreit counsall for examinatioun of Alexander Drummond in Auchterardour.

The said Alexander Drummond being present and examinit and sworne to declair the veritie efter the depositions foirsaidis made be him upoun the xvii day of October 1628 war red over to him and he declairit the saids depositiouns [*word illegible*] trew and ratifeit the samyne.

[*Signed:*] Ad: B: of Dunblane, Thomas Hope, AColville, JElphinstoun.

JC26/9/3/34

[*Endorsed:*] Depositione Alexander Drummont 18 October 1629

G, 6, David Dewaris dochter,

H, 7, Margaret Dog, I[61]

{*p. 1*} 4

At Dunblane the aughtein day of October i^m vi^c tuentie and eight yeiris In presens of Sir James Chisholme of Cromlickis knycht, Mr Alexander Colvill of Blair Justice deput of this realme, James Colvill of Balbedy brother germane to the said Mr Alexander, Mr Johne Grahame minister of Auchterairdour and Mr James Row minister at Muithill.

The whilk day[62] the said Alexander Drummond being reexamined and demandit anent the wordis \that/ he was accustomed to use before the application or at the application of his remeidis for the falling evill and madnes especiallie related this storie together with these uses following saying, That Jesus Christ when he was upon the earth was sent for by his father the God of hevin and took with him his apostles that were eardlisch[63] men unto the mont of Olives, and when he went up he left ane behind him whilk was Sainct Johne whom he commandit to byd still and stay there whill[64] he send him word, now Johne being left him alone behind thoght long and went aff the high way to a by rod wher he fell a sleep, at whilk tyme the Devill came unto him, and because he had forget to say his prayer the Devil cast upon

59 In margin: 'anent his cure with blak woll'.

60 The text in italics is underlined in the MS.

61 'The laird of Corstoun' crossed out.

62 In margin: 'anent the fabulous rymes quhen he practizet his cures and charmes'.

63 'eardlisch': earthly, worldly.

64 'whill': until.

him many diseases but culd not prevaill whill at last he took his tongue from him by the falling evill as these uses schaw.

Sainct Johne lay and sleepet
upon the mont of Olives
and throw a tentation
he forgot his oration
as he was wont him to saive
Then came a fiend with a fals traine
As he lay a sleeping on that hill
and cast on him all kynd of ill
that ever was markit for a man
Since the first hour of the world began
The excess and the parlady
And many other illis for ay
Both the gainscho and the stain
Bate him both throw back and bane
The head work and bainschaw
Other illis that men may know
Right so he cast him untill
the ague and the other ill
Then he culd nether speak nor cry
But thoght on God and his mercy

Then came ane angell fra Christ and touched him with a rod and so he immediatlie rose.[65]

Item[66] confesses that he cured the dochter of David Dewer of Fodrik moores of madnes, for the whilk cure the said David did cast him downe ane angell of gould upon the show[67] in ane token.

Item[68] deponed that he cured ane Margaret Dog of madnes who contracted hir disase after this maner, She being asleep *{p. 2}* in the night lying with her sister Janet Dog in ane closs bed neirest the stock, sche dreamed that sche had copulation with a man, and being affrighted thairby gat upon her feet and ran to the floor with great schowting and crying, haveing gripped a man in her handis whom she fond to be very cold, and continued crying on her father and desyring light till the wholl hous came together, but when the light was come in sche saw nothing but remained still mad whill[69] scho was cured be the said deponer.

65 The illnesses listed in this charm are as follows, as far as we can identify them: 'excess' may be a disease brought on by over-indulgence; 'parlady' may be palsy (paralysis, weakness or tremor); 'gainscho' is unidentified; the 'stain' is kidney stone; 'head work' may be headache; 'bainschaw' is sciatica; 'ague' is fever.

66 In margin: '4G'.

67 'show': possibly 'shaw', a thicket or copse.

68 In margin: '4H'.

69 'whill': until.

[*Signed:*] Jo: Chisholme, AColville, JGrahame at Aughterarder, James Colville, M: Jo: Row minister at Muithill.

At Edinburgh the xii day of Januar 1629 In presens of my lord Bishope of Dunblane, my lord advocate, my lord Justice clerk, my lord Justice deput commissioneris appointit be the lordis of secreit counsall for examinatioun of Alexander Drummond in Aucherardour.

The said Alexander Drummond being presentit befoir the saidis Lordis commissioneris this day sworne and examinat And the depositiounes foirsaidis maid be him the xviii day of October 1628 being red over word be word to him he confessit the said depositioun to be of verritie and ratifeit the samyn in the haill poyntis thairof.

[*Signed:*] Ad: B: of Dunblane, Thomas Hope, JElphinstoun, JColville.

JC26/9/3/22

[*Endorsed:*] At Edinburgh the xii day of Januar 1629 In presens of my lord Bishope of Dumblane, my Lord Justice Clerk, my Lord advocat, my Lord Justice deput, Commissioners appointit be the Lordis of Secreit Councll for examination of Alexander Drummont.

The depositioun within written maid be the said Alexander Drummond upone the xxiiii day of October 1628 In presens of the ministeris within written being red over to him as also be John Hedrig deponent being also red over word be word to the said Alexander, And he being sworne to declair the treuth thairupon, declairit the samyn to be of veritie.

[*Signed:*] A: B: of Dunblane, JElphinstoun, AColville.

24 October 1628

Confession Alexander Drummond the 24 of October

14 Robert Abercrombie

15 Robert Patoun

{*p. 1*} At Waster Tillicutrie the Tuentie fourth day of October i^{m} vi^{c} Tuentie aucht yeiris.

The Quhilk day In presens of Mr Laurance Merser minister of Fossoquhie and Mr Alexander Fotheringhame minister of Muckart and William Alexander at Myln of Tillicutrie.

Comperit[70] Johne Headrig in Waster Tillicutrie and confessit and constantlie affermit that in the monethe of September Last bypast he being Imployit be Robert Abercrombie servitour to the maister of Colvill to go to Alexander Drumond in Ochterardour to Inquyre of him give[71] by his ane meanis he mycht get Intelligence quho hade takine ane ringe of gold from the said Robert, and apppynttit [*sic*] him to give to the said Alexander for his resolutioun fourtie

[70] In margin: 'Robert Abecrombie 14'.

[71] 'give': if.

shillingis money, Went to Ochterardour to the said Alexander Drumond and haveing spokine him thairanent gat this response, haveing givin to him ane Lytill rute lyk ane unyeoun heade in ane clowt,[72] that he sould tak the said Rute and Laye it under the bowster of the auner of the said Ring, quho in his sleip sould sie the persone quho hade takine from him his ringe.

Item he gave[73] to the said berar ane uther Lytill rute of ane Erb and apppynttit [*sic*] it him to put in his mouthe under his towng, and promissit that he haveing sua done it sould mak ony woman thairefter to love or follow him and yeild to ony sute he wald ask of hir.

Item the said tua ministeris haveing examinat the said Alexander Drummond in the Tolbuithe of Striviling the day foirsaid, In presens of Johne Forrester and [*some words blank*] officeris of the burght Upone the forsaidis poynttis confessit the haill depositioun and declaratioun abonwrettin, afferming he gat bot only tua merkis fra the said Jone Headrig and not fourtie shillingis as was apppynttit [*sic*] to be gevin to him.

Item being examinat[74] be the said ministeris anent hellant[75] and curring of Robert Patone at Powmyln of Adie, Alexander Russell of Francie confessit he gave to the saidis persons the powder of the rute of mugvowt quhairwith currit thame of the saidis disaisis. Item that he currit Laurance Russell brother to the said Alexander Russell of the said disas and efter the samyne maner. The quhilk premis is true the saidis tua ministeris abonwrettin Testifeis to be of verritie, subscrivit with our hands At Striviling the xxv day of October 1628 yeirs.

[*Signed:*][76] Mr Laurence Mercer with my hand, AFotheringham with my hand.

JC26/9/3/15

[*Endorsed:*] Depositions Alexander Drummond 25 October 1628

{*p. 1*} At Stirlin the 25 of October 1628.

In presence of Mr Alexander Colville Justice deput, Mr Jhon Rowe Commissar of Dunblane, James Colville of Balbathyr, Mr James Edminstoun minister at St Nynians kirk.

Alexander Drummont[77] being reexamined confessis that he was accustomed to put a Clok about the haid of his patientis to that effect that thay micht not sie quhat he did and that thay micht not tell clatters[78] nor sie the pouders that he did put among the drinks quhen the Ladill was upon the fyr.

72 'clowt': cloth.
73 In margin: 'anent the getting of a womanis favor'.
74 In margin: '15 – Robert Patoun; anent the cureing of dyvers persones of frenacie'. 'Frenacie': frenzy.
75 Word altered; transcription uncertain. Read 'healing'.
76 Three signatures in all, one of them illegible.
77 In margin: 'anent the heid wynking'.
78 'tell clatters': spread rumours.

Further being demanded[79] quhat kynd of curis or remedis he used quhen the clok was about the patients heads, he deponed that he had tuo stoines \callit slaik stones/ of great vertu on[e] of a cleir cullour another of a blakische cullour, quhilk stoinis he put about the neks of his patients and went about thame saying In the name of the father, the sone and the holy ghost I cur the[e].

Moroever confessed he spak uther words quhilk words he wold not repeat for the present tyme.

Morover deponed he had a thrid ston of so great vertu that he wold hav given tua thousand pund, quhilk ston he Lent away and gott never againe as yit.

[*Signed:*] Alexr Colville, Jhon Rowe, James Colville, James Edminstoun.

At Edinburgh the xii day of Januar 1629 In presens of my Lord Bishope of Dunblane, my Lord advocat, My Lord Justice clerk, My Lord Justice depute, Commissioneris appointit to be the Lords of Secret counsall for examinatioun of Alexander Drummond.

The former depositiones maid be the said Alexander upone the xxviii of October 1628 Being red to him Eftir he was sworne, he confessit the samyn to be trew everie word.

[*Signed:*] AColville, Ad: B: of Dunblane, Thomas Hop, JElpinston.

JC26/9/3/21

[*Endorsed:*] 16 William Baveredge, 17 Margaret Porterfeild

{*p. 1*} 10

At Culross the 28 October 1628

In presence of Mr Alexander Colville Justice deput, Mr Robert Colville, Mr Jhon Grahame, Mr Robert Melville ministers, the quhilk day

William Balverage[80] cordoner maryed and aaged about /50/ yeares of auge being demanded anent the maner of his disase quhilk com to him about the year of God i^{m} vi^{c} xxi, confessis that it was a continuall rage of his[81] mynd quhilk keiped him in a tentation to put hand in him selff, and continewing in this troubill and miserie about xii month in end he was counselled be many of his nychtbouris to addresse himself to Auchtererdour to Alexander Drummont, quho is sa notable a curer of all maner of disases, that he could cur all except present death. And the deponer trusting the counsell of the multitud of his nychtbouris in end did addresse himselff to the forsaid Alexander the year of God i^{m} vi^{c} xxii or therby fourtene dayis befor Lambes, and com to the said Alexander above the /12/ hour of the day, quhair he find the said Alexander sleiping in his bed, and quhen the said Alexander raise, he Inquyred the deponer how do ye, quho answered, not weill, to quhome the

79 In margin: 'anent the cure uset be the stones'.

80 In margin: 'anent hoidwinking in his cure'. 'Hoodwinking': blindfolding.

81 MS damaged: 'hi…'.

said Alexander replyed, thow art not weill, disperation dealles with ye and yow art in perill to put hand in thyself and weoman had done ye wrong, to quhom the deponer replyed, quhen did thay that wrong to me, to quhome Alexander replyed, upon Lambes evin Last betuix vi houris and tuelff hours at nicht yow hes bene bewitched, and woemen[82] hes done this to yow (bot heir it is to be weil remarked) that the deponer affirmed that In veritie the siknes and troubill com to him just at that tyme. *Morower the deponer*[83] *affirmed that he com seven sundrie tymes to Alexander Drummont betuix fourtene dayes befor Lambes and Hallow even,*[84] and that everie tyme the said Alexander sett the deponer upon ane stoole beffor the fyr and closed the door, and quhen the deponer was upon the stoole, the said Alexander took the deponeris awine clok and did knit it round about his nek with a string (the tym of this charme was ever {*p. 2*} In the morning about the rysing of the sone), and quhen the clok was about the deponer his nek the said Alexander continewed ever going round about him for the space of ane hour or therby, tinkling with the sound of sum Irons quhich the deponer could never sie.

Morower deponis[85] that the vi tyme he was at Alexander Drummont he told the deponer that he had maid a journay for him and \had/ bene ane errand for him and gave him a warrand (or preservative) for all tymis cumming, viz. the tooth of a bodye and a litill pouder knit in a clout quhilk he desyred him to keip.

Morower confessis that about Bartills day[86] in harvest that same quarter the spous of the deponer called Margaret Thomsone went to Alexander Drummont in Auchtererdour, so soone as sho com in at his door, he knew the deponer his wyf and desyred hir to sitt doun upon a stoole and quhen the said Margaret inquyred how he knew hir quhom he had never seene of beffor, the said Alexander answered I kno yow be your plaid, and deponis that the said Alexander sent sum powder with the deponeris wyf to put in a drink, quhilk procured that he had wors health then ewer if lessor.[87]

Morower deponis that he gave the said Alexander mor then fourtie lib.[88] money for the sevin severall tymes that he went to Auchtererdour.

Morower[89] the deponer affirmis that on the seven tymis as he was going from the said Alexander he commanded the deponer to cum to him upon a Sounday, quhilk quhen the deponer refused becaus he wold keip the kirk and heir the sermon on the Sabboth, the said Alexander replyed, quhat will

82 Possibly read 'ane woeman'.
83 In margin: 'anent the going about with Irnes'.
84 'Hallow even': Hallowe'en, 31 October. The text in italics is underlined in the MS.
85 In margin: 'anent the ammulet of a toothe and sum poulder'.
86 'Bartills day': St Bartholomew's Day, 24 August.
87 *Sic.* The meaning of 'lessor' is not clear. Possibly 'leisure' is meant.
88 *Libri*, pounds.
89 In margin: 'anent the persuasion uset to his patient to be curet on the Sabbath day'.

ye fear in the kirk bot be St Peter and be St Paul Sie if any of the ministers is able to give yow health and cur yow, bot cum to me upon the Sounday, quhilk quhen the deponer refused, becaus of his conscience to keip the Saboth, the said Alexander replyed, Sounday in the morning is the best day of all the oulk to give a charme. {*p. 3*}

Morower[90] the deponer affirmis that he never prospered in his bodie nor his meanes[91] since he conversed and consulted with Alexander Drummont and that it is the offence of all that most trubillis his conscience.

Morower the deponer affirmis that the said Alexander did forbid the deponer to reveale any thing of his doings to the ministers, and incase the ministers wold demand anent the forsaid curis, bad him answer that he did all by the directioun of a print book.

The quhilk day Adam Huttoun Indweller in the Wallis under Gilbert Gourlay being examined if ever he went to Auchtererdour to Alexander Drummont, confessis as efter followis, that he went thrie tymes to Alexander Drummont upon the occasion efter following, viz. Margaret Porterfeild a young woman about 18 yeares of auge being hevilie disased and troubled in her mynd and distracted in hir[92] witts, and hir mother Jonet Trumbill Indweller in Culros being moved with the heavines of hir dochters disase send the deponer to Auchtererdour to Alexander Drummont to Inquyr for sum cur for the forsaid Margarett, and quhen the deponer com first to the forsaid Alexander he enquyred if the deponer \had/ any clothis that apperteined to the patient, quho answered that he had non, bot desyred the said Alexander to repair to the patient in the toun of Culros, *quhilk the said Alexander refused for fear to be apprehended and desyred the deponer to bring the sark, the curch*[93] and the ourlay[94] of the patient with all diligence, quhilk quhen the deponer had done and brocht with him fourtie shillings to Alexander for his paynes, the said Alexander complayned that this was so litill money and took the patients clothis from the deponer and keiped thame about the space of half ane hour or therby, and quhen the said Alexander had considdered of the clothis he com bak to the deponer and said that the patient was troubled with a spirit and that sho had gottin a weaf of wind,[95] for remeid quhairoff the said Alexander {*p. 4*} *ordained and prescryved*[96] *that the deponer should cary bak the sark the curch and the ourlay to the patient and that the patient should put thame all on*

90 In margin: 'anent his directioun to conceill all fra the judges and ministers'.

91 'meanes': resources.

92 'mynd' crossed out.

93 The text in italics is underlined in the MS.

94 'ourlay': collar.

95 'weaf of wind': blast of wind.

96 In margin: 'anent the bringing bak of the claytis to the patient to be worne to cure the seiknes and burning therof therefter'.

and keip thame on[97] for the space of fyve dayes and fyve nichtis and thairefter that they should be takin off againe from the patient, *and put in sum secreit and obscur place quhair non micht sie thame or tuich*[98] thame unto the tyme that the said Alexander com him self, and incase the said Alexander com not off all, he commanded to caus burn thame, and the reason was becaus if ather body or beast happened to tuich the forsaid clothis, the siknes that was upon the patient wold not faill to cease[99] upon thame.

Morower that the forsaid Alexander sent to the patient with the deponer a certain quantitie of a poulder to the bignes of ane eg, quhilk the said Alexander tasted befor he gav it and maid the bailyie of Auchtererdour taist it and his awin sone and also the deponer, and prescryved that als muche of the poulder as micht ly upon the point of a knyf micht be blowen in the patients ear and nostriles, quhill as sho was sleeping.

[*Signed:*] AColville, Ro: Colvill, JGrahame, Robert Melville.

JC26/9/3/1

[*Endorsed:*] Anent John Furd smith in Culros

{*p. 1*} 12

At Culros the xxviiii day of October 1628 In presence of Mr Alexander Colvill of Blaire Justice deput and Mr Robert Colvill, Mr Jhone Grahame and Mr Robert Melvill Minister of Jesus Evangile.

The[100] quhilk day Katherine Furd Indweller in Culros a woman unmaried aidged about threttie yeer on being examined anent the meanes of the sieknes of her umquhill brother Jhone Furd smythe in Culros confessed as efter followes, that the said umquhill Jhone her brother being in suit of a yong woman called Kati Rowen dochter to David Rowen merchant and burges of Culros, and preiving[101] that ane other young man was lykways In suit of the said Katherine took occasione of discontentment with the said Katherine becaus he saw her countenance on that uther yong man called William Guild; and in his anger gave the said Katherine a stroke upon the eare with a rode and not long thereafter the said Jhone Furd was visseid with a paine in his eare and a greevous sieknes that provoked him to such a vehement sweit, that it consumed al his body and trobled his mynd, wherupon the said umquhill Jhone was counselled by many nibors about to send to Alexander Drommond indweller in kirktoune of Achterardore, who as he was informed was able to tell him quhat wrong he had gotten and to cure him of his disease,[102] wherupon

97 The text in italics is underlined in the MS.
98 The text in italics is underlined in the MS.
99 'cease': seize.
100 In margin: 'anent the taking of a sark a ruff and a serviet etc'.
101 *Sic.* Probably read 'perceiving'.
102 MS damaged: 'dis…'.

the said umquhill Jhone took occasione to direct the deponer with al [*start of word obscured*] to go to Achterardore, quhilk acordingly was done.

And when the deponent came to the said Alexander Drommond she told him of the disease of her brother and of the maner therof wherupon the said Alexander took occasione to inquyre if she had brought any of her brothers cloathes in her company, and the deponer answered that she hade brought his sark with his rooff[103] and the serviete wherin he spat his flume: quhilk things the said Alexander received from the deponer and left her in his barne and went over to his owne hous with his owne dochter in law carieying the forsaid sark serviete and roof with him; and after a certane space comming out agane told unto the deponer that her brother was certanly witched and therfor desyred the deponer to give him silver befor he wold use his cure, who answered that she had nocht brought much money for the present but if that the said Alexander wold undertak to cure her[104] brother she would find him cautioun presently to give him xx merkis for his paines. Then the said Alexander replyed, I know ye have some, and the deponer answered, that quhilk I have I wil give quhilk was only xiiii shillings, then the said Alexander affirmed certanly that her brother was witched, and counselled the deponer to desyr her brother to send for the yong woman and her father David Rowen, and to sit downe on his knees to them and byg her healthe of them ilk and of al their kin, And when the deponer sought bak the sark[105] the said Alexander answered he behooved[106] to kep the sark and deale and devyd it at the merches[107] of sevene syndry lords lands {*p. 2*} to see if any healthe could be had to her brother. And morover the said Alexander gave unto the deponer a percel of the rut of a certane herbe quhilk she knew nocht and commanded her to put it under his heade, quhilk the deponer did accordingly, but it did nocht avale for the healthe of her brother who died within two or three days thereafter.

[*Signed:*] AColville, M: Ro: Colvill, JGrahame, Robert Melvill.

JC26/9/3/11

[*Endorsed:*] 20 Margaret Beanis, John Crystie, John Smyth, John Blithe

{*p. 1*} At the Tolbuith of Wester Wemys the 29 Day of October i^m^ vi^c^ and tuentie aucht yeiris In presens of ane great and Noble potent Lord John Lord Wemyss of Elcho, Mr Antoun Murray parson of Wattershome, Mr John Tullus Minister of Easter Wemys.

103 'rooff': ruff.
104 MS damaged: 'h…'.
105 In margin: 'anent the sark'.
106 'behooved': needed.
107 'merches' (marches): boundaries.

Compeirit thir persons Indwellaris in the Toun of Wester Wemys eftir following To beare witnes upone thair conscience Tuiching certaine poyntis Tending to the presumptiounis of witchcraift practized be Alexander Drummond in Auchterarder In thair knawledge and apprehensioun as followis.

Impremis[108] James Broun burges and Indwellar in Wester Wemys compeirit affirmit[109] that about thre yeir since or tharby he past to Auchterarder Twa sundrie tymes, his wyffe being diseassed with a meist fearfull and onNaturall seiknes as appeirit, To seik helpe thairof at the said Alexander, and that at the first tyme Alexander Drummond desyreit him to cum agane and to fetche his wyffis muche with him The quhilk he did, *And eftir his returne Alexander Drummond tuik the muche frome him and keipit the same for the space of Twa houris and restoirit the samyn agane to him, And gave unto the said James sum Litll graines of the quantatie of poulder, desyreand [word crossed out]*[110] him to put thame in quhyte wyne To gif his wyiffe to drink, Efter the quhilk tyme his wyffe Margaret becums convelst of hir diseass, And the said Alexander Drummond said to James Broun that his wyffe had gottin wrong be witchcraift and that it may be that they will cum in and speir[111] quhat scho is doing that did the same to hir, And that the said James Broun gave the said Alexander ane dolour and promeist to gif him meir at meitting.

Secundlie compeirit James Crystie servitour to the said rycht Noble Lord affirming his conscienc that about twa or thrie yeir since or thairby in harvest he past to Auchterarder to the said Alexander Drummond with his bairne Johne Crystie heavelie vexit with diseass of his body desyreand help be advyce of the said Alexander, quha Left the said James without the hous And tuik the boy within ane chalmer,[112] to quhome he knawis nocht quhat was done be the said Alexander, Except the said boy reportit to his father that Alexander Drummond drew and Ledd him be the Lugges[113] throche the chalmer and that the said Alexander said to James that his diseass was oncuirable, And the said James Crystie gave the said Alexander Twa dolouris.

Threidlie compeirit Archbald Smyith[114] servitor to the said Nobill Lord affirming upone his conscience that his sone John Smyith being diseassed in his body and cheifflie in his armes wanting the haill post[115] and powar thairof, that he past to the said Alexander Drummond seikand help and releiffe for his bairne, *Quha counsellit the said Archbald Smyith To wasche his bairnes sark in ane south runing watter or ony furd quhair the king red throw and thaireftir put upone the barne*

108 'firstly'.
109 In margin: 'anent for taking of the patientis mutche for cureing of hir seiknes'.
110 The text in italics is underlined in the MS.
111 'speir': ask.
112 'chalmer': chamber, room.
113 'Lugges': ears.
114 In margin: 'anent the wascheing of patientis sark in ane southe ryning watter etc'.
115 'post': strength, vigour.

agane, And now the bairne hes recovered of his diseass.[116] And the said Alexander Drummond gave to Archbald Smyith ane oyle to rub on the bairne, and the said Archbald gave to the said Alexander Drummond first four pound and nixt threttie four schilings. This was done ane yeir since or thairby. {*p. 2*}

Attour the said James Crystie confessit[117] *that Alexander Drummond gave unto him ane certaine stuffe Lyke ground poulder to put in his sones meate, Togidder with*[118] ane withered heid of ane burde quhilk he advysed to be mixed to the same effect, and counsellit the said *James Crystie that he sould nocht gif out of his awin hous*[119] him selff till he tuik ane salt upone his toung everie morning, affirming that the said James had evill nychtbouris.

Compeirit Janet Airth and Jonet Gell in Wester Wemys,[120] The said Janet Airth spous to John Blyith in Wester Wemys Grantit that scho delyverit to this Janet Gell ane much of Lyning[121] pertening to John Blyith quha wes heavelie diseassed for the tyme, Desyreand him to delyver the samyn to *Alexander Drummond togidder with thrie pundis and to returne the same agane to hir, And that heireftir schortlie scho send Walter Multray taylour (to the said Alexander Drummond) with uther thrie pundis, quha ressavit frome the said Alexander Drummond the said John Blyiths muche togidder with ane Litill quantitie of graine Lyk unto unyoun seid*[122] about twa penny worth thairof To be put among the said John Blyiths drink, And Immediatlie thaireftir the said John Blyth recoverd of his diseass. Thir presentis subscryvit as followis day yeir and place forsaid.

[*Signed:*] Lord Wemys, Mr Jon Tullus Minister of Wester Wemys and AMurray.

JC26/9/3/14

[*Endorsed:*] 23 1 William Scotlandis dochter
[*Addressed:*] To the ryt honorabill Mr Alexander Colvile Justice Deput AColville

{*p. 1*} Honorabill Sir,[123] I resaved your letter bot am informed that suche persones as confessis that thay have delt with the deceaver may incur danger afterward throche thair awin confession, And so I may be compted ane instrument of thair hurt, Bot knowing your honest meaning in suche *a gud purpose*[124] I have tryed some of my parishioneris. Ane William Scotland confessis that he was counselled be a gentil woman besyd us to go to him with his onlie daughter wha had *the falling seiknes to seik remedie, wha cuming*

116 The text in italics is underlined in the MS.
117 In margin: 'anent the taking of salt in the mouth to hinder witchcraift'.
118 The text in italics is underlined in the MS.
119 The text in italics is underlined in the MS.
120 In margin: 'anent delyverit of ane muche to cure the diseas'.
121 'Lyning': linen.
122 The text in italics is underlined in the MS.
123 In margin: '2','23' and 'Anent hoodwinking cutting the belt etc.'
124 The text in italics is underlined in the MS.

thair he tuik his daughter to a kirk, he covered hir face, he cuttit hir belt in 9 pairtes, he Layed hir down on hir bak and drew hir 9 tymes to and fra throche the pairtes of hir belt, he maid her go so oftymes Widdersones[125] about and said sum wordis and prayeris as he thocht And gef hir some Injunctiones streitlie, And so he payit him for his paines and brocht her home. Bot shee was worse then befor and fell into the fyre shortlie after her homcuming and thairefter died. The man is verie sorowfull that he sald nocht have communicat his mynd to me, And promises amendement.

A woman also callit Kathren Whyt that was by hir selff was counsellit to go up to him, and when shee cam, being acquentit with the erll of Montrose folkes, he gef hir the greater creditt and so left hir in his house hir alon till he suld go some erand, and shee *haifing nothing ado confessis that shee looked in oure the chalmer door head and saw some teadis or padokes*[126] *as shee thocht leaderit*[127] and louping up and down the floor quhilk mad[e] her abruptlie run hir way, and quhen shee cam to hir father that was a servand to my Lord of Montrose hous shee told quhat shee had sein, and thay said to hir, he is nocht gratie[128] go nocht neir him agan he will never do ye gud. Otheris whom I have spoken thinkes that he did no ill bot that he tuik unkill[129] gear fra tham. This is all I culd loze[130] for the present. I was to ryd this sam day to Aderay, God willing, to the mariage of my youngest daughter Margarit, If I get occasion quhen I cum home agan I sall persuad otheris to seik out delationes aganst him. The Lord blise to your travellis in this and all suche godlie purposes. Sua making my hairtie commendationes to your bedfellow and commending yow and all youris to Godis grace, I sall remain, Yours in the Lord to be commandit, Mr Jhone Row Minister at Carnok.

Carnok the 3 of November 1628.

JC26/9/3/17 and JC26/9/3/18[131]

[*Endorsed:*] Examinatione Depositiones Concerning Alexander Drummond Warlok 1629

{*p. 1*} Apud Edinburgh xii January 1629 In presens of my Lord Bishope of Dunblane, my Lord Justice clerk, my Lord advocat, my Lord Justice depute, commissioneris.

125 The text in italics is underlined in the MS. 'Widdersones' (widdershins): anticlockwise.

126 'padokes': frogs.

127 The text in italics is underlined in the MS. 'Leaderit': perhaps 'leathered', leathery.

128 'gratie': not found in dictionaries, but apparently meaning 'gracious' (i.e. in God's grace).

129 'unkill': not found in dictionaries, but apparently meaning 'too much'.

130 'loze': not found in dictionaries, but apparently meaning 'learn'.

131 The two sheets with the separate modern numbers JC26/9/3/17 and JC26/9/3/18 are in fact a single document. The first sheet, JC26/9/3/17, has been folded to make four pages. A further footnote below marks the transition between the two sheets.

Alexander Drummond[132] in Auchterairdour Being sworne and examinat, depones that he was in the use to geve directioun to persones visseit with the seiknes callit the falling seiknes and in Greik epilepsis: That thai sould tak thair awin belt and cut the same in Nyne peices and thaireftir to eard[133] the samyn under the dur threshold quhair the patient dwelt, and the patient to pas thaireftir thryse oure and oure the dur in the name of the father, the sone and the holie ghost, And than the patient \upone his kneyis/ to vow to God nevir to eit thaireftir flesche upone Frydayis.[134] Quhilk being sa done the patient sould be frie of the diseas callit the falling evill and in Greik callit epilepsis all the dayis of thair Lyfe and nevir tak the same agane.

The said Alexander[135] being Inquyret of this particular, Gif ane yeir or tua yeir syne or thairby Ane young damesell dwelling in Culrois, quha had hir brother deidlie seik of ane unknawin diseas and with continuall sweitting vanischet away, understanding that the said Alexander had grit skill in cureing of sic diseasis, Come to him and tauld the diseas to him And desyret hir to bring hir brotheris sark and mutche to him and he could tell hir gif he could cure him, And the mutche and sark being brocht, The said Alexander eftir the sicht thairof directit the damesell to pas to hir brother and caus him go to the persone that he suspectit had done him wrang and upone his kneyis to ask thryse of that persone his helth for Godis saik, And to pas with the sark and mutche to ane furd or watter quhair ane Cristiane king had riddin over and washe the sark and mutch thairintill, And becaus the damesell ansrit that the young man hir brother was so waik that he could nocht gang, The said Alexander thairupoun said to hir that he wald keip the said sark and mutche and pas thairwith him self to the said furde or watter and practize the cure him self, The said Alexander declairis that the former turne was of treuth and that he gaif the former counsall to the young woman and keipit the sark and mutche quhilk he put in the said furd and thai past away in the streame, And tauk Litll or na recompance for his cure. {*p. 2*}

Declairis forder[136] anent the falling seiknes, That the people of the cuntrie befoir that thay come to him war in use to tak beist heidis and eit for charmeing the same, But he declairing to thame that that sould nocht availl, Inrespect thay eit them at bankettis or brydells[137] upon Frydayis and uther dayis of the oulk, And thairfoir the only charme quhilk he advyse them to use was to cut thair belt in maner foirsaid, And to vow to abstene fra flesche eiting on Frydayis, and that being done be thame thay sould nevir tak that diseas agane.

132 In margin: 'for cureing the falling evill be cutting the belt etc.'
133 'eard' (earth): bury.
134 In margin: 'and flesche on Frydayis'.
135 In margin: 'anent sark/mutches and useing thairof'.
136 In margin: 'Anent cutting the belt vowis abstenance for flesche on Frydayis'.
137 'brydells': weddings.

Being Inquyret[138] gif ane Colene[139] Eviote sumtyme servand to Sir William Grahame of Braco Come to the deponer And inquyret of him quhat way he micht come to the favour of ane gentilwoman quhome he Lovet, depones that the said Colene Eviote come to him bot rememberis nocht of the tyme quhen. And the deponer shew to the said Colene tua of his buikis, And quhairof he did Reid quhat he thocht was for him, And thaireftir come agane in ane shorte space, And said he behovet to borrow the buik to ane Lady in the northe quhilk he Lent to him, Bot he nevir brocht the buik bak agane to the deponer.

Declaires[140] that [*word crossed out*] the tyme of my Lord Wigtoun his grit seiknes a saxtein yeir syne or thairby, Thair was ane gentileman upone hors bak with ane boy Come to him with ane Letter desyreing the deponer to cum to him to cure his Lordship of his diseas of daftnes, being than hevielie diseasit thairof in his place of Cummernauld, quha was sent to him be his Lordships Lady to bring him thair, At quhais cumming and eftir the knawlege of his eirand be the Letter, The deponer past with the gentilman to Cummernauld upone his awin naig[141] and corsset[142] at Stirling, And cuming to Cummernauld, My Lady Laid doun befoir the deponer ane grit heip of gold Lyk unto counteris and willit him to tak thairof to cure my lord, Quha refuisit to tak ony Bot desyret his Lordship To be instant with his God and to sit doun upone his kneyis and crave God pardoun for burning of tua men, Quha at the deponeris desyre was brocht ower his bed and put doun upone his kneyis being haldin up be tua that wer with him, And thaireftir delyverit to my lady ane quantitie of poulder maid of the rute of mugwart, the halk berrie and the rane tre. At the uptaking of the quhilkis ingredientis of the {*p. 1*}[143] earth he sayde thir woirdis, I tak ye up to cure this seiknes of madnes in name of the father, the sone and the holie ghoist or to ony uther diseas quhilk he was to cure, Accoirding to the quhilk direction gevin be him to my Lady \quhilk was/ for taking the said poulder and to put it in ane foule of brue And to geve it to my lord to drink it, quhilk gif his Lordship refuiset or skunnerit at[144] desyret my Lady hir self to tak thairof with his Lordship for it wald do hir no hurt. My Lady accoirding thairto maid the said brue and put the poulder thairin with thir woirdis, in Name of father, sone and haly gaist, conforme to the deponeris instructioun. And at the saipping[145] thairof to say the lordis prayer thryse over, quhilk was sa gevin be hir Ladyschip to my lord. Eftir the taking quhairof my Lord grew better and arraise and spek perfytlie quhair befoir he could nather speik nor move him self in his bed,

138 In margin: 'Anent favour of wemen'.
139 'N' crossed out.
140 In margin: 'anent rute of mugwart'.
141 'naig': horse.
142 'corsset': crossed (the River Forth).
143 The document's second sheet, numbered JC26/9/3/18, begins here.
144 'scunnerit at': took aversion to.
145 'saipping': perhaps soaking (steeping), or else supping (drinking).

And pat on his claythis, raid furth upone his \hors/ to the hunting; declairis he was sent for a fourtene dayis or thairby thaireftir be my Lady come bak to my Lady with his dochter \Helene dwelland besyde Comerie/, quhilk dochter my Lady was desyreous to sie and speik with, at quhais cuming the deponer ressavit allainerlie ten merkis frome hir, Bot thair was mekill mair gold offerit to him quhilk the deponer wald nocht tak except the said ten merk peace; declairis this secund tyme of his cuming to Cummernauld was fourtene dayis eftir the first, And that he and his dochter stayit thair with my lord a tua nychtis togidder and at his cuming desyret my Lady to remove all his folkis frome his Lordship, And only the deponer with his dochter \and my lady hirself/ in the chalmer to tak up my Lord out of his bed and to Leid him up and doun, Quhilk accoirdinglie was done.

[*Signed:*] Ad: B: of Dunblane, AColville. {*p. 2*}

At Edinburgh the xxvi Januarii 1629 In presens of my lord bishope of Dunblane and my lord Justice depute.

Alexander Drummond rexaminet and sworne[146] demandit quhat is in the kist quhilk he Left at his hous at his away cuming, deponis at his away cuming he Left in his kist certane claythis of his awin togidder with ane buik of his in prent, out of quhilk he reassavit informatioun of all the cures[147] practizet be him for help of ony man or woman of thair diseasis with quhilk thai war visseit. As als[o] thair is ane uthir buik of writt thairin contening certane recepeis extractit furth of the prentit buik, declairis also thair was Left be him In the kist tua Litill stanes callit slaik stanes, the ane blak haifing ane hoill throw the midis with ane red silk string into it and[148] ane cureall beid[149] thairwith, And the uther stane is cleir as Cristall, declairis he Left the key of the kist with his guiddochter John Drummondis wyfe callit Elspeth Burgh quho war in hous with him, as to his sone Thomas he dwelt nocht with him bot is dwelland in ane toun neirby nocht far fra his house in Auchterairdour.

Deponis[150] that quhan John Hedrig [*word crossed out*] had cum twyse to him he gaif him ane peice of herb callit rois bella or daf and dillie[151] to be gevin to Robert Abercrombie quha wantit his ring, That at the ressaveing thairof he sould lay it under his heid and thaireftir In ane vision he sould sie the man that staw[152] his ring, declairis also he delyverit to the said Hedrik ane kynd of herb quhairof he rememberis nocht the name, And desyret him to delyver it ather to his maister Robert Abercrombie or ellis to keip it himself and he wald be better Lykit of thaireftir.

[*Signed:*] AColville.

146 In margin: 'anent the buik'.
147 MS damaged: 'cur…'.
148 'certane' crossed out.
149 'cureall beid': coral bead.
150 In margin: 'anent the stowin ring'.
151 'daf and dillie': daffodil.
152 'staw': stole.

JC26/9/3/23

[*Endorsed:*] 13 Anent Thomas Burne younger. Also anent Robert Abercrombie set doun in the 14 figure.

{*p. 1*} Jhone Hetherig[153] his depositioun befor Mr Andro Rynd minister, Thomas Burne elder and Alexander Harrower two elders.

Imprimis[154] he deponis that he was fowr tymes at Alexander Drumond, twys for his maister Thomas Burne younger and two tymes for Robert Abercromie; the first tyme he gaif him 44 shillings for his maister and asked his \maisteris/ help from him, quho ansred that he culd say *nothing till on[e] of his said frindis is cam and brocht him on[e] of his sarks: the second tyme he cam againe with the seikmans*[155] frind and brocht the sark with them and thei met with Alexander Drumond in this barne, and quhen he saw the seikmans sark he said he haid gotten a blast of evill wind, and said to Jhone Hetherig and Thomas Burne, stay yee heir a litell and I shall tell yow quhat otheris com of him, therefter he went [*rest of line, about 6 words, obscured by a crease*] *almost half ane houir and cam againe with the sark and said goe home and put on the sark* on him: *if he slaik* presently efter he wilbe weill: if he growes wors he will not last, quhilk cam to pas for he presently ramest to dead.[156]

Item[157] Jhone Hetherig confesses that he went the thrid tyme at the comand of on[e] Robert Abercromie quho wanted a ring quhilk he tint[158] of his finger, and gaif to Alexander Drumond 40 shillings 8d. to tell quho haid the ring, the said Alexander gaif him a thing lyk the haid of a gairlik and baid him give to the man quho wanted the ringe and lay it under his heid quha he wos sleiping and he wold see the persone in his sleip quho haid the ring, quhilk quhen Robert Abercromie did and not being the better, he cam to Jhone Hetherig againe and gaif it back againe the thing quhilk he brocht to him, and desyred him to goe to Alexander Drumond and gaif it back again to him and tell that he wos no better and bring him his silver againe or then to tell quho haid his ring, quhen he cam to him and desyred ather the the [*sic*] silver againe or then \sure/ word quho haid the ring. Alexander Drumond answered that if he wold tell, the gentell man wold truble the persone and persew them and thei wold ask quho told him and then he wold be trubled be the kirk, bot desyred the gentell man to come him self and he suld tell him.

Extract out of the session book of Tullicultrie, Mr Andrew Rynd.

xxxi Januar 1629 in presens of my lord Dunblane and the Justice depute.

153 In margin: 'xi'.
154 In margin: 'anent burying of sarks'.
155 Here and later in the paragraph, the text in italics is underlined in the MS.
156 'ramest to dead' (ramished): died in a frenzied manner.
157 In margin: 'anent the tryell of a stollin ringe'.
158 'tint': lost.

This depositioun being red confessis that he sent with this boy the herb callit daffindillie to the use contenit in his deposition, quhilk is sett doun in his Latine buik to be Laid doun under the persones heid quho wanted the ring as his depositioun beiris.

JC26/9/3/9

[*Endorsed:*] 23 Robert Quhyt his sone

{*p. 1*} At the kirk off Fossoquhy the aucht day off Februarie 1629.

The quhilk day in presence off the Minister and Elders off the said kirk, Robert Quhyt elder in Garthquhingans, Androw Gipsone thair, Robert Gib thair, Arthour Patone thair, Alexander Gipsone thair, James Dick at Powemylne, Robert Patone thair, Alexander Russell thair, The saids persons Laufulie summoned to the forsaid day, and cited All off them comperit at except Robert Gib forsaid, Quho being deiplie upon thair kneis sworne and after particularlie examined anent thair dealing with Alexander Dromond sorcerer quhat they also knew and hard off his devilish practeises, deponed as followes.

Imprimis deponed the said Robert Quhyt that he being intysed by Robert Gib forsaid to go to the said sorcerer for seeking helth to his diseased sone went with Androw Gipsone forsaid towards Achterardor to the said sorcerer his house, and carying with them ane sark off the diseased persons, thair arose be the way ane fyr and at tuo severall tymes was sene off[159] the said Androw Gipsone, quho had in careing the said sark drawing men to the sark torre[160] quhairunto the said sark was tyed. The quhich severall vision did not a litell astonish the said Androw Gipsone, bot was not sene off the said Robert Quhyt as instantlie he affirmed.[161]

Item the said Robert deponed that coming to the said sorcerer *his house he tuik the forsaid sark from him and thairwith going in into his house, held him and his said nychtbour without*[162] *by closing the door upon them, And in procease*[163] *of tyme returning and delyviring the said sark to them, appoynted them to put it upon the diseased persone*[164] with assurance that thairefter (give[165] strong death delt nocht with the diseased) he should recover, the quhich the said Robert having obeyed accordinglie it cam to passe, for the diseased persone recovered.[166]

159 'sene off': seen by.
160 'sark torre': might be the pommel of a saddle, a rounded knob of a saddle.
161 In margin: 'SP'.
162 'without': outside.
163 'procease': process.
164 The text italicised here is underlined in the MS.
165 'give': if.
166 In margin: 'anent the resaveing bak of a sark cureing of the patient'.

Item the said Robert deponed that he tuik the said sorcerer to ane brousters house and besyde tuo or thrie peynts off aell gave him xii shillings for his paines and response.

Item the said Androw Gipsone deponed *in omnibus*[167] conforme to the said Robert Quhyt respective his above wrette depositione.

Item the said Arthour Patone, Alexander Gipsone, James Dick, Robert Patone, Alexander Russell as laufull witnesses deponed and testified that they and every one off them hard be relation accordinglie to the said Robert Quhytes and Androw Gipsons depositiones.

Item the said Robert Gib, being Laufulie summoned to the forsaid day and called, compeired not and thairfoir the forsaid Sessione thocht it meit[168] that he should be remitted to be taken ordor with be the civill magistrat. And for certificatione off the forsaids depositiones we the Minister and Elders underwretten have subscrivit thir presents with our hands as followes at the kirk forsaid the xxii off Februarie 1629.

I Laurence Mercer Minister at Fossoquhy for him self and at command off the Elders that can not subscryve as they affirmed.

[*Signed:*] Kynnairde, Chrichtoun.

JC26/9/3/30

[*Endorsed:*] The depositions of Jhon Drummont sone to Alexander Drummont {*p. 1*} At Kirktoun of Auchtererdour the 16 Merch 1629.

Jhon Drummond[169] sone Lawfull to Alexander Drummont now prisoner being examined and demanded if he knew that thair com patients to his father, ansuered he knew that sundry patients and disased person did repair to him.[170]

Being demanded[171] if he had seene thois disased persons [*word crossed out*] send sarks to his father thairby to kno the disases of the absents partyes, ansuered that he had seene sundry sarks cum fra disased persones to his father.

Being demanded if he had ever bene directed by his father to any of his patients, ansuered that he had caryed poulder fra his father to his patients.

Being desyred to cum to be examined judicially to the kirk of Blakford in name of his majestie and his honorable Counsaill, ansuered proudlie that he wold nocht obey.

Elizabeth Brugh spous to Jhon Drummond being urged by the justice deput to ansuer to sum Interogationis anent Alexander Drummont hir father in law, did most proudlie and disobedientlie refuse to depon or to ansuer any

167 'in all things'.
168 'meit': meet, appropriate.
169 In margin: '1'.
170 In margin: 'anent sarkis'.
171 In margin: '2'.

thing at all, nochtwithstanding she was commanded in name of his Majestie his honorable counsaill and his majesteis commissioners thair present, viz. Jhon Hadden of Gleneglais, William Stirling of Ardoch, Jhon Grahame of Orchill, Mr Alexander Colville justice deput, Mr Jhone Grahame and James Grahame of Drumfad.

[*Signed:*] Gleneglis, AColvill, James Grahame.

JC26/9/3/25

[*Endorsed:*] 11 M John Walker in Overgorthie

{*p. 1*} 7M

At Gorthie the /18/ of Merche 1629

The depositions of Jhon Scobye Indweller in Bachilton and Jhone Valker Indweller in Ower Gorthie anent thair consultation with Alexander Drummont, In presence of Mr Alexander Colville Blair Justice deput, Mr Jhon Murray, Mr Jhone Grahame, Mr James Drummond and Mr Jhon Frybairne and Mr James Row.

Jhon Valker aaged about 36 yeares and maried, having contracted a strange and uncouth disaise, quhairby he had a kynd of phrenecie, and had apparitions, creatures of all cullouris appearing to him, and quhill as he was in this great distemper and sicknes quhilk he could no longer Indur without remeid, directed Jhone Scoby[172] his servant for the tyme quhilk was anno 1622 or 1623 or \thairby/ to on[e] Lely Broun ane man renowned in thois places for curing of disaised persons by the sight of thair sarkis, and quhen the said Jhon Scoby find the said Lely Broun to be departed this Lyf at the cumming to his hous quhilk was above Dunning, and Immediatlie thairefter he having the said Jhon Valkeris sark in his company he went to Alexander Drummont at the Kirtoun of Auchtererdour, and finding of the said Alexander at his harvest with his \sone/ Jhon Drummont and his dochter in Law upon the feild, he called upon the said Alexander, quho Immediatlie thairefter com to the deponer and Inquyred at him if he had brocht a sark, to quhome he answered that he had a sark, and told to the said Alexander the maner of his maisters disaise above mentioned, thairefter the said Alexander took the sark fra the deponer, went to his hous thairwith, and within ane quarter of ane hour com out and had the sark hard fallded and commanded the deponer to keip the sark folded and not to opin it till he was at home, and then desyred him to put it upon his maister for the space of thrie dayes or thairby and thairefter to bring it bak againe, quhilk he did accordinglie, and then the deponer confessed that the said Alexander retained the sark the second tyme, and send with the deponer to his maister[173] a litill quantitie Lyk cutted grass or seed in the thoume of his glove, desyring him to direct his maister to append the forsaid grass in a clowt

172 In margin: 'anent him bringing and asking for a sark and taking thairof'.

173 In margin: 'anent the appending of ane ammulet'.

and hing about the patients nek, and Immediatlie the patient confessed that he convulsied[174] and all his apparitions did evanisse,[175] for the quhilk cur he gave {*p. 2*} to the said Alexander Drummont thrie or four lib. for his paynes. The forsaid Jhon Valker being present and heiring the relation of Jhon Scoby messenger and his servant for the tyme, ratifeid all the former deposition of his servant Jhone Scoby.

It is to be noted that the forsaid Jhone Scoby confessed that at the first tyme that he went to Alexander Drummont with the sark of Jhon Valker, his dochter dyed or[176] he come bak againe, and the second tyme that he caried the sark bak againe, his wyf was deceased befor he com bak againe, and he himself was heavilie disased thairefter.

[*Signed:*] Mr Jo: Row minister at Muthill, JDrummond mod:, AColville, JGrahame Min: at Aberuthven.

JC26/9/3/24

[*Endorsed:*] 12 John Hay in Reidfurd
{*p. 1*} 6
At Muthill the 18 of March 1629.

In[177] presence of Mr Alexander Colvill Justice deput, Mr James Drummond Moderator, Mr Johne Graham minister at Aberuthven, Mr Archibald Maklachan at Comrie, Mr James Rowe at Muthill and Mr John Fribairne at Madertie with the rest of the brethren ther convenit, compeirit George Graham in Bellyclon and John Loutfoot *ther and deponit bot*[178] with on[e] voce and consent, that thei bieng at Ridfurd quher the John Hay brother to the said George wes bieng heavily distractit of his witts and mynd, and ther *thei sawe Alexander Drummond use this charme*[179] for curing[180] the said [*word crossed out*] John first he caused transport him bieng syled[181] to ane hearth quher ther wes ane crook over hinging quher he caused sett the said John, and then *he caused bring in a coulter and ane sok and ane pleuch*[182] quhilk he took and thrie sewerall tymes crossed the said John thairwith in his face, breist and all his forpairtes, speiking in the mean quhyll sum wordis quhilk he called holy oratione. Secondly the said Alexander took the crook over his head quhilk he patt also thrys round about his head, speiking also sum words to him.

174 'convulsied': convalesced.
175 'evanisse': vanish.
176 'or' (ere): before.
177 In margin: '6 M'.
178 The text in italics is underlined in the MS.
179 The text in italics is underlined in the MS.
180 In margin: 'anent the cruik and sok and coulter and crossing thairwith and his holy orationis'.
181 'syled': blindfolded.
182 The text in italics is underlined in the MS.

[*Signed:*] Georg Grahame with my hand. Johne Lutfute in Belliclone with my hand tuitching the notaris pen underwrittin becaus I culd not wreit my self. *Ita est Duncanis Aissoun notarius publicus de speciali mandato dicti Johannis scriber nescientis ut asseruit ista hoc meis chyrographum in talibus insertis.*[183]

[*Signed:*] Duncan Aissoun, AColville, JGrahame, JDrummond, JRowe minister at Muithill, Jho: Fribairn.

JC26/9/3/32

[*Endorsed:*] Depositiones, Duncane Aesone, John Balnaves

{*p. 1*} At Muthill the xviii day of Merche 1629.

In presents of Mr Alexander Colvill of Blair justice clerk deput, Mr James Drummond, Maisters John Grahame, Mr John Frebairne, Mr James Row and remanent brethering of the presbytrie of Muthill.

I Duncane Aissoune being examinat upoune my greit aythe Anent my reiding of som buiks pertening to Alexander Drummond now prissoner in Edinburgh, I Be my greit aythe deponis I nevir read upoun ony buik to the foirsaid Alexander except ane Litill buik stylit the Regiment of Lyf,[184] upoun the quhilk buik presentlie I have subscrivit my name the day foirsaid.[185]

And quhenever the said Alexander come to me and desyre me to reid ony thing, I had the place markit of befor by ane Leave of the said buik Laid down thairintill and verrie sindill[186] use that custome except quhen ony stranger come to the toune to colour quhat he intendit wald cause me their reid ony part thairof, and eftir I had red it he wald cause me wreit ane missive to Samuell Jonstone, quhais name I remember not, seing it is sevin yeir and more sen I Left Ochterardour, and the Letter being wreitin, he gave money to ane cadyer[187] to bring home that powder or oyll he causit me reid.

Mairover deponis that I was ane indwellar in Ochterardour ane yeir and moir befor I suspectit the forsaid Alexander of unlawfull and supernaturall healing, and being advertisit be Mr Hary Rollok than my pastour in Abruthven[188] that he was not ane lawfull man, I abstenit from his companye and he from me from thencefurthe.[189]

Mairover deponis that all men judgit him ane deceiver of the people and that I suspectit him my self.

183 'Thus I, Duncan Eason, notary public by special mandate, the said John asserting that he does not know how to write, have inserted my signature in place of his'.

184 [Jean Goeurot,] *The Regiment of Life, wherunto is added A Treatyse of the Pestilence, with the Booke of Children*, trans. Thomas Phayer (London: Edmund Whitchurch, 1544; various later editions).

185 In margin: 'anent the buik'.

186 'sindill': seldom.

187 'cadyer' (cadger): pedlar.

188 Henry Rollock was minister of Auchterarder and Aberuthven from 1617 to 1623.

189 In margin: 'anent his abuse and dissait'.

[*Signed:*] Duncane Aissoun with my hand.

At Abiruthven the xix day of Merche 1629.

In presence of Mr Alexander Colvill of Blair justice deput and Maisters Laurence Merser, George Muschet and Johne Grahame ministers, I John Bannevis reider at the kirk of Ochterarder depones and wretts with my awin hand, my depositionis in maner following. First I enterit to be reider in the kirk forsaid 1622 quhilk wes the first tyme that I had knowlege of Allexander Drummond now prissoner.

Mairover[190] I depone that so shone as I cam to the kirk forsaid, I began to perceave that ther wes a continowell concurs of patients repairing to the said Allexander and principalle upone the Saboth day, and that within ane quarter of ane yeir or thairby thairefter the said Allexander becaus he could not reid himselff did addres him selff to me with a lytill blak buik callit the Regiment of Lyfe, quhilk buik for moir assurance I have subscrivit with my awin hand. {*p. 2*}

Mairover depones that I never reid upone ony uther buik to the said Allexander bot this.

Mairover[191] I depone that I think and am persuadit that altho the forsaid Alexander cam to me to desyre me to reid sum portion of the foirsaid buik, as wes bot policie to cover his secriet doings be that pretext, becaus he did not practeis the directions of the buik quhilk I red to him, bot usit his awin wayis within his awin house secretlie and because sum of the parteis that the said Allexander promist and pretendit to cure declarit to me that he useit nocht these directions quhilk I red out of the buik.

Mairover[192] I depone that I never[193] red the buik unto him nor hauntit his companie sen the tyme that Mr Walter Stewart minister at Blair in Atholl brocht his sone quho wes so mad that he wes drawin with four or fyve persones unto the *forsaid Allexanders house quhom I saw conductit to Allexanders hous in that maner and go in verrie mad, quhom quhen the said Allexander had kepit halff ane hour or thairby secreitlie within his hous he cam out with his patient quha*[194] wes meikill calmer and softer then quhen he went in, to my great admiration.[195]

Mairover[196] I declar thair I think that the foirsaid Allexander wes ane great abuser of his majesteis leiges, and hes hard that hes bein fourtein within him in ane day, and principalle upone the Sabbath day quhilk he did preev[197] and prophane by his drinking with his patientis.

[*Signed:*] Johne Banewis, AColville, JGrahame, Laurence Meser of [*sic*], Mr George Muschett.

190 In margin: 'anent the Sabbath dayis abuse and anent the buik'.

191 In margin: 'anent his fraud and policie to dissave his patientis'.

192 In margin: 'anent the madnes of Mr Walter Stewart his sone and cuir thairof'.

193 'haldit' crossed out.

194 The text in italics is underlined in the MS.

195 'admiration': astonishment.

196 In margin: 'anent the Sabbath dayis abuse'.

197 The meaning of the word 'preev' is unclear. Perhaps the scribe meant to write 'pervert'.

JC26/9/3/13

[*Endorsed:*] Depositiones, Duncane Aesone, John Balnaves

{*p. 1*} At Edinburgh the xxiii of Marche 1629.

In presens of Mr Alexander Colvile of Blair Justice depute and John Bannatyne wryter heirof.

Laurence Russell merchand being examinat quhat he knawis concerning Alexander Drummond in Auchterardour depones that about Witsonday Last 1628 he being diseasit him self, and and [*sic*] haifing socht counsell of dyvers freindis quhat remeid he sould seik becaus he gat na sleip and his fleshe and bluid vanishet away frome him, [*word crossed out*] In end he was advyset be ane Robert Gib in Gartquhunyie within the parochin of Fassowie to addres him self to the said Alexander Drummond than dwelland at the Kirktoun of Auchterardour and now prisoner in the tolbuith of Edinburgh, quha (as the said Robert Gib said to the deponer) had grit skill to cure all diseassis speciallie that soirt of seiknes quhairwith the deponer was visseit. According to the quhilk advyse the deponer raid to Auchterardour aucht dayis eftir Witsonday Last, And came to the said Alexander his hous quha [*word crossed out*] was nocht at hame for the tyme, bot was drinking in ane Robert Ewingis hous quhair the said Alexander had stayit the maist pairt of that day and had bene at the drinking of threttie pyntis of aill, And the deponer haifing spokin with him in the said hous, The said Alexander directit the deponer to cum to his hous upone the morne thaireftir befoir the sone ryseing and thair he sould cure him. Depones upone the morne thaireftir he come to his hous at the appointit tyme quhair the said Alexander Inquyret of the deponer his name verrie instantlie,[198] saying he could nocht help him except he reveillit his name, quhairupone the deponer reveillit his name to him, And thaireftir the said Alexander with ane preface said to him, Laurence gif ye wald go to Edinburgh and get drinkis thair for your helth he wald geve to the physitiones 100 lib. for ane drink, Bot I sall nocht be sa coistlie and sall haill yow and nevir tuitche yow, Nather gif yow drink or draff.[199] Alwayis[200] for your helth I most mak ane voyadge and go ane dreirie way, And thairfoir quhat will ye gif me for my paines. And the deponer being gritlie effrayit and instantlie in his heart and mynd calling to God to assist him, maid answer to Alexander that gif he sould cure him he sould be satifeit for the samyn. Thaireftir at the desyre of the said Alexander the said deponer sat doun upone \ane/ stule befoir the fyre quha Lykwayes ordanit him to cast his plaid over his heid and face becaus, sai he, ye most nocht sie quhat I do, quhilk the deponer {*p. 2*} did.[201] Quhilk being done and the deponer siting upone the stule, The said Alexander past

198 'instantlie': insistently.

199 'draff': residue of malt after brewing, sometimes used as animal feed.

200 'Alwayes': nevertheless.

201 In margin: 'Anent his ganging round about the patient muttering of unknawin wordis sounding with Irins etc.'

dyvers tymes round about, muttering out sum woirdis quhilk the deponer knew nocht, and maid ane sound with the Irnes as gif it had bene the tangis or cutter of ane pleuch, and thairwith as he thocht maid ane hole in the herth of the chymnay. Thaireftir he hard Alexander quihisper out to John Drummond his sone being with him for the tyme, This cure will nocht work for I can get nothing done to him, or the lyk wordis, quhilk as the deponer sayis preceidit upone[202] his secreit In calling upone God in his saule and spreit all that tyme. And haifing rissin af the stule and payit to the said Alexander ane dollour with uther quhyte money[203] quhilk the deponer sayis was about foure pund or thairby, And he haifing tane the samyn, desyret the deponer to cum agane that day aucht dayis[204] for he behovet to cum agane and efter befoir he war fullilie curet, And thairwith desyret the deponer to be verrie secreit and nawayis to reveill the samyn bayth for his awin guid of[205] the said Alexanderis. The deponer thairupoun Left him, Bot nevir fand him self the better, bot rather his diseas and vexatioun of mynd Incressit upone him, For the quhilk causis he nevir returnet bak to him, Bot be prayer to his merciefull God and conference with the ministeris of his blisset woird hes ressavit his helth bothe in body and mynd fra his omnipotent God.

Depones[206] that he being grevouslie vexit eftir his returning frome Alexander, \Robert/ Gib[207] earnestlie delt with \him/ to go bak agane quhilk the deponer altogidder refuiset, quhairupone the said Robert Gib past with ane sark of the deponeris gevin to him be his mother by[208] the deponeris knawlege, and come thairwith to the said Alexander quha bad wasche the same in ane south rynand watter quhair the king had riddin over and to put the sark thaireftir upone him, As also the said Alexander delyverit to the said Robertt ane quantitie of soft fegis[209] to be sewit in the deponeris claithes, quhilk the deponer heiring tell of wald nevir suffer the samyn to be done nor Luik upone the claythis quhilk the samyn was sewit into.

JC26/9/3/12

{*p. 1*} At Edinburgh the first day of Apryle 1629.

In presens of my Lord Bishope of Dumblane, Mr Alexander Colvile of Blair Justice deput.

202 'preceidit upone' (proceeded): arose from.
203 'dollour': Dutch dollar; 'quhyte money': silver.
204 'that day aucht dayis': in one week's time.
205 *Sic.* Read 'and'.
206 In margin: 'with ane litill rutet of the quantitie of ane garlik heid'.
207 'was' crossed out.
208 'by': without.
209 'fegis': figs.

Alexander Drummond[210] in Auchterardour being sworne and examinat this day, depones that John Balnaves was in use only to reid to him upone tua buikis, the ane in Latine and the uther in Inglis, As also that Duncane Aresone was in use to reid to him upone the saidis tua buikis at dyvers tymes as patientis come to him to seik help of their diseassis, and that thay red to him upone na uther buikis bot upone thais tua buikis as he sall ansser to God.

Being Inquyret eftir quhat forme he cureit the dochter of David Dewar in Lessodie quha was diseasit of madnes, Sayis that he send with the said David hir father ane certaine poulder maid of mugwart[211] crope and roote ane peice of rowine trie and of the halkberrie[212] quhilk he band upone the patientis sark quhilk he appointit to be put in hir drink and hir meit for cureing of hir madnes.

Declaris that a tua yeir syne or thairby in the winter seasone Mr Walter Stewart minister of Blair in Athole came to the said deponer to the dwelling hous of Robert Ewing in Auchterardour, quhair the said Mr Walter conferrit with him anent his sones madnes and how he sould be cureit or helpit thairof, And within few dayis thaireftir sayis said Mr Walter come of new agane with his sone that was diseasit to the said Robert Ewing his hous in Auchterardour, with quhome thair was ane or tua men awaitting upone him drugging and drawing him, being bayth hieland men, And fra Robert Ewingis house he was brocht against the deponeris will to his awin house, quhair he stayit nocht ane quarter of ane hour. At quhilk tyme for cureing of his diseas the deponer causit tak ane quantitie of pouder maid of mugwart, rontrie and halkberrie, quhilk being soddin[213] upone the fyre was thaireftir tane af and the drink syvit throw ane clene claith and the patient thaireftir drank the samyn.

Demandit[214] quhy he was in use to blindfold his patientis, declairis he was only in use to cast ane clok or plaid about the patientis heid visseit with madnes or frenizie to put thame frome feir, And being put about thair heid wald with ane scheir tak out ane pairt of the hair of the foirheid and to put thairin ane quantitie of black woll dippit in womens mylk to stay the radge of madnes quhairwith thai war visseit, And that his clok or plaid was put about the patientis heid only to stay thair feir and that thai sould nocht be terrifeit the tyme that he practizeit ony cure upone thame. {*p. 2*}

The samyn day[215] James Buchane now servand of my lord of Lauderdaill being sworne and confrontit with the said Alexander Drummond, affirmet in his face that the tyme of the seiknes of my umquhile Lord Sinclair being

210 In margin: 'anent the reideris reiding upone the bookis'.

211 'mugwart': one of several species of aromatic flowering plants in the genus *Artemisia*. In Europe, mugwort most often refers to the species *Artemisia vulgaris*, or common mugwort.

212 'halkberrie': probably 'hawthorn berry', 'haw', a red berry of the hawthorn bush, also 'haa'.

213 'soddin': boiled.

214 In margin: 'anent heid wynking'.

215 In margin: 'anent the quik cok'.

visseit with ane uncouth diseas, The said Alexander for cureing him thairof was brocht to Ravinscraig quhair the said Lord Sinclair remanit, And at his cuming the cure following be the said Alexander his directioun was put in practize, viz. at his command ane quik cok was gottin and eftir the uptaking of ane payent stane foiranent my lord his chalmer dur[216] The quik cok was put thairintill, and the stane thaireftir put abone it. Depones farder[217] that at the same tyme be the said Alexander his directioun ane David Weddell servand to my lord at that tyme with John Drummond Alexander his sone ane Lang strong fellow past with certane pleuch Irnes frome Ravinscraig to the boig of Oir betuixt the merche of my lordis Landis, and thair ordanit him to Leaf the saidis Irnes for his lordships aire.[218] Quhilkis premissis being constantlie affirmet be the said James Buchane deponer in the said Alexander Drummond his face, As also that at severall tymes be my lady Sinclairis command he had payit to the said Alexander dyvers sowmes of money, viz. ane double angell[219] nixt ten merkis and Last sex pund of silver, The said Alexander maist effrontedlie and malapeirtlie denyit the haill former affirmation except his ressait of ten merkis allanerllie and na forder. The said James[220] forder affirmet that he haifing convoyit the said Alexander fra Ravenscraig hame wardis be the toun of Dysert, he for Love as he sayd he buir to James offerit to geve to him the breif[221] of ane sword that nane sould draw his bluid thairwith quhilk the said James refuisit to tak frome him. The said Alexander denyis the samyn.

Depones the said Alexander Drummond that he was in use to send his sone John at dyvers tymes with poulderis to dyveris patientis for cureing of thair diseassis, bot never with sarkis.

[*Signed:*] Ad: B: of Dunblane, AColville.

JC26/9/3/31

[*Endorsed:*] Deposition of Patrick Grahame[222]

{*p. 1*} Upon[223] the 6 of Apryll 1629 Patrik Graham sone Lawfull to umquhill Patrik Graham of Ridfoord, being voluntarly conveinit befoir Mr James Drummond moderator of the presbytery of Muthill and minister of Fawells, Mr John Graham minister of Abruthven and Mr John Fribairne minister of Madertie at [*sic*] the said Mr Johne his sone in Madertie, he deponit as followes.

216 'ane payent stane foiranent my lord his chalmer dur': a paving-stone opposite my lord's chamber door.

217 In margin: 'anent the earding pleugh Irnes'.

218 'aire': heir.

219 A double angel was a gold coin worth £13 4*s*. It was also known as a 'unit' or 'unite' coin.

220 In margin: 'anent the breif of the sword'.

221 'breif': formal document. In context this may indicate a written charm against sword wounds.

222 Written in pencil in a later hand.

223 In margin: '6M'.

That Alexander Drummond bieng weth his brother Johne Hay in Ridfoord quho at that tyme wes heavily disseased and distracted in his witts, The said Alexander directed, in the audience of the said Patrik[224] that the said John Hay his seik sone be sent to him to Ochterardour that he micht sie it, and that nixt it sould be tain be sum fresch watter foord quhair ane Christain king had crossed, and ther be washed and left ther on sum buss.

Again the said Patrik deponed that he himselff having gone efter that to Ochterardour to inquyre at the said Alexander gif he had any forder direction for the said John Hay his brother, That the said Alexander delyvered to him ane old hors naill, with sum root inclosed in a clout, and directit to incloss it in his sark craig or in sum uther westur[225] efter he did not change, but did wear both night and day, This the said Patrik deponed to be the treuth according to his conscience and knowledg willinglie befor the witnessis forsaid written be Mr John Fribairne forsaid.

[*Signed:*] GBrowne with my hand, Jho: Drummont witness, Tho: Fribairn witness, JGrahame witnes.

JC26/9/3/16[226]

[*Endorsed:*] 24 George Douglas

[*Addressed:*] To his honorabill and deir freind in Chryst, My Lord Justice deput

{*p. 1*} My Lord, My very affectionat deuty rememberit, thes are to shawe yow That the Laird of Keillour[227] and I have usit all dilgence in trying Speidie in Glenalmond, bot have gottin \no/ certantie to build on: bot be a providence in seiking that we have fund ane gritter, and als pregnant as any ye hard of yit. Ther wes on[e] George Douglas quo dwelt in Chappell hill of Loggie Almond, married with on[e] Kirstan Malcolme. This George falleth seik, and eftir Long advys heiring of the brute of Alexander the gritt Sorcerer, he directed his wyfe and hir brother Humfrey Malcolme, quho dwelleth yit in Newrawe of Balgowne in the provests parish, quho cumming to Ochteraudor, fand the said Alexander quho receaved the woman very gladly, bot wold not suffer the man to entrye his hous, quho bieng wearied attending desyred to be in, bot wes repelled be Alexanderis gud dochter quho knew him, and chyded him becaus he wold have cum in so easely, For ye knowe not sayes sho quhat

224 'and Edward Grahame now in Octerardour' crossed out.

225 'in his sark craig or in sum uther westur' (vesture): in the neck of his shirt, or some other garment.

226 This undated letter, and the undated deposition that follows it (JC26/9/3/20), have been placed here because they deal with some of the same people as each other, while the letter also deals with some of the same people as the document after that (JC26/9/3/31), dated at Madderty, 6 April 1629. The writer of this letter, John Freebairn, minister of Madderty, seems to have been involved in all three documents.

227 George Hay of Keillour.

ye ar doing. Bot the man bieng stomached[228] and fearles replyed he desyred[229] the Divell and all his workis, and wold haud furth his sister that thei micht go home, The said Alexander did consult with the seik mans nicht cap and his sark, and inclosed in his nicht cap sum herb \as/ appeared to them, and sum molded earth, and appointed them both to be put on. The woman at hir departur bieng curiouser to understand[230] {*p. 2*} quhidder hir husband wold die or Live, Alexander gave hir this answer that he micht Live long aneuch, if sho and his mother wold follow counsell, Quhilk sho promised to performe. Then sayes Alexander, I will give yow a derectioun, both for his Lyfe and death, If ye wold have him die, ye and his mother sall on your knies friely delyver him to God, and if ye wold have him Live delyver him to the Divell. The woman amased, asked how sho sould know that thes things wer trew quhilk he promised. The said Alexander gave hir this tokin, That since hir away cumming from home, sho had tuo ky calved, and both the calves wer drowned in the moss: Quhilk verily provde trew, the woman conceild all this from her brother, and cum home, and caused use the sark and night cap as wes appointed, Bot he did not convalese, Therfor he grew jealous of his wyfe that sho had not obeyed Alexanders counsell faithfully, did urge hir so straitly to delyver all sho hard of him that at Last he woned[231] that if sho wold not, he sould never eat nor drink in the world, and so did abstein so Long that the pure wyfe is forced to reveill all. Quhilk quhen he had hard, incontinent he sendeth for his mother and causeth them both to sitt doun on their knies, and delyver him hairtfully to God, then he calleth for meat, and quhill he has the spoone in his mouth he fell suddenly by and departed. This is the report of on[e] Johne Malcolme quho dwelleth in Loggie, is brother to the women quho yit Liveth in Keinland maried on on[e] George Crokkart in the bounds of Strathurd, tennent to Mr Robert Nairne. This Johne Malcolme avoweth that he hard his sister depone thus to her {*p. 3*} husband and wes present till he died. Now I have caused summond all the thrie persones, the sister and tuo brethren, I have caused summond Patrik Iviot sumtyme of Bousie in quhous hous I heir ther wes practises doune be Alexander with plew Irones. Mr Jhone Grahame and I did accidently find the messenger quho went betuix Colin Eviot and his maisteris quhom we caused summond in Perth, the assys is summoned and witnessis, Bot all the pepill ar going mad, Mr John Graham will shew yow how in the oppen mercat the gudwyfe of Dubheidis did exclaime and raill agains me, allwayes I defy them in that point, as I defy Alexander in his witchcraft. The Lord knowes I am bussie for no respect bot for his glory. One thing my Lord I would adverteis

228 'stomached': brave.
229 *Sic*. Probably read 'defied'.
230 Reading uncertain at edge of page.
231 'woned': moaned, lamented.

yow of, that I feir ther sall anew[232] not compeir that ar summond, and therfor I wold have yow providing that incais a sufficient assys do not compeir, ye may ather have so many in Lothian as ye may supplie, or thain that ther may be short delay that thei quho ar summond [*rest of line illegible because of fold in page*] assysers and witnessis may be cherged *de novo*[233] and denunced rebellis for dissobedience, and sic as compeir may be summond *apud acta* again the day,[234] For if that purpos be suifted[235] ye neid not hope that any mo sorceris sall sustein the Lawe in your tyme, nether sall ever on[e] Stratherne be challengit efter him,[236] the Lord direct yow and assist us all, so I ever rest, Your honour to serve yow in quhat I can. Jho: Fribairne.[237]

JC26/9/3/20

This the disposisowne[238] at Cirsteine Malacome deponis That Alexander Drowmond spak owt of his awine mouthe to hir for curing of hir huisband George Dowglas befoir thir witnessis, [*word crossed out*] the said Cirsteine retiffies this that he askeit at hir give[239] the said Cirstaine wold have hir husband deid or leveing, and give scho wald have him to leive, sit one hir keines[240] and his mother and give him to the Devill, and the said Cirstaine answeirit him and said that scho wald not do bott that at come be God or guid meines,[241] and the said Alexander Drowmond said to hir, delyver hime to God your self and his motther and he will depairt shortlie fra this wordell,[242] I knaw that, and he answerit to hir, so sertine as ye have twa kye calfit and at home and clois they are both drownit In ane moss, and so it was, and the said Georg Dowglas askeit at hir how it was, and sho tellit hime all that Alexander Drowmond spak and he wald tak in paichens[243] quhill he desyrit them to sit downe one their kneis and refair hime to God and so they deid and so he depairtit schortlie, and this the said Cirstaine depones befoir thir witnessis,

232 'anew': enough.

233 'afresh'.

234 'summond *apud acta* again [i.e. against] the day': formally summoned to appear in court on a specific date.

235 *Sic.* Read 'sisted', i.e. suspended.

236 *Sic.* Read 'nether sall ever on[e] in Stratherne be challengit'.

237 In margin: 'Becaus this depositioun is a gritt on[e], and Johne Malcolme quho reported it dwelleth in the Regailitie of Logie, I wold have yow (for I fearlie sall contempt our summonds) writting again to Keillour because he is bailyie ther and promeis him his expensis tho the presbitery sould pay it'.

238 'disposisowne': deposition.

239 'give': if.

240 'keines': knees.

241 'scho wald not do bott that at come be God or guid meines': she would do only that which came by God or good means.

242 'wordell': world.

243 'paichens': patients.

Johne Malcome in Groane and Georg Croccatt in Keinladis, Michell Browne ther, Downcane Forsyithe ther.

[*Signed:*] John Malcom wittnes, Gorge Crocat wittnes. Jo: Malcolme sworn in judgement in presens of [*sic*]

JC26/9/3/6

[*Endorsed:*] 10. L James Neisch sone to Dubheidis

{*p. 1*} 5

At the kirk of Madertie the 6 of Appryll 1629.

Compeirit Elizabeth Alexander gudwyfe of Dubheids with Elspet Loutfoot hir woman and in presens of Mr James Drummond Moderator of the presbiterie of Muthill, Mr John Graham Minister of Abruthven and Mr John Fribairne Minister of Madertie: and bieng posed upon ther conscience quhat thei could declare touching Alexander Drummond, prisoner in Edinburgh, and suspected and challenged for sorcerie and witchcraft, thei deponed as follows.

First[244] the said Elizabeth Alexander deponed that hir sone James Neish, quha at that tyme wes heavily disseased and distracted so of his witts That skarse sex men could hald him or stay him in his furie, of anything that wold have doone, that sho wes advysed be sum ill instrumenter to send for Alexander Drummond in Octerardor quho wes at that tyme neir by in the cuntrey, Quho com to her also befoir sho send for him, Quho quhen he wes cum, and had sein the young man, he said that he wes possest with ane ill spirit, and bieng askit at[245] the said Elizabeth if he could dryve out the Divell, he ansrit to hir terror and admiratioun that he sould save his soull, And so efter long conference he desyred[246] that ther sould be ane coulter and ane pleuch sok brocht to him and that sum freind micht be gotten to go with him to the chalmer quher he had appointed to charme him, Quhilk wes doone and so efter the hous wes Issued[247] he went in with the seik man and the said Elpset Loutfoot her servand, quho bieng present wes also posed quhat sche saw or hard, quho deponed as followes.

That the said Alexander caused sett ane chair before the fyre quherin he sett the seik man, quhome he blindfolded[248] and directed the said Elspett Loutfoot to stand behind the [*word crossed out*] chair and to hold the cloth {*p. 2*} about the seik mans face, and gave hir this caveat, that [*word crossed out*] sho sould not remove out of the place, And so ye[249] bieng sett and placed the said Alexander

244 In margin: '5 L'.

245 *Sic*. Read 'by'.

246 In margin: 'anent the coulter and sok of a pleuch and charming therwith'. The coulter and sock were the iron cutting parts of a plough, referred to later in the text as the 'plew irons'.

247 'Issued': emptied of people.

248 In margin: 'blind folding'.

249 *Sic*. Read 'he'.

tuik the plew Irons,[250] and risped them[251] befoir the seik mans mouth about a quarter of ane hour and Less, and quhill he thus risped the Irons he muttred him secrett wordis, and \the said Alexander/ wes so horriblie commoned[252] and troubled in the action that all his body trembled and shook and did so sweat that sho wes sure ther wes not ane hair on his body bot it had a drap at it, quhilk also the said Elizabeth does testifie for sho sayes that quhen the said Alexander com furth of the chalmer he wes so weit as if he had bein sprinkled with watter. Lykewayes the said Elspett bieng asked quhidder that sweat did proceid of any Labor or exerceis of his body with the Irons, she replyed that or ever[253] he begane he wes affrayed and trembled, and so terrified her be the fever as sho cald it ane commotion of the body that sho refused ever to be a witnes to the Lyk spectacle. Morover the \said Elizabeth/ deponed that the said Alexander gave directioun to Lay the Iron on the \said James/ in hes bed, quhilk wes doone. And declared that the said Alexander, taking exceptioun at her dochter becaus sho asked his company, said that he knew that sho wes to Leave the cuntrey, bot gif sho wod follow his counsell he suld gif her sum thing to cause her to be loved of any sho pleissed, and bieng asked how he wold effectuat that, he said he wold putt ane poulder in her hair.[254]

Again the saids persones both deponed, that the said Alexander did once iterat thir charme [*sic*] in the Dubheids, efter quhilk thei fand the young man to amend and grew better, bot not fullie, thairfor the said Alexander directed to send him to his owen hous in Ochterardor quher he charmed him the thrid tyme, and gave him an amulett to to [*sic*] hing continuallie nicht and day in his clois,[255] quhilk he yet keipeth very wilfully and superstitiously, alledging that[256] {*p. 3*} his helth consists in the keiping of it, yitt upon the earnest dealing of his minister Mr John Forbairne, he produced the sam befoir him and his mother, quhilk quhen the said Mr John had made a promeis to redelyver, he putt it in his hand, quho having cutt it out ane peice of Lether quherin it wes sewed up, it wes fund to be an roustie broken naill, with a peice of skinne as apperired stikking about the naill and tuo or thrie bitts of stiks or rootes, quhilk the said Mr John redelyvered to him back according to his promeis – This is also to be remembred that quhen the said Elizabeth Alexander asked at him quhat wertew[257] wes in these plew Irons, he replyed that they wer on[e] of on[e] of [*sic*] Gods haly altars. This depositioun tain out of ther owen mouths

[250] In margin: 'anent pleuch Irons and muttering of words'.
[251] 'risped them': rubbed them together.
[252] 'commoned': dealt with.
[253] 'or ever': before.
[254] In margin: 'anent procuring of Love'.
[255] In margin: 'anent the amulett'.
[256] In margin: 'anent the ammulett bieng ane roustie nail and a peice of skyn etc'.
[257] 'wertew' (virtue): power.

and presently penned be Mr Johne Fribairne forsaid, the said day and place, In verification quherof we have all thrie subscrivit the samyn as followes.

[*Signed:*] JDrummond witness, JGrahame witness, Jho: Fribairn writer heirof and witnes.

JC26/9/3/19 and JC26/9/3/8[258]

[*Endorsed:*] 25 Robert Andersone, John Trumble, James Huttone, Margaret Adiesone, umquhile [*1 word blank*] Davidsone, Bessie Stirk, John Colene, Bessie Cuninghame, Thomas Lyell, William Kellok, Merjorie Wilsone.[259]

{*p. 1*} At Dunfermlin the eight day of Aprill 1629.

The quhilk day In presence of Mr Alexander Colvill Justice deputie, Mr Robert Roche Moderatour of the presbyterie of Dunfermlin, Mr Robert Colvill, Mr Hary Makgill, Mr Edmund Myllis, Mr William Pattoun, Ministers of the said presbyterie, The personis eftirspecifeit wer solemnlie sworne and examined concerning such thingis as they know of Alexander Drummond his devilish practisis, quha is apprehendit for ane witch and sorcerer Conforme to ane commissioun gevin be the Lordis of his Majesties previe Counsell to that effect produced befoir the said Brethrene. The depositiouns of the persons sworne and examined ar as followis.

James Andersoun in Pettincreif within the paroche of Dunfermlin about the age of thretty yeiris, sworne and examined, deponit that his Brother Robert Andersoun being heavelie diseased of ane strange disease, he heiring mony resorted to Alexander Drummond in Auchterarder to get help of diseasis went to him to seik help for his brother. And quhen he cam the said Alexander askit him if he haid ane token of his brother quha answerit he haid his sark. The said Alexander tuik the sark from him and bade him come to him again the morne. Quhen he cam the said Alexander sayd his brother haid gotten wronge, And gave him bak the sark saying ye sall dip it thrie tymes in south running water quher ane Christen kinge hes ridden through and therefter put it on him, Quhilk wes done. And therefter he went to the said Alexander quha he being lying down bade the deponer go drink with his sone, quhilk he did and gave him four or fyve merkis of sylver.

James Oswald servand to Andro Trumble in Bromehall within the paroche of Dunfermlin about the age of threttie yeiris, sworne and examined, deponis That he wes send there severall tymes be his Master to Alexander Drummond to seik help to umquhill Jone Trumble sone to the said Andro being heavelie

258 The two sheets with the separate modern numbers JC26/9/3/19 and JC26/9/3/8 have originally been a single document. A further footnote below marks the transition between the two sheets.

259 This endorsement appears on the back of the document's second numbered sheet, JC26/9/3/8. The names are those of the alleged victims of witchcraft, which are not all the same as the names of the deponents.

diseased, And the first tym that the deponer went, The said Alexander asked him if he haid brocht the sark of the diseased persone, quha answerit not, Sa was commandit be the said Alexander to cum back agane to him that same day eight dayis and bring the sark and ane of the diseased personis garteris.

The said James deponis that he went again the samyne day aucht dayis with the diseased personis sark and garter to the said Alexander, quhom he fund in the house of Robert Grahame, And the said Alexander having takin the said sark and garter went out of the deponeris sicht a certane space and cuming back delyverit to him the said sark and garter, bidding put the said sark on the diseased person and wear it aucht dayis and to put the garter about his foreleg the said space, Also the said Alexander commandit the deponer cum again to him within twentie dayis, The sark and garter wes put on the diseased as wes commandit.

Mairour the said James deponis that he went nocht bak to the said Alexander within twentie dayis as he commandit him becaus the patient becam better and {*p. 2*} travelled to mercatis be the space of ten weekis. Yet therefter he fell in his former diseas more heavelie then befor, Quherupon the parentis of the diseased send bak the deponer the third tym with ane sark to the said Alexander, to quhom shewing the estate of the diseased persoun he answerit, if ye haid come bak to me within tuenty dayis as I commandit, althocht the Devill himself haid layd that seiknes on him I suld have helpit him be the grace of God. And the said Alexander gave bak the sark with some brayed[260] powder to be gevin to the patient, Quha wold nather ressave the powder nor the sark saying he defyed the Devill and all his workes and wold tak him to the mercy of God, And within fyve dayis efter the deponer cam bak to the said Alexander the said umquhill Jone Trumble dyed. The deponer sayis that he gave the said Alexander a daller the first tym, And quhat mair he got wes from uther handis.

Catherine Walwod Relict of umquhile James Huttoun within the paroche of Dumfermlin of the age of fourty yeiris, sworne and examined, deponis That nyne yeiris bygone hir said umquhill husband being heavelie diseased went to Alexander Drummond for help, Quha sayd to him he wes wiched and got skayth[261] be one of his Nictbouris that went daylie by his dore, And the said Alexander tuik him to a barne befoir the sun rysing, But quhat he did with the patient he culd nocht tell, he wes so benumed, but the said Alexander wes sene come out all sweating that he wes wett therwith.

Mairour deponis That the secund tym the said umquhill James send up to the said Alexander for sum help, Quha commandit to bring to him the patient his sark and a mutch and a naipkin quhilk the said Alexander sayd he behoved to lay besyd a chapell. These things wer send to him and wer nocht sent bak agane.

260 'brayed': ground up.
261 'skayth': harm.

Farder deponis that the third tym the said James rode up him self by the said Alexander quha tuik him in bane house[262] alone And the said patient came out all sweating but culd nocht tell quhat he did to him, And the said Alexander ressavit at sundry tymes about the sowme of threttie pundis money.

Margaret Edesoun spous to William Mudy masoun within the paroche of Dunfermlin of the age of fourty yeiris, sworne and examined, deponis That she having a bairne heavelie diseased and send a servand to Alexander Drummond to seik help to him, quha send a lock of blak woll bidding meit it[263] with the pape milk[264] and lay it to the open of his head. Also the said Alexander commandit to send the bairnes sark to him, Quhilk being done he send it bak againe bidding put it on the bairne, And efter tua days tak it of[f] him And hyd it it sum place quher no body gois ower, And that they did sa and buryed the sark under the eard under the rute of a wall quher no body may go ower, And ther it lyes.

Robert Davidsone in Dunfermlin of the age of thretty yeiris, sworne and examined, deponis That his umquhill father being heavelie diseasit he went to Alexander Drummond to seik help to him, And understanding that the said Alexander use to ask sum token of the diseased, he caryed his fatheris mutche with him, Quhilk the said Alexander beholding sayd to him, ye ar our long {*p. 3*} in cuming, I can do no guid, he sall die, quhilk shortly cam to pase. Lykewyis deponis that quhen his bairne of tua yeiris of age wes diseased he caryed up his mutche to the said Alexander, quherupoun he luiking sayd his bairne haid gotten wrong be ane that dwelt nocht far from him, And that quhilk wes ordanit for the said Robert himself haid fallen on his bairne.

David Dewer of Lassody in the paroche of Dunfermlin of the age of thriescoir yeiris, sworne and examined, deponis That about sex yeiris since Christen Dewar his dochter of the age of ten yeiris being heavelie diseased, he heiring of mony resorting to Alexander Drummond for help, he went and tuik with him his dochteris mutche, Quhen he came to the said Alexander and told him hir disease, he askit him if he haid ony token off hiris, quha answerit he haid hir mutche, Quhilk the said Alexander tuik from him and went from him out of his sicht, quhen he returned he delyverit the mutch to David and therwith gave ane powder blak colored bidding him put it among hir drink and ailberrie,[265] and efter he had drunken with him he gave him xl shillings. The said Alexander bade him cum agane to him within aucht dayis and tell him how she wes, quhilk David did and gave him uther fourty shillings.

At Dunfermlin the 29 day of Aprill 1629.

262 'in bane house' (ben): in the back of the house.
263 'meit it': join it, mix it.
264 'pape milk': breast milk.
265 'ailberrie': ale boiled with bread, sugar and spices.

The quhilk day in presence of Mr Alexander Colvill Justice depute, Mr Robert Roche Moderatour of the presbyterie of Dunfermlin, Maisteris Edmond Myllis, Johne Cowden, Hary McGill, William Pattoun, Ministeris of the said presbyterie, the persones efterspecifeit wer called, sworne solemlie and examined anent such thingis as thei know of Alexander Drummond his devilish practeisis conforme to the commissioun beformenntionat, Quhilk persones deponit as followes.

James Kellok in the paroche of Bayth of the age of fourtie yeiris, sworne and examined, deponis That Bessie Stirk his wyf being diseased of madnes about Whitsonday[266] 1621, David Dewar of Lassodie and Henry Dick told him that Alexander Drummond haid helpit mony, And persuadit him to go to the said Alexander saying he behoved to cary hir sark and curche[267] to him, Quhilk he did and the said Alexander tuik them fra him but gave them nocht back agane, And the said Alexander sayd sho haid gottin wrong be wichcraft, And he asking him be quhom answerit be a neir freind, And he gave him a broun colored powder to put in hir meat, and going to the drinke he sayd ay quhen he drank to him I find yow God to borrow[268] he sall be weill, Also he bad him ryd hame as fast as he culd, and be nocht fleyd,[269] think on nothing but God, and quhen he cam home he gave his wyf the powder among ane ailberrie, quha instantlie convalesit, rose up and put on hir clothes and wes weill till Dinning day in October[270] efter. Then she fell worse in hir seiknes, And his nichtbouris saying that he haid the wyt[271] quha left hir sark and curche behind him, he went bak and socht them fra the said Alexander, quha answerit he wist nocht quher they were, And he gave him a lock of blak woll and bad him put it in the plaites of hir hear.[272] And quhen it wes in, hir mother cryed, It is death, it is death, And sa being done late at even she dyed the morne efter, he gave the said Alexander first and last xxx lib. {*p. 4*}

Johne Colin younger in the paroche of Dalgatie of the age of threttie yeiris, sworne and examined, deponis That being heavelie tormented went to Alexander Drummond quha sayd he wes witched and that he wold cure him, And first he tuik him to ane house and put his clok about his head and chopit[273] him with sumthing back and foir fra neck to heill at all the Lithes[274] of his body, and wes ay speiking but he understand nocht except the last words, In the name of the father, sone and holy ghost, And quhen he tuik

266 'Whitsonday': the seventh Sunday after Easter.
267 'curche': kerchief.
268 'borrow': pledge, promise.
269 'fleyd': afraid.
270 'Dinning day in October': 9 October, the feast day of St Dionysius (the spelling of whose name varied widely, e.g. Dinnin, Dinnet, Dennis).
271 'wyt': blame.
272 'plaites of hir hear': plaits of her hair.
273 'chopit': struck, tapped.
274 'Lithes': joints.

the clok from his head he saw it wes with ane ax that he choppit him, And asking quhy he coverit his face, answerit that ye suld not tell quhat I do to yow. Therefter he gave him a powder lyk brunt bones and pickellis of the colour of beit[275] seid, quhilk wes bitter as the gall, but it did him no guid. Mairour deponis he saw ther men that haid cum to the said Alexander fra Irving, Glascue and Aberdene.

Johne Rowan in the paroche of Sawling of the age of fyftie yeiris, sworne and examined, deponis That Bessy Cunninghame spous to Andro Rowan in Gask of Dunfermlin paroche being diseasit of madnes, he wes sent to Alexander Drummond to seik help to hir and tuik hir curche to him, and shewing hir disease and delyvering hir curche sayd he feard she wes dead. Alexander answerit I think she sall nocht die, and efter he had promeist him xiiii merkis he gave him a powder lyk brunt bones in the nuke[276] of hir curche, bidding put it on hir head with the powder in the nuke of it. Then he gave him tua daleris, he bad him cum agane and bring the sark that wes presentlie on hir with the rest of the money promeist, And efter she wear the curche with the powder in the nuke therof she becom better. Therefter he caryd the sark that wes on hir but quhat he did with it he can not tell, at that tym he gave him fyve merkis.

Johne Lyell in Sawling of the age of threttie yeiris, sworne and examined, deponis that his uncle Thomas Lyell in the paroche of Cromby diseased of madnes, heiring of divers personis that Alexander Drummond culd help him, And that he wold seik the sark of the diseased man, he caryit his sark to the said Alexander, quha tuik it from him and departed about the space of ane hour and returning gave him the sark agane, bidding put it on him and gave him a powder lyk blak kume[277] quhilk he bad put in a curche and put on his head.

David Stewart in Dunfermlin of the age of threttie yeiris, sworne and examined, deponis that his mother Marjorie Wilsoun being diseasit of madnes he went to the said Alexander, quha sayd he culd do nothing quhill he brocht him hir sark and mutch, Quhilk he caryed them to him, and he keiping them all nicht, on the Morne delyverit them to him, Bidding put them on hir and therefter cast them betuix the post and wall that no body micht tuich them. Then he gave him four merkis, And the said Alexander bad him cum agane and bring more sylver with him, Sa he came the third tyme and gave him ten merkis, And he gave him broun powder and uther thingis lyk skales of Linget[278] quhilkis he bad put among hir meat. Therefter he went to him shewing she wes no better, then he gave him a peic of an hayrie skin bidding him sew it to the cot behind, and sayd that would ather mend hir or end hir.

275 'beit': beet.

276 'nuke': corner.

277 'kume' ('coom'): specks of soot, peat dust.

278 'skales of Linget': linseeds.

William Kellok in Lassody Myln of the age of fourty yeiris, sworne and examined, deponis that having a woman child of fourtene yeiris of age diseased of madnes And heiring of Alexander Drummond that he culd cure, he went to him And caryed hir mutche and collier body,[279] And tuik with him four pundis, But befoir he came to the town of Auchterarder he tuik out {*p. 1*}[280] Tuenty schillings therof and put it in his Napkine, And gave the said Alexander fourty schillings of that wes in his purse, And spendit the uther tuenty schillings in drink with him, And the said Alexander seyd, ye have gewin me over litle sylver, he answerit that he haid no more, To quhom the said Alexander replyed (thocht he shew him his emptie purse), I[281] ye have more, for ye tuik out Tuenty schillings be the way and put it in your Napkine. The said Alexander gave him lyk a peic seyg rute,[282] and bad him put in the weist of hir cott,[283] And bad him cum again, Quhilk he did, And he gave him at that tym another peic lyk a seyg rute to put in the weist of hir cott, And he gave the said Alexander threttie schillings.

[*Signed:*] Mr Robert Roche Moderator of the presbyterie of Dumfermline.

JC26/9/3/2

{*p. 1*} Nicoll[284]

In the house of Dunfermline

Micle Dewar depones as followis – that his wyff being seik was mooved by the good man of Lasyday to goe to Alexander Drummond and took her mutche with him and he asking some token of his wyff, he gave him her mutche, quhilk mutche he receaved and went in quyetly till ane house of his awin quher he stayed about a quarter of ane houre, and quhen he came foorthe he said his wyff haid gotten ill, and that the ill quhilk was Layed upon her was ordained for yow, and that it was Layed on her at that tyme quhen she was travelling[285] and that the persone quha did her the harme was there present with her at her bearing of her bearne, and he gave him a litel powder lyk small sute quhilk he bad give her amongst her meal and she wald be better: and quhen he went back againe he gave him a litle thing Lyk a peece brunt bon[e] and bad him put it upon soume part of her clothis and wear it and she wald be weill anuch. This Micle Dewar being a man of fourty yeare of age deponed after he was sworne and examined the penult of May 1629 yearis befor the minister of Dumfermling and diverse utheris.

279 'collier body': collar body, woman's under-shirt.

280 The document's second sheet, numbered JC26/9/3/8, begins here.

281 'I' (aye): yes.

282 'seyg rute' (sedge root): the root of a grassy rush or flag, possibly wild iris.

283 'weist of hir cott': waist of her coat.

284 In margin: 'Anent his dissait and abuseing of the people'.

285 'travelling' (travailing): labouring, giving birth.

[*Signed:*] Mr Harie Makgill, AColville.
In the house of Dumfermline[286]

Laurie Walker a man of Fyftei yearis, being sworne and examined, depones as followis, that his wyffis sister being seik and pouerly in her bodiei she was carried up till Alexander Drummond, quha quhen he saw her took her Laite at nyht till ane old chappell besyde Auchterarder and bad her seek her healthe for Godis saike quhilk she did: and the morne he broyht her til his house verei tymouslie,[287] and set her downe upon a chaire and took ane old coutter of a pleuche and crossed her breest and bodei diverse tymes and uttered many wordis and mumlingis, and after that dyat[288] gave her some powder and bones to eat and wair with her meal and clothis and he suld warrand hir be weill anuche.

[*Signed:*] AColville, Mr Harie Makgill.

JC26/9/3/7

[*Endorsed*:] William Cuninghames Deposition[289]

{*p. 1*} William Cuninghame his depositione anent Alexander Drummond his dealing with him in his seiknes.

First the said William being in great diseas of bodie and mynd and wanting all power of his left syd, the said Alexander commandit them to send to him William his sark and the garter fra his left lyge[290] quhilk was done and the said William did never sie the same therefter.

Nixt the said Alexander desyret the said William to be transportit to Auchterardor to him and promised to give him ane drink quhilk suld help him to his health: and William cumming to Auchterardor at night desyrit his drink and the said Alexander deferit to give it to him till the morow, Sua to morow Alexander cariet him to ane void hows[291] at the north syde of Auchterardor and caused him sit doune on the herth, Alexander having tainges[292] in his hand, and coverit William his head round about with his clok and laid both his handis upon his head and uttered sume wordis quhilk William hard not bot only his voice, and therefter thair was sutch an ardent heat in his head as if it had bene all on fyre, for the quhilk was givin to the said Alexander tuentie merkis ane double angle and quhen William came home againe Catharine Thomsone [*word crossed out*] said she wald trye him

286 In margin: 'John Smart'.
287 'verei tymouslie': very early in the morning.
288 'dyat' (diet): session of activity.
289 Written in another hand in pencil.
290 'lyge': leg.
291 'void hows': empty house.
292 'tainges': tongs.

and caused gett loch leitches[293] and laid them on[294] William his nek and said, thou terrible devill cum out of the man, after the quhilk [*word crossed out*] William becam wors nor befor and sor trublit and therefter Alexander was send for againe to [*word crossed out*] cum to him againe to his fatheris hows, quho being cum wald doe nothing quhill they promised ane boll of bear or the pryce therof[295] quhilk they promised so sone as William was weill, then the said Alexander caused William sit doune befor the fyre and used sic wordis as he used befor at Auchterardor and immediatlie the seiknes was upon ane mair of Henrie Steinsones quhilk deid.

For certificatione of the which premisses I the said William subscrive the samen with my hand at Aberdour the fourth day of Maii 1629 [*word crossed out*] In presence of Mr William Patoune minister thair and Mr James Patoune his sone wretter heirof.

I William Cuninghame testifis this befor God and man.

[*Signed:*] Mr William Patoune witness, Mr James Patoune witness.

JC26/9/3/28

[*Endorsed:*] Depositiones concerneing Alexander Drummond Warlok

{*p. 1*} Upoun the tuentie thride, Tuentie fourth, tuentie fyfth, tuentie sexth, tuentie sevinth and penult dayis respective off Junii anno i^{m} vi^{c} tuentie nyne yeiris, I Malcolme Browne messenger and ane off the Shereffis in that pairt within constitute Be vertew and att commande of thir our Soverane Lordis letters within writtin direct att the Instance off Sir Thomas Hope of Craighall knycht barronet his majesties advocat for his entres And laufullie commandit and chairgit the particular persones efterspecifeit In maner followeinge, As they wha best knowis the veritie off the within neamit Alexander Drummonde his guiltines off the crymis of sorcerie wichcraft and divilisch chearmingis usit be him thir fyftie yeiris bygane specifeit in the dittay givin in againes him, they are to say, William Stirlinge off Ardoche, James Grahame of Drumfade, Harie Kippen in Drumakellies, Chearles Campbell of Burnesyde off Ogilvy, Johne Thomson in Glenegis, Johne Fute in Glencoy, James Patoun in Ballelisk, Mr Patrike Murray in Ochtertyre, Archibald Campbell off Lagvinshoche, Williame Oliphant att the mylne of Gask, Androw Dow in Drumende of Cowgask, Alexander Buchane in Pitlandie, Johne Dow in Lamrekin, Johne Browne in Thornehill, William Dow in Letterbandoch, Robert Marschell of Pitcarnis, Mr Williame Cuke in Foulis, James Low in Keillour, Williame Stewart in Dalcowie, Walter Stewart in Mephvene, Williame Chapmane in Dunninge,

293 'loch leitches': leeches from a loch. Presumably the sucking of blood by the leeches was meant to indicate the sucking out of the demon.

294 'my' crossed out.

295 The price of a boll of bere (barley) might have been about £5.

David Rolloke in Dynninge, Williame Moncreiffe off Arditie, Alexander Gibson in Rossie, Johne Grahame in Ridfurde, William Gilcreist in the Glene of Glendevin, Johne Gray in Machaine, Thomas Glass of Pittenyen, Robert Quhytt off Dalpatrike, Johne Sanderis burges of Perthe, Antone Dow thair, Androw Meassone thair, Patrike Craigie thair, Johne Woddell in Muirtoune, Hew Ramsay in Dumbarnie, Williame Quhytt in Burnesyde off Diplurge, Hew Moncreife in Magdalaines and Hew Michell in Dubheidis, All personallie apprehendit and delyvrit to ilk ane of theme ane just authenticke copie of the saidis withine writtin letters quha ressavit the samen And Johne Grahame off Urquhill, Robert Grahame of Pennellis, Mr William Murray off Ochtertyre, Johne Walker in Trewne, Lawrene Oliphant of Gask, Finlay Schearer in Abercardny, Mr Johne Malloche of Cardneyis, Johne Quhytt in Currivachter, Williame Quhytt thair and Johne Sinclar in Dalpatrike all att thair dwellinge housis respective abonespecifeit quhair becaus I could not apprehend theme personallie efter knoking sex severall knokes on the maist principall dorris of evrie ane of thair dwelling housis I affixtt and left ane just authenticke copie of the saidis withine writtin letters on evrie ane of theme To compeire before his heines Justice or his deputtis in the tolbuithe of Edinburgh the aucht day of Julii nixtocome In the houre of caus To pas upoun the asysse of the saide Alexander Drummmonde for the saidis crymes ilk persone under the paine of ane hundrethe merkis money This I did efter the forme and tennour of the saidis within writtin letters in all poyntis Beffoir thir witnessis respective Johne Home elder and younger burgessis of Perthe, Mr William Chapman thair, Robert Reiddoche in Foullis, Roger Duncansone in Leithe, James Crystie post in Perthe, William Gilcreist att Cruike of Devin, Alexander Lindsay in Toftewis, Androw Gairdner in Doninge, Mr John Fyff minister att Gask, Lawrence Browne my servitor, Johne Drummond of Colquhylie elder and Lawrence Grahame servitor to John Grahame of Urquhill And for the mair vereficatioun of this my executioun and Indorsatioun subscrivit withe my hand my stampt is heirto affixtt.

[*Signed:*] MBroun messenger.

Upoun the penult and last dayis respective of Junii and first day of Julii anno i^{m} vi^{c} Tuentie nyne yeiris, I Malcolme Browne messenger and ane of the Shereffis in that pairt withine constitute past be vertew and at the commande of thir our soverane Lordis letters withine writtin And laufulie summond warnit and chairgit the persones particularlie withine and under writtin In maner followeinge, they ar to say, Johne Walker in Overgorthie, Johne Stobbie in Bachiltoun, George Grahame in Belliclone, Patrike Grahame burges of Perthe, John Lutefute in Belliclone, Elizabeth Alexander in Dubeittis, Elspethe Lutefute thair, James Guile millar in Tullibardin, Marjorie McClarane in Littil Tullilumie, Lawrence Cutburthe allias Finlaw hir sone, Jonat Cutberthe allias Finlaw spous to [*1 word blank*] Sworde in Blackruthvene and now to Thomas Craigie in Dumbarne, Cristiane Malcolme in Keinlandis and John Malcolme in Logiealmonde, \Umphra Malcolme in Newra messenger/ personallie apprehendit and delyvrit to ilk ane of theme ane just and authentick copie of the saidis withine writtin letters quha ressavit the samen and Patrike Eviott of Tulloche and James Neische in Dubheidis att thair dwelling housis thair quhair becaus I could not apprehende theme personallie efter knokinge of sax severall knokis on the maist principall doris of the saids dwelling housis I affixtt and left ane just and authenticke copie of the saidis withine wrytin letters on ather of theme to compeir befoir the justice generall and his deputis in the tolbuithe of Edinburgh the aucht day of Julii nixtocome In the houre of caus To beir leill and suchefast witnischinge In swa far as they knaw or salbe speirit at theme anent Alexander Drummond within conteanit his proceidingis In the cureinge be diabolicall and unlawfull meanis of divers persones within this kingdome of uncouthe and fearfull deceassis[296] and utheris divilische practiseis committit be him ilk persone under the paine of ane hundrethe merks money This I did efter the forme and tennour of the saidis within writtin letters in all poynts Beffoir thir witnessis respective, Johne Grahame of Balgowne, Williame Strange in Balineblaine, Johne Grahame of Reidfurde, Robert Reiddoche in Foullis, Patrike Walker thair, James Brussone at the Mylne of Bachilton, Williame Millar messenger, James Millar his sone, Malcolme Balmanno in Tullilume, Mr Williame Chapmane burges of Perthe, George Lutefute of Dischaiker and Lawrence Browne my servitor withe divers utheris, And for the mair vereficatioun of this my executioun and Indorsatioun subscrivit withe my hand my stampt is heirto affixitt.

[*Signed*:] MBroun messenger.

JC26/9/3/27

{*p. 1*} The names of the assyseris[297]
X st p David Rollok notter in Dynning
1 st p Williame Stirlinge in Ardoche
p Johne Grahame off Urquhill
2 st p Robert Grahame off Pennellis
2 st p James Grahame off Drumfade
2 st p Henrie Kippen in Drumakellies
3 p Chairles Campbell in Burnesyde of Ogilvy
4 st p John Thomsone in the Glene of Glenneglise
p James Fute in Glencoy
5 p James Patoun in Bellelisk

[296] 'deceassis': diseases.

[297] The meaning of the letters and numbers in front of the names is not known. It is noticeable that the numbers go up to 15, which would be the number needed for a criminal assize; however, the number 2 is written three times against three different names.

d Mr William Murray of Ochtertyre
p Mr Patrike Murray his son of [*sic*]
p Archibald Campbell of Lagvinschoche
6 st d Johne Walker in Trewne
p st Alexander Bucheine in Pitlandie
d Lawrance Oliphant of Gask
7 Androw Dow in Drumende
p John Dow in Lamrekine
x Johne Browne in Thornehill
x Williame Dow in Leitterbandochie
x Finlaw Schearer in Abercardny
p Mr William Cuke in Foullis
p James Lowe in Killour
d Mr John Malloche off Cardny
8 p Williame Stewart of Dalcroe
9 p Williame Moncreife in Arditie
10 p Walter Stewart of Mephvene
11 p Alexander Gipsone in Rossie
p Johne Gray in Meichame
12 p Johne Grahame in Reidfurde
13 p Thomas Glass in Pittentyen
d Johne Quhyt in Curriewachter
d Williame Quhyt thair
14 p Robert Quhyt portioner of Dalpatrike
d Johne Sinclar thair
p Johne Woddell in Muirtowne of Kilgony
p Hew Ramsay in Dumbarnie
15 p Hew Michell in Dubheidis
p Williame [*words crossed out*] Quhyt in Burnesyde of Diplurg
p Hew Moncreife in Morgdelames
p Robert Marschell of Pitcairnis
p Patrike Craige burges of Perthe
p Androw Maissone thair
p Antone Dow thair
p Johne Sanderis thair
p Williame Gilcreist in Glendevin
p Alexander Clark thair
John Sempill proveist of Dumbartren {*p. 2*}

Depositiones concerneing Alexander Drummond Warlok

The names of the witnessis

p Patrike Eviott of Tulloche
p Coline Eviott servitor to my Lord Cessfurde
p John Walker in Over Gorthie

p George Grahame in Balgowme
p John Lutefute thair
p Patrike Grahame burges of the Perthe
d James Neische of Dubeittis
p Elizabeth Alexander his mother
p Elspethe Lutefute thair
p Cristiane Malcolme of Keinlands sometyme spous to umquhill [*1 word blank*] and now to George Crocket thair
p John Malcolme in Logie
p Umphra Malcolme in Newtoun of Balgowne
p James Guild att the mylne of Tullibardein
p Marjorie McClaren in Littill Tillilumbie
p Lawrance Cuthburthe allias Finla hir sone
p Jonat Cuthburthe alias Finlaw some tyme spous to umquhill [*1 word blank*] Sworde in Blackruthven and now to Thomas Craigie in Drumbarnie
P Johne Stobbie in Bachiltoun

JC26/9/3/29

[*Endorsed:*] 8 July 1629, Alexander Drummonds depositione concerning John Maxwell of Stanely.

{*p. 1*} At Edinburgh the viii day of Julii 1629 in the wairdhous of Edinburgh in presens of Mr Alexander Colvill of Blair Justice deput, Mr John Chalmer minister at Archterdyrone,[298] Mr William Levingstoun minister at [*1 word blank*], Mr John Fribairne minister at Madertie.

Alexander Drummond being sworne and examinat, deponit that Letters cam betuix him and John Maxwell of Stanelie[299] anent matteris concerning Staneleis helth quha was diseased of a disperatioun, And that this deponer gaif the said Laird of Stanelie drinkis to provoik Love betuix him and his wyfe, And that Stanelie had beine dyvers tymes at this deponeris hous desyreing the deponer to get to him ane woman, As also deponis that he and Stanelie passit to the woid of Kincardin to confer upone the getting of the forsaid woman, And declairis he ressavit fra the bearar that brocht him the ane ten merkis for him selff and uther ten merk for on[e] John Drummond quha was in use to hold Stanelie the tyme he was in his fate of disperatioun at the deponeris applicatioun of his Cures thairfoir, And sayis that Duncane Aisoune and utheris war the wryteris of his letters.

[*Signed:*] AColville.

298 Auchterderran, in the presbytery of Kirkcaldy.
299 John Maxwell of Stanely, in Renfrewshire.

JC26/9/3/4

[*Addressed:*] For his loving Brother Jhon Bannatyne, Justice clerc deputie and wretter to his Majestie Signet, With hast, At Edinburgh.[300]

{*p. 1*} Loving brother, Thair[301] are to advertiss yow that his Majestie hes beene verie much Informed or rather misinformed of umquhill Alexander Drummont, Quho was brunt ather anno 1628 or 1629 if my memorie faill me not. He hes beene Informed I say that the said Alexander was a perfect physitian and did much good in the contray, and desyres us to give ane accompt of our way of jugement of the said Alexander, and desyrs that with all convenient diligence he may sie the proces and can not rest and be satisfeid till he sie and read the probationis. Thair thairfor to desyr yow, all excuse put asyd, that yow would be pleased to extract the whole proces and cawse wrett it with a good hand that his Majestie may read it with all convenient diligence and send it to me. Direct it to Mr Thomas Hendersone secretarie of his excellence, my trust is that we shall all return about Mertimes[302] nixt, if it plais God if my Lord advocat be in good health acquent his Lordship with this particular, So willing yow all health and happines I rest, Your loving brother to power, AColville. Remember me to all frinds.

Newcastell, 3 8ber[303] 1646. In hast.

JC26/9/3/3

[*Addressed:*] For his Loving brother Jhon Bannatyne, Justice clerk deputie and wretter to his Majestie Signet[304] at Edinburgh.

{*p. 1*} Loving brother, Thair are to advertiss yow that the kings Majestie will not rest satisfeed till he sie umquhill Alexander Drummont his process, this is a busnes that nather yow or I would ever have suspected, Thairfor coment my Lord advocat hearwith Incase his Lordship In good health and with all convenient diligence extract it and cause it be wrettin correctlie with a good hand because his Majestie will peruse it him self in his awen bedchamber. This I will expect with all diligence, as yow would plesour your soverane Lord and prince and oublishe me more and more to Remain, Your Loving brother To power, AColville.

I hope the armye shall come hence at Mertimes with contentment.

Newcastell 6 8ber 1646.

300 This and the next two letters were written from Newcastle in northern England. King Charles was there as a prisoner of the Scottish army occupying Newcastle. He had surrendered to the Scots in May 1646, following the royalist defeat in the civil wars. He seems to have had time on his hands, being able to interest himself in an alleged miscarriage of justice 17 years previously.

301 'Thair' (thir): these, i.e. this letter.

302 'Mertimes' (Martinmas): 11 November.

303 '8ber': October.

304 Several illegible initials here.

JC26/9/3/5

[*Addressed:*] For his loving brother Jhon Bannatyne, Justice clerc deputie and writter to his Majesties Signet, at Edinburgh.

{*p. 1*} Loving brother, I have writtin to yow once or twys bot you never ansuair me, which maks me to feare and suspect your health. Thair are thairfor to Intrait yow to advertiss me of your health and weelfair, and if ever yow receaved my Letters orre not. I dar not go in his Majesties sight becaus I did promise unto his Majestie the sight of Alexander Drummont his proces, which he so much desyres because his Majestie hes beene verie much misinformed by godles men that Drummont was ane notable physitian and did all his wondrous cures by Lawfull meanes, however it be wrett to me of your health. So remembring my Love to your self your sone James Logye and all frinds, I wiss yow all merrye health and happines and shall Remain, Your most Loving brother to power, AColville.

Newcastle, 13 December 1646.

15. PEEBLES WITCHES, 1629

INTRODUCTION

The text edited below is the financial accounts for the trial and execution of a small group of witches in the town of Peebles in 1629. Expenses are listed for various officials in the local court, for the cost of obtaining a commission from the privy council, and for materials and labour costs for the pyre. The execution method may have been unusual. Other information enables us to identify the executed persons as Susanna Elphinstone, John Graham and (probably) Margaret Johnstone.

Serial witch-hunting in Peebles seems to have begun in October 1628, a time when panic over witchcraft was gathering pace in numerous Scottish localities. On the 21st, Marion Greig was suspected of witchcraft by the presbytery of Peebles. John Syd, minister of Newlands, and David Plenderleith, burgess of Peebles, stood surety for her that she would appear when summoned.[1] This investigation evidently turned up the names of further suspects, since on 3 February 1629 the privy council issued a commission of justiciary to James Williamson, provost of Peebles, Alexander Muir and Patrick Thomson, bailies of Peebles, and four named lairds, to try Marion Greig, Isobel Rutherford alias Graham, and Katherine Young, for witchcraft.[2] No record survives of their trial, but they may well have been tried and executed. The accounts edited below show that Isobel Graham, as she was then known, made a 'confessioun aganes the rest of the wiches' that was used in the later prosecutions.

The presbytery of Peebles then seems to have stepped up its involvement.[3] In June 1629, we learn from the privy council records that the presbytery gave in a list of twenty-seven named people from at least six different parishes who were 'vehementlie suspect' for witchcraft. The presbytery seems to have conducted an extensive trawl for suspects. The privy council responded

1 James Walter Buchan (ed.), *A History of Peeblesshire*, vol. ii (Glasgow, 1925), 177.

2 *RPC*, 2nd ser., iii, 32.

3 The presbytery's own minutes do not usually record disciplinary activities in this period, and the witches are not mentioned in them: NRS, Minutes of Presbytery of Peebles, 1624–1644, CH2/295/2.

by issuing an investigatory commission on 11 June to the sheriff of Peebles and his deputes, the bailies of the regality of Dalkeith, and the bailies of the regality of Glasgow. Further research would be required to explain the choice of these commissioners, since neither Dalkeith nor Glasgow were near Peebles. The commissioners were to arrest, imprison and interrogate these suspects – interrogations should take place within fifteen days of arrest – and report back to the privy council who would then give further orders.[4] Unfortunately there is no record of any such report, so we do not have any direct information about what the commissioners did.

Three of the twenty-seven names reappeared in December, and this would lead to the trials recorded in the accounts edited below. On 22 December 1629 the privy council granted a commission of justiciary for the trial for witchcraft of Susanna Elphinstone, John Graham and Margaret Johnstone in Peebles. The commissioners were William Burnett of Barns and James Naismith of Posso (both local lairds), and the provost and bailies of Peebles.[5] In June, Susanna Elphinstone had been described as living in the parish of Peebles, while the other two had been described as John Graham, weaver, alias Jock the Graham, with a blank being left for the parish of his residence, and Margaret Johnstone, alias 'Craweswyffe', in the parish of Traquair. So when the December commission said that all three accused persons were 'in Peebles', this may indicate the sheriffdom rather than the burgh.

The fact that Susanna Elphinstone, John Graham and Margaret Johnstone had all been named in the June investigatory commission may provide a clue as to that commission's activities. It is possible that the investigatory commission did not find enough evidence against the witches, or not enough to convince the privy council. An inconclusive report, or a report that did not lead the privy council to take any action, would not have been minuted. So twenty-four of the twenty-seven suspects may well have survived. However, evidence seems to have emerged later against Elphinstone, Graham and Johnstone. We do not have the minutes of their trial, but a trial was evidently held, since the date of the December commission matches up, at least roughly, with the date of the accounts for the trial and execution edited below.

The accounts do not explicitly name the witches being executed, nor do they even state how many witches there are. Two of the witches are named in passing – John Graham, who is given a loaf of bread, and Susanna Elphinstone, who is given a drink of ale – but without specifying that they are witches or that they are being executed. The name of an earlier witch, Isobel Graham, appears because the burgh had paid a fee for a copy of her 'confessioun aganes the rest of the wiches'. She had been one of the subjects of the February trial commission, and was probably not still alive in December. It is likely that the third accused

4 *RPC*, 2nd ser., iii, 170.

5 *RPC*, 2nd ser., iii, 391.

witch named in the December commission, Margaret Johnstone, was also convicted and executed on this occasion, but there is no definite information.

The accounts make several references to the trial arrangements. Money was paid for a fee for 'the commissioun to burne the witches', showing that the court was held under a specific commission of justiciary, and that more than one witch was being burned. The payment to the servant of James Primrose, clerk to the privy council, and the mention that Thomas Tweedie, burgh treasurer, had spent three or four days in Edinburgh on that occasion, indicate that Tweedie had negotiated to obtain this commission from the privy council. A journey to Edinburgh by the provost was also mentioned, which may suggest that Tweedie's negotiations were not straightforward. The provost and the treasurer had not been among the June commissioners, which provides a further indication that the June commission had ceased to be active.

Although the burgh magistrates organised the trial, the justiciary court that they brought into being with their commission was not simply the burgh court under another name. The burgh court clerk, Patrick Veitch, did not act as the justiciary court clerk; instead, the accounts show that the 'clerk to the wiches proces' was Mr William Dickson, who was the current schoolmaster of Peebles.[6] Nor did the burgh court's dempster act; instead, the role of dempster was taken by the executioner's son. One further official was Mr Andrew Watson, 'procurator in the wiches proces'; he probably led the prosecution. He had at one time been schoolmaster of Peebles, and became vicar and reader of the parish (an assistant to the minister) in June 1629.[7] Dickson's and Watson's titles show them to have been university graduates, but they were probably not legal specialists.

Various details are provided about the process of execution itself. We learn that the venue for the burning was the Calf Knowe. This was an eminence on the Ven Law, the hill to the north-east of the town.[8] The materials for the pyre were itemised: peat, coal, heather, and tar barrels. The specified quantities look plausible if a single pyre was being constructed. A single pyre, if large enough, could have burned three witches.[9]

There is an unusual payment 'for setting wp the gibitt the wichis was hanged wpoun'. The witches thus seem to have been hanged on a conventional gibbet, with their bodies then being burned on a pyre in a separate operation. This would be different from the usual Scottish procedure of tying the witches to a

6 *Charters and Documents Relating to the Burgh of Peebles, with extracts from the records of the burgh, 1165–1710*, ed. William Chambers (Edinburgh: Scottish Burgh Records Society, 1872), 368–9.

7 NRS, Minutes of Presbytery of Peebles, 1624–1644, CH2/295/2, 18 June, 30 July 1629 (unpaginated).

8 Buchan (ed.), *History of Peeblesshire*, ii, 177.

9 For more on the practicalities and costs of executions see Laura Paterson, 'Executing Scottish Witches', in Julian Goodare (ed.), *Scottish Witches and Witch-Hunters* (Basingstoke, 2013), 196–214; Julian Goodare, 'Costs and Profits of Scottish Witch-Hunting', *History Scotland*, 21, no. 4 (July–August 2021), 15–19.

stake that had had a pyre built round it, and strangling them before lighting the pyre. Indeed, no stake appears in these accounts. Instead, there is mention of 'ane cuppill' – a pair of timbers – which could have been used to make the gibbet.

Could the gibbet have been constructed *over* the pyre? Such an arrangement is illustrated in a pamphlet about witches being executed in Roermond, in the United Netherlands, in 1613.[10] However, the Roermond illustration shows an impossibly small pyre, and should not be taken literally. It seems more likely that the Peebles authorities carried out the hanging and burning as two separate operations. This would have saved the cost of a stake, since the gibbet would be reusable. But this cost would have been modest; in the Dundee accounts from *c.*1591 edited above, the stake cost 5*s.* to buy it plus 8*d.* to transport it. Perhaps the two-part operation carried out in Peebles remained uncommon because it provided a less satisfying spectacle than burning at the stake.

The accounts were drawn up by the burgh treasurer, Thomas Tweedie. He had been involved in the arrangements for the trial and the executions, and in the accounts he wrote about himself in the first person. His accounts are laid out in three columns: a left-hand column for dates, a central one for a textual description of each item of expenditure, and a third column giving the amount of money in roman numerals. In the present edition, a fourth column has been added at the right, with figures in square brackets that present the sums of money in a standardised form in arabic numerals.

The dates in the accounts are not precise. Many entries are loosely grouped rather than being listed in strict chronological order, and are not dated individually. The date given should formally be the date at which the treasurer 'discharged' himself for the expenditure (i.e. accepted official responsibility for payment). This may well have some connection with the date on which the event occurred, but the connection is indirect. The 'discharge' date is not necessarily the date on which payment was actually made, either; the tradespeople who supplied materials could well have done so on credit, with payment being made later. Most of the dates given are almost certainly too early, since the trial and the resulting executions probably took place in the week or so after the commission of 22 December.

The accounts were subjected to scrutiny, presumably by the burgh council as a whole or its representatives, after they were written. Two items of expenditure were marked as 'not allowit', one of which was a substantial payment to the provost for a journey to Edinburgh. Tweedie's own expenses in Edinburgh were also reduced from four days to three. The burgh evidently kept a sharp eye on the costly process of executing witches.

10 *Een warachtige beschriivinge van 64 Tooveressen die door haer Tooveryen over de Duysent Menschen ...* (n.p., n.d. [*c.*1613]) (A true account of 64 witches who cast witchcraft on the common people ...), online at <https://www.historieroermond.nl/Heksen1613-1614/heksen1613-1614.htm>.

TEXT

Source: NRS, Accounts of the Burgh of Peebles, 1621–1650, B58/14/2.[11]

{p. 101} The said Thomas Tuedie thesaurer of the burh of Peblis discherges him selff with thir particuallaris efter follouing viz....

November 1629 15	Item to James Haldowne for making for making [*sic*] the Calf Know dwr[12] agreitt be the provest and baillies	xxxiii s iiii d	[£1 13*s*. 4*d*.]
15	Item to the said James Haldowne for making the gibbitt that stands thairupon	iiii lib	[£4]
	[*three unrelated entries not transcribed*]		
19	Item gewin for the commissioun to burne the witches	vi lib xiii s iiii d	[£6 13*s*. 4*d*.]
	Item of drinksilver to James Prymrois his mane[13]	xxx s	[£1 10*s*.]
	Item my awin waigis att thatt tyme for remaining \thrie/[14] dayes in Edinburgh	\4 li 10 s[15]/	[£4 10*s*.]
	Item the provest agred with James Haldowne for setting wp the gibitt the wichis was hanged wpoun	iii lib xiiii s	[£3 14*s*.]
	[*three unrelated entries not transcribed*]		
	Item to Mr William Dikisone for being clerk to the wiches proces [at the] provest baillies and counsallis command	vi lib	[£6]
December 15	[*six unrelated entries not transcribed*]		

11 About two-thirds of the entries below have previously been printed in *Charters and Documents Relating to the Burgh of Peebles, with extracts from the records of the burgh, 1165–1710*, ed. William Chambers (Edinburgh: Scottish Burgh Records Society, 1872), 416.

12 The gibbet on the Calf Knowe hill was probably enclosed by a dyke – a wall of turf or stone. This 'dwr' (door) was presumably a wooden gate or entrance of some kind. James Haddon was evidently a carpenter or wright; the next entry shows that he also made the gibbet itself.

13 James Primrose was the clerk of the privy council. His 'man' – his servant – was evidently the official with whom Thomas Tweedie had negotiated in Edinburgh.

14 'fowr' crossed out here and this word inserted.

15 'vi lib' crossed out here and this sum inserted.

Item directed to conduce with[16] ane lockmane[17] to the wiches my twa dayes waiges allowitt to me	iii lib	[£3]
Item drwcking att his feaing[18]	xxvi s viii d	[£1 6*s*. 8*d*.]
Item gewin be Johnne Robene for fyve laids peittis with ane quartt of aille he gawe to the peitmen coft[19] to burne the wiches	xxxii s viii d	[£1 12*s*. 8*d*.]
Item to Marioun Watsone for thrie laids of coallis	xxxvi s	[£1 16*s*.]
Item to Williame Mwrray for ane twrss of hedder[20]	ix s	[£0 9*s*.]
[*subtotals at foot and head of page not transcribed*] {*p. 102*}		
Item inprimis to Mr Androw Watsone to tak actis of courtt being procurator[21] in the wiches proces	xlv s	[£2 5*s*.]
Item for candill to the tolbuth and chappill compted and rackned with Johnne Tuidies wyfe	xxxii s	[£1 12*s*.]
Item for thrie faldome small towis[22] to bind the wiches hands	xxx d	[£0 2*s*. 6*d*.]
Item for four faldome gritt towis[23] to kitt them up[24] with all[25]	vi s viii d	[£0 6*s*. 8*d*.]
Item to Williame Portews for thrie tar barrellis	xlviii s	[£2 8*s*.]

16 'conduce with': negotiate with.

17 'lockmane': executioner. Tweedie seems to have spent two days searching for an executioner.

18 'drwcking att his feaing': (alcohol) drunk when his (the lockman's) contract was agreed.

19 'coft': bought.

20 'twrss of hedder': bundle of heather.

21 This is the most likely expansion of the MS's 'pro^{r}', but 'pro[secuto]r' is also possible. A procurator was someone who spoke in court, either for the prosecution or the defence. The court would have needed someone to present the prosecution's case, but the accused persons would not necessarily have had anyone to speak for them; they could have been expected to conduct their own defence. Thus, however we understand this abbreviation, Watson is likely to have been the person leading the prosecution.

22 'thrie faldome small towis': three fathoms of thin rope. A fathom was 6 feet (about 2 metres).

23 'gritt towis' (great): thick rope.

24 'kitt them up': tie them up.

25 'with all': also.

Item to Alexander Dikisone ane pair of schowis for wairneing[26] of the ministrie[27] coft from Thomas Lowis att the provestis command	xx s	[£1]
Item to James Haldowne for careing the tarbarrellis to the Calf Know	iiii s iiii d	[£0 4*s.* 4*d.*]
Item to hangmane for his waiges	x lib	[£10]
Item to his sone for being dampster	xii s	[£0 12*s.*]
Item for ane instrument[28] upoun Issobell Grhames [*sic*] confessioun aganes the rest of the wiches att the parsones command[29]	xii s	[£0 12*s.*]
Item gewin to Johnne Robene to carie ane cuppill[30] from Archibald Frankes yett[31] att directioun of the said Archibald	vi s	[£0 6*s.*]
Item to Johnne Grhame[32] and the dampster ather of thame ane loaf	ii s	[£0 2*s.*]
Item Johnne Robene gave Swsanna Elphingsoun[33] ane cheppin[34] aill	x d	[£0 0*s.* 10*d.*]
Item gewin to the provest he being directed to ryd to Edinburgh[35]	ix lib xii s	[£9 12*s.*]
Item att Archibald Frankes directioun for wyne thatt was druckinn befoir my entrie	iii lib vi s viii d	[£3 6*s.* 8*d.*]
Item to Johnne Frank for furnishing the wiches his compt being alowitt and gif neid beis heir presentt to be sene	viii lib xiiii s	[£8 14*s.*]

26 'wairneing': summoning.

27 This may well refer to the other ministers within the presbytery of Peebles. Probably Alexander Dickson would not have needed new shoes simply to summon the minister of the burgh.

28 'instrument': formal legal copy of a document.

29 In margin: 'not allowit'. Dr Theodore Hay, minister of Peebles, was known as 'persone [i.e. parson] and pastour of Peblis': NRS, Minutes of Presbytery of Peebles, 1624–1644, CH2/295/2, 21 May 1629 (unpaginated).

30 'cuppill': pair of timber rafters.

31 'yett': gate.

32 *Sic.* John Graham was one of the accused witches.

33 Susanna Elphinstone was one of the accused witches. Was this ale given to her at the time of her execution?

34 'cheppin' (chopin): a tankard containing about half a pint.

35 In margin: 'not allowit'. This entire entry has been crossed out.

Item to the said Johnne Frank for furnishing lockmane and his sone	iii lib xii s	[£3 12*s*.]
Item for thrie elnes gray[36] to Williame Sowartt	iiii lib	[£4]
Item for threid and making thairof	xii s	[£0 12*s*.]
Item for breid and drink feched furth of David Plendehas[37] to the assytheres[38]	xxx s	[£1 10*s*.]
Item fetched furth thairof to hangmane and wiches	xviii s	[£0 18*s*.]

36 'thrie elnes gray': three ells (about 3 metres) of grey cloth.

37 *Sic*. This name, which appears later in the accounts as 'Plenderlaihas', was presumably the local surname 'Plenderleith'. David Plenderleith may have been an alehouse keeper. He may well also be the burgess mentioned above who acted as surety for Marion Greig in 1628.

38 'assytheres' (assizers): members of the assize.

16. MICHAEL ERSKINE, NEWBATTLE, 1629–1630

INTRODUCTION

Michael Erskine, a miller at Newbyres Mill in Newbattle, was accused of witchcraft and sodomy and investigated by the presbytery of Dalkeith. He was arrested at some point after 15 October 1629 in response to an order that had also named two other men and two women. On this occasion, the presbytery referred to a warrant for arrest which had previously been issued by the privy council.[1] The later documents write of Erskine alone, so it is not clear what happened to the other four suspects.

Erskine was kept in prison in Newbattle for six weeks. He seems to have been tortured with sleep deprivation until he confessed to all the crimes. Then, on 17 December, the presbytery petitioned the privy council, asking for him to be transferred to Edinburgh tolbooth because people in the parish refused to continue guarding him, and the house in which he was imprisoned was insecure. He was then moved to the tolbooth of Edinburgh.

More than three months later, on 2 April 1630, Erskine's trial came up in the central court of justiciary in Edinburgh. The prosecutor was Joseph Miller, substitute to the king's advocate. Dittays from 31 March 1630, based on depositions before the 'Lord Justice' (Alexander Colville, justice depute, who was the judge in charge of the trial), and likewise from the presbytery, were read in the presence of the assize. Erskine denied the crimes. The assize unanimously found him guilty, with the exception of witchcraft committed against Robert Hogg. Whether this was the only witchcraft charge, or whether there were other witchcraft charges of which he was found guilty, was not specified. He was sentenced to be strangled and burned in Newbattle.

Even if we do not have Erskine's confessions, the pre-trial and trial documents of his case give a glimpse of the formal requirements in order to hold a trial, and of the necessity of torture to obtain a confession. The documents also show the importance of his confession as well as the witnesses' testimonies in order to proceed with the trial. The documents also show why the presbytery thought that imprisonment in Edinburgh was necessary, and the role of the central authorities in Edinburgh.

[1] There is no record of a recent warrant in the minutes of the privy council.

TEXTS

Source 1: NRS, Minutes of Presbytery of Dalkeith, 1582–1630, CH2/424/1.

{p. 577} Octobris die xv[2]
The quhilk day the brether desyris the Laird of Costorphin[3] according to the warrand given to thaim be the counsell, and also the Lady Arnistoun,[4] To apprehend and keep in saiff custodie for better tryell Patryk Murray, Thomas Watsoun, Agnes Rannik, Eufayme Skeitchin and Michael Areskin suspect of witchcraft within thair bounds, as also desyris the Laird of Braid and Pennycuik[5] to apprehend and tak Annis Pursell suspect of witchcraft within the parochin of Pennycuik.

Source 2: NRS, Privy Council Register, Decreta, 1627–1630, PC2/11.[6]

{fo. 274r.} Apud Haliruidhous 22 Decembris 1629
Anent the supplicatioun presented to the lords of secreit counsell be the moderator and brethrein of the presbyterie of Dalkeith Makand mentioun that whereafter manie cleere depositiouns givin in to thame agains ane Michael Areskine within thair presbyterie of his guiltines of the cryme of witchcraft and upon diverse pregnant and evident presumptiouns and cleere testimoneis of some other abominable and destestable crymes committed be him not worthe to be heard of they caused apprehend him and committ him to waird in a little hous abone the end of Newbottle kirk quhair they have keeped him under a nightlie guarde and watche thir sax weekes bygane till they sould have gottin ane full and cleere discoverie of all the crymes whairwith he wes burdeinned and now the people of thair parish ar so wearied with the guarding and keeping of the said Michael as they have altogidder refuised anie longer to underly that burdein and the prison hous being ane verie unsure hous not able to keepe the said Michael without ane guarde and watche to attend the same he will not faile to escape and so eschew his tryall and punishment to the great offence of God and to the discredite and scandall of the countrie humblie desyring thairfoir the saids lords that they might *{fo. 274v.}* have thair warrand for transporting the said Michael fra thair waird and jayle in Newbottle to the burgh of Edinburgh in maner and to the intent underwrittn Lykeas at mair lenth is conteanit in the said supplicatioun Quhilk being read heard and considderit be the saids lords and they finding the desyre thairof to be reasonable Thairfoir the saids lords hes givin and grantit and be the tennour heirof Gives and grants thair warrand and commissioun to the saids supplicants to transport and caus the said Michael

2 The year is 1629. In margin: 'Anent apprehending of witchs'.
3 Sir George Forrester of Corstorphine.
4 Mary Home, widow of Sir James Dundas of Arniston.
5 Sir Robert Fairlie of Braid.
6 A summary of this document has been printed in *RPC*, 2nd ser., iii, 385.

saulfelie and surelie to be transported and conveyed fra thair waird and jayle in Newbottle to the burgh of Edinburgh and to delyver him to the provest and bailleis of the said burgh to be committed be thame to thair tolbuith and to be keeped thairin till he be putt to his tryell commanding heirby the provest and bailleis of the said burgh to receave the said Michael fra the said supplicants and suche as they sall direct to make his envoy to Edinburgh and to committ him to waird in thair tolbuith and to deteane him thairin in maner foirsaid as they will answere to the said lords upon their obedience.

Source 3: NRS, Court of Justiciary, Books of Adjournal, 1619–1631, JC2/6.

{fo. 322r.} Curia Justiciarie Supremi Domini Nostri regis tenta in pretorio de Newbottill secundo Aprilis 1630 per magistrum Alexandrum Colvile.[7]

Intran

Michaell Erskine myller at Newbyres mylne

Dilaitit of certane poyntis of witchcraft and filthie sodomie[8] at lenth sett doun in his dittay.

Persewer

Joseph Myller advocat substitute to Sir Thomas Hoipe of Craighall knycht barronet advocat to our soverane lordis advocat [*sic*] Conforme to his Lordships substitutioun and procuratorie producet be the said Joseph in Judgement subscryvit be his Lordship daitit the last of Marche 1630.

The dittay being producet and the pannell accuset of the crymes mentionet thairintill he denyet the samyn.

Assisa

James Brysoun in Quhytehous
Robert Knox in Tempill
Thomas Broun thair
Thomas Steill in Eisthoussis
Johnne Woid thair
chanceller George Harret in Coittis
William Johnestoun thair
James Alexander thair
George Unes in Cokpen mylne
James Unes in Reidheuch
Thomas Greinlaw in Eisthoussis
George Watsone in Eisthoussis
Alexander Ramsay in Caringtoun
Stevin Rannaldsone in Braidwoid
Robert Diksone in Clarkingtoun *{fo. 322v.}*

7 'Court of justiciary of our sovereign lord the king, held in the tolbooth of Newbattle, 2 April 1630, by Mr Alexander Colville'.

8 'sodomie': unnatural sexual intercourse.

The advocat takis instrumentis of the sweiring of the assyse and for verifeing of the pannellis guiltines of the crymes thairin contenit producet dyveris depositiones tane befoir my Lord Justice As also befoir the presbiterie of Dalkeyth maid be umquhile Thomas Watsone, Thomas Smebaird in Stobhill, Patrik Hardie in Carkettil mylne, Robert Robertsone in Stobhill, Thomas Andro the perseweris mother brother, umquhile Malie Turnour, William Waderstoun and John Penman, And upon the productioun and reiding thairof As also upone the Judiciall ratificatioun of the said Thomas Smebaird, Patrick Hardie, Robert Robertsone, Thomas Andro, Robert Erskyne brother to the pannell, Williame Waderstoun and Johnne Penman thair confessiones and depositiones ratifeit in the assyse presens and audience askit Instrumentis and protestit for wilfull error aganis the assyse gif thay sould acquit the pannell of the crymes contenit in his dittay.

The assyse all in ane voce be the repoirt of George Arret chanceller Fyles the pannell of the haill crymes contenit in his dittay except the sorcerie committit aganis Robert Hoge quhilk is deleit out thairof For the quhilk caus the Justice be the mouth of William Borthvik dempster of court decernit and adjudget the said Michell Erskine to be tane to the ordiner place of executioun within the lordship of Newbottill And thair to be wirreit at ane staik quhill he be deid and thaireftir his body to be brunt in asses And all his moveable guidis to be escheit to his majesteis use as convict of the saidis crymes quhilk was pronuncet for dome.

17. STIRLING WITCHES, 1633

INTRODUCTION

The presbytery of Stirling compiled dossiers of evidence against three accused witches early in 1633: Janet Taylor from the parish of Alloa, Marion Mathie from the burgh of Stirling, and Helen Keir from the parish of Clackmannan. All three places were within a few miles of each other. Taylor and Keir lived in Clackmannanshire rather than Stirlingshire, but the presbytery's jurisdiction crossed the county boundary. As we shall see, all three were investigated and tried in Stirling itself. The investigation provides an example of how a presbytery approached community witches and magical practitioners.

Janet Taylor's dossier is the longest, and she also appears again in the dossiers of Mathie and Keir. She was a magical practitioner, or 'charmer', with a wide repertoire of healing practices. Some of her rituals were everyday ones, using nail parings, the client's clothes, or south-running water, but she ranged more widely, and her interrogators took an interest in several details. She recited a verbal charm mentioning a hedgehog, which they wrote down in full. She had a healing stone that she had brought from the Highlands long ago. She named the person who had taught her healing, John Dow Buchanan, who may well have been a Highlander; he had a partly Gaelic name ('Dow', or *dubh*, meant 'black'), and there were Buchanans in the south-western Highlands. Her interrogators questioned her as to how her rituals worked; she explained that she had a special 'charge' to heal. She seems to have had a good reputation, having by her own account practised for thirty years.

The interrogators seem to have been willing to accept some evidence of Taylor's healing without trying to reinterpret it as overtly harmful or demonic. This could nevertheless have made sense in terms of demonic witchcraft; a person who successfully exercised magical or preternatural powers in an unauthorised way could have obtained those powers from the Devil, even if the powers had been used to a good end. However, this reasoning does not appear explicitly in the dossier, and we do see some instances of reinterpretation of Taylor's practices. Some of her clients claimed that they had refused to perform the rituals that she prescribed on hearing that she was a witch. The literal truth of these claims is sometimes hard to reconcile with other aspects of their testimony, and they may have reinterpreted events retrospectively – either through a wish for self-protection, or at the prompting of the interrogators who wanted to hear about witchcraft, or both. Still, the clients' language shows that they recognised lines that charmers should not cross. The dossier also mentioned an occasion in 1629 when Taylor had been in trouble with the kirk session for charming and had promised not to do it again.

Taylor proved particularly vulnerable when it emerged that she sometimes advised clients that they were bewitched, and guided them in identifying the witch responsible for their illness. The interrogators took a special interest in this. Two of the witches whom she identified in this way were Marion Mathie and Helen Keir, who in their turn were formally charged with witchcraft. In Taylor's own mind, and in the minds of her clients, countering bewitchment was a beneficial act, but it did show that her powers were magical or preternatural.

It was no doubt for this reason that one of Taylor's clients, John Sibbet, feared her. It seems to have been his dramatic and unusual case that triggered Taylor's arrest. After negotiating with her to obtain a cure for his wife's illness, Sibbet himself experienced frightening visions of spirits, and attempted suicide by stabbing himself with a knife. He was still unwell when the presbytery began their investigations, and they even urged Taylor to heal him. She replied that she could not perform a healing ritual while in prison, and also claimed that Sibbet was insane (a claim implausibly contradicted by another witness). However, she did predict that Sibbet would recover – which he did. The presbytery seem to have regarded his recovery as evidence of witchcraft.

The dossier of evidence against Taylor, as we shall see, was used to obtain a commission of justiciary for a criminal trial in Stirling, at which she was convicted. Just before her trial, and again between her sentence and her execution, she was questioned again by Henry Guthrie, minister of Stirling. Guthrie acted at least partly in a pastoral role, urging her to confess her sins and repent before she died. By now Taylor was willing to confess to being a witch, but she continued to insist that she had used her powers to defeat other witches. Guthrie took this opportunity to obtain further information about other witches, as well as about Taylor's unwitching practices. It was at this point that Taylor named Helen Keir, prompting the presbytery to launch an investigation of Keir also. This whole episode is recorded at the opening of Keir's own dossier. However, before turning to Keir, we should examine the case of Marion Mathie.

Marion Mathie was investigated together with Janet Taylor. Their activities were not closely linked, but some of the same witnesses testified against both. The case of John Sibbet seems to have prompted Mathie's arrest as well as Taylor's, though in a different way. Taylor was thought to have caused Sibbet to attempt suicide after she had magically cured his wife. Taylor's dossier seems to imply that Sibbet's wife is still alive after this apparently recent cure – but in Mathie's dossier we learn that Sibbet's wife has died of a lingering illness that has allegedly been laid on her by Mathie. Taylor herself testified that Mathie was responsible, which fits with Taylor's willingness to diagnose bewitchment and to accuse others of having caused it.

Mathie seems to have been an independent widow within the burgh of Stirling. She had her own house and yard. No husband was mentioned, but her adult son lived in London. At one point she wanted to send him a letter, with the impression being given that she had written it herself. Her occupation was not specified, but she had business dealings with several craftsmen, and was involved in one transaction for £20, more than the annual wage of a farm labourer. Both Mathie and Keir faced numerous accusations originating in small requests that they had made to neighbours – requests that led to quarrels and resentment when they were refused. This is a familiar pattern in witchcraft studies – but these cases remind us that the pattern was a varied one. Neither Mathie nor Keir were beggars, and they mostly seem to have negotiated with their neighbours on terms of equality.

Numerous neighbours claimed that Mathie had harmed them, usually by inflicting human or animal illness. They usually dealt with these illnesses by seeking reconciliation with Mathie, either politely or aggressively. Some deaths were also attributed to her. She was even accused of having caused the death of a laird, James Forrester of Logie, three years ago – though evidently she had not been accused at the time. Three years ago would have been during the witchcraft panic of 1628–31, so it is particularly surprising that the death of a laird did not lead to a witchcraft accusation. Perhaps his death was reinterpreted retrospectively as having been caused by witchcraft.

Nevertheless, Mathie was sought out by clients for her powers, including in one instance the power to perform love magic – a less common skill than healing. Like Taylor, she had a magical stone. She prescribed one particularly dark healing ritual, requiring a client to refrain from speaking the name of God, and to go round anticlockwise – symbolically the wrong or unlucky way to turn.

Community interactions were often about the everyday business of making a living – but they could also involve strange and magical experiences. One of Mathie's neighbours, John Frissell, experienced visions about her. When he repeatedly saw a magical cat, he suspected that this was Mathie in animal form. Mathie herself responded to this suspicion by saying that the cat was really another woman who visited her, and trying to persuade Frissell that she herself was under magical attack from this other woman. It is not surprising that Mathie had a reputation for witchcraft, and that two neighbours testified that they had threatened to complain about her to 'the judges'. Nevertheless, they had not done so, and had relied on community negotiation to manage their relationship with her.

For Helen Keir there is less evidence of healing or magical practice, though James Hall and Alexander Cousin both seem to have consulted her for advice about small children. She was said to have had a reputation as a witch for thirty years. Her neighbours testified to numerous apparent bewitchments, some of which but not all had been preceded by quarrels or threats. Keir manifested one unusual grievance when she objected to the military recruitment of her son. This event probably occurred during the late 1620s, when regiments were being raised in Scotland to take part in the Thirty Years' War. Most of Keir's difficulties with neighbours were resolved at the time, either by reconciliation rituals or by the allegedly bewitched neighbour consulting another magical practitioner such as Janet Taylor. Keir seems to have known that Taylor had damaging information to reveal about her.

Throughout their investigations, the presbytery evidently had the co-operation of Stirling burgh council. The accused witches were imprisoned, apparently in the tolbooth, while parish ministers and perhaps elders worked in the localities to identify and summon witnesses for questioning before the presbytery. Most of the witnesses testified in person in Stirling, but at least one, Margaret Dawson, submitted a written 'depositioune' instead – presumably written by one of the parish investigators rather than Dawson herself.

Information from these witnesses was then cross-checked, at least in Janet Taylor's case, by questioning the accused witch herself. Some of the incidents about which Taylor was questioned derived from witnesses who, like Dawson, had given information locally rather than testifying before the presbytery in person. The interrogators seem to have limited their questioning to this cross-checking process; there is no sign of any attempt to ask the suspects about dealings with the Devil. Quite possibly the interrogators did not employ torture. They seem to have got little from Helen Keir – mainly an admission that she had spoken angrily about Robert Horne's intention to testify against her – and even less from Marion Mathie. Nevertheless, the tone of calm and polite enquiry presented by the texts should not be misunderstood. Both Taylor and Mathie offered to die if their testimony should be disproved; they knew that their positions were desperate.

The general thrust of the accusations was to present all three suspects as community witches, having wrought magical harm, often in revenge for slights of some kind. Whether the suspects would also have been charged in court with demonic witchcraft is unclear, but there is so little demonic material that this seems unlikely. Unlike some witchcraft dossiers, the text shows little sign of being reshaped into a dittay; a few items seem to function more as background information than as specific charges, and others are so vague that it is hard to see how they could prove malefice. Perhaps such items would have been omitted in writing the dittay. The accusations do, however, paint a rich and detailed picture of everyday life and community interactions, as well as popular magical beliefs and practices.

These accusations occurred in 1633, which was not long after the panic of 1628–31. Prosecutors were sometimes cautious, especially about demonic witchcraft, in the aftermath of panics. In fact, there had not been many Stirlingshire cases in the recent panic. Henry Guthrie, minister of Stirling, may have played a co-ordinating role – but he had been appointed to Stirling only in 1632, having previously served a rural Forfarshire parish (where there had also been few cases in the recent panic).[1] This may help to explain the rarity of demonic witchcraft in these dossiers.

The text of the dossiers has survived by being entered into the regular volume of presbytery minutes. Within the minutes, the dossiers are marked out by the multiple dates in the headings. Taylor and Mathie's investigations are dated between 29 January and 21 February 1633 and recorded together, while Keir's investigation has been entered a few pages further on in the book, dated 3 April to 10 April. These multiple dates indicate that the clerk has not simply recorded the presbytery's business chronologically as it happened, but has brought together all the material relating to each case. Evidently copies of these dossiers were presented to the privy council in connection with a request for a commission of justiciary.

And indeed, on 19 March, the privy council granted a commission to try both Taylor and Mathie for witchcraft. The council noted that the request for the commission had previously been approved by the archbishop of St Andrews. The commissioners were specified as the sheriff of Stirling and his deputes, and the provost and bailies of Stirling.[2] The court was formally constituted in Stirling by virtue of this commission on 23 March; the record of this event, listing all the officers of the court, survives and is printed below in chronological sequence. Formally this court was a one-off event, but the personnel were all members of existing local courts.

As for Keir, who had been identified at a later stage, the council granted a commission to try her for witchcraft on 24 April. The commissioners were specified as the sheriff of Stirling and his deputes, and Sir Robert Bruce of Clackmannan.[3] Keir's dossier itself tells us that Taylor was convicted and burned at Stirling on 3 April. The other two suspects' fate is not recorded, but the fact that all three faced similar accusations, to be heard before similar local judges, is ominous.

TEXTS

Source 1: Stirling Council Archives, Minutes of Presbytery of Stirling, 1627–1640, CH2/722/5.

1 David Stevenson, 'Guthrie, Henry (1600?–1676)', *ODNB*.

2 Louise A. Yeoman (ed.), 'Witchcraft Cases from the Register of the Privy Council of Scotland, 1630–1642', *SHS Miscellany*, vol. xiii (Edinburgh: SHS, 2004), 223–65, at p. 249. Marion Mathie is named here as 'Janet Mathie', but this is evidently an error by the privy council clerk.

3 Yeoman (ed.), 'Witchcraft Cases', 250.

{p. 154} At Sterling the xxix, the xxx and xxxi dayes of Januar, the xx and xxi dayes of Februar 1633, in presens of the brethren thair assembled
The quhilk day compeired Jonet Tailyour in Cambuse, parochine of Alloway,[4] quha in presens of the brethren then assembled *{p. 155}* confessed that schoe lived with ane man called Jhone Mcfarland not being maried, and procreat divers and sundrie childrein for the space of thretie thrie yeirs.

And being accused of charmeing and wther poyntes of Witchcraft confessed frielie, that these 30 yeirs or thairby scho had sett her self to charmeing of sundrie diseases, and in deceaving of the people. Quha became acted in the kirk sessioun buks of Alloway upon the 27 day of September 1629 (for her charmeing of befoir) that give[5] scho used any charmes thaireftir schoe sould be brunt as ane witch,[6] Notwithstanding the said act hes used Witchecraft and charmeing evir since to the 29 day of Januar, quhilk charmes schoe confessed schoe learned of ane Jhone Dow Buchannan quhen schoe was ane yung damosell be handling the hurtchune, the words of the charm ar these as followes.

I handled the hurtchune,[7] I handle yow, naming the persounes name, in the name of the father, the sone and the holy ghost, thrys reipeated. Stocks and stones, thorne busches, aischyn tries and the waves of the seas bear thy soires aff ye. *{p. 156}*

The quhilk day Jonet Tailyour confessed that Jhone Sibbauld and Effie Mcole in Abbay came to her in the Cambus to her awin hous, and desired the said Jonet Tailyour to cure his wife for Gods caus gif she could.

The said Jonet Tailyour confessed that schoe answered that schoe could do no gud to Jhone Sibbaulds wyfe at this tyme, becaus he went into ane uther hous in the toune befoir he come to the said Jonets hous, and that the said Jonet Tailyour could not do gud to the said Jhone Sibbaulds wyfe, becaus the said Jhone had brought none of his wyfes clouthes to her. Quhairfoir the said Jonet bade the said Jhone go home at that tyme, and be at her the morne, and bring with him ane sark,[8] ane curtche,[9] ane coller bodye,[10] and ane mutche[11] of his wyfes.

4 'Alloway': Alloa. This place should not be confused with Alloway in Ayrshire.

5 'give': if.

6 The kirk session of Alloa recorded the following act on 27 September 1629: 'The quhilk day Jonet Tailyor becam actit that gif sche use any charmes here efter the [*sc.* she] salbe birned ae [*sc.* as] ane witch, and John Archibald in Kirkfald is becom cawtioun wnder the pain of ane hunder libs.' Stirling Council Archives, Minutes of Kirk Session of Alloa, 1609–1657, CH2/942/5, p. 236.

7 'hurtchune': hedgehog. The point of this unusual charm seems to be that the practitioner has demonstrated her power by having previously handled a hedgehog. For a suggestion of magical visions of hedgehogs in a witchcraft trial in 1591, see Robert Pitcairn (ed.), *Criminal Trials in Scotland, 1488–1624*, 3 vols. (Edinburgh: Bannatyne Club, 1833), i, part II, 253.

8 'sark': under-shirt.

9 'curtche': kerchief or cap.

10 'coller bodye': shirt-like woman's undergarment.

11 'mutche': hood.

The said Jhone Sibbett the morrow according to the said Jonets directiouns went bak to her and tuk ane sark, ane curtche, ane collarbodie, and ane mutche, of his wyfes, and quhen he mett with her he said for Gods caus do my wife gud and my self no evill, and then he gave the said Jonet Tailyour his wyfes sark, curtche, collarbodie and mutche, the quhilk quhen schoe had ressaived from the said Jhone Sibbett {*p. 157*} schoe speired at him[12] how his wife luiked, and spak to him thes words, I handled the hurtchune I handle yow etc. And that thairefter schoe caused the said Jhone Sibbett to embrace her in his armes and to lay his armes over her shoulders. Lykways the said Jonet Tailyeour imbraced the said Jhone Sibbett and straiked doune his head with her hand thrys, and ridelyvered[13] to him his wyfes sarke, curtche, collerbodie and mutche, and bad him and his wife put on the sarke upon her and wear it 24 hours and efter the 24 hours to put it off her and her seiknes sould leive her, quhilk schoe did and immediatlie recovered, and quhen the said Jhone Sibbet was pairting from the said Jonet Tailyour, desired her to do him self no evill bot rather to lay the diseas upon ane stock or ane stone or gif schoe behuifed[14] to lay it upon some living creatur, that schoe wold spair him self, and lay it upon his awne meare quhilk he had brocht for that end. The said Jonet Tailyour answered, ye ar ane fuile, it appears ye wald have your beasts destroyed. And it is of veritie that efter the said Jhone Sibbets returne from her, and efter that his wife {*p. 158*} according to the said Jonets directioune had worne the sark 24 hours and thairefter put it aff, quhairby his wife become hail of her diseas, Immediatlie the said Jhone become distracted in his mynd in suche ane heigh missour[15] that he ceased not until he put hand in himself and stobbed himself in the bellie with ane knife over the head,[16] the occasione quhairof he efterward being sober[17] confessed to be this, that fra the tyme he returned fra the said Jonet Tailyour he fand himself assaulted be evill spirits quho never ceased to tempt him until they moved him to lift up his hand against himself.

The quhilk day Jonet Tailyour being posed[18] gif schoe could tak in hand to heill the said Jhone Sibbet, answered schoe wold gif they wold sett her at libertie, bot had no power to cuire him so long as schoe was in presone, and said further that nothing ails him bot that he sould recover both of his distractioune and wound, quhilk seamed verie incredible, he having put ane knife of sevin inch long over the head in his bellie and no meanes of remead being used, yet according to her predictioune the said {*p. 159*} Jhone is perfitlie recovered not onlie of his distractioune bot also of his wound, and that without cure.

12 'speired at him': asked him.
13 'ridelyvered' (re-delivered): returned.
14 'behuifed': needed.
15 'heigh missour' (high measure): serious way.
16 'over the head': completely, up to the hilt.
17 'sober': sane, not distracted.
18 'posed': asked.

The quhilk day Jonet Tailyour, being accused for laying on the foirsaid seiknes and distractioune upon the said Jhone Sibbet quhairby he was tempted to put his hand in himself, replyed that the said Jhone was distracted and madde befoir he come to her, and offered that gif Effie Mcole quho brocht him to her wold sweir that he was in his richt witts quhen schoe brocht him to her, in that cace schoe sould tak the cryme upon her and be content to suffer death. And it is of veritie that the said Effie Mcole being called and compeirand did solemlie sweir in presens of the brethrein that the man was in his richt witts, and no ways distracted quhen he met with the said Jonet Tailyour.

Efter this the said Jonet Tailyour said that the said Jhone Sibbett promised to me that the charme sould not be hard of nather efter nor befoir, bot since he has done wtherways it maks not, sayd schoe, let him hold him self as he is, the worse now is his awin, Lett God restoir him to his health gif the Devil hes taken it fra him.[19] {*p. 160*}

The quhilk day Elspet Blak in Tillibodie relict of umquhill Jhone Stein fleschour compeirand and accusing the said Jonet Tailyour conserning the charming of her umquhill husband as followes. The said Jonet Tailyour cumming to her husband required of him twa rumples[20] quhairof he gave her one, and becaus the uther was refused her that schoe went away malecontent, quhairupon the said Jhone Stein Immediatlie become seik, and that for his recoverie schoe was sent for againe, at quhilk tyme schoe returned and handled him and did wasche his feit and hands in sowth running water and paired the nailes of his hands and feit and cuist thame in ane south running water, the said Jonet Tailyour being acused heirupon confessed the samyne in all the circumstances of it, and that by this meanes schoe healed him.

The quhilk day Jonet Tailyour being accused Upon the depositioune given in be Margaret Dawsone in Tilliebodie, parochine of Alloway, against her, confessed the samyne, The tenor quharof is as followeth.[21] {*p. 161*}

Margaret Dawsone speired at the said Jonet gif schoe did any gud to James Thomesones cattell in Rhind, for, sayeth schoe, our calfs dieth[22] everie one. The said Jonet granted schoe gart[23] thame live, and caused everie kow to have ane calf, and said to the said Margaret, will ye do the thing that I bid yow, and I sall caus yours live also, and schoe baid her tak ane litle quantitie of beare,[24]

19 Taylor's implication seems to be that the Devil is punishing Sibbet for breaking his promise to her that he would keep the charm secret. She does not mean to imply that she herself has sent the Devil to do so; indeed it could be godly to believe that the Devil would afflict people who had committed sins. Nevertheless, Taylor is on thin ice here.

20 'rumples': rumps or haunches of meat.

21 This paragraph may give the impression that what follows will be Taylor's confession, but it is actually the 'depositioune given in' by Dawson, to which Taylor has merely assented.

22 Altered from 'deeth'.

23 'granted schoe gart': agreed that she caused.

24 'beare': bere, barley.

and of salt, and ane iron naile, and cast it under the first stak we[25] put in the yaird, and then they wold live.

Also the said Jonet Tailyour confesses the depositione following given in be the said Margaret Dawsone against her, to wit, that at New Yeir day thairefter the said Margaret having taken ane heavie seiknes with suche cauld and trembling in the foir night that schoe was not able to live and was powerles both in legges and armes, and in the end of the nicht with sick sweiting as pyned her away, on ane certane day the said Jonet Tailyour come in to her unluiked for, and layd her hands upon her and spake some muttering words quyetlie to her, and being inquired gif it was the gutt[26] that ailed her answered, her diseas was layed upon her but they repented {*p. 162*} that had done it, and that schoe wold mend againe belyve.[27] Efterward the said Margaret Dawsone continowing in her seiknes, the foirsaid Jonet Tailyour come into her againe, and being inquired gif schoe knew quhat ailed her, schoe answred, in gud faith ye ar witched and Barbara Hendersone has done it to yow. Bot gif ye lyk I sall hail yow againe. Ye must bring me in ane coig[28] full of water yourself that I may wasche your hands and your feit thairin, and pair the nailes of your hands and your feit, and so ye sall be hail. Margaret Dawsone refused to do so, continowed seik quhill[29] Barthole day,[30] mynding then to have complained to the minister upon Jonet Tailyour, quhairupon the said Jonet come to her and foirbaid her gang to the minister, saying, gif ye doubt that I have done yow evill sitt doune upon your kneis and seik your health fra me for Gods saik and ye sall be weill, and fra that further the said Margaret Dawsone recovered. The said Jonet Tailyour confesses this depositioune of Margaret Dawsones in all the circumstances of it.

The quhilk day Jonet Tailyour being accused concerning David Davidsoune parochiner of Clakmannan confessed as followes. That schoe said he {*p. 163*} had gotten wrong and bad[e] his mother for remead of it wasche his hands and his feit with water and pair the nailes of his hands and feit, and to mak ane bannock of thame with ane quantitie of meal, and the said Jonet bade cast the water and lay the bannock in ane busche, and he sould be weill, quhilk come to pas.

The quhilk day Jonet Tailyour being accused gif schoe come to Andrew Reas hous in Clakmannan to cuire his bairne that was heavellie diseased, the said Jonet confest schoe come to his hous and caused his wyfe sitt doune on her knies and seik her bairnes health thrys for Gods saik fra her, and that

25 'we': Margaret Dawson and her household. The scribe has preserved this first-person aspect of her testimony.
26 'gutt': gout.
27 'belyve': immediately.
28 'coig': wooden bowl.
29 'quhill': until.
30 'Barthole day': St Bartholomew's day, 24 August.

schoe caused water the bairnes hands and feit with sowth running water, and pair the nailes of the bairnes hands and feit, and to baik ane bannok with the pairings with ane quantitie of meale and to lay the bannock in ane busche, that no bodie sould gett wrong of it.

The said Jonet Tailyour being posed for charmeing of James Hendersounes bairne in Bowhous of Sauchie, the said Jonet confessed as followes. The said Jonet come to the said James Hendersounes hous, and caused his wyfe sitt doune on her knies and seik the bairnes health thryse for Gods saik fra her, and that {*p. 164*} schoe caused water the bairnes hands and feit with south running water, and pair the nailes of the bairnes hands and feit, and to baik ane bannock of the pearings, with ane quantitie of meale, and to lay the bannock in ane busche that no bodie sould gett wrong of it, and presentlie thairefter the bairne her dochter was restoired to her health.

The said Jonet being posed quhether schoe come to William Chalmers bairne in Clakmannan confest as followes, That schoe come to the said William Chalmers bairne to cure him quho was heavilie diseased, and caused wasche him with faire water, and pair the nailes of his hands and feit, and that the said Jonet Tailyour tuik of her awin meale, and baiked ane bannock of it with the pairings of the nailes, and that schoe caused the diseased bairne eat the bannock, quho was the better thairof after the eating of it.

The said Jonet being accused concerning the charmeing of Robert Horne in Sauchie confest as followes, that the said Jonet come to the said Robert Hornes hous and offered to cuire him, quhilk scho did be this meanes, to witt, be straiking the bak of her hand alongst his syd and muttering some words. This schoe did cumming to him thrie sundrie tymes using the foirsaid charme at everie tyme, saying {*p. 165*} I handled the hurtchune I handle yow etc., and efter he convalesced.

The quhilk day Jhone Demperstoune parochiner of Alloway being solemelie sworne deponit against Jonet Tailyour as followes, That Jonet Tailyour said that he had gotten wrong and baid water his feit and pair his nailes, and thairefter tuik some meale and maid ane kast[31] thairof with the pairings of the nailes and the water, and quhen the said Jhone asked quhat scho wold do with it schoe answered and said, I will tak it and lay it at ane thorne ruite, and quhoever gois by it first will gett your seiknes, as also ther the said Jonet affirmed to the said Jhone Demperstounes wyfe, that he was deadlie witched.

The quhilk day James Thomesoune in Rind compeared and being solemelie sworne, deponis concerning Jonet Tailyour that the said Jonet being desyred to cure his calfes, tuik some meale and water, in the quhilk water schoe put ane certaine litle stone quhilk she affirmed mony yeirs ago she brocht it fra the heiland, and having twtchid the water with the stone schoe kneadit the

[31] 'kast' (cast): mould.

meale and water in deache,[32] and cause tak ane litle quantitie of the said daiche, and muile[33] it amongst the calfes meat and they sould live, quhilk they did alslong as thei gott of it, and that quhen the *{p. 166}* said James understud that the said Jonet was ane witche, he caused cast away the daiche and efter it was cast away they died the nixt yeir.

The quhilk day Jonet Tailyour confest that schoe come about twa or thrie yeirs since to Jhone Cowies hous in Harperhill and asked ane thigging[34] of oates and becaus schoe gott over few[35] schoe said schoe sould gar thame rew it, and quhen immediatlie after that thair dochter grew seik, her mother having soucht upon her knies fra the said Jonet her dochters health, that schoe come to the yung woman and paired her nailes and mumbled some words, efter[36] the yung woman mendit.

The quhilk day William Andirsoune in the Grein deponit that becaus he removed the said Jonet Tailyour out of his bounds at the directioune of the minister of Alloway, the said Jonet threatned the said William Andirsone, and said that he sould repent it and all his, and so it come to pas, for ane dochter of the said William Andirsones being ane woman fell immediatlie in ane heavie seiknes and daylie payned away quhile[37] schoe died, and that same nicht that the yung woman died the said Jonet Tailyour come to William Andirsones hous, ane yung bairne being in the cradle, the said Jonet Tailyeour come and rocked the bairne and twitched[38] the bairne, the quhilk efter the *{p. 167}* twitching died immediatlie, and sundrie bairnes of his thairefter.

The said Jonet Tailyour being asked quhy schoe paired the nailes of the feit of some, of thair hands [*sic*], and baiked ane bannock thairof, and not of all, answered that schoe paired the nails of non of these quho wer witched.

The said Jonet Tailyour being asked quhat is the caus that suppone any wther honest man handled the hurtcheon and paired ther nailes, and wasched thair feit and baiked ane bannock thairof with meale as the said Jonet dois, yet notwithstanding they will be nothing the better, Bot gif the said Jonet handle the hurtcheon, pair thair nailes and wasche thair feit and baik ane bannock thairof with meale they will be the better, the said Jonet answered that ye have no charge to do it.

The quhilk day Alexander and Jhone Chrystie parochine of Alloway being sworne to declair quhat they know concerning Jonet Tailyour deponit as followes, that the said Jonet come, and desyred thame to bring her home ane load of coales upon thair hors, quhilk quhen they refused her schoe said schoe

32 'deache' (and later 'daiche'): dough.

33 'muile': crumble.

34 'ane thigging': a small quantity, requested as a gift.

35 'over few': too few.

36 *Sic*. Read 'after which'.

37 'quhile': until.

38 'twitched': touched.

sould mak thame to repent it, and efter this they apprehendit her hinging on the hors mane in thair stable, quhilk hors died within 24 hours thairefter.

The quhilk day Helen Patersoun being solemlie sworne deponit that Jonet Tailyour come to umquhile Agnes Robertsone spous to John Wilsoun at the brigend of Stirling to cure her diseased leggs, and the meanes that schoe usit for the curing of her leggs is the said Jonet souked her meakle[39] toes with her mouth. *{p. 168}*

At Stirling, the first, the twentie and twentie ane days of Februar In presens of the brethren thair assembled

Marioune Mathie Indwellar in Stirling having not onlie thir many yeirs bygane lived under ane publick and constant sclander of witchcraft, but also professed her self to all the commone people both in brughe and Landwart[40] to be ane witche, and able to do thame evill, that be this meanes schoe micht terrifie thame and mak thame out of fear to acknowledge her with thair guds, In the end waxed so insolent that upon just presumptiounes schoe was taken and compeirand [*sic*] befoir the brethrein of the presbyterie to be tryed. Witnessis of gud fame compeired and deponit upon thair oathes as followeth.

In primis it being allegit against her that schoe, rancountering at the Craigmill with Jhone Sibbetts wyfe in the Abbay of Cambuskenneth, sought meall from her, quhilk becaus schoe refused thairfoir schoe layd ane lingring seiknes upon the said wyfe quharby schoe pyned the space of ane yeir and mair and now is dead.

The said Marioune offered to die gif ever schoe mett with Jhone Sibbetts wyfe at the Craigmill or sought any thing fra her. Notwithstanding heirof at the same dyet quhen witnes [*sic*] wer cum in reddie to prove *{p. 169}* against her the said Marione confest that quhilk under the foirsaid penaltie schoe denyed befoir, namelie that schoe came to the Craigmill, and sought meale fra the said Jhone Sibbetts wyfe quhilk she refused her and it is noturlie knawin that her seiknes followed thairupon. Lykas the wther witche Jonet Tailyour affirmes that it way[41] layd on be Marione Mathie.

The quhilk day Christopher Russell merchand in Stirling being sworne concerning Marione Mathie having given ane lettre to be conveyed be him and delyvered to her sone at Londone, and the said Christew having neglected the delyverie thairof, that at his returne the said Marione come to him and speirit gif he had delyvered the lettre to her sone. The said Christew answered the said Marione Mathie and said he knew not whether he delyvered it or not. The said Marion replyed to him, ye nevir sought my sone, my sone is lying seik. Christew answered, how knaw ye that. Marione scho answered, I knaw it weill enewghe. I knaw said Marione quhair the lettre is, it is in your kist in

39 'meakle': large.

40 'in brughe and Landwart': in town and countryside.

41 *Sic*. Read 'was'.

ane bible that ye bought. The said Christew affirmed befoir the bretherein that he knew it not to be in his kist till twentie days after that his kist came from Leith and then he luiked {*p. 170*} his kist and fand the lettre in his kist in the buik that he had coft[42] as the said Marione Mathie said.

Lykways the said Christew Russell deponit that at his nixt fairing to London thairefter, the said Marione said gif it wer not for the companies saik that is with him schoe sould caus him ly in the ground of the sea[43] for his paines, and quhen his father Jhon Russell come to her to quarrell her for that speache and offered[44] to streik her, schoe said, feare not he sall have foule weather and be in great danger bot he sall returne saife, and sa it fell out, for the said Christew Russell deponit that in the same voyage they suffered ane verie tempestuous storme and hardlie escaped schipwrack.

The quhilk day compeired Walter Blakburne wobster in Stirling and being solemlie sworne deponit against Marione Mathew as followeth. That the said Marione being offendit at him for refusing to be cationer for her for twentie punds, by her witchecraft harmed both his sone and himself. As concerning his sone the said Walter deponit that Marione Mathie having rancountered with him and his sone in Jhone Robertsounes hous in Stirling, schoe maid the said Walters sone to gett some water to wasche her hands. The boy said that thair is no cleane {*p. 171*} water in the hous, Marione said it maters not whether it be foule water or cleane, and when the water was brocht to her schoe did wasche her hands into it, and thairefter did cast the water betwix the boyes feit, and thairefter schoe tuik the bairne be the gairdie of the arme,[45] and nipped him quhill he cryed, and immediatlie thairefter he was stricken with ane heavie disease. Efterward the boyes mother come to the said Marione Mathie and desyred her bairnes health fra her or ells schoe wald complene to the judges. The said Marione answered and said, go your ways, the bairne sall be weill, and according heirto the bairne recovered.

Lykways the said Walter deponit that about six weiks thaireftir schoe come to him on the calsay[46] and chopped[47] him on the arme, and within half ane hour thairefter in the same place quhair schoe chopped him on the arme he brak his arme all in schivers, and that ever since the said Walter is trubled with her maleice and in chaising the boy at everie tyme quhen schoe sies him, saying gif schoe gett ane grip of him schoe sall put him from winding[48] of his bread. {*p. 172*}

42 'coft': bought.
43 'in the ground of the sea': on the sea bed.
44 'offered': motioned or threatened.
45 'the gairdie of the arme': the lower arm, below the elbow.
46 'calsay' (causeway): street.
47 'chopped': tapped.
48 'winding' (winning): earning.

The quhilk day compired Jhone Smith in Castellhill with his wyfe Katharein Livingstone and they being solemlie sworne deponit against Marione Mathow as followes, that the said Marione Mathie being in thair hous and offendit at thame becaus the said Katharein Livingstone wald not lend her silver, quhen the said Katharein Livingstoune past to ane chalmer the said Marione tuik her bairne be the gairdie of the arme and nipped him and immediatlie thairefter the bairne was stricken with ane heavie disease, quhilk seiknes made the bairne to ryse at his hart and syds, blowing as it wer ane pair of bellowes.

The said John Smith being sent for be his wyfe to see his bairne die, he speired quho was last in the hous. The servand woman answered and said that Marione Mathie was last in the hous. The said Jhone desyred to send for Marione Mathie to gif her any thing schoe sought, and quhen the said Marione come againe the said Katharein Livingstoune asked her bairnes health thryse for Gods caus fra her, and the said Marione Mathie said to her, your bairne will be weill within ane schort space, and according heirto the bairne recovered within ane hour and ane half and was als weill as ever he was. {*p. 173*}

Lykways the said Jhone Smith deponit as followes as als the said Katharein Livingstone his spous being sworne depones the same, viz. that the said Marione Mathie immediatlie efter having gon to the castell of Stirling quhair schoe ressawed[49] some beif, schoe returned againe to the said Jhone his hous, and quhen the said Katharein Livingstone craved to know quhat was in her aprone, schoe answered, it was beif, lett me alon till I cum to my awin hous, and I sall send yow bak ane peice of it, and that accordinglie the said Marione sent to thair hous ane peice stincking blak evill favored flesche so deformed that they could not understand of quhat kynd it was, and that they sent it bak to her againe, and immediatlie thairefter the said Jhones meare tuik seiknes. He seing his meare seik went doune to the said Marione Mathies hous, and desyred her for Gods caus to help his meare gif schoe could. The said Marione answered, speak not ane word of God, and bad him gang befoir faur hours in the morning and tak his meare in his hand and tak some body with him that is weill harted and foirbade him let ony bodie witt[50] of the doing of it, and lykways forbade him speak to any body quhome he mett and desyred him to keip it quiet, and bade him gang nyne tymes wothersones[51] about William Thomesones yaird in the quhilk thair is ane quaking esp trie,[52] {*p. 174*} and quhen the said Jhone was going the last tyme about the yaird the said Jhone was cast into ane well and wist[53] not how, and had no power to relyve himself along[54] space, nather his brother to help him quho was with him.

49 'ressawed': received.
50 'witt': know.
51 'wothersones' (widdershins): anticlockwise.
52 'quaking esp trie': the aspen, a tree known for its trembling leaves.
53 'wist': knew.
54 *Sic.* Read 'a long'.

The quhilk day Jhone Frissell smith in Stirling compeirand and being solemlie sworne deponit as followes, that about twa yeirs since or thairby he saw oft tymes ane meakle gray cutt tailed catt, horrible in quantitie,[55] resoirting about Marione Mathies yaird and his quhilk lyeth consigne together,[56] and that he told his wyfe that he wold schoote the catt, quhilk schoe repoirted to Marione Mathie. And the said Jhone and his wyfe Elspet Quhytbrow both deponit that Marione Mathie replyed and said, be it far fra him to schoote that catt for it is ane wyfe in the Carss[57] that cumes to visit me to see quhat I am doing.

Lykways the said Jhone Frissell and Elspet Quhytbrow his wyfe as also Sibilla Drummont deponit, that the said Marione Mathie come unto the said Jhone Frissells hous, schoirtlie thairefter, and said that that ugglie gray catt came the nixt night efter the said Jhone had offered to schoot her to the said Mariounes hous, schoe being lying in her bed, and did lye doune upon her and scarted[58] all her breist, the quhilk schoe schew to thame that her breist was all scarted. {*p. 175*}

Lyke ways the said Jhone Frissell and Elspet Quhytbrow deponit that Marione Mathie brocht ane pair of scheitts, and speired gif the said Elspet could tell gif the[y] wer cutted or not, quhilk quhen the said wyfe refused the said Marione replyed to her, I have ane stone in my bosome quhilk can tell me whether they be cutted or not, I sall caus it tell me, and that schoe tuik out the stone and schew it to the said Jhones wyfe quho depones that schoe saw it and that it was ane browne stone.

Item the said Jhone Frissell deponit that upon ane certaine night in his yaird he saw ane visione lyke ane feltered[59] foale quhilk went throughe his hedge to Marione Mathies hous.

The quhilk day Androw Smith Indwellar of Stirling being solemlie sworne deponit that thrie yeir agoe quhen at the command of umquhile James Forrester of Logye his master he was taking away ane midding[60] of mucke that lay befoir her duire, the said Marione did abuse him in such soirt that his master James Forrester did threaten her, and that he hard the said Marione say to James Forrester that for his paines he sould die ane painefuller death nor his father died befoir him, quhilk according thairto fell out, for it is notourly knawne that the said James Forrester schortlie efter contracted ane dwyneing seiknes quhairin efter ane longsome paine he died. {*p. 176*}

55 'quantitie': size.
56 'consigne together': adjacent to each other.
57 The Carse of the Forth was the low-lying land next to the river. Cambus, where Janet Taylor lived, was in this area. Did Mathie have Taylor in mind?
58 'scarted': scratched.
59 'feltered': shaggy.
60 'midding' (midden): dung heap.

Lykas the said Androw deponit that the same hors quhairwith he was leiding the muck immediatlie efter the said Mariounes threatnings wald not work ane turne 40 dayes thairefter bot perpetuallie drank water and wald eat nothing bot that quhilk violently was put in at the mouth, quhairupon the said James did threaten the said Marione to complein to the judges upon her, and at that tyme his hors recowerit and immediatlie he contractit that Lingring seiknes quhairof he died, quhilk was in many things conforme to the hors seiknes and was judged be all takin aff the hors and laid on upon [*sic*] him.

Lykways the said Andro depones lyk as Robert Cunynghame servant to Androw Alexander being solemlie sworne deponit as followes, that quhen they were going on a certaine tyme to the Inche of Tillibodie to tak furth some hors, they rancountered with the said Marione at the head of the Marie Wynd in Stirling and that they did rune thairefter as fast as they could that so they micht be at the Inche befoir the sea overflowed it, yit they fand the said Marione at the Craigmill befoir thame meiting thame in the way quhilk was impossible to be done be ane ordinar motioune, and that the said Marione said to thame, God speid yow bot the Devill speid some of your companie, and quhen the said Androw Smith said, fals lowne[61] I know thow meanes be me, the said Marione answered, {*p. 177*} thow sall get ane evill foot or[62] thow cume home, I hoip thow sall be hanged in thy awin horshelter,[63] quhilk indied was litle better for in taking of the hors quha had bein always tame and rewlie[64] befoir, the hors ran violentlie upon him, trod him among his feit and trampled on his craig[65] so that verie hardlie his lyfe was preservit.

The quhilk day Helen Patersoune compeirand and being solemlie sworne, deponit that Marione Mathie gave her ane peast,[66] and bade her lay it under her bed, the quhilk quhen schoe did, ane doge of hir maisters tuik the peast from under her bed and eat it, and efter the eating of it the doge rane wode[67] and within aught dayes drowned himself in ane dube.[68]

Item the said Helen deponit that Marione Mathie gave to her ane long small gray stone to lay under Jhone Wilsone her maisters bedhead that be this meanes he might be moved to marie the said Helen Patersoune, bot the said Helen did not use the meanes Marione Mathie gave her, bot gave her the stone againe.

61 'lowne': scoundrel.
62 'or' (ere): before.
63 'horshelter' (horse halter): horse harness.
64 'rewlie' (ruly): well-behaved.
65 'craig': neck.
66 'peast': paste or dough.
67 'wode': mad.
68 'dube': pool.

Source 2: Stirling Council Archives, Minutes of Burgh Court of Stirling, 1627–1633, SBC/37/1/12.

{*p. 236*} At Stirling the 23 Martii 1633
The quhilk day Thomas Craigingelt of that Ilk ane of the shireff deputts of the shirrefdome of Stirling, Thomas Bruce proveist of the burgh thairof, Walter Cowane, David Stevinsone, James Fotheringhame and John Squyar, baileis of the same, justices in that part[69] be our soverane Lords commissioun under his majesties signett of the daitt the nynteine day of Marche Instant for ministrating justice upon Jonet Tailyer in Cambus and Marioun Mathie in Stirling, dilaitt and apprehendit for witchecraft sorcerie, prowyding as the commissioun beirs,[70] Creatt Edward Forrester nottar clerk deputt of the said shirrefdome of Stirling and John Robene commoune clerk of the said burgh of Stirling in clerks commonlie,[71] William Ronald and William Wallace, Messrs Patrik Chrystie and John Huittoune in officiars and serjands, commonlie and severallie, and John Forrester in Dempster, and John Adamsone nottar in procurator fiscall, for all courts to be haldine in the said matter. All and ilk ane of the said persons being present maid faith *de fideli administratione*[72] as use is.

Source 3: Stirling Council Archives, Minutes of Presbytery of Stirling, 1627–1640, CH2/722/5.

{*p. 180*} At Stirling the 3. the 4. and the 10 days of Aprile 1633 in presens of the brethrein thair assembled

The quhilk day Helen Keir in Saquhey in the parische of Clakmannan being delaited for witchecraft be Jonet Tailyeour (quho confessed her self to be ane witche and suffered for it) being also suspect of witchecraft for the space of xxx yeirs and upon wther {*p. 181*} great presumptiounes was in presence of Mr Henrye Guthrie minister at Stirling, Mr Jhone Craigingelt minister at Alloway, Mr Jhone Galbryth minister at Bothkennar, Mr James Spens minister at Avah[73] and Mr Edward Wright minister at Clakmannan, confronted with the said Jonet Tailyour the day of her Impannelling befoir the sentence of assise past against her, the quhitche Jonet having given evident tokens of her repentance, by a frie and cleir confessione of her sinne of witchecraft did constantlie avow in the face of the said brethren that schoe was lykways guiltie of that same cryme of witchecraft, and that the said Helen had done great skaith[74] to sindrie by casting thame in seiknes with her sorceries quhairof the

69 'justices in that part': judges in that case (i.e. the specified case of Taylor and Mathie).
70 In margin: 'Creatioune and aithes of the members of court anent the Witches'.
71 'commonlie': jointly.
72 'concerning the faithful exercise' (of their office).
73 'Avah': Alva.
74 'skaith': harm.

said Jonet had cured many. And particularlie Jonet avowed that Helen had killed Robert Hornes horses and laid diseas on him self, had done skaith to Jhone Melvines cattell and guids, and harmed Jhone Hallye in his persoune and bestiall, and being inquyred be the foirsaid ministers how schoe knew the Inchantments to cum from Helen rather then from ane wther, answered that schoe had learned that her charmes wald not profeit till thair name was named that had laid on the disease, {*p. 182*} for schoe ever Inquyred at the diseased persoune quhome they suspected and caused name sundrie ever quhill the charme wrocht.[75] Sicklyke the said Jonet efter schoe was condemned and at the stack to be executed being posed on her conscience by Mr Henry Guthrie gif that was trew quhilk schoe had befoir avowed of Helen Keir answered on her salvation all was trew.

The quhilk day compeired Robert Hall in Sauchie and being solemlie sworne deponit that upon ane tyme he being desyred by the Laird of Sauchie[76] to tak her gud sone[77] Alexander Dempsterstoune to the warres quhilk he did, for the quhilk the said Helen promised him ane evill turne for it, and thairefter he found himself fyve hundereth merkis the worse, and siclyk to his gudsone for schooting[78] her out of the Lairdes barne promesed him ane evill turne and thairefter ane kow and ane yung oxe stirk[79] died within ane moneth of his gudsones and schortlie efter his gudsone contracted the diseas of the oxe and kow, and died thairof quhilk was betuix Mertimes and Yuile, and quhen his gudsone was deing he layed his death upon her and commonlie said, o that theif is rosting me now.

The quhilk day compeired Jhone Hallie in Sauchie and being solemlie sworne deponit {*p. 183*} that quhen he was hyne[80] to Sauchie he poyndit[81] hir hors, and that the said Helen promesed to caus him rw [*sic*] it and within twentie dayes thairefter he contracted ane heavie diseas quhilk Jonet Tailyour offered to cure quho was brunt at Stirling for witchecraft the iii day of Aprile 1633. And going fra the pleughe with his aix upon his arme his hors skarred, and for fear to learne the hors ane gaid[82] the hors not being used to skar he slang the aix fra him thrie rigges breadth and stak[83] be the hors ane long

75 'caused name sundrie ever quhill the charme wrocht': she got the diseased person to name several names in turn, until the charm succeeded (the point being that it would succeed when the person who had laid on the disease was named).

76 Sir James Shaw of Sauchie.

77 A 'gudsone' is usually a son-in-law, and this may be the meaning here also. However, since Alexander Dempsterton has the same surname as Keir's husband, he may be Keir's stepson.

78 'schooting': shoving.

79 'stirk': ox or cow between one and two years old.

80 'hyne': farm servant.

81 'poyndit' (impounded): legally confiscated.

82 'learne the hors ane gaid': allow the horse to learn a trick.

83 'stak': stuck, remained.

tyme, and being forced to leave the hors he lichted upon the aix,[84] and yet beareth the mark, quhilk Jonet Tailyeour sayes Helen laid upon him.

And withall deponit that having takin ane aiker of land that her husband was wont to occupie, efter that he had tilled it and sowin it schoe come and and [*sic*] rowed[85] up and downe the land lyk ane daft bodie and promesed the land sould never do him gud, and so he fand no gud of it and sicklyk the meare that laboured it died within ane schoirt space.

The quhilk day compeired Robert Horne in Sauchie and being solemlie sworne deponit, that about two yeir bygaine schoe come to his stable quhair he was and desyred twa pocks of draf[86] quhilk he promesed {*p. 184*} and seiking ane peck[87] to missour it with in divers howses schoe told that schoe wald get na peck in that nightbours hous, how know ye that said the said Robert to the said Helen, scho answered I knaw weill eneughe, and thairefter his horses refuised thair meat and died, and lykways upon ane sabbath day in tyme of divine serveice being in his hous cursed him diverse tymes becaus he called her ane witche, and prayed that non of his guds, wyfe nor bairnes sould thryve with him, and his bairne died so it fell out so it fell out [*sic*], for bringing home his malt he assayed ane and thairefter ane wther and could not gett home his malt, and so tryed all his horse and they could do nothing for him nor his wyfe, the said Robert Horne had ten horses and meares deid within two yeirs. And thairefter he going to the mill, the said Helen Keir com running to him and speired how his skabbed beasts did and threatned to do him ane evill turne, and that same syd that the said Helen met him upon[88] he contracted ane heavie diseas that same nicht quhilk remained with him sax weiks, quhairof he was cured be Jonet Tailyeour quho affirmed both befoir her[89] condemnatorie sentence and at her executioune that the said Helen layed it on. {*p. 185*}

The quhilk day compeired Adame Morris in Sauchie deponit [*sic*] that about one and twentie yeir since, he saw Helen Keir cum out of her awin hous upon Pasche[90] day be the greik of the sone[91] in the morning come to ane grein know head,[92] her hair about hir eyes, her coat about her schoulders, and went thryse wethersones about, and went to hir hows againe.

The quhilk day compeired Johne Stirling in Sauchie deponit [*sic*] that efter Helen Keir being taken upon the penult day of Merche the said Helen in the morneing said to Jhone Stirling, Jhone ye ar Robert Hornes nichtbour, deall

84 'lichted upon the aix': stepped on the axe.
85 'rowed': rolled, wandered.
86 'pocks of draf': bags of draff (residue from brewing, used as fodder).
87 'peck': measuring container for a peck (an amount of grain).
88 'that same syd that ... Helen met him upon': the same side (of his body) that Helen had approached.
89 'death' has been crossed out here.
90 'Pasche': Easter.
91 'greik of the sone': sunrise.
92 'ane grein know head': the top of a green knoll or hillock.

thairfoir with him that he may go bak of the things he hes said of me. Siclyk speaking of Jonet Tailyeour, and of that conference that was betuix thame at the ortchard syd of Sauchie, Helen said that Jonet Tailyour wald never tell the thing that was spoken thair for all the world.

The quhilk day Robert Condie deponit that he hard James Dempstertoune Helens husband say that Robert McCole Helens gudsone hard ane great rumbling all nicht in her hous. Schoe answered gif I had bein als wyse as I am auld I sould have had it sattled befoir Robert McCole raiked his eyne.[93] {*p. 186*} Sicklyk her husband said to her, I dar not go in to Stirling with yow, for I fear the ministers will gar me grant,[94] for ye Ladie had almost caused me grant yesternight at supper, schoe answered schoe sould not confes for all the lords of the world.

Sicklyk it being said to her that Robert Hornes dittay wold be her greatest dittay, schoe answered, gif I had witten[95] it I sould have given him seing[96] witchecraft that all the world may sie it, the quhilk the said Helen confessed.

The quhilk day Alexander Michie being sworne deponit that Helen Keir cumming to his hous did seik some fische that was hinging, and being denyed unto her the said Helen said, gif ye will not give me some gif thame to fodds[97] your dochter, quhilk dochter Immediatly thairefter fell deadlie seik, and his wyfe come to Helen Keir with ane drawin knyfe threatning her gif schoe restoired not her bairne to her health (quho sought her bairnes health thryse for Gods caus) that schoe wald kill her, and thairefter Helens dochter went and twitched the bairne quho was immediatlie cuired.

The quhilk day James Hall in Sauchie being sworne deponit that he having ane bairne {*p. 187*} deadlie seck, he went about ten hours at evin about Helen Keir quho come to his hous, and having applyed some herbs to the bairne schoe carried him all night in her armes betuix her paps[98] betuix twa spence[99] duires and muttered some words, and thairefter the the [*sic*] bairne recovered within ane day or twa for the quhilk he gave twa pecks of meall at twa tymes.

The quhilk day compeired Jhone Gilmoir in Alloway and being sworne deponit, that neifering[100] ane kow with ane hors with Helens gudman the said Helen being discontent with Jhone Gilmoir said that his guds would thryve all the worse, and thairefter within ane yeir sewin horses died.

93 'raiked his eyne': let his eyes wander.
94 'gar me grant': make me admit or confess.
95 'witten': known.
96 *Sic*. Possibly an error for 'such'.
97 *Sic* (or possibly 'sodds'). Possibly an error for 'feed', or a miscopying of the daughter's name.
98 'paps': breasts.
99 'spence': storeroom, pantry.
100 'neifering': bartering.

The quhilk day Jhone Mealing in Sauchie being sworne deponit, that thair fell ane therten[101] betuix him and Helen Keir and ever since thairefter he had ane great decay of his guds and geir.

The quhilk day compeired Robert Michie in Sauchie and being solemlie sworne deponit that Helen Keir cumming to the coale hill[102] and taking some coales fra the said Robert, the said Robert teymed her poik[103] quhairupon Helen threatned to do him ane {*p. 188*} evill turne, and thairefter within xxiiii hours he fell heavellie seik quhilk he induired for the space of xiiii weiks duiring whiche tyme Robert fearing her he come to the hellew[104] toune of Sauchie, and drew ane whinger[105] to her and threatned to kill her gif schoe restoired not his health to him. Schoe desyred him to give her ane choppein[106] of aile, quhilk he doing, quhill they wer drinking in comes Helens husband, quhairat Helen chaiffed and fumed and curst him for so doing and desyred Robert to cume to her the morne at ten houres quhilk he did not, bot efter ane schort tyme on ane Sonday on the morning he met her on the rigge head meadow and being so deserted did gif her the first salutatione thryse and sought his health from her for Gods caus thryse on his knies, and thairefter that Sooneday he fand himself recovered, and the said Helen said gif ye be not the better of this cume to me upon Tuysday.

The quhilk day compeired Robert Horne in Parkmill in Alloway and being solemlie sworne deponit that the said Helen and her husband having sauld ane kow to Mungow Dow and having {*p. 189*} ressaived the money the said Mungo cumming to ressaive the kow Helen upon no conditione wald suffer the kow to cum away. Quhairupon Mungo being advysed to lett her be for that day till the morne did so, and cam on the morne, tuik Helen and her husband to ane hostage[107] to drink quhilk quhill they wer doing ane of Helens nightbours advysed Mungo to slip furth and to tak the kow away without her knowledge, the quhilk he did, quhairat Helen efter cuming and finding the kow away and being inraiged used many dispytfull speitches, and Mungo so soone as he had taken home the kow at milking of her they got nothing bot blude and worsume,[108] quhiche Mungo finding sent for the said Helen and desyred the kowis milk fra her for Gods saik, and Helen no suner haveing put her hands to milk her bot scho drew gud

101 'therten': threatening.
102 'coale hill': coal heap.
103 'teymed her poik': emptied her bag.
104 *Sic.* Possibly the scribe should have written 'the said Helen's'.
105 'whinger': dagger.
106 'choppein': mug.
107 'hostage': hostelry, inn.
108 'worsume': pus.

milk from her, bot so soone as schoe depairted schoe gave againe blud and worsume als long as schoe was in his aught.[109]

The quhilk day compeired William Watt in Tellicoulltrie and being solemlie sworne deponit having coft ane kow fra Helens husband in Helens absence he tuik the kow home with him {*p. 190*} and for the space of twa thrie days the kow gave her milk verie peaceablie bot thairefter Helen cumming ever to his byre quhair schoe drew on her hoise,[110] and saying to him gif ye delyver not the money to me the kow sall do yow no gud. He thairefter delyvering the money to her husband fand the kow so far altered that schoe became altogedder untame sa that they could gett no milk drawin fra her in peace bot was forced to lett her go yeild.[111]

The quhilk day compeired William Muire in Sauchie and being solemlie sworne deponit that Helen Keir about thrie quarters of ane yeir since come to his hous upon ane Tysday and gave to ane of his bairns twa apples and bade the bairne eat the ane and play with the wther quhilk the bairne did and thairefter the bairnes parents seiking the aple the bairne played her with all[112] they culd not find it, and the bairne efter that it eat the wther aple never eat maire bot died upon the Saturday nixt thairefter. {*p. 191*}

The quhilk day compeired Thomas Cousing wobster and cuik in Sauchie and being solemlie sworne deponit that he being making ane feast in Androw Orroches hous, Helen Keir cuming to that hous, and seiking some of the meat from him that was in his hands, he refuising Helen said schoe would do him als great ane tort,[113] and within 48 hours he tuik ane fearfull diseas quhilk all bodie called the falling seiknes,[114] and having informatioune that thair was ane Jonet Menteath in Alvah that could cuir him he sent for her, and thairefter schoe be her charmes cuired him, and told him that he saw thame everie day that layd the seiknes upon him, and thairefter within ane yeir being making ane feast in William Jamesounes hous the said Helen cuming thair the said Thomas called her ane witche, and Immediatlie thairefter he fell in his former diseas quhairof he was cuired again be the said Jonet Menteath the quhilk diseas he had never befoir nor efter.

The quhilk day compeired Alexander Cousing wobster in Sauchie, and being solemlie sworne deponit that having ane bairne to be spened[115] and having ane mynd to gif it to Helen Keir about Mertimes[116] last thairefter he

[109] 'aught': possession.
[110] 'hoise' (hose): stockings.
[111] 'yeild': barren, giving no milk.
[112] 'the aple the bairne played her with all': the other apple with which the child played.
[113] 'tort': wrong. This was a technical term from English law, and may not have been current in Scottish popular discourse.
[114] 'falling seiknes': epilepsy.
[115] 'spened': weaned.
[116] 'Mertimes': Martinmas, 11 November.

changed {*p. 192*} his mynd and gave her not the bairne, quhairupon Helen handling the bairne, thairefter the bairne fell deadlie seik for the space of ten weiks, and bringing Jonet Tailyeour the said Jonet cuired the bairne be her charmes and said that Helen was the caus of it and gave lykways charge that Helen Keir sould not sie the bairne in the face.

18. ELIZABETH BATHGATE, EYEMOUTH, 1633–1634

INTRODUCTION

Elizabeth Bathgate lived in the small coastal town of Eyemouth in Berwickshire. Her husband, Alexander Pae, was a maltman, and the couple seem to have been comfortably off, lending money and employing more than one servant. She was caught up in a local witchcraft panic in 1633, but achieved a narrow escape in her 1634 trial with the aid of a supportive husband and effective lawyers. Her case reveals much about community interactions and about sophisticated legal argument.

The Eyemouth panic began in the summer of 1633, and gathered momentum in the autumn with accusations against Agnes Allanshaw, Agnes Wilson, Alison Wilson, Elspeth Wilson and Katherine Wilson. The privy council granted a commission of justiciary for their trial on 26 November 1633, with the commissioners including John Ramsay of Edington, sheriff depute of Berwickshire.[1] Elizabeth Bathgate's own trial record tells us that the confessions of Agnes Wilson and Alison Wilson named Isobel Sinclair, and Bathgate herself, as fellow-witches.[2] On 9 December, the two Wilsons were made to 'confront' Sinclair and Bathgate, and the Wilsons declared that Sinclair and Bathgate had been with them at the sinking of George Huldie's ship by witchcraft. A

1 Louise A. Yeoman (ed.), 'Witchcraft Cases from the Register of the Privy Council of Scotland, 1630–1642', *SHS Miscellany*, vol. xiii (Edinburgh: SHS, 2004), 223–65, at p. 252.

2 Bathgate's dittay provides further information about these and other recent Eyemouth witches. We learn that Agnes Wilson, Alison Wilson and Elspeth Wilson were executed. Her dittay also mentions William Mearns, who committed suicide in prison not long before the prosecution of Allanshaw and the four Wilsons in 1633, and Margaret Bellany ('Balleine'), Agnes Falconer, Janet Liddell, Janet Williamson and Christian Wilson, who had all been prosecuted during a previous panic in Eyemouth in 1629. Bellany was even said to have named Bathgate as a witch in 1629, though no action seems to have been taken against her at that date. To these names should be added William Wemyss, another suspect in 1633, mentioned in the Survey of Scottish Witchcraft. There were also further suspects in 1629.

commission of justiciary for the trial of Isobel Sinclair would be granted on 14 January 1634.[3] But Elizabeth Bathgate proved to be harder to deal with.

The prosecutors imprisoned Bathgate in the tolbooth of Duns, the head burgh of Berwickshire. The leaders of her prosecution were Sir Patrick Home of Ayton and John Home, minister of Eyemouth, who were part of the team that had driven forward the prosecutions so far.[4] Quite possibly the Homes hoped to torture her with sleep deprivation; there was mention at her trial of testimony that had been gathered during the previous 'watching' of Agnes Wilson.

However, Bathgate's husband, Alexander Pae, acted promptly. On 16 December he complained to the privy council, alleging malice and false imprisonment; the council duly summoned the two Homes to appear before them.[5] On 9 January 1634 both Pae and John Home appeared before the council, with Pae claiming that all Bathgate's neighbours recognised her innocence and that her imprisonment was malicious. This did not persuade the council of Bathgate's innocence, but it did persuade them to remove the case from the Homes' hands. Sir Patrick Home was ordered to bring Bathgate to Edinburgh, where she should be imprisoned in the Edinburgh tolbooth and then tried before the central court of justiciary.[6]

Pae's prompt intervention had considerably improved his wife's prospects. The Homes would no longer be able to torture Bathgate into confessing; they would have to rely on the evidence of neighbours, plus the statements of previous confessing witches against her. The Homes had also been deprived of the possibility of obtaining a commission of justiciary that would have enabled them to hold the trial themselves. Moreover, in the Edinburgh court of justiciary, Bathgate would be defended by three professional advocates.

The trial opened formally on 11 February 1634, the date that the council had set in December, but the Homes sought a postponement, blaming the winter weather for delays in assembling witnesses. At some point they had obtained a commission authorising them to summon witnesses to Duns and to record their testimony there, a procedure about which Alexander Pae complained on 27 February. The council did not stop this gathering of evidence, but it did order that all witnesses would have to appear in person at the trial itself if their evidence was to be taken into account.[7] The trial was postponed on 11 February and again on 11–12 March. This second postponement was at the

3 Yeoman (ed.), 'Witchcraft Cases', 253. This commission was also for the trial of Henry Hoggart, another of the accused witches of 1633; he was not mentioned in Bathgate's case.

4 John Ramsay of Edington, mentioned above, acted along with the two Homes as an 'informer' in Bathgate's case, and there were several family relationships among the various Homes and probably others. The two Homes themselves had been active in the 1629 panic in Eyemouth, and had also taken part in the confrontation of 9 December 1633.

5 *RPC*, 2nd ser., v, 572.

6 *RPC*, 2nd ser., v, 176–7.

7 *RPC*, 2nd ser., v, 605–6.

demand of Bathgate's defence team, who protested that they had received a copy of the dittay, listing the charges against her, only the night before. The judges ordered a longer postponement this time, to 4 June. On this day, after six months in prison, Elizabeth Bathgate was finally brought to trial.

The proceedings in the trial are of much interest because the 'pleadings' – the legal arguments for and against each one of the accusations – were conducted in writing and minuted in full. The three defence advocates, Laurence McGill, David Primrose and Alexander Burnett, made a variety of objections to the dittay's eighteen numbered accusations, to which the prosecution replied in its turn, also in writing.[8] Sometimes the defence 'duplyed' with further arguments.

The lack of a confession, and the presence of aggrieved neighbours, meant that most of the accusations concerned malefice rather than demonic witchcraft. There were a few mentions of Bathgate's participation in previous witches' meetings and conspiratorial malefices, in which demonological ideas like shape-shifting appeared. The defence team used demonology to make several arguments about the difference between real witchcraft and the innocent practices of their client. For instance, real witches have no pity; real witches raise storms; real witches may be 'sene fleing lyke crawis, ravens or uther foulis'; and the Devil has 'hornes and clawes' as he is 'prented or represented in comedies or playes'. This last point seems to be a deliberate trivialisation of demonology. The defence could have cited a serious demonologist like Martin Delrio on the Devil's appearance – various other Scottish lawyers cited Delrio – but they chose instead to imply that the Devil belonged in a comedy or play.[9]

Some of the arguments were about the facts of the case. For instance, the defence argued that the death of a young girl had been caused, not by witchcraft, but by her father falling on top of her. The defence could not bring its own witnesses, because the law at the time assumed that it was solely up to the prosecution to prove its case, but the defence could and did 'offer' to prove alternative facts.

There were also arguments about law and procedure. These included arguments about whether certain facts, even if agreed, were sufficient to prove the crime of witchcraft. Bathgate had been seen turning anticlockwise ('widdershins', an ominous direction) in a mill, and was said to have a horseshoe inside her door; were these witchcraft or not? There were arguments about the nature of proof: who had actually witnessed an alleged event? Several of the charges were supported, not by an eyewitness, but by someone else who had been told about the event – effectively hearsay evidence; was this acceptable?

[8] More research could be conducted on defence advocates. McGill and Primrose had also defended Isobel Young in 1629: S. I. Gillon and J. I. Smith (eds.), *Selected Justiciary Cases, 1624–1650*, 3 vols. (Edinburgh: Stair Society, 1954–74), i, 96.

[9] Delrio had written of the Devil at the sabbat that 'His appearance is terrifying, almost always that of a male goat or a dog': Martín Del Rio, *Investigations into Magic*, ed. and trans. P. G. Maxwell-Stuart (Manchester, 2000), 92 (bk. 2, q. 16).

The defence repeatedly objected to such evidence, also asserting that a single witness to an event was insufficient. There were arguments about the status of these witnesses: were they 'prosecutors' or 'informers', for instance?

These arguments were conducted in two phases: before and after the swearing-in of the assize. In the first phase, the defence argued point by point against the 'relevance' of each of the articles of the dittay, hoping to convince the judge to rule them irrelevant. They had a good deal of success in this. Of the eighteen articles, the judge ruled seven of them relevant, three of them relevant with limitations, and eight of them irrelevant. The assize was then sworn in, and the articles of the dittay that remained relevant were evidently read to them (though this was not minuted). The prosecution produced a series of witnesses to prove each article, the witnesses' oral statements were minuted, and the written arguments between prosecution and defence were resumed.

Some of the witnesses confirmed their accusations, but others actually undermined the prosecution's case. George Sprott denied that he had witnessed the alleged events, while John Gray 'wald not tak it upoun his conscience that his bairne deit be witchcraft or sorcerie'. Margaret Home admitted that she herself had caused the death of her ox, and that 'gif utheris had not persewit the pannell [i.e. Bathgate] for witchcraft' then she would never have blamed her. Other pieces of evidence turned out merely to be hearsay. Such testimony, plus the articulate defence arguments throughout the trial, may have been what convinced a majority of the assize. In the end, they returned a verdict of not guilty.

TEXT

Source: NRS, Court of Justiciary, Books of Adjournal, 1631–1637, JC2/7.[10]

{fo. 148v.} Curia Justiciarie Supremi Domini Nostri Regis Tenta in pretorio de Edinburgh undecimo Februarii 1634 per Magistrum Alexandris Colvile.[11]

Anent the dyet appointit be directioun of the lordis of his majesteis secreit counsall be vertew of thair lordships act daittit the[12] nynt day of Januar last bypast For persewing befoir his maisteis justice and his deputis this day and place off Elizabeth Bathcatt spous to Alexander Pae maltman in Eymouth For certane allegit crymes of sorcerie and witchcraft set doun in hir dittay.

10 A summary of much of the text below has been published in G. F. Black (ed.), *Some Unpublished Scottish Witchcraft Trials* (New York, 1941), 14–19. A briefer summary was published in *Spottiswoode Society Miscellany*, vol. ii, ed. James Maidment (Edinburgh: Spottiswoode Society, 1845), 64–6.

11 'Court of justiciary of our sovereign lord the king, held in the tolbooth of Edinburgh, 11 February 1634, by Mr Alexander Colville.'

12 'xix' crossed out here.

The said Elizabeth Bathcat compeirand personallie and being presentit upone pannall be the bailyeis of Edinburght as being wardit within thair tolbuith keipit and detenit thairintil be warrand and directioun of the saidis lordis of secreit counsall quhill[13] scho war tryit of the saidis crymis, As also with hir the said Alexander Pae hir husband compeirand togidder with Mr Laurence McGill, Mr David Prymrois and Mr John Rollok advocattis hir prelocutors, Quha producet the saidis lordis act of secreit counsall off The dait above writtin[14] Appointing and assigneing this ellevint day of Februar instant For hir persute and tryell befoir his majesteis justice and his deputtis for the crymes of sorcerie and witchcraft above writtin, Quhairof the said Elizabeth affirmet hir selff to be altogidder innocent And for tryell thairoff Accoirding to the saidis lordis of secreit counsall thair act and ordinance above specifiet willinglie offerit hirselff to the tryell of the law for all maner of crymes of sorcerie and witchcraft that can be laid to hir charge be ony pairtie quhatsomevir, disassenting simplie to all forder continuation on the ane pairt; And on the uthir pairt Sir Thomas Hope of Craighall knyght barronet advocat to our souerane lord for his hieness intreis compeirand also judiciallie as persewar declairit that be reasone of this tempestuous seasone of the year and foulenes of the wadder Nane of the persones dilaiteris of the said Elizabeth of the crymes foirsaidis nor yit the witnessis to be producet be thame for verificatioun of the dittay war hable to travell to keip this dayis dyet. Desyret thairfoir the justice that the said Elizabeth hir exact and laufull tryell mycht be delayit and continewit to the ellevint day of Marche nixtocum quhairby his lordships informeris and upgevearis of hir said dittay agains hir, togidder with the witnessis and persones to be summoned upone hir assyse, may the mair convenientlie travell, And scho that day to underly hir laufull tryell for the saidis crymes. The Justice Continewis the said Elizabeth hir tryell to the said ellevint day of Merche nixtocum, And ordanit the pannel to be returnet to hir waird be the bailyeis of Edinburgh To remaine thairin quhill the said day of hir tryell Quhairupone my lord advocat askit instrumentis. To the whilk continuatioun the said Elizabeth altogidder disassentit And for tryell and cleiring of hir innocence offerit to find sufficient cautioun actit in the buikis of adjournall That scho sould nocht remove furth of the burgh of Edinburgh Bot to compeir personallie the said ellevint day of Marche nixtocum befoir his majesteis justice and his deputies in the hour of caus To underly the law within the tolbuth of the said burgh for the saids allegit crymis under sic panes It sould pleis my lord justice to set doun, Scho alwayis being fre and relevit furth of the said waird, And thairupone askit actis and instrumentis....[15] {*fo. 154r.*}

13 'quhill': until.

14 In margin: 'Elizabeth Bathcat in Eymouth. Continewit to the xi of Marche nixt hir tryell for sorcerie contenit in hir dittay'.

15 Alexander Pae, Bathgate's husband, made a further complaint to the privy council about this postponement, though without success: *RPC*, 2nd ser., v, 593–4.

Intran eodem undecimo Martii 1634.[16]

Elspeth Bathcat the spous of Alexander Pae maltman in Eymouthe, dilaitit of dyverss poyntis of Sorcerie and witchcraft contenit in hir dittay.[17]

Persewaris
Sir Thomas Hope of Craighall Knyght barronet
advocat to our souerane lord for his hienes intereis
Sir Thomas Hope advocat his lordships sone
Mr John Oliphant advocat
substitutis to his majesteis advocat

Sir Patrik Home of Aytoun
John Ramsay of Edingtoun
Mr John Home minister of Eymouth
Informeris to his majesteis advocat

Prelocutors in defence
Mr Laurence McGill
Mr David Prymrois
Mr Alexander Burnet
advocattis

My lord advocat producet the dittay with the lettres of assyse and executiones thairof and desyret proces.

It is allegit be the pannell that the coppie ressavit be hir and delyverit be hir persewaris Is disconforme to the principall dittay producet in dyvers articles thairof And thairfoir na proces unles thay had delyverit ane autentik coppie of the said dittay and scho wairnit to answeir thairto upone xv dayis warning.

It is answerit be the persewaris that thair is no difference betuix the dittay producet and the coppie delyverit to the pannell *in substancialibus*[18] bot allanerlie in certane circumstances amplifeing the pannellis crymes specifeit thairin.

The justice continewis this dyet to the morne the xii instantio And ordains the pannell to be taine bak to waird to remane thairin And in the meane tyme scho and hir prelocutors to haif ane just coppie of hir dittay and haill articles and circumstances sett doun thairintill. The assyse warnit *Apud acta*.[19]

16 'Entered the same, 11 March 1634'.
17 In margin: 'Continewit to the xii of March instant'.
18 'in matters of substance'.
19 'in open court'.

Curia Justiciarie Supremi Domini Nostri Regis Tenta in pretorio de Edinburgh duo decimo March 1634 Per magistros Alexandrum Colvile et Jacobum Robertoun Justiciarios deputatos.[20]

Intran
Elizabeth Bathcatt spous to Alexander Pae maltman in Eymouthe.[21]
Dilaitit of the crymes of sorcerie contanit in hir dittay.

Persewaris
Sir Thomas Hope of Craighall Knyght barronet
his Majesties advocat for his hienes intreis
Sir Thomas Hope younger his lordships sone
Mr Johnne Oliphant
substitutes to his majesties advocat

Sir Patrik Home of Aytoun
Johne Ramsay of Edingtoun
Mr Johne Home minister
Informeris to his Majesteis advocat

It is alleget as of befoir be the pannellis Prelocutoris That the dyet may be continewit to ane fyftene dayis becaus thay ressavit bot the coppie of the dittay yister nyght in the evening conteining nyntene or tuentie severall articles quhairunto thay ar nocht as yit throuchlie advyset nor prepairet to answer.

The Justice of consent of ather partie continewis this dyet to the fourt day of Junii nixtocum And ordains the pannel to be tane bak to waird to the tolbuth of Edinburgh Thairin to remane in the meane tyme And gif ony thing sall be eikkit[22] to hir dittay Ordains hir prelocutors to haif the autentik doubill of that quhilk sall be additt thairto to the effectis thay may be advyset thairwith fyftene dayis preceiding the said fourt of Junii nixtocum.... {*fo. 160r.*}

Curia Justiciarie Supremi Domini Nostri Regis Tenta in pretorio de Edinburgh Quarto Junii 1634 Per magistros Alexandrum Colvile de Blair et Jacobum Robertoun advocatum Justiciarios deputatos.[23]

20 'Court of justiciary of our sovereign lord the king, held in the tolbooth of Edinburgh, 12 March 1634, by Masters Alexander Colville and James Roberton, justice deputes.'

21 In margin: 'Continewit to the fourt day of Junii nixt'.

22 'eikkit': added.

23 'Court of justiciary of our sovereign lord the king, held in the tolbooth of Edinburgh, 4 June 1634, by Masters Alexander Colville of Blair and James Roberton, justice deputes'. The minutes do not indicate how the two justice deputes divide up their duties, but later it is implied that a single judge is presiding.

Intran
Elizabethe Bathcat spous to Alexander Pae maltman in Eymouthe.[24]

Dilaitit of dyvers poyntis of sorcerie and witchcraft contenit in hir dittay under writtin.

Persewaris
Sir Thomas Hope of Craighall knyght baronet advocat to our souerane lord for his hienes intreis
Mr Johne Oliphant advocat his Lordships substitute

Prelocutors in defence
Mr Laurence McGill
Mr David Prymrois
Mr Alexander Burnet
advocattis
Alexander Pae hir husband

My lord advocat producet the dittay conteining 18 severall articles quhairof the tenour followis. Elizabeth Bathcat spous to Alexander Pae maltman in Eymouth Ye ar indyttit and accuset Forsamekill as nocht only be the devyne Law of almychtie God expressed in his sacred word Bot also be the municipall lawis and actis of parliament of this kingdome Speciallie be the 73 act of the nynt parliament of our souerane lordis darrest guidame Quene Marie of famous and renowned memorie haldin be hir majestie and the estaittis of parliament at Edinburgh upone the fourt day of Junii 1563 It is expreslie provydit, statute and ordanit That na maner of persone or persones of quhat sumevir estait degrie or conditioun thay be of Preswme or tak upone hand at ony tyme thaireftir to use ony maner of witchcraft, sorcerie and necromancie nor geve thame selffis furth to haif ony sic craft or knawlege thairof Thairthrow to abuse the people Nather that ony persone seik ony help response or consultatioun at ony sic usearis or abusearis foirsaids of witchcraft, sorcerie or necromancie under the pane of daith alsweill to be execute against the usear and abusear as seiker of the response or consultatioun as the said act of parliament at lenth proportis.

Nochtwithstanding quhairof It is of verritie

1.[25] That \ye/ the said Elizabeth in the moneth of May The yeir of God $i^{m}vi^{c}$ threttie tua yeiris George Sprote wobster[26] in Eymouth haifing claith of youris quhilk he keiped longer besyde him nor ye desired, ye come to his

[24] In margin: 'Acquit of Sorcerie'.

[25] Here and later, these numbers are in the margin of the MS, repeated in the text, and the text runs continuously. Paragraph breaks have been added editorially for clarity.

[26] 'wobster' (webster): weaver.

house and violentlie reft[27] The samyn away frome him in ane grit spleane and anger thraitning to do him ane evill turne And for that effect upone ane Sonday thaireftir airlie in the moirning ye come in to the said George Sprote his {*fo. 160v.*} hous (he him him [*sic*] selff being out of the toun for the tyme) and nane bot his wyfe Agnes Boncle in hir bed with ane bonny barne And at your incuming saying nothing quhill ye come to hir bedsyde To quhome your first wordis than spokin be yow war thaise, Agnes quhair is your bairne, The said Agnes (strukin with feir) answeired, scho is heir in the bed with me betwix me and the bed stok, quhairunto ye replyed, will ye let me see hir, The said Agnes thairupoun at your desyre turnet up the bed clothes and luit yow see hir face and brest, quhilk quhan scho did ye pat in your hand doun within the clothes till ye come to the bairnes hoche[28] quhilk ye nipped in sic sorte that the bairne did skirle[29] quhilk maid the mother of the said bairne to cry and say, The lord I beteiche my bairne to;[30] And with that (without ony mae wordis) ye tuirned to the dure And went out: And that nip quhilk ye gave to the said bairne was sene ane blae[31] mark in hir hoche quhilk nevir went out of hir flesche so long as scho leveid, bot fra that tyme furth the bairne pyned pitiefullie for the space of thre quairteris of ane yeir and deid by your devillerie and wichcraft laid upone hir, Lyk as in the tyme of the said barne hir pyneing The said Agnes sent to your house to by aucht pennie worth of eggs for hir Quhilk ye refuised to sell Bot your maid Rachaell Hill (unwitting of yow) gave to the said bairne two eggs: quhilk ye threatned sould be dear to thame that gat thame, And thaireftir railed upone the said Agnes, saying goe hame and resset my stollin eggs, Quha said thay haif bene deir eggs to me and my bairne, And so it was For since schoe gat thame The liknes of ane egg did strek out of hir body, Thairfore ye replyed, The Devill tak yow and your bairne bothe, And all this ye haif done be your devillrie and witchcraft and inchantment quhilk ye can nocht *deny, Namelie the pyneing and moirthering*[32] of that bairne.

2. Item[33] ye ar indyted and accused that in the moneth of August The yeir of God i^{m}vi^{c} threttie thre yeiris the said George Sprote being standing foiranent[34] your dur, ye rayled upone him with your devillishe toung becaus he had wyted[35] yow as the causer of his bairnes death, And thairefter taking

27 'reft': tore, snatched.
28 'hoche' (hock): the rear of the knee joint.
29 'skirle': cry out.
30 'The lord I beteiche my bairne to' (betake): I commend my child to the Lord.
31 'blae': livid, bluish.
32 The text in italics is underlined in the MS.
33 In margin: 'Not Relevant'.
34 'foiranent': opposite.
35 'wyted': blamed.

him by the schoulderis ye schote[36] him af your calsay,[37] Saying goe hame and work, For work quhat ye can your teith sall overgang your handis and ye sall nevir get your Sondayis meit to the fore. Since quhilk tyme of that your feirfull threatning and railling Against the said George, he be your sorcerie and witchcraft hes fallen unto extreame povertie and can nevir wyn his meit of his worke thocht he niver work so dilligentlie nyght and day.

3. Item ye ar Indytit and accuset Forsamekill as in harvest bygane ane yeir viz. in anno 1632 yeiris, Williame Donaldsone in Eymouthe being stryveing with George Fultoun your servand, the said Williame bad him gae hame to the witche his goode wyfe, quhairupone within aucht dayis thaireftir The said Williame Donaldsone cuming by yow ye ran eftir him to strek him, And ye persaveing that he did outryn yow, ye in ane rage and furie cryed eftir him in threatning maner, weill so the Devill be in your feit, Eftir quhilk devillish threatning utterid be yow against him The said Williame be your sorcerie and witchcraft became lame and impotent in his feit And sa continewis to this day.

4. Item ye ar indyttit and accused that about sixtene yeir syne your husband Alexander Pae and ye being of intentioun to build upone the gabell of John Gray his byre Bot becaus ye was interupted and stopped in bigging[38] thairof it is of virritie that some few dayis thaireftir the said Johne Gray being frome hame for the tyme Margaret Jaksone his spous cam out saying thir wordis; As my guidman did stope this work quhan he was present So will I stope it in his absence, And schoe haifing hir sone in hir hand bad him roll doun that stane af[f] the work quhilk had bene laid thairupoun; quhilk the young boy did mynt[39] to doe with the pith[40] that he had, And {*fo. 161r.*} becaus of his waiknes scho bad the maesone help him, Quhairupone ye consavet ane grit miscontentment and evill will against the said young boy, quhairthrow immediatlie thaireftir he fell unto a vehement seiknes being feirfullie tormented and distempered baith in body and mynd and nevir convalesced thairof bot deid in ane fraenasie, And sa by your sorcerie and witchcraft laid upone the boy he was pitiefullie murthored and bereft of his naturall lyfe quhairof ye ar airt and pairt.

5. Item ye ar indytit and accused that forsamekill as Margaret Home spous to Mr George Auchterlony Ane four yeir since or thairby, haifing bocht ane hors of hir brothers for fourtie pund to hir husbands knawledge Bot haveing aggreit to pay sax punds mair quhilk he knew not of, And befoir the said Margaret Home cuming ryding hame upone the said hors Scho lichted at your window, at whilk tyme scho cam in to your husband and desyred of him the lane of that sax pund to compleit the pryce of the said horse, lykas your

[36] 'schote': shoved.
[37] 'calsay': causeway, pathway.
[38] 'bigging': building.
[39] 'mynt': attempt.
[40] 'pith': strength.

husband haifing than granted to lend the samyn, ye nawayis wald condiscend thairto; bot flate[41] and skalded upone him for lending thairof without your will and consent, Quhairupone ye in revendge thairof be your sorcerie and witchcraft laid upone the said horse, eftir mony curses and thraitnings utterid be yow that the horse sould nevir doe thame guid, he presentlie contracted ane grevous seiknes and swat to deid in the staw[42] and never thaireftir did thame goode.

6. Item ye ar indytit and accused that forsamekill as within fourtene dayis thaireftir the said Margaret Home haveing of new agane comed to the said Alexander Pae your husband and desyreing of him the borrowing of sevintene pundis for compleiting the pryce of tua oxin boucht be the said Mr George Ouchterlony hir husband fra ane man in the North feild, To the lenning quhairof ye altogidder disassented, saying to your said husband, the Devill ane penny ye sall lend hir, yit he nochtwithstanding thairof did lend it against your will. In revendge quhairof ye (by your sorcerie and witchcraft[)] laid upone ane of the said oxin A strange and suddane diseas, quhairthrow it was nevir able to lay doun, Bot routted[43] continuallie till he deid, And upone the rest of the Cattell the sweit was upone thame all the nyght over lyk the dew of the hare rynd,[44] lykas at that tyme thair was sene be George Purves servand to the said Mr George upone the byre rigging[45] Men and Wemen danceing albeit thay could nocht be knawin: All practised and done be your sorcerie and witchcraft upone the said Margaret Home hir bestial.

7. Item ye ar indytted and accused Forsamekill as the said Margaret Home haveing a thrid tyme cum to your said husband and offering to sell him fyve firlottis of seid aittis to help hir to by ane uther horse withall, yea[46] as of befoir altogidder disassenting thairto and Nawayis being willing that your husband sould let hir have ony thing that was yours, And the said Margaret than saying to yow I nevir gat ony thing of yours with goode will and thairfoir I think it dois me the les guid, Lykas the said Margaret haifing gottin the money frome your said husband althoo against your will And haveing bought ane uther horse and put him to Aill[47] mylne to girseing:[48] It is of veritie that the same hors ran mad and was thaireftir funde stopped[49] in ane hole (It being wounderfull[50] how he sould haif cum thair save only by your sorcerie and witchcraft) and deid, Quhairthrow the said Margaret hes fund be

41 'flate': argued, scolded.
42 'swat to deid in the staw': sweated to death in the stall.
43 'routted': bellowed.
44 'hare rynd': hoar frost.
45 'rigging': ridge of the roof.
46 *Sic*. Read 'ye'.
47 *Sic*. Probably read 'ane'.
48 'girseing': grazing.
49 'funde stopped': found trapped.
50 'wounderfull': extraordinary.

manifold experence that quhanevir scho gat ony thing of yours against your will quhatevir it was imployed upone did nevir thryve nor did hir ony goode.

8. Item ye ar indytted and accused that ye with ane number of your complices, sorceraris and witchis (a tua yeir since or thairby), had ane solemne meitting with the Devill at the heid of the Deid Mans Burne, {*fo. 161v.*} Fra the whilk place cuming downe the brae ye come altogidder by your sorcerie and witchcraft over Mr George Ouchterlony his byre; of purpois to mak it fall in the pot. Bot Elspeth Wilsone (ane of your companie and now execute for witchcraft) being tennent to the said Mr George, did laubour to diswaid yow thairfra, saying cum away, it is our maisteris byre and thair is Cristned saules within it. To whome ye replyid, the Devill mote[51] care, thair is no cristined saule within it bot Thome Burnet, and for him I care not, for whan I had apprysed[52] Mr George his cattell for dett, he brak the lock of the dure quhair thay war and luit thame out. Thaireftir ye (nochtwithstanding of the said Elspeth hir diswaiding) continewid still danceing on the rigging of the said byre; and by your sorcerie and witchcraft caused it to fall in the patt, within whilk byre was a man, a boy, and xvii heid of cattell; all wounderfullie preserved by Godis providence save ane young souking calff. All this ye did by your sorcerie and witchcraft quhilk ye can not deny. And sua by your keiping tryst and meiting with the Devill at the place foirsaid and doun throwing of the said byre and smoreing[53] the young ox \or calff/ in maner foirsaid, ye have declaired your selff to be ane sorcerar and ane witch and consulter with the Devill to the hurt of your nychtbouris and distructioun of thair guidis.

9. Item[54] ye ar indyted and accused that about foure yeir since ye being grinding malt in the mylne of Haymouth, all the servands being out and nabody in the mylne bot your selff at that tyme, ye than addressit your selff to the making of your devillish conjurationes and consultationes with the Devill your maister, And for that effect ye war sene rynning witherschynes[55] about ane wane eave;[56] at whilk tyme Johne Andersone myller cuming in, whome quhen ye perceaved to spy and behold your doingis ye stayed and stoode still, And this ye did by your devillrie and witchcraft quhilk ye can not deny.

10. Item ye ar indyted and accused Forsamekill as ye upone sum occasioun haveing conceaved ane deidlie malice and hattred agains Stevin Allane in Eymouth, ye be your sorcerie and witchcraft sought his lyfe and wrak, the ane by laying grevous seiknes upone him quhairthrow he was muche trubled and vexed, the uther by your devillish charmes and witchcraft inflicted upone his

51 'mote': may.
52 'apprysed': confiscated by legal process.
53 'smoreing': smothering.
54 In margin: 'Not found relevant'.
55 'witherschynes': anticlockwise.
56 'wane eave': the eaves of a building.

cattell quhairby ane grit number of thame in ane shorte tyme shote to deid.[57] The said Stevin nevir understanding thairof, untill the tyme that Aliesone Wilsone ane confessing witch and execute for witchcraft a littill before hir convictioun confessit the same to the said Stevin him selff in the heiring of James Levingstoun befoir the dome of death was gevin out against hir.

11. Item[58] ye ar indyted and accused that at myd somer last Robert Flint and Symone Wilsone servitours to James Wedderburne in Coldinghame being sent to Eymouth for wyne to thair guid wyfe than being seik: In thair returning hamewardis frome Eymouth (lait in the nicht whan all men was at rest and sleeping in thair bedis) ye was seine and vivelie[59] discovered be thame to be sark wylicoit allane[60] and bareleggid standing at the bak of your awin yaird conferring with the Devill in the liknes of ane man, haveing on gray claithes upone him, And whan thay bad yow godspeid nather ye nor he did speik or answer, whairat the saidis tua youthes was affrayed And said the ane to the uther, God bliss us quhat can this woman be doing heir with this man at this tyme of night, The uther replyed let hir allane for scho is callid not luckie, quhairupone thay come away in ane grit feir and dreddour for that thay had sene of yow and that ye did nocht speake.

12. Item[61] ye ar indyted and accused Forsamekill as four since [*sic*] or thairby Margaret Ballaine being prissoner at Aytoun for witchcraft was weill tret and {*fo. 162r.*} interteaned[62] be Helene Tait spous to Robert Warrand in Aytoun, and that by your comand and directioun, For no uther caus bot only to conceale and suppres your name in not delaiting yow to be ane witch, Quhilk Margaret Ballain in hir examinatioun be your minister (being perticulerlie demandit quhat schoe knew concerning your sorcerie and witchcraft) Denyed that schoe knew ony thing concerning yow, And nocht withstanding thairof scho declared that ye war a sicker[63] witch, whilk wald be sene and hard whan scho was brunt, quha evir leived thre or four or sevin yearis eftir hir. Be the quhilk affirmatioun maid be the said Margaret Balaine a notorious witch in the tyme of hir imprissonment above writtin affirmeing yow to be ane sicker witch, wha without all questioun understuid of your devillisch and secreit practizes in that your devillish airt of witchcraft, and the causeing hir be interteneid be the said Helene Tait upone your charges for eschewing your dilatioun to the minister to have knawledge of witchcraft and medling thairin, Albeit it be knawin sufficientlie that ye and the said Margaret Ballaine war practizeris of that wicked and devillish airt of sorcerie quhilk ye can not deny.

57 'shote to deid': died suddenly.
58 In margin: 'Not found Relevant'.
59 'vivelie': clearly.
60 'sark wylicoit allane': (wearing) only a shirt and under-petticoat.
61 In margin: 'Not found Relevant'.
62 'weill tret and interteaned': well treated and supplied.
63 'sicker': certain.

13. Item ye ar indyted and accused for being in company with Jonet Liddell, Agnes Falconer, Jonet Williamesone and Cristiane Wilsone at ane meitting quhilk ye and thay had with the Devill within the teynd yaird of Eymouth sevin yeiris since or thairby under silence and clud of nyght, frome the whilk teynd yaird be the Devillis directioun ye all went togidder in propper persone to the mylne of Eymouth and brunt the samyn be your sorcerie and witchcraft.

14. Item ye ar indyted and accused for being in companie with the said Jonet Lyddell, Agnes Falconer, Jonet Williamesone and Cristiane Wilsone, Notorious witches, in the moneth of September the yeir of God $i^{m}vi^{c}$ tuentie six yeiris, Quha be your convening togidder in the schore of Eymouth under silence and clud of nyght, ye thair crewallie murthoret amongst yow umquhile David Hynd, wha was than watching the boattis be night in the tyme of the hering drave.[64] And your reasone of his murthoreing was only to prevent his out putting of yow for convening togidder at sic ane unlawfull tyme and godles meitting, And thairthrow ye ar airt and pairt of the murthor of the said David be sorcerie and witchcraft quhilk ye can not deny.

15. Item[65] ye ar indyted and accused That ye had ane horse schoe in a darnet[66] and secreit pairt of your dur, keiped be yow thairupoun As ane devillish meanis and instructioun frome the Devill, receaved be yow to mak your guidis and all uther your effairis quhilk ye tuik in hand to prosper and succeid weill speciallie within your houss, As for being in companie with Jonet Williamsone and utheris notorious witches at ane meitting in your awin stack yaird quhair the Devill was present amongst yow. Lykas ye your selff hes dyvers tymes confessit it to be ane worlds wounder gif Jonet Williamsone war ane witche That ye war not ane witch also, seing ye had mony privat deallingis togidder quhilk few knew bot your selffis, Bot sa it is that schoe confessit hir selff to be ane witch, And thairfoir ye most[67] be conscious to your selff that ye ar also ane witche quhilk is nottourlie knawin and ye can nocht deny.

16. Item[68] ye ar indytted and accused That forsamekill as Williame Mearns ane notorious warlok Quha confessing his awin guiltnes of sorcerie and witchcraft in presense of dyvers commissioneris appointit be the secreit counsall as his examinatoris and for his tryell at Eymouth be ane assyse affixt to be upone the sixt day of September The yeir of God 1633 yeiris, And being than Interogat in his examinatioun be the saidis commissioneris anent your knawlege and practizes in sorcerie and quhat he knew concerning yow in that matter, He for answer thairto than declairit that ye war nocht sonsie[69] In regaird that ye had grit socieatie (as he affirmet) with ane Patrik Smyth in

64 'hering drave': herring fishery.
65 In margin: 'Not fund relevant'.
66 'darnet': hidden.
67 'most': must.
68 In margin: 'Not fund relevant'.
69 'nocht sonsie': ill-omened.

Lammertoun Quha was knawin to be ane notorious warlok, And quha being conscious thairof to him selff afoir his challenge and taking and to eschew his lawfull and publict tryell, overcum with the temptatioun of the Devill his maister, Pat violent handis in him selff {*fo. 162v.*} for feir of taking, lykas the said William Mearns for perticuleris that he knew against yow He did refer yow to Aliesone Wilsone hir depositiones, Quhilk Aliesone (as he declared) could tell of yow strange thingis gif scho pleased, And so by your familier correspondence with thease sorceraris and professid witches ye haif declairet yourselff to be ane manifest witch and sorcerar quhilk is nottourlie knawin and ye can nocht deny.

17. Item ye ar indytit and accused that in the moneth of Marche in the yeir of God i^m^vi^c^ threttie thre yeiris ye with a number of your complices, witches and sorcerares, had ane solemne meitting with the Devill upone the schore of Eymouth: Frome quhence the Devill convoyed yow all unto that schip quhairin George Holdie in Eymouth was with his companie, And thair by your sorcerie and witchcraft ye maist crewallie sank and distroyit the schip and so perisched the said George with his schip and guidis with the haill companie being within the samyn, quhairof ye ar and was airt and pairt quhilk ye can nocht deny.

18. Item ye ar indytit and accused that upone the Nynt day of December The yeir of God i^m^vi^c^ threttie thre yeiris ye being confronted in judgement (in presence of his majesteis commissioneris) with Aliesone and Agnes Wilsones, Thay than confessing thair awin guiltines of witchcraft befoir thair convictioun befoir thair dome and at thair executioun eftir thair convictioun and dome dilaited yow to be guiltie of the same cryme of sorcerie and witchcraft for the quhilk thay war to geve thair lyves, And in particuler they avowid in your face that ye was present with thame at the away casting of the said George Huldie his schip with him selff his companie and guidis, And sua be your keiping tryst and meiting with the Devill at the place foirsaid and perishing of the said schip be your sorcerie and witchcraft in maner and at the tyme foirsaid ye haif declaired your selff to be ane sorcerar and rank witch and ane consulter with the Devill for venting of your crewaltie and hurt of your nychtbours nocht only in thair guidis bot also in thair persones and lyves, quhilk is notourlie knawin and ye can nocht deny the same, For the quhilkis crymes of sorcerie and witchcraft abone writtin ye aucht and sould be pwneist conforme to the lawis of this realme etc.

Eftir reiding of the whilk dittay and accusatioun of the said Elizabeth Bathcat be virtew thairof of the crymis rexive[70] above specified in sort thairintill, It was alledgit be the said Elizabeth and hir prelocutors Against the first article of dittay quhilk consistis of tua pairtis, viz. first that George Sprote wobster in

70 'rexive': respectively.

Eymouth haifing claith of the pannellis quha keiped the samyn langer nor schoe desyred, And nixt that the pannell violentlie tuik it frome him and promeist thairfoir to doe him ane evill turne etc. as the dittay beiris, It is answerit to the first poynt that the samyn can infer no poynt of witchcraft, Nocht beiring ony soirt of inchantment or sorcerie done be the pannell quhilk procuret the bairnes daith, bot only that scho Nippit the bairne quhilk wald rather infer the cryme of Murther, Quhairof gif schoe war accused scho wald offer to prove be sufficient honest witnesis at the bar That the daith of the bairne was procuret be the awin father George Sprote who haiveing the bairne in his airmes went to George Purvis his nychtbours hous to borrow ane pan, And cuming back to his awin house with the bairne and the pan, his fute slippit in ane hole before the dure quhilk moved him to stumble and fall and the bairne under him, sua that the bairne being crusched with \that/ fall pyned and deceist, Lyk as to the secund poynt of the said article the samyn is na wayis relevant Nocht condiscending upone[71] ony sorte of sorcerie, {*fo. 163r.*} witchcraft or inchantment or that ony drogis was applyit to the eggis, Quhair be the contrair the lybell beiris that the eggs war delyverit be the pannellis maiden to Rachaell Hill[72] and war nevir tuiched or handillit be the pannell thaireftir.

To the quhilk it is answerit be my lord advocatt that the alledgance maid againes the first article of the dittay aucht to be repellit inrespect of the dittay[73] quhilk is relevantlie consavet *super minis precedentibus maleficio et damno imediate sequunto*[74] quhilk be the common law and consent of all doctors[75] and continuall practique of this judicatorie is relevant to infer witchcraft and the practise thairof, lykeas the dittay beires that this fact was done be the pannels devilrie, sorcerie and witchcraft, and it was nevir urget in ane lybell of witchcraft that the persewar sould condiscend upone any devilrie or inchantment quhilkis ar only knawin to the Devill himselff and his suppostis or counsall,[76] Nather is it contrair to the dittay that it beires Murthor, becaus murthor and witchcraft may verie weill concure togidder, the ane as the end the other as the midis,[77] And as to that pairt of the alledgance maid againes the father quha was author of the bairnes murthor, that is plaine contrair to the dittay and againes the presumptioun of that naturall love and cair that a father hes to his bairne.

71 'condiscending upone': specifying.

72 *Sic.* According to item 1 of the dittay, Rachel Hill *was* Bathgate's maid. This error may have been made either by the defence team or (perhaps more likely) by the clerk. It did not materially affect the defence's argument.

73 'inrespect of the dittay': with regard to the dittay (i.e. the defence objection should be rejected because it contradicts what is said in the dittay).

74 'upon a preceding threat of witchcraft, with harm following immediately'.

75 'doctors': learned writers, i.e. lawyers.

76 'supposts or counsall': supporters or advisers (i.e. witches or other demons).

77 'midis': means.

Item as to the second article The persewar repeitis the former answer with this eik that it beires ane outward signe of the malefice and witchcraft be the stryking furth of ane lumpe in liknes of ane egge.

It is duiplyit thairto be the pannell and hir prelocutors that the former exceptioun standis relevant notwithstanding of the reply, Becaus in all criminall dittayes Speciallie concerning witchcraft the malefice aucht to be lybellit, bot heir thair is no malefice lybellit quhilk may infer witchcraft bot only the nipping of ane bairne, No minatorie[78] speiches being utered of befoir quhilk may be paraleld to the subsequent malefice, lykeas the first pairt and the second doe admitt ane contradictioun, For the first pairt beires that the bairne pynit and died of the nipe and the second by the inchantment of the eggis. Lykeas it is newir lybellit that ony sorcerie was applyit to the egge bot be the contrair that the egge was given by[79] the pannells knawledge and thair is nothing lybellit of witchcraft bot a minatorie speich utered to hir servand. Nather is it liklie or probable that scho wold keip inchanted eggis in hir hous and leive thame open to hir servand quhairby hir husband might haive gotten of thame. And as to the wordis adjectit to evrie article, subjoineing the crymes sett doun thairintill to be done be sorcerie and witchcraft, not condiscending upone any particular lybell of sorcerie and witchcraft quhilk may haive any contingence or affinitie with the malefice, The samyn is nawayes relevant to infer the pannells guiltines of witchcraft.

To the whilk duply it is answerit be the persewar that the samyn aucht to be repellit inrespect of the dittay as altogidder contrair thairto.

It is allegit be the pannell and hir prelocutors agains the secund article of the foirsaid dittay that the samyn is no moir relevant nor the first, Nocht condiscending thairintill upone ony sorcerie or inchantment quhilk procuret the said George Sprote his povertie nor upone the tyme quhan the pannell sould haif utterit the minaceing speiches lybellit, nather yit of the progres, tymes, periodis and circumstances of his said extreame povertie, And nocht condiscending quhat guidis and geir he had quhan scho tuik him be the schoulders and what he had to the foir in stok[80] or how the samyn was diminishet, For it is notouirlie knawin that he was ever ane poore man And could skairse intertine him selff be his work quhilk is nottour and manifest to his haill nychtboures, And albeit he had meanis Nathing is lybellit to haif procuret his distres bot only ane soirt of rayleing or flyteing[81] whilk is comoun to wemen who ar steired up by thair malicious nychtbouris, And speciallie be wobsteris as commoun objectis to wemenis spleane, And thair is nothing heir lybellit bot only minaceing speiches quhilk is nocht contenit in the propositioun or act of

78 'minatorie': threatening.
79 'by': without.
80 'what he had to the foir in stok': what assets he possessed.
81 'flyteing': quarrelling.

parliament speicifiet in the dittay, And thairfoir the samyn being altogidder irrelevant as it is lybellit it can nawayis be put to the knawlege of ane assyse.

It is answerit thairto be the persewar that the allegeance foirsaid maid agains the secund article aucht to be repellit inrespect of the dittay, and secund article thairof maist relevant in it selff beiring the said George Sprote his meanis and moyane to haif bene tane fra him be the pannellis sorcerie and witchcraft. {*fo. 163v.*}

As to the third article of dittay concerning Williame Donaldsone, It is allegit be the pannell and hir prelocutors that the samyn is nawayis relevant, Nocht condiscending upone ony poynt of witchcraft quhairby the said Williame Donaldsone become lame and impotent of his feitt, bot be the contrair the said article beiris in it selff ane manifest absurditie and contradictioun, That the said Williame did outrwne the pannell and that he presentlie fell lame, For gif he did outrwne hir he could not be lame And gif than he had fallin lame schoe wald have outrwne him And mycht haif overtakin him and strukin him becaus it war hir intentioun sa to haif done for sclanddering hir in hir Name, And it is notourlie knawin and offerit to be provein at the bar be honest and famous witnesis that the said William Donaldsone was of befoir sumquhat impotent of his legis and continewis yit in the same estate as he was of befoir unchanget, lykas the dittay in that article is nawayis relevant as proceiding upone minaceing speiches And na sorcerie adjoynet or applyit to the subject.

To the quhilk it is answerit be the persewar That the alledgeance foirsaid is nowayis relevant Inrespect of the dittay quhilk beiris nocht only minatorie speiches bot sorcerie and witchcraft adjoynet thairwith, And thairfoir that article as relevant in the selff aucht to pas to the cognitioun and tryell of ane assyse.

As to the fourt article of dittay Anent the injurie and bewitching of John Gray his bairne, It is allegit be the pannell and hir prelocutors That the samyn fourt article is na wayis relevant, Nocht condiscending upone ony poynt of witchcraft quhilk procured the bairnes pyneing and deiing, Nor na preceiding minatorie speiches against him, And thairfoir the said article is maist ridiculus and fabulus in the selff agains the bairne to infer ony sorcerie or witchcraft practizet agains or upone him, Bot be the contrair as the dittay beiris That the bairne was forceing and preising him selff manfullie and curagiouslie to cast doun ane stane, to quhome the pannell did na harme nather be word or deid *et cogitationis pena non inflictitur*,[82] And thairfoir the article above writtin anent the allegit injurie done to the said Johne Gray his bairne can nocht pas to ane assyse.

To the quhilk it is answerit be the persewar that the said alegeance aucht to be repellit in respect of the dittay and the pannellis minaceing speiches specifiet thairin.

As to the fyft article of dittay Anent the allegit bewiching of Margaret Home the spous of Mr George Ochterlony hir horse, It is alledget be the pannell and

[82] 'and punishment is not inflicted for thought'.

hir prelocutors That the samyn fyft article is altogidder irrelevant and ridiculus Nocht condiscending upone ony poynt of sorcerie whilk maid the hors to die, Nor quhat speiches schoe utterid bot only luiked upone the hors as gif hir eyis had bene the eyis of ane cokcatrice[83] to strek the leving object with present daith by the poysoneable aspect of the serpentis eyis, And as gif thair war nocht mony diseases following horses,[84] And quhilk hors is confessit to be presentlie coft[85] frome umquhile William Home, lyk as it is nottour and manifest that the said George Ochterlony uset the said horse thaireftir in his work and raid upone him to Edinburgh And thaireftir that he deyit as ane auld horse most die in some manis handis, *Secundo nullo modo relevat*,[86] nocht condiscendand that evir the pannell tuiched the hors or that {*fo. 164r.*} evir the hors lybellit pyned thaireftir Nor being speciall at quhat tyme the said hors deid, And thairfoir the said fyft article as altogidder irrelevant and ridiculous can nawayis pas to the knawledge of ane assyse.

To the quhilk it is answeired be the persewar That the fyft article is maist relevant and urgent, Speciallie inrespect it is confessit be the pannell as the dittay beiris that the pannellis husband lent the money agains hir will to the said Margaret Home quha was the byer of the hors, And that the hors being bund to the wyndow the pannell come furth and utterid thir speiches Saying the hors sould nevir do thame guid, And at that tyme threatined and minaced the said hors, Quhairupone the said hors immediatlie thaireftir contracted his grevous seiknes and deceissit thairof.

To the quhilk it is duplyet be the pannell that the former answer aucht nocht to be respectid bot sould be repellit inrespect of the pannellis former \defence or/ answer maid to the said fyft article.

As to the sixt article of dittay Anent the said Margaret Home hir allegit deid ox, It is allegit be the pannell and hir prelocutors that the samyn sixt article is lykwayis maist irrelevant and absurd And conteins thairin nather charmeing, sorcerie nor minassing speiches, Bot only ane refuisall and unwillingnes of the pannell that hir husband sould lend the money lybellit, quhilk is comoun to wemen Quha usuallie ar nocht so liberall as thair husbandis and speciallie that thair husbandis sould len thair geir to uther mens wyfes, And thair is nothing lybellit quhilk may infer the unthryveing or disease of the ox lybellit upone theis words adjectit, the Devill ane penny (saying to hir husband) ye sall len, For it is ane virrie evill consequence that becaus scho discharged or diswaidit hir husband to lend the money quhilk coft the oxen

83 'cokcatrice' (cockatrice): a mythical animal, a combination of a serpent and a rooster, with lethal gaze or breath.

84 'mony diseases following horses': many diseases to which horses are vulnerable.

85 'coft': bought.

86 'The second is in no way relevant'.

Ergo[87] that scho was the caus of the tracking[88] or daith of that ox seing it is nocht lybellit that scho ather saw thame or utterid ony minaceing speiches tending to ane subsequent malifice, And it is ane usuale thing that oxin taks the routting evill[89] and ane sweiting seiknes quhilkis ar both lybellit, and quhair it is lybellit that thair war wemen sene danceing upone the riging of the byre that nyght, The samyn is irrelevant, nocht condiscending that the pannell was ane of thame, And it is offerit to be provin gif neid beis at the bar that the ox lybellit deid in the band.[90]

To the whilk it is answerit be the persewar that the said sevint [*sic*] article is maist relevant nochtwithstanding of the alledgeance maid in the contrair, Because it is confessit be the pannell that the moneyis was lent against hir will to the said Margaret Home, And than uttering thir speichis to hir husband, The Devill ane penny ye sall lend hir, scho thaireftir practizet hir sorcerie and witchcraft upone the saidis tua oxin quhilk was bocht be the said Margaret Home for the said money quhairupone ane of thame contractit ane disease and nevir lay doun bot dyit in the routing evill quhilk was done be the pannellis witchcraft. As to the secund part of the alledgeance quhair thair was men and wemen sene danceing upone the byre quhilk was sene be George Purvis servand to the said Mr George, the samyn is confessit be ane of the pannellis associatis.

It is duplyit be the pannell that the sixt article of dittay above writtin *nullo modo relevat*[91] Becaus it is nocht foundit upone the act of parliament Nor subsumes nocht conforme thairto that ony sorcerie was applyit to that ox Or that ony minaceing speiches was utterit or thraitnet agains him quhilk procuret his daith.

As to the sevint article of dittay Anent the said Margaret Home hir cuming to the pannellis husband offering to sell him fyve firlottis of seid aittis[92] to help hir to by ane uther hors withall, quhilk the pannell disassentit {*fo. 164v.*} unto etc. as the sevint article beires, It is alledgit be the pannell and hir prelocutors that the said sevint article is nawayes relevant bot maist absurd in it selff, Nocht condiscending upoun any minatorie speiches utered be the pannell or that ewer scho saw that madd hors specifyit in the said article, For it is not liklie nor probable that the said Margaret Home sould haive come the thrid tyme to the pannells husband gif scho had suspectit that scho sould haive recaivet skaith,[93] and that this hors sould haive fallin in ane ditch be the pannells occasioun it is altogidder ridiculus.

87 'therefore'.
88 'tracking': struggling, suffering.
89 'routting evill': a cattle disease characterised by bellowing ('routting').
90 'in the band': in harness (while working).
91 'is in no way relevant'.
92 'fyve firlottis of seid aittis': five firlots of oats for sowing as seed. A firlot was about 36 litres.
93 'skaith': harm.

As to the aucht article anent the pannellis alledgit being in companie with certaine sorcereris and witches at ane solemne meitting with the Devill at the heid of the Deid Manes Burne etc., It is alledgit be the pannell and hir prelocutors that the said aucht article is nothing bot a ridiculus and absurd calumnie and prayeth my lord Justice to advert thairto quhilk importis ane meir unlikliehoode, Viz. That Elspeth Wilsone quha was brunt for ane witch out of piti and compassioun quhilk is unusuall in witchis did offer hir counsall to dissuade the pannell to cast doun Mr George Auchterlony his byer, Lykeas the samyn is nawayes relevant, nocht condiscending quhither the danceing lybellitt was in the day tyme or in the nyght, for to haive bene in the day it is not probable becaus witches meitinges ar clandestine and in the night, And gif in the nyght it is not qualifiet nor lybellit that any persone was thair present quha did see the danceing or quho knew of that meiting and thair is nothing lybellit upoun Elspeth Wilsone hir depositioun bot that scho saw hir.

To the quhilk it is answerit be the persewar that the said aucht article is maist relevant in it selff beiring that the said Elizabeth Bathcatt was danceing upoun the byer of Mr George Auchterlony, and as it is confest be the pannell that it was not in the day time thairfoir of necessitie it behoved to be in the nyght, Thomas Burnet being lying in his bed within the said byer for the tyme quhilk is confest be ane of the pannells associattis the tyme of hir imprissonement, Viz. be Elspeth Wilsone, And thairfoir that article being maist relevant in the selff aucht to be put to the knawlege of ane assyse.

Anent the nynt Article of dittay beirand the pannell to haif bene sene dancing and making conjurationes be rynning widdershynis about ane Wane eave within the mylne of Eymouth etc., It is allegit be the pannell and hir prelocutors that the said Nynt article is altogidder ridiculous, Nocht beiring any poynt of sorcerie or witchcraft at all Nor na malifice following thairupoun, bot only that schoe was playing hir selff and thocht schame whan schoe saw the myller, Quhome quhan schoe saw schoe left hir former postoure (quhilk scho had reasone to doe) To sie hir stuff than grinding in the mylne, And thairfoir the said article as altogidder irrelevant sould na wayis be put to the knawlege of ane assyse etc.

To the quhilk it is answerit be the persewar That the nynt article is maist relevant as is [*sic*] confessit be the pannell that schoe was danceing about the wane eave, And it is the custome of witches to haif thair meittings and danceings within mylnes, lyk as the dittay beiris that the pannell was danceing and going widderschynis about within the said mylne of Eymouthe, And quhan schoe saw the myller schoe stuid still feiring that he sould reveill the same It being ane comoun posture and custome of witches to doe.

As to the tent article of dittay Anent the seiknes allegit laid upone Stewin Allane in Eymouth and his cattell etc., It is allegit be the pannell and hir prelocutors That the samyn is irrelevant and generall, Nocht condiscending how and in quhat maner the pannell harmet Stewin Allane in his persone or guidis aither be word or deid, For na Muttering speiches ar lybellit quhairupone ane malifice followit or that thair wer ony sorcerie practizet or applyit, It being the only the [*sic*] {*fo. 165r.*} assertioun of the lybeller That Aliesone Wilsone deponit that the pannell was the caus of the said Stewin his diseas and sua *non relevat*[94] nocht condiscending that the said Aliesone Wilsone befoir hir convictioun, eftir hir convictioun and the tyme of hir daithe deponit as the article beiris.

To the quhilk it is answerit be the persewar That the Tent article is maist relevant condiscending in speciall upone the pannellis sorcerie and witchcraft and the effectis of the samyn quhilk is confessit be the said Aliesone Wilsone quha confessit hir witchcraft with grit penitence and remorse a littill befoir hir convictioun And deid ane penitent woman.

As to the ellevint article Anent Robert Flynt and Symon Wilsone servandis to James Wedderburne thair seing of the pannell conferring in the nyght at the bak of hir yaird with the Devill in the liknes of ane man having gray clothes etc., It is allegit be the pannell and hir prelocutors that the said Ellevint article is altogidder irrelevant as the former article beirand that the tua boyes saw ane man cloathed in gray quha was the Devill as is lybellit, bot how could they know the man to haive bene the Devill unles they had bene sorcereris thaimselffes, seing thay saw him in ane humane chaipe[95] nocht chyngeing his forme at all, nor that he did assume to himselff any uther uglie chaipe with hornes and clawes as the Devill uses to be prented or represented in comedies or playes, as is confest of sundrie witches to be, lykeas it is maist notoure that quhair God is named with reverence the Devill evannischeth away, and thairfoir the said article of dittay as it is consevet is maist ridiculus and irrelevant.

To the quhilk it is answerit be the persewar that the said Ellevint article standis relevant nochtwithstanding of the alledgeance becaus as the lybell beiris scho was sene be the tua boyes lybellit sarkwylicoat alone standing at the bak of hir awin yaird conferring with the Devill in liknes of ane man at that tyme of the nyght quhen uthers was in thair bedis and the tua boyes biding thame God speid they maid no answer bot evanishet away.

As to the tuelf article anent Margaret Balleny hir interteainment the tyme of hir imprissonement at Aytoun for Witchcraft and that be Helene Tait spous to Robert Warrand in Aytoun by the pannells alledgit directioun and command only to suppres the pannells name in not dilaitting hir to be ane witch etc., It is alledgit be the pannell and hir prelocutors that the said tuelf article is nawayes relevant, nocht condiscending that Margaret Balenie quha was brunt for ane witch did dilaitt or fyle the pannell of witchcraft in judgment befoir or eftir hir convictioun, and as to the rest of that article the samyn is bot a frivolus narotioun [*sic*] without any probabilitie or coherence and resolves upoun the

94 'is not relevant'.
95 'chaipe': shape.

testimonie of Dame Issobell Ker Lady Aytoun. Secundo the foirsaid article is nawayes relevant in thes wordis quhair it is said be the said Margaret Balenie that the pannell was a sikker witch nawayis condiscending in quhat poynt of witchcraft the pannell was guiltie.

To the quhilk it is answerit be the persewar that the foirsaid tuelff article is maist relevant not withstanding of the alledgeance abovewrittin as the samyn is lybellit, in sua far as Helene Tait be the pannell hir directioun went to Aytoun to Margaret Balleny than being wairdit in Aytoun and geave to hir all necesser intertenement To the effect scho sould conceill the pannellis witchcraft as is lybellit, And notwithstanding of the samyn intertenement gevin be the pannell to hir scho confessit and affirmet that the pannell was and had bene ane notorious witche, And farder said that scho sould suffer for the samyn within thrie or four of[96] sevin yeiris thaireftir.

As to the threttene article of dittay anent the pannellis allegit being in cumpanie with Jonet Liddell, Agnes Falconer, Jonet Williamesone and Cristiane Wilsone notorious witches at ane meitting quhilk thay had with the Devill within the teynd yeard of Eymouthe, and thairfra be the Devillis directioun passand to the mylne of Eymouthe and burneing the samyn be sorcerie as the said article beiris, It is alledget be the pannell and hir prelocutouris that the said threttene article is not relevant *ut concipitur*,[97] nocht beiring that the associat witches lybellit confessit at thair daith dieing Christianlie that the pannell was ane of thair associattis.

The persewar for answer thairto opponis the dittay and threttene article thairof as it standis being maist relevant in it selff to pas to ane assyse. {*fo. 165v.*}

As to the fourtene article anent the murthour of umquhile David Hynd be sorcerie and witchcraft in September 1626 yeiris being watching the bottis be nyght in the schore of Eymouthe the tyme of the herring drave, It is alledget be the pannell and hir prelocutouris That the said Fourtene article is nawayis relevant as it is consavet, and repeittis the alledgeance maid to the threttene article immediatlie preceiding. Secundo *non relevat*[98] nocht condishending quhat way David Hynd was murthourit, quhider be knyff, quhinger,[99] suord or uther offensive wapone.

To the quhilk it is answerit be the persewer that he opponis the dittay thairto as maist relevant and contingent.

As to the Fyftene article of dittay, Anent the pannellis alledgit haveing ane horse schoe in ane darnit or secreit pairt of hir dur keipit be hir thairuppoun as ane instructioun ressavit from the Devill to mak hir prosper in warldlie meinis etc., It is alledgit be the pannell and hir prelocutouris

96 *Sic*. Read 'or'.
97 'as it is conceived'.
98 'is not relevant'.
99 'quhinger': dagger.

That the samyn is nawayis relevant, beiring nather witchcraft, sorcerie nor malifeice following nor na depositioun judiciallie taikin and reiterat be the pannellis alledgit assosiattis nominat in the said article, The tyme of thair daithe, Bot only beiris ane consequence quhilk nawayis followis ether premissis Having na coherence thairwith.

The persewar for answer thairto oppones the said Fyftene article.

As to the saxtene article, Anent William Mearns warloke his confessioun maid be him confessing the day of his tryell his guiltines of sorcerie and witchcraft quha than sowld have declairit that the pannell was not sonsie, And referrit the pannallis guiltines and knawledge thairof to the relatioun of Aliesone Wilsone witche etc., As the said article beiris, It is allegit be the pannell and hir prelocutouris that the said article is nawayis relevant, nocht beirand That Williame Mearnes confessit in judgement that the pannall was ane witche hir selff or that schoe had any consort or familearitie with witches as being positive ane of thair number, Bot that article beiris allanerlie the persones lybellis declarationes[100] quhilk never was suorne in judgement.

To the quhilk it is answerit be the persewar that the said saxtene article is maist relevant becaus William Mearns the day of his tryell at Eymouthe in presence of the commissioneris his judges Confessit his awin guiltines of witchcraft and delaitit the pannell in maner specifyit in the said article.

As to the sevintene article Anent the away casting and perisching of George Huldeis schip in Eymouthe be the pannell and hir allegit complices insert in the said article, It is allegit be the pannall and hir prelocutouris that the said Sevintene article is na wayis relevant, nocht condiscending how, in quhat maner or at quhat tyme the pannall and hir assosiattis did sink George Huldeis schip or quha war present at the sinking and perisching of the same, Or that ony tempest was raised be the saidis associatis witchis or that thay war sene fleing lyke crawis, ravens or uther foulis about the schip as use is with witchis, Or quhat sorcerie or inchantment thay uset or quhat wordis thay utteritt, Nather ar the associat witches thair depositiones lybellit, in respect quhairof the said article is nawayis relevant to pas to the knawledge of ane assyse.

To the quhilk it is answerit be the persewaris that the said Sevintene article is maist relevant condiscending boithe upoun the tyme, place and monethe, And opponis the said article as is lybellit to the pannellis alledgeance abovewrittin.

As to the Auchtene article, Anent the pannellis confronting with Aliesone and Agnes Wilsones witches and thair delaiting of the pannell to be guiltie of the same crymes of witchcraft confessit be thame for quhilkis thay war to suffer and geve thair lyffe, It is allegit be the pannell and hir prelocutouris that the said Auchtene article is nawayis relevant *ut concipitur* and repeittis the alledgeance above writtin maid agains the said Sevintene article of dittay,

100 *Sic.* The sense is: 'the declarations of the persons libelled', i.e. Mearns and Wilson who had been named in the 'libel' or dittay.

adjoyneing thairto That the said Agnes and Alisone Wilsones be thair allegit confessiones constant and uniforme in judgement befoir and eftir thair convictiones and the tyme of thair daithe did not constantlie aver the pannell to be ane of thair associattis and that thay deit Cristianlie.

The persewer Opponis the said Auchtene article as maist relevant in it selff notwitstanding of the pannellis alledgeance maid in the contrair. {*fo. 166r.*}

The Justice be interloquitour[101] Findis the first, thrid, Fourt, fyft and sixt articles of dittay relevant, The haill aucht article also relevant *Conjunctim*,[102] Findis in lykmaner the tent article relevant to pas to the knawledge of ane assyse with this advyce to the assyse to cognosce and considder upone the tyme of the committing of the cryme and haill remanent circumstances mentionet in the said tent article, Findis the threttene article relevant, As to the fourtene article remittis the samyn to the assyse and findis the samyn to be relevant as airt and pairt of the murthour contenit thairuntil with this adverteisment to the assyse to try gif David Hynd was murthouret at the tyme and in maner lybellit in the said xiiii article and gif he be deid or leveand as etc., Findis the sevintene article relevant, As to the Auchtene article Findis the samyn nawayis propper to be cognoscet be the justice As being ane qualificatioun of the 17 article immediatlie preceiding, And thairfoir remittis the said 18 article to the assyse to be considderit be thame as accoirdis, And as to the remanent articles of dittay, viz. the secund, Sevint, Nynt, ellevint, Tuelff, Fyftene and sixtene articles, Findis the samyn and ilk ane of thame Nawayis relevant to pas to ane assyse, Quhairupone ather partie alsweill persewar as defender askit actis and instrumentis.

Assisa

Mark Home in Chirnesyde[103]
Thomas Broun in Eymouth
James Levingstoun thair
Phillope Nisbet thair
Johne Dunlope in Flemyngtoun
James Wight in Aytoun
Patrik Greive thair
James Hopper in Coldinghame
Adame Dunlope in Eymouth
Bartill Polwart in Coldinghame
Nicoll Ramsay in Foulden
Williame Haistie in Quhyterig
Johnne Daill in Foulden
Samwell Gray in Gwnnisgrene
George Lyddell in Edingtoun

101 In margin: 'Interloquitour'.

102 'joined'. The article could not prove guilt on its own, but it could be considered along with another one.

103 In margin: 'Chancellour'.

The Persewar takis instrumentis of the sweiring of the assyse, And for verificatioun of the pannellis guiltines of the severall crymes contenit in the severall and perticuler articles remitted to thair knawlege and determinatioun uses and produces the probatioun following, And first For preveing of the first articles of dittay produces George Sprote wobster in Eymouth and Agnes Boncle his spous, desyreing thame to be sworne be the judge and thair declaratioun to be tane Judiciallie and writtin, off the quhilk declaratioun the termes followis. George Sprote sworne judiciallie and demandit be the justice quhat he knawis concerning the first article of dittay beirand the pannell to haif Nipped his bairne quhairof the bairne deceissat within thre quarteris of ane yeir thaireftir, As also Anent the inchantet eggis gevin to his bairne quhilk come out of the pannellis hous And that the bairne deceissat be hir sorcerie and witchcraft, Eftir reiding of the haill first article of dittay The said George Sprote be his grit aith declairet that at the tyme specifiet in the said article, viz. upone the Sonday at morne he was absent frome his hous, And thairfoir he knew nothing thairof, quhairupone the pannell with hir prelocutors askit instrumentis.

Agnes Boncle judiciallie sworne and examinat deponis Eftir reiding judiciallie of the said first article of dittay unto hir Conforme thairto That about Michaelmes[104] bygane ane yeir on the Sonday thaireftir Elizabeth Bathcat Come to the deponeris hous airlie in the morning and askit for the deponeris bairne being tua yeir auld, To quhome the deponer maid answer, My bairne is heir betwix me and the bedstok, At quhilk Elspethe pat hir hand in the bed and nipped the bairne in the hoche quhilk movet the bairne to skirle and greit[105] vehementlie, quhilk nip being sua gevin to the bairne the said Elizabeth immediatlie thaireftir past furth of the deponeris hous, Fra the quhilk tyme the bairne pynet and dwynet[106] away the space of thre quarteris of ane yeir and than deceissat. Farder depones That about Yule eftir the geving of the former nip to hir bairne, Ane lass of Elspeth Bathcattis hous come and brocht fyve eggis with hir to the deponeris hous Ane of the quhilkis fyve eggis was tane frome hir be the deponer quhilk scho roisted and gave to hir bairne, Eftir the bairnes {*fo. 166v.*} eating of the quhilk egg The bairne was sa visseit with hevie seiknes That the haill matter quhilk come throw hir was lyk unto rottin egis, As also that in the tyme of hir seiknes thair arraiss ane gritt lumpe under the bairnes okster[107] to the liknes of ane guise eg[108] bot of ane gritter quantitie, And sayis that about Pasche[109] thaireftir The auld Lady Cranstoun cuming to Johnne Brownes hous in Eymouth, The deponer past to the said

104 Michaelmas was 29 September.
105 'skirle and greit': cry out and weep.
106 'dwynet': dwindled.
107 'okster': armpit.
108 'guise eg': goose's egg.
109 'Pasche': Easter.

lady with hir dochter in hir airme and demandit gif thair was ony help for hir, To quhome the said lady answerit (eftir sighting of the bairne) Thair is no herb that growis in the garding will help that bairne, For schoe is bewitched.

It is alledgit be the pannall and hir prelocutors Agains the said Agnes Boncle hir declaratioun That the samyn sould nocht [*sic*] respectit nor ressavit for tua reasones, First, becaus it is ane declaratioun of pairtie Quhais assertioun can not mak faith And can nocht be admittit for fyve penneis far les in prejudice of the pannellis lyfe and estate. Secundo, it can nocht be respected Becaus scho is *testis singularis*[110] quhairas in the expres word of God na man may be condempned upone the depositioun or testimonie of one persone[111] Bot aither *ore duorum* or *trium testium.*[112] Tertio, let it pleis the assyse to considder That hir husband hes alreddie deponet judiciallie (being solemnelie sworne[)] That he knawis nothing of that first article. Quarto, That the kings advocat can nocht draw up informationes be him selff, Bot schoe only being informer and the dittay being gevin up be hir Scho most byde be it or ellis underly hir deserved puneishment, And in effect this is bot ane asseveration to hir knawledge that the lybell is trew As gif the pannell had desyred the deponentis aith of calamnie[113] quhidder or no scho had reasone to persew the lybell quhilk scho hes now declared scho had reasone nochttheles Nather in ane civil nor criminall judicatoreis [*sic*] is approbatioun without uther probatioun respectit.

It is answerit to the first allegeance be the persewar That the said Agnes Boncle is nather pairtie nor informer bot only is ressavit as witnes to give informatioun to the assyse upone the article of dittay anent the daith of hir bairne, And schoe being sworne judiciallie hes be hir grit aithe declairit that the pannell was the only daithe of hir bairne be hir sorcerie and witchecraft inflictid upoun hir said bairne, likas the said Agnes Boncle schoe could nocht be informer nather hir husband quha hes compeirit and declairit he knew nothing of the bussines. Secundo quhair it is allegit that schoe is bot only *singularis testis et unicus testis*[114] quhilk sould not be respectit, It is answerit thairto that in lesemajestie[115] and witchecraft in siclyke haynous and odious crymes wemen ar admittit witnes. As to the fourt reassone alledgeing that the kingis advocat cannot draw up informationes be him selff without ane informer, The persewer denyis the same lykas the samyn dittay is persewit without any informer, And gif the pannell was allegit[116] that thair war any

110 'a sole witness'.

111 Deuteronomy 17:6: 'At the mouth of two witnesses, or three witnesses, shall he that is worthy of death be put to death; but at the mouth of one witness he shall not be put to death.'

112 'by the testimony of two or three witnesses'.

113 An 'oath of calumny' was an oath that could be required from either the prosecutor or the defender, swearing that they had just cause to pursue or defend the case.

114 'singular witness and sole witness'.

115 'lesemajestie': treason.

116 *Sic.* Probably read 'would allege'.

informer here it is answerit that the wyffe the bairnes mother is na informer at all bot only is producit and examinat for geveing information to the assyse of the verritie of the fact. As to the last pairt of the alledgeance beirand that the said Agnes aithe is only gevin *tanquam juramentum calumnie*,[117] Aucht to be repellit in respect the caice is nocht alyke *in criminalibus judiciis* as in *civilibus*.[118]

It is duplyit be the pannall that the foirsaid alledgeance standis relevant nocht withstanding of the former answer or reply, be reassone the said Agnes Boncle is ane speciall pairtie as is constant and cleir be the verrie dittay, And as to that pairt of the reply quhairby it is allegit that ane woman may be witnes in witchcraft and lesemajestie as is set doun in the act anent treassone and witchecraft, Answeris thair is na suche warrand nather of law nor practique, And thair is na law nor practique exprest against the law or word of God Be the quhilk it is speciallie statute that na man sall die upoun the depositioun of ane witnes, And as ane witnes wald not mak faithe in ane civile caus far les in ane criminall It being expreslie statute be the law that probationes *in criminalibus causis debent esse luce meridiana clariores*.[119]

Item the persewar for proveing of thrid article of dittay, Anent the sorcerie and witchcraft inflicted and laid upone William Donaldsone quhairby he is maid criple and lame of his feit, Produces the said William Donaldsone quha being judiciallie sworne {*fo. 167r.*} and the thrid article of dittay red to him He be his grit aithe affirmet the haill article to be of verritie as it is sett doun, quhairupoun the persewar askit instrumentis.

The pannell with hir prelocutouris repeittis the former alledgeance maid agains Agnes Boncle for answer thairto baithe that William Donaldsone is pairtie informer et *unicus testis singularis*.[120]

Item for proveing of the fourt article of dittay the persewar producet Johnne Gray in Eymouthe, Quha being judiciallie sworne and the fourt article of dittay red to him declairit the samyn to be of verritie as he is informet be his wyfe, And that within fourtene dayis eftir the tyme lybellit that the boy his sone fell seik and deid, Bot wald not tak it upoun his conscience that his bairne deit be witchcraft or sorcerie, quhairupoun the pannell askit instrumentis.

Item for proveing of the fyft article of dittay Anent the sorcerie and witchcraft laid upoun Margaret Homes horse quhairby he swat to deid, produces the said Margaret Home quha being sworne judiciallie and the said fyft article red over to hir, declairit That schoe come to Alexander Pae the pannellis husband to borrow sax pund quhilk was lent be him to hir agains his wyffis will and consent and that within ane monethe thaireftir hir horse swat to deid in the stall, bot will not say upoun hir conscience that he deid be

117 'as an oath of calumny'. See above for an explanation of this procedure.

118 'in criminal trials as in civil ones'.

119 'in criminal trials must be clearer than the light of midday'.

120 'a sole, singular witness'.

sorcerie or witchcraft, And thairfoir desyret the assyse to Judge thairupoun, Quhairupon the pannall askit instrumentis.

Item for proveing of the saxt article of dittay Anent the daithe of Margaret Homes oxe quhilk deid of the routing evill be the pannellis sorcerie and witchcraft laid thairupoun, Produces the said Margaret Home quha being lykwayis sworne judiciallie and the said saxt article red over to hir declairid that hir ox deid within fyftene dayis eftir the tyme lybellit and sayis gif utheris had not persewit the pannell for witchcraft schoe wald nevir have accuiset the pannall of witchcraft, for that the ox lybellit had deid in hir default, quhairupoun the panel also askit instrumentis.

Item for proveing of the aucht article of dittay Anent the pannellis being in companie with certane witches at ane soleme meiting with the Devill at the heid of the Deid Manes Burne and thairfra cwmming togidder to Mr George Auchterloneis byre and making it to fall in the pott, Elspethe Wilsone being in thair cumpanie and dissuaiding the pannell thairfra, And for the daithe of ane young calff perteneing to the said Mr George than being within his said byre, Produces George Home in Eymouthe servand to the Ladie Blakhill quha being judiciallie sworne and the said Aucht article red to him declaired that the said aucht article was sua repoirtit to him to be of verritie be Agnes Wilsone the tyme that he was watching and keiping the said Agnes in hir prissone or waird quhairin schoe was detenet to the day of hir tryell or convictioun.

It is allegit be the pannell and hir prelocutouris agains the declaratioun maid be George Home That the samyn sould nawayis be respectit be the assyse becaus the said declaratioun is nocht positive frome him selff and upoun his awin knawledge bot only upoun the repoirt of umquhile Agnes Wilsone quhan he was watcheing hir, And consequentlie the said depositioun proves nathing nor sould be respectit unles it war secundit by the productioun of the criminall proces led and deducet agains the said Agnes Wilsone beiring hir to have fyllit the pannell in judgement befoir hir convictioun, eftir hir convictioun and at the tyme of hir daithe, schoe alwayis deing constantlie and Christianlie, quhilk was practizet in ane criminall proces persewit befoir my lord Justice at the instance of his majesteis advocat agains Issobell Young,[121] lykas be the civile law and all lawis in all courttis criminall and civile na faithe can be gevin to witnessis be ane uther manes relatioun.

Item for proveing of the threttene article Anent the burneing of the mylne of Eymouthe be the pannall and hir associattis nominat in the said article The persewar referris the knawledge and notorietie thairof to the assyse.

The pannell takis instrumentis that thair is nathing producet to verifie the said article of dittay bot only the malicious naked assertioun of the persewaris informeris.

[121] For this point in Isobel Young's 1629 trial see Gillon and Smith (eds.), *Selected Justiciary Cases*, i, 114–15.

Item for proveing of the Fourtene article anent the murthour of David Hynd be sorcerie and witchcraft as the article beiris, The persewer referris the knawledge and notoretie of that article lykwayis to the knawledge of ane assyse.

The pannell takis instrumentis that thair is nothing producet be the persewar for proveing of the said Fourtene article bot his informeris assertioun.

Item for proveing of the sevintene article and auchtene article following thairupoun, produces the depositiones of Aliesone and Agnes Wilsones maid in judgement in presence of the judge nominat and constitute be the lordis of his majesties secreit counsall thair comissioun anent thair {*fo. 167v.*} tryell, of the quhilkis depositiones the tennour followis. At Eymouthe the Nynt day of December 1633 yeiris in presence of Sir Patrik Home of Aytoun knyght, Johnne Ramsay of Edingtoun, Mr Johnne Home Minister of Eymouthe, Mr George Home Minister at Aytoun, Mr Cristopher Knollis Minister at Coldinghame and utheris under subscryvveris, Alisone Wilsone confessing hir awin guilt of witchcraft being confrontid in judgement befoir the commissioneris, assyseouris and multitude of peple thair present, avowed upoun Elspethe Bathcate and Isobell Sinclair That thay war guiltie of the samyn cryme for quhilk schoe was to give hir lyffe and in perticuler declairet that the said Elspeth and Isobell was present at the perisching of George Hooldie and his cumpanie. Agnes Wilsone confessing hir awin guilt and being confrontit withe the said Elspeth and Issobell avowit the samyn upoun thame and that thay war boithe present at the perischeing of the said George and his cumpanie. The quhilkis premiss is witnessit be the under subscryveris *Sic subscribuntur*[122] depositiones, Pa: Hume, Johne Ramsay, Mr Jo: Home Minister at Eymouthe, G. Home Minister at Aytoun, Mr Christopher Knolles Minister at Coldinghame, Maister Patrik Home, Be the quhilkis depositiones the saidis Alisone and Agnes Wilsone hes affirmet in the pannellis face being confrontit with thame befoir thair executioun that schoe was in cumpanie with thame at the perischeing of the said George Huldeis schip. Upone the productioun and publick reiding of the quhilkis tua depositiones verefeing the saidis sevintene and Auchtene articles of dittay in maner foirsaid, The perseweris askit instrumentis And protestit for wilfull errour agains the persones of assyse gif thay acquit the pannell thairof.

It is alledgit be the pannell and hir prelocutouris agains the verificatioun of the sevintene and auchtene articles That the samyn sould nawayis be respecttit be the assyse, Becaus it is na judiciall act of Agnes and Aliesone Wilsones depositiones takin in judgement, Nather beiris it (albeit it war autentick as it is not) That the said Aliesone and Agnes Wilsones being sworne in judgement did constantlie depone that the pannell was accessour to thair cryme or that thay being confrontid with hir eftir thair convictioun did constantlie abyde be the depositioun maid befoir thair convictioun, Nather beiris the said subscryvit writt that \thay/ deid Christianlie and penetentlie abyding be thair

122 'Thus they have subscribed'.

said depositiounes, And sua nathing being producet to verifie the premissis That article is nawayis provein, Quhilk writt is all writtin be Mr John Home his awin hand quha is informer and is only ane assertioun of tua witches agains the pannell quha is ane honest woman without hir awin confessioun bot denying the same.

It is answerit be the persewar to the first pairt of the said alledgeance That thir depositiones maid be Aliesone and Agnes Wilsones man[123] have faithe and be respecttit Becaus thay war takin Judiciallie in ane court haldin at Eymouthe the Nynt of December 1633: be vertew of ane comissioun direct frome the lordis of secreit counsall to the honourabell pairteis undersubscryveand, Viz. Sir Patrik Home of Aytoun, John Ramsay of Edingtoun, Mr Alexander Lauder of Gunnisgrene and Patrik Home of Wastrestoun comissioneris abovenamet quha war present at the confronting of the pannall Elizabethe Bathcat with Agnes and Aliesone Wilsones in the court haldin at Eymouthe the day foirsaid, and the said Mr John Home was not commissioner bot only ane witnes to the saidis depositiounes with dyverse utheris Ministeris of that presbetrie, And as to that pairt of the said alledgeance beiring that the saidis Agnes and Aliesone Wilsones deid not Christianlie nor penetentlie etc., it is answerit thairto that the said Agnes and Aliesone Wilsones went to the daith with the same confessioun befoir thair convictioun, eftir thair convictioun and at the staik, and as for the rest Remittis the knawledge thairof to the assyse, And as of befoir inrespect of the probatioun producet for verefeing of the saidis poynttis of dittay, protestis for wilfull errour agains thame gif thai sall acquit the pannell thairof.

The pannell with hir prelocutouris protestit in the contrair gif thay sould find hir guiltie or culpable of the former crymes quhairof schoe is maist frie and Innocent.

Quhilkis persones of assyse being ressavit, solemnelie sworne and admittit eftir accusatioun of the said Elizabeth Bathcat of New agane be dittay in the presence and audience of the severall and perticuler articles of dittay \above specifiet/ and crymes thairin contenit fund relevant be the Justice, Thay removet altogidder furthe of court to the counsall hous {*fo. 168r.*} of the said tolbuithe quhair being incloiset thairintill Thay first be pluralitie of voittis electtit and choiset the said Mark Home In Chancellour, Thaireftir ressonet and voittit upoun the poyntis of dittay above writtin Fund relevant be the Judge and referrit to thair knawledge, Togidder with the probatioun uset and producet be the persewer for verificatioun thairof with the objectiones and alledgeances maid be the pannell and hir prelocutoures agains the said probatioun, And withe the severall answeris maid be the persewar thairto,

[123] 'man': must.

And being ryplie and at lenthe advyset thairwith,[124] Reenterit agane in court quhair thay be the repoirt and Judiciall declariatioun of the said Mark Home chancellour, For the maist pairt and be pluralitie of voittis, Fand, pronuncet and declairit The said Elizabethe Bathcat To be cleane, innocent and acquit of the haill crymes rexive and perticulerlie above writtin fund relevant be the Judge and referrit to thair knawledge as said is, Quhairupoun the said Alexander Pae spous to the said Elizabeth Bathcate and in hir name askit actis and Instrumentis.

124 In margin: 'Acquit'.

19. BARBARA BOWNDIE, ORKNEY, 1643–1645

INTRODUCTION

Barbara Bowndie, living in Kirkwall in Orkney, was accused of witchcraft and interrogated before the presbytery in 1643.[1] She was accused in a linked trial, being denounced for witchcraft by another woman. Bowndie's case had a prehistory, and it is necessary to go back to 1642 to see why she came under suspicion of witchcraft. In that year, the presbytery began enquiring into the alleged witchcraft of Marjorie Paplay, whose name would repeatedly be linked with Bowndie's for the next few years. The minister of Shapinsay, Henry Smith, raised the initial case against Paplay; as we shall see, this would spark off a complex local power struggle. The case against Bowndie started during this struggle in November 1643.[2]

When Bowndie was 'incarcerat for witchcraft' late in 1643, this was the worst year of witchcraft accusations in Orkney, and a national panic was going on in mainland Scotland. She mentioned several demonological ideas in her confession: witches' meetings, dancing at witches' meetings, the Devil in diverse shapes, sexual intercourse with the Devil, destruction of corn fields with the help of the Devil, and denunciation of several women suspected to be witches. She was first interrogated informally, in a 'privat' questioning by ministers and a ruling elder, and five days later was formally interrogated before the presbytery. She confessed during the informal interrogation, and retracted her confession later. The formal interrogation consisted of nine

1 The records usually name her as Boundie or Bowndie, but a few entries in late 1644 name her as 'Lauchtane alias Bundie' (variously spelt). Both these surnames are rare, but in 1615 there is a record of 'Nicoll Lauchtane alias Bounde, fisher in Kirkwall': *Court Books of Orkney and Shetland, 1614–1615*, ed. Robert S. Barclay (Edinburgh: SHS, 1967), 52–6. This man may well have been related to Barbara; perhaps he was her father. For other Lauchtanes at this time, see *Orkney Testaments and Inventories, 1573–1615*, ed. Robert S. Barclay (Edinburgh: Scottish Record Society, 1977), nos. 128, 188.

2 For detailed accounts of this case see Liv Helene Willumsen, *Witches of the North: Scotland and Finnmark* (Leiden, 2013), 178–90; Peter Marshall, 'The Minister, the Merchant and his Mother: Politics and Protest in a 17th Century Witchcraft Complaint', *New Orkney Antiquarian Journal*, 9 (2020), 56–70.

points which all related to the Devil, use of demonic witchcraft or witches' meetings. Bowndie now denied all points, and refused to denounce other women. Then several witnesses gave their declarations, much of which concerned what had happened during her imprisonment. It became clear that she had been offered means to hang herself.

Since Bowndie continued to deny witchcraft, the presbytery ordained two men to supplicate the privy council for a commission to put her to torture. The presbytery asked the sheriff to retain her in prison until the council's answer was received, to which he agreed. This shows the co-operation between the presbytery and the sheriff in witchcraft cases. This is the last that is recorded about Bowndie in 1643; presumably the council failed, or refused, to grant the torture warrant that the presbytery had requested.

Bowndie's case came up again on 3 April 1644, when there was an entry that they would wait for more information about her from Shetland. She had stayed for some time in Shetland, where she travelled with an unbaptised child. During this stay, it was said that she had been speechless for twenty-four hours, and it was believed that she had been with the fairies.[3] The need for information about this led to a delay in finishing her investigation. On 3 August 1644 it was reported that she stood to her former declaration, and three ministers and one ruling elder were ordained to bring her to a confession. On 6 November, the sheriff gave in some new depositions from Shetland, which the brethren examined and returned to the sheriff. In December 1644 the brethren met with the sheriff to examine these depositions. The final fate of Barbara Bowndie is not known, but the absence of subsequent references to her makes it likely that the presbytery abandoned its attempt to prosecute her.

Meanwhile, the presbytery dropped Marjorie Paplay's case in 1643, but she was still under suspicion. On 1 May 1644, James Baikie, her son, declared that he wanted an extract of Bowndie's examination, which was granted to him, in order to protest against the slandering of his mother. He continued his protests until 1645, which gave rise to divisions within the presbytery. After this there is no further mention of Paplay in the records. Although she escaped formal prosecution, her case is a good illustration of the reputation of witchcraft clinging to a person for years.

In the records of Bowndie's case, we find several narrative voices entangled in each other. The voice of Bowndie herself is heard first confessing to witchcraft and then retracting her confession. Other voices, sometimes introducing further conflict, include the voice of a previously executed witch, Elspeth Cursiter, as it is rendered by witnesses as well as the minister Henry Smith; the voice

[3] For the experience of encounters with fairies see Julian Goodare, 'Emotional Relationships with Spirit-Guides in Early Modern Scotland', in Julian Goodare and Martha McGill (eds.), *The Supernatural in Early Modern Scotland* (Manchester, 2020), 39–54.

of James Baikie; the voices of the other Orkney presbytery ministers and elders, collectively and sometimes individually; and the voice of the sheriff.

Witchcraft accusations against Marjorie Paplay play an important role in Bowndie's case, so some material relating to Paplay has been included in the text below. Henry Smith tried to organise a prosecution of Paplay from 1642 onwards. Paplay's son James Baikie, a wealthy man with influential supporters, tried in several ways to clear his mother's name, objecting to improper procedure and attempting to bring a counter-prosecution for slander. The presbytery generally supported Smith but was itself divided, with the minister Patrick Waterston and the ruling elder John Pottinger supporting Baikie; another minister, James Morison, intervened on Baikie's side in 1645. Smith repeatedly cited a declaration made by Elspeth Cursiter, a woman previously burned for witchcraft, saying that Marjorie Paplay was a witch.[4]

Thus Smith, together with some other ministers, tried to make Barbara Bowndie denounce Marjorie Paplay and some other women. Bowndie was initially interrogated 'in privat' by Patrick Waterston and Patrick Wemyss; they seem to have given her ale in order to get her to talk. John Aitken, commissary and son of the sheriff depute, was also involved in some aspects of this informal interrogation. Bowndie denounced several women informally – but later, in her formal interrogations, she withdrew her confession and insisted on her own innocence and that of the other accused women. This led to claims and counter-claims about what had been said and done earlier; Wemyss sought to uphold the accusations, while Waterston encouraged Bowndie not to denounce Paplay nor any other 'honest woman'. The focus on Paplay, the factional disagreements, and the interplay between the presbytery and the sheriff create a complex and multi-layered discourse.

TEXT

Source: Orkney Archives, Minutes of Presbytery of Orkney, 1639–1646, OCR/4/1.[5]

{p. 195} Presbyterie holdin at the kirk of Kirkwall November 2 1642. session 1....

The ministers and ruling elders present, viz: Mr Walter Stewart Moderator, Mr James Morisone, Mr Patrick Graham, Mr George Johnston, Mr Henrie Smith, Mr George Graham, *{p. 196}* Mr Alexander Sommervall, Mr James Haigie, Mr Williame Watsone, Mr Robert Persone, Mr James Aitkin, ministers:

4 For the political context of this struggle see Marshall, 'The Minister, the Merchant and his Mother'.

5 Digital images of this manuscript volume can be seen in the Virtual Volumes section of the ScotlandsPeople website, using the reference CH2/1082/1.

Hew Halcro of Cruke, Patrick Smith of Braco, Williame Sinclair of Saba, Alexander Johnston, John Beaton, Robert Chalmer, John Williamesone, Gilbert Mirland, ruling elders.... *{p. 202}*

Tertio Novembris,[6] Session 2.

The whole Brethren and ruling elders above nominat in the first session, were present, and John Germeston, ruling elder for Firth.... *{p. 203}*

Compeired Mr Henrie Smythe minister at Shapinshay and protested as followis:[7]

1. I protest that the Law and former practice of this presbytrie be remembred and keeped, which have still been used in matters of this kynd, viz. That no person delated to the civill Judge, as guiltie of witchcraft, be any who hes been convict and execut for witchcraft should be heard to complaine that they are slandered, Neither any be ordained to make satisfaction as slanderers of them, But that they be referred to the civill Judge to whome they were delated, there to be clensed, where they were fyled, or els to be and stand enacted till further tryall, as the Law and custome is.

2. I protest that no determination of this Judicatarie anent the scandall of Marjorie Paplay pursued be her or any in her name against Agnes Sinclair spouse to Magnus Cromartie in Diernes be prejudiciall to mee or any other adherent to this protestation wronged or pursued be the said Marjorie as a preparative to urge us, or any one of us, to satisfie as slanderers of her in respect of the suddaine death of Katharine Thomesone my mother in law after some hard speeches uttered be the said Marjorie to her *quinto Martii*[8] 1632; and of Elspeth Culsetter the witch her deposition anent the samyne in the moneth of June, 1633 yeers; as also in respect of some other points which I or any other person damnified or unjustlie pursued be the said Marjorie or any other in her name may Lay to her charge.

Which protestations forsaids the Brethren allow as reasonable. *{p. 204}*

Maister Harie Aitkin Shirref deput being desired for cleiring of Mr Henrie Smith his protestations to declare if Elspeth Culsetter witch did delate that Marjorie Paplay mother to James Baikie of Tankernes was a witch; Answered that the said Elspeth did indeed declare that the said Marjorie was the greatest witch of them all. Quhairupon Mr Henrie Smythe requyred act of presbyterie and protested *ut supra*.[9] And protested further against the said Shirref-deput That the said Marjorie might be enacted in the Shirref court bookes to underly the Law, as others who were delated be the said Elspeth Culsetter as guiltie of witchcraft, were, when she should be requyred, And that the said act might stand against her, untill further *{p. 205}* tryall were made anent

6 '3rd November'.
7 In margin: 'Smythes two protestations'.
8 '5th March'.
9 'as above'.

her witchcrafts, and that such meanes might be used for tryall and searching thereof as is usuall and accords of the Law.... {*p. 207*}

Compeired James Baikie of Tankernes, and desired a summonds against some certaine persons whome he alledged to be slanderers of his mother, which the Brethren could not condescend unto, In respect of Mr Henrie Smythe his protestations, and their approbation thereof. The said James protested the extract of[10] the said Mr Henrie his protestations, which the Brethren condescended unto.... {*p. 208*}

Master Henrie Smythe protests,[11] 1. That Marjorie Paplay her selfe should compeir and pursue her slanderers by giving in a bill of complaint conforme to the order seeing the said Marjorie is still resident in Kirkwall. 2. That whensoever the said Marjorie compeirs and complaines he adheres to his former protestations, earnestly requyring the presbyterie to take the samyne to their serious consideration, in case of his absence, which the Brethren condescended unto.... {*p. 250*}

Tertio Novembris [1643] Session 4

Sederunt, Master James Morisone moderator, Mr Walter Stewart, Mr Patrick Grahame, Mr George Johnston, Mr Patrick Weemse, Mr George Grahame, Mr William Watsone, Master James Aitkin, Mr James Haigie, ministers, Patrick Smythe of Braco, Magnus Tailyour, ruling elders....

Ordaines Barbara Bowndie, who is incarcerat for witchcraft to be examined in face of presbytrie, the nixt Weddensday *octavo Novembris*/.[12] Ordaines to motion unto the Brethren of the presbytrie that {*p. 251*} they would take some course anent the ordering of the house, for avoyding of confusion and tumult....

Presbyterie holden *octavo Novembris* session 1....

Sederunt, Master James Morisone moderator, Mr George Johnston, Mr Walter Stewart, Mr Patrick Waterston younger, Mr James Haigie, Mr Patrick Grahame, Mr Henrie Smythe, Mr George Grahame, Mr James Aitkin, minister[s]: Patrick Smythe of Braco, John Pottinger, Patrick Miller, Magnus Spence, Walter Houstoun, Alexander Cumyng, ruling elders.... {*p. 252*}

As touching the examination of Barbara Boundie continued the last meeting to be done this day, the Brethren ordaines it to be continued till the morrow: Wherupon John Pottinger skipper protested that so many as had relation unto John Aitkin shall not be her accusers, as namely, Mr James Aitkin, Mr George Grahame, Mr James Haigie, Master Walter Stewart, and

10 'protested the extract of': demanded a copy of.

11 In margin: 'Smyth his other two protestations'.

12 '8th November'.

Master Henrie Smithe:[13] becaus the said Barbara reported and said that John Aitkin had seduced her to slander some honest women in the toun, such as Elspeth, Marjorie, and Marion Paplays, to whom the said John hath relation, as being sonne in law to the forsaid Elspeth Paplay.

As for answer unto John Pottinger his protestation the Brethren present against whom he hath not excepted, declare that they think themselves to be so few, that if the rest should be removed, whom he desired, that they acknowledge themselves unable to give ane answer in name of the presbyterie, quhilk they can warrand.

Wherupon the persons fornamed against whom the said John excepted, protested that neither this protestation of the said John, nor any other anent this business of Barbara Bowndie and Marjorie Paplay, shall be allowed be the presbyterie, till they be orderly cited to answer for themselves unto these reasons which are to be given in against them.

It is ordained that at the examination of Barbara Boundie quhilk is continued unto the morrow, that three Brethren shall be examinators of her in face of the presbyterie and that every brother shall give information unto these *{p. 253}* three, and if any Brother that thinks his Information not fullie acted, shall have Libertie (having protested for Lieve) to examine her himselfe, upon the points to be Laid unto her charge.

Ordaines Master George Johnston, and Master Patrick Waterstoun younger to concur with the Moderator, in the examination of the said Barbara Boundie....

Nono Novembris[14] Session 2[d].

Sederunt, Master James Morisone moderator, Mr Walter Stewart, Mr William Watsone, Mr Patrick Grahame, Mr James Aitkin, Mr George Grahame, Mr Patrick Waterstoun younger, Mr James Haigie, Mr Thomas Cok, Mr David Watsone, ministers: John Pottinger, and Magnus Spence, ruling elders.... *{p. 254}*

The Brethren present thought good to send the Moderator with Mr George Johnston, and Mr Patrick Waterstoun unto Barbara Boundie, who was then presently in ward, to deall with her in privat, by prayer, and conference before they came in publick;[15] whereunto they condescended provyding, that Mr David Watsone Minister and Patrick Smythe of Braco ruling elder would assist them, quhilk they willingly did undergo.

After prayer and conference with the said Barbara in privat, she was presented publickly before the presbyterie and accused upon the points following:

[13] For Pottinger's connection with James Baikie and others see Marshall, 'The Minister, the Merchant and his Mother', 62.

[14] '9th November'.

[15] This informal questioning of Barbara Bowndie came to form the backdrop for the formal interrogation, as it is often referred to.

1. *primo*,[16] concerning her saying, that the Devill told her that if she should be put to death, the whole cornes should be blowne in the ayre by him. Answred she spoke of it for weaknesse of her owne flesh, and for feare of her Lyfe.

2. *Secundo*, Being asked, if she upon occasion of necessitie in Zetland, did condescend to serve the Devill. Answered, That being travelling with ane unhoven[17] childe four yeers[18] {*p. 255*} and being fainted by the way she became speechless, and so remained for the space of 24 houres, and was sore tormented, and the people said, that she had been with the Farie. She answered, she saw no Farie.

3. *Tertio*, Being asked concerning her giving her selfe out for a discoverer of witches. Answered That she denyes the same.

4. *Quarto*, being posed[19] in particular, concerning the Devill his apparitions in diverse shapes upon the ball-Ley,[20] and his having carnall copulation with Marjorie Paplay at that tyme, as a man hes adoe with a woman, Answered That Steven Anguson brought stark aill[21] to her, which made her to speake these wordes in Mr Patrick Waterstoun, and Master Patrick Weemse their hearing. Wherupon Mr Patrick Waterstoun replyed that she spake these words in presence of the Brethren, before Mr Patrick Weemse did speake with her and repeated it over againe before the brethren in both their audience, being as yet sober, and that it was afterwards, that a drink of small aill was brought unto her by Steven Angusone at her earnest requyst, to quench her thirst, and she[22] did take but take one drink of it, all the quhyle that the said Master Patrick was with her, reserving the rest in the stoup:[23] And being oftentimes in publick exhorted be Master Patrick Waterstoun, that she should not lie upon[24] Marjorie Paplay, nor no honest woman, did at that tyme reply unto him, God forgive you that beares over much with them, All which was spoken before she got that drink of aill.[25]

16 '1st'. Subsequent Latin numbers in this list correspond to the numerals: '2nd', '3rd' and so on.

17 'unhoven': unchristened (to 'hove' here means to raise a child to the font).

18 This probably implies that the child was four years old.

19 'posed': asked.

20 'ball-Ley': field for ball games. The idea of a ball-Ley (Ballvollen), as a meeting-place for witches, also appears in confessions in witchcraft trials in Finnmark, northern Norway, in 1621–5, most likely introduced in leading questions during interrogation by the Scotsman John Cunningham, who was in the service of the Danish king and district governor in Finnmark: Liv Helene Willumsen, 'Exporting the Devil across the North Sea: John Cunningham and the Finnmark witch-hunt', in Julian Goodare (ed.), *Scottish Witches and Witch-Hunters* (Basingstoke, 2013), 49–66, at pp. 60–2.

21 'stark aill': strong ale, with a high alcohol content, unlike the 'small aill' mentioned later which was a normal thirst-quenching drink.

22 This word inserted above the line.

23 'stoup': jug.

24 'lie upon': accuse falsely.

25 It seems important to establish a timeline for when she was given ale to drink: if this was before or after she confessed to witchcraft. Whether the ale was 'stark' (strong) or 'small' (weak) is also in dispute.

5 *Quinto*, Being asked againe whither she knew it to be of veritie, that she had seen the Devill Ly with Marjorie Paplay on the ball-Ley? Replyed that she knew nothing of it, but such as she was tryed upon, And being asked what that meant to be tryed upon? Replyed that the young commissar John Aitkin had said to her, Tell mee about Marjorie Paplay what ane woman she is, and thou shall never want thy Life,[26] spake more then enough of the said Marjorie at that tyme, and of sundrie other honest women, such as Elspeth and Marion Paplayes, and Elspeth Baikie and the good wife of Essinquoy. But Barbara Boundie said that she never knew no ill {*p. 256*} to these women.[27]

6. *Sexto*, being asked concerning Thomas Lentron his being put to death by Marjorie Paplay her witchcraft, by putting a quhyte thing Lyke calk[28] in his drink. Answered that what she had spoken therof was put in her mouth by Master Patrick Weemse.

Master Patrick Waterstoun replyed that that could not be, in respect he was beside and knew the contrair, and declared further, that it being inquyred be Master Patrick Weemse if she knew that Thomas Lentron had gotten any wrong, after long entreatie made to her to declare the same, if she knew ought of that matter, did at length declare that the said Thomas was witched be Marjorie Paplay; and upon his demaund she told the manner of it, by scraping in etc. Barbara Boundie answered That she had never spoken[29] concerning Thomas Lentron, if she had not been spired at,[30] be the said Master Patrick Weemse.

7 *Septimo*, The said Barbara being asked now againe, concerning the realitie of it, whither the said Marjorie had witched the said Thomas Lentron, as she had spoken before? Denyed the same.

8 *Octavo*, Being asked if she having been desired be Mr Patrick Weemse, to tell if she was one of the fourscore and nynteen that danced on the Links of Munes in Hoy?[31] At first denyed, but therafter confessed that she said it, which being conferred with her first words in saying that it was but sixe yeers, since the Devill deceived her, is found to varie in her speeches, for it is elleven yeers, or thereby, since the dancers in Munes were first spoken of.

9. *Nono*, Being asked what questions John Aitkin spired concerning Marjorie Paplay? Answered he spired about the hand of the dead man, that lay above her bed head and stired about her aill; But spired not, if the Devill Lay with her upon the ball Ley; Neither yet spired he about any of her sisters, nor of

26 This is an oral expression, exemplifying how features of orality are woven into the written court records.

27 This double negative indicates an oral expression.

28 'calk': chalk.

29 'had never spoken': would never have spoken.

30 'spired at': asked.

31 The narrative of ninety-nine persons dancing with the Devil in the fields of Moaness in Hoy had been told and retold in the local community for several years: Liv Helene Willumsen, 'The Ninety-Nine Dancers of Moaness: Orkney Women Between the Visible and Invisible', in Goodare and McGill (eds.), *The Supernatural in Early Modern Scotland*, 72–85.

Elspeth Baikie. Patrick Smythe of Braco declared that Barbara Boundie had said unto persons of respect, that they should have {*p. 257*} a care to bid the officers keep away some folk from her, In respect that offer had been made unto her by a Ladder of a tow[32] to hang her selfe, or of a knyfe to stick her selfe, quhilk would be ane easier death for her, then to be burnt. Denyed that either she said it, or yet that it was true.

Master Patrick Grahame reported that Barbara Boundie said that short after she was put in ward, John Baikie his woman came unto her, and said false common thief Looke that thou Lie not upon honest women, Denyes.

Master Patrick Grahame also declared that Barbara Boundie said unto him, that the Farie appeared unto her beside the ball-Ley coming out of Essinquoy, and told her all that she had spoken of Marjorie Paplay unto the Ministers. Denyes this also.

Shee being inquyred further be some of the Brethren (becaus John Pottinger had said that John Aitkin had seduced her to speake ill of Marjorie Paplay) whither John Aitkin had come to her himselfe alone, at any tyme, or not? Answered that he never came himselfe alone to her, without two or three with him, except one tyme that he came with ane officer.

Master James Aitkin for cleiring of his brother John Aitkin said that she had spoken these speeches of Marjorie Paplay, in Fubister, before she met with John Aitkin after her taking. Denyed it, and said that when she was taken, she ran into the sea, to her craig,[33] and was flyed[34] out of her wit. And being further delt with be Master James Aitkin anent his brother, said that if he had not first lifted that purpose,[35] she would not have lifted that purpose to him.

Being asked touching Cummer Dyk, if she knew any witchcraft to her? Denyed. Ordaines the Brethren to conveene to morrow after the morning prayers. {*p. 258*}

Decimo Novembris[36] 1643. Session 3.

Sederunt, Master James Morisone moderator, Mr Patrick Grahame, Mr Walter Stewart, Mr David Watsone, Master Henrie Smythe, Master Williame Watsone, Mr James Aitkin, Mr George Johnston, Mr Patrick Watersoun younger, Mr Thomas Cok, Mr George Grahame, Mr James Haigie, Mr

[32] 'tow': rope. This sentence is confused. The meaning is probably something like this: 'Considering that an offer had been made to her of a ladder and a rope to hang herself, or a knife to stab herself, which would be an easier death for her than to be burned.' The word 'by' in the sentence as written may mean that the scribe was thinking about the person who made the offer, and considered writing something like this: 'an offer had been made to her by a neighbour of a ladder and a rope'. Neighbours sometimes tried to stop imprisoned witches from confessing and naming names. Alternatively, the offer could have come from a compassionate or cynical prison guard.

[33] 'to her craig': up to her neck.

[34] 'flyed': afraid.

[35] 'lifted that purpose': raised that subject.

[36] '10th November'.

Thomas Abercrombie, ministers: Patrick Smythe of Braco, Thomas Traill, John Pottinger, ruling elders....

Ordaines Master Walter Stewart, and Mr David Watsone to conceave and forme a supplication to the secret counsell for purchasing a commission, to put Barbara Boundie to tortures, upon grounds publiklie declared in the presbyterie.

Ordaines Master Thomas Cok and Master George Johnston to go to the Shirref, and desire him that Barbara Boundie now in firmance, should be still retained unto such tyme as all lawfull meanes of tryall that can be thought upon, be used towards her.... {*p. 260*}

Master Thomas Cok, and Mr George Johnston report that the Shirref hath promised to retaine Barbara Boundie in prison, till the answer of his letter returne from the South concerning the said Barbara; And that he should doe nothing thereanent but be the Brethren's advyse.... {*p. 278*}

Presbyterie holden *tertio Aprilis*, 1644....

Sederunt, Mr James Morisone moderator, Mr George Johnston, Mr Walter Stewart, Mr Henrie Smythe, Master Patrick Grahame, Mr James Aitkin, Mr Patrick Waterstoun younger, Mr George Grahame, Mr William Watsone, Mr James Haigie, ministers: Hew Halcro of Cruk, David Heart of Rusland, John Cromartie elder, Walter Heddell, Patrick Smythe of Braco, Patrick Halcro of Wyre, Edward Halcro of Howton, ruling elders....

As touching Barbara Boundie, whom the Shirref promised to retaine in firmancie, according as the presbyterie should advyse him; the Brethren thought good this day that she should be retained still, untill such tyme as they expected dittaes against her to come from Zetland, and the Shirref to be advertised of this be Mr George Johnston[37] and David Heart[38].... {*p. 282*}

Presbyterie holden *primo Maii*, 1644, Session 1....

Sederunt, Mr James Morisone moderator, Mr Walter Stewart, Mr George Johnston, Mr Patrick Grahame, Mr David Watsone, Mr George Grahame, Mr Patrick Waterstoun younger, Mr Henrie Smith, Mr William Watsone, Mr James Haigie, Mr James Aitkin, ministers: Patrick Smythe of Braco, David Heart of Rusland, Hew Halcro of Cruk, John Cromartie elder in Cara, John Clerk, ruling elders.... {*p. 286*}

James Baikie protested[39] that he might have ane extract of Barbara Boundie her examination, quhilk was granted.

The said James protested also, that he might have the extract of the Law, and practice of this presbyterie, wherupon the condescent of the brethren

37 Minister of Kirkwall.

38 Ruling elder, Kirkwall.

39 In margin: '1. Baikie his protestation anent Boundie. 2. His protestation anent ane extract of the Law etc'.

unto Master Henrie Smythe his protestation *tertio Novembris* 1642. Sess. 2. was grounded, viz. That no person delated unto the civill Judge, as guiltie of witchcraft, should be heard to complaine that they are slandered etc.

Secundo Maii, 1644, Session 2.

Sederunt, Mr James Morisone, moderator, Mr George Johnston, Mr Walter Stewart, Mr Patrick Grahame, Mr Henrie Smythe, Mr Patrick Weemse, Mr David Watsone, Mr George Grahame, Mr Patrick Waterstoun younger, Mr James Haigie, Mr James Aitkin, Mr William Watsone, ministers: Patrick Smythe of Braco, David Heart of Rusland, John Cromartie elder, Hew Halcro of Cruk, Thomas Sinclair of Campstane, John King.... {*p. 289*}

Compeired James Baikie, and being desyred be the moderator, in a friendlie way, to declare whither or not, he had occasioned that scandall upon the presbyterie, in the matter of ruling elders: Answered that he thought he had given satisfaction unto the brethren commissioners directed unto him for that effect; and further he would not.

Mr James Haigie[40] protested that for a friendlie setling of all controversies betwixt him and James Baikie, he hath referred in the said James Baikie his power to chuse presentlie newtrall men to settle, wherof the said James accepted and nominats David Heart and Magnus Tailyour, who should settle the same within eight dayes, Referring the day and place unto the commoners.[41]

James Baikie compeired againe, and renewed his former protestation for ane extract of the law and practice of this presbyterie, *ut supra*.

The said James further protested[42] that he might have a just extract of the ground, wherupon Mr Henrie Smythe his protestations against Marjorie Paplay, or others in her {*p. 290*} name, and the brethrens condescent thairunto was taken.

The brethren answer that these bookes whence the ground of etc. are not in their hands, and that therfore they desyred him to use his best meanes for finding out of these books.

James Baikie protested that since the Brethren have not the books, that therfore their condescent unto the protestation is unlawfull: wherunto he added more, that except there be a lawfull delation against Marjorie Paplay, she cannot be frustrat of Justice.

The brethren present declared unto James Baikie that umquhile Mr Harie Aitkin Shirref deput delated unto them that Elspeth Culsetter, when she was burnt for witchcraft declared that Marjorie Paplay was the greatest witch of them all....

40 In margin: 'Haigie his protestation anent setling all controversies betuixt him and Baikie'.

41 'commoners': arbitrators.

42 In margin: 'Baikie his protestation'.

Tertio Maii, 1644. Session 3.
Sederunt, Mr James Morisone, Mr Patrick Weemse, Mr Patrick Grahame, Mr Walter Stewart, Mr George Johnston, Mr David Watsone, Mr George Grahame, Master Patrick Waterstoun younger, Mr Henrie Smythe, Mr James Aitkin, Mr James Haigie, ministers.... {*p. 291*}

James Baikie protested that any declaration made be umquhile Mr Harie Aitkin of ane alledged delation made be one Culseter,[43] against his mother Marjorie Paplay was no Lawfull delation, and ought not to hinder her of justice of any that has, or shall slander her, except the alledged delation be Lawfullie provin and condescended unto in particulars. And further the said James offers him selfe to prove that the said umquhile Mr Harie Aitkin did acknowledge and confesse that the said alledged delation made to him, be the said Culsetter was no lawfull delation, and that he as Judge, could no way proceid against the said Marjorie, be a Law, upon that delation.... {*p. 298*}

Sess: 3 *Agusti* 8 *post meridiem*
The Presbyterie meiting at the tyme appoyntit the Bretheren sent to the women in firmancie reported that Barbara Lauchtane alias Bundie stood to her former declaratioun 9 November 1643.

Ordains Mr George Jonstoun, Mr Patrick Grahame, Robert Peirsoun ministeris and David Heart Ruling eldair to go to morrow at sevin horis and deal furder with the said Barbara and Labour earnestly to bring hir to a Confessioun as also to heir Mr Patrick Weymis vindicate from these vyle imputationis and calumnies put upon him be the said Barbara.

Sess: 4 *Augusti* 9
Mr Patrick Weymis protestit that notwithstanding of the unjust calumnies Laid against him by Barbara Lauchtoun alias Bundie quho had deponed hir owin dittay and utheris also befoir ever he saw hir, yit by manifest and opin confessioun befoir the judge and ministeris, yit he was content that the shirriff and his bretherinis desyre to confront hir, especiallie for trying of some sinister and secret suggestionis quhich the said Mr Patrick alleadges to have being used by some imprejudice[44] of hir former confessioun and his credite.... {*p. 301*}

Presbyterie holdin 6 *Novembris* 1644 ... Sessio: 2. 6 November: *post meridiem* ... {*p. 303*}

The Sheriff clerk gave in some new depositions from Zetland against Barbara Laughtoun alias Bundie to be revised and marked be the presbyterie to morrow.

[43] Elspeth Cursiter.

[44] *Sic.* The scribe may have meant to write 'in prejudice'. The grammar of this whole paragraph is confused, but it seems to mean that Patrick Wemyss is agreeing to a recommendation by the sheriff and the presbytery to have Bowndie 'confronted', perhaps by himself. He thinks that someone has used 'sinister and secret suggestionis' to induce Bowndie to change her confession.

Sessio: 3. *Novembris* 7 1644
The Bretheren having examined and markit the depositionis givin in the nycht befoir against Barbara Lauchtoun alias Bundie did returne them unto the Shirreff Clerk subscrivit be the Clerk of Presbyterie.... {*p. 305*}

Sessio: *decimo quarto Novembris*[45] 1644
Sederunt, Mr George Jonstoun moderator, Mr Patrick Weymis, Mr Walter Steuart, Mr Patrick Grahame, Mr David Watsone, Mr Patrick Waterstoun younger, Mr Robert Peirsoun, Mr James Strikin.

The Bretheren foirsaid occasionallie being in the towne meat[46] upoun the Shiriff his intreatie to examine and merk some depositionis givin in of Late against Barbara Lauchtoun alias Bundie quhilk they did accordinglie.... {*p. 318*}

Presbyterie holdin *ultimo Aprilis*[47] 1645
Sederunt, Mr George Jonstoun moderator, Mr James Morisone, Mr Walter Steuart, Mr Patrick Weymis, Mr James Hagie, Mr James Aitkin, Mr George Graham, Mr Patrick Waterstoun younger, Mr William Watsoun, Mr Robert Peirson, Mr Henry Smyth, ministers, James Baikie, {*p. 319*} John Cragie, William Cragie, James Traill, John Scott, ruling eldaris.... {*p. 322*}

John Baikie gave in a paper concerning his mother Marjorie Paplay subscrivit with his hand and took instrumentis that he had given in the same....

Session 2^{d}. *Maii* 1 1645.
Sederunt, Mr George Jonstoun moderator, Mr Patrick Weymes, Mr James Morison, Mr Walter Steuart, Mr Henry Smyth, Mr Patrick Grahame, Mr George Grahame, Mr James Aitkin, Mr James Haigie, Mr Patrick Watersoun younger, Mr Thomas Abercromie, Mr William Watsone, Mr Robert Peirsone, ministeris, William Cragie, John Cragie, William Sinclair {*p. 323*} of Greinwall and Hew Sinclair of Dumhay ruling eldaris....

The bill given in be John Baikie yesterday[48] being read and found full of foul imputatiouns on the presbyterie and visitoris of the kirk of Kirkwall, Mr James Morisone was posed quhither he had any hand in it, quho confessed that he margined it[49] with his owin hand and the presbyterie findis furder collationing that peper with otheris givin in under his owin hand that they ar all of one hand wreat and thairupoun judges him in one voice to be manifastlie accessorie thairunto. The Presbyterie after mature deliberatione and one occasioun of more frequent writing of the Brethren and reading of Mr James

45 '14th November'.
46 'occasionallie being in the towne meat': happening to be in the town, met.
47 'last [30th] April'.
48 In margin: 'John Baikie his bill given in, was read and considered'.
49 'margined it': annotated it in the margin.

Morison his peperis, of new laying to heart the many foul affrontis and gross calumnies layd upon the Presbyterie by these peperis such as sclandering them of perjurie, corruptioun and partialitie every quhair throughout his paperis and of creueltie and circumventioun in one speciall place, As also his uther gross faultis as seditioun, renewing of jares composed,[50] kendling of discordis, instigating and informing of utheris to upbraide and to lay heavy and unjust reproaches and calumnies on the presbyterie, his manifast ambitioun and presumptioun in his whole cariadge befoir us this tyme, his vehement and unmanerly passioun quhich he would not compesce[51] being oftin admonished and rebuiked, bot in speciall his lying and declyning of the presbyterie, decernes him worthie to be suspended and be thir presentis suspendis him.[52] And becaus thair is ane ringing sclander of many gross oversightis {*p. 324*} committed be him in his calling, thinks good nothwithstanding of his present course to proceid to the visitatioun of the kirkis that upon furder sight and knowledge, they may proceid to furder censure if neid b[e]. This sentence being read in the said Mr James audience he declares that as he had befoir appealed, so he now appealed Lykwayis from the said sentence and protestit it sould be null till such time as it sould be rectified be the generall assemblie, Affirming with all[53] that he sould prove all that he had said or wreatten.

50 'jares composed': arguments (jars) that had been resolved.

51 'compesce': restrain.

52 For more details of the suspension of James Morison, see Marshall, 'The Minister, the Merchant and his Mother', 66–7.

53 'with all' (withal): moreover.

20. HELEN CLARK, NEWHAVEN, 1643–1645

INTRODUCTION

The initial prosecution of Helen Clark, the wife of a fisherman from Newhaven, occurred during years of intense witch-hunting in Scotland. A witchcraft panic took place during 1643 and 1644, in which 162 women and eleven men were accused.[1] Clark's prosecution stalled in 1643, but was resumed in 1645. Her case contains many details of neighbourhood interactions and problems in a fishing community.

The documents related to Clark's case come from the court of justiciary in Edinburgh. The first one is a pre-trial document produced in the locality. The other documents were produced centrally once a decision to hold a trial had been made – though, as we shall see, there is no evidence that the trial was pursued to a conclusion. The presentation of the documents below follows a chronological line. Some undated documents have been placed in their most likely order.

On 16 October 1643, Clark was brought before the burgh of Newhaven and the kirk session of North Leith, combined local secular and religious authorities, suspected of witchcraft. She was said to have consulted with a woman called 'Elspeth the spae wife' twenty years previously, who had since been convicted for witchcraft and burned. Various neighbours, male and female, also told stories of quarrels and misfortune. There had been at least three attempts at reconciliation rituals. One of these, involving an 'enchanted mackerel', had been successful at the time. Another reconciliation, involving the sickness of James Bissett, was supported by neighbours, who collected a financial 'contributione' for him and sent Clark herself to deliver it – though Bissett died in the end. However, Clark denied witchcraft. There seems to have been no attempt to interrogate her under torture; instead, on 18 November, she was pricked by a witch-pricker from Musselburgh, who

1 Liv Helene Willumsen, 'Seventeenth-Century Witchcraft Trials in Scotland and Northern Norway' (University of Edinburgh PhD thesis, 2008), 40, Table 2.

duly found a Devil's mark on her arm. A report about all this was sent from the presbytery to the lord advocate on 23 November.

Then there was a summons from the justiciary court in Edinburgh dated 22 December 1643, as Clark was now formally accused of witchcraft. The summons incorporated the entire text of what was intended to become the dittay in court. Versions of the neighbours' testimonies were converted into accusations directed against her. The summons ordered Clark to be arrested, and set a trial date: 12 January 1644. She was duly imprisoned, but no trial was held. No reason for this is given in the documents, but perhaps the central authorities were distracted by their efforts in assembling the army of the Solemn League and Covenant, which would cross the border into England on 19 January 1644. This was the beginning of more than one year in the Edinburgh tolbooth for Helen Clark.

The prosecution was resumed in March 1645. A number of men were summoned to form the assize: forty-one from North Leith, two from Edinburgh itself (the West Port), and five from Newhaven. Presumably an assize of fifteen members would have been chosen from this larger group. Twelve 'wemen witnessis' were also summoned. A document dated 12 March gave another witness's testimony against her. There was a petition from Clark, asking for a postponement of the trial so that her defence advocate could return; the petition mentions Andrew Fairfoul, minister of North Leith, as the main person promoting the prosecution. A postponement was ordered by the judge on 19 March, the last dated document that we have. As part of the trial proceedings, we have a group of brief but important documents written by the judge, rejecting five of the prosecution's nine accusations outright, and ordering the assize to treat the other four accusations with various degrees of caution. This judge, Alexander Colville, was a long-serving justice depute who tried numerous other witchcraft cases.

One of the rejected accusations was a classic instance of a quarrel followed by misfortune. Clark had quarrelled with Barbara Purves about a debt and threatened her, following which Purves' child had died by falling into a boiling cauldron. Many judges and assizes treated such sequences of events as straightforward proof of witchcraft, but here Colville ordered that the assize could not even consider it, on the grounds that the 'accident', as he called it, *could* have had some cause other than witchcraft. He treated the Devil's mark cautiously, too, ordering that it could not stand alone as evidence for conviction.

These sources show the development of the case as well as Helen Clark's own voice, both in the petition and in the rendering of her voice in the witnesses' testimonies. Ideas of *maleficium* as well as demonological ideas come to the fore in this trial. Traditional beliefs of malefice and weather magic surface along with demonological ideas like the Devil's mark. The trial documents give a glimpse of the ideas of witchcraft and the mentalities of the common people in a fishing community. There is no record of whether her trial was pursued to a conclusion.

TEXTS

Source 1: NRS, Court of Justiciary Process Papers, 1643–1650, JC26/13.

JC26/13, bundle 1, no. 3.[2]

{*p.* 1} *Apud Leithe decimo sexto mensis octobris anno millesimo sexcentesimo quadragesimo tertio.*[3]

The quhilk day in presens of Maister Androw Fairfull minister at the North Kirk of Leith George Craufurd baillie of Newheavin and maister Allexander Wardrop reidar at the said North Kirk Compeirit personallie Helene Clark spous to George Boyll fischer in Newheavin Quha being accuset befoir us as ane witche and upon the poyntis of witchecraft givin in be the persones under writtin To wit the said Helene being accused [*about 2 words crossed out*] for verrifeing thairof George Cunynghame Johne Cunynghame Jealis Hunter[4] Being solemnelie sworne befoir us with consent of the pairtie accused and in presence of hir selffe deponed that when scho wes seik about tuentie yeires syne or thairby that Ellspeth the spae wyff[5] quha wes brunt in South Leith for witchecraft did wasche the pairtie accused, and whan the said Ellspeth did wasch hir scho cawsit ane pair of sheitis to be pult about the tub that nane of the watter sould skayll[6] and efter the samyn wes finishit gave strait cumand to toome[7] the watter upon sum privat place quhair no repair wes,[8] And they that toomed the watter transportit the samyn to the sea syd and toomed it thair and thairefter cumeing home they declairit that the watter wes cassin in the sea, Quhairupon the pairtie accused with the spae wyff sayd that they war grieved, and thairefter thair arose ane gritt storme of wether and took away ane yole[9] of Newheavin and wes nevir seine thairefter And be the storme four houssis in Newheavin war blowin doun.

As also for verrifeing of the poyntis of witchecraft against the said Helein Clark accused Jeane and Christiane Thomsones tua persounes reputt to be of gude lyff and conversatioun[10] within the parochin being solemnelie sworne befoir us in presens of the partie accused depones that efter the pairtie accused

2 All the documents edited here from the box numbered JC26/13 come from the same bundle, which has no overall label, but some individual documents carry notes calling it bundle 1. The bundle also contains some documents on other cases.

3 'At Leith, 16 October 1643'.

4 'and sundrie utheris inhabitantis within the parochin of North Leith' crossed out here.

5 'spae wyff': prophetic or fortune-telling woman. Elspeth was a common name. No accused witch known as 'Elspeth the spae wife' has so far been identified, but one possibility is Elspeth Baird, accused in Leith in 1628 (SSW). This accusation was less than 20 years previously, but the incident with the water and the storm could have been earlier.

6 'scayll': spill.

7 'toome': empty, pour out.

8 'quhair no repair wes': where nobody would go.

9 'yole': yawl, small boat.

10 'conversatioun': behaviour.

wes waschin be the spae wyf bein inquyrit how the pairtie accused wes hir reply wes scho will be weill for they neidit not to send for hir seing thair wes nothing that wes done bot the pairtie accused could doe the samyn hirselff.

And siclyke for verrifeing of the poyntis of witchecraft against the said Helene Clark pairtie accused Ewfame Randell and Jonet Mckenlay nichtboris to the pairtie accuset being solemnelie sworne befoir us and in presence of the pairtie accused depones that the said Heleine pairtie accused affirmit to James Bissett (thair being ane contraversie betuixt hir and him anent hir sones sailling with the said James for bying of ane pairt of ane boit that hir sone had ane mynd to) that the said James sould nevir saill ane uther yeir thairefter Quhairupon the said James Bissett imediatlie thairefter took seiknes dwynet[11] and died.

Jonet Anniesoun spous to the said James Bissett for verrifeing of the poyntis of witchecraft against the said Helene pairtie accuset being solemnelie sworne befoir us and in hir presence depones that the said Helene cam upon Pasche Mounday[12] (quhen the defenderis husband wes lying seik and dwyneing) with tuentie schillings in hir hand that wes contribut be the nichtboris for supplie of his present necessitie The said Helene and the deponer haveing ane long tyme befoir that space not speking togidder in respecte of the former contraversie betuixt the deponers husband and the pairtie accused,[13] And beholding him in the face said that scho wissit that it war undone that is done,[14] Lykeas the deponer depones that haveing cumet in to the pairtie accuset hir hous and scho haveing sayd to Jonet Cunynghame the pairtie *{p. 2}* accused guid dochter that scho had provydit meikill salt, The pairtie accused replyit Tuty tuty thair wes more salt provydit nor wald be watt[15] this yeir, whairupon followit that their wes no tak of heiring[16] this yeir.

Margaret Burges indueller in Wairdie being sworne depones that thair being ane contraversie betuixt the deponer and the pairtie accuset anent ane pair of plaids quhilk wes impignorat[17] to the pairtie accused, And lowsing[18] the samyn frome hir scho sayd that scho sould repent it, And thairefter the deponeris husband cumand by the pairtie accused hir hous contractit such ane deidlie diseas that throw the pairtie accused hir invective malice to him took bed dwyned and died.

Margaret Boyll indweller in Leith sworne depones that thair being ane veriance betuixt the deponer and the pairtie accuset anent sum oysteris the pairtie accuset affirmit that the deponer sould rew it at that tyme And

11 'dwynet': wasted or pined away.
12 'Pasche Mounday': Easter Monday. In 1643 this was 3 April.
13 In margin: 'Witness James Bissit Couper'.
14 'scho wissit that it war undone that is done': she wished that what had been done was undone.
15 'more salt provydit nor wald be watt': more salt supplied than would be wet (i.e. used for preserving fish).
16 'tak of heiring': catch of herring.
17 'impignorat': given in pledge (for a loan).
18 'lowsing': redeeming.

thairefter the deponer tuik seiknes and lay auchtene oulkis[19] seik dwyneing And the pairtie accused haveing sent in ane mccrell[20] about Fasterence Evin[21] with Helene Sword now deid scho then recoverit heir health and became weill, and when the said Helene brocht in the mcrell scho gave the deponer ane strait comand that scho sould under the paine of hir lyff nocht eit of it that nicht bot to eit it the morne neirest hir hairt.

Barbara Purves indweller in Leith being solemnelie sworne befoir us and in our presence depones that about ten yeir syne or thairby the pairtie accuset hir husband being addettit to the deponer Sevin pundis And the deponer haveing cumet to hir and inquyreing hir money the pairtie accused sayd go home go home, tho sould go worse home nor scho cam afeild[22] Quhairupon scho haveing cumet home the deponer hir bairne wes taikin out of ane seithing kettill.[23]

Helene Thomsone spous to Williame Craig in Newheavin being solemnelie sworne befoir us and in our presence that Johne Smith haveing cumet in to hir hous and affirmeing the pairtie accused wald be his deathe seing that he had not maried the pairtie accused hir dochter contractit seiknes and suspecting the said Helene Clark pairtie accused to be the occasioner thairof went to the pairtie accuset at the direction of the deponer to crave his healthe and send about ane pynt of aill To the quhilk the pairtie accused gave him tua eggis quhilk he eittit and quhen he wes telling the pairtie accuset that he wold go to ane doctor to mend his back scho sayd that he could not doe it And ane schort tyme thairefter he died. {*p. 3*}

Apud Leith decimo octavo novembris anno domini 1643.[24]

The same day in presens of Mr Andro Fairfull minister at the North Kirk of Leith George Craufurd baillie of Newhaven and Mr Allexander Wardrop reidar and sundrie of the elderis of the said kirk Williame Stobie in Musselburght haveing sichtit the pairtie accused and scho haveing cassing af hir clois of hir left airme thair wes fund thair upon ane mark Quhilk the said Williame persaving thrust ane prene being ane insche and ane half of lenth thairin quhairof the said Helene wes nowayes sensible nor no blood followit efter the preine wes taikin out haveing remaynit ane half hour within hir airme.

Signed: Mr William Dalgleische moderator.

At Edinburgh the 23 of November[25]

Recommends to the Lord advocat to peruse thir depositions and to report his judgement thereanent.

[19] 'auchtene oulkis': eighteen weeks.

[20] 'mccrell': mackerel.

[21] 'Fasterence Evin': Shrove Tuesday. In 1643 this was 14 February.

[22] 'tho sould go worse home nor scho cam afeild': you will go home in a worse state than when you came out. The scribe has mixed the second-person 'thou' with the third-person 'scho'.

[23] 'seithing kettill': boiling cauldron. It later emerges that the child died.

[24] 'At Leith, 18 November 1643'.

[25] This note is in a different hand from the main text.

JC26/13, bundle 1, unnumbered document.[26]

Charles be the grace of God king of Great Britaine France and Ireland defender of the faithe To our Lovittis [*blank*] Messingeris our Shereffs in that pairt conjunctlie and severallie speciallie constitute greitting. Forsameikle as[27] it is humlie meanit and complenit to us our trustie and weilbelovit counsallors Sir Thomas Hope of Craighall barronet our advocat for our intreis and Robert Robiesone William Dunkiesone parochiners in North Leithe for thame selffis and in name and behalf the remanent sessioun of the said kirk informeris to our advocat in the mater underwrittin,

Upoun Helene Clerk spous to George Boyle fischer in Newheavin that quhair albeit be the devyne law of almychtie God mentionat and set doun in his sacred word all useris and practizeries of witchcraft sorcerie charming suithsaying and inchanting ar ordanit to be puneist to the daith As also be diverse actis of Parliament of this our kingdome Speciallie be the 73 act of the Nynth parliament of our darest goodame queane Marie of good and nevir deing memorie It is expreslie provydit statute and ordanit that na maner of persone or persones of quhatsumevir estait conditione or degrie thai be off presume nor tak upone hand to use any maner of witchcraft sorcerie or nicromancie Nor gif thame selffis to have any sic craft or knawledge thairby to abuise our good subjectis As also that na persone or persones seik any help responce or use consultatione with any sic useris or abuseris foirsaidis under the payne of deathe Alsweill to be execute againe the user abuser and sorcerer as the seiker of the responce or consultatione As in our saidis lawis and actis of parliament at lenth is contenit,

Nothwithstanding[28] quhairof It is of veritie that the said Helene Clerk a tuentie yeir since or thairby being veseit[29] with ane heavie seiknes and deseis, schoe for hir cure and releiff thairof expres againe the lawis of almychtie God and our actis of Parliament preferring the cure and help of the Devill and his devillische and wicked instrumentis witcheis and sorceris befoir the help and cure of the omnipotent and almychtie God and the ordiner meanes appoyntit be his sacred word, Addressit hir selff and consultit with ane Notorious witche callit Elspethe the spay wyfe quha was convict and brunt for witchcraft be quhus devillische directiones the said Helene did wesche hirselff with water charmet and inchantit be the said spay wyfe, in the practeizeing quhairof ane pair of scheittis was put about the tub in the quhilk the water was put that nane of the charmit water sould spill or ryn over with this express injunctione gevin be the said witch that eftir the said Helene hir wascheing thairwith the

26 This document carries a note saying that it is from bundle 1, but it forms a separate item in the box JC26/13 because it is larger than the other documents in the bundle. The text runs continuously, with breaks indicated by words in bold and numbered marginal notes. Here, paragraph breaks have been added editorially for clarity.

27 'forasmeikle as': because.

28 In margin: '1. Anent the pannells cure be the spae wyfe'.

29 'veseit': visited, afflicted.

said charmet or inchantit water sould be careit to some private place quhair na repair of peaple was and thair to be cassin furth and tumed, Bot sa it is that the said inchantit water being transpoirtit and careit to the sea syde and castin in the sea be the careyers thairof Be that occasione and be the sorcerie and witchcraft of the spay wyfe and of the said Helene Clerk quhilk was cured thairby, Ane horrible and grivous storme and tempest of wind and wether arrais[30] quhilk tuik away ane bot or yole out of the harburie of Newheavin quhilk nevir was sene agane As also four severall houssis within the said toun war blawin doun and distroyit to the ground to the greit loss of the awneris and heritouris thairof. Eftir the practeizeing of the quhilk devilissche cure upone the said Helene Clerk in maner foirsaid the said spay wyfe being inquyret be certane nychtbouris how the said Helen was and wald be, schoe for answer thairto declairit that schee wald be weill aneughe for thai neidit not to ask at hir sic questiones becaus all that was doun for cureing of hir could have bene alsweill practeizet and doun be the said Helen hirselff as be the said spay wyfe.

Item[31] schortlie thaireftir ane contraversie haveing fallin out betwix the said Helene Clerk and James Bisset for bying over his head of ane pairt of ane bot that the said Helene hir sone had ane mynd to, the said Helene in revenge thairof threatnit maist maliciouslie the said James Bisset that he sould nevir prosper not saill ane uther yeir thaireftir, According to the quhilk devillische threatning and be the said Helene Clerk hir devillische sorcerie and witchcraft, he immediatlie thaireftir contractit ane seiknes quhairin he remanit bedfast with contenuall sweiting ane lang space thaireftir And in end deceissit thairof, lykas the said Helen a litle befoir his daith viz. at the Pace Monday immediatlie preceiding came to Jonet Anisone spous to the said James Bisset quha had not spokin with hir ane lang tyme of befoir And behalding the said James Bisset being in bedfast and looking in his face utterit thir words to the said Jonet his spous, I wische that war undone that is done, declairing thairby that he was bewitchit be hir and be hir devilrie and witchcraft casin upone him that feirfull seiknes quhairof he deceissit as said is, And siclyk schortlie thaireftir the said Jonet Anisone haveing come to the said Helene Clerk hir hous and forgaddering[32] with Jonet Cuninghame dochter to the said Helene declairit to hir that schoe had provydit meikle salt meaneing for the herring at Dumbar drave,[33] Quhairunto the said Helen replyet in thir wordis in maist threatning and bitter maner, Tuty tattie thair is mair salt provydit nor will be wat this yeir, Quhairupone and according to the said Helen hir devillische predictione and be the sorcerie and witchcraft practeizet be hir and hir devillische assosiattis thair was no tak of herring that yeir.

30 'arrais': arose.

31 In margin: '2. Anent James Bissett his daithe be hir sorcerie'.

32 'forgaddering': meeting.

33 In margin: '3. Anent her sorcerie upone the Dumbar herringe drave'.

Item[34] Margaret Burgess the spous of umquhile [*2 words blank*] in Wairdie haveing laid ane pair of plaidis in wad[35] to the said Helene upone ane sowme of money, quha haveing schortlie thaireftir lowset the samyn plaidis, The said Helene at the redeameing and louseing thairof in great splayne[36] and anger threatnit to the said Margaret and said to hir schoe sould repent the louseing thairof quhairupone the said [*2 words blank*] spous to the said Margaret Burges shortlie thaireftir cuming by the said Helene hir hous, contracttit be the said Helen hir sorcerie and witchcraft ane heavie and greavous seiknes that was laid be the said Helene upone him, past hame to his hous tuik bed and remanit in great dollour[37] payne and torment with continuall switing ane lang tyme and in end decessit thairof, And sua be hir sorcerie and witchcraft was crewallie murdreist and slane.

Item[38] ane discord and varience haveing fallin out betwix Margaret Boyle indweller in Leith and the said Helene Clerk for sume oisters The said Helene out of ane devillische dispositione and mad humour threatnit with cursed speiches the said Margaret saying to hir thir wordis that schoe sould repent and rew it or it war lang,[39] according to the quhilk wiked and devillische threattning ane grevous seiknes was laid upone the said Margaret Boyle be the said Helene Clerk hir sorcerie and witchcraft quhairin schoe lay dwneing in great dollour and payne the space of auchtene oulkis thaireftir or thairby, Quhairupone the said Helen being upbraidit be hir nychtboris quha affirmit that be hir devillische meanes sorcerie and witchcraft the said Margaret Boyle was sua paynet and tormentit, the said Helene for cure and help of the said Margaret be hir [*damaged, word partly legible*[40]] witchcraft and charmeing sent in to the said Margaret Boyle ane inchantit or charmet makrell quhilk was careyit be [*damaged, word partly legible*[41]] Sword now deid with the strait injunctione and directione that the said Margaret sould [*damaged, word partly legible*[42]] eat thairof that nycht under the payne of hir lyfe, According to the quhilk injunctione and be the said Helene Clerk hir charmeing sorcerie and witchcraft abonewrittin the said Margaret Boyle was cured of hir said deseis.

Item[43] at a ten yeir since or thairby Barbara Purves indweller in Leith haveing cume to the said Helene Clerk and craveing payment fra hir of ane debt of sevin pundis money awand be hir husband to the said Barbara, The said Helene in great wreathe and anger brak furthe in thir wordis Saying to

34 In margin: '4. Anent the daithe of the husband of Margaret Burges'.
35 'in wad': in pledge (for a loan).
36 'splayne' (spleen): resentment.
37 'dollour' (dolour): sorrow.
38 In margin: '5. Anent Margaret Boyle hir malifice and cure thairof'.
39 'or it wer lang': ere long, before long.
40 The word is probably 'sorcerie', as this is a common combination in other sources consulted.
41 The word is probably 'Helene'.
42 The word is probably 'nocht'.
43 In margin: '6. Anent the bairnes daithe of Margaret Purves'.

hir goe hame goe hame thow sall goe wars hame than thow hes cume a feild at quhilk tyme be the said Helen hir sorcerie and witchcraft practeizet be hir ane of the said Barbara hir bairnes at the said Barbara hir hame cuming was brunt to dead in ane seitheing caldrone or kettle and was tane dead furth thairof.

Item[44] the said Helene Clerk haveing consavit ane deadlie heatret malice and evill will aganes John Smyth in Newheavin becaus he refuiset to joyne him selff in mariadge with Issobell Boyle hir \dochter/ the said Helene hir dochter [*sic*] the said Helene in revenge thairof and be hir sorcerie and witchcraft laid ane heavie and greavous seiknes upone the said Johnne Smyth quha haveing thaireftir for his releiff of the said desease and be directione of Helene Thomesone spous to William Craig in Newheavin come to the said Helene Clerk the unlayer[45] of the said seiknes upone him to crave his health, the said Helene Clerk for his cure and releiff gave to him tua eggis quhilk he than eattit at hir desyre Eftir his eatting of the quhilkis eggis the said Johnne Smyth finding him selff no better come bak agane to the said Helene and said to hir that he behouvet[46] to goe to some doctor of phisick to be cured, To the quhilk the said Helene replyet and affirmet that thair was na doctor could mend him thairof, sua that within few dayis thaireftir he deceissit of the said seiknes, And sua the said Johnne Smyth was crewallie murdest and slane be the said Helene hir sorcerie and witchcraft practeizet be hir upone him at the tyme foirsaid.

And finallie[47] upone the auchtene day of November last bypast the said Helene Clerk being presenttit and examinat be Mr Andro Fairfoull minister at the Northe Kirk of Leith George Crawfurd baillie in Newheavin and sundrie of the sessione of the kirk concerneing hir witchcraft and sorcerie abonewrittin And demandit gif schoe had the devillische mark upone hir quhilk schoe denyet, William Stobie in Mussilbrught[48] being present haveing sightit the said Helene and hir claithes tane aff hir thair was thane fund upone hir left airme the said mark quhilk the said William Stobie knawing and perseaveing for tryell and cleiring thairof thrust in ane lang great preine being ane insche and ane halff of lenthe in the said mark quhairof the said Helene was noways sensible, quhilk preyne remanit thairin the space of halff ane hour and eftir drawin furthe thairof na blood followit Off the quhilkis cryme of sorcerie and witchcraft and distructione and away taking of the persones foirsaidis thairby the said Helene is airt and pairt for the quhilkis crymes schoe aucht

44 In margin: '7. Anent the daithe of John Smyth be hir sorcerie verifeit be Margaret Thomsone the spous of William Craig in Newheaven [*words crossed out*] Kathreine Smyth sister to [*'David' crossed out*] John Smyth uset as witnes'.

45 'unlayer' (on-layer): layer-on.

46 'behouvet': needed.

47 In margin: '8. Anent the devillis mark upone hir left airme Tryit and fund thairupone be William Stobie in Mussilburch etc.'

48 William Stobie in Musselburgh was a witch-pricker who travelled around to prick suspected witches.

and sould be puneist conforme to the lawis and actis of Parliament abone writtin to the terour and example of utheris to commit the lyke gif sua be.

Our will is heirfoir and we chairge yow straitlie and commandis that incontinent thir our Lettres sene ye pas and in our name [*about 10–12 words damaged*] committer of the cryme abonespecifeit in maner foirsaid and the said George Boyle fischer in Newheavin hir spous for his entreis to compeir befoir our Justice and his deputtis And underly our lawis for the samyn In our tolbuithe of Edinburgh the twelff day of Januar nixtocum in the hour of caus to the effect that upone hir tryell and convictione of the said crymes schoe may be puneist in hir persone and guidis conforme to the lawis of this realme, Attoure[49] that ye in our name and aucthoritie lawfullie summond ane assyse togidder with witnessis quha best knawis the veritie of the said Helene Clerk hir guiltienes of the crymes foirsaidis Nocht exceiding the Number of fourtie fyve persones to compeir befoir our Justice and his deputtis the saidis day and place to pas upone the said Helene hir assyse and to heir witnessing in the premissis ilk persone under the payne of Ane hundrethe merkis According to justice as ye will answer to us thairupone, the quhilk to doe we commit to yow conjunctlie and severallie our full power be thir our Lettres delyvering thame be yow dewelie execute and indorsat agane to the beirer, Gevin under our signet Att Edinburgh the twentie tua day of December And of our Rigne the nynetene yeir 1643.

Ex deliberatione duorum consilii etc.[50]

[*Signed:*] Jo: Bannatyne.

Penultimo Decembris 1643.[51] [*Fragment of seal on verso.*]

JC26/13, bundle 1, no. 2.[52]

Additiounis to Helene Clerk hir dittay

Item in the moneth of [*1 word blank*] the year of God i^{m}vi^{c} [*1 word blank*] yeiris Ye the said Helene haveing sauld to Margaret Runsieman than servant to Lucres alias Luse Cokburne indweller in [*1 word blank*] ane laid gallone[53] full of oisteris And cuming at that tyme to the said Lucres hous thairwith, ye set doun the laid gallone and bad the said servand namitt Margaret Runsieman to toome the leid gallone Quhilk servand ansring yow in ruche and hard woirdes, I haif nothing to toome it, ye marking that hir misbehavior and angrie countenance ye come and toomed the lead gallone your selffe Quhairupone the said servand woman tuik up the said lead gallone and slang it frome hir and thairwith brak

49 'Attoure': also.

50 'Decided by twelve of the (privy) council'.

51 '30 December 1643'.

52 This document has no complete date, and it is unclear whether it was written in the 1643 phase of the proceedings or the 1645 phase.

53 'laid gallone': cauldron or vat, made of lead or copper.

ane of the girthes[54] thairof Quhilk being sa done be hir in your presence and in sic dispyte, ye than said to the said servand woman, hes thow done this I sall gar the[e] rew[55] and repent the same, Accordingly to the quhilk malicious thraitining sua utterit be yow the said Margaret Runsieman the same verie nycht be your sorcerie and witchcraft laid be yow upoun hir, hir leg was brunt. Quhilk sho hes affirmit to be of veritie in presence of the Laird of Benholme, James Halyburtoun, Robert Robertson, John Luikup and Mr Alexander Wairdrope.

Item ane aucht yeir syne or thairby Ye the said Helene haveing come to William Oswale [*sic*] cordiner in South Leith the husband of Jeane Grahame ye than desyrit him to mak ane pair of guid buittis \to your sone/ thraitining him at that tyme gif the buittis war nocht guid and sufficient he sould nevir make ane uthir pair to ony in Newheavin thairof, According to the quhilk thraitining he nevir mad ony thaireftir Bot within aucht dayis thaireftir be your sorcerie and witchcraft ye laid ane heavie diseas and seiknes upone the said William Oswale Quha dwynet and pynet away dyveris dayis and nychtis with grit dolloris and payne thairintill And means be your sorcerie and witchcraft deceissit thairof And sua was crewallie murdreist and slane by your sorcerie and witchcraft laid be yow upone him as said is.

As to the daith of John Smyth be your sorcerie and witchcraft in maner specifeit in the 7 article of the first dittay For verification thairof uses Katharene Smyth his sister as witnes quha declaires that she hard hir brother upone his deid bed leave his daith and causis thairof upone the said Helene Clerk be hir sorcerie and witchcraft.

JC26/13, bundle 1, unnumbered document.

{*p. 1*} Roll of the names of Inquest for Helene Clerk in Newhevin

North Leith

James Ramsay metster[56]	John Tailyefeir wever
Robert Bar wriyt	James Home mailmaker
John Bar timberman	John Waldie timberman
Alexander Rankene	James Rob cordiner
Elias Wilsone couper	John Seatoun baxter
James Powis wriyt	James Clerk metster
Adame Or couper	Thomas Hude sailer
John Ginkene sailmaker	James Cunyinghame
Alexander Low wever	Robert Blyth

54 'girthes': hoops.

55 'gar thee rew': cause you to regret.

56 'metster': official who checks weights and measures.

John Buchan cordiner
Robert Hendersone wriyt
Mongo Wriyt
Robert Wilsone
James Mathie
James Pantoune
John Maistertoun
John Campbell quheilwriyt
James Ramsay metster
Mathow Campbell wever
John Mathesone couper
Alexander Inglis balmaker [*sic*]
John Inglis
John Gordoune smyth
Robert Blak husbandman
John Aire smyth
Androw Maisone timberman
Malcome Bar timberman
John Lindsay tailyeor
William Stewart mailmaker
William Mitchell younger
George Rae merchant
William Castrum mailmaker
James Bisset at Wastport of Edinburgh
Thomas Dowglas tanner thair

For Newheavin

Thomas Gudlet fermer
John Sword thair
William Crystie thair
George Taite thair
John Cunyinghame boteman

Wemen witnessis

Jeane Thomsone dead[57]
Crysteane Thomsone
Ewphame Randell
Barbara Purves
Margaret Thomsone
Jean Grahame dead
Margaret Boyll dead
Margaret Runzeman
Jeane Cunnyinghame in Newhevin dead
Margaret Burges in Wirdie
Katharene Smyth dead
Jonet Makinle in Gruntounend {*p. 2*}

Upone the tent and ellevent dayes of Mairche I^{m}vi^{c} fourtie fyve yeirs I James Douglas Justice maiser past and lawfullie warnit and chairget the heall persones of Inquest within specifeit to compeir befoir the Justice and his deputes within the tounis tolbuith of Edinburgh upone the Inquest of Helen Clerk under the paines contenit in the act of Parliament to compeir all the tuelf day of Mairche instant. This I did befoir thir witnessis, James Douglas my sone, Hairie Balfoure in North Leith. Subscrivit with my hand JDouglass Jwsteice offiessar.

JC26/13, bundle 1, no. 1.

[*Endorsed:*] Jonet Mcinlay depositione concernes the witch of Newheavin tane up the xii of Mairch 1645.

{*p. 1*} Apud Edinburgh xii Martii 1645 In presence of Mr Alexander Colvill of Blair his majesties Justice deput.

57 Here and later, the word 'dead' has been added in a different hand. It may mean that the woman is to testify concerning someone's death.

Jonet Mcinlay spous to John Smetoun cowman in Brunteilland for the present and quha dwelt at Newheavin 1643 yeiris being examinat upone hir oathe depones as eftir followis That about the end of August or thairby anno 1643 Robert Haddin burges of Edinburgh was possessor of tua cobillis[58] quhich always belongit to Newheavin quhairof James Bisset a seafaring man indweller in Newheavin was skipper of the one And \not long/ eftir the tyme the said James Bisset bocht the halff of one of the cobbilis (that he possesit and quhairof he was skipper) frome the said Robert Haddin in the deponers hous to the quhilk bargane the deponers husband John Smeatoun and hir selff war eare witnessis.

Farder depones that upone the morow immediatlie eftir following[59] Hew Boyle[60] fischer in Newheavin and sone to Helene Clerk the pannell came in to the deponers hous And demandit the deponer gif schoe had hard of a bargane maid betwix Robert Haddin and James Bisset concerneing the buying of ane coble (the said Hew Boyle being accumpaneit with Jonet Fortoun his mother in law) and callit for ane pynt of aill[61] that he myght inquyre of the bargane To quhom the deponer answerit that it was trewth that the bargane was endit and subscrivit and schoe saw and hard it To quhom the said Hew Boyle replyet, how hes that beggar loun gottin money to buy the coble, Unto quhom the deponer replyet that the sowme was payit for the coble and ane dischairge gevin. Farder depones that Helene Clerk now upone panell came to the deponers hous the nixt morneing immeditalie following and callit for ane chopping[62] of aill And demandit the deponer gif it was of veritie that James Bisset had bocht the halff of[63] one of Robert Haddins cobles, quha answerit It was verie trew, quhilk words the said Helene Clerk heiring utterit thir speaches to the deponer, Hee James Bisset boucht the halff of that coble he sall nevir goe to Dumbar in hir For my sone boucht the uther halff of hir And he sall have hir all And depones upone hir great oathe schoe said farder he will pyne away lyk ane head hair,[64] Quhairupone it followit that within fyftene dayis thaireftir the said James Bisset tuik bed and lay pyneing with seiknes the space of 29 weikes eftir and wald have swat sumtymes thrie sarkis[65] in a day And soe dwynet and deit. Farder depones that some few days befoir the said James Bisset his depairtour The nychtbouris in Newheavein gatherit ane contributione among tham selffis to help and supplie the necessitie of the said James in his seiknes quhilk contributione the said Helene Clerk ressavit brocht in to the said James Bisset his hous and sit doun befoir his bedsyd And

58 'cobillis': rowing-boats.
59 'James Bissett botman' crossed out here.
60 'sone' crossed out here.
61 'And dem…' crossed out here.
62 'chopping' (chopin): tankard.
63 'Ro…' crossed out here.
64 This simile seems to refer to men's hair loss while ageing.
65 'sarkis': shirts.

lookit in his face he being than sweating And utterit thir speaches to him, Hoes me gossop gif it war to doe that is done,[66] to quhom James replyet, Lord tak me ather aft this warald[67] or els grant me my healthe, unto quhom the said Helene replyet, Ill warand gossop[68] your days not be long now, And in effect the said James Bisset within aucht days thaireftir deceissit.

[*Signed:*] AColville. {*p. 2*}

Farder depones upone hir oathe that umquhile John Smyth smyth in Newheavin quha sould have mareit Helene Clerkis dochter quha buir ane bairne to him About ane 15 days befoir his daith, being in the deponers hous sit doun at the fyre syd with his goodsister in cumpanie with him And being wonderfullie pynet spak thir wordis to the deponent, schoe haveing regratit[69] his waiknes and present estait, In good faith Jonet thair is none ye wyt[70] of my waiknes bot Helene Clerk and schoe will be my daith for I am trublit with hir in the nycht and uther thrie women with hir.

[*Signed:*] AColville.

JC26/13, bundle 1, unnumbered document.

{*p. 1*} First anent the Inchantit watter and hir wasching be the spae wyfe repellit.[71]

Secund anent James Bissetis daith *relevat*[72] in the first member thairof and nocht of the secund.

Thrid anent Margaret Burges *relevat* the persewar condiscending[73] how long scho was seik and quhen sho deceissit.

The fourt anent the seiknes of Margaret Boyle laid on hir and the said Helenes cure of it, the Inchantit mccrell fund relevant with this caveat that the assyse tak heid to the probatioun.

5. The fyft anent the Injurie done to Barbara Purves bairne and falling in the sething caldroun deleit[74] be ressone the accident mycht have fallin out *aliunde*[75] not be witchcraft.

6. The saxt article anent John Smyth and his seiknes and daith and Inchantit egs nocht relevant as is conceaved.[76]

66 'Hoes me gossop gif it war to doe that is done': Well now, my friend, if only what has been done were still to do (i.e. I wish that this had not happened).

67 'aft this warald': off (away from) this world.

68 'Ill warand gossop': I'll assure you, my friend.

69 'regratit': regretted, deplored.

70 'wyt': blame.

71 'repellit': refused.

72 'is relevant'.

73 'condiscending': specifying.

74 In margin: 'deleit'.

75 'from another (cause)'.

76 In margin: 'repellit'.

The first and second eikit[77] articles bayth repellit.

The Last article anent the Devillis mark and hir bruit of witchcraft[78] findis it may be conjoinet with ony of the articles fund relevant per se. {*p. 2*}

1. The first article nocht relevant.

2. Finds the secund relevant in the first pairt thairof anent James Bisset his bewitching and daithe.

3. As to the thrid article concerning the bewitching of Margaret Burges hir husband and his daithe Finds it relevant, The persewer condiscending how long he remanent seik and of the tyme of his daithe.

The \fyft/[79] ordainit to be deleit over the bairnes falling in the ketill and burning to deid be reassone the accident thairof myght haif probablie fallin out *aliunde* nocht be witchcraft.

As to the \fyft/[80] finds it relevant with this caveat that the assyse be adverteist to tak heid to the probation.[81]

JC26/13, bundle 1, unnumbered document.[82]

1. First article[83] nocht *relevant.*

2. Secund finds relevant in the first member bot nocht in the secund anent the hering drave.

\4. Fourt/[84] relevant with this caveat that the assise be adverteist to teak heid to the probatioun becaus the mint[85] ar nocht specefeit \nor/ [*2 words illegible*] persones.

\5./[86] Deleit be ressone that the accident be falling in the seithing caldrone myght probablie haif come *aliunde* nor be witche craft.

3. As to the thrid article anent the pannells bewitching of Margaret Burges quhairby scho contractit ane lingering and sueitting seiknes and thairefter deceissit, *relevat* the persewer condiscending how long scho lay seik of that seiknes and how sone scho deceissit.[87]

The first eikit article nocht *relevat.*

The secund eikit article nocht *relevat.*

77 'eikit': added.

78 'bruit of witchcraft': reputation for witchcraft.

79 In margin: '5 deleit. Margaret Boyles bairne'.

80 'fourt' crossed out here.

81 In margin: 'Relevant fyft'.

82 This document has no heading, endorsement or date. On the back are written the first four lines of an incomplete and apparently unrelated text about the widow of a burgess of Linlithgow.

83 'anent Elspet' crossed out here.

84 '3. Thrid' crossed out here.

85 Reading uncertain. Perhaps an abbreviation for 'minatory' (threat).

86 '4' crossed out here.

87 In earlier documents, it was Margaret Burgess's *husband* who was said to have died.

Anent the article and[88] common bruit to Joyne that with ony other poyntis fund relevant.

Item anent the article of the Devills mark to be Joynet with ony of the poyntis fund relevant per se.

As to the sixt article gif it quar lybellit that the tua eggis war Inchantit and charmet for, Nocht relevant as is conceavet.[89]

JC26/13, bundle 1, unnumbered document.[90]

My Lord Justice and his majesties advocat unto yow humelie menis and shawis I your pure crature Helene Clerk spous to George Boyle fisher in Newhevin that quhair I am incarcerat keipit and detenit in waird within the tolbuith of this burgh of Edinburgh \be the space of this yeir bygane/ for allegit being airt and pairt of the cryme of witchcraft quhairof I am most innocent and to that effect haif offerit at divers tymes to abyd tryell Lyke as I haif bene sundrie tymes convenit befoir yow for that effect And now quhair as maister Williame Maxwell advocat my procurator is absent furth of this burgh and may not attend upoun me maister Andro Fairfule minister and uthers my dilatoris and accuseris takand and suteand[91] thair advantage quhair as my said procurator is absent and that no uther will compeir for me insistis most maliciuslie and crullie agains me for suteing of my Lyfe he haveing defendit me in tyme bygane and knawing the haill secreitis of the caus And seing my said dilatoris and accuseris haif oft and divers tymes procureit continewatiouns[92] fra tyme to tyme quhair as I wes willing to insist and that thay now suteis thair advantage be the absence of my said procurator I will most humelie intreat yow for the favor of God to grant me ane continewatioun for the space of xv dayis and I sall caus my procurator be heir to attend upoun the defending of me and I shall sute no forder continewatioun but sall pray for yow.

JC26/13, bundle 1, no. 4.

[*Endorsed:*] xix Martii 1645. Helene Clerk the spous of George Boyle in Newheavin For witchcraft. Continewit to the first Wednisday of Junii nixt. The dittay with the eik, hir examinatioun and ane depositioun, 4 peces gevin up.

88 *Sic.* Probably read 'on'.

89 A line has been drawn through at least part of this paragraph, and 'deleit' written in the margin.

90 This undated document was evidently written shortly before the postponement of 19 March 1645, recorded below.

91 'suteand': seeking.

92 'continewatiounis': postponements.

{p. 1} Curia Justiciarie Supremi Domini Nostri Regis Tenta xii Martii 1645 Per Magistrum Alexandrum Colvile justiciarium deputatum.[93]

Intran
Helene Clark spous to George Boyle fischer in Newheavin
Dilatit of dyverss poyntis of sorcerie and witchcraft contenit in hir dittay.

Persewar[94]
Sir Thomas Hop his majesteis advocat....[95] *{p. 2}*

Curia tenta in pretorio de Edinburgh 19 Marche 1645 Per Magistrum Alexandrum Colvill.[96]

Intran
Helene Clerk spous to George Boyle in Newheavin
Dilaittit of the cryme of witchcraft.

Persewer
My lord advocat

The Justice contenowis the dyet to the first Wednisday of Junii nixt.

Source 2: NRS, Court of Justiciary, Books of Adjournal, 1637–1650, JC2/8.

{p. 431} Curia Justiciarie Supremi Domini Nostri Regis Tenta in pretorio de Edinburgh xix Martii 1645 Per Magistrum Alexandrum Colvile.[97]

Intran[98]
Helene Clerk spous to George Boyle fischer in Newheavin
Dilatit of dyverss poyntis of sorcerie and witchcraft specifeit in hir dittay.[99]

Persewar
Sir Thomas Hoip of Craighall knyght barronet his majesteis advocat for his hienes intres.

93 'Court of justiciary of our sovereign lord the king, held 12 March 1645, by Mr Alexander Colville, justice depute'.
94 'Mr John Oliphant substitut to his majesties advocat' crossed out here.
95 The remainder of the page contains a draft minute of a different case.
96 'Court held in the tolbooth of Edinburgh, 19 March 1645, by Mr Alexander Colville'.
97 'Court of justiciary of our sovereign lord the king, held in the tolbooth of Edinburgh, 19 March 1645, by Mr Alexander Colville'.
98 In margin: 'Sorcerie'.
99 In margin: 'Continewit to the 4 of Junii nixt'.

The Justice at the earnest suplicatioun of the pannell concerning continuatioun of hir tryell of the crymes contenit in hir dittay affirmeing hir self to be Innocent of the samyn And that Mr William Maxwall hir procurator Is absent quha is upone the counsall of all the defenss scho hes against the dittay and hes compeirit for hir sen the begyning of this proces As also with advyse and consent of his majesteis advocat and of Mr Andro Fairfoule minister at North Leith and of the elderis and deacones of the sessioun thairof Continews the pannellis tryell to the first Wednisday of Junii nixtocum with this caveat and of suretince[100] that na forder continuatioun sall be grantit in this matter heirefter.

The witnessis and assysours are warnet thairto *apud acta* ilk persone under the pane of tua hundreth merkes. Quhairupone the persewairs askit Instrumentis.

[100] Reading uncertain. The meaning is evidently 'assurance'.

21. MARION PARDOUN, SHETLAND, 1644

INTRODUCTION

Marion Pardoun, also known as Marion Peebles, was accused of witchcraft in Shetland in 1644. She was denounced by Janet Fraser, who had recently been executed for witchcraft, and she herself was tried along with Margaret Guthrumsdochter. The records of the other women's cases have not survived, but for Pardoun's own case a copy was made, both of the pre-trial and the trial records. It contains many details of neighbourhood quarrels and bewitchments, as well as some more unusual elements – shape-shifting into the form of a porpoise, and the ritual of cruentation or corpse-touching as a means of determining guilt or innocence.

Marion Pardoun lived in Hillswick in Northmavine. She was said to be over sixty years of age. Her husband was Svend Iverson, and she had adult children. She also had a servant, so she apparently was no poor woman. She was well known in the local community. Her neighbours testified that she had caused many bewitchments in connection with quarrels – but most of these bewitchments had been followed by successful reconciliations, and most of her alleged victims seem to have recovered successfully. There are instances of transference of disease from one person to another, and from a human to an animal. The cures all seem to have followed previous allegations of bewitchment; a few of them involved actions resembling healing rituals, but Pardoun does not seem to have practised as a healer.

Pardoun was initially investigated by members of the presbytery of Shetland. This investigation mainly involved questioning her neighbours, and dealt with harmful magic that had resulted in various misfortunes, particularly human sickness and animal sickness and death. A draft dittay produced after this investigation was presented to the presbytery on 15 March 1644. Then additional investigations were made, including 'waking' her – torture by sleep deprivation. The apparent aim was to make her confess to the overturning of a boat in which four people had drowned. Pardoun and her husband were asked to lay hands on the corpses; when blood issued from them, the interrogators regarded this as a proof of murder. Pardoun's 'confession' appears in the document almost entirely in the form of marginal annotations in which she responds to allegations gathered against her. Demonological ideas entered into the trial, when for instance she was seen with two ravens that were alleged to be demonic. There was, however, nothing about the making of the demonic pact (except in the first vague charge), nor about witches' meetings.

The presbytery declared Marion Pardoun and Margaret Guthrumsdochter 'guiltie, worthie of death', and 'required' the secular authorities to bring them to trial and 'minister justice upon them' – unusually assertive language for a church court. On 21 March, the two were duly tried for witchcraft at a justice court, a version of the sheriff court, in Scalloway. Guthrumsdochter's dittay does not survive, but Pardoun's dittay is printed below. It is packed full of hostile and aggressive words: witchcraft is not just witchcraft, but the 'wicked and devilish airt of witchcraft ... quhilk ye rank witch can not deny'. The assize found all the points of the dittay, except two, proven. The death sentence was given for both women on 22 March 1644.

TEXT

Source: *Sir John and Wendy Scott, Gardie House Archive, Bressay, Shetland.*[1]

Intrat upon pannall Mareoun Peipbles alias Pardone, spous to Swane Iversoun in Hildiswik.

In the first, the said Mareoun Peblis alias Pardone is indyttit and accusit for the fearfull and damnable renunceing of God, your faith and baptisme, giveing and casting of your selff, bodie and saull, in the hands of the Devill, following, exerceing, using and practiseing of the fearfull and damnable craft of witchcraft, sorcerie and charmeing, in maner following, viz.:

In the first,[2] ye ar indyttit and accusit for cuming in the moneth of [*1 word blank*], the yeir of God I^{m} VI^{c} threttie [*1 word blank*] yeris, to the hous of John Banks in Turvosetter, and Jonet Robertsone, his spous, of a wicked, divilish and malicious intentioun to cast witchcraft and seiknes upon hir, and missing the said Jonet thair for going to Suenasetter, quhair sho then wes, and efter your cursing and outskolding of hir, telling hir that sho sould repent

1 A previous version of this text has been published by Samuel Hibbert, *A Description of the Shetland Islands* (Edinburgh, 1822; reprinted Lerwick, 1891), 280–6. Hibbert's transcription varies from the present one at several points; some of these are clearly errors, but some of his readings might suggest that he had used a different manuscript. His text is partly modernised, and omits most of the marginal annotations. An abbreviated, revised and modernised version of Hibbert's text has been published by G. F. Black and Northcote W. Thomas (eds.), *Examples of Printed Folklore Concerning the Orkney & Shetland Islands* (County Folk-Lore, vol. III: Printed Extracts, no. 5; London: Folk-Lore Society, 1903), 88–99.

2 In margin: 'Fylls / 1 witchcraft'.

quhat sho haid done to your doughter and gudsone,[3] and imediatlie with the word for that, by your devillish airt of witchcraft, ye cust seiknes upon the said Jonet, quha imediatlie upon your departure fell in ane extraordiner and unkyndlie[4] seiknes, and lay aught[5] weikis, ever taking hir shours[6] and panis by fittis at midday and midnycht, and sa continewit most crewellie tormentit in the said seiknes, castin upon be your said devilish witchcraft during the said space, quhill the said Johne Banks cam to yow and threattned yow, at quhilk tyme ye gave him a gulyeoun[7] of silver to hold his peace, and conceill the same, promeising to him that nothing sould aill his wyff, and thairefter for that ye sent hir ane cheis of the breid of anes looffe,[8] composed by your said devilish airt of witchcraft, with ane Jonka Rolland, desyring the said Jonet to eat the same, quhen (tho the said Jonet refuisit to eat) yit imediatlie thairefter grew weill, bot tua of hir kyne[9] died, the said seiknes being castin upon them be your said wicked and devilish airt of witchcraft.

Lyk as also[10] ye ar indyttit and accusit for that by your said airt of divilish witchcraft ye did upon the recoverie of the said Jonet cast the same seiknes upon Marjorie Banks, sister to the said Johne Banks, quha continewit thairin efter the same maner tormentit tuentie dayis, till that on[e] Elsa in Ulnafirth cuming to yow, by directioun of the said John Banks, and warned yow thairof, quhairupoun by your said divilish witchcraft the said seiknes wes taken af the said Marjorie, and castin upon a young kow of the said Johnes, quhilk took woddrome[11] and died within 24 hours thairefter, quhilk ye can not deny.

Item,[12] ye the said Marioun is indyttit accusit for that ye being [*1 word blank*] yeiris syne or thairby suspected and comonelie bruted[13] as a comone and rank witch, ye cuming along upon sum your said divilish and wicked intentioune to umquhill Eduard Halcro in Overure, quhair he wes dichting bear to steip for malt,[14] ye being of wicked intentioun be your said divilische craft to undo the said making of malt, and he suspecting yow, efter he had reproved yow for cuming thair at that tyme, ye said to him all sould be well tuitching the said making, as it so fell out, sa taking upon yow and acknawledgeing be your wordis your power in the said wicked and devilish airt of witchcraft, yit for that lykwyis ye following throw and persisting in your said wicked and

3 'gudsone': son-in-law.
4 'unkyndlie': unnatural.
5 'dayis' has been crossed out here.
6 'shours': pangs.
7 'gulyeoun': guilder (Dutch or German coin).
8 'the breid of anes looffe': the breadth of one's palm.
9 'kyne': cows.
10 In margin: '2 witchcraft'.
11 'woodrome': madness.
12 In margin: '3'.
13 'bruted': rumoured.
14 'dichting bear to steip for malt': preparing bere for soaking in order to make malt.

devilish intentioun to undo and wrack the said umquhill Eduard, did thairby marr and undo tua other makingis of the same bear, quhilk never did good, quhilk ye rank witch can not deny.

Item,[15] ye the said Marioun is indyttit and accusit for that in Aprile 1641 the said umquhill Eduard, cuming to your hous, quhair efter ye haid urged him to tak meat, he took resolutioun to go to the war[16] (being not of intentioun befoir), and going with Swene, your husband, to the Geo Heid[17] quhair they wer usit to go doun, he being affrayit to go doun first desyrit your husband to go befor him, quha refuising to go, the said Eduard went, quhair in the going doun and steping upon a stone, quhilk wes ever a sure step befoir, ye the said Marioun, be your said wicked and divilish airt of witchcraft, maid the said stone to lows[18] and fall doun with him, quhairby his lyf wes in great perell, yit saved to the admiratioun[19] of all the beholderis, and ye being accusit thairfor, taking the said occasioun and cryme upon yow, answerit that it wes not for his gud bot for Helen Clousta his spous good that he wes saved.[20]

Item,[21] ye the said Marioun is indyttit and accusit for that ye, by your said wicked and devilish airt of witchcraft, did cast ane terrible and feirfull madnes and seiknes upon ane Madda Scudda, sumtyme your awin servand, becaus sho wald not byd with yow, quhairin sho continewit most terriblie tormentit, and throw the torment of the said diseas sho wes caryit many tymes to run upon hir awin sister that keipit hir, and divers utheris, to have devorit them in hir madnes, and sa continewit a yeir and half ane yeir, till sho, being counsallit be the nychtbouris of Hildiswik, ran upon yow the said Marioun, and drew blood of yow, in James Halcrois hous, bytting tua of your fingers till they bled, quhairupoun thairefter the said Madda Scudda recoverit of hir diseas, and cam to hir rycht sences, thairby maniefestlie showing and approveing[22] your said trade and exerceing of you the said Marioun Pardoun your said divilish and wicked craft of witchcraft, tormenting and abuseing thairby of poore waik Christianes, Goddis people, aganes quhom ye carie evill will and malice, quhilk ye, rank witch, cannot deny.

Item,[23] ye the said Marioun Pardoun is indyttit and accusit for that [*1 word blank*] yeiris syne or thairby, James Halcro in Hildiswick haveing a kow that ye alledged haid pushed a kow of yours, ye in revenge thairof, be your said

15 In margin: '4 witchcraft / fyllis'.

16 'go to the war' (ware, sea-ware): go to collect seaweed.

17 'the Geo Heid': not a place-name, but the head or summit of a 'geo', a cleft or ravine in a coastal cliff.

18 'lows': loose.

19 'admiratioun': astonishment.

20 In margin: 'confest words spoken to the said Helen'.

21 In margin: '5 witchcraft / confessit Jhones mid and that sho run on hir and thairefter wes weill / fyllis' ('mid': maid).

22 'approveing': proving.

23 In margin: '6 witchcraft / confesyt but that sho did not work it / fyllis'.

divilish airt of witchcraft, maid the said James his kow milk nothing bot blood, quhairas your awin kow had no harme in hir milk, quhairupoun thay suspecting yow, shew the said bloodie milk to Marioun Ketle, your servand, quha desyrit of them the same bloodie milk for Goddis caus to show yow, and said sho hoipit the kow sould be weill, quhilk haveing gottin and cuming thairwith to your hous, and shawing it to yow thairefter, the kow grew weill, thairby showing and proveing your said divilish practise of the airt of witchcraft.

Item,[24] ye the said Marioun is indyttit and accusit for that ye haveing in anno 1642 yeirs hyrit ane kow fra Andro Smyth younger in Hildiswick, quhilk ye keipit fra the bull quhen sho wald have taken bull, and becaus the said Andro getting knawledge thairof causit the same to be brought to the bull, and bullit aganest your will, the nixt yeir quhen sho calved, ye by your said divilish airt of witchcraft took away hir proffeit and milk, sa that sho milked nothing but watter, quhilk stinked and taisted of sharne[25] a long tyme, till that ye cuming by the said Andro his hous, he suspecting yow, caused yow to milk hir and look to hir, efter qutthick[26] doing imediatlie the said kowis milk come to its owne nature, thairby indicating and showing your said divilish and wicked and abhominable airt and practise of witchcraft, quhilk ye cannot deny.

Item,[27] ye the said Marioun is indyttit and accusit for that in anno I^{m} VI^{c} [*1 word blank*] yeiris, ye cuming by ane peice grass quhair Andro Smyth elder in Nidesetter haid sex kyne tedderit,[28] quhairunto ye clameit entres,[29] out of quhilk grass ye and your sone, efter ye haid lousit and callit the kyne, ye fell in skolding with and abusit the said Andro, and said to him that he sould not have sa mony kyne to eat grass and milk the nixt yeir, according to the quhilk words it sa fell out thairefter, that by your said wicked and divilish airt of witchcraft, the saids haill sex kyne died befoir Pash[30] the nixt voir,[31] all fat and gudlyk, by that same ordour as they wer lousit be yow on tedder, begineing at the first kow, quhilk wes ane blak kow, quhilk ye lousit, quhilk died 20 dayis befor Yule, fat and tydie, and sa furth successive the rest, be your said divilrie and witchcraft, conforme to your said veneficall,[32] wicked and malicious promeis, quhilk ye cannot deny.

Item,[33] ye the said Marioun is indyttit and accusit for that [*1 word blank*] yeirs syne ye cuming to the said Andro Smyth elder, and desyring the len[34] of

24 In margin: '7 fyllis / witchcraft / referrit to Andro his ayth be hir quha maid fayth'.

25 'sharne': cow-dung.

26 *Sic.* Read 'quhilk' (which).

27 In margin: '8 witchcraft / deponit and sworne / fyllis'.

28 'tedderit': tethered.

29 'entres': permission or right to enter.

30 'Pash': Easter.

31 'voir': spring.

32 'veneficall': concerning witchcraft or poison (Latin *veneficium*).

33 In margin: '9 witchcraft / deponit hes confest / fyllis / tuitching in cursing and death of the calf throw madnes'.

34 'len': loan.

ane hors to go to Urafirth, to lead peattis,[35] quhilk he refusing to do ye, out of a wicked and malitious hart, said to him that he sould repent it, quhairupoun ye be your said wicked and divilish airt of witchcraft, and for outting of your malice and keiping of your said divilish promeis, within aught dayis thairefter did kill ane of his best wark hors, and within half ane yeir thairefter uther thrie of his said hors, thairby shawing boith by your words and deids your wicked and divilish skill, cunneing and practise of the foirsaid divilish and abhominabill airt of witchcraft, quhilk ye cannot deny.

Item,[36] ye the said Marioun is indyttit and accusit for that [*1 word blank*] yeris syne ye being suspected to have cassin seiknes upon the said Andro Smyth elder his mother, quhairof sho lay long benume[37] and sensles, ye cuming tyme foirsaid to thair hous of Overure, and thay challengeing and quarrelling yow thairfoir, ye fell in cursing and skolding and went to the dore, quhair ane calf wes standing in the dore befor yow, quhairupon, in your said wicked and divilish malice, be your said detestable craft of witchcraft, ye did cast seiknes, that it presentlie than ran mad over a craig and died.

Item,[38] ye the said Marioun is indyttit and accusit for cuming to Andro Erasmussones hous in Eshenes, [*1 word blank*] yeirs, quhair he haveing ane kow a thrie dayis calved befoir, quhairupon as ye luikit sho imediatlie, be airt and divilrie, cust seiknes, that sho imediatlie crap[39] togidder, that na lyf wes looked for hir, till they sent for yow, and causit yow lay your hand upoun hir, quhairupon sho than imediatlie recoverit, and wes weill, quhairby manifestlie and cleirlie appeiris your foirsaid wicked, devilish and detestable lyf, cariadge, trade and practise of the foirsaid abhominable airt and craft of witchcraft, quhilk ye cannot deny.

Lyk[40] as ye the said Marioun, to cullour and extenuat the said craft, alledgeing that ye wantit[41] the proffeit of your kyne, quhilk wes not trew, bot onlie to tak occasioun, by your said wicked and divilish airt the proffeitt, the said Andro his kyne come to his hous,[42] and efter causing his wyf shaw yow the milk of hir kyne, desyring hir to caus Issobell Sinclair, hir servand woman, to go with yow to kirne,[43] quhilk sho did, quhairby and by your said wicked and divilish airt ye tuik away with yow the proffeit of the said Andro his kyne and milk, the space of tuentie dayis, till the said Andro his wyf went to your hous and shew yow the milk and butter, and maid publicatioun thairof to the

35 'lead peattis': transport peat.
36 In margin: '10 witchcraft / sworne / fyllis / tuitching the calf and cursing'.
37 'benume': numbed.
38 In margin: '11 witchcraft / sworne / fyllis'.
39 'crap': crept.
40 In margin: '12 witchcraft / sworne / fyllis'.
41 'wanted': lacked.
42 In margin: 'in July thairefter'.
43 'kirne': churn.

nychtbours, imediatlie thairefter gat back the proffeit of boith his milk and butter, quhairby maniefestlie appeirs and is shawin your guiltines in taking away the same, be your said wicked and detestable airt of witchcraft, and your restoring again of the samen upon thair challenge, quhilk ye can not deny.

Item,[44] ye ar indyttit and accusit for that [*1 word blank*] yeiris syne ye cam to Thomas in Orabister, and desyrit a quyak[45] kow of his, of four yeir ald, to hyre, quhilk wes with calf then, quhairof he maid yow half a grant bot not the full untill he sould advys with his mistres the gudwyf of Urafirth, quha wald not consent, and becaus ye gat hir now[46] ye outskoldit him, and wes verie angrie, and in revenge of his said refusall imediatlie thairefter ye cust seiknes upon the said kow, quha being at the hill with the rest of hir kyne scho tuik a wodrame[47] or madnes, and cam runeing home fra the rest to the byre dore, brack up the samen and went in, haveing hir head throwen backward to hir back, that four people could not get it drawin back, and thairby died, throw the said deseas cassine on hir be your said airt, working and witchcraft, quhilk ye cannot deny.

Lyk[48] as ye not being in your divilisch and wicked mynd eneugh revengeit and sattisfeit, ye be the samen your craft, divilrie and witchcraft, within sex ouckis[49] thairefter cust the lyk seiknes upoun ane uther kow of the said Thomas his kyn, quhairby sho also died mad and in woddroum, and for the quhilk ye ar also indyttit and accusit, and can not deny the samen.

Item,[50] ye the said Marioun is indyttit and accusit for that in anno 1634, at Michelmes,[51] quhen the cornes wes taking in,[52] the said Thomas in Orabister having aught peices of horss and meirs[53] going on the riggis[54] of Ulnesfirth, ye cam furth with a staff to ding[55] away the hors, quhair ye fell and hurt your knee, quhairupoun ye to revenge your selff of to assyth[56] your wicked and malitious hart and mynd did by your foirsaid airt of witchcraft and divilrie caus that within aught dayis thairefter his best hors died, and thairefter befoir Candlmes[57] uther sex horssis and meirs.

44 In margin: '13 witchcraft'.
45 'quyak': heifer (young cow).
46 *Sic*. Read 'not'.
47 'wodrame': madness.
48 In margin: '14 witchcraft'.
49 'ouckis': weeks.
50 In margin: '15 witchcraft'.
51 Michaelmas, 29 September.
52 'quhen the cornes wes taking in': when the grain was being harvested.
53 'aught peices of horss and meirs': eight animals, horses and mares.
54 'riggis': cultivation ridges.
55 'ding': strike.
56 'assyth': satisfy, compensate.
57 Candlemas, 2 February.

At Scalloway the 15 Marche 1644 yeiris
Wee the moderator and remnant brethren of the presbytery of Yetland being conveined, day and place forsaid, and having examined the doun wreattin proces, doe find and declare the poyntis formar markit in the margine being lawfulie provin to be witchcraft, and therfor the pairtie guiltie, worthie of death, be the law of God and the law of the kingdome, and requyris yow judgeis to put them to the[58] knowledge of ane assyse, and minister justice upon them accordinglie, as ye wil be anserable to God his majestie and counsel, and the discharge of your dewtie heiranent.

Nicol Whyte, moderator.

M. Robert Murray, clerk.

Item,[59] ye the said Marioun Peibles alius Pardoun is indyttit and accusit for that at Candlmas or thairby, 1643, on ane Sonday, ye cuming in to the hous of James Halcro in Hildiswick, quhair Andro Broun thair wes for the tyme, and falling in contest and flytting[60] with him, tuitching ane boat, ye being inraged with your veneficall malice aganest him, cursed him with many wicked and execrable words, and by your damnable and veneficall heart wisching and craveing evill to befall him, quhairupoun by your divilisch airt and craft of witchcraft bewitched him and cust seiknes upoun than imediatlie that he fell in ane deidlie seiknes and diseas. That upoun the Monday nixt thairefter he did sa contract sa vehement and deidlie diseas and seiknes, tormentit thairby fra the croun of his head to the sole of his fute,[61] that thair wes no lyff expectit of him, for quhairfoir his nychtbours, knawing your detestable brute[62] of witchcraft, and your power usit thairof and practise thairin, and that quhansoever ye cursed thair fell sum notable and extraordiner mischeiff and evill to thame, they did advys him to send for yow to shaw that thair wes na lyff for him, and that thay all suspected yow for casting the same upon him, quhairupoun eftir many denyellis to cum and sie him, at last ye cam to him, quha shew yow his deseas and seiknes, togidder with the occasioun thairof imputtit be him and uthers to be the occasioun thairof, and thairfoir prayit yow to lay your hand upoun him, quhilk ye wald not do, nor be na intreattie, nather of him nor of your nychtboris, moved thairto till that they all that wer in the hous be weried of your refusalls went furth, quhaireftir he prayit yew for Goddis caus to lay your hand upoun him, and ye at last being moved

58 'inquest' crossed out here.

59 In margin: 'fyllis / witchcraft / confest ane tyme sho pat hir finger to …hir … / confest hir … in judgment and cursit him … / Item, confest sho sent the bannok'.

60 'flytting': arguing, scolding.

61 This is an expression often used in Scottish witchcraft confessions in connection with entering the Devil's pact: Liv Helene Willumsen, *Witches of the North: Scotland and Finnmark* (Leiden, 2013), 145. However, here the expression refers to the body of a bewitched person.

62 'brute' (bruit): rumour, reputation.

thairto, useing your said veneficall and damnable charmes and witchcraft, ye did uncover his leg and pat your finger thairon, and on the ground, thrie severall tymes to and fra, quhairby than imediatlie, be your said airt of witchcraft and charmes, he felt and fand his pane and diseas to desolve, fra the croun of his head to the sole of his fute, at quhilk tyme he wes befor hir tuitch sa heavilie diseased, fra top to too, throw all his bodie, with a swelling in his handis, lithis,[63] armes, leges and knees, that he wes unable to move or turne himselff in the bed, bot efter the said tuitch he became able to sit up and turne him, and within tua dayis wes fullie recoverit, and went furth, quhilk sudden recoverie, togidder with your forme and maner of charmeing and cureing of be your said tutche and charmes, being spred abroad among the nychtbours, and the same cuming to your earis, about 14 dayes efter his recoverie, ye said to the nychtbouris unhoall[64] on them that haid bewitched yow that wald not witche yow over the bankis, quhairupoun imediatlie agane he fell again in the said seiknes, wors then befoir, and pyned away with sick[65] extreamitie of seiknes that he sent to yow agane, desyring meat out of your hand, and efter long intreattie ye wald not cum to him with it, least[66] your witchcraft and charmes agane sould cum to lycht, bot send with Swane [*1 word blank*], your husband, ane bannock, efter long stryveing betuix the said Swane and yow, quhilk of yow sould give the same to him, quhilk he haveing eattin he agane recoverit presentlie thaireftir, and the said seiknes wes cassin be yow upon ane kow pertening to the said Andro [*1 word blank*], quhilk than died, quhilk haill premisses wes wrought and done be your said deteastible and divilish airt of witchcraft and charmeing, quhilk ye cannot deny.

Item,[67] ye the said Marioun is indyttit and accusit for that ye bearing ane deadlie and veneficall malice in your heart againest the said \umquhill/ Eduard Halcro in Overure, as in your former dittayis and accusatiounes appeiris, persisting in and incressing your malice and divilish intentioun of your wicked heart, and taking occasioun to renew and bring your wicked intentioun, by your said wicked airt of witchcraft, to work his rwyne and death, being set on edge throw a speitch spoken be him to the said Swane [*1 word blank*] your husband, quhen he wes casting peittis[68] to him in voir last, quhair as the said Andro Broun also wes casting peittis to him, he haveing said to your said husband and bade him go to yow to desyre yow to go to your pobe[69] the Devill, and bid him lowse ane knot, that the said Andre Broun mycht be able (being then bot verie waik) to cast out his bank of peittis, quhairupon ye and the said

63 'lithes': joints.
64 'unhoall': bad luck.
65 'sick' (sic): such.
66 'least': lest.
67 In margin: 'fylls'.
68 'casting peittis': digging out peats.
69 'pobe': father or foster-father.

Swane, being angrie, awaitting your occasioun to put your said abhominable airt and craft of witchcraft to distroy and put doun the said Eduard Halcro, and haveing covenantit and convenit with the Devill to bring the same to pass,[70] as ane declaratioun of \umquhill/ Jonet Fraser, witch, quhom ye desyrit the Devill to move hir to assist yow, doeth record, quhilk she boith befoir and efter hir convictioun did testiffie, ye, be your said wicked, detestable, abhominable and divilish airt of witchcraft, being transformed in the lyknes of ane pellock quhaill,[71] at the least or rather be your consent and wish the Devill, cloithing your spirit with in the said quhaill,[72] and the said Eduard being at sey with Malcolme Smyth, sone in to Helen Clousta, his spous, and Nicoll Smyth, sone to Grissell Bruce in Glus, and [*1 word blank*] Kneland, servand to the said Eduard, all four in ane fisher boat, cuming fra the sey at the north bankis of Hildiswick, on ane fair morneing, the [*1 word blank*] day of [*1 word blank*], last bypast, ye did cum under the said boat and overturne hir with thame, and drowned and devoirit thame in the sey, rycht at the shore quhair thair wes na danger utherwayes, nor hazard to have cassin thame away, it being sick[73] fair wedder, as said is, lykas quhen the said \umquhill/ Eduard wes fund with the said umquhill [*1 word blank*] and ye and said Swane [*1 word blank*] your husband wer send for, and brought to sie thame, and to lay your handis on thame, [*1 word blank*] dayis efter the said death and away casting, quhen all thair bluid wes evanished and disolveit frome any naturall course or caus to ishue and rune, the said \umquhill/ Eduard bled at the coller bane or craig[74] bane, and the said [*1 word blank*] in the hands and fingeris guishing out bluid thairat,[75] to the greit admiratioun of the beholderis, and revilatioun of the judgement of the Almytie, and by quhilk lyk occasiounes and miraculous works of God maid manief[est] in murdours and the murdereris thairby, be many frequent occasiounes brought to lycht, and the murdereris by the said proof brought to judgement, convict and condemned, not onlie in this kyngdome also this countrie, bot lykwayis in all forren Christiane kingdomes, as by many frequent precedentis and practiqus of and tuitching murderis and murdereris[76] is notorlie knowin, sa that the foirsaid murder of the saidis persones with the rest of thair company throw yow and your said

[70] This seems to be the closest approach in this document to the concept of the demonic pact. It refers, not to the initial agreement between witch and Devil, but to the witch calling upon the Devil to cause bewitchment.

[71] 'pellock quhaill': porpoise.

[72] An attempt to interpret this act of shape-shifting in demonological terms.

[73] 'sick': such.

[74] 'craig': neck.

[75] This was the ordeal-like test known as cruentation or corpse-touching. See Malcolm Gaskill, 'Reporting Murder: Fiction in the Archives in Early Modern England', *Social History*, 23 (1998), 1–30, at pp. 8–13.

[76] In margin: 'and witchcraft'.

husbands deid, airt, part, red[77] and counsall, is maniefest and cleirlie provin, not onlie throw and by the foirsaids precedencies of your malices, wicked and divilishes practises by witchcraft, confessioun and declaratioun of the said umquhill Jonet Fraser, witch, reviled to hir as said is, and quha wes desyrit be him to concur and assist with yow to the doing thairof, bot lykwayis be the declaratioun and revilatioun of the justice and judgement of God, throw the said ishueing of bluid frome thair bodies, quhairby with ye and your said husband ar fund, takin and provin in the act of your said witchcraft and murder, and speciallie quhen the said Marioun Peibles alias Pardoun, now on pannall, quhilk ye boith rank witch and murderer can not deny.

Lykas ye the said Mareoun, indyttit and accusit as ane comone rank witch, charmer and deceaver, and quha hes ever all your dayis, this lx years and moir, bein sa reput and haldin, bearing and behaveing yourselff sa, and ane covenanter, consulter and convener with the Devill, \he being/ in divers shapes and lyknesses, apering to yow speceallie, for that ye being coming fra Brekone to Hildiswik, in the moneth of [*1 word blank*] last, quha wes to be apprehendit and sent in for the foirsaids crymes, to suffer the do...[78] thair, in the way did convene and appeir to yow, boith in your going to and fra Br[ekone] and Hildiswik, in the lyknes of tua corbies,[79] ane on everie syde of yow, clos at your sydes, going and happing alongis the way with yow to Hildiswik, and stayit with yow, never leving yow, thrie quarters of a myle, till Mr Robert Ramsay overtuik yow, that the ane tuik flyght to the sey and the uther to the land and hill, and than did challenge yow anent the saids corbies, and the caus of thair so far accompanying yow sa neir and sa far way, it not being the nature of wyld foulles to follow sa far, keip fute sa neir appropriating[80] ony man or women, ye than did cast a gloss upon it, saying they smellit bread on yow, quhilk maid them, to quhom ye said ye was casting bread to thame, quhilk wes only a lie maid be yow, considering at your returne they convenit with yow and conveyit *ut supra*[81] als far back again, also sene and proven.

As lykwayis ye have not onlie behaved your selff as said is as ane comone rank witch, never giveing your selff to learne nor know the trew God and quhom he haith sent Jesu Chryst, no not so mutche as to learne the Lords prayer, nor to repeat the same in all your lyftyme, bot as reprobat frome God hes given your selff baith[82] saull and bodie to serve the Divell, and sa bund up be him that ye will not nor hes power nor will cast aff the Devill sa mutche as

77 'red': advice.

78 Word illegible. Hibbert, *Description*, 285, reads this passage as 'quhen you wir to be apprehendit and sent in for the foirsayid crymes to suffer, the devill there in the way, did converse and appear to you'.

79 'corbies': probably ravens.

80 Hibbert, *Description*, 285, reads 'approaching', and this seems to be the meaning.

81 'as above'.

82 Reading uncertain.

to follow, learne and repeat the Lords prayer efter ane of Goddis ministeris and childrene, bot is and hes bene all your dayis ane wicked, divilish, fearfull and abhominable curser, and quhome ye ever ye cursit and quhom ye discordit and wishit evil[83] unto, everie evill, seiknes, harme and death followit thairupoun, throw your pry...able[84] diabolicall tongue, witchcraft and cursing and hes ever behaveit your selff as a comone witch and charmer, taker away of your nychtbours profeits, of thair rowmes, lands, cornes, grass, cattell, ky, sheip and utheris, and a charmer and healer of sum and caster of seikness upon uthers, and everie way liveing a damnable, wicked and diabolicall lyff, contrair to God and his comandementis, quhilk ye cannot deny, and thairfoir ye the said Marioune aught and sould undergo the tryell of ane assyse, and being convict adjudgitt thairfoir to the death, and your haill lands, if ony ye have, foirfaltit, and your moveable guds escheit and imbrocht to his majesties use, conforme to the lawis and daylie practiquis of this realme.

The brethren considering the premisses *ut supra* in the former sheet of paper
Nicol Whyte, moderator
M. Robert Murray, clerk
Provin f.[85]

Curia justiciarie ac vicecomitatus de Yetland, tenta apud Scallowaybankis, in castro ibidem, per venerabiles viros magistrum Jacobum Mowat de Olaberie, Joannem Stewart de Bigtoun et Patricum Umphray de Sand, vicecomitates ac justiciares deputates eiusdem, vigesimo primo Martii 1644.

Curia tenta et legitime affirmata.[86]

The quhilk day comperit James Gray, procurator fiscal, and produceit the dittayis of witchcraft given aganes Mareoun Pardoun and Margaret Guthrumsdochter, witches, pannallit, and desyrit they sould be accusit thairupoun, and the saids dittayis put to the tryell of ane assys, quhome the judges present ordanit to be callit, quhairupoun the procurator fiscal askit acts of court.

83 MS damaged: 'ev...'.

84 Word partly illegible.

85 In margin: 'Provin also be Mans Finlasone and [*torn*] Erasmussone quhen they wer waking hir sho speirit quhair the husband wes quha ansering hir speking concerning hir husbound sho answrit he lay under hir heid and wald not suffer hir to confess'. Hibbert, *Description*, 286, reads 'tutching her hand' instead of 'under hir heid'.

86 'Court of justiciary of the sheriff of Shetland, held at Scallowaybanks, at the castle of the same, by the venerable men Mr James Mowat of Ollaberry, John Stewart of Bigton and Patrick Umphray of Sand, sheriff and justice deputes of the same, 21 March 1644. Court held and legally fenced.'

Assisa

James Mowat of Hamnavo
Ola Mansone of Ilisbrucht
Andro Mansone in Mangasetter
Thomas Williamsone in Brewik
Harie Christophersone in Tangwik
Mans Finlaysone in Burraland
Mans Suanesone in Tongone
William Tulloch in Skelberie
Ola Williamsone in Glus
Jon Erasmussone in Enisfirth
James Gregorisone in Setter
Ola Harra in Sulem
James Boduelsone in Uyea
Andro Smyth younger in Hildiswik
Laurens in Stow thair

The assyse being ressaveit, sworne and admittit, and efter reiding of the dittayis and examinatioun of the pannalls thairupoun, and haveing ressaveit the depositiounes of divers famous[87] witnesses, quha wer suorne tuitching the saids dittayis, proveing them, as lykwayis in consideratioun of the confessiounes and circumstances markit and set doun in and upon the saids dittayis, they passing out of judgement and reviseing the saids dittayis, togidder with the saids depositiones of witnesses, haveing nominat Ola Manssone of Ilisbrucht in chancellor, and efter examineing of the haill poyntis and consideratioun of the depositiounes and confessiounes of the said Marioun[88] fyllis hir of the haill poynts of dittay led aganes hir, baith generall and speceall, except those of Thomas of Orabister, not proven, and anent Eduard Halcrois malt, quhairin they rest *clauso ore*,[89] and tuitching Margaret Guthrumsdochter they all in ane voice fylls hir of the haill poyntis of dittay produceit, and remittis sentences to the judgis, and dome to the dempster. In witnes quhairof subscribit be the said chancellor
Ollaw Magnussoun.

Continewis sentence to the murne
xxij Martij 1644
The judgis adjudges and decernis the pannalls to be takin be the lockman to the place of executioun, to the west hill of Berrie, and thair wyryt[90] at ane staik and brunt in ashes, betuix and 2 efter none, quhilk Andro Chappie, dempster, gave for dome.

87 'famous': reputable.
88 In margin: 'Pardoun'.
89 'with closed mouth'.
90 'wyryt': strangled.

22. JEAN CRAIG, TRANENT, 1649

INTRODUCTION

Jean Craig lived in the parish of Tranent in Haddingtonshire. She was married to William Steill, a coal-miner; she herself also worked in a coal-pit, probably as a coal-bearer. Her mother was Beigis (Margaret) Wallace, who had been burned as a witch in 1629, during the panic of 1628–31.[1] Wallace had named her daughter as a witch shortly before her execution. Family relations among women came to the fore in this trial, as one of the witnesses against Craig was her sister-in-law. The voices of the witnesses, the accused and the judiciary come to the fore.

Craig's investigation and trial took place in March and April of 1649, which was another period of panic over witchcraft. Our earliest dated evidence, from 17 March, is a letter from James Baillie, brother of the politician Sir William Baillie of Lamington who was a member of the committee of estates that then governed Scotland.[2] Lamington was in Lanarkshire, but Sir William Baillie also owned a coal-mining estate at Penston in Haddingtonshire, which James Baillie seems to have managed. Craig had worked at Penston when she had allegedly bewitched Beatrix Sandilands; James Baillie's letter outlined this incident, which would soon be investigated in much more detail. He also mentioned Craig's association with the witches of the 1620s. He wrote his letter, to the minister of Tranent, in response to an enquiry from the parish elders; we do not know what prompted these elders to open the investigation.

By 28 March, Craig had been arrested and imprisoned in the tolbooth of Tranent. This was by warrant from the chancellor, according to the presbytery record. Local secular authority, in the form of the baron bailie of Seton and

1 A commission of justiciary for the trial of Beigis Wallace in Preston and Margaret Matheson in Prestonpans for witchcraft was issued on 21 August 1629: *RPC*, 2nd ser., iii, 271. Matheson too was mentioned in Craig's trial, as was Janet Reid in Prestonpans, who seems to have been caught up earlier in the same panic. A commission for Reid's trial, along with three other women, was issued on 3 July 1628: *RPC*, 2nd ser., ii, 353.

2 In June 1649, Sir William Baillie himself received a commission of justiciary to try three Lanarkshire witches, Margaret Dickson, Agnes Hunter and Isobel Murray: SSW.

Tranent, was also operating in co-operation with the ministers. On 31 March and 2 April, Craig gave non-demonological 'confessions' in which she either denied her alleged malefices or attempted to explain them without admitting to witchcraft; she had been reconciled with Beatrix Sandilands, for instance. However, soon after that (on 12 April, according to one document), she gave a full demonological confession, presumably after torture or other coercion. She confessed that she was the Devil's servant, described the Devil's appearance (unusually, he initially appeared as a cat), spoke of the Devil's promise and repeated meetings with the Devil, and admitted that she had renounced her baptism. She acknowledged her guilt 'with teares as it seemit'.

The investigators also gathered information from numerous neighbours about episodes of maleficent witchcraft. One accusation was that Craig had caused the death of the baby of her sister-in-law, Agnes Steill, by stroking the baby with stones. This may have been an attempt at healing that failed. Craig's mother Beigis Wallace had also confessed in 1629 that she had wanted to dedicate this baby 'to her Lord' (the Devil). Another accusation was that Craig had killed Beatrix Sandilands by threatening her and blowing in her face. Most of the accusers were ordinary folk, but one, Jean Cockburn, was the sister of a laird. Cockburn, Sandilands and some other accusers claimed that Craig had inflicted some form of 'madness' on them, and graphic details were related of what may have been psychotic episodes. A few of the accusers, of whom Cockburn was one, retracted their accusations later. Some accusations named Agnes Affleck as a 'scholar' to whom Craig had taught witchcraft, and Affleck would later be prosecuted herself.[3]

On 11 April, the presbytery resolved to seek a commission of justiciary from 'the Counsell or whom it concernes'. They were evidently unsure who was in charge of the administration in the unsettled and revolutionary weeks that followed the execution of Charles I on 30 January 1649. It would eventually be the committee of estates, not the privy council, that authorised Jean Craig's trial on 20 April. They did this, unusually, by sending the two justices depute, the Edinburgh judges, to Tranent, to hold the trial in the locality.

The committee's decision responded formally, not to the presbytery, but to a supplication from Thomas Crawford and four more of Craig's alleged victims. The supplicants addressed the committee of estates directly, noting that the privy council was not functioning. Their demand for prosecution suggests that they may have been offering themselves, not as witnesses, but as private prosecutors; this would have been unusual, since public prosecution was normal in witchcraft trials. The lord advocate, Thomas Nicolson, did not go to Tranent, but on 26 April he commissioned a depute to do so, George Ramsay (the commission has a blank in which Ramsay's name has been

3 A commission of justiciary was issued for the trial of Agnes Affleck on 22 May 1649: SSW. The documents below sometimes call her Nanz Fleck.

inserted); in the end it was Ramsay who led the prosecution. Meanwhile, on 25 April, the presbytery commissioned some ministers to attend the trial. The trial itself took place on 27 April.

The documents edited below come from four different sources. First there are extracts from the presbytery minutes. Second, the largest group of documents comes from the justiciary court process papers. Third, there is a brief order to hold a trial from the records of the committee of estates. Fourth, the formal minutes of the trial, on 27 April, are edited from the books of adjournal.

These documents are printed below in roughly chronological order, but such order cannot be precise. Some of the documents in the process papers are undated, while others have more than one date, having been written at one stage and then either updated later or used for a further purpose later. In the process papers we see stories of malefice told and retold, but the investigators seem to have little concern for chronology. The long dittay (there is more on the dittays in a moment) accuses Craig of having pursued her 'sorcerie' for 'twelf yeiris', yet the bewitching of Agnes Steill's child is said to have been twenty-two years previously. Other dated malefices are the bewitching of Beatrix Sandilands in 1636, and Craig's ominous words about John Cowan, son of James Cowan, which she is said to have spoken after her imprisonment. But most of the incidents are undated. One small but striking inconsistency is the story of James Smith's herd boy, who, says the short dittay, 'be hir sorcerie and witchcraft deceissit, at the leist was nevir sene thaireftir'. This seems to be a clumsy attempt to combine two different stories.

The documents include at least three attempts to systematise the charges against Jean Craig. A list of 'accusations' with sixteen itemised charges (JC26/13/B/11) is probably the earliest; several of its charges are later combined or dropped. Then there are two dittays: a long dittay with nine itemised charges (JC26/13/B/1, /2), and a short dittay with five itemised charges (JC26/13/B/7/2, JC2/8). The long dittay is evidently earlier than the short one. It has marginal notes about the relevancy of individual charges, which match up to some extent with the way in which certain charges have been either rewritten or dropped entirely in the short dittay. Charges that the judge ruled irrelevant would not normally be presented to the assize. The short dittay itself exists in two versions, one of which (JC26/13/B/7/2) is heavily abbreviated and is evidently a draft; the two versions are textually independent even though their content is similar. The fact that the short dittay was recorded in the books of adjournal (JC2/8, Source 4 below) might seem to indicate that it was the one that was actually presented to the assize in court.

However, the long dittay continued in use, as marginal notes were made on it about whether Craig had been convicted or acquitted on its individual charges. Other documents with notes on relevancy and verdicts on individual charges tell an even more complicated story (JC26/13/B/7/1, JC26/13/B/9 and

JC26/13/B/8). For instance, one charge, the bewitching of Jean Cockburn, did not appear in any of the three itemised lists – but it was still considered by the assize, who acquitted her of it. They also acquitted her of some charges that can be seen to have been included in the long dittay but not the short one. Further study of these documents would be desirable. The short dittay may perhaps represent an attempt, after the trial, to create a record only of those charges of which Craig had been convicted. Convicted, however, she was, and the court ordered that her execution should take place on 1 May 1649.

TEXTS

Source 1: NRS, Minutes of Presbytery of Haddington, 1648–1661, CH2/185/6.[4]

{*p. 25*} At Humby March 28 [1649] … {*p. 26*}
Mr Robert Balcanquall[5] reporting that one Jeane Craig in Tranent is apprehended and putt in firmance by warrant from the Lord Chancellour and that for the scandall of witchcraft desyred the Presbyterie to nominate some brethren to assist him in dealing with her that shee may be brought to a Confession The Presbyterie ordeines Masters Johne Oswald and Archbald Duglass to concure and assist him thairin….[6] {*p. 27*}

April 11 … {*p. 29*}
Mr Robert Balcanquall[7] exhibiting a copie of the depositiounis and dittayes of Jeane Craig in Tranent of witchcraft, which being redd the Presbyterie gives advyce to supplicate the Counsell or whom it concernes for a Commission to try her and judge her according to Law…. {*p. 34*}

April 25 …
Mr Robert Balcanquall[8] desyreing some of the brethren to be nominated for being present at Tranent upon Friday nixt at quhich tyme the assyse is to sitt upon Jeane Craige for witchcraft ordeines Masters Johne Oswald and William Trent to be present the said day.[9]

4 A summary and paraphrase of these extracts from the presbytery records has been printed in David M. Robertson, *Goodnight My Servants All: The Sourcebook of East Lothian Witchcraft* (Glasgow, 2008), 160–1.

5 'In margin: 'Jeane Craig accused of witchcraft'.

6 Robert Balcanquhal was minister of Tranent, while John Oswald was minister of the adjacent parish of Prestonpans. Archibald Douglas was minister of Saltoun.

7 In margin: 'Jeane Craig'.

8 In margin: 'Jeane Craig ass…ed' (word or words damaged).

9 In margin: 'Ordinance thairupon'.

Source 2: NRS, Court of Justiciary Process Papers, 1643–1650, JC26/13, bundle B.[10]

JC26/13/B/10/3

[*Addressed on cover:*] For The rycht reverent in the Lord Mr Robert Mackanquell [*sic*] minister of Gods word at Tranent, thaisse.

{*p. 1*} Rycht reverent

Sir I haifing resavit ane letter out of Tranent fra sum of your folkis in Tranent disyring me that I wold acquent you with the behaviour of Jean Craige spous to William Steill treullie that shee gaite ane verry ill word for sho frequentit the company of witchis as Margrat Mathiesoune and Janet Reid quho was brunt both at Prestoune Margrat Mathiesoune Jean Craige keippit a long tyme till I pat[11] hir away out of Penstoune And ane passage I remember of Jeane Craige thair was a puir man ane of our colheueris[12] and to \my/ memorie that \they/ called his wyf Beatrix Sandilandis ane Tranent women [*sic*], Jean and sho discording at our pat[13] in Penstoune shee alledgit that Jean Craige blew in hir face and treullie the woman went maid[14] that four or fyf of us cold skairslie had[15] hir the women told me that Jean Craige had blayne in hir face and withall sho utrit sum speitch to hir quhilk was to my memorie that sho mycht sie a blak sicht of hir, telling me that I sent for hir sho at the first refuissit for to cum I sent againe for hir and causit hir husband bring hir quhilk he did and then I did Accuse hir upon that quhilk treullie sho did not denye thaisse wordis that the puir woman acussit hir upon, I caussit hir sitt doune on hir kneis and seik the puir woman forgivnes and I told hir if the woman continuit any Langer so that I shold put hir to ane farder tryell quhilk treullie efter that the woman greu prettie weill and recoverit so that bissines seisit and so soune as my brother com I telling him he gaif ordour to put thir[16] away quhilk I did for the maist pairt of the Lairdis tenentis kneu this to be of verratie and as I am informid John Parkie him self is Living yet quho will declair this to be of treuth, So haifing no farder for the present wishing you and youris all health and happines, I rest, your affectionat freind to pour, JBaillie.

Edinburgh the 17 March 1649.

John Dicksoune in Penstoune knois this to be truth for the puir folkis dwelt in a housse pertining to him.[17] {*p. 2 blank*} {*p. 3*}

10 A summary and paraphrase of most of these documents has been printed in Robertson, *Goodnight My Servants All*, 364–75.

11 'pat': put.

12 'colheuris' (coal-hewers): coal-miners.

13 'pat' (pit): coal-pit.

14 'maid': mad.

15 'had': hold.

16 *Sic*. Read 'hir'.

17 This sentence, a postscript in the same hand, ends the letter. A fragment of a seal remains.

At Tranent the Last of March 1649[18]
Alexander Baillie elder in Penstoune deponed and witnessed that he knew the within written Beatrice Sandilands, become mad, and \being grivouslie tormented by sore [*sic*]/ a Little after did die, but of the way and manner how he knew nought.

The said day Johnne Diksone in Penstoune deponed just as Alexander Baillie did.

The said Alexander Baillie yonger deponed that in the verrie meane time that the poore woman Beatrice Sandilands became mad shee confest clearly to him that Jean Craig blew in hir face and this he depond upon his salvation and damnation.

Item, The said day James Winla in Penstoun depond that many a tyme he had heird the woman say that Jeane Craig had blowin in her face, and that he hard Jean Craig say or that day 8 dayes[19] shoe sould see a blak sight on Beatrice Sandilands, as also that he had seen after that.

Jeane Craig[20] on Monday at morne the 2d of April befor the minister of the Parish of Tranent and the Barron baillie Mr James Ramsay confest that she was acquainted with Margaret Mathesone and Jennet Rid specifeit in the Letter.

Item she confest that she cwst out[21] with Beatrice Sandilands.

She confest that she asked Beatie Sandilands forgivenes for the ill she had done her.

Confession.[22]
Jean Crage confessit hirself to be a wicht [*sic*] and cravit pardone of God for the sin of wichtcraft and being inquirit what meanes she cum in his the Divles servantis answerit by ane Margrit Mathesone quha cam to hir in Penston and entyse hir [*word unreadable*] in [*word unreadable*] being Inquirit what shaipe the Divle apparit to hir she answerit in the Lyknes of catt, being inquirit what she requirit of the Divle and what he gave hir she answerit that Be upone a peice of coole or ony thing with the words (a blak sight upon the face) wich words haveing said to ane Beatrix Sandilands presently she went mad. Moreover confessit that the words spokin to James Smith servant in Litl Falsyd and that the Divle was ones with hir many tymes to renunce hir baptisme and with teares as it seemit acknowledgit the gultiness of hir and pryet for mercie for the sin of wichtcraft and she repent this day in the ministers presence and many elders.

18 The text on this page is in three separate hands, none of which are the same as the hand of the letter. Evidently a blank page of the letter has had later notes added to it.
19 'or that day 8 dayes': within eight days' time.
20 This paragraph begins a different hand.
21 'cwst out' (cast): fell out.
22 This heading begins a different hand.

JC26/13/B/10/2

[*Endorsed:*] xxvii Aprilis 1649. Jeane Craig spous to William Steill coilyear in Tranent, convict of witchcraft and sorcerie the said day at Tranent and Brunt thairfoir.

{*p. 1*} The depositions [...][23] declarit befoir the minister [...] eldris within the said paroch [...]

James Baillie deponeit that Jeane Craig Falling on [...] ...trix Sandalandis upoun the colhill of Painestoun [...] that the said Jeane Craig blew in hir face and [...] said Beatrix went mad And quhane shoe blew [...] speiches Ane blak sicht be upone that face [...] quhairof he sent for the said Jeane and shoe cwm... [...] ...ned home And according to [...] eache ane another And bein... [...] turned in hir agonie That shoe [...] Imediatlie the violence of [...]

Alexander Ballie [...] suddenlie [...] way and [...]

Johne Dick... [...]

Alexander [...] the tym [...] blew [...] foirse [...]

James Winlaw depones that he hard the said Beatrix in the tyme befoir hir deceis depone that the said Jeane did so blaw on hir face the tyme and place foirsaid And that he hard the said Jeane Craig say That or that day aucht dayes shoe suld sie ane black sicht of hir As also he had seine thairefter.

James Smithe in Litle Fawsyd depones that his[24] servand fallin seik and dieing suddenlie within twentie fowr houris constantlie affirmeit befoir his dathe that meitting with Jeane Craig in the morneing quhen he was going to his work with his masteris horsis airlie in the morning Saluted the poore man with thess words, Quhat Devill[25] do ye so soone up in the morneing. Crost the way befoir him with his said thrie horssis And the thrie horsis never cuttit gras agane bot died and the servand man also. The wther servand and his horsis quhilk shoe did nocht sie at that tyme no harme befell tham. {*p. 2 blank*} {*p. 3*}

Jeane Craig hir confessione maid this xii of Apryle 1649 In presens of Mr James Ramsay barron baillie in the Lordschip and barrony of Seatoun and Tranent, Mr [*1 word damaged*] Balcanquell minister at Tranent, Mr Walter Balcanquell his sone, James Cowane [...] Alexander Weir nottar.

First shoe confest That befoir shoe dwelt in Pa... [...] fell in contraversie with Beatrix Sandilands [...] with Margaret Mathesone and Jonet Reid in [...] both brunt as witches.

Said Margaret severall tymes visitit hir [...] sume nichtis with hir.[26]

23 This document is badly damaged, with about one-third of the paper having been torn away. Ellipses in brackets thus '[...]' indicate long discontinuities, often with 5–15 words missing.

24 'man' crossed out here.

25 Probably this should be understood as an expletive, 'What the Devil are you doing?'

26 In margin: '9 article. This haill confessioun of Jeanes Is Includit heirintill in the haill perticularis set doun heirin'.

Confest that Beatrix Sandilands haveing [...] hir worss And that shoe kne... [...] shoe [...] James [...] better.

Also shoe [...]

Being [...][27]

Being enquyred In quhat schaip or lyknes the Devill did appeir to hir Shoe answered First at Painestoun In the lairds kitcheing In the lyknes of ane katt And nixt in hir awin hous In the lyknes of ane man And quhilk tyme he had carnall copillatione withe hir And that he caussid hir renunce hir baptisme and become his servand.[28]

And being Inquyred quhat shoe craveid of the Devill, Answered revenge and hairt sythe[29] of thes that offend hir.

And being askit quhat he gave hir, Answered that be casting ane peice of coll or stane and saying (ane black sicht upoun that face) sould have hir desyre. Quhiche wordis haveing said to Beatrix Sandilandis and ane peice coll also lykwayes castin at hir That the said Beatrix Become imediatlie mad. This confessione was emitted be Jeane Craig the twentie sevin day of Appryll [*1 word damaged*] Mr James Ramsay Barrone ballie of the Lordship and baronie of Sea...[30] and Tranent, Mr Robert Balcanquall Minister at Tranent, Mr Walter Balcanquall his sone, James Cowane colgreiv[31] [...]

JC26/13/B/11[32]

[*Endorsed:*] [*2 words illegible*] Elphingston of Prestongrange, Mr Robert Ramsay, Trimboll of Scottiston, William Robertson, Mr George Hamilton.

{*p. 1*} Accusations against Jeane Craig spous to Williame Steell in Tranent First the said Jeane Craig is accused by John Naeper, and his wyf Helen Cowane of the Death of James Wilsone, the said Helens first husband, as also of the Death of James Broedie in Elfinstoune, of John Crawfoord in Tranent, and of William Eckfoord there.

2. The said Jeane Craig is accused by her owne Good sister Nanz Steell for never suffering Beigges Wallace her mother rest, from solliciting and begging of her night and day the Gift of a Childe quhilk at that tyme was in the said Nanzes Bellie and unborne. That the said Jeane Craig might give

27 In margin: '9 article'.

28 In margin: '10 article'.

29 'hairt sythe': satisfaction, revenge.

30 Word damaged; probably 'Seatoun'.

31 'colgriev' (coal-grieve): manager of a coal-pit.

32 There exists a second copy of this document, numbered JC26/13/B/6. It is word for word the same as JC26/13/B/11, with the exception of some apparent copying errors, and lacking the endorsement and the final note dated 20 April. Textual differences between the two documents are noted in footnotes below.

it to her Lord, as soone as ever he should come in the world. This, the said Beigs confest to be trew, a little before her Burning at Prestoune Pannes.

3. the said Jeane Craig is accused by the said Nanz Steell after the Childe was borne for touching and rubbing all the Liths[33] and Parts of his Bodie, with three litle staines, quhilk three staines, the said Jeane had gotten from her mother Biegs; after which touching and rubbing, the Childe daylie dwyn'd and pin'de away till hee dyed.

4. The said Nanz Steell, on her great oath with Teares depon'de, that one tyme Jeane Craig had told her, that shee knew well that Bairne not to be hers, but her Lords; and that nought was fite for him, but Foxtree[34] leafes and Southrunning water, and thir things she promist to get, but never did it. Item after this Childe the said Nanz bare sex to whom shee had never a drop of milk.

5. The said Nanz Steell and her Husband and her sonne diverse Nights saw going about a knocking staine[35] that stood in her Howse great numbers of black uglie Beastes like litle whelps[36] after which terrible sights her husband and her sonne being wonderfully affrighted, both of them pyn'de away, and at last, of long and lingiring Sickenesse did die.

6. The said Jeane Craig is accused by John Parkie of many Poyntes of witchcraft, as first of blowing on his wifes face, and at that tyme, of uttering some divellish words unto her, whereat presently shee becomes so mad, that foure or fyve strong men were not able to had[37] her.

7. The said Jeane is accused for entring John Parkies howse in the Night and putting upon his staff, some ugly thing lyke a Cat, quhilk all that night shee rosted, at the poor Mans Fire.

8. The said Jeane is accused for making a number of Cats skip and trip round about Johne Parkies Fire side and hee to rid himself of such a horrible sight, taking up a Tree[38] to chase them away, as the Cats went out at a hole neare the chemnie, the last turn'd about his head and cryes forth, Ai what ailes Beatie now. In this meane tyme, the poor mans wife Bettie Sandilands whose face Jean Craig had blowne on, was lying bound hand and foot[39] because of her Madnesse.

9. The said Jeane Craige is accused for overlaying all places of the said John Parkies howse, with uglie Lumps of rid[40] raw flesh, and for besprinkling all the

33 'Liths': joints.
34 'foxtree': foxglove.
35 'knocking staine': a stone with a hollow in which barley was placed for 'knocking', removing the husks.
36 'whelps': young dogs.
37 'had': hold.
38 'Tree': piece of wood.
39 JC26/13/B/6 omits 'and foot'.
40 'rid': red.

Floore and ground thereof with horrid Blood, all which Places and Ground foresaid, seem'd to all that looked thereon to swime with flesch and blood.

10. The divellish malice of the said Jeane Craige never left the said poore Man John Parkie till she had kild the said Beatie Sandilands his wife, by her Divelryes, even in the verry Colepot, and that without either mark or wound, as many in Tranent Paroch can testifie.

11. The said Jeane Craig is accused by Thomas Crawfoord for killing his Brother John Craufoord, who at his Last howre, left his Death upon Jean Craige only, \Mr Robert Balcanquell being witnesse/: Item the said Thomas, discording one day with William Steell her husband, perceived presently all power and strenth to stand or walk taken from his sonnes Leggs, and of them ever since hath had no abilitie nor Power.

12. The said Jeane Craig is accused by James Cowan Colyear[41] in Tranent, who, one night interchangeing some words with her husband he gott his face so rent be Nanz Fleck one of the said Jeans Schollers,[42] that the blood sprang and still everie Night nill hee will hee[43] hee is enforced, as one not able to rule himself, to rive and rent himself and chiefly in the face till the bloud come. {*p. 2*}

13. The said Jeane Craige is accused by the foresaid James Cowan of appeareing nightly before him in his howse in his Bed, and at his fireside, yea when hee should rest himself hee is tumbled and hurld up and downe his hall[44] floore, Item for causing run out from an under[45] his Bed, and a thort[46] his howse Numbers of ill spirits, Lyke uglie black Tykes,[47] at quhilk, and such like fearfull sights, the said James Cowane is oft tymes seen to creep in an under[48] Beds and lurk quyetlie in holes heer and there, and somtymes will climb up upon Bedheads and hyde himself between the verrie lofting and the Geasts[49] of his howse[50] as Nighbours who have seen it can testifie.

14. The said Jeane Craig is accused by the said James Cowane, of some words spoken by her since shee was imprisoned, which words, upon this occasion, she spoke. James Cowan having a sonne named Johne Cowan, who had his Legg lately broken in the Colepot was carried home to his fathers howse, throw Patrick Craigs, whereof the said Jane [*sic*] Craig, hearing tell,[51] demands of

41 'Colyear' (collier): coal-miner.
42 'Schollers': scholars. The implication is that Jean Craig has taught witchcraft to Agnes Affleck ('Nanz Fleck').
43 'nill hee will hee': whether he will or not.
44 JC26/13/B/6 omits 'hall'.
45 *Sic*. JC26/13/B/6 has 'run out under'.
46 'a thort': across, throughout.
47 'Tykes': ill-bred dogs.
48 *Sic*. JC26/13/B/6 has 'creepe in under'.
49 'geasts': joists.
50 JC26/13/B/6 omits 13 words here, having only 'upon bedheads as nighbours'.
51 'whereof the said Jane Craig, hearing tell': when the said Jean Craig heard of this.

Patrick, when hee came to visite her, what way the youth John Cowan was carried home; what way said Patrick, in deed Jeane hee was carried throw my howse, I rew that said shee, and why sa replyed hee, Jeane,[52] I ken my sell said shee, I wish rather hee had rather come throw Katherin Smiths. This the said Patrick Craig, James Crafoord and William Johnstoun can testifye.

15. The said Jeane Craig is accused By James Smith in Litle Faside for having been seen airely[53] one morning in his Byre, among his Ky[54] and oxen cambeing[55] her head, After which immediatly his Ky, in stead of milk gave Blood, and oxen went wood[56] and the Boy that keept them, and had seen her, dyed shortlie after.

16. The said Jeane haveing verry earlie at morne mett with a servant Man of the said James Smiths who had with him sex Horses, To whom shee used these words for a Salutation, What Deell[57] dow yee so soone up at morne, she having crossed the way the man was on with the last three hors, they never cutted grasse againe but dyes, and so did the Man a litle space after; as also the three Horsse that were formest dyed[58] some days after.

Depositiones

On Saturday the last March 1649 in the Tolbooth of Tranent, Before the minister, the Elders, and many honest men of the said Towne, compeared Alexander Baillie younger in Penstoune who being taken deeplie sworne did witnes, that the for mentioned Beatie Sandilands said to him at that verrie instant tyme that she was turnd mad, The Jean Craig had blawen on her Face.

The said day James Winla in Penstoune, upon his great oath did likewise depone, that hee had hard the said Beatie say many a Time, that Jeane Craig had blawen in her Face; as also that hee had hard Jean Craig herself say, that shee should see a blak sight on Beatie Sandilands, or that day eight dayes which fell out accordingly as shee had said.[59]

The said day Libra Smith, an old servant woman to the foresaid James Smith depon'd on her oath, that shee knew her Maisters Ky to give in stead of milk nothing but Blood, his oxen to goe wood and his hors shoot to dead,[60] as also his two men servants that keepit them never to be well, fra that morning they saw her, till they dyed.

52 'and why sa replyed hee, Jeane': and why so? he replied to Jean.
53 JC26/13/B/6 omits 'airely'.
54 'Ky': cows.
55 'cambeing': combing.
56 'wood': mad.
57 'Deell': Devil. Again, this should probably be understood as an expletive, 'What the Devil are you doing?'
58 'also' crossed out here.
59 JC26/13/B/6 omits 'as shee had said'.
60 'shoot to dead': die suddenly.

Item the tenth of Aprill, Jeane Cockburne, sister to the Laird of Butterdane,[61] testifes, and declars, that Jeane Craig coming one Day, through her Howse in Prestoune takes her by the Shakell[62] Baines of her Armes, and withall utering some wordes, she becomes so mad and distracted, that for many a Day after, Shee was not at her self, and even to this day is not, as is well knowne both by her Nighbours and many of the Paroch, as is witnessed by her Brother, subscribed by her self.[63] {*p. 3*}

Jeane Craigs Confession taken the said last March 1649

First shee confest before the ministers of Tranent and the Pannes, before Mr James Ramsay the Barron-Baillie, the Elders, and many other honest men of the Towne, that she had been acquaint with Margaret Mathesone and Jennet Rid who were both burnt for notorious witches. This is witnessed by a Missive from the Lard of Lamintouns Brother, to Mr Robert Balcanquell.[64]

2. She confest that Beatie Sandilands in Penstoun had one day angerd her, for the quhilk shee had angerd her worse and that shee had at the command of Lamintouns Brother fallen downe on her knees, and sought the said Beatie forgivenesse for the wrong shee had done her, wherupon presently after the woman became somewhat better.

3. She granted that she knew James Smith when she dwelt beside him, to have Ky that gave blood, oxen that went wood, horse that shot to dead,[65] the men that keept them to be ill at ease, But she was not the wite of that.[66]

At Hadintoun Apryll 11th 1649

The whilk day the presbytrie of Hadintoun having redd and considered the accusations depositions and confesson abovewriten thinke it incumbent to the pairties persewers to supplycate his Majesties counsell or whom it concernes for a Commission to sitt upon and try the said Jeane Craig and the process against her and to judge according to law.

[*Signed:*] JMakghie Clerke.

20 April 1649

The Co ...[67]

61 Robert Cockburn of Butterdean.

62 'shakell': wrist.

63 In margin in a different hand: 'which be not relevant per se bot to be joynt with ane of the malefices in the dittay'.

64 This 'Missive' is the letter of 17 March printed above.

65 'shot to dead': died suddenly. JC26/13/B/6 has 'shot them to dead'.

66 'she was not the wite of that': she was not to blame for that.

67 *Sic.* This last entry is in a different hand, the same hand that wrote the equivalent note at the end of JC26/13/B/4, printed below. Perhaps the scribe began to write his note here, then changed his mind and wrote it on JC26/13/B/4 instead.

JC26/13/B/4

[*Endorsed:*] Thomas Crawford etc. in Tranent.

{*p. 1*} Unto the Lords and others of the Committee of Estates humble[68] means and shewes your Lordships servitors Thomas Crawfoord John Parkie John Neper, James Couan in Trannent and James Smith in Litle Fausyde, That where wee and divers others in the Countrie have been heavelie wronged by Jean Craig a notorious witch who hes also been accused and examined before the Presbiterie of Haddington of manie high and execrable[69] poynts of witchcraft as the accusations produced before the said Presbiterie will testifie and after tryall of the matter shall better appeare, Our humble desire theirfore is that seing their is no Quorum of the Secreet Counsell for the present your Lordships wold be pleased to grant warrand and command to his his [*sic*] Majesties Justies Deputts to repaire unto the place where the said crymes and Malefices were committed and their with the concurrence of such Gentlemen upon the bounds as they shall think fitt to take tryall of these accusations and Minister Justice upon the Partie and[70] \inflict upon/ her such condigne Punishement as she shall deserve.

20 April 1649.[71]
The Committee of Estats doth give warrant to his Majestyes Justice deputs to repair to the place and minister justice as is desyred.

[*Signed:*] Loudoun Cancellarius, JPr com.

JC26/13/B/1, JC26/13/B/2[72]

{*p. 1*} Jeane Craig spous to William Steill Indweller in Tranent

Ye are Indytit and accuset Forsameikle as be the devyne law of almychtie God contenit in his sacreid word Speciallie set doun in the xviii chapter of Deuteronomie and xx chapter of Leviticus Against the useris and practizeris of Witchcraft Sorcerie charmeing and south saying And against the seikeris of help and responssis fra thame thretining to the comittaris of all sic devillische practizes the puneischement of daith As also be dyvers lawis and actis of parliament of this kingdome Speciallie be the 73 act of the Nynth Parliament of our soverane lordis darrest grandame Queane Marie of good Memorie It is expreslie provydit statute and ordanit That no maner of persone or persones of quhatsumevir estait degrie or conditioun thay be of

68 *Sic.* Probably read 'humbly'.

69 'execrable': detestable.

70 'put' crossed out here.

71 This heading begins a different hand.

72 This document, on two sheets of paper, has been given two separate archival numbers. The first sheet is JC26/13/B/1. The beginning of the second sheet is noted below.

Presume nor tak upone hand at ony tyme thaireftir To use ony maner of witchcraft Sorcerie or Necromancie nor geve thame selffis furth to have ony sic craft or knowledge thairof thairthrow to abuse the people nather that ony persone seik ony help respons or consultatioun of ony sic abusearis forsaidis or usearis of sorcerie witchcraft or necromancie under the pane of daith To be execute als weill against the usear and abusear as the seiker of responsis or consultatioun as in the saidis Laws and acts of parliament at Lenth is contenit Nochtwithstanding quhairof It is of verritie that ye the said Jeane Craig expres against the saidis Lawis and acts of parliament, schaiking aff all feir of the almychtie and omnipotent God hes thir mony yeiris bygane be your sorcerie and witchcraft and be the advys and counsell of the Devill your Lord and maister Laid on and tane af dyvers horrible diseassis and seiknessis upone sundrie persones our soverane Lordis guid people and subiectis als also upone thair bestiall and guidis.

1. And namelie[73] be the space of [*1 word blank*] yeiris bygane or thairby ye haveing conceaved ane devillisch haitrent[74] and malice against umquhile James Wilsone husband to Helene Cowan for the tyme \one quhom schoe causet ane coll[75] to fall/ now the spouse of John Naper In [*1 word blank*] As also against umquhile James Bradie in Elphingstoun and againse umquhile Johne Crawfurd in Tranent and Lykwayis againse umquhile Williame Ekfurd thair ye be your sorcerie and witchcraft efter consultatioun with the Devill your maister Laid upone the saidis James Wilsone James Bradie John Craufurd and umquhile Williame Eckfurd dyvers feirfull seiknessis and diseasses off the quhilkis thay all deceissit and sua war crewallie murdeist be your sorcerie and witchcraft Laid Be yow upone thame Quhilk is nottourlie knawin to the nychtboures and haill cuntrie people quhair ye dwelt and ye can nocht deny. {*p. 2*}

2. Item[76] ye ar Indytit and accuset For the devellische and continewall consultatioun with Beiggis Wallace your mother ane notorious witche and quha was brunt for witchcraft at Preston pannes be the space of \xxii/ yeris syne or thairby And namelie In your continewall deilling with the said Beigis Wallace your mother And for your nycht and day solisting and begging The gift of ane man chyld quhairwith Agnes Steill your goode sister was than with and undelyverit of To this effect that ye the said Jeane Craig sa sone as the said chyld sould come in the world ye mycht offer and geve him to the Devill your Lord and maister quhilk the said Beigis confessit to be of verritie a Litill befoir hir burning at Preston pannes, And siclyk eftir the said chyld was

[73] In margin: 'Findis this Article Relevant *conjunctim* with the thrid Article and with the second pairt of the 5t Article'.

[74] 'haitrent': hatred.

[75] 'coll': (piece of) coal. The coal seems to have fallen on James Wilson. The phrase about it is interlined, with no precise indication of how it should be read in connection with the rest of the text.

[76] In margin: 'fylit'.

borne be the said Agnes Steill your sister in law and scho delyverit thairof ye be your sorcerie and witchcraft for distructioun of the said chyld Rubbed and sleiket him over with thre Littill Inchantit stanes in his Lithes and pairtis of his body Quhilk thre stanes was gottin be yow frome the said Beigis Wallace your mother Eftir your quhilk Tuiching rubbing and sleiking over and over at dyvers tymes of the said chyld with the saidis thre devillisch Inchantit stanes gottin fra your said mother The said chyld be your sorcerie and witchcraft daylie dwynet and pynet away till the tyme of his deceis[77] And sua the samyn was crewallie slane and murtheriet be your sorcerie and witchcraft quhilk is nottourlie knawin Lyk as all the tyme fra the beiring and delyverie be the said Agnes Steill your guid sister of the said chyld ye evir frequenting the hous ye delairet to the said Agnes that ye knew the chyld was nocht hirs Bot was your Lordis meanying thairby the Devill your maister And that thair was nothing fitt for him bot fox trie Levis and south rynning watter Quhilk ye promeissit to gett and apply to him \albeit/[78] ye nevir did it Eftir the deceis and bewitcheing of the quhilk chyld be your sorcerie and witchcraft in maner foirsaid The said Agnes Steill your guidsister haveing borne and brocht furth sax severall childrene ye the said Jeane Craig beiring ane secreit grudge and hie malice agains the said Agnes Steill ye Be your sorcerie and witchcraft practizet be yow upone hir[79] causet hir milk altogidder to vanish out of hir breist and palpes Sua that scho nevir had ony milk quhairwith to nureis ony of thame.

3. And finallie ye still continewing your crewall haitrent and malice Against the said Agnes Steill hir husband and childrene ye by your sorcerie and witchcraft practizet against thame maid dyvers feirfull sichtis[80] to appeir dyvers nychtis within thair duelling hous Namelie ye causet grit Numberis of uglie beistis nychtlie rynning about ane knoking stane standing in thair hous The said Agnes Steill William Hekfurd hir husband and William Hekfurd hir sone contracted feirfull seiknessis and diseassis quhilk be your sorcerie and witchcraft was Laid upone thame And thai thaireftir dwynet and pynet away in grit dollour and payne And in end deceissit And sua thai were both murthereist and slane be your sorcerie and witchcraft quhilk ye can nocht deny.[81] {*p. 3*}[82]

4. Item[83] ye the said Jeane Craig Ar Indytit and accuset Quhairupon ye haveing contracted ane deidlie haitrent and evill will Against Johne Parkie in Tranent and Beatrix Sandilands his wyfe In the moneth of [*1 word blank*] The

77 In margin: 'findis this Malefeice practizet be witchcraft Relevant'.

78 'Quhilk' crossed out here.

79 In margin: 'finds not this relevant per se bot joynes with the 2d or 3d Article'.

80 'sichtis': sights.

81 In margin: 'finds this Malefeice Relevant hir husband and sonnes names being condiscendit upone' (i.e. specified). A marginal note in a different hand adds: 'William Hekfurd and hir sone is also namit [*'William' crossed out*] \Robert/ Hekfurd'.

82 The second sheet, JC26/13/B/2, begins here.

83 In margin (as three separate items): 'confest'; 'findis this article Relevant being Joynt with the [*'aucht' crossed out*] \9/ article'; 'fylit'.

yeir of God I^mVI^c Threttie sex yeiris or thairby ye Come to their dwelling hous And eftir some devillische speiches utterit be yow against the said Beatrix Sandilands ye be your malicious and devillische sorcerie and witchcraft with grit violence blew upone hir face Quhairupone the said Beatrix be that devillische Blast blowin upone hir face and be your horrible and devillische speiches quhilk yow utterit furth against hir Immediatlie Became mad and bereft of hir naturall witt sua that foure or fyve strong men war nocht of habiltie to hald hir Quhik was done be your devillrie and witchcraft Laid upone hir. Lyk as shortlie thaireftir ye still persewing in your devillische malice ye Come under silence of nycht to the said John Parkeis hous And haveing upone your stalff[84] some devillische Inchantit beist Lyke as a Catt And remaining all that nycht within the said house ye past to the fyre and roistit the samyn Inchantit uglie beists thair at Thaireftir be your sorcerie and witchcraft practizet be yow within the said John Parkeis hous ye causet ane grit number of uglie Cattis ye[85] rather devillis in the Liknes Come danceing \and triping/ about the pure man John Parkeis fyre Whairupon the said John to rid him selff of that horrible and feirfull sight Tuik up ane trie to chaise thame away Sua that the haill number of Cattis than being in the hous past out at an hoill neir by the chymnay At thair quhilk away passing furth at the said hoill The last of thame Turnes about and Cryis out with ane audible voce and speich (Hay quhat ailes Beatie now) In all this tyme the said Beatie Sandllands[86] on quhome ye the said Jeane Craig in your devillische maner had blowin was lying bound hand and fute becaus of your devillische madnes Laid upone hir in maner foirsaid Lyk as be your devillrie and witchcraft practizet be yow within the said John Parkeis house ye strawed and cuist doun in all the places thairof dyvers uglie Lumpis of reid raw flesche Sua that be your sorcerie and witchcraft the haill floore and ground thairof was besprinkellit with horrible Reid bloode And all that Looked thairupone be your sorcerie seamed to swoone with flesch and bluid And Lykwayis ye nevir being satisfeit unto the tyme be your sorcerie and witchcraft ye had bereft the said Beatrix Sandilands of hir naturall Lyfe Sua that scho was tormented with continuall feiris and horrible paine quhair evir scho repairet ye in the verrie Coill pott In end be your sorcerie and witchcraft ye bereft hir of hir Lyfe quhilk is nottourlie knawin to the haill parochin of Tranent and Contrey people thairabout.

5. Item[87] ye haveing conceaved ane deidlie malice and evill will against the said umquhile John Crawfurd in Tranent Quha be your sorcerie and witchcraft Laid upone him in maner foirsaid was maist feirfullie bewitchet and bereft

84 'stalff': staff.

85 'ye' (yea): indeed.

86 'was lying' crossed out here.

87 In margin (as two separate items): '*Non relevat* and is first pairt of the 5 article'; 'findis this pairt of the [*'sex' crossed out*] fyft article relevant *conjunctim* with the first and 3 article'. '*Non relevat*': is not relevant; '*conjunctim*': conjoined.

of his naturall Lyfe Quhlk at the hour of his daith he affirmet in presens of dyvers famous witnessis Namelie in presens of Mr Robert Balcanquell Minister To be of verritie And left his daith and the only caus thairof upone yow Ye Lykwayis continewing your malice against Thomas Crawfurd his brother becaus of some contraversie and discord that fell out betwix William Steill your husband and him ye for revenge thairof be your sorcerie and witchcraft Laid ane heavie diseas upone Thomas Crawfurd his sone Sua that the haill power of his tua Leggis is tane frome him and he unhable to walk or travell thairupon continuallie sensyne. {*p. 4*}

6. Item[88] ye the said Jeane Craig Ar Indytit and accuset Forsameklill as ye haveing conceavet ane deidlie haitrent and malice Against James Cowan Coilyear in Tranent Becaus of some outragious speiches that past betwix the said James Cowane and Williame Steill your husband be the space of ane yeir or thairby, ye in revendge thairof be your sorcerie and witchcraft and speciall counsall and command gevin be yow to Agnes Affleck Ane of your devillishe scolleris Informit sa the said Nans Fleck \to vex, trubill and affray him/ That the said James Cowane that nycht was sa vexit and trubillit in dyvers pairtis of his body speciallie in his face That the blood sprang out thairof in grit abundance, Lyk as every nycht sensyne be your sorcerie and witchcraft Laid upon him he is sa bereft of his naturall wittis That he hes no power nor habilitie To reule him selff Bot be your sorcerie and Incantatioun Is forced and compellit Nill he will he To ryve and rent him selff and cheiflie in the face Till the blood spring out in grit quantitie, And farder the said James Cowane be your devillische sorcerie and witchcraft Is sa terrified be your appeirance nychtlie in his hous at his fyresyde and at his bedsyde and within his bed quhan he should sleip That he is hirrellit[89] out thairof and drawyn and tumbled up and downe his floure be wickit spreittis[90] That comes ryning out frome under his bed in gritt numberis Lyk unto uglie blak tykes at quhilks and sic uther feirfull apparitiones The said James Cowane is oft tymes sene to creip under the bedis and Lurk quyetlie in holes heir and thair And sometymes To clymb upon the bed heidis And to hyd him selff betwix the Lofting and geistis and cuples of his hous weill knawin and sene be his nychtbouris And finallie ye synce your Imprisonement still continewing in your malicious haitrent and evill will agains the said James Cowane he haveing a sone namit Johne Cowane Be your sorcerie and witchcraft practizet upone him and utheris your associattis at your command he being working in the Coilpat The saidis John Cowan his Leg be your devillische witchcraft was brokin thairintill And thair \eftir/ he was carreit hame to the said James Cowane his fatheris house, upoun the

[88] In margin (as two separate items): 'aquit [*sic*]'; 'findis the 6t poynt Relevant being Joynit with any of the sevint or 8t'.

[89] 'hirrelit': hurled.

[90] 'quhairby he is for feir' crossed out here.

occasion quhairof certane freindis of the said John Cowan cummand to the prisson to visseit yow fell furth in dyvers discourses with yow And in end upone the hurt ressavit be the said John Cowane be his brokin Leg in the Coill heuch[91] ye the said Jeane Craig did thairupon demand of thame Be quhat way was the said John Cowane cayreit [*sic*] hame to his fatheris house It was answerit to yow that aftir breking of his Leg he was brocht hame and caryeit throw Patrik Craigis house to his fatheris house quhairupone and upone that repoirt maid to yow of his hamebringing ye replyed to the said Patrik Craig (quha war ane of thais that come to visseit yow in the prissone) The way sayis Patrik to yow was Indeid Jeane That the youth was cayreid throw myne the said Patrik Craigis hous To the quhilk ye maid answer to the said Patrik Craig I rew that Patrik The said Patrik thaireftir replyed and answerit to yow in thir woirdis And quhy sa Jeane ye answerit bak againe to him in thir woirdis I ken my selff Patrik And I wish he had rather bein caryeit and come throw Katherene Smythis house quhilkis discoursis ar to be provin and verifeit be the said Patrik Craig and be James Craufurd and be William Johnstoun In all quhilkis premissis ye have declairet your selff anent the said James Cowane and John Cowane his sone for the feirfull witchcraft practizet be yow against thame To be ane manifest sorcerar and witche conversant with the Devill and his scolleris and servandis for thair distructioun. {*p. 5*}

7. Item[92] ye the said Jeane Craig Ar Indytit and accuset Forsameikill as ye haveing conceavet ane deidlie haitrent and evill will against James Smyth in Litill Fawsyde did thir divers yeiris bygane be your sorcerie and witchcraft do quhat in yow lay to distroy him his cattell and goodis and put him to extreme povertie And namelie In the moneth of [*1 word blank*] in the yeir of God [*1 word blank*] Last bypast Ye seing the said James Smyth his ky and oxin standing airlie in the moirning in his byre ye enterit within his said byre And thair eftir cambeing of your heid and hair thairof thairintill ye be your sorcerie and witchcraft (eftir your passing throw the saidis oxin and ky) Tuik frome the haill ky thair haill mylk sua that at the milking of thame nathing bot bloode come frome thame in stead of mylk And the haill oxin Immediatlie thaireftir Ran mad Lyk as the boy or hird that keiped and waitted upone thame and upone the ky and \had/ sene yow that moirning within the said byre he shortlie thaireftir be your sorcerie and witchcraft schot to deid of quhais daith ye war be your [*word crossed out*] sorcerie and witchcraft speciall actrix[93] and airt and pairt and of the bewitching of the saidis oxin and ky in maner forsaid.

91 'Coill heuch': coal-pit.
92 In margin (as two separate items): 'The 7t poynt relevant'; 'fylit'.
93 'actrix': feminine form of 'actor'.

8. And siclyke[94] ye haifing schortlie thaireftir Airlie in ane moirning met and rancountered with ane servant man of the said James Smyth in Littill Fawsyde quho had by his gyding and Leading sax horssis pertening to his maister To quhome for ane salutatioun ye utterit thir wikked woirdis Quhat devill dois thow man sua sone at morne ye be your devillisch sorcerie and witchcraft first crossed his way quhairin he was with the saidis horssis Sua that Immediatlie thaireftir the [*words crossed out*] thre horssis of the sax horssis schortlie thaireftir schote to dead and nevir eitit grase thaireftir And the man him selff with the saidis uther thre horssis within a littill space thaireftir Lykwayis be your sorcerie and witchcraft deceissit off quhais daithe and distructioun be your devillisch and unlaufull meanes ye war speciall airt and pairt.

And finallie[95] ye ar Indytit and accuset as ane commoun witch and sorcerar hanting[96] and keiping conference and familiaritie with the Devill your Lord and maister and with dyvers witches his sworne servandis speciallie with Beigis Wallace your mother ane notorious witche And quha for hir devillrie and witchcraft was tryet convict and brunt for witchcraft at Prestoun pans and quha declairet befoir hir daith yow to be the only caus and instrument [*word crossed out*] of the daith of the chyld of Nans Steill your sister in Law in maner befoir expressit by your sorcerie and witchcraft abone written The quhilk devillische tred[97] of sorcerie ye have exerceissit thir twelf yeiris bygane For the quhilk ye aucht and sould be puneist to the daithe Conforme to the Lawis of almychtie God and actis of parliament of this kingdome to the terror and example of utheris etc.

JC26/13/B/5

Be It kend till all men be thir present Letters Me Mr Thomas Nicolsone advocat to our soverane Lord Quhair as Jeane Craig the wyfe of William Steill in Tranent Is delaittit and to be accuset and persewit be dittay befoir his Maiesteis Justice deputis within the tolbuth of Tranent upone Fryday nixt the xxvii day of Apryle instant of dyvers poyntis of sorcerie and witchcraft committit be hir against dyvers persones his majesteis subiectis specifeit in hir said dittay To have thairfoir maid and constitute And be thir presentis mak and constitutes \George Ramsay/ My depute in that pairt geveand grantand and committand to him my full power expres bidding and charge as depute to me his Majesteis advocat To compeir in the said Justice court to be keipit the saidis day and place And thair for me and my name as my depute foirsaid To persew the said Jeane Craig of the crymes specifeit in hir said dittay And

94 In margin (as two separate items): 'The 8t poynt relevant'; 'fylit'.

95 In margin: 'thir xxii yeiris hes beine the servand of Margaret Mathesoune and Jonnet Reid. The quhilk Beigis Wallace your mother declairet'.

96 'hanting': resorting to.

97 'tred': trade, occupation.

to doe all thingis neidfull Anent hir tryell and persute of the crymes foirsaidis Quhilk I promit to hald ferme and stable as gif I war present my selff In witnes quhairof I haif subscryvit thir presentis with my hand at Edinburgh The xxvi day of Apryle The yeir of God I^{m}VI^{c} fourtie nyne yeiris Befoir thir witnessis James Chalmers inserter of the witnessis and James Douglas my servitores.

[*Signed:*] TNicolson, JChalmers witnes, JDouglass witnes.

JC26/13/B/10/1

{*p. 1*} [*3-4 lines torn away*] ... substitut to his majesties advocat quha producit his lettres and commissione to that effect.

Assisa
Archibald Purves in Tranent
Peter Wylie thair
John Craig thair
Richard Trumble thair
James Congeltoun in Langnidrie
Ritchard Wadell in Seaton
Adame Waddell in Seaton
Robert Heriot in Langnidrie
Robert Gilmour in Seaton
James Alane in Wintoun
James Carfra in Wintoun
Patrick Spence in Preston pans
John Read thair
[*1 word damaged*] Fleck thair
[*1 word damaged*] Wood thair[98]

Dilatours[99]
Thomas Crawfurd in Tranent sworne the 2d and of the 5t article.[100]

Agnes Steill[101] sworne the dittay and the malifice done to hir husband And sone contenit in the 3 article. As also the 2d article.

John Parkie[102] sweiris the 4t article to be trew concerning the malifeice done to his wyfe.

98 These names appear elsewhere as Thomas Affleck and Hector Wood.

99 The 'Dilatours' (accusers) are separate from the witnesses who are listed next. This list may relate to the supplication for a trial printed above, from five men of whom Thomas Crawford and John Parkie were two. Here, the third 'dilatour' is a woman, Agnes Steill; was she also being treated as a formal prosecutor?

100 'Helene Cowane' and 'John Napier hir spous' crossed out here.

101 In margin: '3d acquit'.

102 In margin: '4t'.

Witnes

James Winla dwelland under Lamingtoun[103] sworne depones he saw raw flesh in the hous, depones he hard the panell promeis ane blak sight sould come upone Beatrix Sandielands or that day aucht days quhilk fell out accordingly bot cannot tell the panell {*p. 2*} [*3-4 lines torn away*]

Alexander Bailyie elder in Penstoun \under Lamington/ sworne depones he saw Betie Sandielands goe mad bot knawis nocht quhairby schoe went mad or how schoe come by hir madnes.

John Dikesone in Penstane under Lamington sworn depones Betie Sandielands went lycht bot knawis[104] how shoe cam by it bot that Betie Sandielandis gave the panell the wyt[105] of hir madnes.

Jeane Hunter[106] wedow in Penstoun sworne depones shoe knawis nocht anent Agnes Steills bairne hir bewitching bot only sayis schoe saw hir come in [*1 word damaged*] quhill the woman was delyverit [*1-2 words damaged*] schoe hard hir thryse say [*1-2 words damaged*] hous at hir In cuming [*2-3 words damaged*] war afryght that war [*2-3 words damaged*] cannot say that Jeane [*2-3 words damaged*] \upone/ saying of thaise blasfem...[107] was the caus of the bairnes dai....[108]

James Smith in Litle Fawsyd sworne depones by Jeane Craig hir witchcraft about 15 yeir since at the Witsondy Jeane Crag was sene his[109] byre betweene his ky and oxin about 4 hours in the morning and that presentlie thairefter the oxin went mad And the ky gave blood thairefter instead of mylk, And depones that schoe thretnit the boy saying ye suld be als fremed[110] to the hous as I, And fra that time since the boy was nevir sene agan and can evir[111] be fund albeit he was borne in the paris.[112] {*p. 3*} [*3-4 lines torn away*]

... began bot went a beging and deit shortly eftir and reportit to the deponer that the pannell ly behind him \in the bed and knew the boy deid be hir witchcraft/.

Libra Smyth wedow in Tranent sworne depones that shoe mylkit the ky that gave bluid ane day and that the oxin was sald for thair skyne and the horsis deid quhen thay war lousit fra the pleuch that nycht, And the hird boy ran away and was nevir sene agan, and the wther boy[113] nevir thrave thairefter bot begit and deit in Tranent.

103 'dwelland under Lamingtoun': he was a tenant of Sir William Baillie of Lamington.
104 *Sic*. Possibly 'not' has been omitted here in error.
105 'wyt': blame.
106 In margin: '2d acquit'.
107 After this partly damaged word, another word is missing. Before it, the scribe has written 'spe...' and crossed it out. The complete text may well have read 'thaise blasfemous speeches was the caus'.
108 Word damaged, probably 'daith'.
109 *Sic*. Probably read 'in his'.
110 'fremed': foreign, unrelated.
111 *Sic*. Probably read 'nevir'.
112 'paris': parish.
113 'begyt and' crossed out here.

James Cowane[114] in Tranent sworne depones all the evill cam upone his sone was be Nans Afflekis Menes only.

Cristiane Merstoune sworne depones [*1-2 words damaged*] 3 or 4 nyghts efter hir goodman gat the [*1-2 words damaged*] schoe saw Jeane Craig sits behind [*1-2 words damaged*] the bed.

Jeane Cokburne sworne depones shoe was no weill befoir Jeane Craig gripit hir be the armes and that schortly eftir within 3 dayis shoe fand hir selff wors ane long tye eftir bot will nocht say it was throw hir sorcare and witchcraft.

Alexander Forrestar in Carberie knawis nothing.

JC26/13/B/7/1

The first article finds relevant conjoynt with the 3d article and secund part of the 5t article.

The assyse[115] clenges hir of the first 3d and fyllis hir of the 2d and of the 5t And that clengit.[116]

The 2d article relevant per se.

The assyse fyllis hir of the 2d article.[117]

The 4t article relevant.[118]

The assyse fylls hir of the 4t article.[119]

The 6t Article Relevant joynet ather with the 7t article or the 8 article.

The assyse clenges hir of the 6t article and fyllis hir of bothe the 7t and 8t.[120]

Sevint article fund relevant.

The assyse fylls hir thairof.[121]

8t article fund relevant.

The assyse fylls hir thairof.[122]

The tent the assyse fylls.[123]

JC26/13/B/9[124]

1. Anent the 1 article:[125] Concerning James Wilsones daith and John Crawfurdis daith brother to Thomas Crawfurd and James Bradies daith clengs hir thairof In respect thair is no confessione probatione nor aith of panel producet.

114 In margin: '6 acquit'.
115 'fyll' crossed out here.
116 In margin: 'acquit'.
117 In margin: '2 Fylit'.
118 'conjoynit with the 5t article' crossed out here.
119 About 6 words crossed out here. In margin: '4 Fylit'; 'acquit' crossed out.
120 In margin: '6 acquit'.
121 In margin: '7t fyllit'.
122 In margin: '8t fyllit'.
123 In margin: '10 fylit'.
124 This document, on a small slip of paper, is in the same hand as JC26/13/B/8 (printed here below), and the two items are probably intended to be read together as a single document.
125 In margin: 'Clengis'.

JC26/13/B/8[126]

{*p. 1*}[127] 5t. Fyllis hir [*2 words crossed out*] of the bewitching of Thomas Crawfurd sone \to Thomas Crawfurd,/ hes done in the second pairt of the 5t article anent the taking away the power of his 2 legs In respect of the said Thomas his fatheris depositione.[128]

2 article. Fylles hir lykways of the 2d article Anent the daith of Agnes Stellis bairne in respect of the probatione producit and of Agnes Steills aith insuering that poynt of dity to be trew.[129]

3. Anent the 3d article Concerning the daith of William Heckfurd and Robert Hekfurd his sone Clengis hir thairof as not proven.[130]

4. Anent the 4t Article: Concerning Beatrix Sandilands and hir daith be witchcraft and hir madnes fyllis hir thairof in respect of hir Confessione.[131]

6. Anent the 6 article: Concerning James Cowan and the malefeice ressavit be him and done to his sone John Cowane Clengis hir thairof Becaus thair is no Probatione producet for verifeing thairof[132] only the said James Cowane declairs any wrang he ressavit was done to him be Agnes Affleck and not be Jean Craig.[133]

7, 8. Anent the 7 and 8 articles: Concerning James Smyth the bewitching of his goodis and serwandis fyles hir thairof In respect of the said James Smyth awine aith and the witnessis probatione produced.[134]

9t article: Anent Jeane Cokburne sister to Butterdane Concerneing the wrang allegit done to hir clengis hir thairof In respect of Jean Coburnes awin declaratione.[135] {*p. 2*}

10. Anent the 10 article: Concerning hir confessione to be a witch and that sho becum the Devillis servand and renunceing of hir baptisme and having copulatione with the Devill And his appeiring to hir in severall shapes Fyllis thairof in respect of hir awin confessione.[136]

[126] This document is in the same hand as JC26/13/B/9 (printed here above), and the two items are probably intended to be read together as a single document.

[127] The paragraph numbers 1–10 below are written in the margin, but here they have been taken into the main text because they clearly form part of it. Further marginal numbers have been added later, as follows: '1' opposite paragraph 2; '2' opposite paragraph 4; '3' opposite paragraph 7–8; '4' opposite paragraph 10. These numbers may represent an attempt to align these items with equivalent items in the short dittay. For discussion of the long and the short dittays, see the Introduction above.

[128] In margin: 'Fyllis'. This whole paragraph has had two lines drawn across it.

[129] In margin: 'Fylls'.

[130] In margin: 'acquit'. This whole paragraph has had a line drawn across it.

[131] In margin: 'Fyllis. This is joynt with the 9'.

[132] 'declaring' crossed out here.

[133] In margin: 'acquit'. This whole paragraph has had a line drawn across it.

[134] In margin: 'Fylls'.

[135] In margin: 'acquit'. A further note has been added at the foot of this page, printed in the present edition at the end of the main text; see a later footnote below.

[136] This whole paragraph has had a line drawn across it.

Last. And fyllis hir as ane comone sorcerer and witch.

Mark Boustean.[137]

Jeane Craig To be tane to the Mure brow upone Tysdy [*2 words crossed out*] being the first of May 1649.

JC26/13/B/7/2

{*p. 1*} The quhilk day Jean Craig spous to William Steill in Tranent wes entirit upone panell delaitit accusit and persewit be dittay at the instance of George Ramsay the advocate substitut to the right honourabll Mr Thomas Nicolson advocate to our soveran lord for his hienes interes conforme to his lordships procuratorie and substitutione subscribit with his hand to that effect with dyvers poynts of sorcerie and witchcraft at lenth specifiet and set doun in the said dittay.

1. Speciallie for the murthour and distructione of ane young chyld borne be Agnes Steill hir sister in law shortlie eftir hir beiring thairof and that be hir sorcerie and witchcraft in maner specifeit in hir dittay.

2. Item for hir devillish onlaying of ane feirfull deseis upone[138] Beatrix Sandielands[139] be hir sorcerie and witchcraft in causing the said Beatrix Sandilands become mad and to be bereft of hir naturall wit be the said Jeane hir sorcerie and witchcraft in maner specifeit in hir dittay and for the said [*sic*] to hir dath and distructione.

3. Item being also chergit for bewitching with hir sorcerie and witchcraft of James Smith in Lytle Fawsyd his ky and oxin in cuming arly in an morne to his byre and passing throw the samyn quhair his ky and oxin war than standing And be hir sorcerie and witchcraft making the said ky ky [*sic*] thairefter to gif nothing bot blud instead of mylk and his haill oxin thairefter to ryn mad and schut to daith and the boy or hird he being than being [*sic*] within the byre wes never thairefter fund be hir sorcerie and witchcraft in maner specifeit in hir dity.

4. Item the said Jean Craig continwing in hir malice against the said James Smith in Litle Fasyd rancountering[140] with ane servand of his airlie in ane morning leading furth sax of his viz. James Smiths horsis and crosd his way said to his servand man quhat Dewill dois thow up soe sone at morne and thaireftir thrie of the his [*sic*] horsis be the said Jeane Craig hir sorcerie and witchcraft laid upone tham Imediatly shot to dead and the man him selff with the uther thrie horsis be hir sorcerie and witchcraft lykwayis decessit in maner specifeit in hir dity.

137 This name and the short paragraph below it have been added at the foot of p. 1, after the rest of the document was written, in a different hand. This may well be the hand of Mark Boustean, the dempster of the court, himself.

138 'John Parkie in Tranent and' crossed out here.

139 'his wyfe' crossed out here.

140 'rancountering': meeting.

Item the said Jean Craig being Indytit that schoe being interrogat upone the 27 of Apryle instant in presence of dyverss famous witnesis confest that shoe was ane witch and craweit Gods pardone thairfor, And also being interrogat be quhat meanes the said Beatrix Sandilands becum mad, Answeret be na good mater[141] {*p. 2*} bot be witchraft [*sic*] laid upone hir, And also being Interrogat for becuming the Devils servant And be quhas intyisement, the said Jean confest It wes be the intysement[142] of Margaret Mathiesone for malice borne to the said Beatrix Sandielands.[143] The said Jean declairing hir selff thairby to be ane manifest witch And finallie the said Jean being indytit as ane comone witch, hanting and beiring cumpanie with dyverss witches speciallie with the said Beigis Wallace hir mother, Margaret Mathesone and Jonet Read all witches and brunt in Prestoun Panes for witchcraft and that shoe had confest the samyn to be of veritie as also that shoe had dyverss meetings with the Devill at dyvers tymes and in dyvers places quha wald appear to hir in the liknes of ane cat and at tymes in the lyknes of ane man and that he had carnall copulatione with hir and maid hir renunce hir baptisme and becum his servand, the said Jean Crag ratefeit hir depositiones thairanent and that shoe cravet of the Devill revang and heart syth of tham that offendit hir, as at lenth is set doun in the said dity, quhilk perticuler poynts of dity abonespecifiet being fund relevant be the Justice and Judges foirsaidis the samyne was refarit be the tham [*sic*] to the knawledg of an assyse of the persones following, thai ar to say, ø[144] quhilk persones of assyse being ressavit, sworne and admittit, Affter acqusatione [*sic*] of the said Jeane Craig be dittay of the perticuler crymes abonespecifiet and instrumentis tane thairupone and protestatione maid be the said George Ramsay advocat substitute abonewrittin for wilfull errour against the said assyse Incaice thai sould acquit the said Jean Crag of the crymes specifiet in hir dity, removet altogethir furth of court to an secret place be tham selffis within the said tolboth thair thai be pluralitie of vots electit and chessit the said James Carfra ane chancellor And thair ressonit and woitit upon the poynts of dity perticularly abonespecifiet [*about 3 words unreadable*] and at lenth adwysset thai reenterit again in court quhair thay with ane voce be said James cravet declaratione of [*word crossed out*] James Carfra chancellour.[145]

141 Reading uncertain.

142 'intysement': enticement.

143 Matheson had been executed in 1629, yet Craig's quarrel with Sandilands had occurred, according to other documents, in 1636. Either there had been a previous quarrel, or else the interrogators did not regard this chronological inconsistency as important.

144 This symbol is evidently the scribe's reminder to himself to add these names when writing the final version of the text.

145 This is the very end of this small sheet of paper. It may also be the end of the text, but it seems inconclusive. Perhaps the text continued on a second sheet, no longer extant. The whole document is written in a small and cramped hand, and a few readings are uncertain.

Source 3: NRS, Minutes of the Committee of Estates, 1649, PA11/8.

{fo. 46r.} Twentieth of Apryle 1649

Lord Chancellor Pr.	Toftis	Sir James Hope
Argyle	Hartrie	Sir John Smith
The Lord Generall	Colonell Scott	Hew Kennedy
Balmerino	Busbie	James McCalloch ...[146] *{fo. 49r.}*
Burghlie	Duddingstoun	
Craighall	Sir James Hacket	

Warrand to the Justice Deputtis concerneing Jeane Craig

The Committee of Estates gives Power and Commission to his Majesties Justices deputtis to repaire to Tranent, and try and examine Jeane Craig there against quhom diverse accusations of the Cryme of Witchcraft are given in, And to administrat and do justice upon hir according to the Lawes of the Kingdome and practique thereof in the like Caices.

Source 4: NRS, Court of Justiciary, Books of Adjournal, 1637–1650, JC2/8.[147]

{p. 660[148]} Curia Justiciarie Supremi Domini Nostri Regis Tenta in pretorio[149] ville de Tranent vigesimo septimo Aprilis 1649 Per honorabiles et discretis viros Magistres Alexandrum Colvill de Blair et Jacobum Robertoun de Bedlay justiciarios deputatos. Curia legitime affirmata.[150]

Intran

Jeane Craig spous to William Steill coilyear in Tranent.

146 These members of the committee of estates were: John Campbell, first earl of Loudoun, chancellor (presiding); Archibald Campbell, marquis of Argyll; Alexander Leslie, lord general; John Elphinstone, third Lord Balmerino; Robert, second Lord Balfour of Burleigh; Sir John Hope of Craighall; Sir Alexander Belsches of Toftis; John Dickson of Hartree; Colonel Walter Scott of Hartwoodburn; John Dickson of Busbie; George Dundas of Duddingston; Sir James Halkett of Pitfirrane; Sir James Hope of Hopetoun; Sir John Smith of Groathill; Hugh Kennedy, provost of Ayr; and James MacCulloch, burgess of Whithorn.

147 A transcript of almost all of this document has been printed in S. I. Gillon and J. I. Smith (eds.), *Selected Justiciary Cases, 1624–1650*, 3 vols. (Edinburgh: Stair Society, 1954–74), iii, 812–15. A summary and paraphrase of it has been printed in Robertson, *Goodnight My Servants All*, 362–4.

148 This is the modern archival pagination. Some sources, including the SSW, use the volume's original pagination, by which the case is pp. 740–2.

149 '*burgi de Edinburgh*' crossed out here.

150 'Court of justiciary of our sovereign lord the king, held in the tolbooth of the town of Tranent, 27 April 1649, by the honourable and discreet men, Masters Alexander Colville of Blair and James Roberton of Bedlay, justices depute. Court legally fenced'.

Dilaittit of contraveneing the actis of parliament maid against the committeris of of [*sic*] sorcerie and witchcraft, speciallie the 73 Act of the nynt parliament of Queane {*p. 661*} Marie, dischairgeing all maner of persone or persones to use any maner of witchcraft, sorcerie or necromancie, or to gif thame selffis furth to have any sic craft or knawledg thairof, thairby to abuis the peiple, or to seik any help, response or consultationne at any sic useris of abuseris etc. under the payne of daith, as at lenth is contenit in the said act. Contrair the tennour[151] of the quhilk act of parliament, the said Jeane Craig,[152] thir many yeiris bygane, be hir sorcerie and witchcraft and be the advyse and counsall of the Devill, hir lord and master, with quhom schoe was conversant at all tymes, keipand trystis and meittingis with him and with Beigis Wallace, mother to the said Jeane.

And namelie,[153] a twentie twa yeir since, Agnes Steill hir sister in law being with chyld and neir the tyme of hir delyverie, schoe solistit earnestlie the gift of the chyld quhairwith the said Agnes was for the tyme, And for this effect eftir the beiring of the said chyld be the said Agnes Steill, the said Jeane be your[154] sorcerie and witchcraft for destructione thairof rubbit and sleikit over the said chyld with thrie inchantit stanes quhilk was gottin frome the saidis [*sic*] Beigis Wallace, hir mother, be occasione of the quhilk rubbing of the said chyld with the saidis thrie inchantit stanes and be the said Jeane hir sorcerie and witchcraft, the said chyld thaireftir deceissit And sua was crewallie murthourit and slane be the said Jeane hir sorcerie and witchcraft.

Item, being dilaittit of the onlaying of ane feirfull seiknes upone Beatrix Sandielandis, the spous of John Parkie in Tranent, be hir sorcerie and witchcraft sua laid upone the said Beatrix a tuell yeir since or thairby, causeing hir become mad and bereft of hir naturall wit, and in and be occasione of the said madnes, sua laid upone the said Beatrix be the said Jeane hir sorcerie and witchcraft was bereft of hir naturall lyfe.

Item, being dilaittit that schoe, haveing ane deadlie heatret against James Smyth in Litlefawsyd, schoe be hir sorcerie and witchcraft come airlie in ane morneing to his byre in Litlefawsyd, and passing throw the said byre quhair his oxin and ky stand for the tyme, and be hir sorcerie and witchcraft laid be hir upone the said ky and oxin, tuik away the mylk fra the ky sua that thai gave nathing but bluid thaireftir instead of milk, and his said oxin ran immeddiatlie mad, and the boy or hird that keipit thame, being also within the byre and seing hir thairintill, the said boy be hir sorcerie and witchcraft deceissit, at the leist was nevir sene thaireftir.

151 'tennour' (tenor): meaning.

152 In margin: 'Jeane Craig in Tranent, convict and burnt for witchcraft'.

153 Here and later, paragraph breaks are added editorially for comprehension. The original text runs continuously, with breaks signalled by larger letters.

154 The text slips momentarily here from third person to second person.

Lykas airly in ane uther morneing schortlie thaireftir, the said Jeane, contenowing in hir former malice borne be hir against the said James Smyth, haveing rancounterit with ane servand man of his leiding furth sax of the said James his horsis, saluttit him with thir wiked words, Quhat Devill does thou man soe sone up at morne, and croseing his way the said Jeane be hir sorcerie and witchcraft laid upone thrie of the saidis horssis, thay presentlie schot to dead, and uther thrie horsis with the man servand himselff schortlie thaireftir deceissit be hir sorcerie and witchcraft sua laid upone thame.

And fynallie being dilaittit as ane commone sorcerer and witche, and keiping trystis and meittingis with the Devill and utheris witches, the said Beigis Wallace hir mother ane notorious witche, as also with Margaret Mathiesone and Jonet Reid, baithe witches, convict and brunt for witchcraft at Preston Panes, and seiking counsall fra the Devill how to be avainget upone dyverse persones be witchcraft, speciallie against the said Beatrix Sandielandis, and making become [*sic*] mad as said is, and for becomeing the Devillis servand and ressaveing his mark, quha dyverse tymes appeirit to hir in dyverss schaipis, at the first tyme in Penstoun, in the lairdis kitching in the lyknes of ane cat, and at ane uther tyme be the Devillis appeirance in hir awin hous in the lyknes of ane man, quhair he had carnall copulatione with hir and causet hir renunce hir baptisme and to become his servand, {*p. 661*} all confessit be hir this 27 of Apryle to be of verritie in presence of the Minister of Tranent and dyverse famous witnesses at lenth specifeit in hir dittay and severall poyntis thairof abonewrittin.

Persewer

George Ramsay sone to umquhile Mr Symone Ramsay of Quhythill, substitute to Mr Thomas Nicolsone, his majesteis advocat for his hienes intreis, conforme to his lettre of procuratorie subscryvit with his hand daittit the 26 day of Apryle 1649 yeiris.

Efter reiding of the quhilk dittay and severall articles thairof abone writtin, the justice, finding the samyn relevant, referrit the tryell of the factis and deidis thairin contenie to the tryell of ane assyse off the persones following, lauchfullie summond to that effect.

Assisa

Archibald Purves in Tranent
Peter Wylie thair
John Craig thair
Ritchard Trumble thair
James Congletoun in Langnidrie
Ritchard Waddell in Seatoun
Adame Waddell thair
Robert Gilmour thair
James Allane in Wintoun
Robert Heriot in Langnidrie

James Carfra in Wintoun
Patrik Spence in Prestoun Panes
John Reid thair
Thomas Affleck thair
Hectour Wood thair

Quhilkis persones of assyse being ressavit, sworne and admittit efter accusatione of the said Jeane Craig be dittay of the perticuler crymes of sorcerie and witchcraft abonewrittin and protestatione tane be the said George Ramsay persewer of the said dittay and instrumentis tane be him of the sweiring of the said assyse and of wilfull errour to be committit be thame in cais thai clene or acquit the said Jeane Craig of the crymes of Sorcerie and Witchcraft contenit in the dittay abonewrittin, Removet altogider furth of court to the assyse hous or secreit part within the said tolbuith Quhair thai for the maist pairt Vottit and choyset the said James Carfra In chancellour in thair number, thairefter ressonet and voitit upone the poyntis of the foirsaid dittay and perticuler articles thairof rexive[155] and particulerlie abonewrittin, and being ryplie and at lenth advyset thairwith and with the depositiones of dyverss witnessis suorne, ressavit and admittit and reponeing[156] Judiciallie anent the pannellis guiltines of the crymes specifeit in the said dittay and with the said Jeane Craig hir confession maid be hir this day in presence of the Witnessis subscryveris thairof, Reenterit agane in court quhair thay all in ane voce be the report and declaratione of James Carfra chancellour Fand, pronuncet and declairit the said Jeane Craig to be fyllit, culpable and convict of the severall and perticuler crymes of sorcerie and witchcraft specifeit and contenit in hir said dittay. For the quhilk caus the Justice be the mouth of Mark Boustene dempster of court adjudget, decernit and ordanit the said Jeane Craig to be tane upone Tewsday nixt, being the first day of Maii 1649 yeiris, to the place of hir executione, viz. to the Murebrow, and thair first to be wirreit at ane staik quhill schoe be deid And thaireftir hir bodie to be brunt in assis, And hir haill moveable goodis belanging to hir to be escheit and Inbrocht to our soverane lordis use, as culpable and convict of the saidis crymes, Quhilk was pronuncet for dome.

155 'rexive': respectively.
156 *Sic*. Probably read 'deponeing'.

23. INVERKEITHING WITCHES, 1649

INTRODUCTION

Margaret Martin, Katherine Grieve and Isobel Leitch were accused in a witchcraft panic in 1649 in the burgh of Inverkeithing in Fife. The document edited below is a partial record of their investigation in June and their local trial in July. It forms a small but vivid and detailed part of a much broader story that can only be summarised here.[1] The minister of Inverkeithing, Walter Bruce, was a keen witch-hunter whose activities divided both the elite of the burgh itself and the members of the presbytery of Dunfermline. By the time of these prosecutions, he had already been suspended once by the presbytery and then reinstated. He later tried to arrest the wives of several Inverkeithing magistrates for witchcraft. Further research could well be carried out on Bruce's supporters and opponents. Those who helped him to interrogate these three women were clearly among his supporters.

Parliament issued a commission on 23 May 1649 to arrest and interrogate witchcraft suspects in Inverkeithing; two of the commissioners later reappeared as trial commissioners.[2] The suspects were not specified individually, but they evidently included Margaret Martin, Katherine Grieve and Isobel Leitch. Walter Bruce and his colleagues interrogated these women over four days in June, presumably with the aid of sleep deprivation since they obtained compliant and stereotypical confessions to the demonic pact. The confessions duly recited the ideas of renouncing baptism, getting a new name, entering into a pact with the Devil, the Devil's mark and copulation with the Devil. Margaret Martin entered the Devil's pact when she was at a meeting in another woman's house, and the Devil asked her to be his servant. As part of the ritual, she put one hand on her head and the other hand under her foot, signifying

1 For what is known of the broader panic see Stuart Macdonald, *The Witches of Fife: Witch-Hunting in a Scottish Shire, 1560–1710* (East Linton, 2002), 100–8.

2 RPS, 1649/5/309. These commissioners were John Bardie of Salvedge, William Blackburn, John Davidson, John Douglas, Thomas Thomson, John Anderson and James Brown, burgesses of Inverkeithing. Walter Bruce himself was not named as a commissioner, but he was evidently able to take part in interrogations.

that her whole body would be in the service of the Devil. Witches' meetings were said to have taken place in a field and in a witch's house.

One of Walter Bruce's targets was the wealthy heiress Margaret Henderson, Lady Pittadro, who seems to have been among the faction of his enemies.[3] In the interrogations, Bruce and his colleagues shaped the confessions to show Henderson as the witches' ringleader and as Bruce's personal enemy. Thus, Margaret Martin confessed that Henderson had wanted to buy Bruce's house, explaining that 'the said Lady Pittadrow was the caus of all his truble'. Henderson had convened a witches' meeting 'that sho might compleane to the Divill upone Mr Walter Brusse', and was 'ring laider of that meitting' of witches against him. Martin even urged Bruce to stand firm in his godly determination against his enemies: 'the said Margaret intreated the said Mr Walter to be earnest with his God For he had many ivill willeris and many snairs laid for him'. It is remarkable to find a witch's confession being shaped to deliver such a godly, if partisan, message. Katherine Grieve emphasised Henderson's higher status in the Devil's service: 'being interrogat iff the Lady Pittadrow was ane witch, The said Katharine answered, Faith scho is ane and mor gultie then I ame For I was bot as ane slave to thame and ane out cast'. These confessions were weapons in a local struggle.

Margaret Martin named a further twenty-three persons as witches. A few of them seem to have been previously executed, but most of the names represented a broadening of the panic. Katherine Grieve named eighteen names, all but one of which had also been given by Martin. Isobel Leitch, in her briefer confession, named only five names, but three of these were unique to her. All the names were of women.

The three suspects were brought before the court in Inverkeithing on 11 July. This was a local court of justiciary, constituted, as the record below states, by the authority of parliament itself ('the estaites of parliament'). Parliament had issued the commission for the trial on 5 July.[4] The document edited below is an extract from the minutes of the trial, made by James Smeaton who was clerk of the court and also the burgh clerk. The formal constitution of the court is noted. The three women's dittays, entirely constructed from their prior confessions, are recited. However, the court's decisions are not included. The outcomes of these trials are not known.

3 For more on this see Louise Yeoman, 'Hunting the Rich Witch in Scotland: High-Status Witchcraft Suspects and their Persecutors, 1590–1650', in Julian Goodare (ed.), *The Scottish Witch-Hunt in Context* (Manchester, 2002), 106–21, at pp. 118–19.

4 *Acts of the Parliaments of Scotland*, vi, II, 463.

TEXT

Source: *NRS, Court of Justiciary Process Papers, 1643–1650, JC26/13/5.*[5]

Curia Justiciaria Tenta in pretorio burgi de Innerkething dominum Joanem Erskane de Otterstoune, Alexandrum Spittell de Lequhat, Joanem Bardie de Selvedge, Gulielmum Blaikburne et Malcum Duncan, burgenses prefati burgi, undecimo die mensis Julii anno domini Millesimo sexcentesimo quadragesimo nono. Sectis vocatis, curia legittime affirmata.[6]

The quhilk day the said persones abonenamit Commissioneris appoyntit be the estaites of parliament to the effect underwryttin Electit and chusit James Smetoune clerk of the said brugh to be clerk to thame Johne Broune messenger procurator fiscall Williame Dewer officer and Thomas Gay dempster, Quha being all lawfullie sworne gaiff their aithes *de fideli administratione*[7] quhairupone this act etc.

The same day[8] comperit personallie Johne Broun procurator fiscall foirsaid and gave in befor the saidis Commissioneris ane clame againes the persones efternominat for the particular caussis efterspecifeit Quhairoff the tennor followis. Margaret Mairtine, Katharin Greive and Isobell Litche ye ar indyttit and accusit of your lyves in sua far as ye haiffin schakin off all the fear and dreid of our eternall and dreidfull God and of his sone Jesus Chryst and of the kingis majestie viz. the said Margaret Mairtine upone the nynth day of Junii i^{m}vi^{c} fourtie nyne yeiris In presens of Mr Walter Brusse minister at the said brugh of Innerkething, Androw Dicksone ane of the baillies thairoff, Mr Johne Weymes scolemaister thair and Johne Douglas burges thair Efter incalling upone the name of God being interogat In presens of God and as shoe sould answer to God at the great day did with tears confess hir abominable sine of witchcraft And that it was Beatrix Thomsone[9] quha first learned hir and drew hir away from hir God and that the Devill did first appear to hir in the said Beatrix hous in the licknes of ane gentill man and desyred hir to be his servand quhich shoe did accept and he caused hir put hir put hir [*sic*] hand upone hir head and hir uther hand upone the sole of hir foott and delyver hir selff ovir to him and renunce hir baptizme and he

5 This is a single, long document within the box numbered JC26/13. It bears the pencil number JC26/13/5, and effectively forms a single-document bundle, separate from the other bundles in the box.

6 'Court of justiciary held in the tolbooth of the burgh of Inverkeithing by John Erskine of Otterstone, Alexander Spittall of Lequhat, John Bardie of Salvedge, William Blackburn and Malcolm Duncan, burgesses of the said burgh, 11 July 1649. Suits called, court legally fenced'.

7 'concerning the faithful exercise of their office'.

8 In margin: 'Margaret Mertene'.

9 In 1623, the privy council had issued a commission for Beatrix Thomson's trial for witchcraft along with six other Inverkeithing women: *RPC*, xiii, 192–3.

gave hir his mark upone the right syd of hir nose beneth hir eye. Lykwayes shoe did confese that she had severall meittingis with the Divill and the last meitting was since Rossina Oswald and the rest was takin quhilk was upone the Hilfeild and the meitting was desyred be the lady Pittadrow and ane of the principall caussis of the meitting was that sho might compleane to the Divill upone Mr Walter Brusse for buying of the hous quhilk he is in and quhilk sho wald haiff had to hir goodsone and that the said Lady Pittadrow was the caus of all his truble and that sho had desyred the Divill that he might never cum to his place againe[10] and the said Margaret intreated the said Mr Walter to be earnest with his God For he had many ivill willeris and many snairs laid for him Lykwayes sho declarit that the lady Pittadrow was ring laider of that meitting[11] and thair was present in it Marjorie Durie, Marjorie Fergoie, Marjorie Hutsone, Katharin Grive, Bessie Wilsone and hir dochter Marione Thomsone quha was officer[12] and warned thame all to the meitting and being intreated to frie hir awin saule for Chrystis saik and tell iff sho had any mae[13] to tell of in the toune or paroche Sho did serouslie confess that Janet Mitchell, Margaret Grive, Hellen Duglas, Hellen Stanous, Emie Angus, Jannet Smeittone, Agnes Kellok and Katharin Smyth in Toun end war as gultie as shoe was and in that same service with hir, And in the paroche shoe delaited Issobell Mitchell in Scotismylne, Barbra Chattow in Caldsyd, Issobell Paickok and Bessie Wilsone in Maistertoune. Morover the said Margaret did confess that the said Lady Pittadrow did keep Elizabeth Broune in hir hous the space of ane moneth efter shoe was delaited as gultie of witchcraft and filed for the same and thair efter sho was brunt in Dalketh. Moreover Junii twelf In presens of Mr Walter Brusse, Mr Johne Weimes and Johne Douglas the said Margaret Martine confessis that Beatrix Douglas and Joannet Grege was present at the forsaid meiting.

And siklyke[14] upone the tenth day of Junii and year of God foirsaid In presens of the saidis Mr Walter Brusse, Mr Johne Weimes and Johne Douglas the said Katharin Grive Efter incalling upone the name of God being interrogat in presens of God and as sho sould ansr to God at the great day did with tearis confess that about four or five yeiris agoe Margaret Blaikburne sent for hir to hir hous quhair the Devill was sitting with the said Margaret clothed in buff broun cullored clothes and they had ane pynt of aill and ane caik and the Devill drank to hir and asked if sho wold be his servand and scho accepted

10 A reference to Walter Bruce's recent suspension by the presbytery of Dunfermline.

11 The idea than one participant was a 'leader' of a witches' meeting was known elsewhere, for instance in Finnmark, Norway. See Liv Helene Willumsen, *Steilneset: Memorial to the Victims of the Finnmark Witchcraft Trials*, trans. Katjana Edmundsen (Oslo, 2011), 29.

12 The idea of an 'officer' who would 'warn' (summon) the witches to meetings evidently derived from local courts, whose 'officers' performed this function.

13 'mae': more.

14 In margin: 'Katharene Greive'.

and renunced hir selff to him and he had copolatione with hir and gave hir his mark quhilk is a littell abone hir knie in hir left legg and being interrogat iff thair was any mae with thame scho answered thair was non mae in the hous Bot schoe hard sum wemenes toungis in the chamber And being fardder interrogat if schoe had any ma meittingis since she answered that sho had bein at thrie or four quhairoff the last was in the Hilfeild and thair mett with the Devill, Hellane Stanhous, Emie Angus, Joannet Grege, Margaret Grege, Bessie Wilsone, Marjorie Fergie, Joannet Smetoune, Katharine Smyth in Toune end, Issobell Mitchell in Scotsmylne, Barbara Chattow in Caldsyd, Hellen Douglas and the Lady Pittadrow. And being interrogat iff the Lady Pittadrow was ane witch, The said Katharine answered, Faith scho is ane and mor gultie then I ame For I was bot as ane slave to thame and ane out cast. Morover scho affirmed that thair was such a court of thame thair that it wold haiff filled the hous Bot scho hir selff being seeklie stayed at ane out syd and could know no mor of thame bot quhen scho was aquanted with ane they war all dancing and reilling throw uther.[15] And being interrogat quho was officer scho answered Marione Thomsone was officer and warned thame all to the meiting. As Lykwayes upone the threttine day of Junii the year of God abonewryttin befor the abovenamit witnessis the said Katharin confest thair war also present at the foirsaid meiting Beatrix Douglas, Marjorie Durie, Agnes Kellok, Marjorie Hutsone.

And lykwas upone the first day of Junii the yeir of God foirsaid In presens of [*1-2 words torn away*] Walter Brusse, Androw Dicksone, Alexander Henrysone and Mr Johne Weymes [*1-2 words torn away*] Issobell Leitch efter incalling upone the name of God being interrogat in presens of and as sho sould answer to God at the great day did with tearis confess that about four yeiris agoe sho met in Margaret Blaikburns closs with Rossina Osit and Margaret Aytoune and the Devill askit at hir if sho wold be his servant and sho accepted and the Devill desyred hir renunce hir baptizme quhilk shoe confessis sho did and he gave hir ane new name viz. Lydia and he gave hir ane nipp in the neck quhich sho confessis to be hir mark. Morover sho confessis sho was at the meiting in Margaret Blaikburnes barne and that Issobell Guthrie and Christiane Thomsone war with hir, Lykwayes sho confest that about Yull last the Devill, Margaret Blaikburne and sho met togidder in the said Margaretis closs in the evining tyme and Christiane Thomsone was with thame and being interrogat quither the Devill had copolatione with hir or not sho answered lett me alone I think schame to confess it. Extracted *de libro actorem dicti curie justiciarie per me Jacobus Smetoune notarium publicum ac scribum ejusdem sub meis signo et subscriptione manualibus.*[16]

[*Signed:*] JSmetoune.

15 'all dancing and reilling throw uther': all dancing a reel, in and out among each other.

16 'from the book of the acts of the said court of justiciary by me, James Smeaton, notary public and clerk of the same (court), under my sign and subscription manual'.

24. JANET SAWYER, AYR, 1651–1652, 1658

INTRODUCTION

The trial of Janet Sawyer took place in 1658, during the English military occupation of Scotland. Sawyer was a middle-aged woman in Ayr, married to John McAdam. Her husband was a messenger, and had stables. The years 1658 and 1659 saw a considerable number of witchcraft trials in Scotland, with a total of eighty-two in 1658 and 100 in 1659. Several of the alleged witches came from parishes in the south and west of Scotland. Whereas the bulk of Scottish witchcraft trials took place in the south-eastern part of the country, the trials of Sawyer and some others took place in Ayr, on the west coast. Circuit courts played an important role in carrying through the trials.[1]

Both Janet Sawyer and her husband had previously been mentioned in the Ayr kirk session minutes in December 1643. They were accused of flyting (quarrelling), and her husband was accused of abusing his spouse. Both had previously been privately admonished by the kirk session. They both confessed, and were publicly admonished to behave better.[2] Then, in January 1647, Sawyer was again brought before the kirk session, this time accused of slandering another woman for theft and harlotry. She denied the accusation, and a group of five elders were appointed to investigate the case and report.[3]

Janet Sawyer was first accused of witchcraft by another witch, Helen Garven. She was in prison in Ayr on 7 October 1651 together with three other women: Janet Crawford, Janet Sloan and Elizabeth Cunningham. This is briefly mentioned in the records of Ayr burgh council. Pricking was used to provide circumstantial evidence.

However, no witchcraft trials were held in 1651, which was a time of warfare and political turmoil. The English army invaded Scotland in 1650, and had largely completed its conquest by the end of 1651. Scottish central

1 Liv Helene Willumsen, 'Seventeenth-Century Witchcraft Trials in Scotland and Northern Norway' (University of Edinburgh PhD thesis, 2008), 273, Table 55.

2 NRS, Minutes of Kirk Session of Ayr, 1620–1646, CH2/751/2, fo. 411r.

3 NRS, Minutes of Kirk Session of Ayr, 1646–1653, CH2/751/3/1, fos. 16r., 263r. No report has been found in the minutes.

government institutions collapsed during 1651, leaving local authorities with no central direction apart from the English army, until the English established their own governmental institutions during 1653. One result of all this was a hiatus in witchcraft trials after the panic of 1649–50.

Then, almost six years later, on 6 April 1658, several women from Ayr were brought before the Ayr justice court, accused of witchcraft. Among them was Janet Sawyer.

Janet Sawyer never confessed to witchcraft. Her pleas of not guilty are recorded. Many witnesses were brought before the court to testify. The testimonies of witnesses are recorded in seventeen articles, all containing accusations against her. Some of these neighbours confirmed their accusations before the court, but others cautiously qualified their statements or even claimed to know nothing. The court records document her trial to the end, including verdict and sentence. In addition, full information is given on the formalities of the officials in charge of the court and the members of the assize.

Maleficium as well as demonological ideas are activated during the trial. Most of the accusations have to do with *maleficium*, casting spells causing sickness and death on humans and animals. Several motifs related to folk belief are activated, including weather magic, raising of storms and mentioning of traditional days like Lammas Eve. In addition, Sawyer had allegedly been seen dancing with cats, which afterwards went to her house. And she is reportedly seen with the Devil. Article 13 contains clear demonological ideas: becoming the Devil's servant, the Devil's pact, renouncing baptism and the Devil's mark. This mixture of *maleficium* and demonological ideas seems to characterise many witchcraft trials taking place in the mid-seventeenth century, not only in Scotland, but in most European countries.

When rendering the testimonies of the witnesses, sometimes Janet Sawyer's own voice is heard, particularly in spells and threats that she had uttered and that were retold by the witnesses. Thus, orality sheds light on her individual way of expression, and her words, as they are recorded by the scribe in 1658, contribute to the personification of a verbally strong woman.

Janet Sawyer was found guilty of witchcraft and sentenced to be strangled and burned. Very unusually, a letter survives from a witness to her execution, stating that she denied witchcraft at the point of her death. This letter is printed below.

The text below comes from five sources. The first two are local sources, from the council minutes and kirk session minutes of Ayr. They concern the earlier, inconclusive phase of the investigation in 1651–2. The third and fourth are the records of Sawyer's trial on 6 April 1658. The dittay has been preserved in the process papers of the justiciary court, while the minutes of the trial come from the circuit court minute book. Finally, the fifth source is a letter from an English eyewitness to Janet Sawyer's burning on 23 April.

TEXTS

Source 1: Ayrshire Archive Centre, Minutes of Council of Ayr, 1596–1669, B6/18/2.

{fo. 80r.} 7th October 1651
Hew Kennedy John Craufurd and James Chalmer tuik instrumentis The four prisouneris Jonet Craufurd, Jonet Sawer, Jonet Slowan and Elizabeth Cunynghame delait and accusit for witchcraft war in waird and firmeance and maid protestatioune as magestratis for thair exoneratioune.... *{fo. 91r.}*

13th July 1652
The Commissoun[4] anent the four Imprisouned challengit persounis for witchcraft to wit Jonet Craufurd, Jonet Sawer, Elspeth Cunynghame and Jonet Sloan delyvered to the counsall to be sent a feild with the minister[5] wha hes the haill proces delyvered to him be the clerk and soe he is exonered[6] of the haveing of the same.

Source 2: NRS, Minutes of Kirk Session of Ayr, 1646–1653, CH2/751/3/1.

{fo. 263r.} 27 December 1652
Jonet Sawer, Jonet Slowan, Elspet Cunningham and Jonet Crawford wer ordaned to be summonded to compeire befor the session the nixt day for the scandall of witchcraft.... *{fo. 264v.}*

3 January 1653
This day the session concluded in regard they could not all wait upon it, that the ministers Hew Kennedie, James Chalmer, John Adamsone, Donald Smyth, William Hunter or more or any wther five or six with the ministers should sit upon the processes concerning the witches and summon call and tak the depositiones and examine the witnessis judiciallie and appoint the dyet of thair meiting from tym to tym as they shall think fit till the sam be prosecut.

Source 3: NRS, Court of Justiciary Process Papers, 1658, JC26/25.

Air Court Air Dittays 6 Apryle 1658
Assyse Margaret Sawer
present Jonet Sawer
present Jonet Slowane
present Elspeth Cuningham
and first
Jonnat Sawer

4 In margin: 'Anent proces of prisouneris'.
5 William Adair was minister of Ayr throughout this period.
6 'exonered': relieved from.

Thow[7] art indyted and accused quhairas thow art indyted and accused [*sic*] about the spaice of [*blank*] yeiris or thairby thow did quarrell Johne McConnell for taking stables from thy awine husband and miskeneing of the[e] and thair withall (said they should be dear stables to him) thow took the kye[8] of ane of the stables quhilk thow then keiped and when Johne McConnell strave to goe downe the closae to get that kye out of the stable, thow thy sone and thy daughter strook and bled him and swor thow should be his death, and that sam day about ane hour or thairby thaireftir when Margaret Turk Johne McConnelles wyf said to the[e] that God and thow would reckone for the wrong thow had done to hir husband, thairupon Margaret McAdam thy dochter swor by the Eternall God shoe should be Johne McConnell his dead and his wyfes boathe, And also thow said immediatlie to Margaret Turk thow should gar hir rew it,[9] thaireftir within two or thrie dayes shoe fand the[e] in the stable where thy husbands horse was with thy armes about the horse neck and undir his bellie and goeing about him laughinge, of the quhilk horse Johne McConnell gat litle or no good and sold him for eight merk Scottis and within twentie dayes he died, As lykwayes the said Johne McConell himself in persoune was a long tyme seik in agues and sweitinge and so faint that he was altogidder waik and unable for workeing and sumtymes knew not quhair he was and was treulie impowereshed, which does evidentlie appear to proceid from thy devilische airt of witchcraft threatninges and minaceing Quhilk thow cannot deny.[10]

present Hew Blair of Blairstoune

Secundlie[11] thow art indyted and accused for that in Marche last thow cam to the goodman of Blairstoune and craved ane sixpence for thy sister soone[12] for fetcheinge of ane horse to the said Blairstoune, quhilk he refuised sayeinge the man that aught him was dew the money to Hew Dook, thow replyed hea will be little the ritcher in keipeing of it, And immediatlie when he went hom to Blairstoune he fand the self same horse stricken in the nose and haveing lost ane great deall of blood he nevir did him good, quhilk did proceid from thy deveillishe airte of witchecraft whilk thow cannot deney.[13]

Thirdlie[14] thow art accused for that becaus thow art suspected that the dochter of Helleine Garven ane confessing witche that killed ane chikene of thyne that thairfoir thow did wronge ane [*sic*] hir dochters ky[15] by taking

7 In margin: 'Witnessis to the first article present Johne Mcconnald present Margaret Turk his spous'.

8 'kye': key.

9 'gar hir rew it': cause her to regret it.

10 In margin: 'denyes'.

11 In margin: 'Witnessis of the 2'.

12 'sister soone' (son): nephew.

13 In margin: 'denyes'.

14 In margin: 'Witnessis 3 article present Helen Garveins daughter Mr William Adaire excusit Jonet Burnes'.

15 'of hirs' crossed out here. Probably the word 'ky' should also have been crossed out. It is clearly Helen Garven's daughter herself who has been wronged.

from hir the power of hir feet so that shoe lay ane bedrell[16] the space of six or seveine weekes, Eftir Quhilk spaice the said Helleine came to the[e] and did heavilie compleine of hir, sayeing allace womane I have no meanes to sustaine this young on[e], I will be forced to tak hir upon my bak and begge, what neided yow doe this herschip[17] to me for ane egg, it was bot the pryce of ane pynt of aill, quhairupon sho[18] went to hir house and rubbit the said Hellein hir dochters legges and thaireftir that same night sho came hirpling[19] to the doore and was perfytlie recovered within ane short spaice, which does evidentlie appear to proceid from thy devillishe airt which thow cannot deny.[20]

Fourtlie[21] about Lambmes[22] 1649 Mairteine Walker haveing tyed thrie horse neir the entrie of thy cloase haveing brought home ane gang[23] of coalles with thame to Adame Cunynghame and his wyfe with whom thow was at variance and said to Martein Walker, young man tak your horse by the gait[24] and let us have the foot rod[25] frie, The quhilk thow said in great Anger and immediatlie on[e] of the thrie beastes quhilk was ane meir lay downe seik and eat no moir and with great dificultie was got home and within fourtie aught hours died, And within ane moneth the uther two also died and he got service of non of the thrie albeit they wer found to have no ordinar disease of horsses Eftir they wer sighted be ferriers,[26] Quhilk cleirlie proved it proceided from thy devillische airt Quhilk thow cannot deny:[27]

Fyftlie[28] thow art indyted and accused for that about Wittsonday 1649 yeirs Adam Cunynghame smyth was goeing up his awin stair with ane lap: full of salt Thow said seing him thair is some stolne geir comeing from the shoare, he replyed it is my awin weill woone geir, Then ansyred Marione Walker spous to the said Adame, if yow wer in bed with your husband yow wold not be visiting your nighbores so oft, Quhairupon sho[29] ran up the said Adam his stair with ane mad countenance and took Adam his bairne quhilk

16 'ane bedrell': a bedridden person.
17 'hership': damage, devastation.
18 'sho': presumably Janet Sawyer. The scribe has failed to convert the third-person 'she' of the pre-trial document into the second-person 'you' required for a dittay.
19 'hirpling': limping.
20 In margin: 'denyes'.
21 In margin: 'Witnessis 4 article absent Johne Rid Chyrurgeone present Cuthbert Mcgrein'.
22 'Lambmes': Lammas, 1 August.
23 'ane gang': a load.
24 'gait': street.
25 'foot rod': footpath.
26 'sighted be ferriers' (farriers): examined by horse doctors.
27 In margin: 'denyes'.
28 In margin: 'Witnessis 5 article present Johne Gairner merchant present Adame Cunninghame present Marioune Mcwhitter his spous'.
29 *Sic.* This pronoun appears to refer to Marion Walker, but from the context it is clearly Janet Sawyer who is being said to have run up the stair. This is another failure to convert the third-person 'she' to the second-person 'you'.

was upone the mother hir breast and shook him by the cloathes and handled him roughlie, Quhairupone the mother of the chyld said Lord save my chyld, avoyd the[e] Sathan,[30] doune the stair witche theife, thairefter thow went doune the stair with many injurious words and great anger and flait[31] up the stair for ane good spaice, And so thaireftir the chyld fell downe the stair and brok some of his ribbes, as als the said Marione Walker fell downe the stair being with chyld which killed the chyld in hir bellie, Thaireftir hir husband and childreine fell seik and becam mightilie impowerished, As als Hellein Garven ane confessing witche declaired that thow had taken the fuisoune[32] of hir aill quhilk manifestlie appeared to proceid from thy devellishe airt of witchcraft And quhilk thow cannot deny.

Sixtlie[33] thow art indyted and accused for that thow about fyftein yeiris since or thairby said to Agnes Murdoche spous to Robert Hutchesoune couper that thow should gar hir rew the takeing of the ingle[34] frae the aquavitie pot[35] and that it should be a deir pot to hir, The quhilk Agnes Murdoche fand Eftirwards for eftir thow had straikeit the bak and breist of Robert Hutchisoune youngar ane chyld to the said Agnes, Quhilk straikeing was within fourtein dayes eftir the threatineinge, the said young chyld died of ane uncouth and sudden siknes and that within thrie dayes Eftir the said grippeing, cryeing still in his siknes Oh my bak my face my breast bellie and legges Jonnat Sawer hes grippet me, also within ane moneth or thairby Eftir the forsaid threatninge Jonnat Broun thy mother cam in to cam in to [*sic*] the said Agnes Murdoche hir house and sought ane pynt of aill from hir dochter Jonnet Hutchsoune, And becaus Jonnet Broune had not money the said Jonnet Hutchisoune emptied the drink into the aill butt againe, quhairwith Jonnet Broune depairtit displeased, immediatlie thaireftir the said Agnes Murdoche cam into hir awin hous and suddenlie fell downe deafe and dumbe and lost power of hir leges and contineweit so the matter of ane quartar of ane yeir or moir, dureing Quhilk tyme shoe fand as if ane spitt wer stopeit[36] throw hir head hir heart and bak quhilk keiped hir in a continuall heat and torment without sleipe and with suche drouthe that she drank excessivelie and yit hir tongue and lipps scortcheit with heat so that shoe becam exceidinge leane lyk

30 'avoyd thee Sathan': get away from me, Satan.

31 'flait' (from 'flyte'): scolded.

32 'fuisoune': goodness or nutritive quality. This accusation, relating to Helen Garven, is clearly a separate point from the previous accusation in this paragraph, relating to Adam Cunningham and Marion Walker. More careful drafting would have given the Garven accusation a paragraph of its own.

33 In margin: 'Witnessis 6 article present Agnes Murdoch absent Jonet Hutchsone absent present James McKindare'.

34 'ingle': fire.

35 'aquavitae pot': whisky pot. Presumably this was an apparatus for distilling whisky, which would have needed a fire.

36 'stopeit': stabbed.

ane atomie,[37] bot beinge desyrous to be carried ben[38] to hir foir stair[39] in ane cleir moone light nycht about allevein hours in the night she with uthers saw four cattis as it wer danceing the reill dance and admired[40] how they keiped such ane methed,[41] thaireftir they went by twais as it wer in uthers armes up the stair to thy hous who was Agnes Murdoches nixt nighbour, wher eftir they [*word crossed out*] enterit thair was a great din and the sellar door oft tymes oppeneing and seikeing where thy drink stood, thaireftir betwixt 12 and 1 hours in the night cam down the sam stair quhair the cattes went up ane man with his face and neck covereit with blak and his wholl boddie cled in blak also, togidder with 3 women two of them the two Neveingis and the uther ather Jonnet Gardner or Jonnat Sloand and Eftir tham thow cloaseit the doore that night the said Agnes Murdoch gat moir sleip nor shoe had gottin half ane yeir befoir, bot about 5 hours in the morneing betwixt sleipeing and wakeninge she apprehendeit shoe hard the[e] sayeinge haist on the fyre to rost hir sho hes bein over long sleipeinge, Quhairupon sho beigit[42] to be takine out of the bed for fear and that samyn day she beige [*rest of line illegible*] awin foirstair she sees ye at the foirstair foot to whom she sayes Lord forgive yow Jonnet Sawer for keiping ane ingle undir me for I am rostit and tormentit, thow ansyrit hir laugheinge, [*word illegible*][43] faceit theif thow shall be bettir rostit yit, quhairupon Agnes Murdoche cryeit to tak hir down the stair And being caried down the stair sho cryeit let gar the doges leap ye[44] witche blood and thairwith all gat blood of ye, And ye [*sic*] the said Agnes Murdoche went up againe the stair upon hir awin feet ellso[45] the paine and heat left hir from that tyme bot Eftir that tyme hir papes[46] and breast brak out in boylles, quhen the torment ceased the said Agnes Murdoche hir dochter about that tyme bled thy head with ane cap:[47] Lykwayes thow is suspect to be the deathe of the said Robert Hutchesoune who died suddenlie of ane unknowen siknes haveing formerlie said he sould rew ye[48] not mendinge of thy fleckstane,[49]

37 'atomie': skeleton.
38 'ben': through.
39 'hir fore stair': her house's external stair.
40 'admired': was astonished.
41 'methed': method, rhythm.
42 'beigit': begged.
43 This word must be an insulting adjective applied to Murdoch's face.
44 *Sic*. Murdoch's utterance was evidently something like 'Let the dogs lap the witch's blood' or 'Let the dogs lap your witch blood'.
45 *Sic*. Perhaps read 'also'.
46 'papes': breasts.
47 *Sic*. Drawing blood from an alleged witch's head was a recognised method of counter-witchcraft. The nature of the weapon or implement that Murdoch's daughter used is unclear.
48 *Sic*. Read 'the' (i.e. Hutcheson's own failure to mend Sawyer's flake-stand).
49 'fleckstane': flake-stand, a framework for displaying goods for sale.

Quhairby it is most clear and evident that the premissis[50] did proceid from thy devillische airt of witchcraft and quhilk thow cannot deny.

Seventlie[51] thow art indicted and accused for that about two yeiris since or thairby Quhen the ship callit the shipp of Balfast cam to the raid[52] of Air to get ane takell to serve hir for the voyage to Barbadus, thair cam ane sudden storme upone hir in the raid so that the ship drave and brak upon the shoar and perished, the quhilk day thow was declaired by Helein Girvane ane confessing witche now burnt to be lyeing within the sea mark with thy mouth up sukeing the air lyk ane adder, As also it was verified by Adam Dalrymple befoir his death in the audience of sundrie famous[53] witnessis that he fand the[e] the self sam day within the sea mark in the shoar at fyve hours in the winter morneinge and said to ye it was for little good thow was thair, Bot thow affirmed thow went onlie to tak the sea air bot the self sam day the ship was cast away as said is, And so soone as the ship was loast the storme immediatlie ceassed and becam fair weather with the wind at ane East bloweing af the shoar, Quhairby it is most evident that the premissis did proceid from thy devellishe airt and Quhilk thow cannot deny.[54]

Eightlie[55] thow art indicted and accused for that fra the tyme that Adam Dalrumple had spoken of his findinge of ye upon the shoar and had spoken to ye as he did that thow sought all oppurtunities to tak his lyfe becaus thow malicted[56] him thairfoir Quhilk ye[57] rather appeires that becaus whilles[58] the said Adam being a searcher on the sabath day fand ye out of the kirk and threatned ye to thy face that he wold delait ye to the sessioune, Thow said he might not doe so, he replyed he wold do it, Thow ansyrit againe ye shall nocht sie me there, And trew it is that upon Monday quhilk was the sessioune day the said Adam Dalrumple took his bed with ane uncouth and unkyndlie siknes swatt and continuallie meltit away insensiblie and upon Saturday at night died and declaired the foirsaid conference[59] and thy answer upon his death bed and oftin tymes declaireit that if there was a devill out of hell thow was on[e], quhair it is most clear and evident that the premissis did proceid from thy devillishe airt of witchcraft quhilk thow cannot deny.[60]

50 'premissis': above-stated events.

51 In margin: 'Witnessis 7 article present Elisabeth Smith present Johne Howstone'.

52 'raid': roadstead, anchorage.

53 'famous': reputable.

54 In margin: 'denyes'.

55 In margin: 'Witnessis 8 article present John Kennedie in Touneheid present John Hustoune messengere absent Charles Dalrymple absent Alexander Aichsler present Williame Campbell'.

56 'malicted': not found in dictionaries, but evidently meaning 'cursed' (cf. 'malison').

57 *Sic.* The clerk seems to have begun to phrase the next clause beginning 'Quhilk ye ...', then changed his mind to write 'Quhilk rather appeires ...', but forgot to delete the 'ye'.

58 'whilles': once, formerly.

59 'conference': discussion.

60 In margin: 'denyes'.

Nyntlie[61] thow art indicted and accused for that about the spaice of nyntein yeirs since or thairby thow fell in malice and contraversie with Margaret Miller spous to umquhill Johne Houstoune callit meikill Johne about ane lang settle[62] bought frae Johne McAdam thy husband quhairupone thow and shoe fell in flytteinge thow alledgeit that Margaret Millar with fals keyes had stollne wort and aill from hir nighbors for the Quhilk cause the said Margaret summond ye to the sessione Bot befoir the day of compeirance thow rownded[63] sumthing in Margaret Millars lugg[64] Quhairupon she fell immediatlie seik and was caried to the kirk to and fro be two persones and thaireftir hir seiknes increased with extream sweateing and could nevir abyd to sie ye and within few dayes thaireftir dyed Quhilk is most evident hes followed from they devellishe airt of witchcraft quhilk thow cannot deny.[65]

Tentlie[66] thow art indicted and accused for that thow cam to Mr Williame Smyth reader to crave the rent of the hous he dwelt in and becaus the said house maill was in contraversie he refuiseit to pay, Quhairupon thow upbraided him with many injurious words and said he should not byd thair, thow wold gar him flit out of that house, Quhairupon he offereit[67] to put ye to the door and thow returned as gif thow wold have strucken him till Jeane Smyth dochter to the said Mr Williame overawed ye that thow durst not, so thow depairtet in wraith, At ane uther tyme thow being flyteing with the said Mr Williame neir thy awn dwelling house, Helleine Garven declaired that shoe forbad ye in these words, morover said Jonnet[68] meddell not with that man for he is man of kirk, Bot thow ansyrit hir with angrie words and slighet[69] hir, and shortlie Eftir this when Mr Williame was comeing to the minister neir that verie place quhair thow gave him the injurious and malicious words, Thair fell ane great pak of wooll upon him and dang him to the ground, Eftir quhilk tyme he took a languisheinge seiknes sumtymes sweateing and oft tymes a roasteing heat utterlie loast his stomacke[70] and shortlie thaireftir died, quhilk did proceid from thy injurious words and devillishe airt quhilk thow cannot deny.

61 In margin: 'Witnessis 9 article present Johne Houstoune'.

62 'settle': bench.

63 'rownded': whispered.

64 'lugg': ear.

65 In margin: 'denyes'.

66 In margin: 'Witnessis 10 article present Charles Dalrymple'.

67 'offereit': showed an intention.

68 *Sic.* This would make more sense if the name was Helen, since it is Helen Garven who is speaking here. Alternatively, if 'said' has been written in error, Helen's reported words could be understood as 'Moreover, Janet, meddle not …'.

69 'slighet': scorned.

70 'stomacke': appetite.

Elleventlie[71] thow are indicted and accused for that thow being in the house of Charles Dalrimple fell in conference with Charles wyfe, thow askeit quhat sho thought of the proveist rughe handlinge of ye about the giveing infeftment to Williame Campbell in the land quhairof thow was portioner, Charles wyf ansyrit I saw it not bot hard of it, quhat had thow to doe thairwith for it did ye no hurt, thow ansyrit thow hoped in God to sie a reveing[72] upon the proveist for it, and thaireftir shortlie thow straiked the chyldes heid and the proveists young boy called David died of a sudden siknes, and by the report of all that did sie him he was wronged for his head swelt exceidinglie and his flesh grew black and blae and quhilk is most evident did proceid from thy devillishe airt and quhilk thow cannot deny.[73]

Twelltlie[74] thow airt indicted and accused for that thow did oft tymes frequent the house of James McGraine taillyour and buir in thy selfe upon his wyfe[75] contrairie to his mynd quhairwith he was greatlie displeased and for that cause usit all meanes to keip ye out of his house and from any compayneing with his wyfe, as namlie[76] he bosted[77] ye and called ye a witche and told he desyred nocht thy companie, as Lykwayes finding that thow had lent a caldroune to his wyfe to brew, that he might tak away that ground he bought ane caldron to [*words crossed out*] serve himself, for this cariage[78] of his thow was greatlie in anger and displeaseit with him and shoreit[79] oftin to put him to the sessioune[80] for that scandall, and oft tymes said to his wyfe thow wold gar hir rew war it nocht for hir saik, about the quhilk tyme thow beinge in the house of the said James McGrain quhair his lad was seik, his wyf said to ye allace quhat shall I doe with my lad I think he shall die, thow speired quhair is he let me sie him, and haveing sein him thow said that nothing wold aill him bot, said thow, the first tym that the bairne that is in my arme called Bessie tak seiknes she will nevir overput it,[81] The quhilk followeit for within two or thrie dayes thaireftir the said young bairne took an flux[82] and within fourtein dayes or thairby died, As also the said James McGraine about the sam tyme took a flux and contineweit wors and wors till the chyld was buried and Eftir the bairne died he begane to recover, So

71 In margin: 'Witnessis 11 article Jonet Caldwal servant to Charles Dalrymple [*words crossed out – rest of line unreadable*] present Margaret Smith'.

72 'reveing': revenge.

73 In margin: 'denyes'.

74 In margin: 'Witnessis 12 article by dieing witches'.

75 'buir in thy selfe upon his wyfe': you put pressure on his wife.

76 'namlie': in particular.

77 'bosted': threatened.

78 'cariage': behaviour.

79 'shoreit': threatened.

80 'put him to the sessioune': complain about him to the kirk session.

81 'ovirput it': recover from it.

82 'flux': discharge from the bowels.

lykwayes his wyfe had the sam seiknes for the spaice of seventeine weekes so that shoe was neir to deathe and in the tym of thair seiknes thow cam oft tymes in, quhairwith he[83] said James was still displeaseit and dischairgeit hir[84] companye quhairby it is most clear and evident that the premissis did proceid from thy devillishe airt and Quhilk thow cannot deny.

Thretteintlie[85] thow art indicted and accused that thow is to becom the Devill his servant and enterit in pactioune with him renunceit thy baptizme and in signe and taken[86] thairof thy bodie being searched be the ordinar joynar[87] befoir severall famous witnessis Sathan his insensibl mark[88] was found in divers parts of thy bodie by stabeing of the samen and as yit remaineth, the quhilk does evidence thy guiltines of the said horrible cryme of witchcraft Quhilk thow cannot deny.

Fourteintlie[89] thow art accused for comeing to the house of Mathew Drippes at Wittsonday was a yeir[90] and sought thrie cannes of aill frae his wyfe quhilk she refuised ye, and Eftir much urgeing for it thow sought an chapein[91] of aill quhilk was given ye and thow drank it in that house, and as thow was goeing away thow took the said Mathew Drrippes [*sic*] his wyfe by the hand and gave hir thrie scarts in the luif[92] the dindling[93] quhairof remained in hir luif for six hours thaireftir, and immediatlie thaireftir Mathew Dripes his wyf loist the good of 3 breweingis of aill each of tham eftir uther.

Fyfteintlie[94] thow are accused that about sevein or aught yeirs since thow cam to the house of umquhill James McAdam to borrow barm Quhilk was given ye, a great pairt quhairof thow split by the way as thow was takeing it home and immediatlie thaireftir they lost thair Chainge[95] so that albeit many persones useit to frequent thair house befoir to give tham severall of thair drink,[96] yit thair was not ane Eftir that who com to thair house altho it was in the tyme of midsumer fair, the quhilk being remarked be the goodwyf of the house she declaireit it was Jonnet Sawer Becaus shoe had wronged tham as said is, quhairupone the goodwyf of the house and hir servant went to the house of the said Jonnet Sawer and borroweit barm fra hir againe quhilk they

83 *Sic*. Read 'the'.
84 *Sic*. This is another instance where the pronoun should have been changed from third to second person.
85 In margin: 'Witnesses 13 article by dieing witches'.
86 'taken': token.
87 'the ordinar joynar': the local carpenter.
88 The Devil's mark was supposed to be insensible and did not bleed.
89 In margin: 'Witnessis 14 article [*words crossed out*] present Mathew Drips present Agnes Miller his spous present Margaret Miller his servant'.
90 'was a yeir': a year ago.
91 'chapein' (chopin): half a pint.
92 'scarts in the luif': scratches on the palm.
93 'dindling': trembling.
94 In margin: 'Witnessis 15 article present Margaret Miller present Jonet Mcadame'.
95 'thair Chainge': the customers in their inn ('change-house').
96 This phrase seems to mean that they sold a lot of drink (to customers).

gat frae the[e] and tak hame, and immediatly thaireftir the house was fillit full of severall persones quho maid severall of thair drink [*sic*].

Sixteintlie[97] thow art acused about 16 yeirs since thow gave twa feather bedes in keipeing to Marion Mitchell, and quhen thow sought tham againe she retained tham for the house maill,[98] quhairupon thow in wraith thow compleaned to Margaret and allegit she had stolne sum of the featheres out of the beds, and notwithstanding that Margaret gave ordour to Marion Mitchell to get hir hous maill and thow thy bed, yit thow insistit in thy contending words and said to Marion Mitchell sho should have haird newes of hir husband, the quhilk followeit according to thy predictione for in the voyage immediatlie thaireftir was takin by a pirret[99] and keipeit in prison ane yeir.

Seveinteinthlie[100] thow art accused that about 3 yeirs since or thairby becaus Walter Bell had strukin ane bairne of thyn, thow went in to John Laughlands house quhair the said Walter then dwelt and useit injurious words againest him, and within the spaice of fourtein dayes thairreftir his wyfe being delyvered of two bairnes, thow went in to the womane lyeing in chyldbirth, and immediatly the milk went out of hir breast quho had sufficient milk befoir thow went in to hir, ane of the bairnes died the uther vanuished away Lyk ane atomie, the quhilk proceidit from thy devillish airt, the quhilk is so much moir evident becaus quhen the said Walter Bell within ane moneth thaireftir was watching ye, thow said to him doe ye not remember quhen ye strak my bairne, he ansyrit I have forgottin yit thow declaireit out of thy mouth that thow had him long tyme at ill will bad[e] him be good to his wyfe and let hir be gud to him for the discords betwixt thy husband and ye said thow hes brought ye to this shame.[101]

Denyes all.

Source 4: NRS, Circuit Court Minute Books, 1655–1666, JC10/1.

{*fo. 173v.*} The justice court haldin within the Tolbuith of Air the sext day of Apryll 1658 be the right honorabill judges Lawrence and Gudeere.[102] The Court lawfullie fencit.

Mr Alexander Hamilton clerk
Robert Barringer officer
Johne Speir dempster …[103] {*fo. 174v.*}

97 In margin: 'Witnessis 16 article present Marione Mitchell'.

98 'maill': rent.

99 'pirret': pirate.

100 In margin: 'Witnessis 17 article present Jonet Huntar present Robert Patoune present David Mcellvell present Margaret Laughland'.

101 In margin: 'denyes'.

102 Henry Lawrence and Henry Goodyear, two of the English judges on the council of state.

103 Here and later, text about other cases being tried by the court has been omitted in this edition.

Assyseors 6: Apryle 1658

Chancellor William Wallace of Burnebank gg[104]
John Hog in Arnes cg
James Galt in Coustounend gg
William Wylie in Warnokland gg
Thomas Thomsone in Knokintiber gg
William Steill in Jaksthorne gg
James Gordoun in Inschmark gg
Alexander Auld in Gersmylsyd gg
Robert Tailyeor in Boigsyde gg
Thomas Legat in Warnik gg
Adame Creuks in Halkhill gg
John McGawn in Kilmarnock gg
Robert Fergussone in Holl gg
John Mortoun in Burnebank gg
William Stevinsone in Rottinraw gg … *{fo. 175v.}*

Efternone: 6: Apryle 1658 … *{fo. 176r.}*
Jonet Sawer
Jonet Slowane
Elspeth Cuninghame
Witches

Witnessis to Jonet Sawer
John McConnell, Margaret Turk, Hew Blair of Blairstoun, Helene Garvans dochter, John Reid: absent seik, Cuthbert McGrane present, John Garner present, Adame Cuninghame and his wyff both present, Elizabet Smyth present, John Houstoun present, John Kenedy present, Charles Dalrimple present, Alexander Aitchler seik, William Campbell present, Margaret Smyth present, Jonet Caldwall present, Mathow Drips present, Agnes Myller present, Margaret Myller present, Jonet McAdame present, Marion Mytchell present, Jonet Hidber present, Robert Patone present, David Mcaillvell present, Margaret Coughlane present.

Witch Assyse
Jonet Sawer 1 article: anent John McConnells hors deid and himselff,[105] pleads not guiltie.

Witnes
John McConell says he tuk stables against hir will quhairupone hir dochter and schoe fell upone him and thereftir schoe and hir dochter sweir thai sould

[104] This and other annotations in this list presumably indicate some procedure, perhaps to do with how the assizers were summoned or sworn, or how they voted.

[105] 'anent John McConnells hors deid and himselff': concerning the death of John McConnell's horse and harm to himself.

be my daith, says he was Impoverished thaireftir and trublit in seiknes, says schoe was gottin in the stable with his hors.

Witnessis 1 article[106]
Margaret Turk says schoe saw hir about hir hors nek and he nevir did good bot will not blame hir for the hors.

Witnes 2 article[107]
Hew Blair to the 2: article says he bocht the hors fra Captan Colvene says within 2: days schoe came to him and socht ane sax pence and scho said eftir he sould repent it, and thereftir his hors ressaved a strok in the plough and bled to daith.

Witnes to the 3d article[108]
3 article: pannell pleadis not guiltie.

Jonet Burne witnes thereto concerning the powr tane frome hir legs says schoe does not remember.

4: article: denys the samen, witnes thairto.[109]

Cuthbert McGrane concerning Martene Wilkies hors knawis nothing bot heirsay.

Adame Cuninghame says he band the horsis to hir yet[110] and schoe bad lois thame or els thai culd goe hame in ane wors tyme, and ane of thame presently fell doun and the uther 2 deid within 20 days.

Marion McNator[111] knawis nothing.

5 article: anent Adame Cunynghames bairne and his wyff and himselff.[112]

Adame Cuninghame says as schoe thretnit it fell out eftirward bot will not say schoe was the caus of it. {*fo. 176v.*}

John Garner elder sworne to the said article: knawis nothing.

6: article anent Agnes Murdoch chyld quhich schoe groped[113] and hir selff.[114]

106 In margin: '1: article: guilty x'.
107 In margin: '2: article: clenged'.
108 In margin: '3: article: clenged'.
109 In margin: '4 article: guilty x'.
110 'yet' (yett): gate.
111 Probably the scribe's spelling of the Ayrshire surname McNider/McNedar.
112 In margin: '5 article: 'guilty x'.
113 'groped': handled, touched with the hands.
114 In margin: '6: article guiltie x'.

Agnes Murdoche says schoe was 15: oulkis[115] def and dom[116] and affirmes the haill Article to be trew anent hir seiknes and hir chylds daith.

James McNider kenes nothing bot *ad comone clamora*.[117]

7: article anent the schip casting away.[118]

Elspeth Smyth says hir husband told hir schoe was [*sic*]

Adame Dalrimple says hard Elspeth Smyth and hir forsaid [*word crossed out*] sua he saw hir \rathe/[119] and said to hir it was for it that it was for litle good shoe was.[120]

8: article anent Adame Dalrimple daith done be hir witchcraft.[121]

John Kennedy knawis nothing.

John Houstoun says Adam Dalrymple hard him say theas words one his daithbed.

Charles Dalrimple depones to the treuth of the 7 article And to this article deponis conforme thairunto And that [*word crossed out*] his brother told him if evir there was a deill[122] schoe was ane and says ane witch told him shoe was his brothers daith and wald be his to[o].

William Campbell says he hard all concerning the 7 article and also the 8 be Adame Dalrimple except only he saw him not in his daith bed.

Nynth article:[123] John Houstoun says Margaret Myller told hir all the words contenit in the article.

10 article concerning [*blank*] Smyth his daith[124] Charles Dalrimple knaws there fell ane pace[125] of wooll upone him bot no further or that schoe was the caus of his daith.

11 article anent the provest chyld quhich deid be hir.[126]

115 'oulkis': weeks.
116 'def and dom': deaf and dumb.
117 'according to the common report'.
118 In margin: '7 article x guiltie una vote'.
119 'rathe': early.
120 In Sawyer's dittay below, item 7, we are told that Adam Dalrymple 'fand the[e] the self sam day within the sea mark in the shoar at fyve hours in the winter morneinge and said to ye it was for little good thow was thair'. The present paragraph seems to be a slightly garbled preliminary version of that information. Perhaps it is the scribe's rough notes written at the time, rather than a later fair copy.
121 In margin: '8 article x guiltie una vote'.
122 'deill': devil.
123 In margin: '9 article guiltie'.
124 In margin: '10 article clenged'.
125 'pace': pack.
126 In margin: '11 article clenged'.

Jonet Caldwall says schoe knawis nothing thereof.

Margaret Smyth knawis nothing thereof bot hard hir thretin the provest that he sould repent.

12: article no witnes.[127]

13: article anent the Devillis mark no witnes.[128]

14 article anent Mathow Drips.[129]

Mathow Drips knawis nothing bot quhat his wyff told him.

Agnes [*word crossed out*] Myller depones conforme to the article and that schoe lost 3 browings of aill eftir and anent the scraps of hir luiff.[130]

Pannell confessis the scraping of hir hand bot that it was out of mirriement. {*fo. 177r.*}

15 article the borowing barme fra James McAdame.[131]

Margaret Myller depones conforme to the article in absens anent Jonet McAdames schaming.

18 [*sic*][132] article[133] anent Marion Mitchells husband and hir speiche to [*word crossed out*] the said Marion concerning that scho sould heir hard news of hir husband.

Marion Mitchell says schoe spak the wordis contenit in the said article.

19 [*sic*] [*word crossed out*][134]

Jonet Huie says conform to the article in everything, says nothing against hir concerning the chyldis daith bot that there was mylk in hir breist[135] befoir.

Robert Patone ignorant.

David McIllvaill nothing.

Jonet Lauchlane nothing.

The court adjourned to morow at aucht a clok.

Eftirnone: 6: Apryll 1658[136]

127 In margin: '12: article guiltie delay clenged'.

128 In margin: '13 article delay guiltie x'.

129 In margin: '14 article x guilty'.

130 'luiff': palm.

131 In margin: '15 article clenged'.

132 There is a gap between Article 15 and Article 18 in the original document. Articles 16 and 17 are missing.

133 In margin: '16 article clenged'.

134 In margin: '17 article guiltie'.

135 'breist': breast.

136 In margin: 'Witchcraft Jonet Sawers convict and brunt'.

The assyse Lykwayes be pluralitie of votes be the mouthe of thair said Chancellor finds the pannell Jonet Sawers guiltie of bewitching John McConnells hors mentionat in the first article of hir dittay, Also thai all in ane voce[137] finds hir guilty of the bewitching of Mertene Walkers hors mentionat in the fourth article of the dittay, And of the fyfth article anent the daith of Adame Cuninghame chyld the harme ressaved be hir selff and hir husband, Also of the 6 article In bewitching Agnes Murdoche, And of the tent, {*fo. 177v.*} Aucht and nynth articles of hir dittay Anent the schip casting away and the daith of Adame Dalrimple and Margaret Myller spous to umquhile John Houstoun, Also thay be pluralitie of votteis[138] finds hir guiltie of haveing the devills mark mentionat in the thretene article of hir dittay, And of the 14 article Anent the bewitching Agnes Myller mentionat thairintill In scarting hir luiff And causing it to dinnell for sax hours thaireftir, And last finds hir guiltie all in ane voice of the 17 and last article of hir dittay In bewitching Margaret Lauchlane spous to Walter Bell [*words crossed out, one of the words is 'bewitching'*][139] In taking frome hir of the mylk out of hir breist, And be pluralitie of votes Assoilzeis hir of the Remanent article of hir dittay.

[*Signed:*] WWallace.

Air 7 Apryll 1658

Sentence Contra Jonet Sawers as convict of witchcraft ordanet to be brunt 23: Apryll 1658.

As also the Commissioners adjudges Jonet Saweris as fund guyltie of the severall actis of witchcraft mentionat in hir dittay and verdict of the assyse To be tane to the ordinar place of executioun of the burgh of Air upoun Fryday the twentie thrid day of Apryle instante And there betuix tua and foure houris in the afternone to be strangled at a stak till she be deid thaireftir hir bodie brunt to asses and hir gudis esheit.

Source 5: Worcester College, Oxford, manuscripts of William Clarke, Colonel Robert Sawrey to [blank], Ayr, 26 April 1659 [sic for 1658], xxx.85.[140]

Uppon Fryday the 23th instant was one Janett Saers late an Inhabitant in this towne according to a sentence passed by the Judges (the Assize having found her guilty of witchcraft) strangled at a stake and after that her whole body burnt to ashes, She did constantly deney that she knew any thing of witchcraft, and at her death made a very large confession of her wicked life

137 'voce': voice.

138 'votteis': votes.

139 It is not possible to read the other words crossed out.

140 From microfilm 'Sir William Clarke Manuscripts, 1640–1666', edited by G. E. Aylmer (Hassocks: Harvester Press, 1977); copy in Edinburgh University Library. This letter is also printed in C. H. Firth (ed.), *Scotland and the Protectorate* (Edinburgh: SHS, 1899), 382.

and had good Exhortations to the liveing but remained to affirmed [*sic*] that she knew nothing of witchcraft, and as I was informed by those that heard her when the Minister was urgeing her to confesse she had these words, Sir I am shortly to appear before the Judge of all the Earth and a lye may damne my Soule to hell, I am cleare of witchcraft for which I am presently to suffer and so with a seming willingnesse submitted herselfe to death, the people in this country are more sett against witchcraft then any other wickedness, and if once a person have that name and come upon an Assize it's hard to get of[f] with lesse then this poore Creature.

[*Signed:*] Ro: Sawrey.

25. MARGARET BEVERIDGE AND JOHN CORSE, DYSART, 1657–1658

INTRODUCTION

Margaret Beveridge and John Corse were a wife and husband living in the burgh of Dysart in Fife. They were first suspected of witchcraft during a panic in 1643, but came under more sustained investigation between December 1657 and January 1658. Their case is notable for this long back story, but even more for the unusual way in which their confessions were negotiated.[1]

Beveridge and Corse were named as witches on 25 October 1643 by another alleged witch, Isobel Propp, at a time when many witches were being accused in the parish. We learn this in the text below because the kirk session clerk, writing in 1658, provided extracts from the earlier records for the use of the prosecutors, but the original 1643 record also survives for comparison.[2] Another extract shows that Beveridge and Corse had both been named as witches on 16 December 1647 by another woman accused of witchcraft, Grisell Rankin. But in December 1657 John Corse himself claimed that his wife was a witch.

John Corse evidently suffered from nightmarish visions of some kind. He probably had difficulty even in making sense of the visions for himself, let

[1] There is an account of this case in P. G. Maxwell-Stuart, *Abundance of Witches: The Great Scottish Witch-Hunt* (Stroud, 2005), 22–30. This account suggests that Beveridge and Corse were indeed witches and that Corse had become a witch in about 1651 (e.g. p. 25), but this interpretation of the case is not followed here.

[2] The original kirk session record, under the date 25 October 1643, has Isobel Propp naming 'John Corss and his wyfe' among a long list of other alleged witches: NRS, Minutes of Kirk Session of Dysart, 1643–1653, CH2/390/2, p. 48. There is a great deal more about the prosecution of these witches in the Dysart kirk session records around this time, on which more research is needed. The Survey of Scottish Witchcraft did not include this episode. Stuart Macdonald, too, in his account of the panic, apparently relied on the presbytery records rather than the kirk session records for this period: Stuart Macdonald, *The Witches of Fife: Witch-Hunting in a Scottish Shire, 1560–1710* (East Linton, 2002), 81–3, 228–9. Macdonald mentions Beveridge and Corse's 1657–8 case briefly on p. 84. Unfortunately, the Dysart kirk session records are not extant for 1657–8.

alone in explaining them to other people.[3] His interrogators placed him under pressure – how much pressure we do not know, but there were suggestions of torture – to shape or convert his visions into a narrative of having made a pact with the Devil. They succeeded to some extent, but one striking feature of this case is that Corse tried repeatedly to tell alternative versions of his story.[4] Sometimes he told of resisting the Devil's temptations and assaults, or of the Devil himself rejecting him because he was a godly man. Sometimes he told of assaults by *witches*, raising the question of who these witches might be. In his initial confession on 16 December 1657, he named Margaret Williamson, but in January 1658, if not before, he added the names of two more witches: Agnes Halkett and his own wife, Margaret Beveridge.

Did Corse accuse his wife in order to deflect the interrogators' attention away from himself? Such an interpretation is probably too simple. He said that he wanted to 'convince his wyfe Margret Bevarage of her sin of witchcraft' – the language that Scottish ministers used when they sought to persuade sinners to repent. He added that he 'desyred his wife to confess that shoe might get here [*sic*. her] soule saved'. So he seems to have been trying to tell a godly story of sin and repentance. In one of his nightmarish visions, he had encountered his wife in the shape of a rat – a story that he made sense of by having yet another witch, Janet Ross, explain it to him. His 16 December confession has a breathless quality. It shifts between past and present tenses and between the first and third persons; it includes direct speech; and some actions (such as opening his door to let the Devil out) are merely implied, with the narrative running on too fast to state them explicitly. These narrative qualities, plus the shifting perspective on Corse's own guilt or innocence, mean that his reported words call for particularly careful reading.

After her husband's revelations, Margaret Beveridge was interrogated too – again probably under torture. She confessed to several classic demonological ideas: having renounced her baptism, having entered into the Devil's pact by placing one hand on the top of her head and the other beneath the sole of her foot, and also having received the Devil's mark, which made her afraid. She also confessed to meetings with the Devil. She said that the Devil had black clothes and a cloven lip. She named Margaret Williamson as a witch, as her husband had previously done. Finally, the record stated that she had withdrawn her confession. It was said that she had confessed before the session without any torture, but pressure of some kind had evidently been placed on her to make her confess.

3 For a study of visionaries and their difficulties see Julian Goodare, 'Away With the Fairies: The Psychopathology of Visionary Encounters in Early Modern Scotland', *History of Psychiatry*, 31 (2020), 37–54.

4 For an analysis of Corse's changing self-presentation see Ciaran J. M. Jones, 'Spiritual Roles in Early Modern Scotland' (University of Edinburgh PhD thesis, 2020), 158–63.

The two documents edited below, one each for Corse and Beveridge, compile information about their confessions in 1657 and 1658, and all the previous denunciations back to 1643. There are thus many dates in the documents, and unfortunately not all of these dates are clear. As noted in footnotes below, the scribe has altered one or two dates, and even the easily readable dates may not be correct. Corse's second confession as it appears in his document, which names only Margaret Williamson, may have been given before the third one, which also names Agnes Halkett and Margaret Beveridge, as its placement in the text would imply – yet the second confession is dated 17 January and the third one is dated 7 January. Beveridge's own recorded confession is dated 14 January, and the document recording it also mentions that Corse had named her as a witch on 17 December – a date that does not appear in Corse's own recorded confessions at all.

Although Beveridge's document ends with a note of her retraction of her confession, both documents seem to have been written with the aim of continuing the investigation. The documents' location among the justiciary papers suggests that they were presented to the central authorities to support a request for further authorisation. They are signed by two bailies and two ministers, a mixture of secular and religious authority. These local authorities either wanted a commission of justiciary, or else at least a commission authorising them to interrogate the suspects further under torture. Nothing further has been found about the case, however, so the request, if made, may have been refused.[5]

TEXT

Source: NRS, Court of Justiciary Process Papers, 1658, JC26/24.

JC26/24, bundle 6, no. 7

[*Endorsed:*] 2 Februar 1658. Confessione John Corse warlok.

{*p. 1*} At Dysert 25 October 1643
The quhilk day In presens of Alexander and William Simsones bailleis, James Guthrie, Johne Scott elders with Mr James Craig precentor, being conveined in the tolbooth of Dysert. Issoble Prop being incarcerat for the hynous cryme of witchcraft who compeired and confest, the same, Lyke as schoe deleated Johne Cors and his wyfe Margret Beverage to be witches. Extract forth of the sessioun book by Mr James Craig clerk.

5 Maxwell-Stuart, *Abundance of Witches*, 27, states that Corse was executed, citing 'a further record', the nature of which is not specified.

At Dysert 16 December 1657
Quhilk day after exhortatioun and prayers by Mr James Wilsone minister: Johne Cors frielie confest as followes, he being at Babirnie[6] milne about 18 yeirs agoe or therby declared ther came tuo men to him and the ane of them had a buik in his hand in and I bade him put my name in his buik and he answered he would not till he saw whatt gate I would goe[7] and within 10 dayes they both came againe to me at the same place and they sought sundrie things of me at that place which I refused them, and the Devill answered me that fleshe and Blood had not gevin me that,[8] and therafter I come I come [*sic*] to the Gallow towne[9] about 9 or 10 hours at night and ther I mett with a company of women, and I said I would goe to Robert Lesels hous and they answered they had bein ther befoir and therfra,[10] I was caried to the west end of the town, And how I come I can not tell, and when I come to my awin hous I fand Agnes Halkeit and Margret Williamsone (Robert Swynes wyfe) sitting therin, and the doore barred upon them, and I asked how came yee in, and they said throw the hole of the doore, and Margret Williamsone called me out of my hous (the Divell Lyke a black man being in my hous) and I speired[11] at Margret Williamsone if that was here[12] housband and she answered I,[13] and he vanished out of my sight and the said Margret bad him oppen the doore and the said Johne bade him goe forth as she come in, therafter shoe took me to the 3 trees[14] and the Divell said to them at the 3 trees, what is that you have brought me now, and schoe sayes a man that was counted ane good man upon the earth, and the Divell sayis why have ye brought me that old fellow here, he wall[15] returne back againe, and they asked what they should doe with me, and he said carie him back the way he come for he would shame them all, then the women cryed, the tyme is passing, mark him, and the Divell marked me in my right theich and then I renunced my babptisme [*sic*], putting the one hand to the crowne of my head and the other to the sole of my foote, and delyvred all betuixt my hands to the Devill. This was confest befoir Mr

6 Perhaps Balbirnie in Forfarshire. It is some distance from Dysart, but Corse seems to have travelled for work; see his later mentions of Auchtermuchty.

7 'whatt gate I would goe': what direction I would take (i.e. what decision he would commit himself to).

8 'Flesh and blood have not given you that' seems to mean something like 'No mere human being should have the ability to refuse my demand as you have done'.

9 Probably Gallatown, about 1km north-west of Dysart.

10 'they had bein ther befoir and therfra': they had (already) been there and come back. The comma after 'therfra' is in the MS.

11 'speired': asked.

12 Here and later, the scribe repeatedly writes 'here' for 'her'.

13 'I' (aye): yes.

14 This place may have been near the present-day Three Trees Lane, about 1km to the west of Dysart.

15 *Sic*. Probably read 'will'.

James Wilsone minister, Mr Andrew Briand schoolemaister and Mr James Craig precentor with James Jonstoune wright.

[*Signed:*] JWilson minister at Dysert, ABriand schoolmaster at Dysert witnes, Mr James Craig witnes. {*p. 2*}

At Dysart Januray 17 1658

Johne Cors declared in presens of the sessioun of Dysert that the said Margret Walliamsone complained upon him to the Divell, and shoe called him out of his awin hous and went with him to the 3 trees where the Divell and a company of witches wair.

And further when he delyvered him self to the Divell the Divell askit him, what he would have from him for that gift, which he had gevin him, he answered that he would have no thing, and the rest of the company desyred him to dance, he said he could not dance, and ane cryed out, the tyme runnes, mark him mark him, the Divell cast him downe at his foot and markit him.[16]

And further he declared befoir the Eldership of Dysert at one of thes tymes when the Divell come to him at Balbirny milne the Divell turned away frome him Lyke a brussell coke.[17]

Januar 7 1658

The quhilk day Johne Cors confest in presens of Mr James Wilson and William Gay that his wyfe was a witche and was among that wicked company of witches, and that shoe and Margret Williamsone came to his bed syd in Auchtermoughtie in the night tyme sevin yeir bypast and further that his wife was that night with the Devill and Nans Halkat and Margret Williamsone when he first entered in covenant with the Divell and that same night efter he had delyvered him self to the Divell, the Devill said to him what will ye have of this gift yow have gevin me, he himself answered nothinge, but his wyfe said at that tyme as he thought, what will you doe with your dyvers debtoris. Witnessis Mr James Wilson, Walter Hegie, Johne Keir, Andrew Gay.

[*Signed:*] JWilson witnes, William Gay witnes, Johne Keir witnes.

Further he confest that the morrow after he had entered covenant with the Divell and was so betrayed, his wyfe said to him now shoe had gotten ane mends of him.

And that Jonet Ros who was deleated for a witch did one day ask him if ther was any rottens[18] in his hous after that his wyf had goin out of the hous from him and bidden him tarie in the hous till shoe come againe, he answered he saw no rottens in it except on[e] wpoune the kist[19] end quhich was vearie greatt and when he went to streik it, it went from him, she answered that rotten was your wyfe.

16 This is an unusual narrative use of the idea of the Devil's mark.

17 'brussell coke': perhaps a turkey.

18 'rottens': rats.

19 'kist': chest.

[*Signed:*] William Gay witnes. {*p. 3*}

Januar 27[20] 1658
Johne Cors declared further to convince his wyfe Margret Bevarage of her sin of witchcraft that about tuo yeiris since the Devill was in ther hous in the shape of a man who had ane cloven Lip, and he stayed all night in the house, and shoe said to him that man was here good brother,[21] and shoe caused him Lye with the said Johne all night, and the said Johne affirmed that it was not here good brother but the evill man and he had once sein him before at ane evill turne when they were tempting him. The said Johne further desyred his wife to confess that shoe might get here soule saved. Witness William Smith, William Hegie.

Further the said Johne Cors declared that his wyfe cam once to Auchtermoughtie to him when he was receiving corne in another Licknes then here owin quhich he said was more then evir he had spoken, and being asked what shoe was Lyke, he said here Liknes shoe appeared in was much marker[22] then here owin and sho said to him, knitt your sackis mouth erre ever yow pay the corne.[23]

The said Johne Cors further confest that he haid fallen in double adulterie, once with ane woman in Dundie whos housband wes alyve, And againe with one Kathrine Boss in Dysert whos housband was also alive and the said Johne Cors wyfe being alive also, and that he \did/ ather twyce or thryse committ adulterie with the foirsaid Kathrine Boss. Further he confest that he comitted tuo severall fornicationes Lykwayes which all was formerlie conceilled and never knowen.

Thes affoirsaid confessiones were once and againe declared by the said Johne Corse in presens of the minister and elders of Dysert undersubscryving.

[*Signed:*] PSimsone Baillie witnes, JWilson minister at Dysart witnes, MRt Honeyman minister at Dysert wittnes, William Gay elder witnes, Jo: Melvill Baillie witnes, JGay. {*p. 4*}

At Dysert 21[24] Januar 1658
Quhich day Crispune Swyne in Stroore compeired befoir the sessioun and upoun his oath deponed that about fyve yeiris since he mett with Johne Cors in Falkirk and wher he said that he should doe him ane ill turne wheron the said Crispune became distracted.

[*Signed:*] Mr James Craig clerk to the sessioun.

20 This number has been altered, and the reading of the '7' is not certain.
21 'good brother': brother-in-law.
22 'marker' (from 'mirk'): darker.
23 This phrase, meaning 'Tie up the mouth of your sack before you pay for the corn', seems to have been a proverb.
24 This number has been altered, perhaps from '24'.

JC26/24, bundle 7, no. 1

[*Endorsed:*] Fyff: Margaret Baveradge hir confessione of witchcraft 1658.

At Dysert 25 October 1643
The quhilk day in presens of William and Alexander Symsones Bailleis, James Guthrie, Johne Scott elders and Mr James Craig reader being convened in the tolebooth of Dysert, Issoble Prope compeired and having confest her self to be a witch deleatt Johne Cors and Margret Beverage to be witches, as her self was as shoe confest and was thaireafter brunt for the foirsaid hynous cryme.

At Dysert 16 December 1647
Quhilk day Girsell Rankin having confest her self to be a witch, for the which hynous cryme was brunt, sho declared openlie and plainlie that Johne Cors and his wyfe Margret Baverage were witches.

At Dysert 17 December 1657
Quhilk day Johne Cors compeired befoir the sessioun and having confest him self to be a witch deleatt his owin wyfe Margret Baverage and Margarett Williamsone to be witches as him self was.

At Dysert 14 Januar 1658
Quhilk day Margaret Baverage wyfe to Johne Cors being incarcerat for witchcraft compeired befoir the session and confest sho was a witch and that schoe mett with the Devill at the thrie trees and that he had black clothes, and more sho said shoe mett with the Devill in her awin hous with ane cloven[25] Lippe as also sho confest that shoe was affrayed when the Devill give her the mark, and then sho putting the one hand to the crowne of here head and the other to the sole of here foott and give all betuixt to the Devill and then renunced her baptisme. More shoe deleats Margret Williamsone to be a witch and said schoe vanished from here[26] tuo tymes, once at the moore nixt at the thrie trees dancing, and it was Light that night.

Albeit now schoe denyes the premissis and passeth frome here former confessioun yet schoe declared it befoir the sessioun without any tortering as is witnessed by the undersubscrybers.

[*Signed:*] PSymsone Ballie, JWilson minister, Jo: Melville Baillie, MRt Honyman minister.

[25] 'Foott' crossed out here.

[26] 'shoe vanished from here': Margaret Williamson vanished from her (i.e. from her sight).

26. THREE LISTS OF WITCHES, 1658–1659

INTRODUCTION

The document edited below as Source 1, with the contemporary title 'Names of the Witches 1658', is a list of names of 113 accused witches connected with the witchcraft panic of 1658–9. It covers eight counties, of which six are in the south-west, and two (Stirlingshire and Perthshire) are in central Scotland. These counties probably represent one of the 'circuits' of the regional circuit courts that tried serious crimes in this period. It is printed below alongside two documents edited as Source 2 and Source 3, for Ayrshire alone, listing forty-two almost identical names for that county but giving additional contextual information.

'Names of the Witches 1658' does not state what purpose its list is intended to serve, but some physical details may help to elucidate this purpose. The manuscript is a single booklet with sixteen pages, neatly written in three different hands. Once written, the booklet has been folded up very small. The outside leaves are dirty, showing that it has been much used, probably by a messenger or messengers on horseback. Messengers sometimes carried such documents in their riding boots, where dirt could enter.

The three different hands often relate to specific counties or groups of counties. Perhaps different administrators took responsibility for certain areas within the region covered by the court. However, the different hands may also or instead indicate that different parts of the list were written at different times. The first writer may have co-ordinated the document's production; he certainly took a continued interest in it, since he made edits to later parts of the document (as also did the second writer). More study of these hands might well be revealing. The first writer, for instance, was also the clerk who minuted the circuit court trials of March 1659, on which more in a moment. Some notes on the three hands are made in footnotes below, though further study would be required to disentangle all the alterations and annotations.

In between some of the parish lists, several blank spaces and even pages have been left, evidently in the expectation of adding more names. There have indeed been some later additions and deletions. These features are indicative of gradual compilation. The mentions of confessions to be sought, and the discussion of 'delators' (accusers), show that the list was begun at an early stage in the process, before trials had been held. As we shall see, the resulting trials were held at different dates, so the messenger or messengers probably made several different rides around the Scottish counties. Later annotations reveal an updating process.

The 'Names of the Witches' list thus seems to have been written to be used by messengers sent by the court to travel around the parishes listed, summoning assizes of local men for forthcoming trials. Such assizes would be needed for all of the accused witches, so the messenger would need all of their names. A circuit court tried all serious crimes, not just witchcraft, but perhaps the lists are of accused witches alone because the messenger was to summon specific assizes for the witchcraft cases. The lists for Lanarkshire and Renfrewshire are not organised by parish; perhaps these are interim lists that would later have been broken down by parish, or perhaps the intention was to summon just one assize for the whole county.

Additionally, and perhaps at an earlier stage, a messenger seems to have been expected to collect evidence against the accused witches in at least some of the parishes he visited. At two points there is mention of witches' confessions said to be in the possession of parish ministers. There are also a few names of 'delators' – accusers of witches. The messenger would thus have been expected to obtain written statements from them, or to summon them to testify in person, or both. Was the messenger expected to collect evidence only in the parishes where specific evidence was mentioned, or would he ask for evidence in all the parishes that he visited? And would the evidence-gathering ride be combined with the assize-summoning ride, or would two or more separate visits to the parish have been made? The document does not say; presumably some knowledge of this kind was a matter of custom and practice, not written down, while some summonses would have been recorded in separate documents that may no longer survive. We do at least know that the document was not used to summon the accused witches themselves; that function was fulfilled by Sources 2 and 3, as we shall see.

Altogether there are names of 113 accused witches in 'Names of the Witches 1658'. They can be broken down by county as follows:

Stewartry of Kirkcudbright: 12 witches (and 4 delators and 2 ministers)
Dumfriesshire: 5 witches
Lanarkshire: 3 witches
Renfrewshire: 13 witches
Ayrshire: 41 witches (not counting 1 crossed out and 1 erroneous duplicate)
Dunbartonshire: 21 witches (and 2 delators)
Perthshire: 6 witches
Stirlingshire (also including Clackmannanshire): 12 witches
TOTAL: 113 (104 women, 9 men)

The list includes only a small proportion of the parishes in each county (and none at all in Wigtownshire, which must have been within the remit of the 'circuit'). Evidently these are the parishes from which local information has been received. Some of this initial information (and perhaps all of it) has evidently come from ministers or their kirk sessions. Witches in two parishes are designated 'poor', indicating receipt of poor relief. Only the kirk session would have been concerned by that.

Occupations or other identifying features are given for a handful of the witches. For instance, one woman from Perth is designated a midwife. Two men from Dumbarton are designated sailors, and some women are sailors' wives. Three witches are designated 'poor'. One witch from Kippen is 'ane young damsell'. But most witches are designated only by their place of dwelling, plus marital status in the case of many of the women.

The document's interest for the administrators did not cease with the trials. The first of the writers later annotated it with the outcomes of some trials – those of suspects listed below as being in Stirlingshire. There is much more information about these witches below in the present volume, under the title 'Alloa and Related Witches, Clackmannanshire, 1658–1661'. They were all tried at a circuit court in Stirling on 22 and 23 March 1659, when the verdicts noted on the list below were delivered. The writer of these notes did not mention the sentences that were then passed on those convicted, even though some of these were unusual, as noted in footnotes below.

Overall, despite the modest size of the 'Names of the Witches' document, it represents the fruits of an extensive process of bureaucratic information-gathering. The information thus gathered would sometimes prove to be lethally effective, though it is beyond the scope of the present edition to trace the fate of all the people named in the list. We can at least see that the information was then further updated for the county of Ayrshire with the second and third documents.

These two Ayrshire documents, printed below as Source 2 and Source 3, are similar to the first one, and evidently related to it. Source 2 is headed 'Porteous Roll of Ayr 1658' – a 'porteous roll' was a list of alleged criminals who were to be summoned before a court – while Source 3 is headed 'Air Court Air Dittays 6 Apryle 1658'. These two almost identical lists cover only Ayrshire, and they give an almost identical list of names for that county only – forty-two names in total in Source 2, forty-one in Source 3. Detailed comparison with 'Names of the Witches', Source 1, shows four substantive differences in names between the lists. Source 3 has one extra name for the parish of Craigie; one name in Irvine (Isobel Henderson) has been crossed out in Source 3 (but not Source 2); the parish named Dalry in Source 1 is called Dunlop in the other lists; and one name is different in that parish (Janet Walker in Source 1, John Walker in the other lists). Apart from that, not only are the names the same, but the ordering of the names within each parish is the same. However, the two Ayrshire lists carry extra information and are evidently later. Even when the first Ayrshire list, Source 2, is being written, it has more information than Source 1 about some of the witches. By the time of the later Source 3, a messenger has already visited all the parishes, and has returned with the information that, for instance, some individuals are 'deid', and others are 'not to be found thair'. Some of this information seems then to have been added retrospectively to Source 2.

These lists make clear that they have been created for the purpose of summoning the accused witches themselves to the court, shortly before trials are due to be held. This becomes even clearer with a further document, not transcribed in full below, but discussed in footnotes. This document is almost identical to Source 2, but it is an order to the sheriff of Ayr and his administrators to summon the witches. Source 2 itself bears a note stating that these summonses have been carried out.

A further observation can therefore be made about the 'Names of the Witches' list, Source 1: it covers a long period of time, more than twelve months. It was begun very early in 1658; even in the spring of 1658 the Ayrshire lists could provide extra information, and those Ayrshire witches who could be found were all brought to trial in April 1658. But the 'Names of the Witches' list remained in use by the circuit court administrators, or was brought back into use. The Stirlingshire and Alloa witches that it listed did not even come to the authorities' attention until later in 1658, and their trials were held in March 1659. Yet the administrators were still using and annotating the list at this later date.

Overall, these lists can tell us much about the activities of the witchcraft prosecutors. Even the fact that the lists are of 'witches' is significant. The circuit court was responsible for all serious crimes, but the administrators evidently thought that 'witches' needed special attention.

The lists show us different stages of information-gathering – and also reveal some of the limits of the administrators' knowledge. When the Ayrshire lists report that some alleged witches are 'not to be found' or that there is 'non suche thair', does this indicate that the people named had fled, or that they had never existed and that the initial information was therefore faulty? Further local research may shed more light on this. The present edition shows how much more can be found about the Alloa and Stirlingshire witches, for instance. There is also a lot of information in the archives about Dumfriesshire at this time, to give only one example.[1]

In the edition below, the 'Names of the Witches' list is printed on the left-hand side of the page, with the Ayr porteous roll list and the 'Air Court'

1 The Survey of Scottish Witchcraft would form a good starting-point for such local research. The Survey did not know about the 'Names of the Witches' document itself, but it did survey the justiciary court records in NRS, where most of the surviving manuscripts giving more information about these accused witches can be found.

list added to it in two parallel columns. These columns appear only for the middle one-third of the text below – the Ayrshire section of the 'Names of the Witches' list. In the three columns, the headings and names almost always correspond, though differences of detail are visible. One difference of ordering of the parishes is noted in footnotes.

TEXTS

Source 1: Wellcome Library, London, MS 3658.[2]

{*p. 16*}[3] Names of the Witches 1658
Witches
Witches[4] {*p. 1*}

\Kirkculbryght/

Witches in Troqueir paroch

Margaret Lawry in Preistland
Ewphame McChyne thair
Margaret McCheane in Craiginbrig

Ironegray Paroche

Helene Murhead hir confessione Is in the hands of Mr Patrik Broun lait minister at Ironegray

Lochruttoun

Agnes Clerk in Lawstoun

Partoun Witches

2 This document has a bookplate of the nineteenth-century book collector T. Dawson Brodie (which the separate document numbered as Source 6 in 'Alloa and Related Witches, Clackmannanshire, 1658–1661', edited below in the present volume, also has; the two documents also have similar bindings). Attached to the document is a draft transcript dating apparently from the early twentieth century. The Wellcome Library has digitised the document itself and the draft transcript, and made them available on the internet: <http://wellcomelibrary.org/item/b19111319>.

3 This is the cover page, evidently intended to be read first. The cover, and the first three internal pages, are in the hand designated here as Hand 1.

4 These two words appeared on opposite sides of the cover of the document when folded.

Katharene Gordoun spous to Alexander McGill

Kirkpatrike Durhame

Issobell Rodgersone in the Mylne of Kirkpatrik

Cowend and Swthik witches

Jonet Murray in Madinpap
Helene Blair in Cowend
Jonet Slauder in Maybeg
Nicolas Wilsone in Brekinsillis
Bessie Thomesone spous to Charles Blair

Dilators of the said witches of Cowend and Suthik

James Lyndsay of Sawgirth
David Cairnes of Kip
Rodger Aikin of Achinhay
Thomas Gibbesone in Bakerbuss {*p. 2*}

The confessione of the witches of Cowend and Suthik ar said to be in the custodie of Mr Alexander Smyth minister of Cowend.[5]

Dumfries

Witches in Dumfreis

Margaret Gunyeone in Dumfreis
Elspeth Maxwell Elder in Dumfreis
Catharene Edyer thair
Georg Lokhart in Kelwood thair

Witches in Glencairne parish

Janet McKinot[6] in the Maynes {*pp. 3–4 blank*} {*p. 5*}[7]

Witches dillated in Lanerkshyre

Marion Carruthers spouse to George Findlay in Glasgow
Jonet Lochheid spouse to William Tulloch skiper in Glasgow

5 Half a page is left blank for more names at this point.
6 The last two of these letters are blotted and uncertain.
7 Hand 2 begins at this point, and continues until part of the way down page 8.

Margaret Gay[8] servitrix to John Mure in Kingland

Witches in Renfrew[9]

Jonet Tulloch in Renfrew toune[10]
Jonet Findlaysone spouse to John Patersone in Yocker
Jonet \Gemill/[11] in Renfrew toune
Malie Knock thair
Jean Gilmour wedow thair
Agnes Greinlaw[12] wedow thair
Margaret Stewart weidow thair
Issobell Simpsone in Calderheuch in Lochwhinoch parish
Jonet Aitkin in Cairnehill
Jonet Orr in Corheid
Espeth Fouls in Neilstone {*p. 6*}
Bessie Craufurd thair
Margaret Smith thair

	Source 2: NRS, Court of Justiciary Process Papers, 1658, JC26/25.[13]	*Source 3: NRS, Court of Justiciary Process Papers, 1658, JC26/25.*
Witches in the shirrefdome of Ayre[14]	Perteuies Roll[15] of Ayr 1658 …[16]	Air Court Air Dittays 6 Apryle 1658

8 'spou…' crossed out here.
9 About six lines are left blank for more names at this point.
10 In left-hand margin, in Hand 1: 'brunt'.
11 The scribe has crossed out a name here and inserted 'Gemill' above the line.
12 The scribe has changed this from 'Grein' to 'Greinlaw'.
13 The box numbered JC26/25 contains numerous bundles, mostly not individually numbered, and only loosely sorted. This document is from a bundle bearing a note on the wrapper saying '21 items', while the paper itself bears the pencil annotation 'JC26/25 Item 2'. The same bundle also contains another copy of this list, with the pencil annotation 'From JC26/25'. It has not been transcribed in full in this edition, as it is mostly word for word the same as the document edited here as Source 2, but it has the following differences: (i) the annotations 'Dead' against individual names have been added in a second hand; (ii) the notes in Source 2 against some names saying that a person is not to be found are absent in this list; (iii) at the very end of the list, a further heading 'Air Witches' has been written and then crossed out (which may suggest that this list was copied directly from 'Names of the Witches 1658', Source 1, which has the Ayr witches in this position); (iv) a different note, ordering the summons of the suspects, has been written at the end, transcribed in footnote 35 below. This document thus occupies an intermediate position between our Source 1 and Source 2.
14 Source 1, 'Names of the Witches 1658', continues here in the left-hand column, while the two Ayrshire documents, Source 2 and Source 3, are placed in the middle and right-hand columns. See the Introduction above.
15 'Perteuies Roll' (porteous roll): list of alleged criminals to be summoned.
16 This document begins by listing the names of ten alleged criminals other than witches. One is charged with murder and the other nine with adultery. These names have been omitted here.

Tarboltone witches	Tarbowltoune witches[17]	Tarboltoune witches[18]
Jonet Reid spouse to James Smith	p: Jonnett Reid spous to James Smyth thair	Jonnat Reid spous to James Smythe thair: per:
Margaret Sinderland wedow thair	p: Margaret Sunderland widow thair	Margaret Sudderland widow in Parkmylne thair: per:
Jonet McSkiming thair	p: Jonnet MacSkiming thair	Jonnat McSkyming in Blakdyk per:
Agnes Patersone in Tarboltone	D: Agnes Patersoune thair	Agnes Pattersoune in Tarboltoune d:
Jonet Gillespie thair	P: Jonnet Gillespie thair	Jonnat Gilespie in Privik thair: per:
Cragie witches dillated	Cragie Witches	Craigie witches
John Lourie in Borland	P: Johne Lowrie in Borland thair	Johne Lowrie in Bordland thair: per:
Marrion Millikin	p: Marion Millikine thair	Marione Millikin thair: per:
Hew Dumbar thair[19]	p: Hew Dunbar thair	Hew Dumbar thair: per:
Christian Hunter thair[20]	p: Cristian Huntar thair	Cristiane Huntar thair his spous: per:
John McKie thair[21]	p: John McKie thair	Johne McKie thair: per:
Agnes Wasone	p: Agnes Wasowne thair	Agnes Wassoune thair per:
Jonet Simpsone thair	p: Jonnet Symson thair	Jonnat Sympsoune thair: per:
	p: Jonnet Murdoch thair	Jonnat Murdoche thair: per:[22]

17 Before the 'Tarbowltoune witches', Source 2 gives a list of three 'Ayr witches'. They have been moved to a later position editorially in order to align them with Source 1.

18 Before the 'Tarboltoune witches', Source 3 gives a list of three 'Air witches'. They have been moved to a later position editorially in order to align them with Source 1.

19 An 'x' has been added after this name, perhaps in Hand 1.

20 An 'x' has been added after this name, perhaps in Hand 1.

21 An 'x' has been added after this name, perhaps in Hand 1.

22 This name is not in the 'Names of the Witches' list.

Agnes Robisone[23]	p: Agnes Robesone thair	Agnes Robisoune thair: per:
John McKie[24]		
Marione Sympsone	Marion Symsoune thair	Marioune Sympsoune thair: per:
Jonet Tait {*p. 7*}	Jonet Taitt: Dead	Deid. Jonnat Tait
Rickhartone witches	Rickkertowne witches	Rickartoune parishe witches
Catharen Morsland spouse to Robert Steill[25]	D: Catheren Mogersland at Haining	Kathreine Mongersland spous to Robert Steill at Hayneing thair: d:
Marrion Lie spouse to John Adam	p: Marion Leyes weidow now in Tarbowton	Marione Leyes spous to umquhill Johne Adam now in Shawwood in Tarboltoune parishe: per:
Agnes Mortoune spouse to Thomas Mortoune	Agnes Mortowne spows to Tomas Morton non such thair	Agnes Mortoune spous to Thomas Mortoune not to be fund thair:
Kilbryd witches	Kilbryd witches	Kilbryd parishe witches
Bessie Woodsyde at the Kirktoune of Kilbryde	p: Bessie Wodsyde at the Kirk Towne off Kilbryd	Bessie Woodsyde at the Kirktoune of Kilbryd per:
Jonet Grahame in[26] Fairlie	p: Jonnet Grahame in Fairley	Jonnat Grahame in Fairlie per:
Jonet Wilsone thair	Jonnet Wilsowne thair Dead	Deid Jonnat Wilsoune thair
Jonet Boyd thair	p: Jonnet Boyd thair	Jonnat Boyd in Hartcraige thair per:
Helen Thein thair	p: Heline Thorne thair	Helleine Thain thair: per:

23 An 'x' has been added after this name, perhaps in Hand 1.

24 *Sic.* This and the next two names have been squeezed in at the foot of the page, perhaps in Hand 1. 'John McKie' himself is an erroneous duplicate; his name has already been given earlier in the Craigie list.

25 Above this name, another name has been crossed out, and is now only partially legible: 'John E... in L...'.

26 Word altered, perhaps from 'thair'.

Ardrossan	Ardrossan witches	Ardrossan witches
Margaret Lorimer spouse to Thomas Robisone thair	Margat Laurymer spous to Thomas Robesone thair dead	Deid Margaret Lowrimer spous to Thomas Robisone thair:
Dalrye[27] witches	Dunlope witches	Dunlop witches
Margaret Allan spouse to John Montgomerie	Margaret Allan spows to Johne Mackgomery thair Dead	Deid Margaret Allane spous to Johne Montgumrie
Margaret Cunnyngham weidow thair	Margaret Cuinyngham widow thair: non such thair	Margaret Cunyghame widow thair not to be found nor summoned:
Wiolat Guililand weidow thair	Wiolat Guillieland widow thair: none such thair	Violet Gulliland widow thair not to be found nor summoned
Jonet Hamiltone wedow thair	Jonnet Hamiltowne widow thair: non such thair	Jonnat Hamiltoune widow thair not to be found nor summoned:
Margaret Patone wedow thair	p:[28] Margaret Patowne widow thair: now in Lurat in Dalry parish	Margaret Pattoune in Howret in Dalry per:
John Guililand in Kilbirnie	p: Johne Guillieland in Kilburnie: nou in Dalray parish	John Gulliland sumtyme in Kilburnye now in Dalry: d: ressaved ane act for his appearence quhen requryrit
Jonet Walker in Ardrossan {*p. 8*}	Johne Walker in Ardrossan non such thair	Johne Walker in Ardrossane not to be found nor: summoned
Largs witches	Larges witches	Lairges witches
Margaret Jamisone in Largs	Margaret Jamesone in Largs non such thair	Margaret Jamesoune in Lairges non suche nor summoned:

27 *Sic.* All the other lists say 'Dunlop'. Dalry and Dunlop were both parishes in northern Ayrshire.

28 This 'p:', and the similar 'per:' in the third list, may both be abbreviations for 'personally summoned'.

Jonet Holmes thair	Jonnet Holmes thair: non such thair	Jonnat Holmes thair non suche thair nor summoned:
Irwine witches	Irving witches	Irwing witches
Anable Gothray weidow in Irwine	p: Annabell Gottray widow thair	Annable Gottray thair: per:
Agnes Wallace weidow thair	p: Agnes Wallace widow thair	Agnes Wallace widdow thair: per:
Bessie \Fullarton/[29] wedow thair	Bessie Fullertown widow thair Dead	Died Bessie Fullartoune widdow thair
Christian Neving weidow thair	Cristian Neving widow thair Dead	Deid Cristiane Neving widdow thair[30]
Issobell Hendersone wedow thair	p: Issobell Hendersone widow thair	
Air witches[31]	Ayr Witches[32]	Air witches[33]
Jonet Sauar in Air[34]	p: Johnett [*sic*] Sawer in Ayr	Jonnat Sawer spous to Johne McAdam messenger per: tryal assyse convict and brunt
Elspeth Cunninghame thair	p: Elspet Cuninghame thair	Elspethe Cunynghame thair: per under actit be the nixt court
Jonet Slowane thair {*p. 9*}	p: Jonnet Slowand thair	Jonnat Sloand thair: per:
	Wpon[35] the threttie and last dayes off March And first second thrid fourt and fyft dayes of	

29 The scribe has crossed out a name here and inserted 'Fullarton' above the line.

30 'Issobell Hendirsoune widdow thair: per:' crossed out here.

31 With this heading, and until the end of page 11, Hand 1 resumes.

32 This heading, and the list of three names that follows it, comes at the beginning of the list in Source 2. It has been moved to this position editorially in order to align it with Source 1.

33 This heading, and the list of three names that follows it, comes at the beginning of the list in Source 3. It has been moved to this position editorially in order to align it with Source 1.

34 Janet Sawyer's case is edited above in the present volume.

35 In place of this final note, the otherwise similar document 'From JC26/25' (on which see footnote 13 above) has the following note: 'Schireff of the sherefdome of Air your deputts

Apryle 1658 yeires, I Thomas Aitone officer Lawfullie sumoned the abovenamed persones personallie and att ther duelling Howses as they ar above marked above sic be: P: p: D: To compeir befoir the Honorable Lawfullie sumoned the abovenamed persones personallie and att ther duelling Howses as they ar above marked above sic be: P: p: D: To compeir befoir the Honorable Judges in cawses Criminall At Ayr upon the sixt day off Apryl 1658 yeares To answer to the Indytment Given Wp against them In all Poynts with certiffication This I did befor these wittneses, Alexander Izack in Irving, Robert Simmpsone In Kilbryd and Steven Wilsowne in Largs, Mathew Crawfurd in Dalray, Henry Rankine in Kilvinning, William Mirrie in Wodheid, And for the Mair verification subscryvit with my hand, Thomas Aittoun officer.[36]

---

and officers ye sall upone sight heirof caus laufully summond the haill abovenamet delinquents to appear befoir the honourabll commissioners in criminall caussis in tolbuith of [*'Glasgow' crossed out*] Aire the saxt day of Apryle nixt to answer to thair Indytments with certificatione thay sall be declared fugitives. And that ye report this precept with your executione upone the said summonds of the said delinquents against the dounsitting of the court As ye sall be answerable to the said …ners [*word damaged, probably 'commissioners'*]. Subscrivit be me Mr Alexander Hamiltoun clerk to the criminall court At Edinburgh the 15 of Merch 1658 at comand of the saids comissioners. [*Signed:*] Alexander Hamilton.'

36 This is the end of the columns for the Ayrshire lists, Source 2 and Source 3. 'Names of the Witches', Source 1, continues below.

\Dumbartonshire witches/[37]

Jonet McClintok spous to Robert Watsone in Dumbarton
Jonet Park thair spous to William McKeane sailler
Jonet Stewart thair spous to Patrik McMayne couper
Agnes McKeane spous to John Glen cordiner thair
Jonet McEvin thair[38] spous to Robert Porterfeild thair
Elspeth Cwik spous to William Auin[39] sailler thair
Robert Semple sailler thair
John Gilchreist sailler thair
Agnes Watsone spous to umquhile George Buchannan bailyie thair
Marione McEwin spous to William Clerk thair

Bonill parish Witches

Cristiane Dunlop thair
Jonet McKinla thair
both poor

Wasterkirkpatrik parish Witches

Jonet Tower (poor) in the Maynes of Wasterkirkpatrik
Jonet McKie in Chappeltoun parish Wasterkirkpatrick
Jonet Mitchell thair
Jonet Leitch in Comiltoun spous to Walter Findla thair in the said parish
Katharene Somervell in Dammuir in the said parish[40] {*p. 10*}

Kilbarchan parish

Katharene Stevinsone in Caldsyd
dilator
John Low smyth
To inquyr of James Stevinsone in Caldsyd[41]

Kilmaronok parish[42]

Jonet Buchannane in the Aber of Kilmaronok
Jonet Bilsland in Meikle Portnelland spous to James McKeane Weaver thair

37 This heading, originally 'Dumbarton witches' and then altered, appears to have been added after the main text was written.
38 The scribe has initially written 'in Dum…', then crossed it out and written 'thair'.
39 Reading uncertain.
40 The same scribe has written 'Par:' in the left-hand margin here.
41 It seems that James Stevenson and John Low are both 'delators'.
42 This is modern-day Kilmarnock, not Kilmaronock.

Effie Neillie spous to umquhile Robert McKeachny in the Waird in the Maynes of Kilmaronok[43] {*p. 11*}

Witches Pearth shire

Issobell Myller Midwyff in Pearthe
Cristane Young spous to John Myller in Pearth
Marjorie McClaren spous to Lawrence Cuthebert thair
Jeane Bell Wedow thair
Issobell Huttoun wedow thair

Monyvaird parish

John McEwin in Laworgane[44] {*p. 12*}[45]

\Witches in Stirling shire And first in Stirling toun/[46]

Bessy Steinson relict of the deceist Alexander Lennox gairdner in Stirling[47]
Isabell Bennet spouse to William Mungall in Stirling[48]
Magdalen Blair in Stirling[49]

Alloway Witches[50]

Kathren Black spouse to Thomas Measson in Alloway[51]
Elspeth Black spouse to John Demperstoun there[52]
Barbara Arskein thair[53]
Elisabeth Crocket thair[54]

43 Half a page is left blank for more names at this point.
44 Half a page is left blank for more names at this point.
45 This final page of the text is written in Hand 3. There are annotations in Hand 1. Documents for all the witches listed on this final page are included below in the present volume under the title 'Alloa and Related Witches, Clackmannanshire, 1658–1661'.
46 This heading, in Hand 1, may have been added after the main text was written.
47 Annotated in Hand 1, in two different places: 'Convict'.
48 Annotated in Hand 1: 'Convict'. (Isobel Bennett was in fact convicted of charming but *acquitted* of witchcraft. She was sentenced to be whipped.)
49 Annotated in Hand 1: 'Assoilyeid'.
50 This is Alloa in Clackmannanshire, not Alloway in Ayrshire. Clackmannanshire, a small county, seems here to have been grouped administratively with Stirlingshire. The five names that follow are all bracketed in the left-hand margin, and annotated in Hand 1: 'Witches'.
51 Annotated in Hand 1: 'Convict'. (Katherine Black, Elizabeth Black and Isobel Crockett, although convicted, were sentenced to banishment rather than execution. They then spent three years in prison and were eventually freed.)
52 Annotated in Hand 1: 'Convict'.
53 Annotated in Hand 1: 'Convict'.
54 Annotated in Hand 1: 'Convict'.

James Kirk thair[55]

Witches in Kippen parochin

Isabell Keir spouse to Androw Ritchie in Kippen parochin[56]
Margaret Harvie in the said parochin[57]
Margaret Gourlay widow thair[58]
Janet Miller ane young damsell thair[59] {*pp. 13–15 blank; p. 16 is the cover page, here printed above*}

[55] Annotated in Hand 1: 'Clenged'.
[56] Annotated in Hand 1: 'Convict' – but this word has then been crossed out. (Isobel Keir was in fact convicted and executed.)
[57] Annotated in Hand 1, in two different places: 'Clenged'.
[58] Annotated in Hand 1, in two different places: 'Assoilyeid'.
[59] Annotated in Hand 1: 'Assoilyeid'.

27. ALLOA AND RELATED WITCHES, CLACKMANNANSHIRE, 1658–1661

INTRODUCTION

This large group of documents concerns a panic over witchcraft centred in Alloa, near Stirling. It was a chain-reaction hunt for witches, in which one suspect named others and these were then investigated in their turn. There were at least twenty-seven suspects overall. At least sixteen were brought to trial, and seven were executed; there was also one death in prison. The detailed and varied documentation of the panic enables us to see how ideas of demonic witchcraft and malefice were developed and refined over several months. Repeated interrogations of the suspects created different versions of many stories – stories of meetings with the Devil, and stories of collective malefices. There were also depositions from aggrieved neighbours that told of individual malefices.[1]

Alloa was a small town, with a population of perhaps one thousand. Some of the accused witches lived in the town itself, while others were from nearby settlements like Cambus and Tullibody. Some witches from two locations further afield, Stirling and Kippen, were also drawn into the panic. The Alloa prosecutors came partly from the burgesses and bailies of the town, and partly from the landed elite of the surrounding area. The local justices of the peace, all lairds, played prominent roles. The presbytery of Stirling was involved

[1] Several scholars have discussed the Alloa witches in print. None have used the full range of sources edited below; in particular, hardly any use the large dossier of March 1659 (Source 6 below). R. Menzies Fergusson, 'The Witches of Alloa', *Scottish Historical Review*, 4 (1907), 40–8, is mainly a précis of the presbytery records from May and June 1658 (Source 2 below). The fullest narrative of the panic is by P. G. Maxwell-Stuart, *Abundance of Witches: The Great Scottish Witch-Hunt* (Stroud, 2005), 91–107, 203; this is based on the records of the presbytery and of the justiciary court (the sources numbered 2–5 and 7–8 below). The case is used to make a number of points about magical healing in Joyce Miller, 'Cantrips and Carlins: Magic, Medicine and Society in the Presbyteries of Haddington and Stirling, 1600–1688' (University of Stirling PhD thesis, 1999), 172–8 and *passim*. This too uses the presbytery and justiciary court records. One article uses *only* Source 6 to make illustrative points about women and witch-hunting: Julian Goodare, 'Women and the Witch-Hunt in Scotland', *Social History*, 23 (1998), 288–308.

early on, and the panic also drew in the Stirling burgh authorities and even the military officers in Stirling Castle.

The panic occurred in two phases, broadly May to August 1658 and November 1658 to March 1659. The initial suspect, whose confessions seem to have launched the panic, was Margaret Douchall. She was arrested and interrogated by local authorities in Alloa in early May 1658. She confessed to harming others, to making a pact with the Devil, and to attending several meetings with the Devil and six other witches. Four of these, Janet Black, Bessie Paton, Katherine Rainie and Margaret Taylor, were rapidly arrested and confessed in their turn. It is not clear why the other two, Elizabeth Black and Margaret Dempsterton, were not arrested immediately, but we shall see that Elizabeth Black was prosecuted later. Douchall herself died in prison soon after her confessions; she is first mentioned as having died on 10 June. She seems to have been subjected to sleep deprivation, and the other suspects made allegations of torture; this will be discussed below.

This first phase may have had roots further afield. Bessie Paton mentioned Sybilla Drummond, a witch from Dunblane, as having already been executed at some date before 26 June 1658. Drummond's relationship to the Alloa witches is not clear; either or both may have accused the other. Drummond's case may well have preceded Douchall's, in which case we might see the panic as initially spreading from Dunblane to Alloa – perhaps via the town of Stirling, which lay between the two. At any rate, once the evidence had been gathered, the four chief suspects who were still alive at this point, Janet Black, Bessie Paton, Katherine Rainie and Margaret Taylor, were tried in the central justiciary court in Edinburgh on 3 August. They were all found guilty and ordered to be executed on the 11th. This brought the first phase of the panic to an end.

By now, however, the prosecutors had acquired various names of further alleged witches, and had heard various stories about them. Fourteen further names had been given in the confessions of the first phase: Elizabeth (or Elspeth) Black, Katherine Black, Elizabeth (or Elspeth) Crockett, Margaret Dempsterton, Barbara Erskine, Bessie Harlaw, James Hudston, Katherine Kay, James Kirk, Janet Mason, Janet Miller (in Tullibody), Janet Paterson, Janet Reid and Katherine Wightman. For some of these suspects, the prosecutors had a good deal of information.

The second phase of the panic, therefore, began by pursuing some of these suspects. Five prominent names gradually emerged from among the fourteen suspects who had been named in May: Elizabeth Black, Katherine Black, Elizabeth Crockett, Barbara Erskine and James Kirk. Two more of the fourteen, Bessie Harlaw and Janet Reid, were mentioned briefly in the dossier of March 1659 that provides much of the evidence for this phase (Source 6 below), but do not seem to have been brought to trial. One entirely new Alloa suspect emerged in the second phase: Marie Cunningham, who may or may not be the same person as the late Marion Cunningham, also named in the dossier though not as a witch. Again, there is no record of her having been brought to trial.

The chronology of the second phase is hard to reconstruct. On 15 December 1658, Katherine Black had been in prison for over three months, while Elizabeth Black had been in prison for over eighteen weeks at about the same date (Source 5). This might well date their arrests to early September and early August respectively. Elizabeth Crockett was interrogated at about the same time, on 6 September, but her confession was brief and indecisive (Source 6). Thereafter the prosecutors seem to have slackened their efforts; there was no more recorded action until 15 November, when several witnesses testified against Elizabeth Black, Katherine Black, Elizabeth Crockett and James Kirk. The pace then intensified with the interrogation of Barbara Erskine on 14 March 1659; she poured out a great deal of evidence, not only against herself but also against these other four suspects. These then were the five suspects from the Alloa area whose cases went all the way to trial in the second phase.

In the meantime, in early 1659, the panic spread to Stirling and beyond. Accusations in the town of Stirling were first recorded on 13 January, when Magdalen Blair was accused of having bewitched Helen Ker to death. The prosecution initiative seems to have been taken by the minister of Stirling, Matthias Simson, who had been involved in the first phase of the Alloa panic and now discovered cases in his own parish. The secular authorities of the burgh, the provost, bailies and burgh clerk, were also active. They gathered evidence, not only against Blair, but also against Isobel Bennett and Bessie Stevenson. Unlike the Alloa investigators, the Stirling investigators do not seem to have used torture or to have sought the demonic confessions that torture would have elicited. All three of the Stirling suspects were magical practitioners, and the investigators mainly asked them about their practices. They also gathered evidence from neighbours about malefice.

Then, at some point before March 1659, the military authorities in Stirling Castle also moved into action against witches. This investigation seems to have been led by Colonel Thomas Read, the English military governor of Stirling. The investigation focused, not on the town, but on Kippen, a rural parish some distance to the west. The fact that Kippen was part of the presbytery of Dunblane, not the presbytery of Stirling, may indicate that it was not the church which brought the Kippen witches to the military officers' attention. Nevertheless, the Kippen witch-hunt was soon being recorded alongside the ongoing Alloa and Stirling witch-hunts.

The Kippen investigators began with Isobel Keir, a well-known magical practitioner who had an existing reputation for witchcraft. They also pulled in three more suspects from that parish, Margaret Gourlay, Margaret Harvie and Janet Miller.[2] These three seem to have been named by Keir's accusers; all four had some kind of association with each other. Keir's daughters Christian Ritchie and Elizabeth Ritchie were also named as having been involved in some of her alleged malefices, but there was no explicit statement that they were suspected of witchcraft. Christian would even be summoned to testify against her mother.

Colonel Read and his fellow-officers thus summoned to Stirling, not only the suspects from Kippen, but also a large number of witnesses. The beginning of their investigation cannot be dated precisely, but there is one clue. Although some of the witnesses' stories about Isobel Keir went back many years, one accusation against her narrated an episode of 15 December 1658, showing that she had not yet been formally accused at that date. The outcome was a dossier of evidence against the four suspects – particularly against Isobel Keir – dated 16 March. This dossier (part of Source 6 below) has less against Margaret Gourlay, Margaret Harvie and Janet Miller; evidence against them was gathered separately (Source 5). As with the Stirling investigation, the Kippen investigation did not use torture, and focused on neighbours' evidence of malefice and suspects' own statements about their magical practices – though Janet Miller's evidence had an ambiguous character, as we shall see.

Neither the Stirling town witches nor the Kippen witches seem to have had personal connections, either with each other, or with the Alloa witches. Rather, it was the prosecutors who connected the three groups. The connection appears in two ways. Much of the Kippen evidence appears in the same March 1659 dossier as the main evidence against the second-phase Alloa witches; and the suspects from all three places were all tried together in the same court.

Thus we come to the trials of the second phase. The Stirling military authorities completed their investigations on 16 March, while the justices of the peace in Alloa completed theirs on 14 March. After their evidence had been gathered, twelve witchcraft suspects were brought to trial before a circuit court – a travelling version of the justiciary court – in Stirling on 22 and 23 March. The accused persons were divided into three groups, with three separate local assizes, for the Stirling, Alloa and Kippen witches. All three groups were tried before just one panel of judges, who passed sentences at the very end.

The outcomes were severe, but less severe than in the first phase. Barbara Erskine, Isobel Keir and Bessie Stevenson were convicted and executed – one execution from each of the three groups. Elizabeth Black, Katherine Black and Elizabeth Crockett were convicted by the Alloa assize, but, unusually,

[2] This Janet Miller, in Kippen, should be distinguished from Janet Miller in Tullibody, who had been named in the first phase of the panic but was never brought to trial. A third Janet Miller, the wife of Andrew Fairlie in Arnprior, was not an accused witch but a witness against Isobel Keir.

the judges sentenced them to banishment from the country rather than execution. Magdalen Blair, Margaret Gourlay, Margaret Harvie, James Kirk and Janet Miller were acquitted, though Blair and Kirk, who had both been suspected as magical practitioners, were ordered to find caution for future good behaviour; Blair and Gourlay were also ordered to be whipped. Isobel Bennett was acquitted of witchcraft but convicted of charming, and also sentenced to be whipped. Overall, then, the Stirling assize acquitted two out of its three witchcraft suspects, the Alloa assize acquitted one out of five, and the Kippen assize acquitted three out of four. This was a much lower conviction rate, and an even lower execution rate, than in the first phase, when all the suspects brought to trial had been convicted and executed. There were arguments in court, and protests afterwards, when the Alloa assize convicted some of the suspects on the basis of evidence that the judges had ordered them to ignore. This was probably why the judges passed non-capital sentences on three of the witches.

These three witches, Elizabeth Black, Katherine Black and Elizabeth Crockett, were not in fact banished. The judges had probably intended them to be transported to the English colonies in America – a voyage that might take some time to arrange. National events may have distracted the authorities thereafter: the collapse of the Protectorate government later in 1659, and the restoration of the monarchy in 1660. The three women were still in prison in the summer of 1661, when they petitioned the privy council, asking for a retrial and to be liberated on caution in the meantime. The council ordered Alexander Colville and John Cunningham, the justice deputes, to investigate. On 5 July they recommended a retrial, as the previous proceedings had contained 'materiall errors'. The council approved this recommendation on 2 August, adding that the trial should take place before 1 September.[3] The three prisoners petitioned again in November 1661, as no trial date had been set. This time the privy council ordered that the trial should take place before 1 January 1662.[4] This was at the height of the national panic of 1661–2, when witches were being executed in large numbers.[5] However, the final documents below show that the justice deputes were given the alternative option of liberating the women on caution – an option that they took up, presumably because they had no intention of reopening the prosecutions. They had to find caution to appear before the court if summoned, but this was probably a formality; if the authorities had seriously intended to prosecute them, they would have kept them in prison. Thus, after three years in prison, these three women were finally liberated.

3 *RPC*, 3rd ser., i, 26.

4 *RPC*, 3rd ser., i, 75.

5 Brian P. Levack, 'The great Scottish witch-hunt of 1661–2', in his *Witch-Hunting in Scotland: Law, Politics and Religion* (New York, 2008), 81–97.

The prosecutors

Who was behind the prosecutions overall? No single individual took the lead, and indeed the documents below are remarkable for the large and diverse range of interrogators and other investigators they name as co-operating in the prosecutions. Still, it may help to highlight a few individuals here, either because they come up repeatedly or because of their prominence among the local elite generally. The involvement of different local authorities can also be indicated.

The first name to mention is Thomas Mitchell of Coldon. He had bought most of the town of Alloa in 1653.[6] He was also a ruling elder in the parish of Alloa. The witches were accused of having killed two of his children – an episode to which the interrogators, including Mitchell himself, returned again and again. Further research might reveal more about Mitchell's role in the governing of the parish and the town – the extent to which other interrogators were beholden to him personally, for instance.

The earliest investigators, listed in Source 1, seem to have been local men from the secular administration; a constable is named but no minister, for instance. On the other hand, we are told in Source 2 that Margaret Douchall was first denounced to the parish minister by the elders, who then brought in the constables to arrest her. It may not be possible to establish a secure chronology for these events.[7]

In the church, Matthias Simson, minister of Stirling, and John Craigengelt younger, minister of Dollar, became active in the early investigations.[8] They acted on behalf of the presbytery, but the presbytery may well have chosen them for their commitment. Simson reappeared when the second phase of the panic spread to Stirling itself. However, by March 1659 both ministers were being cautious, pointing out inconsistencies in Margaret Douchall's initial testimony (Source 6, section IV). If this represents a change of mind, there may be a broader pattern of growing caution. For instance, Alloa men John Arthur and Henry Towart were among the witnesses to the initial

6 *RMS*, x, no. 81. Coldon was in Kinross-shire, but Mitchell clearly lived in Alloa at the time of the panic, and had probably done so even before he bought Coldon in 1649: *RMS*, xi, no. 89.

7 Source 2 seems to say that Douchall was first summoned before the kirk session on 11 May, and was later arrested and imprisoned. Source 1, by contrast, dates her initial confession to 10 May, and implies that she was already in prison at that point. Neither of these documents seems actually to have been written until June.

8 Alloa's parish minister was John Craigengelt elder (*c.*1595–1664); he had been minister of the united parishes of Alloa and Tullibody since 1626. He was present on 19 May 1658 at the initial presbytery meeting that discussed the witchcraft accusations. However, at the next meeting he was noted to be sick, and he seems to drop out of the records thereafter (Source 2). His son continued to be involved; this was John Craigengelt younger (1629–59), minister of Dollar, who had previously (until 1656) been schoolmaster of Alloa. See Hew Scott (ed.), *Fasti Ecclesiae Scoticanae*, 7 vols. (2nd edn., Edinburgh, 1915–), iv, Presbytery of Stirling, pp. 292, 306.

confessions in June 1658, but by December they were testifying to Elizabeth Black's illness in an effort to delay her prosecution. Craigengelt, too, supported them in this effort.

The justices of the peace of Clackmannanshire became involved early on, and seem to have become even more prominent during the second phase of the panic. The largest component of the March 1659 dossier below, which as we shall see comprised much of the evidence for the second phase, comes from them. And when Elizabeth Black and Katherine Black submit petitions in this phase, it is the justices of the peace who are keeping them imprisoned, in the tolbooth of Alloa itself. These justices were Harry Bruce of Clackmannan, Robert Bruce of Kennett, Sir Charles Erskine of Alva, James Holburne of Menstrie and Robert Meldrum of Tullibody. Erskine was a younger brother of John Erskine, fourth earl of Mar, the principal local magnate. It was from Erskine's father, the third earl, that Thomas Mitchell had bought Alloa in 1653. Further research could be carried out on these men and their connections. Overall, the panic seems to have been a general one, commanding broad support among the local elites, both clerical and secular. The secular authorities, such as the justices of the peace, may have taken more of a lead, but the interlocking nature of local elites meant that church and secular authorities were probably not two different groups.

Interrogations and demonology

The Alloa authorities placed heavy pressure on the suspects to obtain confessions. The constables kept Douchall 'in closs prison and ane guard night and day attending her', which indicates that she was subjected to sleep deprivation, and she confessed 'at last' after numerous visits from the minister and elders (Source 2). Her death in prison, within a month of her arrest or less, may be indicative of further ill-treatment.

Specific allegations of actual torture were recorded on 23 June. Margaret Taylor named her torturers as John Thomson, Thomas Kidston and John Kidston in Cambus; Katherine Rainie named her torturers as David Vertie, John Short and Robert Archibald; Bessie Paton named her torturers as David Vertie, James MacNair and James Nicoll. The women gave slightly different accounts of what had been done to them, and indeed there seem to have been three separate episodes. Burning with hot stones featured in all three accounts. Taylor said that she had been made to stand on a high stool while two men burned her feet, while Paton said that the burns on her legs had still not healed (Source 2). On 19 July, five men were summoned to deny that they had tortured these three witches: John Thomson baxter in Alloa, Thomas Kidston and John Kidston in Cambus, James MacNair and James Nicoll (Source 3). The fact that they denied the torture on oath is noteworthy, and the women's stories may not be entirely true. However, it is hardly likely that their formulaic confessions to demonic witchcraft had been given entirely voluntarily, so the men's denials do not carry complete conviction either. It might be noted that three of the alleged torturers, those named by Katherine Rainie, were not summoned. Of these three, David Vertie may well have been related to Bessie Vertie, one of the alleged victims of Margaret Douchall's malefice, and to John Vertie, one of the members of the assize that convicted these tortured witches on 3 August. In court on that day, Margaret Taylor named another alleged torturer, Andrew Thomson, who was present as a witness, and had previously been recorded in Source 1 as one of the interrogators.

There are other indications of pressure by the interrogators to obtain specific pieces of information. Bessie Paton tried to retract most of her confession, saying that 'some bade her say quhat sche haid said that the rest might therby be induced to confess'. She added that she had been carried in spirit in her sleep, evidently hoping that the interrogators would agree that this was not witchcraft. Similarly, Margaret Taylor said that she had spoken about one point in her confession because 'James Lindsey bade her say it and promeist her shelter for her lyfe to say so' (Source 2). The intensity of the prosecution's efforts also appears in the fact that several of the suspects were pricked for the Devil's mark, apparently by a professional witch-pricker. We learn little about the pricking process itself, but various locations of the marks on the witches' bodies are noted.

The confessions themselves reveal something of the way in which questioning was carried out, and the different ways in which suspects could respond. Barbara Erskine and Elizabeth Crockett, whose confessions are prominent in the March 1659 dossier (Source 6), provide contrasting responses, and it is hard to know which one to be more sorry for. Erskine initially tried to drown herself when she was accused, so she must have been highly distressed. However, once in the interrogators' hands she became articulate and co-operative, accusing others in a desperate attempt to retain the interrogators' approval for herself. She can be seen using folkloric story-telling motifs in order to create her stories, in particular the idea of the limited powers of the witch against someone of strong faith. Having used this to create one story, she then used it again in a context where it was clearly illogical.

Crockett reacted differently to the pressures of imprisonment, interrogation and probable torture. Instead of becoming articulate, she descended into incoherence. Both of her confessions were brief and confused, and she had to be guided with leading questions. The basis of her confession was evidently an episode of sleep paralysis, a sleep disorder in which the experient feels an anomalous and sometimes terrifying presence in the room.[9] Having been persuaded to convert this experience into an episode of having had sex with

[9] Margaret Dudley and Julian Goodare, 'Outside In or Inside Out: Sleep Paralysis and Scottish Witchcraft', in Julian Goodare (ed.), *Scottish Witches and Witch-Hunters* (Basingstoke, 2013), 121–39.

the Devil, Crockett then said that 'he wes nether cold nor hott' – a detail evidently responding to an interrogator asking 'Was the Devil's body cold?' The correct answer to this question was 'Yes', since the Devil was thought to have no blood and thus no body heat; but the interrogators seem to have been satisfied with Crockett's vague reply. Questioned next about the Devil's mark, she was recorded as saying 'shoe knew not whether the Devill gave hir ane mark or not that night he lay with hir, but if it wer found wpon hir, shoe should be content to die the death of a witch'. This was clearly the interrogators' way of recording the following conversation:

Q. Did the Devil give you a mark that night when he lay with you?

A. I know not.

Q. If a mark is found on you, will you be content to die the death of a witch?

A. Yes.

It will be seen here that it is the interrogators who do most of the talking. They go on to ask another question about the Devil's mark, eliciting the recorded answer that 'if shoe had the Devills mark it was on hir privie member'; this too is probably a response to a leading question in which Crockett says no more than 'Yes'. Her answer makes little sense when set beside her earlier statement that she did not know whether she had a mark. Quite possibly many other witches' confessions besides Crockett's were initially incoherent, but hers stands out because the interrogators left it at that, rather than continuing until a coherent story was constructed. They may have tried to tidy it up – they interrogated her twice, on 6 September and again on 14 March – but Crockett remained incoherent and confused.

The interrogators gathered intriguingly ambiguous testimony from Janet Miller in Kippen, a young, unmarried woman – 'ane young damsell'.[10] Was she a witch, or was she accusing others of witchcraft? She related that she visited Margaret Gourlay's house one night and found her, Margaret Harvie and Isobel Keir sitting together with a black man (the Devil was implied). Gourlay offered Miller some of the food that they were eating, but she refused it. In another story, Miller told of how she had avoided the black man and committed herself to God instead. The record nevertheless stated that Miller herself was 'suspect of witchcraft', so she seems to have been poised between the status of a guilty witch and that of an innocent person who had inadvertently encountered some witches. In this she may be compared with Elizabeth Anderson, a young woman in the later Bargarran case who was originally suspected of witchcraft, and who testified to having attended witches' meetings, but who was converted into a prosecution witness.[11] Miller's prosecution, unlike Anderson's, went all the way to trial, but she was acquitted.

10 This description of her comes from 'Names of the Witches, 1658', edited above in the present volume.

11 See 'Bargarran Witches, Renfrewshire, 1697', edited below in the present volume.

From the start, the interrogators were well aware of the standard features of demonology expected from a confessing witch. The time and place of the first meeting with the Devil, what he looked like on that occasion, the renunciation of baptism, his having sex with the witch and his body being cold (all the detailed confessions are from women), his giving the witch a mark, and his promises to the witch about their relationship: all these motifs come up repeatedly.

There is also a good deal of popular demonology in the confessions: the Devil's riding of the witches, his interest in unusual sexual positions, his promise that a witch should not be burned, his asking the witch what malefice she wanted to inflict, his calling a roll of attendance at meetings, his observance of social hierarchy by keeping a gentlewoman next to him, his treating the demonic pact like a contract of employment, and so on. The whistle played by James Kirk at a witches' meeting can be heard only by those at the meeting, according to Barbara Erskine. Witches can overhear anything that anyone says about them on a Friday, according to Elizabeth Black. Katherine Black gifts her newborn daughter to the Devil, for which he rewards her with many men's and women's goods, according to Bessie Paton. Margaret Taylor has the remarkable idea that the witches speak a special language among themselves which they can understand only at meetings with the Devil. All this is congruent with learned demonology, but not prominent in it; it seems to arise more from folkloric ideas about the Devil. Taylor's statement that Janet Miller in Tullibody had met the Devil 'and yet the said Jonet knew not that sche wes ane witch' reveals a conception of involuntary witchcraft that is alien to learned demonology.

One folkloric feature of the Devil in these confessions is that he usually remains in the background and rarely wields much power. In Katherine Rainie's confession, the Devil and the witches all flee in different directions when their meeting is interrupted by James Morris. The interrogators do not seem to have summoned Morris to confirm this. According to Rainie, the witches' parting words at another meeting are 'Our god be with yow' – yet in learned demonology the Devil is never a 'god'. This meeting is a notably festive one, with the witches singing, dancing and holding hands. We even hear the name of a popular song: 'Besse Paton led the ring and sang Walli Fa our Bridgarme'. Janet Black shows more interest in Paton's power than in the Devil's power: 'scho said that Besse Paton was a great witch and had moir strenth in hir fingar nor scho had in all hir bodie'.

Shape-shifting was a theme in which popular and learned demonic ideas could interact. The confessions tell of various instances of shape-shifting, none of which seem dramatic. Witches go over a dyke in the shape of cats, although shape-shifting hardly seems necessary to achieve this feat. Some witches enter a byre through a hole in the door, but others seem to have entered in human shape. The mention of dragons ('corbies and dragones') is a rare appearance of belief in a magical creature. Shape-shifting appears mainly in the confessions, but there are also instances of it in witness testimony. Donald Ferguson sees Janet Black in the form of a sow that follows him home, while Bessie Miller sees unnatural cats sitting ominously on an ale vat before disaster strikes. Most of this seems to be popular demonology. Some of the interrogators ask Margaret Douchall to explain her shape-shifting into the form of a corbie (raven or crow), but neither their question nor her answer addresses the key intellectual issue of whether flight takes place bodily or in spirit.[12]

Malefice

Many stories of malefice are told and retold, throughout the suspects' confessions and throughout the witnesses' testimony. This gives rise to an important distinction. The witnesses, with hardly any exceptions, speak of instances of harm done to themselves, and attribute this harm to a specific named witch – often someone with whom they have quarrelled. The confessions, by contrast, speak mainly of conspiratorial malefice by groups of witches, not all of which is directed against specific individual victims. Conspiratorial, collective malefice was a less common idea than individual malefice – but, from the very start, the Alloa investigators thought of witchcraft as conspiratorial. They recorded numerous stories of individual malefice, but witches' meetings and collective malefice appeared at the beginning of Margaret Douchall's first confession, and retained their prominence throughout the panic.

One important early instance of collective malefice was the sinking of a ferryboat at Blackgrange, in which five men drowned. This tragedy was a live event in the community's consciousness; there was no need to summon witnesses to prove that it had happened. Bessie Paton, or her interrogators, attached the sinking to one of the witches' meetings, saying that Barbara Erskine had been present. The story was soon elaborated, with Janet Black confessing that the witches had taken the form of corbies. The prosecutors carefully collated these details, which all appeared in Paton's dittay.

Social hierarchy appears in various community interactions, and even among the witches themselves. Katherine Black was Margaret Taylor's employer, for instance. Social hierarchy is also important when the witches commit malefices against members of the elite. One such malefice was the drowning of the earl of Mar's coal mines. Alloa was a coal-mining area, and Margaret Douchall herself was a coal-bearer. Malefices against the elite seem to have been particularly likely to be thought to be collective: it would take more than one witch to strike at an earl. It might be added that, although

12 Cf. Julian Goodare, 'Witches' Flight in Scottish Demonology', in Julian Goodare, Rita Voltmer and Liv Helene Willumsen (eds.), *Demonology and Witch-Hunting in Early Modern Europe* (London, 2020), 147–67.

Douchall gave poverty as her motive for making the demonic pact, this may have been a response to a leading question. It is unlikely that she was really impoverished; one of her neighbourhood altercations concerned a loan of ten merks that she had made. She remains an enigma, despite her talkativeness or even perhaps because of it. She seems to have thought of herself as to some extent a victim of others' witchcraft.

One key act of malefice against the elite, already mentioned above, was the bewitching to death of two of the children of Thomas Mitchell of Coldon, in December 1657. This event comes up again and again in the confessions, with an effort to establish the details of what happened, and the participation of a number of witches. This bewitching, like several of the other malefices, was never thought of as the act of an isolated witch. The interrogators made no effort to establish a motive, as they often did for individual malefices; no prior quarrel or grievance was suggested. The main dittay of August 1658 accused the witches of 'haveing conceaved ane crewall and devlish hatred against Thomas Mitchell off Coudoune', but gave no reason for such hatred. We gather that conspiratorial witches are simply 'crewall and devlish'. The dittay repeated a similar phrase for all the other collective malefices. Yet when it went on to accuse Bessie Paton of two individual malefices, it did attribute specific motives to her.

There were alarming hints that members of the elite had joined the witch conspiracy. Margaret Douchall, in her second recorded confession, declared ominously that 'if they sould tak and burne her there sould better wyves in Alloway nor herself be burnt with her' (Source 2). The interrogators asked her for the names of these women, but did not pursue the question when she drifted away from the point. They did however become interested in another gentlewoman who appeared in several early confessions. This was an incognito woman with a black 'pock' – a hanging appendage to a hat – which disguised her, hiding her face. The interrogators gathered further details of this woman's appearance, and finally elicited a name for her: Katherine Kay.[13] However, they did not try to arrest her, and we may even wonder whether the woman with the black pock was a real person. She reappeared in the second phase of the panic, when Barbara Erskine said that Katherine Black might know who

[13] A Katherine Kay in the parish of Newburgh, northern Fife, was suspected of witchcraft in 1653 and 1655. On the former occasion the charges were not pursued, and on the latter she was made to do penance for having cursed the minister. Some details of apparent curses and reconciliation rituals were noted. She acted as a wet-nurse, so presumably had borne a child, but no husband was mentioned. See John Ewart Simpkins (ed.), *County Folk-Lore: Printed Extracts nos. IX, X, XI: Examples of Printed Folk-Lore Concerning Fife, with some Notes on Clackmannan and Kinross-shires* (Folk-lore Society: County Folk-Lore, vol. 7; London, 1914), 98–9. Newburgh was over 40km from Alloa, and the Alloa 'woman with the black pock' was thought of as a gentlewoman, while Katherine Kay in Newburgh was clearly no gentlewoman. Still, perhaps the witches' use of the name was based on something that they had heard from Newburgh.

she was; the identification with Katherine Kay had been dropped or forgotten. A second incognito gentlewoman, described as the woman with the bonny white coat or the gross woman with the white coat, remained anonymous throughout (there was a hint that she was Elizabeth Black, but this was not taken up). Both of these incognito gentlewomen seem to play similar roles in the confessions. The idea that a group of ordinary women might be joined by a gentlewoman in disguise may have been a folkloric motif.

Not all the evidence supported the prosecution, and contradictory voices were raised. The witnesses to the witchcraft of Magdalen Blair disagreed about a past conversation in which Blair might have implied that she had caused harm to Helen Ferguson. Blair herself offered a third version of the conversation. William Lindsay's testimony about the loss of his household's ale brewing offers a rare insight into how people thought about natural and unnatural events. His wife and servant had previously testified that the contents of the ale vat had vanished unaccountably through Katherine Black's witchcraft. Lindsay, however, explained that he had searched the brewhouse with a candle, finding a hole in the vat and a drainage channel down which the liquid had flowed (Source 5).

Vengeful fire-raising appeared repeatedly in Janet Miller's testimony. Arson was a rare but fearful crime. Although it could be thought of as a women's crime, arson was usually considered separate from witchcraft – but Miller's stories seem to conflate the two (Sources 5 and 6). Perhaps Miller herself was the arsonist, but she may have been a fantasist. Her stories mainly accused Margaret Gourlay, and the judges initially ordered both Miller and Gourlay to be banished for fire-raising, but they changed their minds (Source 7).

The documents reveal various episodes of healing and other magical practice, particularly concerning Isobel Keir (Source 6). The 'charms' of Bessie Stevenson, Isobel Bennett and Magdalen Blair are arranged under headings of the diseases that they cure, almost in the way that one might find them in a book of medicinal recipes (Source 5). The university graduate James Cunningham related a detailed story, full of oral speech, of his attempts to obtain healing from Elizabeth Black and her husband. Black advised him that he had been bewitched by Marie Cunningham and told him how he could break the spell that she had cast (Source 6). Here and elsewhere, magical practice extended into the field of unwitching.

The documents and their editing

The edition below brings together numerous documents from four different archives. Together they provide a detailed picture, first of the pre-trial investigations, then of the two sets of trials themselves, and finally of the aftermath in 1661. Here some notes may be given of the eight individually numbered '*Sources*' into which the documents have been arranged.

Chronologically, the earliest document is *Source 1*: a note of the confessions of Margaret Douchall and other witches, dated 10 June 1658 but referring back to events in May. Presumably rough notes were made of the confessions at the time, and written up later. The interrogators seem to be local Alloa men, including a constable. There is no obvious involvement from the church, and it may have been the local secular authorities who sparked off the panic. The document does not specify what prompted Douchall's arrest. Within the first few sentences we are already being told, not only of charming that she had carried out, and not only of malefices that she had committed, but also of her coven – a rare appearance of this word – and of meetings with the Devil.

The presbytery of Stirling soon heard of what was going on, and *Source 2* consists of the relevant passages from the presbytery minutes. They co-ordinated the gathering of more evidence during the first phase of the panic, and this source thus contains more confessions and other evidence. Again, some of the confessions are recorded retrospectively. Several later sources also refer back to the interrogators' memories of these early confessions. In the presbytery record, we find the ministers working, not just with the Alloa townsmen who may have begun the investigation, but also with the justices of the peace; the early involvement of the kirk session is also mentioned. The source concludes in late June with the presbytery deciding to approach the higher secular authorities to arrange a criminal trial.

The panic thus moved to the criminal courts. *Source 3* consists of loose papers from the 'process papers' of the justiciary court – papers that are additional to the main series of minutes and court books. These mostly come from July 1658. They include more confessions of suspects, a note about alleged torture (discussed above), and a note about summoning the members of the assize for the trials of the first phase. The formal record of these trials in the justiciary court, in Edinburgh on 3 August 1658, constitutes *Source 4*. This includes a composite dittay that recapitulates some of the key charges against the witches, plus the guilty verdicts and death sentences.

With *Source 5* we enter the second phase of the panic. This consists of more process papers from the justiciary court. Again, this includes confessions, but there is a wider range of types of document than before. Some of the confessions come from the new Stirling group of suspects rather than from Alloa itself. Opposition to the trials also appears; there are several petitions and other documents in favour of Elizabeth Black and Katherine Black.[14] It might be added here that the process papers are by their nature miscellaneous in character, and have never been fully catalogued, item by item; they are thus hard to search. The edition below cannot guarantee to have found every document concerning the panic, but it is hoped that most of them are included.[15]

14 These two women may well have been related to each other, and perhaps to Janet Black too, but the documents never state this explicitly.

15 One document not included below is a bundle labelled 'Stirling Court 1659 (witchcraft)' in NRS, JC26/26, which was 'unfit for production' when the volume was being edited, but was conserved and became available at proof stage. It is a roll with witness lists, dittays of Bessie Stevenson, Isobel Bennett, Magdalen Blair and Katherine Black, and summary

The dossier of March 1659, already discussed above, forms *Source 6*. Like *Source 5*, it is a collection of pre-trial papers for the second phase of the panic. Unlike *Source 5*, though, it is a large single item that requires analysis as a unit. The dossier has been assembled from four unequally-sized components, editorially numbered *Sections I–IV* in the edition of the text below. Each of the sections began as a separate document, but they have been bound together, probably at the time.

To take each section individually: *Section I* is a letter of 28 June 1658. It belongs to the first phase of the panic, and all the witches mentioned in it were already dead when the dossier was compiled, but the compilers presumably thought that it was useful background information. *Section II*, the longest and most complicated, is a booklet compiling evidence of various kinds, with various dates, against Elizabeth Black, Katherine Black, Elizabeth Crockett, Barbara Erskine and James Kirk. *Section III* is a booklet about the Kippen investigations. It mostly contains detailed witnesses' statements against just one suspect, Isobel Keir, but one section of it deals also with three further suspects, Margaret Gourlay, Margaret Harvie and Janet Miller. Finally, *Section IV* returns to Alloa itself, being a posthumous record of statements by Margaret Douchall against Elizabeth Black, framed with the evident intention of discrediting Douchall's testimony. It is dated at Stirling, 22 March 1659, the same day that the trials of the accused witches opened in that town.

It may be helpful to supplement the above summary of the dossier with a more detailed breakdown of the contents of each section. This breakdown (with editorial numbers) is as follows:

Section I. Letter of 28 June 1658

1. Letter to the commissioners for justice about Margaret Douchall, Margaret Taylor, Bessie Paton, Janet Black and Katherine Rainie, 28 June 1658 (fo. 1r.)

Section II. Evidence against Barbara Erskine, Elizabeth Crockett, James Kirk, Katherine Black and Elizabeth Black

2. Confession of Barbara Erskine, Alloa, 14 March 1659 (fo. 4r.–4v.)
3. Witnesses' statements against Elizabeth Crockett, Alloa, 15 November 1658 (fo. 5r.)
4. Confession of Elizabeth Crockett, Alloa, 14 March 1659 (fo. 5r.)
5. Confession of Elizabeth Crockett, Alloa, 6 September 1658 (fo. 5v.)
6. Witnesses' statements against James Kirk, Alloa, 15 November 1658 (fo. 6r.)
7. Statements of Barbara Erskine against James Kirk, Alloa, 14 March 1659 (fo. 6r.)
8. Confession of James Kirk, Clackmannan, 19 March 1659 (fo. 6r.)
9. Witnesses' statements against Katherine Black, Alloa, 15 November 1658 (fo. 7r.–7v.)

dittays of eight others. We hope to include it as an appendix to the companion volume to the present one: Julian Goodare (ed.), Scottish Witchcraft Narratives and Tracts.

10. Witnesses' statements against Katherine Black, Alloa, 14 March 1659 (fos. 7v.–8r.)
11. Statements by Barbara Erskine and Margaret Taylor against Katherine Black, Alloa, undated (fo. 8r.)
12. Witnesses' statements against Elizabeth Black, Alloa, 15 November 1658 (fo. 8v.)
13. Witnesses' statements against Elizabeth Black, Alloa, 14 March 1659 (fos. 8v.–9v.)
14. Posthumous record of statements by Bessie Paton against Elizabeth Black, Alloa, undated (fo. 9v.)

Section III. Evidence against Isobel Keir

15. Witnesses' statements against Isobel Keir, Stirling, 16 March 1659 (fos. 10r.–14v.)
16. The above includes statements by Janet Miller, witchcraft suspect, against Isobel Keir, Margaret Gourlay and Margaret Harvie (fo. 12v.)

Section IV. Testimony concerning Margaret Douchall and Elizabeth Black

17. Posthumous record of statements by Margaret Douchall against Elizabeth Black, Stirling, 22 March 1659 (fos. 15r.–16v.).

Within this broad framework there are occasional overlaps and interpolations. On fo. 5v. there is an 'X' which provides a cross-reference to Elizabeth Crockett's other confession.

Thus, apart from the introductory letter, the dossier comprises three main types of document:

1. Confessions by witchcraft suspects about their own witchcraft.
2. Statements by innocent neighbours about someone else's witchcraft (typically saying that a given witchcraft suspect had harmed them).
3. Statements by witchcraft suspects about someone else's witchcraft.

Type 1 sometimes overlaps with type 3, when a confession also mentions other witches. However, some statements by witchcraft suspects are entirely about other witches, and these seem distinct. The document even concludes with an unusual fourth type:

4. Statements by witchcraft suspects about someone else's witchcraft, which the interrogators disbelieved.

This arose when several of those who had interrogated Margaret Douchall (who had died between 11 May and 10 June 1658) recalled on 22 March 1659 that Douchall had made statements about Elizabeth Black's alleged witchcraft that they believed had been made out of malice.

Source 7 is the minutes of the trials of the second phase – those of 22 and 23 March 1659 in Stirling. The minutes do not preserve everything; the dittays that would have given details of the accusations are absent, and only two of the three local assizes are listed. But there are brief notes of much of what happened in court. Numerous witnesses were brought in to testify to specific points, some of which seem to be additional to the points made in the pre-trial documents. Most of the witnesses adhered to their previous testimony, but a few of them retracted it in whole or in part. The accused persons' replies to the accusations were summarised, as were their comments on their own previous confessions. Thus Elizabeth Crockett, given another opportunity to speak about the uncanny nocturnal encounter that formed the main evidence against her, at last found herself able to say categorically that the Devil had had nothing to do with it, and to have this statement recorded. The minutes noted all the verdicts, stating which were unanimous and which were not, and all the sentences. The sentences were all pronounced on the 24th, not without some changes of mind by the judges. Crockett, along with Elizabeth Black and Katherine Black, was convicted only by a majority, which may have influenced the judges' decision to pass non-capital sentences on them. Walter Sword, the chancellor of the assize that decided on these verdicts, had previously been one of the interrogators, with his name appearing repeatedly ever since the first document.

Finally, *Source 8* consists of documents, again from the justiciary court process papers, that come after the trials. The first one is dated 22 March 1659, the same day as the first day of trials, but it was written after the trials of Elizabeth Black and Katherine Black that had occurred on that day, and thus should be read as a post-trial document. The two women petition against unjust trial proceedings and demand a retrial. They allege partiality in the jurors: eight local jurors had voted for conviction, whereas seven jurors who did not know the accused persons had voted for acquittal. Moreover, the jurors had relied on the confessions of previous witches, which the judges had directed them to ignore. As noted above, the two women were not granted a retrial, or at least not at the time, but they escaped execution. Along with Elizabeth Crockett, they remained in prison until 1661. One of their petitions from that date is printed below, along with a warrant to the justice deputes, and the latter's decision to let the three women go free.

TEXTS

Source 1: National Library of Scotland, Edinburgh, Confessions of Margaret Douchall and others, 1658, MS 1909.[16]

[*Endorsed:*] Confessionis, Margret Duchell And utheris Junii 1658.
The Confessiones of Margaret Duchell and uthers witches in Alloway 1658.
1658.[17]

[16] Three sheets, written on one side only. A previous edition of this document has been published: George F. Black (ed.), 'Confessions of Alloa Witches', *The Scottish Antiquary*, 9 (1895), 49–52.

[17] The first two of these endorsements are on the verso of folio 1, and the third on the verso of folio 3. At that point, the words 'Anent McNachtan' have been crossed out.

{*fo. 1r.*} At Alloway the tent Day of Maii 1658 yeiris, The delationis, Dittees, and confessionis of wmquhill Margret Duchall \and/ Margret Tailyeor, Bessie Paton, Jonet Blak and Kathren Renny, and otheris as followis.

In first wmquhill Margret Duchall quho died laitlie in prison, being accused for charming and other great presumptionis of the sin of witchcraft, Did freelie confes hir paction with the Dewill, how he appeared first to hir in the liknes of a man in broun cloathis, and ane blak hat, who desyred hir to be his servant, to quyt God and renunce hir baptisme, all quhich scho granted scho did, as lykwayis scho granted he gawe hir his mark quhich was on hir eye lid, Scho lykwayis granted the death of thrie woman[18] with hir own handis, Scho lykwayis declared that ther was sex woman moir besyd hir self that was in thair cuwing,[19] Whois names scho declared to be, Margret Tailyeor, Besse Paton, *Jonet Blak*, Kathren Renny, *Elspit Blak*,[20] and Margret Demperstoun; Scho lykwayis declared, that scho and thes said woman, was at \ane/ meeting, at the bletching burn abowe Jean Lindsayis yaird, with ane other long las with a blak pok,[21] quhom scho said scho knew not, bot the rest knew hir, And after they war turned all in the liknes of cattis, they went in over Jean Lindsayis yaird dyk and went to Coudonis hous, whair scho declared, that the Dewill being with tham went up the stair first with Margret Tailyeor, Besse Paton and Elspit Blak who had ane pok with som thing[22] in it lyk peas meall, and they strawed[23] it on tuo of Coudons bairnes, quhich scho granted was the death of tham both. Scho lykwayis granted, they altogidder had on[e] meeting to Tullibodie, quhair they kild a child, ane other to Clakmanan, quhair they kild ane other child, ane other meeting to the Grang of Alloway, quhair they kild ane milk kow, ane other to the Bowhous, quhair they kild ane horse and ane kow: Margret Tailyeor[24] being in prison hes confessed hir self to be the servant of the Diwell be paction, quho appeared to hir in the liknes of a young man with gray cloathis and a blew cap, quho desyred hir to renunce her baptisme quhich scho did, and quho gawe hir his mark, as scho confesses in hir secret member, Scho lykwayis confessed that scho was at thair meeting, quhen they destroyed Cowdonis tuo bairnes, and that ther was on[e] thair with ane blak pok with tham, and ane

18 *Sic*. Here and later, 'woman' should be read as 'women'.

19 'cuwing': coven.

20 This name, and several others in the document, have been either underlined or overlined (as indicated here by italics). 'Elspit Blak' has lines both under and over the name.

21 'long las with a blak pok': tall young woman with a black hanging appendage to a hat. ('Pok' can also mean 'bag', but that is not the meaning here.) This woman is often mentioned hereafter, usually anonymously, often as 'the bony las with the blak pok'. She is sometimes identified in Sources 2 and 3 as Katherine Kay.

22 Conjectural restoration of damaged letters.

23 'strawed': scattered.

24 In margin: 'Margret Tailyeor'.

other with ane bony quheit coat,[25] and *Besse Paton, Jonet Blak, Kathren Renny* and Margret Demperstoun: Scho lykwayis confessed that they wer \at/ ane meeting in the Bowhous whair scho hir self was thair with Besse Paton, Jonet Blak and Kathren Renny, quhair they destroyed ane horse and ane kow, and scho declared that Besse Paton yeardit[26] raw flesh and salt wnder the horse stall, Scho lykwayis confessed ane meeting in the *Cuningar*,[27] quhair they war altogidder dancing, to wit, Jonet Paterson in Craigward,[28] Barbara *Erskin in Cambus, Jonnet* Millar in Tullebodie, Besse Paton, Jonet Blak, Kathren Renny, James *Hudston*, And James Kirk[29] who plaid on the quhisle to tham, and that the Diwell was present with tham.

Besse Paton[30] hes not as yit confessed hir paction with the Dewell, Bot scho is delated be Margret Duchall, *Margret* Tailyeor, *Jonet Blak* and *Kathren Renny*, that scho is guiltie of the sin of witchcraft, and that scho hes bein with tham at severall meetingis with the Dewill, and speciallie at the destroying of *Cowdonis bairnes*, Edward Turnoris kow, and at the destroying of William Monteathis horse and kuy,[31] and that scho yeardit raw flesh wnder the stall, quhair newer a beast liwed yit that stood in that place, with many horrible dittes[32] and great presumptionis giwen in against hir: And scho hir self confessed that Margret Tailyeor and the bony las with the blak pok, and Elspit Blak[33] was the thrie that went in that \night/ to Cowdonis hous that the tua bairnes war destroyed, to that token as scho said, that the first bairn that died, ther died ane bitch with him, and the second bairn quhen he died thair died ane cat with him: Scho lykwayis declared that *Kathren Blak*[34] *and Jonnet Reid* was {*fo. 2r.*} as guiltie as hir self, for scho said scho hard *Kathren Blak* say on[e] night to Jonnet Reid quhen they discordit, away common theiff, ye hawe the windingscheittis of all Margret Mastertounis sex bairnes in your kist[35] lyand, and yow was the dead of tham all. Scho lykwayis declared that Barbara Ersken in Cambus, was guiltie lykways for scho was at the casting away of the boat at Blakgrange,[36] quhair ther was fywe men cast away.

25 The woman with the bonny white coat, presumably thought of as another gentlewoman, is mentioned several times hereafter but never seems to be named.
26 'yeardit': buried.
27 The 'Cuningar' (a word meaning 'rabbit-warren') was near the southern edge of the town.
28 Conjectural restoration of damaged letters.
29 In margin: 'J. K.'
30 In margin: 'Besse Paton'.
31 'kuy' (kye): cattle.
32 'dittes' (dittays): accusations.
33 In margin: 'Eliz'.
34 In margin: 'Kat'.
35 'kist': chest.
36 Blackgrange was on the north shore of the Forth, west of Cambus and Tullibody. The sinking of this boat is often mentioned hereafter.

Jonet Blak[37] confessed the meeting with the Diwell among the quhinis[38] as scho went to *Sunisyd*, in the liknes of a dog with a sowis head, who cam hom[e] to hir hous and baid[39] with hir, quhich was ay since the great storm of snaw. Scho confessed severall meetingis with the abowenamed cuwing, confessed all thair names, and lykwayis that ther was ane bony las with ane blak pok with tham that went ay nixt the Diwell with Margret Tailyeor, and that scho was with tham at the destroying of Coudonis bairnes, quhair the Diwell, Margret Tailyeor with ane long rok[40] and Kathren Renny with the short rok and the bony las with the blak pok all went up the stair togidder, and that they took somthing out of thair putches befor they went wp from the bak door, quhich was the death of the bairnes: Scho said that since scho begud[41] to confes, the Diwell had taken hir thrice away, Scho declared lykwayis that Besse Paton was at the drouning of the boat at the Blakgrange, quhair the Fywe men was lost, and that the said Besse wold hawe had hir with tham bot scho wold not goe: Scho wold newer ceas in the tym of hir confession bot spak ay of the Diwell, Margret Tailyeor and the bony las with the blak pok, whom scho said was ay togidder. All this is besyd many horrible dittes and great presumptionis, quhich wold tak ane great wolum to expres.

Kathren Renny[42] hes confessed freilie hir paction with the Diwell, that scho hes bein this long tym in his service, and that he first appeared to hir in the *Bodis Medow* in the Liknes of a man with \gray/[43] cloathis and ane blew cap. Scho confessed he took hir be the hand and desyred hir to be his servand quhich scho granted, and that he desyred hir to renunce hir baptisme, quhich scho grantis [scho did,][44] And scho being asked quhat meetingis scho had with the Diwell, and the rest of hir cuwing, scho ansuered scho had severall meetingis with all tham abowenamed, som *tymis at the Cuningar quhair they* danced and sang, somtymis at Androw Erskins litle hous quhair they war skard on[e] night with James Moreis, And scho confessed they had a meiting wp the burn, quhair ther was ane bony las with ane blak pok, who went befor ower Jean Lindsayis yaird dyk and Margret Tailyeor with hir, and Besse Paton, Jonet Blak, Margret Duchall and hir self stayed at the stair foot, till they went wp to Cowdonis hous and destroyed tua bairnes. Scho also declared that Elspit Blak was at the sam meiting with tham, with many great dittes, and horrible presumptionis against hir besyd.

37 In margin: 'Jonet Blak'.
38 'quhinis': gorse bushes.
39 'baid' (abode): dwelt.
40 'rok': distaff.
41 'begud': began.
42 In margin: 'Kathren Renny'.
43 'blew' crossed out and 'gray' written over it.
44 Conjectural restoration of damaged words.

All thir last four mentioned in the marien,[45] ar in prison, and heir followis the names of the personis delated and som of thair dittes and presumptionis, quhich ar not as yit apprehendit.

Elspit Blak[46] delated, be Margret Duchall, Be Besse Paton, be Jonnet Blak and be Kathren Renny to be guiltie, and that scho hes bein at all thair meitingis, with many other great dittes and horrible presumptionis against hir.

Margret Demperstoun is delated be Margret Duchall and Bessie Paton: we hawe not as yit hard of any ditte or presumption against hir.

Kathren Blak[47] is delated be Besse Paton, and Kathren Renny, to be guiltie, and that scho was at thair meetingis, scho hes bein of ane ewill nam thir twentie yeiris bygain and wpward, and many fearfull dittes and horrible presumptionis against her.

James Hudston is delated be Margret Tailyeor, to be guiltie and that he was at ane meeting with tham {*fo. 3r.*} in the Cuningar, And ane great ditte giwen in against him besyd.

Jonet Reid is delated be Besse Paton and Margret Tailyeor to be guiltie, with sundrie great ditties against hir.

James Kirk[48] is delated be Margret Tailyeor to be guiltie, and that he was at ane meeting with tham in the Cuningar, quhair the Diwell and they war altogidder dancing, and the said James Kirk playing on the whisle to tham, with many great dittes and fearfull presumptionis against him, besyd ane ewer[49] name of ane warlok and ane great charmer all his lyftym.

Barbara Erskin is delated be Besse Paton to hawe bein at the casting away of the boat at the Blakgrang, scho is lykwayis delated be Margret Tailyeor, quho declairis scho was at ane meiting with tham in the Cuningar, quhair they danced altogidder with the Diwell, and James Kirk quhisling to tham.

Jonet Paterson in Craigward \is/ delated be Margret Tailyeor to be a great witch, and if scho be not spedilie taken, Margret Tailyeor sayis scho will doe the toun of Alloway ane ewell turne.

Jonet Millar in Tullibodie is delated be Margret Tailyeor to be guiltie, shoe hes the report of a great charmer, all hir lyftym, and many great dittes against hir.

All thir abowe wrettin confessionis delationis and dittes exprest we wnder-subscryweris testifie to be of trewth as witnes our handis at Alloway the said tent day of Junii 1658 yeiris, as followis:

[*Signed:*][50] Alr. Ritche, J. Sinklair, Johnn Kirk constable, James Lindsay, Kinhorne, J. Cucklone, Walter Suord, A. R., William Dryisdall, James Mitchel

45 'marien': margin. The 'four' are Margaret Taylor, Bessie Paton, Janet Black and Katherine Rainie. The other marginal names are in a different hand.

46 In margin: 'Eliz'.

47 In margin: 'Kat'.

48 In margin: 'J. K.'

49 *Sic.* Presumably this is a copying error for 'ewel' (evil).

50 A few of these holograph signatures are not decipherable with certainty.

cowpeir, Henry Towar, Willam Symmer, John Murray, Andro Thomson, Johne Hunter, John Short, Rot. Archibald, Johne Mackenzie, Johne Valke, Johne Arthowr, James Cwninghame.

Source 2: Stirling Council Archives, Minutes of Presbytery of Stirling, 1654–1661, CH2/722/6.

{*p. 89*} At Stirline the 19 day of Maii 1658
Sederunt Masters Archibald Muschett moderator, George Bennett, Robert Wright, Matthias Symson and Masters Johne Craigingelt elder and youngar. Mr Alexander Callendar absent, his excuse being declarit wes admittit....

The said day[51] Mr George Bennett and Mr Matthias Symson ar appoynted to goe to Alloway and conferr with the persones quho ar thair apprehendit for witchcraft and to endevor to bring them to confessioun and convictioun....[52] {*p. 90*}

In regaird that the Committee of the Synod appoyntit for trying of Jonet Dicks scandallis quhich is to be at Stirline the 7 of Junii nixt and that most pairt of the brethren of the presbyterie ar members of the said Committee, therefore the nixt presbyteriall meitting is appoyntit to be the 23 of Junii nixt at Alloway[53] for emergent occasiounes thair, particularlie for trying and examining those quho ar thair apprehendit for witches and endevoring to bring them to confessioun and convictioun.

At Alloway the 23 day of Junii 1658
The said day the Brethren of the presbtyrie eftirnamit conveined according to thair former resolutioun anent the particulars relating to these emergents[54] that occasioned thair coming heire at this tyme, more speciallie for trying and examining those persones who ar apprehendit for witches in Alloway.

Sederunt Masters Archibald Muschett moderator *pro tempore* (in absence of Mr Johne Craigingelt eldar last chosen moderator who is now seik), George Bennett, Robert Wright, Matthias Symson, Johne Craigingelt youngar Ministeris, The Laird of Clakmannan, The Lairds of Menstrie and Tullibodie[55] and Mr Robert Bruce of Kennett justices of peace who were present be virtew of thair offices anent the trying of the witches and Thomas Mitchell of Coldon ruling eldar of Alloway, Also Mr James Cunningham and some other gentlemen being present....

51 In margin: 'Witches'.

52 To bring the suspects to 'convictioun' probably means to bring them to an awareness of their sin, but the word can also imply conviction by a criminal court.

53 In margin: 'Nixt dyett of the presbyterie at Alloway'.

54 'emergents': occurrences, recent events.

55 Harry Bruce of Clackmannan, James Holburne of Menstrie and Robert Meldrum of Tullibody.

Efter solemne prayer and invocatioun of the name of God, The saids brethren and justices of peace present having receavit and at lenth heard and considerit ane paper under the hand of Mr James Meldrum Session clerk of Alloway bearing the confessioun of Margaret Duchill (who is now dead) of witchcraft, and dilating[56] others, the tennor of which paper is heirby appoyntit to be insert and is accordinglie done as followes.

At Alloway the elevinth day of Maii 1658 yeires, Margaret Duchill indweller in Alloway for syndrie dilatiounes agaynst her to the Minister be severall eldaris of her scandalous cariage in the sinne of witchcraft wes cited before the Sessioun the said day, and eftir the dilatiounes wes read to her before the Sessioun sche denyit them all except that sche confessid that sche haid said to William Moresone eldar that if they sould tak and burne her there sould better wyves in Alloway nor herself be burnt with her. Upon which confessioun with many presumptiounes agaynst her the Minister and eldaris sends ane letter to the justices of peace with ane of the eldaris and clerk of the Sessioun, who returned ane order, direct to the Constables of Alloway, to secure her persone in closs prison and ane guard night and day attending her, and eftir severall visits maid be the Minister and some eldaris with many gude exhortatioues and pithie prayeris with severall demands concerning that sinne of witchcraft, so did at last confess as followes. {*p. 91*}

First[57] that sche hes beine in the Divellis service thir tuentie yeiris bygane, and being askit quhair sche mett first with him, who [*sic*] answerit in Issobell Jamesones litle house quhair sche dwelt her self all alone, and who came in to me to the said house in the likeness of a man with broune cloathes and ane litle blak hatt, who asked her, what ailleth yow, sche answerit I am ane poore bodie and cannot gett quhairon to live, he said ye sall not want if yow will doe my bidding and he gave me fyve shilling and bade me goe buy ane pek of meill with it, and I went to the tron[58] and bought ane pek of peis meill with it, and it wes gude money.[59] I brought it home and bakit bannoks, and he sent me for ane chopine[60] of aill and wee did eate and drink togither, and thaireftir I went to the Calsey and span on my rok[61] till night. And quhen I came in, he wes in the house and bade me close the doore and quhen I went to my bed he came in over to me and lay with me all night and he causit me to ly on my face and he gatt on abone me and haid to doe with me, and grunkled[62] abone me lyke a kow. Thereftir he said to me, Magie will yee

56 'dilating' (delating): accusing.
57 In margin: 'Margaret Duchill her confessiouns of witchcraft'.
58 'tron': public weighbeam, here considered as the venue for a market.
59 More often, the Devil's gifts were not 'gude money' but vanished or turned to leaves or dung.
60 'chopine': tankard.
61 'rok': distaff.
62 'grunkled': grunted.

be my servant, And I said I wold be his servant, then he said ye most quyte God and your baptisme, which I did, and he gave me his mark on my eyebrie by ane nip and bade me quhensoevir ye wold have me, call upon me by my name Johne and I sall nevir leave yow but doe any thing to yow that yow bide me; Thereftir in the greek of morning[63] I convoyed him doune the bowrig where he vanisched from me.

Secondlie sche being asked what evill scho haid done in the said service the said 20 yeires, sche answerit the first wrong that evir sche did wes to Bessie Vertie, and being askit quhat wrong sche did to her, sche answerit sche took her lyfe, and being asked what way sche took her lyfe and for quhat cause, sche answerit that sche and I discordit at the Pow of Alloway bearing coalles, and I went to the Divell and sought a mends of her, and he said to me, quhat will yow have of her, And I said her lyfe, then said he goe to her house the morne and tak her be the hand and sche sall nevir doe any more gude, which I did and sche presentlie took seiknes quhairof sche died.

Thridlie sche confessid sche wes the death of Jonet Houston spous to Johne Duthie wobster, and being asked quhairfore sche did that to her, who [*sic*] answerit sche wes aughtand[64] me ten merks and wold not pay me, and quhen I craved her sche said sche cared not for me, I went and complained to the Divell and sought her lyfe who bade me goe to her the morne and crave her agayne, and if sche pay yow not tak her a dunsh[65] upon the back and sche sall nevir doe no more gude which I did and sche pyned away ay and quhill[66] sche died.

Fourthlie sche confessid sche wes the death of Johne Demperstounes daughter who wes about tuelf yeires of age or thairby, who [*sic*] being asked what ailled her at that young lass, sche answerit I going allongs the bridge of Alloway sche running by me touched me, and I said quhat ailleth the lass to touch me, sche answerit, away witch theiff, I went to the Divell and socht a mends, he bade me the first tyme I saw her to tak ane tug of her arme and sche sould blood to death which I died [*sic*] and the lass went home and presentlie bled to death, and sche being asked be the Minister how could ane tug of ane arme or ane dunsh on the back or shaking of hands be the death of any bodie, scho answerit that eftir sche gatt the word from Johne her master sche wold have done it to the greatest man or woman in the world.[67]

Fyftlie sche being askit what were the wemen that sche said if sche were burnt sould be burnt with her, sche answerit that sche haid beine at severall meittings with the Divell and syndrie wemen with her, and being asked

63 'in the greek of morning': at daybreak.

64 'auchtand': owing.

65 'tak her a dunsh': give her a thump.

66 'ay and quhill': until.

67 Douchall's answer here fails to engage with the minister's question, probably because she does not know enough about how he thinks that witchcraft is supposed to work.

who they were, sche answerit that one night at twelf a cloak at night Elspett Black came to her house and took her out to the Crafts[68] of Alloway quhair they mett with the Divell and sche did declair and constantlie bydes be that the Divell read[69] them both that night. Sche did lykewyse declair that Jonet Black came one day to William Moresones house desyring tuo pennyworth of snuff, and because sche haid no money to pay for it he wold not give her the same, and for which cause the same night sche conveined with her self, Bessie Paton, Margaret Talyeor, Kathrine Rainy and me the said Margaret Duchill, and wee all being togither fand the said William Moresone at his owne baksyde[70] whom wee did violentlie draw by armes and shoulderis throuch yce and snow to Walter Murrayes barne where wee thought to have drowned him in ane holl, but he crying God be mercifull to me, they all fled from him but my self, who came home at his back lyke a black dog but he saw me not, all which the said William Moresone did divers tymes long tyme before this declair that he wes mightilie fearit but nevir knew till this confessioun.

Sixthlie sche did lykewyse declair that sche wes at ane meitting in the Cunningar with Jonet Blak, Bessie Paton, Margaret Talyeor, Katherine Rainy, Margaret Demperston, Elspet Black, quhair they dancit in others hands[71] with the Divell present {*p. 92*} going up and doune among them some of them singing and some of them dancing and Bessie Paton leading the ring, sche did lykewyse declair that the haill said wemen abovementioned haid many severall meittinges in the Crafts of Alloway with the Divell, and that Elspet Black warnit them ay[72] to thair meittinges, and thair last meitting wes at Androw Erskynes brewhouse doore within this ten dayes, and being chased be ane James Moreis about elevine a cloak in the night wee went by Walter Murrayes barne and went all home. Sche confest ane meiting in the Cuningar of all the sevine with the Divell in the likeness of catts who went to the Gran[ge][73] and destroyed ane kow to Edward Turnour, Ane other meitting ane night and they went to Tullibodie and killed ane bairne, Another meiting and went to the Bow house and killed ane hors and ane kow to William Menteith, ane other meitting and they went to Clakmannan and killed ane chyld of Thomas Bruce, another meiting and they went to Coldones and wes the death of tuo bairnes of his. Subscryvit this JMeldrum Session clerk of Alloway.

There wes also another paper presentit by Mr Johne Craigingelt youngar and subscryvit be him bearing the confessioun and examinatioun of the four persones following who were apprehendit by ordor of the justices of the peace, partlie on the depositioun of the said deceist Margaret Duchill and partlie on

68 Probably read 'Crofts', as in Source 6 below.

69 'read': rode (in the sense of magical travel).

70 'at his owne baksyde': behind his house.

71 'in others hands': holding each other's hands.

72 'warnit them ay': always summoned them.

73 Conjectural restoration of damaged letters.

the presumptiounes and partlie upon *mala fama*,[74] To witt, Margaret Talyeor, Bessie Paton, Jonet Black and Kathrine Rainy, all in the paroch of Alloway, the tennor of which paper is heire also sett doune as followes.

At Alloway the thrid day of June 1658, Present the Laird of Clakmannan[75] and the Laird of Kennett[76] justices of peace, Mr Harie Guthrie Minister of Kilspindie, Mr Robert Wright Minister of Clakmannan, Mr Johne Craigingelt Minister of Dollor wreitar heirof, Mr James Cuningham and Thomas Mitchell of Coldon eldaris of the kirk sessioun of Alloway and Johne Keirie elder of the said sessioun,[77] Eftir prayer and exhortatioun It being asked whither Margaret Talyeor wes guyltie of the sinn of witchcraft, scho answerit yes and it wes about thrie yeires since in the winter tyme in the day tyme without the house[78] in the way to the heuch,[79] Margaret Duchall being with her at Bagrie burne, the Divell appeired in the likenes of ane young man in blak cloathes, And bade her renounce her baptisme, which she condiscendit[80] to doe, quhairupon he promised that sche sould nevir want, and bade her call him quhen sche stood in neid by the name of Johne, Acknowledges eftir that sche did renounce her baptisme upon her knees, that he gave her his mark on the privie parts, And that within ane quarter of ane yeire since that he haid carnall dealling with her as ane man uses to doe with a woman, his bodie wes cold. It wes the same place quhair he first came to her and that thair wes present with her Bessie Paton, Kathrine Rainy, Margaret Duchall, Jonet Blak, Barbara Erskyne; and that Margaret Duchall came to her in the likenes of ane catt and thaireftir appeired in her owne shaip and said sche behovit to goe with her ane errand, and that also Elspett Crockett in Gaberstoun mett with them, and that the nixt meitting wes about 12 hours at night in Bodsmeadow about one quarter of ane yeires since, there being in company Jonet Blak, Bessie Paton, Kathrine Rainy, Elspett Crockett, Barbara Erskyne, And that he lay with her agayne and that they onlie danced, and that James Kirk at the back of the greine wes present and played on ane whistle, And that thair language wes not our ordinarie language, sche wes inducit to this service of Sattan because sche wes abused by Kathrine Black her goodwyfe,[81] and that sche wes in the Bowhouse in the forderend of eateseid tyme,[82] and that thair wes present Jonet Blak, Bessie Paton and Margaret Duchall, and the reason of thair going thair wes because Jonet Back [*sic*] was angrie for straw,

74 'bad reputation'.
75 Harry Bruce of Clackmannan.
76 Mr Robert Bruce of Kennet.
77 In margin: 'Margaret Talyeor her first confessioun of witchcraft'.
78 'without the house': outside the house.
79 'heuch': crag, ravine or quarry. Possibly a coal-pit, since Margaret Douchall worked as a coal-bearer.
80 'condiscendit': agreed.
81 'her goodwyfe': her mistress, employer.
82 'the forderend of eateseid tyme': the end of the time of sowing of oat seeds.

they mett in the waird yeard and went to the Bowhouse, and Jonet Blak and Bessie Paton went in at ane holl in the byre doore, and that the nixt day ane hors and ane cow died, and that sche wes in the Cuningar this winter in the tyme of snow, the Divell being present in his former likeness as ane man, and thair wes present Bessie Paton, Jonet Black, Kathrine Rainy and Margaret Duchall. Jonet Black she affirmes said that sche wes the death of ane bairne in Tullibodie of Marie Moreis and that Margaret Duchall told her that they were at Clakmannan and killed ane bairne to Thomas Bruce, and that quhen they meit Sathan calls the roll, and her name was Jonet given to her at the first quhen scho renouncit her baptisme and interest in Jesus Christ, And that Satan mett with her in the likeness of ane rouch dog that night quhen Jonet Grott died, and Margaret Duchall, Kathrine Rainy and Jonet Grott wes with him, and they came to her in the night in the loft quhair sche lay, and they went in to Androw Thomsones house at his back doore and they took out the fusson[83] out of his wheat bread, and that Jonet Groatt who died that night took the bread and gave evrie one of them ane peice bread, which sche took with her and did not eate nor ken quhat came of it, {*p. 93*} and that she wes at the head of Thomas Mitchellis yeard eftir they haid comed from the burne, being present Bessie Paton, Kathrine Rainy, Margaret Duchall, Jonet Black, and that the Divell went first up in the likeness of ane litle man, Bessie Paton nixt and Kathrine Rainy and Jonet Blak in at ane holl at the back doore, and that sche and Margaret Duchall stayed doune the stair and went not in, and that also thair wes ane gentlewoman with ane blak pok quhom sche knew not and wes nixt the Divell, and that Bessie Paton knew her and that the Devill appeired lyke ane bissome[84] to her since sche came to this house and that he promised that sche sould not be burnt. That sche wes thair but once and that Jonet Blak haid the meall to be casten first on the dog, then on the bairnes, and that Jonet Millar in Tillibodie told her that the Divell haid appeired to her, yet the said Jonet knew not that sche wes ane witch. And being furder prest concerning that gentlewoman that haid the blak pok, greine waistcoatt and gray tailles, answerit that she could not tell quhat sche wes because her face was covered but that Bessie Paton knew her because sche wes nixt to her, and being agayne prest and earnestlie exhorted by syndrie present that without fade[85] or favor of any that she wold be frie in her confessioun and not conceall quhat that woman wes, sche answerit that sche could not tell what sche wes, but said that quhat sche heard uthers say concerning that woman with the pok. It wes agayne desyrit that if sche fearit to tell out publictlie her name that sche wold whisper it in the Laird of Clakmannans eare and

83 'fusson': goodness or nourishing power.
84 'bissome': broom.
85 'fade' (feud): enmity.

the Laird of Kennetts, sche answerit that sche could tell nothing but quhat utheris said to her and that sche sould whisper which sche did.

The forsaid day Eftir incalling on the name of God,[86] Bessie Paton wes exhorted by Mr Robert Wright and syndrie present that sche would be frie in her confessioun, being posit[87] if sche wes ane witch answered, No, except that sche haid beine caried in spirit while asleepe, and if so that sche knew not. And denyed all that wes formerlie writtin, and that sche nevir spoke of ane gentlewoman with a blak pok but that some bade her say quhat sche haid said that the rest might therby be induced to confess.

The said day Jonet Black[88] being posit if evir sche did any gude to man or beast by charmes, answered that sche did nevir any evill to man or beast by charmes, yet that she found ane whelp when she wes going up by Bagra burne and in her returne took up the whelpe which sche hid quhen sche went by, And brought it bak to her house and that it did eate nothing but drank water and it wes blind; Sche caried it in her lap and because it wes not lyke to be ane whelp she buried it; And that sche saw six weomen at Johne Dowes yeard and went to Bodsmeadow, the women were Margaret Talyeor, Margaret Duchall, Bessie Paton, Kathrine Rainy and ane gentlewoman with a blak pok but knew not quhat sche wes, and that Bessie Paton brought her up frae the house about bedtyme and that they played up and doune that night and thaireftir sindered,[89] And the nixt meiting wes the nixt night and the same women that were before and went up to Dickies Land and quhen sche came to the bridge sche saw thrie going up Thomas Mitchells forestair, the woman with the blak pok, Margaret Taylyeor and Bessie Paton, and that sche stayed doune with Margaret Duchall and wes about the bridge quhen sche saw them goe up; the thrid tyme before the kirk doore they mett and these onlie that wes before and danced throuch the yeatt,[90] Agayne that thair wes ane gross round woman unknowne to her, the nixt meitting at Bagraburne tuo nightes eftir and that Bessie Paton brought her and that they danced thair and did no more that night.

The said day Kathrine Rainy[91] confest sche mett with Bessie Paton, Jonet Black and Margaret Duchall and that Bessie Paton said that thair wes uther thrie before that wes at Thomas Millars barne, and that they went to Thomas Mitchellis house and returned to Bodsmeadow, and thair sche saw ane man in gray cloathes with ane blew bonnett, and that sche saw ane woman with ane blak pok, ane gray gowne and ane greine waistcoatt but knew not what she wes because she was covered with ane blak creape over her face, and also

86 In margin: 'Bessie Paton'.
87 'posit': asked.
88 In margin: 'Jonet Black'.
89 'sindered' (sundered): separated.
90 'yeatt': gate.
91 In margin: 'Kathrine Rainy'.

that thair wes ane gross woman with ane whyte coatt, but that sche knew not quhat sche wes except that she might guess and that it wes lyke Elspett Blak but could not say that it wes sche; Next wes coming from Androw Erskynes and that they were chased be James Moreis and that sche only saw Bessie Paton, Jonet Blak and Margaret Duchall; Sche confessid that the man with gray cloathes and the blew bonnett took her by the hand and asked her if she would be fied,[92] sche said that she cared not, this wes at that meitting up in Bodsmeadow, and that his hand wes cold and quhen sche fand it cold, that she wes feared and took out her hand agayne, sche thought he wes not righteous, she thought that it wes the Divell and sche said that she sained[93] herself. This is the truth of quhat wes confessid by the forsaids persones before the foirnamit judges and persones present which I Mr Johne Craigingelt Minister at Dollor appointit by this meitting to write doe testifie by this my subscriptioun Subscryvit thus Johne Craigingelt. {*p. 94*}

Upon the whilkes forsaides dilatiounes and confessiounes the saids four persones alreadie apprehendit were for further tryall by ordour of the saids justices callit for and re-examined judiciallie as followes, and first compeired

Margaret Talyeor[94] who being posit whither she wes guyltie of the sinn of witchcraft yea or not? Answered and confest that about thrie yeires agoe the deceist Margaret Duchall tystit[95] her to goe to Bagraburne, where the Devill appeired to them in the likeness of a young man in blak cloathes and promeist to her that sche sould want nothing that she stood in neid of, sche asking it at his hands, and bade her renounce her baptisme which sche did by putting one hand on her head and the other on her foote and renuncit her baptisme from God to that man which sche knew not at first to be the Divell but that sche knew him to be the Divell before they partit at that tyme, And that the Divell bade her call him by the name Johne and named her Jonet, and eftir she knew that it wes the Divell sche haid covenanted with, which she knew before they partit with him at that meitting, sche did keipe her to her former covenant, and confest that the Devill gave her at the said tyme ane mark upon her private pairts by a nip with his hand which wes at that tyme painfull, Furder confest that the Devill struglit with her and did cast her doune on her back and haid adoe with her as a man haid to doe with a woman, and in that tyme of thair copulatioun sche thought his bodie wes coldryfe,[96] Furder confest that she haid a meitting with the Devill about ane quarter of a yeire thaireftir at Thomas Millaris barne about twelf houris at night, and that Kathrine Rainy, Bessie Paton and the deceist Margaret

92 'fied': employed.
93 'sained': blessed.
94 In margin: 'Margaret Talyeor her second confessioun before the presbyterie and justices of peace'.
95 'tystit': enticed.
96 'coldryfe': cold.

Duchall and Jonet Blak wes with the Devill and her the said tyme; sche being posit who warned her to that meitting, answerit Margaret Duchall quho came in at the window in likenes of a catt and said to me, Jonet yee most goe ane errand which wes to meitt with Sattan, and said that she went out at the window in the likeness of a catt, and thaireftir wes in the likeness of a woman, and that they went up to a burne where they mett and thaireftir they came to Thomas Mitchell of Coldon his house and went in over the yeard dyke and that Bessie Paton, Jonet Blak and Kathrine Rainy went up to the said Thomas his house in at a holl of the doore in the lykeness of catts and destroyit one of his children, and that the Divell went up with them and that she and Margaret Duchall and one Elspett Crockett in Gaberstoun (quho wes also with them) stayed at the stairfoote till they came back. Being posit if thair were any moer persones with them nor she hes named, particularlie a woman with a blak pok, Answered sche knew none other person thair nor she hes alreadie named. Being posit why she did formerlie say that thair wes a woman with a blak pok in thair company, Answered that James Lindsey bade her say it and promeist her shelter for her lyfe to say so, And that he said he caired not whither sche told her name or not, because the rest that were tane haid said it wes Kathrine Kay, as lykewyse that seing the rest haid fylled her[97] that Captane Crichton came to her and said quhat wes the cause she wold not fyll Kathrine Kay also and that he did so severall tymes, and sicklyke that Johne Thomson bade her also fyll Kathrine Kay.

Also confest that she haid another meitting with the Devill at Bodsmeadow in the night tyme and that Kathrine Rainy, Jonet Blak, Margaret Duchall and Bessie Paton wes with her and the Divell at that tyme, and that Margaret Duchall came to her in the night tyme and bade her ryse and goe ane errand, and that she went with them and went as she thought out at the window, and that the Divell at that tyme wes in the lykenes of a feltered[98] beast, and that Kathrine Rainy, Bessie Paton and Jonet Blak wes then trysting[99] to goe some errand but she knew not quhat it wes, And that the Divell at that tyme shook hands with Kathrine Rainy, and that the Devill bade them all welcome, and that they haid a language among them quhen they mett which sche cannot speake nor understand nor could, except at such meittinges as they haid with the Devill. As also confest that in eatsyde tyme last, Margaret Duchall came to her at tuelf houris in the night and bade her ryse and goe ane errand to meitt with Sathan, which she haid not powar to refuse, and that she arose and went with her to Bowhouse, and that Jonet Blak, Bessie Paton and Margaret Duchall were with her, and that the occasioun of thair going thair wes that Jonet Blak or Bessie Paton haid taine anger at William Menteiths folk, and

97 'fylled her': accused her, said that she was guilty.

98 'feltered': shaggy.

99 'trysting': making an arrangement to meet.

that the said other tuo women went in at the stable doore, and that ane hors and cow of the said William Menteiths died within 20 dayes thaireftir. Also confest that sche haid another meitting with the Devill at the Cuningar, and that Kathrine Rainy, Bessie Paton, Jonet Blak, Margaret Duchall and Barbara Erskyne in Cambus wes with the Divell and her at that time, and that James Kirk eldar in {*p. 95*} Alloway wes also with them and played on a whistle and that they all dancit, As also that sche saw other wemen in companies going by them that tyme. Also confest that quhen she renouncit her baptisme sche renouncit also her interest in Chryst Jesus. As lykewayes the said Margaret Talyeor confest that the night in which Jonet Groatt wes buried, the said Margaret Duchall, Kathrine Rainy and her self togither with the said Jonet Groatt went to Androw Thomsones house quho is the sone of the said Jonet Groatt, And that the said Jonet Groatt opened a kist and took bread out of it and gave them to eate quhairof they did eate; Also confest that since she wes imprisoned sche sayes sche saw lyke a long bissome going up and doune the house at which she was afrayed.

Sche furder declarit that Johne Thomson did torture her by making her stand up high on a stooll and causit Thomas and Johne Kidstones in Cambus putt hott stones to her feete, which wes eftir her first confessioun, bidding her tell of the woman with a blak pok. All which her forsaides confessiounes being read over to her sche acknowledgit that all the samen wes of truth in face of the ministeris of the presbyterie and justices of peace forsaid.

The forsaid day the said Bessie Paton[100] (who is dilated by the deceist Margaret Duchall and the said Margaret Talyeor to be guyltie of witchcraft as thair saids depositiounes and declaratiounes specifies) wes called before the brethren and justices of peace forsaid, who being gravlie and seriouslie exhorted to declair the truth and being posit particularlie whither scho is guyltie of the sinn of witchcraft and hes maid any pactioun with the Devill yea or not, sche did absolutlie deny that she is guyltie of witchcraft.

Sche being posit whither at the desyre of any seik person sche went to Sybilla Drummond in Dunblane who wes burnt for a witch, answered that at the desyre of Kathrine Blak spous to Meassone in Alloway she went to the said Sybie Drummond and desyrit her to come and helpe Elspett Bryce who wes than travelling[101] in chyld birth about 19 yeirs since and that the said Sybie refusit to goe with her because said she the said seik woman wold doe no gude, But bade putt a look[102] salt in her mouth and a soup[103] south running water and a look of a molehill on tilled Land and give her, and that the deponner told this cure to Jonet Baxter servant to the said seik woman and David Carron her husband and that the seik woman forsaid died shortlie thaireftir.

[100] In margin: 'Bessie Paton her examinatioun'.
[101] 'travelling' (travailing): in labour.
[102] 'look': handful.
[103] 'soup' (sup): drink.

The said Bessie Paton being posit whither she wes at any tyme in the company and at the meitting of witches and whither she wes caried in her sleepe and dreamed of witches, sche said sche cannot tell.

The saids Bessie Paton and Margaret Talyeor being confrontit togither, the said Margaret did averr in the said Bessie her face that sche wes at a meitting with her and other witches at Thomas Millars barne where they came in at the yeard[104] head, and the said Bessie came in first and that Kathrine Rainy and Margaret Duchall with them, the said Bessie denyit the same and affirmit that she wes nevir at any of these meittinges bodilie. Also the said Margaret affirmit before the said Bessie that she wes with the Devill and her at another meitting in Bodsmeadow but the said Bessie denyit the same.

The said Bessie being further posit confest sche wes once on a Sabbath in James Kirkes house the sabbath before the said Bessie wes tane, The quhilk James is dilated *ut supra*.[105] Lykewyse the said Margaret affirmit in her face that the said Bessie wes at another meitting with the Devill and her in the Bowhouse, but she denyit it.

The forsaid 23 of Junii compeired before the brethren of the presbyterie and justices of peace foresaid Kathrine Rainy,[106] who being apprehendit for witchcraft wes conveined for tryall and examinatioun, and being posit whither sche wes guyltie of the sinn of witchcraft yea or not? Answered and declarit as followes, To witt that in winter last sche mett with Bessie Paton, Jonet Blak and Margaret Duchall at the coall gate syde[107] bewest[108] Thomas Millars barne, she going home from Alloway quhair she wes seiking her husband, and that she went alongs with them till sche came to Jeane Lindseyes yeard dyke, and because she fell, in going over the dyke, sche went no further, but that the said women came back and that woman with a blak pok and a gross round woman with a whytte coatt wes thair the said tyme which last tuo {*p. 96*} sche knew not, and they tuo did not come bak but the said uther thrie came bak to Bodsmeadow with her where she saw a man in gray cloathes and a blew bonnett, and Bessie Paton as she thinkes wes the woman that speired at her[109] if she wold be fied with[110] the said man, Sche said she cared not, and thaireftir the said man took her by the hand which she fand to be cold and pulled hers out of his hand and sained herself and thought he wes the Divell and not righteous. And the forsaid Bessie being callit in and confrontit with the said Kathrine, the said Kathrine averd in the said Bessie her face, Nevirtheless the said Bessie adheres to her denyall. The said

104 'dyke' crossed out.
105 'as above'.
106 In margin: 'Kathrine Rainy examined'.
107 'the coall gate syde': the side of the path to the coal-pit.
108 'bewest': to the west of.
109 'speired at her': asked her.
110 'be fied with': be employed by.

Kathrine furder declarit that she wes tortured by David Vertie, Johne Schort and Robert Archibald by putting hott stones to her feete and putting thir on hers pressing her feete to the hott stones.

Furder Margaret Talyeor being callit in and confrontit with the said Katherine, did averr that the said Katherine wes with the Devill and her at a meitting in the Cuningar and dancit with the rest which wes on Hallow evine, and James Kirk did whisle to them, Nevirtheless the said Kathrine denyit the same, Also sche averd that the said Kathrine wes with the Devill and her in Androw Thomsones house that night that Jonet Groatt wes buried and appeired agayne *ut supra* etc., but she denyes that also.

The said day compeired before the presbyterie and utheris beforenamit Jonet Black[111] who being apprehendit for witchcraft wes conveined for tryall, and sche being posit whither she wes guyltie of witchcraft or had any meittings with the Devill, confest that she haid thrie meittinges with the women following, To witt Bessie Paton, Margaret Talyeor, Kathrine Rainy, Margaret Duchall and a woman with a black pok whom sche knew not, The first meitting being at Bodsmeadow short while before Yule last, and the 2d meitting at the end of the teynd barne at 8 houris at evine, and the thrid at Thomas Mitchellis staires, and that sche saw Margaret Talyeor, Bessie Paton and another woman whom she knew not goe up Thomas Mitchellis staires in the night tyme, Also confest that she fand at Bagraburne about 20 dayes before Yule last a litle living blind beast lyke a mordewart[112] whilk she brought home with her and keipt it in her house 25 dayes at her fyreside but it wold eate none, and that she nevir loott[113] any sie it, but thaireftir she took it away and laid it in a thorne bush and a broad stane on it and thought it haid beine dead, but eftir tuo dayes it mett her besyde her owne house, and then she took a mell and feld it als bread as a bonnett[114] and buried it in a watt fur[115] in the waird.[116] Furder sche said that Bessie Paton trystit her[117] to all the saids meittinges, and being confrontit with her averd the same in her face, yet the said Bessie denyes the same; Furder the said Jonet Blak confest that she haid sinned in going to these meittinges, Furder the said Bessie Paton declaired that David Vertie, James Maknair and James Nicoll did torture her by putting stones on her bak and feete and burnt her legs with fyre (which sche sayes ar not yet whole) and that they did it to mak her confess.

The Brethren of the presbyterie and justices of peace forsaids, having heard and considerit the confessiounes and declaratiounes of the persones

[111] In margin: 'Jonet Black her confessioun'.

[112] 'mordewart': mole.

[113] 'loott': let.

[114] 'she took a mell and feld it als bread as a bonnett': she took a hammer and crushed it (so that it was) as wide as a bonnet.

[115] 'watt fur': wet furrow.

[116] 'waird' (ward): perhaps the name of a field or cultivated area. There has previously been mention of 'the waird yeard'.

[117] 'trystit her': invited or summoned her.

beforenamit, and finding that Margaret Tayleor hes clearlie confest witchcraft and express pactioun with the Devill and some malefices, and that thair ar great presumptiounes that the other thrie ar guyltie of witchcraft, doe thairfore judge it expedient that a letter be writtin in name of this meiting to the judges competent in criminal causes,[118] representing the case forsaid unto them, and desyring that they may tak cours with the saids women as accords of the Law, and Mr Matthias Symson is appoyntit to draw up the said Letter and he to subscryve it in name of the Brethren, and the Laird of Menstrie to subscryve it in name of the justices of peace in this shyre, and the said letter is to be sent away with dilligence.[119] {*p. 97*}

It is recomendit to the Brethren especiallie to Mr George Bennett and Mr Archibald Muschett before they remove out of this toune to goe to the saides four women apairt and seriouslie and gravlie by prayer and exhortatioun to deall with them towards confessioun and endevor to convince them of thair haynous offencis and report thair dilligence the morrow to the presbyterie….

At Alloway the 24 of Junii 1658…
Repoirt maid[120] that Mr George Bennett and Mr Archibald Muschett went and dealt seriouslie with the witches towards a confessioun as they were desyrit yester night, but fand no more from them nor wes formerlie confest be them.

Source 3: NRS, Court of Justiciary Process Papers, 1658, JC26/24, JC26/26.

JC26/24, bundle 7, no. 2.

[*Endorsed:*] 19 July 1658. Testificatione of the Justices of Peace that the witches was not tortoured.

At Alloway the ninteen day of Julii 1658 yeiris we the justices of peace of Clakmanan schyr having hard, that Kathe Reny, Bessie Paton and Margret Tailyeor did affirm that John Thomson baxter in Alloway, Thomas and John Kidstounis in Cambus, James Maknair and James Nicoll sowld have tortured and brunt tham with hot stonis and for that we caused summond the said parties above designed befor us the said day and confronted tham befor the saidis thrie witches who could mak furth nothing against them, and therafter we called tham on[e] by on[e] and after they war deeplie sworn to tell the trewth they all deponit that they never tortured nor brunt on[e] of tham, which we testifie to be done by thir presentis subscrivit with our handis day and place above specifeit.

[*Signed:*] Harie Bruce, RBruce, Ja: Holburne.

118 In margin: 'Letter to be writtin to the Criminall Judges'.

119 'with dilligence': with urgency. A letter to this effect, written by James Holburne of Menstrie and Matthias Simson from Stirling on 28 June, is printed below as part of Source 5.

120 In margin: 'Witches'.

JC26/26, bundle 3, no. 20.

{*p. 1*} At Clakmanan the 22 day of Julii 1658. In presence of Harie Bruce of Clakmanan, Mr Robert Bruce of Kennet, Justices of the peace of Clakmananschyr, compeiret the witnessis of the witches of Alloway thair confessionis delationis and ditteis and being sworn deponit as followis.

In first[121] compeirit James Lindsay, James Crightoun, John Thomson baxter, David Wertie litstar, William Horn merchant and Robert Moreis coupar, who all being deiplie sworn be the said Justices of peace to tell the trewth and conceill nothing, quhat they hard Margret Tailyeor confes of the sin of witchcraft, they did declair that scho did confes, that the first tym that ever scho saw the Divell was in Thomas Measonis brewhous, quho appeared to hir in the liknes of a young man with gray cloathis and ane blew bonnet, and that he gave hir his merk on hir secret member,[122] and that scho promised to be his servant, scho lykwayis confessed that scho was at ane meeting at Cowdonis hous quhair thair was with hir ane bony las with ane blak pok and ane with ane bony quheit coat, and Besse Paton, Jonet Blak, Kathren Renny and Margret Duchall, quhair they destroyed tuo of Cowdonis bairnes, scho lykwayis confessed the death of William Monteathis hors and kuy.

Secondlie compeirit James Crightoun, Walter Sword, James Lindsay and William Monteath kirk elder who all being sworne, declared that Margret Tailyeor declared and confessed that Kathren Key[123] and no other bot scho, was the woman with the blak pok that was with tham at the destroying of Cowdonis tua bairnes, and that scho wold goe to death with it.

Thridlie[124] compeirit William Moreson kirk elder, Mr James Meldrum, John Thomson baxter, James Anderson baxter, John Kirk constable, and James Crightoun who all being sworn declared that they all hard Margret Duchall delait Margret Tailyeor to be a witch[125] and that scho was at the destroying of Cowdonis tua bairnes and at the destroying of ane bairn in Mari Moreis hous in Tullibodie and at the destroying of ane other bairn in Thomas Bruce hous in Clakmanan, and at the destroying of ane kow to Edward Turnor and at the destroying of ane hors and ane kow to William Monteath.

Fourtlie[126] compeirit John Anderson \kirk/ elder, John Mitchell constable, John Thomson baxter, James Maknair and James Crightoun, who did all swear and depon that they hard Margret Tailyeor delait James Hudsoun and James Kirk to be warlokis, Jonet Paterson in Craigward, Barbara Erskin in Cambus and Jonet Millar in Tullibodie, who war all at ane meiting in the Cuningar and the Divell with tham, and James Kirk playing on the whisle to tham. {*p. 2*}

121 In margin: 'Margret Tailyeor.'
122 In margin: '1. The mark in hir secret member confesset be hir selff and particularlie.'
123 In margin: '2. Delaited Katharene Kay.'
124 In margin: '3.'
125 In margin: '5 malefices contra Margaret Tailyeor.'
126 In margin: '4. Persones delaitted be Margaret Tailyeor to be at a meitting with hir in the Cuningar.'

Fiftlie[127] Margret Tailleor declared Jonet Read to be a great witch and said that if thay had looked hir kist in tym ye wold have gottin the winding scheittis of all Margret Mastertounis bairnes, Witnessis deponit and sworn: James Crightoun, John Thomson baxter, Robert Mitchell younger, John Mitchell constable and James Maknair and John Anderson kirk elder. *{p. 3}*

Compeirit[128] James Crightoun, James Lindsay, Robert Moreis couper, David Wertie, John Main younger and James Millar and being all sworne deponit and declared that Kathren Renny being asked how long scho had bein in the Divillis service scho ansuered ever since befor Lentron[129] and scho being asked quhair scho had first seen him, scho said in the Bodis medow in the liknes of a man with gray cloathis and ane blew bonnet, And being asked quhat he said to hir, scho ansuered he took me be the hand, and asked me if I wold be his servant, and I said, yes, and being asked quhat moir he said to hir, scho said he bad me renunce my baptisme and I did it,[130] and being asked quhat was his name, and scho said John, and being asked quhat meetingis scho had had with him and the rest, scho said the first meeting was that night that we went in to Cowdonis hous,[131] and we mett up the burne and ther was ane long small woman with ane blak pok on hir head, and scho and Maggi Tailyeor gead befor with the Divill, in ower Jean Lindsayis yeard dyk, and scho, Besse Paton, Jonet Blak and Maggi Duchall followed tham, and ther they gaid up to Cowdonis and scho and Jonet Blak and Maggi Duchall stayed at the stair foot till they cam doun again and thairafter the long las with the blak pok went away with Maggi Tailyeor, and scho hir self with Besse Paton, Jonet Blak and Maggi Duchall cam with the Divill to Bodis medow,[132] and Jonet Blak delyvered Kathren Renny to the Divill, quho took hir be the hand, and scho said his hand was lyk other hand,[133] bot it was veri cold, and they danced in otheris handis,[134] and Besse Paton led the ring and sang Walli Fa our Bridgarme,[135] and after they had danced and sung a long tym they all pairted, and at pairting ewri on[e] said to a nother, our god be with yow, and being askit quhat habit the long las with the blak pok was in, scho said in a gray gown and a grein wastcot, and being asked quhat other meetingis scho had with tham, scho ansuered they had ane other meeting with tham at Androw Erskeinis litle hous, bot being skard be James Moreis we went all sundrie gaits[136] and pairted.

127 In margin: '5. Delaited Jonet Reid.'
128 In margin: '1. Kathren Renny confessione.'
129 'Lentron': Lent. In 1658, the season of Lent had begun on 24 February.
130 In margin: 'Renunciatione baptisme.'
131 In margin: 'Meiting anent Cowdonis.'
132 In margin: 'Meiting with the Devill at Bodismedow quhair Bessie Paton and 3 utheris was.'
133 'lyk other hand': like an ordinary (human) hand.
134 'in otheris handis': holding each other's hands.
135 'Walli Fa our Bridgarme': May our bridegroom have good fortune. Evidently the name of a popular song.
136 'we went all sundrie gaits': we all went different ways.

Secondlie[137] John Main kirk elder, James Crightoun, James Meason and John Fairlie compeirit and deponit that on the xi day of Maii 1658 they askit Kethren Renny if scho had any mor to say nor scho had, scho ansuered scho had on[e] thing to tell bot scho had no will to doe it, they desyred hir to tell freilie any thing scho knew as scho wold wish mercie to hir soull, scho ansuered again scho had no will to speak of gentilfolk, and they told hir that gentilfolk wold be far to seek quhen scho behoved to ansuer befor the tribunall of \God/ to give ane accompt, scho ansuered that Kathren Key was with tham at Cowdonis, quhen the tua bairns was destroyed, and that Kathren Key, Margret Tailyoer, Besse Paton and one with a quheit coat went up the stair, and the rest stayed at the stairfut till they cam doun. {*p. 4*}

Thridlie[138] compeirit James Chamberis, Johne Thomson and Walter Sword quho deponet that Kathren Renny confessed that Kathren Blak, Elspit Blak and Margret Tailyeor was at ane meeting at Androw Erskeinis litle hous,[139] and being skard with James Moreis, Elspit Blak went in ower the grein dyk with the Divell, and Margret Tailyeor and Kathren Blak went through David Measonis.

Fortlie[140] compeirit Allexander Main and Robert Archibald and deponit that Kathren Renny delated Kathren Wightman, Besse Harla, Elizabeth Crokit and Jonet Meason to be witches.

Fyftilie compeirit Androw Drffen[141] and James Robertsoun quho deponit … Besse Harla was … [*four lines mostly worn away here, and parts of the next two paragraphs*]

6. Sextlie compeirit James Lindsay, John Thomsone, Robert Archibald, William Moreson elder, who all deponit that Kathren Renny was delated be Margret Duchall, be Margret Tailyeor, be Jonet Blak, and be Besse Paton to be at … meitingis … destroying of bairnes, horse and kuy.

7. Seventlie compeirit William Moreson, Patrik Chamberis kirk … Meldrum skoolmaster who declared that … and tryed wpon Kathren Renny in hir hind head[142] befor officeris Thomas Nepper bailyie of Alloway, Alexander Stewart and James Mitchell yowngar kirk elder.

We the Justices of peace undersubscryving doe declare that all the witnes conteined in thir four leaves war convened befor us and being deeplie sworne, did evrie ane of tham deponit as befor and above set down in evrie particular, quhich we testifie to be trew be this our subscription at Clakmanan the 25 of Julii 1658 yeiris.

[*Signed:*] Harie Bruce, RBruce.

137 In margin: '2.'

138 In margin: '3. Kathren Renny.'

139 In margin: 'A meitting at Andro Erskens litle hous with Katherene Blak and Elspet Blak.'

140 In margin: '4. Persones delaited be hir to be witches.'

141 This name has been damaged, but the opening 'Drff' or perhaps 'Drss' is fairly clear.

142 This is where the Devil's mark was found by the pricker, as is stated in Source 4 below.

JC26/26, bundle 3, no. 21.[143]

{p. 1} In first[144] compeirit Thomas Mitchell of Cowdon, Walter Suord, James Lindsay, Mr William Lindsay, David Vertrie and John Thomson, who all being sworn deponit that Jonet Blak confessed her ingadment in the Diwillis service,[145] and that scho met first with him at Demperstounis Loan Head, quhen scho was going to Sinnisyd, and that he cam hom that night with hir, quhilk was in the great storm of snaw, he appeared to hir in the liknes of ane blak dog with ane sowis head.[146] Scho confessed severall meetingis with Margret Tailyeor, Besse Paton, Elspit Blak, Margret Demperstoun, Kathren Renny and Margret Duchall and speciallie on[e] at Cowdonis hous, quhair ther was with tham ane bony Las with ane blak pok, who went up Cowdonis stair with Margret Talyeor, Besse Paton and Kathren Renny and Margret Tailyeor had ane long rok and Kathren Renny ane schort Rok and they had sum thing in thair putches, that was the death of the tua bairnes, Scho confessed that the first that ewer Intysed hir to the Diwillis service was Besse Paton.

Secondlie[147] Compeirit William Moreson and John Stein kirk elderis and deponit that Jonet Blak declared that Besse Paton knew of the blak dog as weall as hir self and that scho banished the blak dog from hir sex weekis, and quhen scho went to Leith, Besse Paton and Margret Tailyeor went both with hir, Scho confessed scho had the thing that slew Cowdonis Bairnes bot Besse Paton gat it from hir, Scho confessed many meetings quhair Margret Tayleor, Besse Paton, Kathren Renny, Elspit Blak and Margret Demperstoun was ay togidder, And that thair was ay ane bony Las with a blak pok with Margret Tayleor and the Diwill togidder.

Thridlie[148] compeirit Mr James Meldrum, Robert Formand and David Keir, quho deponit that Jonet Blak confessed that ther was ane dog that lay with hir in hir bed, all the Last winter, and therafter confessed befor tham, that it was the Diwell and that scho put up ane deall[149] betuixt hir and him, becaus scho was ay trowbled with him.

Fourtlie[150] Compeirit David Wertie, Thomas Beiny and Robert Drysdaill who deponit that they told Jonet Blak[151] that Margret Duchall said that scho was with tham that war at the casting away of the boat at Blakgrange, *quhair*

143 This undated document was evidently written in about July 1658.

144 In margin: 'Jonet Blak.'

145 In margin: 'Confessed pactione.'

146 In margin: '1. Confesses the severall meitings with the rest Especially at the distroying Cowdounes barnes.'

147 In margin: '2.'

148 In margin: '3. Confessed the Devill lay with hir in Lyknes of ane dog.'

149 'ane deall': a wooden plank.

150 In margin: '4. At the casting away the boat.'

151 *Sic.* Perhaps Janet Black told them.

fyve men died and all in the liknes of corbies, they asked hir how they could be[152] in the liknes of a corbie, scho said weall enewgh, bot Il warrant yow I was not ther my Lain.[153]

Compeirit[154] William Moreson kirk elder, Patrik Chamberis kirk elder and Mr James Meldrum who declared that the Diwillis merk is fund on Jonet Blak hir right oxster,[155] and that befor Mr Thomas Nepper bailyie of Alloway, Allexander Stewart and James Mitchell yownger kirk elder. {*p. 2*}

Ditties against Jonet Blak

Donald Forgison[156] deponis that on[e] night being duelling wnder Janet Blak, that they hard hir say about midnight, scho being all alon in the hous abowe tham, awoid Satan,[157] get out of my bed, and with sum thing in hir hand rumbling abowe and under the bed, com out foull theiff and mak me quyt of yow.[158]

Donald Forgisone[159] deponis that John Boidis wyff now duelling in Leith said to him, that on[e] day quhen scho was tuo myllis be wast Leith comming hom, schoe saw a woman comming towardis hir from the skap quhair thay tak the mussellis,[160] and presentlie bot looking about scho saw nothing bot a sow, quhich followed and persewed hir to the bak of hir own hous, and thair in the tuinkling of ane eye, saw no sow, bot Jonet Blak standing thair, And asking hir quhat scho was doing thair, scho said scho was comd to get the hous meall[161] that scho was aughten hir.[162]

Compeirit William Moreson and John Stein kirk elderis and James Lindsay who deponit,[163] that Margret Duchall, Margret Tailyeor,[164] Besse Paton,[165] and Kathren Renny,[166] did all of tham confes and declair that Jonet Blak[167] was ane witch and *that scho was with* tham,[168] at the *distroying of* William *Monteath his horse and kuy*, Edward Turnouris kow, at *killing of ane bairn in Marie Moreis*

152 Here and later, the text in italics is underlined in the MS.
153 'my Lain': alone.
154 In margin: '5. The mark found one hir rycht oxster.'
155 'oxster': armpit.
156 In margin: '1.'
157 'awoid Satan': go away, Satan.
158 'quyt of yow': free of you.
159 In margin: '1.'
160 'skap quhair thay tak the mussellis': coastal mussel-bed.
161 'hous meall' (mail): rent for a house.
162 'that scho was aughten hir': that was owed to her.
163 In margin: '3. Confessiones of Margaret Duchell, Margaret Tailyeor, Bessie Patone, Katharene Rany, mair of the malefeices thai and Jonet Blak witch ratefeis to.'
164 '1' written above this name.
165 '2' written above this name.
166 '3' written above this name.
167 '4' written above this name.
168 In margin: 'Malefeices against Jonet Blak.'

in Tulliebodie, at killing of ane *bairne in Thomas Bruce his hous* in Clakmanan And at killing[169] of tua bairnes in Cowdonis hows. {*p. 3*}

In first[170] compeirit James Crightoun, Thomas Lindsay, David Wertie litstar, Robert Moreis couper, James Paterson and William Millar who being all sworn, deponit and declared that they hard Bessie Paton confes[171] that the night they went all in to Coudonis hous to destroy the tua bairnes, that ane of ws fell in the [*sic*] in owergoing of Jean Lindsayis yaird dyk, and all the rest lewgh at hir, Scho confessed lykewayis that the night the first of Cowdonis bairnes died, ther died ane Bitch with him, and the night the second bairn died *ther died* ane cat with him:[172] And scho declared *that the* woman with the blak pok and Margret Tailyeor and Elspit Blak who caried the meall that was strawed on the bairnes went first wp the stair, Scho lykewayis declared that Kathren Blak and Jonet Reid war both witches And that scho hard Kathren Blak say to Jonet Reid, quhen they discordit, ga ham comon theiff and tak out the winding scheittis of Margret Mastertounis bairns out of your kist, for ye was the dead of tham all, Scho lykewayis declared that Barbara Erskin was ane witch, and that scho was at casting away of the boat at Blakgrange quhair Fywe men lost [*sic*].[173]

Secondlie[174] compeirit, Androw Thomson baxter, Robert Archibald litstar and David Wertie litster, and all being sworn did depon that Besse Paton delated Kathren Blak to be a witch and that scho gifted hir doghter to the Diwell quhen scho was a child And for that gift the Divell gawe hir the gift of many a man and womanis goodis and gear.

Thridlie[175] compeirit James Crightoun, Walter Sword, and James Lindsay, who all deponit that Besse Paton confessed that the woman with the blak pok was Kathren Key, and that the said Kathren Key, Margret Tailyeor and Elspit Blak who caried the pok with the meall that was strawed on the bairnes went first wp Cowdonis stair, quhen the bairnes was destroyed And scho said scho wold goe to death with it.

Fourtlie[176] compeirit Patrik Chamberis kirk elder, William Moresone kirk elder, Mr James Meldrum skoolmaster, Allexander Stewart, James Maknair, James Moreis and John Thomson baxter, who declared that Besse Paton being asked if scho had the Diwills merk, did absolutlie deny that ewer scho knew

169 '5' written above this word.
170 In margin: 'Besse Paton.'
171 In margin: 'Confessis scho wes at Cowdones hous at the distruction of his tua bairnes.'
172 In margin: '1. Delaittis Katharene Kay, Elspeth Blak, Jonet Reid, Barbara Erskene.'
173 In margin: 'Confessis schoe wes at the casting away the Boat at Blakgrainge.'
174 In margin: '2. Delaits Katharene Blak.'
175 In margin: '3. Anent Cowdonis bairnes.'
176 In margin: '4.'

any thing of the Divill or his merk, at last scho being tried for it, It was found wpon hir in hir secret member, befor all the said witnesses.[177] *{p. 4}*

Ditties against Besse Paton

Robert Formand[178] deponit that quhen he was wronged be Besse Paton, in that peece of the ward quhich he Labored[179] and payit for, he summondit hir to the court, and the said Besse said it sould be a deir summonding to[180] me and werie schortlie after I contracted seeknes, and was rosted with heat, the half of each tuentie four houris and pyned away quhich lasted with me about half a yeir, and both my hors died being both lustie[181] and fat.

Compeirit[182] William Moreson \kirk/ elder, James Lindsay, John Dow wobster and James Anderson baxter all being sworne deponit that they hard Margret Duchall *delait Besse Paton* to be a witch and that scho was at \the/ destroying of Cowdonis tua bairnes, destroying[183] *of ane bairn in* Clakmanan and[184] ane other in Tullibodie, and[185] ane kow to Edward Turnor, and that scho went to William Monteathes stable and put in Raw *flesch under the stall and within* tuentie four howris, ther died the best horse and his best kow. The said witnes deponit lykwayis[186] that Margret Duchall said that Besse Paton put in a clout[187] in a holl of William *Hepbronis wall of his hous*, and sua lang as it sould be thair, William Hepbron sould newer win him self ane meall of meat and this scho did becaus William Hepbronis wyff wold not sell her draff.[188]

Thridlie[189] compeirit William Moreson elder who deponit that he hard Jonet Blak declair that Besse Paton cam to hir and bad hir goe with hir quhen scho cast away the boat at Blakgrange quhair the fyve men was lost, and scho said that Besse Paton was a great witch and had moir strenth in hir fingar nor scho had in all hir bodie, and scho said lykwayis that Besse Paton was at all thair meitingis at destroying the bairnes, horse and kuy.

Fourtlie[190] compeirit William Moreson kirk elder, James Crightoun, James Lindsay, John Thomson baxter and Robert Archibald, quho all deponit that Kathren Renny and Margret Tailyeor hes in all thair confessionis \delatted/ Besse Paton to be a witch and that scho was at all thair meitingis at killing of children, horse and kuy.

177 In margin: 'The mark on hir secreit member.'
178 In margin: '2.'
179 'Labored': ploughed, cultivated.
180 'him' crossed out.
181 'lustie': sturdy, healthy.
182 In margin: '2.'
183 '2' written above this word.
184 '3' written above this word.
185 '4' written above this word.
186 In margin: 'Malefices Against hir.'
187 'clout': cloth.
188 'draff': residue of malt after brewing, sometimes used as animal feed.
189 In margin: '3. Jonet Blak confessis schoe was at the casting away the bott at Blakgrang with Bessie Paton.'
190 In margin: '4.'

JC26/24, bundle 15, no. 9.

[*Endorsed:*] Roll of Assyse, August 1658. Assise for the Witches of Alloway, 3 August 1658.

John Scobie yow ar to summond the personis wnderwrettin to appear befor the Judges at Edinburgh the thrid day of August nixtocum 1658, to be wpon the assise of the Witches of Alloway wnder the pain of ane hundreth merkis of penaltie ewrie ane of tham Who sall not appeir the said day according to ane ordor direct to ws from Georg Lokart adwocat to his hienes the lord protector of the dait the tuentie second day of Julii 1658.

-x John Wertie skipper in Alloway[191]
-x John Thomson skipper thair
-x Robert Moreis merchand thair
- Thomas Harrowar cordinar thair
-x James Spalding thair
-x James Huntar weawer thair
-x John Murray thair
- Androw Stein flescheour thair
-x Allexander Ritchie yowngar thair
-x James Mitchell yowngar thair
-x Androw Ros tailyeour thair
-x Patrik Formand thair
- John Nukoll cordinar thair
-x Androw Henderson tailyeour thair
-x David Thomson thair

/ James Blak thair
- Hendrie Towart thair
- Thomas Fotheringham thair
/ William Johnstoun smyth thair
* Thomas Mitchell maltman thair
/ David Fergus in Rasselloch
- William Burn in Gracornhill
- Thomas Millar in Grange of Alloa
/ Robert Thomson in Hilton
- John Galloway in Tullibodie
- John Renny smyth thair
* James Burn in Blakgrange
- Malcom Alexander in Menstrie
/ John Moreis in Clakmanan
- Archibald Quheit flescheour thair

- Hendrie Hutcheon cordinar thair
-/ Thomas Burne smyth thair
John Thomson in Ferritoun
James Dikie in Sauquhy
* John Anderson maltman in Alloway
Thomas Thomson in Grange of Alloa
- Edward Wightman in Arnes
Allexander Drysdaill in Balhairtie
Symon Drysdaill in Ferimaill
Patrik Burne thair
- John Anderson yowngar in Blakgrange
John Allexander in Powhous
- William Allexander in Menstrie
James Millar smyth in Sauquhy
- John Cowie yowngar in Cobilcrook

[*Signed:*] Charles Erskine, RBruce.

191 The symbols annotating this list are evidently the messenger's system for keeping track of the summoning process.

JC26/24, bundle 6, no. 5.

Causes, to be called the 3d off August, 1658.

[*This document consists of ten one-line summaries of prosecutions to be brought, the ninth of which is:*]

Lord advocat, contra, foure wiches off Alloway.[192]

Source 4: NRS, Court of Justiciary Minute Books, 1655–1659, JC6/5.

{*fo. 272r.*} Witchcraft
Margaret Tailyeor
Bessie Patone
Jonet Black
Katharene Rany
Prissoners

Persewer
Lord Advocat

Witnessis
To attest the Justices of peace Subscriptione
James Lindsay in Alloway[193]
William Moreis kirk elder thair
Androw Thomsone bakster thair

3 August 1658

Margaret Tailyeor alledgit Andro Thomeson did tortour hir at hir confession.

Eodem die post meridiem[194]

[Procu]retouris[195] for the pannell sayed the witnessis depositions are not to be respectit except they are present.

Ye and ilk ane of yow ar Indyted and accused For that Notwithstanding be the devyne Law of Almytie God and actes of parliament of this Natione, the committers of the crymes of sorcerie and wichcraft ar punisheable by deathe, Nevertheles It is of verritie that yee having shaken aff all fear of God, reverence and reguard to his devine Law and Lawes of this Natione hes thir many yeirs bygane betaken your selffes to the service off Satane the enemy of your salvatione, keiped many trystes and meetings with him, had carnal

192 In margin: 'Witchcraft'.
193 'Thomas Mitchell of Cowdoun' crossed out above this name.
194 'The same day, after noon'.
195 Conjectural reading of indistinct word partly obscured by binding.

copulation with him, entred In pactione and covenant with him, renunced your Baptismes, received his marks in your bodies and promised to be his servantes, Lykas Be the Devills assistance yee and evrie on[e] off yow by your sorcerie and witchcraft hes comitted severall malificies Laid one and tane aff uncouth diseissis and seiknessis upone the people of this natione ocassioneing thairby sundrie of thair daithes And yee laid one seiknes one bestiall cattel and goods As be your depositiones and confessiones taikin in presence of his hienes Justices of peace and of dyvers uthers famous[196] witnessis moir manifestly will appear.

1. And first ye and ilk ane of yow haveing conceaved ane crewall and devlish hatred against Thomas Mitchell off Coudoune, ye accompanied with the deceast Margret Duchell and Elspet Black In the moneth of December Last I^{m}vi^{c} fiftie seavine yeires came under silence and cloud off night about tuelve houres at even to the duelling hous of Coudone, carreing along with yow ane pock with some Inchanted meall therin quhilk the Devill your maister had givine yow, and haveing all gone up the stairs *{fo. 272v.}* the Devill going formest ye went all at the hole of the doore In thee [*sic*] Licknes off catts, And be your devilrie and witchcraft strawed the said Inchanted meill upone tua of the said Thomas his childring so that schortlie efter thay evanisched and pyned away to daith, the nycht that the first chyld died thair haveing deid ane bitch with hir, and that nycht the secound deid thair haveing ane cat deid with him, Off the quhilk crewall murder of the said tua childring by your Inchantment, sorcery and witchcraft ye ar airt and pairt.

2. Secoundly ye and ilk ane of yow ar Indyted and accused For that ye haveing consaved ane devillishe heatret against Marie Moreis in Tilliebodie upone the [*1 word blank*] day of [*1 word blank*] ye by your devillrie and witchcraft at ane consultatione had be yow with the Devill your maister laid ane grevous seiknes upone ane chyld of the said Moreis, quhairof the chyld did deceise within ane schort space thairefter, off the quhilk crewall Murder of the said chyld by your sorcery and wichcraft ye was airt and pairt.

3. Thirdlie ye and Ilk ane of yow ar Indyted and accused for that yee haveing conceaved ane hatred against Thomas Bruce in Clackmanane upon the [*1 word blank*] day off [*1 word blank*] yeirs ye also Laid on ane greivous seeknes upon his chyld sua that by your sorcery and wichcraft he duynet[197] pynet away and dyed off the said seeknes within a short space thairefter, of the quhilk murder ye ar lykwyse airt and pairt. *{fo. 273r.}*

4. Fourthlie yee and ilk ane of yow ar Indyted and accused For that ye haveing conceived ane crewall hatred against Edward Turner In Grange, ye by your sorcerie and wichcraft killed and destroyed ane kow of his, off the quhilk yee was Lykewayes airt and pairt.

[196] 'famous': reputable.

[197] 'duynet': dwindled, wasted.

5. Fyfthly ye and Ilk ane of yow ar Indyted and accused for that yow haveing conceaved ane devlish hatred against William Manteith In Bouhous In Alloway, haveing received some Inchanted raw flesh from the Dewle your maister ye went thairwith to the said William his stable and pat the samen underneath the stall quhair by your devillrie and wichcraft within 24 houres efter your doun Laying theroff the said William his best hors and his best kow both dyed.

6. Sexthlie yee and Ilk ane off yow ar Indyted and accussed for being at 5 severall trystes and meetings with the Devill your maister, First at Thomas Millers barne, befor yee went to Coudounes hous and bewicht his 2 children, Nixt meeting ye hade was at the place called Bodsmedow quhair the Devill appeared to yow In the Licknes of ane feltered[198] foall, and ye all danced togither in utheris hands,[199] Bessie Patone leading the ring and sayeing Walifall our bridegroome, Third meeting at the Cuniger at Hallow even last quhair ye all lykewayes did daunce togither, the Devill leading the ring, fourth meeting ye had at the Bowhous, and the fyfth at Androw Erskines litle house quhair ye being scarred be James Moreis then fled away, all which meetings {*fo. 273v.*} yee have confessed be youre depositiones to be off verritie.

7. Sevinthlie ye the said Bessie Paton in particular, Is Indyted for that haveing conceaved a devlish hatred against Robert Formane In [*1 word blank*] becaus he had summondet yow to the court for wronging him, In a piece off waird, which he had in laboring,[200] ye said to him that it should be a dear summonding to him, sua that be your sorcerie and wichcraft, he Immediatlie thairefter contracted a fearfull seeknes, and was rosted with heat the ane halff off evrie tuentie four houres, and pyned away In his bed, the which lasted with him about half ane yeir, Lykas ye then bewiched tua off his horses to death, they being both fat and lustie at that tyme quhen they dyed.

8. Sicklyke ye the said Bessie Patone haveing conceaved ane crewall \hatred/ against William Heapburne In Alloway becaus his wyff wold nocht sell yow some draff, yee in revenge thairoff pat ane Inchanted clout In a holl off the house wall, quhich so long as It continowed there he never schrew[201] nor was able to win himselff a meal of meat.

9. Sicklyke ye the said Bessie Patone was In company with Janet Black and Barbara Erskeine at the casting away of the boat at Black Grange quhair be your devilrie and wichcraft ye sank and pat to death 5 men that were In the boat, haveing all than appeared In the Licknes off corbies. {*fo. 274r.*}

And Lastlie all of yow hes the Devill your maisteres mark on your bodies, viz. the said Margret Tailyeor in your secret member, ye the said Bessie Patone in your secret member, ye the said Jonet Black in your right okster[202] and

198 'feltered': shaggy.
199 'in utheris hands': holding each other's hands.
200 'laboring': cultivation.
201 *Sic.* Probably read 'threw' (thrived).
202 'okster': armpit.

ye the said Kathren Rainy in your hindhead, quhlk is proven and tryed be the pricker and searcer of the said marks In presence off famous witnessis.

3 August 1658

All pleadis not guyltie to all the dittay.... {*fo. 275r.*}

The Witches of Allowa assyse 3d August 1658

John Vertie in Alloay	James Hunter weater[203] thair
John Thomsone skipper	John Murray thair
Robert Morice merchand	Andro Stewin thair
Thomas Hamilton cordiner	Alexander Ritchie younger thair
James Spalding cordiner thair	James Mitchell younger thair

Andro Ross tailyeor thair
Patrike Forman thair
Andro Henrysone tailyeor thair
David Thomesone thair

Assyse sworne for the witchs. {*fo. 275v.*}

Edinburgh 3 of August 1658

The assyse all in ane voce be the mouthe of James Mitchell younger thair chancellor finds the pannell Margaret Tailyeor guiltie of the syn of witchcraft In renunceing hir baptisme with the Devill haveing carnall copulatione with him And of airt and pairt of the haill malefices mentionat in hir dittay.[204]

[*Signed:*] James Mitchell.

3 August 1658

Also the said assyse all in ane voce be the mouth of thair said chancellor finds the Pannells Jonet Blak and Katharene Rany guiltie of the syn of witchcraft and of the haill malefices mentionat in thair dittays.[205]

[*Signed:*] James Mitchell.

3 August 1658

And Last the said assyse By pluralitie of voices[206] finds the pannell Bessie Patone guiltie of the syn of witchcraft and of airt and pairt of the rest of the malefices quhairof the uther thrie abonewrittin ar fund guiltie.[207]

[*Signed:*] James Mitchell.... {*fo. 276r.*}

203 'weater' (tide-waiter): customs officer.

204 In margin: 'Witch: Margaret Tailyeor convict and Brunt'.

205 In margin: 'Jonat Blak, Katharine Rany convict and Brunt'.

206 Although the assize convicted three of the four witches unanimously, its members were divided over Bessie Paton – even though she faced additional charges (numbered 7, 8 and 9 in the dittay). Perhaps some of the assizers found these charges unconvincing.

207 In margin: 'Witch: Bessie Patone convict and Brunt'.

Sentences …
3 August 1658
The Commisioners adjudges Margaret Tailyeour, Bessie Patoun, Janet Black and Catherin Rennye as being found guiltie of the sin of witchcraft specified in their Instruments to be taken upon Weddinsday the elevinth of this instant to the Castell hill of Edinburgh, And their betwixt two and three houres in the afternoon to be strangled at stakes till they be dead and their bodies to be brunt to ashes and their goods eschiet.[208]

Source 5: NRS, Court of Justiciary Process Papers, 1658–1659, JC26/24, JC26/26.

JC26/26, bundle 3, no. 2.[209]

[*Endorsed:*] Testificat in favour of Katharene Blak.
We undersubscryveares Be thir presenttes Testifie and declaire That Katherene Black spous to Thomas Maissone indueller in Alloway by reasone of her heavie sicknes and infirmitie occasioned throw her straite imprisonement and want of foode, coall, candle, beddeing and utheres necessars Is Recommendit to the publict prayeres of the parochiners of Alloway. And accordinglie thairto wes publictlie in the church prayed for efter sermone as use is: Quhilk we declaire to be of treuth be thir presenttes subscrivit with our hands Att Edinburgh the sevinth day of December i^{m}vi^{c} Fyftie eight yeirs.[210]
[*Signed:*] Johne Strwler, Robart Dillie, JSandies.[211]

JC26/26, bundle 3, no. 19.

[*Endorsed:*] Supplicatione, Catharene Black.
Unto the Honourable the Commissioners for administration of justice to the people in Scotland The Humble Supplicatione of Catharene Black prisoner at Alloway, Sheweth,
That where be Instigatione of certaine ewilldisposed persones to your petitioners honestie she is most maliciouslie branded and delaited and committed to prison upon Suspition of Witchcraft, Wherein schoe hes remained prisoner above three moneths bygane, And albeit your petitioner be maist innocent of that Cryme Yet schoe is maist maliciouslie keiped in prisone without either offering to present her to ane Legall tryall or Liberating her upon Cautione, Albeit earnestlie sought for by her freinds,

208 In margin: 'Witches, Margaret Tailyeor, Bessie Patone, Jonet Blak, Kathrene Rany, Brunt [*day obscured by binding*] August'.
209 Three separate documents have this number.
210 The day and month have been filled in later.
211 The reading of these holograph signatures is far from certain, but the third name is John Sands, who later stands caution for Katherine Black.

Throw whilk hard and unchristian ussage your honours petitioner hes contracted heavie Sicknes, Licklie to dye of the samen.[212]

May it therfore please your honours in Consideration of the premissis to tak your petitioners sad sufferings to Commiseratione, And to give warrand to the Justices of Peace of Clakmannan shyre (upon your petitioners Giveng Baill) to cause put her to Libertie furth of prisone, And your Petitioner shall ever pray for your honours everlasting Happiness.

Edinburgh the 14th December 1658.

The Commissioners (upon the Petitioner Catharene Black her finding good caution for her appeareance before Them the first day of the Circuit for the shyre of Clakmannane to answer to such things as shall be Layd to her Chairge) doe heirby give order to the Justices of peace for the said shirefdome To cause put the said Catharene Black immediatly furth of their prisone, And ordaines the saids Justices To bind over the witnesses wha knowes any thing of her guiltines and to send in whatsoever depositiones, examinationes of Bands to be takne be them thereanent against the said first day of the Circuit, or else to showe ane reasonable Cause in the contrair betuixt and the First day of Januar nixtocum.

[*Signed:*] Will: Laurence, Mosley.

Edinburgh the 14 December 1658.

The abovewrittin supplicatione with the honorabll commissioneris delyverance at the end therof Was produced be Edward Nisbet wryter in Edinburgh and registrat in the buiks of adjornall be me.

[*Signed:*] Alex: Hamilton.

JC26/24, bundle 6, nos. 10, 4.[213]

[*Endorsed:*] Band, Johne Sands and Robert Measone, to Mr George Stirling, 1658.

Be it kend till all men Be thir presentis lettres Wee Johne Sands of Langsyde within the lordship of Culroiss and Robert Measone sone to Thomas Measone Indueller in Alloway For sameikle as Katherine Black spous to the said Thomas Measoune Haveing petitiouned The Honorabill Commissioners for administratioune of justice to the people In Scotland To give warrand to the Justices of peace of Clackmannane shyre For putting of the said Katherine Black to Libertie as being Imprisoned by them above thrie monethis bygane upon suspitiouns of Witchcraft, Wpon the quhilk petitioune It pleased the Commissioners afoirsaid To give ordor to the Justices of peace of the said sherefdome To caus put the said Katherine Black Imediatlie furth of thair prisone schoe finding good

212 The words 'And is prayed for in the Church' have been crossed out here.

213 This single-sheet document has been cut into two pieces, damaging a line of text, as noted below. The pieces have the separate modern numbers 10 and 4. The first part of the text is on number 10.

catioune For hir appearance befoir them the first day of the circuit for the shyre of Clackmannane To answer to such chargis as sould be laid to her charge, As the said petitioune and and [*sic*] the Commissioners ordor and warrand thairto dated the fourtene of December instant Registerat be Mr Alexander Anietone clerk to the Court In caussis criminall at mair lenth beares, Lykeas upon sight of the foirsaid petitioune and ordor and warrand abovewrittin Sir Charles Erskyne of Alveth \and James Holburne of Menstrie/ tua of the Justices of peace of the said shyre of Clackmannane Be ther lettere dated the fyftene of December Instant direct to Mr George Stirling thair clerk Desyred him as clerk foirsaid to take sufficient cautione for the said Katherine Black hir appearance In maner above mentionat And cautione being fund To give ordor to the constables For putting of hir to Libertie As the said lettre hirby be proports And now sieing the said Mr George hath given warrand to the constables of the paroche of Alloway For putting of the said Katherine Black to libertie Thairfor wit ye ws the saidis Johne Sandis and Robert Measoune To be bund and obleist Lykeas we be the tenor heirof Faithfullie binds and obleissis ws conjunctilie and severallie our airis executoris and Intromitters with our guids and geir quhatsumevir as cautioner and sovertie for the said Katherine Black That schoe sall compeir befoir the right honorable Commissioners In Criminall causes the first day of the nixt circuit to be haldin for the shyre of Clakmannane thair to answer at the Instance of quhatsumevir pairtie To all such things as salbe laid to hir charge wnder the paine of Ane thousand pundis scots money To be peyit to any who the saids Commissioners sall appoynt and nominat For receaving of the samen And for the [*about 4 words damaged*] content and consents [*about 4 words damaged*] Justice[214] court, binkes of Justice[215] or any uther laufull Judicatorie binkes within this natioune To have the strenth of ane declarator of any of the Judges thairof That all executioune on ane simple charge of six dayes mey pass heirupon And constitutis [*1 line blank*] Our laufull procurators and In witnes quhairof (writtin be James Kincaid servitor to David Moir shereff clerk of Striviling) and subscrivit with our hands att Striviling the eightene day of December $i^{m}vi^{c}$ fiftie eight yeirs Befoir thir witnessis the saidis David Moir and James Kincaid.

[*Signed:*] JSandeis, Robt. Mesone, JKincaid witnes, DMoir witnes.

JC26/26, bundle 3, no. 2.[216]

[*Endorsed:*] Coppie of the Suplicatione, Elspethe Blak, With the delyverance one the end thairof for hir appearance at the circuit for Clakmannane shire anno 1659.

[214] The document now numbered 10 ends here, with its last line having been damaged when the paper was cut into two pieces. The text continues on the document now numbered 4.

[215] 'binkes of Justice': benches or seats of justice (i.e. courts).

[216] Three separate documents have this number.

Unto the honourable commissioneris in criminall causis to the peaple in Scotland The humble supplicatione of Elspeth Blak prissoner at Alloway, Sheweth,

Wheras be the instigatione of certane Evill disposed persones your petitioneres unfrendes Schoe is dilaitted and committed to prissone without any ground upone suspition of witchcraft Quhairin schoe hes contenowed prissoner thir 18 weiks and above And albeit schoe be most Innocent of the said cryme And for cleiring hir selff thairof hes earnestly beged for ane tryell \yit/ the Justices of peace by quhais ordour I was[217] committed altogidder refuissis to doe the same or yit to liberat me *pro tantum*[218] Without your honours ordour to that effect I for the present being in grit mesery and throw my restreint hes contracted heavie seiknes being lying in the fluxes lykly to die thairof As an testificat under the hands of dyverss honest men heir to schaw will testifie.

May it thairfore pleass your honour in consideration of the premissis to tak your petitioners sad suffering to comiseratione And upone your petitioners finding caution to the clerk of the criminall court for hir appearance befoir your honours the first day of the circuit for Clakmanan shire to underly the law for the said cryme or any thing can be laid to hir chairge at the Instance of quhatsomevir parties to gif heirby ordour to the Justices of peace to put your petitioner to Libertie furth of prissone And your petitioner sall evir pray.

Edinburgh the 6 day of \January 1659/[219]

The commissioneris upon the petitioner Elspeth Blak hir finding cautione to the \justices of peace of Clakmanane/[220] for hir appearance befoir thame The first day of the circuit for Clakmannan shire to answer to all sutch things as sall be laid to hir chairge doe heirby gif ordour to the Justices of peace for the said shire efterward To caus put the said Elspeth Blak to Libertie furth of prissone And thir presentts sall be thare \warrand/ And ordanes the said Justices to Bind over the witnessis quha knawes any thing of hir guiltienes And to send in quhatsumevir depositiones, examinationes or bands to be tane be tham thairanent against the dounsitting of the said circuit or elss to schaw ane causs in the contrar.[221]

JC26/24, bundle 6, no. 6.

[*Endorsed:*] Testificat of Elisabeth Blak hir seiknes, 1658. [*In another hand:*] Stirling Court, 1659, Clakmanan.

We Johnne Mitchell elder, Hendrie Towart, Thomas Ronnald, indwellers in Alloay, and others undersubscryvand, doth be thir presents declair and

217 At this point the text shifts temporarily from the third to the first person.
218 'for so long' (i.e. until the trial).
219 Date altered from 'December 1658'.
220 Several words crossed out here, and this phrase added above the line.
221 'betuix and the first herof' crossed out here.

testifie, To anie whome it may concerne, That Elizabeth Black prissoner for the aledged sinn of witchcraft Is for the present mightilie trubled with ane disease called, the bloodie flux, quhilk sho hes in the baddest sort, And by reassone therof Is verie unweill in hir bodie. This wee declair (haveing sein the same) to be of veritie, As witnes our hands Att Alloway the 28 of December 1658.

[*Signed:*] A. S., Henry Towar, Johne Arthour, J. Cragingelt witnes to Andro Slevine and Henrie Towarts subscriptione.

JC26/26, bundle 3, nos. 4 and 5.[222]

[*Endorsed:*] Depositiones annent Magdalen Blair attacht[223] for witchcraft and charming.

{*p. 1*} Sterling the 13 January 1659

Mr Matthias Simpsone and Robert Russall baillie haveing mett in Duncan Buchannans house for visiting of Helen Ker quhais spous who [*sic*] for the present is heavilie deseased and supposed her self to have gotten skaith by witchcraft And supposeing Madlan Blair to be the persone She is conveened and the persons following being examined depones as followes.

James Anderson baxter[224] declard that about an yeare since or thairby There was a horse belonging to Richard Kidstone in Spittell standing before Madlane Blairs doore after he was disburdeened of a load of whins and there being some scolding words past betuixt the said Richard and her, schee strake the said Richards horse saying, God nor he shoot to death[225] And the horse died suddenlie the same day after he was taken home.

The said Magdalane hereupon examined confest that shee strak the said horse and uttered the foresaid words.

The said Helen Ker[226] depones that shee challenged the said Magdalene about those words and told her the horse was dead and Magdalen answered, it was litle enough although[227] it had fallin upon the man himself, and shee never gave a malison but what shee saw light.

The said Magdalen hereupon posed, acknowledges that shee sayed then That shee once prayed \for/ a malison upon John Steill who had gotten a bairn with her and would give her nothing to help it, and he lay long sick and spent much of his geir.

[222] The two sheets in this bundle with the separate modern numbers 4 and 5 are in fact a single document. Both sheets have been folded to make four pages, with the second sheet being inserted within the first to make a booklet of eight pages. Only the first three pages have been written on. A further footnote below marks the transition between the two sheets.

[223] 'attacht': arrested, imprisoned.

[224] In margin: 'James Andersone witnesse annent Magdalen Blair'.

[225] 'shoot to death': die suddenly. This phraseology might appear to be a preventative charm rather than a curse, but it is evidently being presented as a curse.

[226] In margin: 'Helen Ker'.

[227] 'although': even if.

The said Helen farder sayed that the said Magdalen at that tym sayed to her, what had shee a doe to come speake with her since her husband and shee were not friends, and that \sam/ night[228] the said Helen going in to her bed which was made, found a lump of dead sand betuixt the sheets like a modiwort hillok[229] It being ten hours at ewin, and altho shee was weell in health at that tym yet that night shee tooke siknesse which hath continowed with her ewer since, the extremitie of it seazing upon her at that houer of the night till the last Saturnday when told[230] the minister that shee suspected the said Magdalen had wronged her, and since her paines come not to her till midnight.

The said Magdalen[231] hereupon posed declares that shee onelie sayed to Helen, What have ye adoe to come to me for I have nothing to do with yow, And being asked about the dead sand how it came in to Helens bed, shee answered ye should aske that of the leuve,[232] For that is als much as ye would make me doer of all.[233]

[*Signed:*] M. Symson, Robert Russall. {*p. 2*}

Sterling the 14 January 1659

In presens of Master Mathias Simpson minister and Robert Russell baillie and divers uthers Helen Ker being desired to tell if ewer shee made use of any charme for obteaning her health, Shee confest that shee was charmed by one Katharine McGregor in Dunblane, with a drink of water, and that the same Katharine charmed Mr Thomas Lindsay minister at Dunblane and his wife.

And being desired to tell if shee thought that Magdalen Blair had wronged her by witchcraft, Shee held upe her hand in a signe that shee did think soe, Shee being desired soe to doe in regaird shee was speechl[ess][234] throw the extreamite of her desease, and the neernesse shee was to her death being but about tua houres before.[235]

[*Signed:*] M. Symson, Robert Russall.

Sterling the 18 Januarii 1659

The quhilk day Duncan Nairn provest, Andrew Buchanan and Robert Russell baillies, being conveened for farder tryall of the said Magdalen Blair annent the cryme of witchcraft whereof shee is suspected, and haveing conveened before them the persones following for giveing informatione thairanent, They deponed as followes, viz.

228 'or the next night after' crossed out here.

229 'modiwort hillok': molehill.

230 *Sic.* Read 'when she told'.

231 In margin: 'Magdalen'.

232 'the leuve' (leave): the others. Before 'leuve', the probable word 'rest' has been crossed out.

233 In margin: 'James Norie clerke of the said burgh being like wise auditor to the foresaid depositiones attests the same'.

234 Conjectural restoration of damaged letters. MS 'speechl…'.

235 In margin: 'James Norie clerke of Stirling and writer hereof attestis the same'.

Helen Fergusone[236] spous to Andrew Toward wright declares that about the moneth of March 1658 shee being goeing upe the way to her husbands workhous, Margaret Paule spous to John Allan skinner mett with her and desired her to goe in to Marjorie Wingyets seller next to Magdalen Blairs house (being on the afternoone) and when they had gone in togither to drink a choppin of ale, the said Magdalen came in to them without any desire[237] and sayed to Margaret Pawle That shee was kinde when her husband was sike But since shee had not been kinde, And imediatlie therafter shee sayd to the deponer That since shee gave her not meat as shee did formerlie The deponer never threave,[238] and the deponer replyed That it was too true.

The said Margaret Pawle[239] declares the like except annent the last part therof, which to hir memorie was that Magdalen sayed that Helen had no moir in her amrie[240] than formerlie that[241] shee got meat fra her.

The said Magdalen[242] hereupon examined declared that to the best of her knawledge shee went not in to the said Helen Ferguson and Margaret Paule, And nather that shee spoke any thing to the said Margaret as Helen depons, But about that tyme shee sayed to Helen That shee would not be a boll of meale the richer at the years end that the deponer got none of her meat.

I James Norie comon clerk of Stirling subscribes as notary for the said Magdalen at her comand Becaus shee cannot write. JN. {*p. 3*}[243]

William Luckisone[244] maltman declares that about six yeres since or thairby he contracted a sore sicknes and in the meane tyme haveing occasion to visite Katharine Luckisone \his sister now/ spous to James Andersone, and finding her and Magdalen Blair sitting togither in the foot of Andrew Cowans yaird The said Katharine asked at Magdalen what shee thought aled the deponer, And Magdalen thereupon asked at the deponer if there was any enmitie or discord betueen Issobell Bennet and him, and he answered that there was none that he knew of, except that at sometimes when her fowles would be in his fathers victuall, he would throw stones at them to call them furth of it, Whereupon Magdalen desired that he would goe to Issobell Bennet and take a grip of hir coat taile and drink a pint of ale with her and crave his health from her thrie tymes for the Lords sake, and he would be weell, But he did it not.

The said Katharine Luckisone hereupon examined declared the same to be true.

236 In margin: 'Helen Fergusone'.

237 'without any desire': without any invitation.

238 'threave' (thrived): prospered.

239 In margin: 'Margaret Paule'. This whole paragraph has been squeezed in as an afterthought.

240 'amrie' (almery): cupboard, locker or other storage place.

241 *Sic*. Probably read 'when'. The issue is what had happened after Helen Ferguson stopped giving 'meat' (food) to Magdalen Blair.

242 In margin: 'Magdalen Blair'.

243 The text continues on the next page, a separate sheet with the modern number 5.

244 In margin: '3. William Luckison'.

I James Norie notary and comon clerk \of Stirling/ subscribes for the saids William and Katharine at thair comand Becaus they cannot write.

The said Magdalen[245] hereupon examined declared that about the foresaid tyme shee[246] was sitting with the said Katharin Luckison when William Luckison came to them and when Katharin asked at her what would doe good to Williame and shee answered that a rose cake was good for[247] him and bad him take it, But denyes the rest, And this shee denyed at the first Till shee was confronted befor the saids Williame and Katharine.

James Andersone[248] baxter declares that when he was in sute of Katharine Luckisone his present spous, There being a discord betuixt him and her quhairupon he went in sute of an other, In the mean tyme he mett with Magdalen Blair as he was goeing to meet with the woman that he was in sute of, And shee sayed to him, That he would never get an other woman but Katharine Luckison his present spous.

[*Signed:*] James Andersone.

The said Magdalen[249] hereupon examined declares that shee onelie sayed to him, stay at home, For ye neid not seeke an other woman but Katharine seing shee is as good as an other.

JC26/26, bundle 3, no. 3.

[*Endorsed:*] Depositions against Margaret Gourlay and Janet Miller, 1659.
[*Endorsed:*] Depositiones against Margaret Gourlay and Janet Miller, Witches, Stirling Court, 1659.
[*Endorsed:*] Confessiones and depositiones of Margarat Gourlay and Jonet Miller.

{*p. 1*} Att Stirling the [*number altered, illegible*] Februarii 1659 In presence of Colonell Read, Luetenant Collonel Cloberie, Major Matlo, The Lairds of Touch, Banokburne and Harbertschyre.

Jonet Miller in Kippen declairit that she went in to Margrett Gourlayes hous six weiks since or thairby the same nyght the fyre becum in Androw Wryghts hous efter the sun set quhair sche found Isobell Keir and Margrat Harvie quhair she saw ane blak man with thame and ane tabill coverit with ane whyt cloth, With sum boylet beif and bread, the said Margaret offeret to hir ane part of the meat, Which she refused to eat, and then Margret Gourlay had hir goe about hir bussines, and imediatlie thairafter the fyre

245 In margin: 'Magdalen Blair'.
246 'saw' crossed out here.
247 'it' crossed out here.
248 In margin: 'James Andersone'.
249 In margin: 'Magdalen Blair'.

begun in Margret Gourlay[250] in the little hous quhilk they were at meat, and then Androw Wryght and Georg Wordie in Banokburn quenshet the fyre.

Wpon the nixt morning in the tuaylyght she saw ane glans of woman[251] in Androw Wryghts hous quhair Margrat Gourlay was kendling the fyre in the chimnay And imediatlie the lint on the top of ane bedd in the hous syd was in fyre, which was extinguishet be the saids Androw Wryght and Georg Wordies aforesaid.

Also she sayes that Jonet Wryght oye[252] to Margrat Gourlay hard tuo nyghtes befoir the sound of ane thunderspeall at Margrat Gourlays window And at bed tyme thair wes a great truble at the dore and stones cast of[f] the top of the wall.

The next nyght at the tueylyght when Androw Wryght wes puting in the horsses he saw fyre burning in Margrat Gourlayes hous in the other bed and wes extinguishet be Androw Wryght and his wyfe, Thairefter the same nyght fyre wes tuys or thrys brok out in the said Androwes hous in thrie places and wes extinguishet be the cuntrie people, And within ten dayes fyre brok wp on the north syd of the \outsyd/ hous afoirsaid in the morning efter the sun reas, And that John Knox in Rampherlie preyet quhen they extinguishet the fyre.

Tuo dayes thairefter quhen the people were windoing[253] cornes in the barne the said Jonet Miler cam in the byre at the tueylyght quhair she saw Margrat Gourlay speiking to ane woman not knowen to hir haveing ane whyt coat on and ane plad about hir, Within half ane hour thairefter Euphame Wryght spous to the said Androw saw the fyre rys in the servant mens bed in the byre, which wes extinguishet be Androw Wryght and his wyf and servant namet Patrik Manoch, And thairefter the said Margrat Gourlay and hir oye afoirsaid waket the hous.

Imediatlie thairefter the fyre wes extinguishet John Wryght and the said Jonet wes tareing but the burnt strae they saw ane mekill woman clothet in whyt standing at Margrat Gourlayes doore.

Thairefter within tuo dayes fyre wes fund in the morning on the bak of the hous the said Margrat being about ane myle fra the hous And than she said to Cristane Shaue, hard ye if thair wes ane fyre in our hous this day, she said no, then said Margrat Gourlay to hir Thair wilbe fyre in our hous this day And it wes so and the fyre extinguishet before she returnet.

Within tuo dayes thairefter Walter Buchanen was going to the mos and his man with him, in the morning he saw as he said tuo weomen with Margrat Gourlay in the stak yaird, The said Jonet Miller declaires she saw the said Margrat Gourlay and Isobell Keir and Margrat Harvie with hir And the said

250 After 'Gourlay', another word has been written and then illegibly altered. It may have been intended to be 'bed', the word found in a comparable passage in Source 6 below.

251 'ane glans of woman': a glimpse of a woman.

252 'oye': grandchild.

253 'windoing': winnowing.

Margrat putting in foure hanks of wolen yairn in one stake, Thairefter John Wryght went out and fund the fyre kendlet in fyve places on the bak of the hous in the barne yaird and they took out fyve burning coles out [*sic*] of the hous quhair it wes burning and they put them in the hous fyre quhair all of thame craklet extraordinerlie And quhen they were taking out the coles ane blak corbie cam flieing above the hous too and agane[254] And imediatlie the same stak quhair Margrat Gourlay wes standing took fyre Which wes extinguishet be all the cuntrie And that at no occatioun the said Margrat Gourlay assistet to extinguish the fyre.

The said day in the tueylyght Jonet Miller wes going to hir father Thomas Miller his hous and quhen she wes gone about half ane quarter of ane myle fra Androw Wryghts hous ane blak man met hir and said, quhair are yow going, she answeret, to hir father, quhair is it said he, she said wp bay,[255] she being afrightet and not able to speik, said he, What neid ye be afrayet, I will doe yow no evill, and laid his hand on hir shoulder being heavier nor ane other mans hand, and he inquyret if Margrat Gourlay wes at home, she said yea, And he inquyret if ever {*p. 2*} Margrat Gourlay desyret hir goe anie quhair out with hir, she answeret No, then said he she will speik to yow, and bid yow doe sum thing for he wes hir master And he being removet he lookit bak often bot she beteachet hir[256] to God and durst not returne to her mistres that nyght.

Thairefter within tuo nyghts \on ane Wednisday nyght/ she wes cuming home to Arcumrie, she met a litill eftir the sun set the same man, bot she removet out of the way and beteachet hir to God, And so he went bay and spok not to hir.

And on the Saturday at nyght thairefter Isobell Keir came to hir she being binding the kye and speiret if she wald have ane coill bot did not shaw it to hir and then she show hir ane burning peit coill and inquyret if she wald tak it and kiendill the hous quhilk hir mistres leye stook they being removet to duell in ane other hous, And she refusing it she went auay and saw Patrik Monoch cuming with hay to the kye And quhen they enteret the hous with the haye they saw the hous burning, Which wes extinguishet be nychtbours.

Wpon the Sabath thairefter in the morning Margrat Gourlay wes kendling the fyre in the hous and desyret hir to goe barrow ane busom[257] fra John Wryght, And not getting the busom the said Margrat met hir in the doore and put ane burning peit coill in hir hand and desyret hir to lay it on the wall end above the kye, and the said Jonet confeses she laid the coill quhair

254 'too and agane': to and fro.

255 'wp bay': up by. This should be understood as an incomplete reply: 'Up by …' a place that she cannot name.

256 'beteachet hir' (betook): committed herself.

257 'barrow ane busom': borrow a broom.

she wes desyret. Thairefter Margrat went to the west end of the hous quhair Alexander Mcilhais fund hir on hir knies as if she had bein prayeing.

Thairefter John Wryght went to the byre and saw the coall blinking bot it haid not kendlet anie of the hous, And then he brought in the coill and speiret quha had done it, And then Jonet Miller confeset she did it.

The confesioun afoirsaid is signet by the justices of peace at Stirling the 15 March 1659 efter it wes red to the deponent and acknouledget be hir.

[*Signed:*] Thomas Reade, Ja: Mutlow, WStirling.

JC26/26, bundle 3, no. 6.

[*Endorsed:*] Depositiounes against Margarat Harvie.
[*Endorsed:*] Depositions against Margaret Harvie, Witch, 1659.

The depositioun of witnesses examined in presence of Colonell Thomas Read, Liuetenent Cloberie, Major Matlo, Williame Stirling of Harbertshyre, Captane Callant and Captan Hunt, at Stirling the 16 March 1659, Against Margrat Harvie in Kippen paroch.

Agnies Dinoven in Kippen depones that hir dochter Margrat Milne being seik she tauld Margrat Harvie thairof Wha bad hir goe to Isobell Keirs hous and take thrie rugis of the thak[258] above the said Isobell hir doore heid and seik the bairnie health for Gods caus, which she refuset to obey and the bairn diet.

Jonet Miller now in the prisoun suspect of Witchcraft declaires that about the 15 of December last by past, she went in to Margrat Gourlay hir hous efter the sun set quhair she saw Isobell Keir and Margrat Harvie and ane blak man with thame, all siting at one tabill covered with ane whyt cloth and sum boylet beif and bread thairon, And that the said Margrat \Gourlay/ offered to the deponer ane pairt of the meat Which she refuiset to eat, And then Margrat Gourlay baid hir goe about hir bussines, And imediatlie thairefter ane bed in the hous quhair they were at meat took fyre, Which wes extinguishet be Androw Wryght and Georg Wordie.

Also Jonet Miller declaires that within eyht dayes or thairby thairefter she saw Isobell Keir, Margrat Harvie and Margrat Gourlay in Androw Wryghtis stak yaird and Margrat Gourlay puting in four hanks of wolen yairn in ane stak, And thairefter imediatlie Johne Wryght went out and fand fyre kenilet[259] in fyve severall places on the bak of his hous nearest the barne yaird, And that they took out fyve burning colis out [*sic*] of thes places of the hous quhair it wes burning and put thame in the hous fyre quhair they craked extraordinerlie, And that ane blak reaven came flieing too and again above the hous And imediatlie thairefter the said stak quhair Margaret Gourlay wes standing took fyre, Which wes extinguished by the cuntrie people.

258 'thrie rugis of the thak': three bundles of the thatch.
259 'kenilet': kindled.

The depositiounes afoirsaid are taken in our hearing and signed by ws. [*Signed:*] Thomas Reade, John Clobery, WStirling, Ja: Mutlow.

JC26/26, bundle 3, no. 9.

[*Endorsed:*] Supplication, Kathren Black, 1659.

{*p. 1*} Unto the Honorable Commissioners for administration of Justice in causes criminall to the people in Scotland, The Humble Supplication of Kathren Black for the present prisoner at Alloway, Sheweth,

That where upon ane Supplication presented to your Honors the 14 December last 1658 yeirs That your petitioner was branded and most maliciouslie calumniated of the cryme of Witchcraft and Incarcerat thairfor within the tolbuith of Alloway, It pleased your Honors then, (nothing being made out by the depositiones of witnessis against her to mak her guiltines appeare,) to grant Warrand by your Honors deliverance, direct to the Justices of Peace for the shyre of Clakmannan to put your petitioner to libertie upon her finding caution, to appeare the first day of the Circuit at Stirling, to answer to all such things as should be layd to her chairge, as the samen supplicatione and delyverance subscryved under your hands, Heirwith to show will testifie. And albeit conforme to your Honors ordinance sufficient Baill was given by your petitioner to the Justices of peace for the said shyre of Clakmannan for your petitioner her appearance at the said Circuit, under the payne of ane thousand pounds Scotts money, quhilk Band was accepted, and your petitioner accordinglie then released out of prisone, being most willing to conforme to the Condition therof, to have made her appeirance, Yet nevertheles out of malice and splene, notwithstanding of the said baill, your petitioner is latelie seased upon, and of new Incarcerat without any ground or warrand, floweing from your Honors, quhich is meerlie done in contempt of your Honours ordinance,

May it therfore please your Lordships, In consideratione of your petitioners hard and malitious usage, as being ane Innocent persone, quhich shall be made out before your Honors at the said Circuit, Yet as of before, upon new Baill, to give order to the saids Justices to liberat your petitioner upon her appearance in maner forsaid, And for the favor of God Allmightie to tak course with your petitioners malitious accusers and dilators, And that the Justices may mak it appeare, upon quhat sufficient grounds they have reincarcerat your poor petitioner, and if they cannot, to censure and fyne them for the samen In example of uthers to contemne your honors ordinance in tyme comeing, And your poor petitioner shall ever pray for your Lordships everlasting Happines. {*p. 2*}

Edinburgh the 16 March 1659

The Commissioners gives heirby warrand to the Justices of the Peace for the shyre of Clakmannane and Stirling, or magistrats thairof, in whose prison the petitioner is for the present Incarcerat, to put her to libertie, upon the former baill allready given, and to be given in corroboration thereof, for her appeirance before ws at Stirling the 22 of this Instant utherwise if they doe not, to be answerable under perill.

JC26/26, bundle 3, no. 22.

[*Endorsed:*] Precept and executione Against the witnessis led against Bessie Stevinsone, Issobell Bennet and Magdalen Blair accused for witchcraft, 1659.

{*p. 1*} Officers of the burgh of Sterling Ye or any of yow shall pas this present seen And laufullie Sumond warne and charge Jonet Henrie, Margaret Mershell spous to Corporall Biggs, Patrike Wright cordinare, George Wright fischer and Issobell Smart his spous, Christian Chrystesone spous to James Chrystesone wright, Jonet Chrystesone sometime thair servant, Margaret Matson spous to Williame Lawrie, Bessie Burn spous to Robert Wingyet messenger, Jonet Bennie relict of the deceast Thomas Gilfillan weaver, Jonet Gilfillane [*1 word blank*], Marjorie Wingyet spous to John Wilsone baxter, Katharine Thomsone spous to Peter Easeman Englishman, Katharine Wright spous to Thomas Mitchell maltman, Jeane Watson spous to John Morisone customer,[260] Helen Fergusone spous to Andrew Cowane wright, Thomas McAulay fleshour, Jonet Wright spous to James Buchanan wright, Margaret Cowane spous to Edward Luckison cordinare, Elspet Miller spous to Robert Adame taylyer, Thomas Miller merchand, John Gib cultellare,[261] James Patersone at the bridge and Isobell Willieson his spous, \James Andersone baxter,/ To compeir before the honourable Commissioners for administration of justice to the people in Scotland in causes criminall In ane Justice court to be haldin be them within the tolbuith of the said burgh of Sterling the twentie tua and Twentie thrie dayes of Marche instant, To beare leall and suithfast[262] witnessing in so far as they know or salbe asked at them annent the crymes of witchcraft and charming quhairof Bessie Stevinsone, Issobell Bennet, and Magdalen Blair in Sterling are dilated to be guiltie, and for the which they are for the present attached \and/ arrested that Justice may be administred against them the foresaids dayes, Ilk witnes under the paine of ane hundereth pounds Scotts money, According to Justice etc., Be this precept Given at Sterling the sixteen of Marche 1659.

Of comand of the Provest and baillies of the said burgh of Sterling. James Norie, Clerk. {*p. 2*}

260 'customer': customs officer.

261 'cultellare': cutler, maker of knives.

262 'leall and suithfast': honest and truthful.

Upon the sevintene day of Merch I^{m}vi^{c} fiftie nyne years, I Patrik Fergusone ane of the ordinar officers of the burgh of Sterling past at comand of this within wreatine precept And be vertew thairof laufullie sumonded the haill within named and designed persones all personallie apprehendit and delyverit to ilk ane of them a copie of this within wreatine precept To comper before the honorabll commissioners, dayes, place, for the cause, and under the paynes within rehearsit. This I did Before ther witnessis, Williame Wilsone, Alexander Jeills and Walter Aissone, officers of the said burgh of Sterling, And for the more witnesing heirof subscrivit as followes my stampt is affixt.

[*Signed*:] P. F. [*Wax seal.*]

JC26/26, bundle 3, no. 12.

[*Endorsed:*] Precept For sumonding witnessis againes Bessie Stevinsone and Issobell Bennett befoir the court, 1659.
[*Endorsed:*] 18 Merch 1659. James Suord messenger. Wytnesses Alexander Chrystiesoun and Walter Aisone.

{*p. 1*} Officers of the sherefdome of Sterling, ye or one of yow sall pass this precept sene And laufullie sumond warne and charge Alexander Chrystisone in Craigforth, Jonet Wilisone his spous, To compeir befoir the honorabll Commissioners for adminisratione of Justice to the people in Scotland in caussis criminall att Sterling the twentie tua and twentie thrie dayes of Merch Instant To bear suthfast witnessing In sua far as they know or salbe speirit at therin Anent the crymes of witchcraft and charmeing For the which Bessie Stevinsone and Issobell Bennett Induellers in Stirling ar for the present attacht and Imprisoned within the Tolbuith of the said burgh And that under the paine of Ane hundreth punds Scots, Be this precept Given att Sterling the sixtene day of Merch 1659.

Att comand of the shereff principall.

[*Signed:*] JNoir. {*p. 2*}

Upon the eightine day of Merch 1659 years, I James Suord messenger Laufullie sumond the within designed Alexander Chrystiesone and Jonet Williesone his spous personallie apprehendit and delyverit to them a copie of this within wreatine precept, To comper before the honorabll Judges within specified, dayes, place, for the cause, and under the paynes within rehearsit, This I did before thir witnessis, Alexander Chrystiesone tenent in Wester Lovyland, And Walter Aissone ane of the ordinare officers of the burgh of Sterling And for the more witnessing heirof Subscrivit with my hand my stampt is heirto affixt.

[*Signed:*] JSuord messr.

JC26/26, bundle 3, no. 14.[263]

[*Endorsed:*] Names of the witnessis sumond to depone against the witches in the Town of Sterling.

Names of the witnessis who hes given thair depositiones to the magistrats of Sterling annent Bessie Stevinsone and Issobell Bennet \and Magdalen Blair/ attached for the crimes of witchcraft and charming.

Names of those residing in the towne[264]
Jonet Henrie
Margaret Mershell spous to Corporall Biggs
Patrike Wright cordinare
Issobell Smart spous to George Wright x
George Wright
Christian Chrystesone spous to James Chrystesone wright
Jonet Chrystesone thair servant x
Margaret Matson spous to William Lowry
Bessie Burn spous to Robert Wingyet
Jonet Bennie relict of Thomas Gilfillane weaver x
Jonet Gilfillane
Marjorie Wingyet spous to John Neilsone baxter
Katharin Thomsone spous to Peter Easeman Englishman
Katharin Wright spous to Thomas Mitchell maltman
Jean Watson spous to John Moresone customer
Helen Fergusone spous to Androw Cowan wright
Thomas McAuley fleshour
Jonet Wright spous to James Buchanan wright
Margaret Cowan spous to Edward Luckison cordinar x
Elspet Miller spous to Robert Adam taylor x
Thomas Miller merchant x
John Gib culteller x
James Patersone at the bridge x
Isobell Willison his spous
James Andersone baxter
\William Luckisone maltman
Katharin Luckison spous to the said James Andersone
Margaret Paule spous to John Allane glover/

[263] This undated document is written in the same hand as the body of the two preceding ones, and evidently belongs with them.

[264] 'Helen Ker, dead' has been crossed out at the head of this list.

Names of those residing in Perth shire
Issobell Stewart spous to Malcome Ferguson at the bridge of Turke

Names of these residing in Sterling shire
Alexander Chrysteson younger in Craigforth
Jonet Willison his spous

All these witnesses abovenamed are personallie ceited ilk ane of them under the paine of ane hundereth pounds. We Williame Wilsone, Patrik Fergusone, Walter Ayssone, and Alexander Geills officers of the burgh and James Sword meser conforme to the executiones producit.

JC26/26, bundle 3, no. 11.[265]

[*Endorsed:*] The maner of the charmes of the Stirling witchs.

The maner of Bessie Stevinsones Charming and takeing off deseases and laying them on uthers.

Shoe declares shee knowes blasted persones (which is meant persons bewitched) by the gogling of their eyes and turning hither and thither to ather side.

For charming thairof shee receaves certane of their cloathes and weets them in Sct Ninians Well and causeth them to be put on the persons soe deseased. This cure shee declares will ather end them or mend them in a suddaine, And shee learned it of the Lady McFarlans dochter 24 years since.

For the transmitting this desease from one to another It seemes by her declaratione being this That as shee goes to the well to weet the cloathes or comes from the same If shee meet noe bodie by the way There is noe health for the sike persone, and if shee meets any There is health Swe that it would seeme whomesoever shee meets shee transmitts the desease to them, utherwayes the sike persone cannot be cured.

Beside the weeting of cloathes for the said desease, Schee useth to lay twa foxtrie[266] leaves under their head, twa under their midle and twa under their feet.

For charming of maw turning.[267]

[265] This undated document may have been written at any point up to the commencement of the trials of these accused witches on 22–23 March 1659.

[266] 'foxtrie': foxglove.

[267] 'maw turning': nausea or vomiting, here considered as a disease of children.

Shee declares shee leads such persones thrie tymes round about an oaken post and utters these words, 'oaken post stands thow, bairns maw turns thow, God and St Birnibane the bright, turne my bairns maw right, in Gods name.'[268]

For charming persons forespoken.[269]

Shee declares shee charmes them thus, 'Three bitters hath thee bitten, heart and ill eye, tongue all the maist the bitt must bee', In the name of the father, sone and holie ghost shee delyvers all to him, And in the meane time of the useing this charme, shee declares shee assumes a pairt of the sike bodies desease upon her self, but not soe sore, and it continowes with her about the space of a quarter of an hower, and shee declared there was noe good in the charme.

For tryall and charming of the heart fevers.

Shee declares, That shee takes a belt and tua threeds and puts one threed without the belt and an other within the same, and rolls the belt togither with the threeds, and puts the same under the ockster[270] of the pairtie soe deseased, and if they be soe deseased baith the threeds turns to one side of the belt.

The maner of Isobell Bennets charming.

For charming blasted persones Shee declares that shee washes such persones with watter brought from the hollow groundes of the sea,[271] and takes a litle quantitie of meale and strawes it in the foure corners of thair bed, and layes under them the caker of a horse shoe,[272] that hes ridden over our good neighbours[273] and a houke[274] and a peece raw fleshe, and utters these words thrie tymes, 'The father, the sone, and the holy ghost'. And this being done, the sike persone will suddenlie ather end them or mend them that they lye not in paine.

For charming those that are mawturned.

Shee declares shee leads them thrice round about an oaken post, expressing these words thrice, 'Oaken post stands thow, Bairns maw turns thow, God and St Birnibane the bright, turne the bairns maw right'.

For cureing one that is wronged by an other at variance with them.

268 Here and later, the words placed editorially in quotation marks have been written in larger, more formal letters.

269 'forespoken': bewitched.

270 'ockster': armpit.

271 'hollow groundes of the sea': tidal pools.

272 'caker of a horse shoe': iron pin inserted in a horseshoe to prevent slipping in icy conditions.

273 'our good neighbours': the fairies.

274 'houke': sickle.

Shee bidds them goe to such persones as they are at variance with or suspects hes wronged them and crave their health fra them for Gods sake and they will be weill.

For keeping folks fra harme.

Shee bids them take a quike modiewort[275] and put it in a box and burie it, under the outside of the threshold of their doore.

Magdalen Blairs maner of imprecation and quhat followed thereon, with the maner of her cureing persons wronged by others.

A horse standing before her doore, shee strake him, saying God nor he shoot to death, and that same night after he was tane home he died.

And it is deponed against her That shee sayed, schee never gave a malison but what shee saw light.

And for persones wronged by others, shee bids them goe to such and crave their health from them thrie tymes for Gods sake and they wilbe weill.

JC26/26, bundle 3, no. 13.[276]

Witness against Isobell Keir

Johne Wright
Androw Dougall
Cristane Ritchie
Agnes Dinoven
Johne Gow
Jeane Gilespie
John Wre
Marjorie Dinoven
John Harvie
Johne Fairlie
James Harvie
Robert Foster
Johne Harvie
John Makilhoise
Jonet Miller prisouner
Duncan Foster
Jonet Miller spous to Androw Fairlie

Witnesses against Margrat Gourlay

[275] 'quike modiewort': live mole.

[276] This undated document was presumably written shortly before the commencement of the trials of 22–23 March 1659.

Androw Wright
James Maklay
Patrik Manoch
Jonet Miller prisouner
Georg Wordie
Cristane Shaw

Witnesses against Margrat Harvie
Agnis Dinoven
Jonet Miller

JC26/26, bundle 3, no. 18.[277]

[*Endorsed:*] Names of the assysers sumond out of the Towne of Sterling.
[*Endorsed:*] John Sands of Langsyd.[278]

Names of those within the burgh of Sterling that are sumonded to be upon the assise of witches and uthers.

Johne Baird merchand
Coline Lapslie merchand
Gilbert Robertsone merchand
Walter Stirk merchand
Alexander Young merchand
Johne Donaldsone merchand
Johne Andersone elder baxter
James Gib glover
James Robertsone cordiner
Johne Henrie hamerman
Robert Pirnie weaver
James Espleene taylor
John Luckiesone maltman
James Murhead maltman
Thomas Turnbull litster
James Moriesone couper
Johne Thomsone in Whins

The above named persones are all personallie sumond be the ordinare officers of the burgh of Sterling personallie apprehendit Ilk persone under

[277] This undated document was presumably written shortly before the commencement of the trials of 22–23 March 1659.

[278] John Sands of Langside had previously petitioned on behalf of Katherine Black. Perhaps this document is a copy that he requested.

the payne of Ane hundreth pounds Scotts. The names of the officers are William Wilsone, Patrik Fergusone, Walter Aissone and Alexander Geills and are present to affirme the same.

JC26/26, bundle 3, no. 7.

[*Endorsed:*] Assyse Roll for Alloway, 1659. Anent exceptions against as infamous [*3-4 words illegible*].

Assyss off Clakmanan sshyr
p William Alexander in Menstrie
p John Kirk in Alloway
p Paitrik Brown in Shelldell
p Johne Rid in Gilland
p James Cowsstown in Parkmill
p Johne Samsson in Feritown
p Thomas Famie in Cllakmanan
ex William Moriss in Allawa[279]
p Androw Samsson in Allawa
p James Twrner in Allawa
Thomas Miller in Grenge
p Johne Doog in Mistown
Donolld Forgisone in Allewa
Walter Sword ther
Johne Chrystie in Comers
Johne Andersone[280] constable
Patrick Chalmers in Alloway[281]
John Steven in Craigtoune

This Lisst is drawen be the Shiraff and two of the Justice of peice of Clakmanan Shyr. Swbscrywit at Starlling the 22 of Mairch 1659.

[*Signed:*] WBruce, Harie Bruce, RBruce.

JC26/26, bundle 3, no. 17.

[*Endorsed:*] 22 March 1659. Names of the prissoners in Stirling, 1659.

Names of those that are to be arraigned before the Justice court within the burgh of Sterling.

[279] 'James Chalmers merchant in Allawa' has been crossed out here.

[280] 'in Hauchrie' (reading uncertain) has been crossed out here.

[281] This and the next name have been added later in a different hand, the same hand that has written 'constable' above.

Stirling Witches
x Bessie Stevinsone
x Issobell Bennet
x Magdalene Blair

In the shyre of Sterling
Margaret Gourley
Jonet Miller
James Jervey
Issobell Keir
Margaret Harvie
Jonet Mackley

In Clackmanan shyre
James Kirk
Kathrine Black
Barbra Erskeene
Elizabeth Crocket

JC26/26, bundle 3, no. 15.

[*Endorsed:*] 22 March 1659. Doubell of the Roll of assysers For the shirefdome of Clakmanane. 1659. Stirling toun. Clakmanan shire.

These list of thes in Clakmanane shyr nomenat be the justice of peace of the shyr under subscrivit is to be somond be the sheriff oficeres in Clakmanane parich To be wpone the asyss of the delinquentes in the said Shyr at the Crimenall Courtt to be holdine at Stirling the 22 and 23 dayes of March Instant 1659 By the Judges for crimenall caussis.

Out of Doller pairish
Symone Drysdill constabell x
William Houtoune constabell x
James Drysdill elder x
Patrik Burne in Sheedell x
Thomas Scotland x

Out of Clakmanane parich
William Philp in Linmill
Johne Reid in Hilend x
Robert Millner in Forest
Hendrie Houchoune constabell
Thomas Combie x

Thomas Burne smith x
Archibald Quhyt x
Johne Moris x
Johne Thomsone in Feretoune x
Mathow Carfar
Johne Horne Shauboodie
James Hall Startoune
William Miller in Harsholl x
Johne Dickie Sachie x
Allexander Harravar Orchardhead

Out of Tillicutrie
William May x
Johne Harrawar constabell
William Drysdill constabell x

Out of Allaway parich
\Duncan Forgues in Resaloch/[282]
Johne Krystie in Cambus
William Morisone sesioune elder
Donald Forgisone
Walter Suord in Allavaye
James Shalmers thair
Androw Thomsone thair
Robertt Morisone merchand thair
Johne Stwine in Craigtoun
Thomas Miller in Grange
Patrik Shalmers in Allan
James Turner thair
Johne Cairdson Banchrie x
Allexander Ramsay Orchard
Johne Andersone constabell
\John Kirk constabell/[283]

Out of Logie
Johne Dougein in Ayetoun
Harie Houchoune constabell
Williame Alexander Menstrie
x Walter Robe in Ballquhain
Archbald Gellespie x
Johne McBeid

[282] This name has been written over another name beginning 'Johne', which is crossed out.
[283] This name has been written over another name, illegibly crossed out.

JC26/26, bundle 3, no. 2.[284]

[*Endorsed:*] March 22 1659. Mr William Lyndsays Against his wyff. Stirling Court.

I Mr William Lyndsay spous to that Adulterous Helen Sibbald In reference to ane scandall Laid on Katheren Black prisoner, Anent hir actions in Loosing ane Mask of Malt to the said Helen Sibbald my said spouse, Doe Faithfullie and Christianlie Declaire to all whom these may concerne, Especiallie to the Right Honourabll the Commissioners of the peace off Clackmanane shyre, That the trewthe thairof is, The first Mask[285] after our sad Mariage, The Maid of the howse Bessie Millar rysing to lett the fatt goe,[286] seing all wrong, came to my bed syd and told Helen Sibbald my spouse the Mask was lost, shoe Arose and went to the brewhowse and saw soe, And came to me saying shoe never knew the Lyk, And declaring to me iff shoe saw what came off it shoe cared not, Therafter I Arose And went to the brewhowse And saw nothing in the fatt but Draff, No Appearance off losse on the floore; quhich maid me searche with ane candle befor them both round about the fatt, At last I fand befor bothe thair faces ane hole in the Maskin fatt, at the neathermost pairt thairoff, quhich isswed out all the wirt[287] in ane syver[288] quhich ran throw the howse and downe the streets as was knowen to ws all and many neighbours, This is the trewth off what I know or saw as testifies my hand.[289]

[*Signed:*] Mr William Lyndsay, RMklaran witness to William Lindsays subscription, TMorison witnes to the subscriptioun.

Source 6: British Library, London, Dossier on Witches of Alloa, 1658–1659, Egerton MS 2879.[290]

Source 6, Section I. Letter of 28 June 1658

[*Addressed:*] For the right honourable the commissioners for administration of justice in criminal causses to the people of Scotland. these Humbly.

284 Three separate documents have this number.

285 'Mask' (mash): batch of ingredients for brewing ale in a vat.

286 'lett the fatt goe': strain the contents of the vat.

287 'wirt' (wort): ale in the process of brewing.

288 'syver': drainage channel.

289 This account of unsuccessful brewing, with the wort (liquid) leaking away naturally through a hole and a drainage channel, has evidently been given to contradict the witchcraft-related story of the episode that Helen Sibbald and Bessie Miller had told one week beforehand. See Source 6 below.

290 A note inside the cover of this volume states that it was purchased at Sotheby's, 18 March 1909, Lot 201. It has a bookplate of the nineteenth-century book collector T. Dawson Brodie (which the separate document 'Names of the Witches, 1658', edited above in the present volume, also has; the two documents also have similar bindings).

{*fo. 1r.*} My Lords, There were lately five women apprehended in the parish of Alloa in Clackmannanshire upon suspicion of Witch-craft: One of them who was first under restraint confessed the renunciation of her baptisme, and that she did enter into Covenant with the Devill and committed many murders and other mischiefs; but she died in the place of her restraint.[291] The other four (whom she detected with some others not yet apprehended) were examined the last Wensday before some justices of peace, and the presbytery of Sterling, and some of them confesse their guiltinesse.[292] It remaineth therfore that your lordships take it into your serious consideration, what course to take, for the further discovery and punishment of that Devilish crime, that the accursed may be destroyed from amongst us, lest wrath be upon us from before the Lord. To which effect the justices and ministers abovesaid, did appoint us to signifie thus much to your lordships and to report to them your determination in the businesse; in the humble expectation wherof we remaine, Your lordships most humble servants, Ja: Holburne, Matthias Simson. Stirling, Junii 28th 1658.

[*Endorsed:*] Lettre fra Major Holburne to the Judges concerning the witches of Alloway, 1658.

[*Endorsed:*] 8 Julii 1658. Contenowed to the thrid of August 1658.[293]

Source 6, Section II. Evidence against Barbara Erskine, Elizabeth Crockett, James Kirk, Katherine Black and Elizabeth Black

{*fo. 3r.*}[294] The confessiones and depositiones of witnesses upon oath before his heighnes justices of peace of Clackmananshyre: Against Barbara Arskine, Elizabeth Crokett, James Kirk, Kathren Blak, Elizabeth Blak, imprisoned for the aleadged sin of Witchcraft.

March 1659.

Depositions against the Alloway witches, Stirling Court, 1659. {*fo. 3v. blank*} {*fo. 4r.*}

291 This was Margaret Douchall, whose confessions recur throughout these documents.

292 These were Janet Black, Bessie Paton, Katherine Rainie and Margaret Taylor. Several of their examinations and confessions are recorded under the date 23 June, which was 'the last Wensday', in the presbytery records (Source 2 above).

293 These two endorsements, on fo. 1v., are in different hands, both different from the hand of the letter itself. The address, printed above, is the only text on fo. 2. The trials of Janet Black, Bessie Paton, Katherine Rainie and Margaret Taylor took place on 3 August 1658 (Source 4 above).

294 This section has a wide left-hand margin, in which are entered (i) paragraph numbers: these are taken into the text to create paragraph breaks (the text itself sometimes runs on continuously); (ii) marginal comments, mostly in a different hand: these are placed in footnotes at the point in the text where they begin or to which they relate. Poor handwriting and tight binding make some of these marginalia hard to read; short illegible passages are indicated by [...].

Barbara Erskine hir confessione in presence of Sir Charles Erskine, Harie Bruce, James Holburne, Mr Robert Bruce, justices of peace of Clakmananshyre. Alloway, 14 day of March 1659.[295]

1. The said day the said Barbara did confess that shee had pactione with the Devill: And that about 18 yeirs or theirby Margaret Duchell brought the Devill to hir house and come to hir bed and lay above hir heavier then two men: And after that shoe[296] was ever still trubled with him, and hir spirit was ever caried with him, and shoe was ever still tempted with him:[297] And when shoe would goe to the kirk to heare the Word of God he was with hir trubling hir and would cause hir fall on ane step *and closed hir eares that shoe heard not the Word of God at all: And the*[298] first meiting that they had was in the cuning yaird:[299] And the number of them that was thair, was first the Devill and then Margaret *Talyeour*, Jonet *Blak, Bessie* Paton, *Kathren* Ranie, Jonet Read, Elizabeth Crokett, Kathren Blak *and James Kirk* that *played on a whisle: And thair was with* Kathren Blak ane gentle woman with ane blak poak[300] and ane blak scarf about hir craig,[301] but shoe could not knaw hir, for hir blak poaks was over hir face, and if any bodie knew who shoe was Kathren Blak knew wha shoe was: And the Devill shooke hands with the said Barbara in the cuning yaird and said to hir, Will yow be my servant and shoe said, I will: And the Devill put his hand on hir head and the other hand on hir breast and said, I will have a promise of yow, and shoe said, quhat promise will you have of me: And he said to hir, yow must renunce your baptisme and forsaik God and Christ Jesus and be my servand: And the Devill did promise hir monye but shoe refused it and sould have none of his *mony at all*: And he would have hir bund to him both soule and bodie for ever, and shoe did so:[302] And then the Devill shoke hands with hir and called hir Jonet: And when shoe had any evill to doe, call on his name Johne: And he was in the lyknes of ane man but he had evill favored feit, rough and harie: With ane stand[303] of gray clothes and ane blew bonet on his head.

2. And in that same yeir shoe band hir self with the Devill they had ane great meiting againe in the cuning yaird, all the companye, and they danced all togither and the Devill in the midst of them and James Kirk playing on the whisle to

295 In margin: 'Barbara Arskine hir confessione against hir selff.'

296 'shoe': she.

297 In margin: 'And first hir confessione of hir first meiting in the Cunningard quhair was Elizabet Croket, Katharene Blak, James Kirk and gentlewoman with the blak pok. [...] Also shoe confesses hir to be [...] with the [...] Also confesses [...] in the same place and the said James Kirk playing to thame one the quhissill.'

298 Here and below, the text in italics is underlined in the MS.

299 'cuning yaird': Cuninghar, a place near Alloa.

300 'poak': hanging appendage to a hat.

301 'craig': neck.

302 In margin: 'denyed' (written in a different hand from other marginalia).

303 'stand': suit.

them (and declared that none would heare the whisle but these of the company): And after they had danced a long tyme they all come in to the toune of Alloway.

3. And about thrie yeirs since or thairby Margaret Talyor, Jonet Blak, Bessie Paton and Margaret Duchell did goe to the Blak Grainge and perished a boat thair with fyve persones thairin, but shoe and Margaret Duchell stayed in the Cambus till they had done: And they wer in the lyknes of corbies: And after it they did goe to William Mitchells in Bowhouse and killed a kow to him thair: And then they went to Edward Turnours in the Graing and killed ane other thair.

4. Also declared that when shoe was delatted for a witch the Devill came to hir and would have[304] hir to drowne hir self {*fo. 4v.*} in the Watter of Doven, quhairunto shoe did consent and did goe to the watter and the Devill did goe in first and shoe after him, and plunged lyk a dog besyd hir in the watter, but shoe wan to the dry land againe by the help of William Miller in Cambus who did rescue hir.[305]

5. Also declared that about 8 or 9 yeirs or thairby Kathren Ranie, Jonet Blak, Bessie Paton, Margaret Talyor and Kathren Blak wha was the maine actor did sitt upon my Lord of Marr his coall workes *lyk corbies and dragones and stopt the workes and drowned them, and shoe hir self was*[306] within half ane bow shot[307] and less from them but was not with them:[308] All which tyme they thocht to have killed Cowdons[309] but could not gett it done because his faith was stronger then so:[310] And declared that they assayed to doe it tuyce but bewarr with the third tyme.[311]

6. Also declared that Elisabeth Croket had hir doughter in Johne Kirk his service in which tyme they wanted[312] some monye and did blame the lass for it, for which cause the said Elisabeth thought to have wronged Johne Kirk and his wiff, but could not gett it done,[313] so shoe threw ane lass child of his with ane blast of wind in the bark pott[314] and drowned the child.[315]

[*Signed:*] Charles Erskine, Harie Bruce, RBruce, Ja: Holburne.

304 'drowned hir self' crossed out here.

305 In margin: 'Witness William Miller who did rescue the said Barbra from drowning hir self.'

306 The text in italics is underlined in the MS.

307 'half ane bow shot': a measure of distance.

308 In margin: 'Barbara Erskine hir confessioun against Catherine Blak anent the drowning of my Lord of Mar his works, and destroying of Cowdoune.'

309 'Cowdons': the children of Thomas Mitchell of Coldon.

310 'stronger then so': too strong.

311 'bewarr with the third tyme': watch out for the third time. The children eventually died in December 1657.

312 'they wanted': John Kirk's family lost.

313 This was illogical, since Crockett had obviously succeeded in 'wronging' Kirk's family. Erskine here was evidently repeating the 'could not get it done' motif that she had used in the previous story about Mitchell of Coldon.

314 'bark pott': a large pot for tanning leather.

315 In margin: 'Barbara Erskine hir depositione against Elisabeth Croket anent the destroying of Jone Kirk his bairne in the bark pott.'

7. The said Barbara confesses that shoe did charme bairnes, women and other persones, and being asked how shoe charmed them, shoe ansred, I say in the name of the father son and holy ghost thryce over I begin this work, Elredg King and Elredg Queine[316] quhat ever Yow gett rest in kirk or kirkird[317] burneth till this bairne become well againe.[318] {*fo. 5r.*}

Alloway 15 November 1658

The depositiones off witnesses upon oath in presence of James Holburne, Mr Robert Bruce, justices off peace of Clakmanan shyre against Elisabeth Crokett imprisoned for the aledged sin of witchcraft.

1. The said day Robert Archibald, Walter Suord, Alexander Maine, did declare wpon oath that they heard Kathren Ranie declare that the said Elisabeth Crokett was ane witch and after shoe heard shoe was delated shoe fled the bounds and since shoe heard of some respit and quyetnes shoe came home agane and now of late hearing of new talking is fled againe.[319]

[*Signed:*] RBruce.

Alloway 14 March 1659

Elisabeth Crokett hir confessione before Sir Charles Erskine, Harie Bruce, James Holburne, Mr Robert Bruce, justices of peace of Clakmanan shyre.

2. The said Elisabeth did confesse that in Lentron last,[320] shoe being lying in hir bed wnwell in the dawning of the day, found ane \thing/ come on hir in the bed wnder the clothes and lay above hir very heavie, having nether armes nor lygs, hot nor cold as shoe thought, clothed with old gray clothes, but shoe saying (as shoe affirmed) Christ be heir it evanished away and shoe knew not how it come nor how it went away.[321] X[322]

316 'Elredg King and Elredg Queine': the Elf King and Queen.

317 Reading uncertain; it could also be 'kirkue'. This would make little sense, however, and the meaning 'churchyard' seems probable. Erskine may originally have said something like: 'I say the following words: "In the name of the Father, the Son and the Holy Ghost." Then, thrice over: "I begin this work. Elf King and Elf Queen: whenever you seek rest in church or churchyard, you should burn until this child becomes well again."' This is not a precise translation of the text as we have it, but it is the closest one that makes sense. The interrogators may not have grasped the intricacies of the charm, and may have garbled it.

318 In margin: 'Barbara Erskine hir confessione of charming and the witnesses thairto: Walter Sword, James McBrair, Jone Kirk, Thomas Stowpard: to Barbara Erskine hir confessioun of charming.' The scribe of the main text initially wrote 'witnesses Walter Sword, James McBrair, Jone Kirk, Thomas Stowpard', and this has been amplified in the second hand. Later there are several further instances of this practice.

319 In margin: 'Witness to Katharene Rany hir confession of Elisabeth Croket to be a witch.'

320 'Lentron': Lent. This was evidently the Lent season of 1658, as becomes clear later when the same story is recorded with the date 6 September 1658.

321 In margin: 'Elisabeth Crokett hir confession before the justices and to the witness that is sett on the 6 article of the Devill being in bed with hir.'

322 In margin: 'the next page'. This is a marginal note to the 'X', in the same hand as the main text.

3. In the presence of the saids justices Barbra Erskine being confronted with the said Elizabeth \Barbara/ did declare that shoe was with the Devill and them at twa severall meitings in the cunyng yard (as is manifest in Barbra Erskines first and second article of hir confession).[323]

4. As also the said Barbra did declare that the said Elisabeth was the death of Johne Kirk his bairne by causing ane blast of wind blow the child in the bark pott and so drowned, as is sett downe in the 6 article of the said Barbara hir confession.[324]

5. The said Johne Kirk did depone wpon oath before the saids justices that his child did drowne in the bark pott but knew not quhat was the cause of it but thought it was the wind that blew the child in.[325]

[*Signed:*] Charles Erskine, Ja: Holburne. {*fo. 5v.*}

Alloway, 6 September 1658

6. The quhilk day Elisabeth Croket did confess and declare that in Lentron last bypast, shoe lying in hir bed in the dawing found ane come in to hir bed and lye in hir right arme, and thairat shoe thocht he had carnell copulatione with hir, and that he wes nether cold nor hott, and declared that shoe knew not when he come in nor when he went away:[326] As also declared that shoe knew not whether the Devill gave hir ane mark or not that night he lay with hir, but if it wer found wpon hir, shoe should be content to die the death of a witch.

The same day the said Elisabeth did confess that if shoe had the Devills mark it was on hir privie member.[327] {*fo. 6r.*}

Alloway, 15 November 1658

The depositiones of witnesses wpon oath in presence of James Holburne, Mr Robert Bruce, justices of his heighnes peace of Clakmanan shyre, against James Kirk imprisoned for the aledged sin of witchcraft.[328]

323 In margin: 'Barbara Erskine hir declaratione against Elisabeth Croket being confronted together anent twa meitings together in the cunyng yaird.'

324 In margin: 'Barbara Erskine hir depositione against Elisabeth Croket anent the death of Johne Kirk his bairne.'

325 In margin: 'Johne Kirk his awne depositione anent the trueth of the same.'

326 In margin: 'Elizabeth Croket hir confessione of carnall deill with the Devill, and *Witnesses* thairto *Alexander Richie younger, fleshor in Alloway, Andro Thomsoun thair* to the said Elisabeth hir confessioun of carnell copulatioune with the Devill.' Words italicised here are apparently in the same hand as the main text.

327 In margin: 'Elisabeth hir confession of the Devills mark. *Witnesses* thairto *William Moris, Johne Thomsoun, James Lyndsay, Robert Archibald.*' Words italicised here are apparently in the same hand as the main text.

328 In margin: 'James Kirk: witnesses to Margaret Talyour and Katherine Ranie thair deposing against James Kirk, viz. James Lyndsay and 3 utheris.'

1. James Lyndsay, Andro Thomsoun, Johne Kirk did depone that they heard Margaret Talyour declare that the said James Kirk was ane warlock and that he was at ane meiting with them altogither in the cuning yard with the Devill present and that he played on the whisle to them quhen they all danced in a ring.

2. William Moris, kirk session elder, did depone wpon oath that he heard Kathren Ranie declare severall tymes in the tolbuith of Edinburgh before hir executione that James Kirk did severall tymes play to them on his whisle in Bods meidow.

[*Signed:*] Ja: Holburne, RBruce.

Alloway, 14 March 1659

3. In presence of Sir Charles Erskine, Harie Bruce, James Holburne, Mr Robert Bruce, justices of his heighnes peace, Barbara Erskine being confronted with the said James Kirk did most boldly affirme that the said James was at twa severall meitings with them in the cuning yaird and plaed on his whisle to them and they all danced but shoe and Margaret Duchell for they wer but twa waly dragles:[329] as is sett downe in the first and second articles of the said Barbray hir confessioun.[330]

[*Signed:*] Charles Erskine, Harie Bruce, RBruce.

Clakmanan, 19 March 1659

4. In presence of Harie Bruce and Mr Robert Bruce, justices of peace of the shyre: James Lindsay, Johne Thomsoun and Alexander Moris did depone wpon oath that wpon 10 September 1658 James Kirk did confesse the Devills mark to be on his left shoulder and being tryed at his awne desyre was found clearly to be the Devills mark and for which he was content to die the death of a witch, and he being asked how long he had that mark, he said he could not well remember, it was so long since.[331]

5. Also he confessed the charming of Johne Demperston his kow with ane thrid of red silk, and that Helen Nicoll had learned him to doe it.[332] {*fo. 6v. blank*} {*fo. 7r.*}

Alloway, 15 November 1658

The depositiones of witnesses wpon oath before James Holburne, Mr Robert Bruce, justices of his heighnes peace of Clakmanan shyre, against Kathren Blak imprisoned for the aledged sin of witchcraft.[333]

[329] 'waly dragles': woeful stragglers.

[330] In margin: 'Barbara Erskine hir depositione being confronted with James Kirk ratifyet hir former depositione against him.'

[331] In margin: 'Witnesses, James Kirk, proving his confessioun of the Devills mark.'

[332] In margin: 'James Kirk his confessioun of charming John Demperstouns kow before thir *Witnesses, James Lindsay, Johne Thomsoun, Alexander Moris*.' Words italicised here are apparently in the same hand as the main text.

[333] In margin: 'Kathren Blak.'

1. The said day Andro Thomsoun, James Lindsay, William Moris did depone wpon oath that they heard Bessie Patoun declare that Kathren Blak was a witch and that shoe would goe to death with it: and that shoe lykwayes declared that shoe heard Kathren Blak say to Jonet Read when they discorded, Goe home, common theiff, and tak out the windingsheits of Margaret Maistertouns bairns, for yow was the death of them all.[334]

2. James Lindsay, Johne Michell deponed that they heard Kathren Ranie declare that Kathren Blak was at ane meiting with them at Andro Arskines litle house and being skarred be James Moris shoe went home throw David Measones.[335]

3. Johne Hunter, Andro Arskine and Robert Archibald did depone that Kathren Ranie did declare that if Kathren Blak and Bessie Harlaw wer not takine they would doe the toune of Alloway more harme nor ever they gott yet.[336]

4. William Moris did depone that he heard the said Kathren Ranie declare the same at the fyre when shoe was going to be brunt.[337]

5. Andro Thomsoun, David Vertie[338] did depone wpon oath that they heard Bessie Patoun declare that the said Kathren Blak gifted hir doughter to the Devill on the second or third night after shoe was borne: And for that the Devill gifted hir many a man and womens goods and geir.[339]

6. Johne McKenighie deponed on oath that in July 1648 or thairby David Measoun, Kathren Blak hir sone, being drinking with him, the said Kathren come to them and was angrie that he should be drinking with the said Johne (who had desyred the said David to stay with him all night), and said, God send yow ane ill wakneing or[340] the morne, for he shall not stay with yow all night: And the said Johne going that same night to lett the fatt goe quhilk he had masked,[341] he was almost destroyed with cattis without the house, and ane catt lap on his bairne who was lying in the credle within the house, thairafter he took the bairne out of the credle and laid him in besyd his mother, shoe being asleip, and shortly after he going to the bairne found him lying as he left him but dead.[342]

334 In margin: 'Witnesses to Bessie Paton hir confessioun against Kathren Blak declaring hir to to [*sic*] be a witch.'

335 In margin: 'Witnesses to Kathren Ranie hir depositione against Katherine Blak that shoe was at a meiting with them at Andro Erskins house.'

336 In margin: 'Witnesses of Kathren Ranie hir declaratione against Katherine Blak.'

337 In margin: 'William Moris his declaratione of the former depositione at Kathren Rainis death.'

338 The scribe initially wrote 'Andro Thomsoun, Robert Archibald ...' but then crossed out the second name.

339 In margin: 'Witnesses to Bessie Paton hir declaratione anent Katherine Blak hir gifting hir dochter to the Devill.'

340 'or': before.

341 'to lett the fatt goe quhilk he had masked': having earlier 'masked' a 'fatt' (vat) by mixing malt with hot water for brewing, he now had to strain the contents.

342 In margin: 'Witness to Katherine Blak hir imprecatione against Jone McKenigie and the efect quhilk followed thairon that same night.'

7. Agnes Akine deponed on oath that shoe being serving the said Kathren betuixt Martimes 1657 and Whitsonday 1658, that Margaret Talyour wha hes now suffered as a witch being serving with hir, and wpon some words of wreath passing betuixt them, the said Margaret took hir be the plettis of hir hair going to thair bed and drew hir bak and immediatly shoe lost hir speach[343] {*fo. 7v.*} that shoe could not speak from that tyme in the evening the ane day till foure at night on the morow, at quhilk tyme the said Kathren came but [*sic*] from Margaret Talyour and took hir ane skelp[344] on the brow and said, quhat devill is that that aileth thee, and immediatly shoe spoak and sweare shoe should goe and tell the minister, but they disswaded hir from goeing.

As also deponed that on the 30 of October last, Thomas Measoun hir housband offerred hir ten pound Scots not to depone any thing against his wyff, and bade hir say that the tounes people bade hir say it.[345]

[*Signed:*] Ja: Holburne, RBruce.

Alloway, the 14 March 1659

8. In the presence of the said Sir Charles Arskine, Harie Bruce, James Holburne, Mr Robert Bruce, justices of his heighnes peace of Clakmanane shyre, Barbara Arskine being confronted with the said Kathren did most boldly affirme that shoe was at twa meitings with them and the Devill in the cuning yard, as is sett downe in the first and second articles of the said Barbra hir confessioun.

9. As also declared being confronted with hir that about 8 or 9 yeiris since or thairby, Kathren Ranie, Jonet Blak, Bessie Paton, Margaret Talyour and the said Kathren Blak, wha was the maine actor, did sitt wpon my Lord of Mar his coall workes lyk corbies and dragones and stopped his workes and drowned them, and shoe hir self was within half ane bow shott to them but was not with them: At which tyme they thocht to have killed Cowdoun but could not gett it done because his faith was stronger then so: And declared that they assayed to doe it tuyce but bewar with the third tyme: As is sett doune in the fyft article of the said Barbra hir confessioun.[346]

10. The said day Bessie Millare, Helen Sibbalds servant, deponed that about foure yeiris since, having masked hir mistres fatt as shoe used to doe and in the morning when shoe arose to lett it goe shoe saw twa catts sitting on the fatt lid, and when they saw hir they went and cryed in the yaird, and when shoe took aff the fatt lid shoe found nothing therin but draff and all the

343 In margin: 'Agnes Aikine hir depositione anent the wrong shoe gott be Margaret Talyour, and how shoe gott hir speach be Katherine Blak hir stryking hir on hir brow.'

344 'skelp': blow.

345 In margin: 'And Thomas Measoun his offer of monye to the said Agnes not to reveill the same.'

346 In margin: 'Barbra Erskine hir confessioun against Katherine Blak being confronted together anent the drowning of my Lord of Mar his coall works and assaying to destroy Cowdoune Thomas Michell of Cowdoune sett downe in the fyft articles of Barbra Erskine hir confessioun declaring the same to be off trueth.'

ground both beneath and about the fatt dry, and when shoe called hir mistres to sie it hir mistres said, thair hes beine no good heir: And in the greik of the morning[347] the said Kathren Black came downe the baksyd[348] and asked, if shoe had good wort,[349] and shoe said ay, and the said Kathren said thair is not meikle of it, and the said Helen said shame fall that leill gesser,[350] and the said Kathren said quhat is the matter and did laugh, and said hold your toung and be quyet, yow shall never miss it[351] {*fo. 8r.*} for I dreamed that your wort was all gone, and shoe came never before nor thereafter to ask such a question.

This Helen Sibbald and hir servant Bessie Miller did depone before the said justices wpon oath.[352]

[*Signed:*] Charles Erskine, Harie Bruce, RBruce.

Barbara Erskine did declare[353] that Kathren Blak, when shoe sent Margaret Talyour hir servant, wha is now brunt, to tak wp geare[354] that shoe had bought from any cuntrie man, bade hir, when shoe went from hir, remember yow tak up the chiretie[355] with it, and being asked at the said Barbara quhat the cheritie was, shoe said it was the fusione[356] or substance of that mans wholl barne and barne yaird.[357]

Margaret Talyour wha was servand to the said Kathren Blak, being in prison in Alloway, did declare to Sir Charles Arskine that the said Kathren hir mistress was ane witch.[358] {*fo. 8v.*}

Alloway, 15 November 1658.

The depositiones of witnesses in presence of James Holburne, Mr Robert Bruce, justices of his heighnes peace of Clakmanan shyre, against Elisabeth Blak in prisoun for the aledged sin of witchcraft.[359]

347 'in the greik of the morning': at daybreak.

348 'the baksyd': the boundary of the town, delineated by the back fences of the inhabitants' yards.

349 'wort': ale in the process of brewing.

350 'shame fall that leill gesser': shame on that true guesser.

351 In margin: 'Witnesses against Kathren Blak for taking away and bewitching Helen Sibbald hir wort.'

352 One week later, a very different account of this episode of unsuccessful brewing was given by Helen Sibbald's husband, Mr William Lindsay. See Source 5 above.

353 In margin: 'Witnesses, William Moris, Alexander Stewart, Alexander Richie.' Written in the same hand as the main text.

354 'to tak wp geare': to collect goods, here probably grain.

355 'chiretie': a small extra amount added to some grain measures. Here the word is not used literally.

356 'fusione': goodness or nourishing power.

357 In margin: 'Barbra Erskine hir confessione that Katherine Blak commanded hir servant Margaret Talyour to bring the substance of any mans barne with hir when shoe was sent to receive the gear shoe had bought.'

358 In margin: 'Margaret Talyour hir declaratione to Sir Charles Erskine anent hir mistres Kathren Blak that shoe was as great a witch as hir self.'

359 In margin: 'Elisabeth Blak.' Written in the same hand as the main text.

1. James Lindsay, Johne Kirk, Andro Thomsoun, deponed on oath that Margaret Duchall did declare, and did constantly byd be it till the houre of hir death (wha died in prison), that the said Elisabeth Blak was at all meitings with them, at destroying of bairnes, horses and kyne, and that ane night the said Elisabeth Blak came to hir at midnight and took hir out of hir awne house to the Crofts of Alloway, quhair the Devill came to them, and as shoe said, rede[360] them both.[361]

2. Robert Archibald, Walter Suord, James Crightoun deponed on oath that Bessie Patoun declared that Elisabeth Blak was the woman that had the bonie whyt coat that was at the destroying of Cowdoune his twa bairnes, and that shoe carried the meall that was strawen on the saidis bairnes when they wer destroyed.[362]

3. Hendrie Towart did declare on oath that Margaret Duchall said that Elisabeth Blak was hir brother Thomas Duchall his death and that shoe was as great ane witch as hir self, and that shoe laid seiknes on hir awne son and came to hir to tak it aff againe, quhilk the said Margaret did and laid it on the said Elisabeth hir awne horse, who died immediatly, and thairafter the said Elisabeth did exclame against hir and called hir witch for doeing thairoff.[363]

4. William Lindsay deponed on oath that Kathren Ranie declared that Elisabeth Blak was at thair meiting at Andro Arskines litle house, and being skarred be James Moris shoe went in over the greine dyk with the Devill.[364]

5. Robert Archibald deponed on oath that Kathren Ranie declared that Elisabeth Blak went wp Cowdounes staire with the Devill and Margaret Talyour, when his twa bairnes was distroyed.[365]

[*Signed:*] Ja: Holburne, RBruce.

Alloway, 14 March 1659

In presence of Sir Charles Arskine, Harie Bruce, James Holburne, Mr Robert Bruce, his heighnes justices of peace of Clakmanan shyre.

6. The said day Mr James Cunynghame younger[366] did depone wpon oath that about the beginning of October 1657, he being lying reading neir by the

[360] 'rede': rode. For a discussion of the Devil riding witches see Julian Goodare, 'Flying Witches in Scotland', in Julian Goodare (ed.), *Scottish Witches and Witch-Hunters* (Basingstoke, 2013), 159–76, at p. 163.

[361] In margin: 'Witness to Margaret Duchall hir depositione against Elisabeth Blak declaring hir to be at all meitings with the Devill.'

[362] In margin: 'Witnesses to Bessie Patoun hir declaratione against Elisabeth Blak anent the destroying of Cowdons bairnes.'

[363] In margin: 'Witnes against Elisabeth Blak anent the death of Margaret Duchall hir brother. *Witnesses, William Moris, Patrik Chambers*.' Words italicised here are apparently in the same hand as the main text.

[364] In margin: 'Witnesses against Elisabeth Blak.'

[365] In margin: 'befoir repeited to him'.

[366] In margin: 'Witnes against Elisabeth Blak.'

Hauk Hill in Alloway, the said Elizabeth Black came to him and said, shoe knew by his countinance that he was not well, and said that he had that same disease quherof hir son James had beine seik thrie quarters of a yeir, and if he pleased shoe and hir housband would cure him, he thanked hir and pled for that tyme,[367] and a lytle after he accidentaly mett hir at the bak of Andro Dickie his yaird, wher shoe said to him he would kill himself unless he spoak to hir housband, so by hir perswasiones finding himself wnwell he spoak to him and foolishly condiscending to tak some drinks from him (without letting any bodie know of it) and after severall drinks for the {*fo. 9r.*} which he largly gott monye from him and finding him self still worse and worse and apprehending shoe was but cheating him for more monye, he went to hir awne house about the beginning of November and told hir that nether shoe nor hir housband did keip promise to him because he found himself rather worse than better. Shoe told him the fault was his awne because he did not belive the drinkes could cure him. Then shoe asked if he did sweat at any tyme and if he was still sad. He answered yea. Then said shoe, yow are certanly witched and that in a siker[368] sort, and no less will slaik[369] them nor your lyff if they can gett it. Then said he how can it be, and shoe smyling said, a ha, joy,[370] yow know not thair trikes, yet they can tak any disease aff ane man and put it on whome they please, yea more then that (betuixt me and yow), if they can not gett it put wpon the bodie they would have it on, they will seik to gar the bodie think it and trow it and that will doe the bodie as much ill as if the disease wer laid wpon the bodie they would have it on. But Ile tell yow a way, said shoe, how to be fried of it, if yow will tak my advise and promise to tell it no bodie, sie that yow keip it to your self, for I would not for any geare that folkes heard of it. Say on said he. When yow goe then to the colledg (said shoe) goe to Marie Cunninghame and tak hir in to ane house and drink ane chopine of aill with hir and when yow have done lett hir goe out before yow, and when hir bak is to yow tak ane grip of hir coat betuixt your finger and your thoumb, or betuixt twa of your fingers, and clap doune on your kneis and say give me my health for Gods saik thryce over, it matters not whether yow speak it lowd or not, it will be anough if yow speak it quyetly in your awne mynd, and when yow have said it, shoe will presently know and look about to yow and mak to seik some thing from yow, a pin ore any lytle thing lyk that, sie yow give hir it not but say God be betuixt me and yow, and have no more medling with hir, for if yow give hir any thing or tak any thing from hir after this, all the rest will doe no good. Then shoe asked him quhat day of the weik it was, which he told hir.

367 'pled for that tyme': excused himself on that occasion.
368 'siker': certain, serious.
369 'slaik': satisfy.
370 'joy': mate, pal.

I would not for a pound, said shoe, that it wer Fryday, for then shoe would know all that we are speaking of hir. How so, said he. Because the Devill, said shoe, gives all witches that power that quhatsoever is said of them on a Fryday, be they never so farr aff, they will know evine as well as yow and I who are speaking together.[371]

7. The said day Helen Sibbald deponed upon oath that about nyne yeirs or thairby since, shoe duelling in Elisabeth Blak hir house, and hir brewhouse being wnthaiked,[372] the said Elisabeth came to hir [and] desyred help of hir woman to cast wp the divetts to the house, and shoe said that shoe could not spare hir in regard shoe was going to the kirk to be kirked,[373] and the said Elisabeth said, The Devill send yow ane ill foote, and shoe going to the kirk fell so seik {*fo. 9v.*} that shoe was not able to say thrie words in the kirk, but was helped home agane, and went to hir bed and hir lyges swelled and was not able to goe to the kirk for ane yeir and thrie quarters of a yeir, and ever since not able to travell a myll of gate[374] as all hir neighbors knowes, but quhat shoe is helped by horse.

[*Signed:*] Charles Erskine, Harie Bruce.

Bessie Patoun (wha is brunt) did declare whill shoe was in prison at Alloway[375] that Elisabeth Blak, wpone ane anger against hir awne sone James Demperstoun, did lay on ane heavie seiknes wpon him, and after he had lyne wnder the same thrie quarters of ane yeir, the said Elisabeth came to the said Bessie and bade hir tak aff the seiknes aff hir sone, for he was over long tormented, quhilk shoe refused to doe but bade hir goe to Margaret Duchall and bid hir doe it, which shoe did as is before sett downe[376] in the third article.[377]

Source 6, Section III. Evidence against Isobel Keir

Depositions against Isobell Keir, 1659.

[371] Here Friday seems to be thought of as an unlucky day. The opposite view could be taken, and one demonologist thought that the demonic power of diviners failed on Friday and Sunday: Pierre de Lancre, *On the Inconstancy of Witches: Pierre de Lancre's Tableau de l'inconstance des mauvais anges et demons (1612)*, ed. and trans. Harriet Stone and Gerhild Scholz Williams (Tempe, Ariz., 2006), 134.

[372] 'wnthaiked': unthatched.

[373] 'to be kirked': to rejoin the congregation formally for the first time after giving birth.

[374] 'myll of gate': mile of road.

[375] In margin: '*Witnesses, James Lindsay, Johne Thomsoun* against Elisabeth Blak.' Words italicised here are apparently in the same hand as the main text.

[376] In margin: 'This set doun befoir'.

[377] This is the end of the text of fo. 9v., which ends the dossier against Barbara Erskine, Elizabeth Crockett, James Kirk, Katherine Black and Elizabeth Black. There is then a further blank folio, unnumbered. The next section was originally a separate booklet, and is written in a different hand.

Depositiounes contra Isobell Keir.[378] {*fo. 10r.*}

The depositioun of witnesses examined wpon oath in presence of Colonell Thomas Read, Liuetenent Johne Cloberie, Major James Matlo, Williame Stirling of Harbertshyre, Captain Callant and Captan Hunt. Att Sterling the 16 March 1659. Aganst Isobell Keir spouse to Androw Ritchie in Arnfinlay of Kippen paroch.[379]

1. Johne Wright of Pousyd haveing takin his oath deponed that he being verie seik and no lyfe expected of him six yeir since, Isobell Keir spous to Androw Ritchie in Arnfinlay came to visit him and for recovering of his health desyred him to take tuo spindiles and put one of thame in ilk one of his oxters or arme holes, which he refused as not being ane laufull medicin, nevertheless she sayeing he wald be weill, he recovered shortlie thairefter.[380]

2. And farder the said Johne deponis that he came to the abovenamet Isobell Keir ellevin yeir since in the moneth of Junii, at the breking of day light, in the burn of Arnpryor, casting watter over hir head with hir hands severall tymes: And being inquyred quhairfor she did it, hir answer was, that the watter wes not cleane: Also the deponer declaires he saw no thing she haid to wash or carie watter away in.

3. And sicklyk the said Johne Wright declaires that he wes informed be his wyf named Elizabeth Makfarlane and be his miller named Androw Dougall that his milne in \Arnpryor[381]/ wald not grind: And being repaired be Williame Chalmer milnewright, the milne wald not yit grind: And then the milnewryt declared he could doe no more to mak hir grind: Thairefter the deponer declaires that the afoirsaid Elizabeth Makfarlane went to Isobell Keir and spok to hir anent the milne and imediatlie thairefter the milne grand without reparatioun.

Androw Dougall miller deponet according to Johne Wright his deposition anent the milne.[382]

4. Moreover Johne Wright afoirsaid depones he saw Elizabeth Ritchie dochter to the said Isobell Keir come to his kill logie[383] fyve yeir since in the nyght tyme, and take fyre furth thairof, and that his malt wald not mak thairefter till he went to Androw Ritchie husband to the said Isobell Keir

[378] These two titles to the booklet that follows are written, in different hands, on the cover page, now numbered fo. 14v. The text of the booklet begins on fo. 10r.

[379] Annotated: 'Depositiones of the witnesses against Issobell Keir', in a different hand from the main text. It is not the same as the hand of the annotator of the previous section. Subsequent marginalia are also in this new hand.

[380] In margin: 'Johne Wright'.

[381] The scribe originally wrote 'Pousyd', then crossed it out, added a caret and wrote 'Arnpryor' in the margin.

[382] In margin: 'Andro Dowgall'.

[383] 'kill logie': the lower portion of a kiln, underneath the drying chamber.

and threatned him that if the malt wald not make he wald challeng his wyfe for the sam: And thairefter the malt mead kyndlie[384] as it sould doe. {*fo. 10v.*}

5. Also Johne Wright deponet that he haveing boght ane kow 6 or sevin yeiris since,[385] Cristane Ritchie dochter to the said Isobell Keir came wpoun the first day of Maii callet Beltane day and milked the kow, and being accused thairof, said she haid warrand fra him to milk the kow, bot had no such warrand: And also the said Johne deponet that kow gave no more milk till November thairefter: And then quhen she wes killed wes no fatter nor when she was milked: And that he had sixtein kows and horsses deit the same yeir. Johne Wricht.[386]

Cristane Ritchie aforesaid declaires she milket the said kow bot does not remember if it wes wpon Beltane day or not: And that at directioun of the people that were in hir fathers hous she toist[387] out the milk at the doore bot remembers not if hir mother wes in the hous or not.[388]

6. Agnis Buchanen spous to Johne Harvie in Armoir deponed ane servant woman belonging to Johne Wright of Pousyd namet Jonet Rioch came \wpon Thursday/ to the deponent hous with ane child of Johne Wrightis of ten weiks old to get suke,[389] the mother of the child being in Glasgow: And that Issobell Keir being in the deponents hous took the child in hir armes and said to Jonet Rioch, be carefule of the child he will not have manie dayes: And wpon the Sonday nixt thairefter in the morning the child died: And that they never perceaved the child to be seik at all till the same instant that the barne diet.[390]

Jonet Rioch deponet as said is concerning the child in all thinges, with this addition, that she inquyred at \Isobell Keir/ how she knew that the child wald die, she answeret that she knew by the childs face and the smell of its clothes.[391]

Isobell Keir, being inquyred heirof, allegit that Jonet Rioch said to hir the child haid ane lump in its haiss[392] sum dayes befoir: Bot Jonet Rioch being examined if she said so, the said Jonet, and also Agnis Buchanen, deponet that thair wes no such words spok at all, bot that the child wes then in good health.[393] {*fo. 11r.*}

7. Agnis Dinoven spous to Thomas Milne in Armoir haveing takin hir oath depones that Johne Gow in Gartmoir wes verie seik, and it being reported

384 'kyndlie': naturally, properly.
385 'fra Johne Wright' crossed out.
386 Not a signature, but perhaps a copy of one.
387 'toist': tossed.
388 In margin: 'Cristeane Ritchie dochter of Issobell Reid [*sic*]'.
389 'to get suke': to be breastfed.
390 In margin: 'Agnes Buchanan spous to John Thornton [*sic*]'.
391 In margin: 'Jonet Rioch'.
392 'haiss': possibly a variant of 'hals, hause', neck.
393 In margin: 'Issobell Keir'.

that he wes dead and straght,[394] the deponent went to the lyk wake,[395] and that Isobell Keir lay with the said Johne Gow the space of the night wnder one playd:[396] And the nixt morning about the sun rysing the aforesaid Johne Gow yawned tuyc[397] verie heavilie and imediatlie recovered and wes in health within eght dayes: And that Duncane Dinoven being the first that entered the hous (quhair Johne Gow was seik) fell seik imediatlie efter he entered the hous and continoued seik the space of thrie yeires and then died.[398]

8. And when Duncane Dinoven wes seik that the afoirsaid Johne Gow came to visit him and said to him, Yow are seik of the same seiknes that I haid: And thairefter Margrat Forgisoune mother to Duncan Dinoven went to Isobell Keir and tauld hir that Johne Gow said that the seiknes that he haid wes wpon Duncan Dinoven, Isobell Keir replyet and said to Margrat Forgisone, What Duncan wantis sall cum on hir, and so strak and bled the aforesaid Margrat.

And also depones that efter Duncan Dinoven haid bein seik thrie yeires, Isobell Keir cam to visit him and took him out of the bedd, and that he diet within thrie dayes thairefter.

9. Also the said Agnis Dinoven depones that tuo yeiris agoe hir dochter namet Margrat Milne wes verie seik and the deponent tauld Margrat Harvie thairof, wha baid hir goe to Isobell Keirs hous and take thrie rugis of the thak[399] abone hir doore and seik hir dochters health of Isobell Keir for Gods saik,[400] bot she refuset to obey hir desyre, hir dochter diet.

10. Also the deponent declaires she hard the deceaset Elizabeth Foster spous to the afoirsaid Johne Gow saye that the said Isobell Keir broght to hir ane peice leven[401] to eat, bot refuising to eat it, she gave it to ane dog and to ane hen and chikens: And imediatlie the dog, the hen and chikens diet.

Johne Gow abone namet depones that he wes exceiding seik and expected death, and that Isobell Keir came and satt the space of one nyght wnder his head and that imediatlie thairefter he recovered.[402]

Isobell Keir being examined thairanent denyed that she satt wnder his head at all more nor the rest of the companie did.[403]

11. Jeane Gillespie in Kippen deponet[404] that fyve yeir since hir deceaset dochter of sevin yeirs old came to hir and tauld that Isobell Keir said to hir,

394 'straght' (stretched): laid out before burial.

395 'lyk wake': festive watch kept at night over a dead body.

396 'playd' (plaid): cloak.

397 'tuyc': twice.

398 In margin: 'Agnes Dinnoven'.

399 'thrie rugis of the thak': three bundles of the thatch.

400 'seik hir dochters health of Isobell Keir for Gods saik': ask Isobel Keir to restore her (Agnes Denovan's) daughter's health, for God's sake.

401 'ane peice leven': a piece of leaven (fermenting dough).

402 In margin: 'John Gow'.

403 In margin: 'Issobell Keir'.

404 In margin: 'Jean Gillespie anent hir dochters daith'.

Thow art a weill threiven great headit child since thy father diet: And imediatlie thairefter the bairnis head becam verie sore and loset the pouer of one hir armes and hir leg and diet[405] within the space of thrie dayes: And that the bairn affirmed all the tyme of hir seiknes that Isobell {*fo. 11v.*} Keir wronget hir.

Also depones that within thrie dayes efter the bairne wes dead the said Isobell Keir cam and beged the bairnes shoes.

12. Johne Wre in Armanell depones[406] that \tuo/[407] yeirs since Isobell Keir cam to his hous and no persone being in the hous she stayet siting at the baksyd of his hous byres fyve houres space: And wpon the nixt morning at the sun rysing the said Isobell came and satt at the same place quhair she satt the preceiding day, and at hir removeing thens the kow that stood within the byre opposit to the place quhair Isobell sat wes wood[408] and diet presentlie: And imediatlie thairefter his wyfe fell seik for nyne weiks space.

13. Marjorie Dinoven in Armoir deponet that six yeirs agoe she haid ane child of six yeirs old playing befoir hir doore: And as she was informed Isobell Keir cam by the bairn: And within half ane hour the bairne diet without[409] the hous.[410]

14. Johne Harvie in Armoir depones that thair wes sum differ[411] betuixt his wyfe and Isobell Keir ten yeres agoe, and imediatlie thairefter his wyfe wes seik for the space of thrie moneths: And after she convalesed, Androw Ritchie husband to Isobell Keir came to him desyreing the lean of his malt kill[412] to dry oates wpon, which he refused to len: And imediatelie thairefter he haid fyve makings of malt spoyled evrie one efter ane other, that when the malt wes put in the rott heap and sould have bein sueit, all of it becam sour and altogidder wsles,[413] quhairby he wes prejudget in[414] fyve hundreth punds and wes necessitat to leif off that trad: He declaires he caused maltmen and other skilet[415] men look the bear[416] wha affirmed it myght be good malt.[417]

And thairwpon he wes wnwilling that Isobell Keir sould cum in his hous thairefter.

405 'diet': died.

406 In margin: 'John Ure'.

407 The scribe initially wrote 'fyv', then crossed it out and wrote 'tuo'.

408 'wood': mad.

409 'diet without': died outside.

410 In margin: 'Deposition, Marjory Dinnoven, anent the daith of hir chyld'.

411 'differ': quarrel.

412 'lean of his malt kill': loan of his malt kiln.

413 'wsles': useless.

414 'wes prejudget in': lost.

415 'skilet': skilled.

416 'look the bear': examine the bere (a kind of barley, used to make malt for brewing ale).

417 In margin: 'Depositione, John Harvie, for his brewing 5 makings of malt and the gane never pertaneing to him'.

15. Nevertheles tuo yeir since the deponer declaires[418] he cam one day to his awin hous and broght in ane mear:[419] And finding Isobell Keir in his hous he wes angrie with his wyfe that sufferet Isobell to cum in, quhairwpon Isobell Keir went out: And imediatlie thairefter within the space of ane quarter of[420] ane hour the mear diet \presentlie/.[421]

He declaires Isobell Keir hes bein suspect of witchcraft thir manie yeirs bypast.

Agnis Buchanen spous to Johne Harvie aforesaid depones according to the said Johne Harvie in maner foirsaid.[422] {*fo. 12r.*}

16. Johne Fairlie portiouner of Arnfinlay deponet that he wes cuming bay[423] Isobell Keirs hous tuo yeir since and quhen she hosted,[424] the deponer said, this is ane evill tyme for old wyfis and old meares, quhairat Isobell being offendit, tuo of his meares diet shortlie thairefter: And a little space thairefter the deponer declaires he wes again cuming by the said Isobell and inquyred of hir how she did, she replyed and said with a laching[425] countenance: this is not ane good tyme for auld wyfis and old meares.[426]

Isobell Keir confesses she said thos words afoirsaid.[427]

17. James Harvie in Eistercarden depones that thair being sum differ betuix him and Isobell Keir, she cam to him wpon the 8 of Maii comonlie callit Littil Beltan day, and desyret him to shoot ane hair wpon the pasturatt of his cattell, which he refuset to doe: And shortlie thairefter his hird[428] wes pasturing his kye and ane kow fell doun dead in the same place quhair \Isobell Keir told him/ the hair wes.[429]

18. Also the deponent declares that 17 or 18 yeirs agoe the said Isobell Keir being duelling in ane hous that belonget to him, he put thrie horssis in the hous to preserve thame from pairties of souldiers: And shortlie thairefter all the thrie horssis diet and did him no service.[430]

19. Robert Foster of West Polder deponed that he haveing ane kow belonging to [*1 word blank*] Foster in Kilmoir pasturing with his kowes, the said Isobell Keir causet the deponent his wyfe put in sum milk that she milket from [*1 word blank*] Foster his kow with hir awin milk: And that thairefter all

418 In margin: 'Death of John Harvies meir'.

419 'mear': mare.

420 The main scribe has added 'ane quarter of' for a second time above the line.

421 This word has been added in the margin. It may be intended to come earlier: 'thairefter presentlie within the space …'.

422 In margin: 'Depositione, Agnes Buchanane his spous conforme'.

423 'bay': by.

424 'hosted': coughed.

425 'laching': laughing.

426 In margin: 'John Fairlie, 2 mears'.

427 In margin: 'Issobell Keir'.

428 'hird': herdsman.

429 In margin: 'Deposition, James Harvie, anent hir bewitching ane kow of his and 3 horsses'.

430 In margin: '3 horss belonging to him'.

that yeir his heall milk[431] wes not wsefull for him: And a littill thairefter ane child of his of thrie yeir old diet in the whey.[432]

20. Also depones that the said Isobell came evrie first day of Maii thir eghtein yeir bypast, airlie in the morning east the north syd of his toun quhair he duelt and west the south syd thairof quhair his cattell pastor, since which tyme he hes not haid the benefeit of \the milk of/ his cattell as formerlie he haid.

21. Johne Harvie in Carden deponet that sevin yeir syne, Isobell Keir came to his wyf and boght ane pund of butter in Julii: And that he haid no good of his milk thairefter for that yeir and that neither men, weomen or doges myght teast it.[433]

Also depones that at Lambes[434] last, Isobell Keir cam to his hous and gatt sum whey of his wyfe: And thairefter he haid no wse of his milk, it wes so evill teastet. {*fo. 12v.*}

22.[435] Johne Makilhous deponet that thare being sum difference betuix his wyfe and the said Isobell Keir eightein yeirs agoe, she strak and bled his wyfe: And thairefter his wyfe wes seik the space of half ane yeir: And at his wyfis recoverie, all his cattell diet.[436]

23. Jonet Miller within the tolbooth of Stirling suspect of witchcraft declares that about the 15 of December last she went in to Margrat Gourlay hir hous in Kippen paroch after the sun sett, quhair she fund Isobell Keir and Margrat Harvie and ane blak man with thame, all siting at ane tabill covered with ane whyt cloath, and sum boyled beif and bread thairon: And that the said Margrat Gourlay offered to the deponer ane pairt of the meat, which she refuset to eat, and then Margrat Gourlay baid hir goe about hir bussines: And that imediatlie thairefter the bed in the hous quhair they were at meat took fyre whch wes extinguishet be Androw Wright and George Wordie.[437]

24. Also the deponer declaires that within eght dayes or thairby thairefter she saw Margrat Gourlay, Isobell Keir and Margrat Harvie in Androw Wrightis stak yaird,[438] And the said Margrat Gourlay puting in four hanks of woulen yairn in ane stak: And thairefter imediatlie Johne Wright went out and fand fyre kindlet in fyve severall places on the bak of the hous in the barn yaird: And that they took out fyve burning coles out [*sic*] of \that place of/ the hous quhair it wes burning and put thame in the hous fyre quhair they craked extreaordinerlie and that ane blak corbie came flieing too and again[439] above

[431] 'his heall milk': his whole milk, i.e. all his milk.
[432] In margin: 'Deposition, Robert Foster, anent hir bewitching his milk and cattell'.
[433] In margin: 'Deposition, John Harvie, anent hir witching his butter and quhay'. 'Quhay': whey.
[434] 'Lambes': Lammas (1 August).
[435] Altered from '21' in the same hand. The next four numbers, 23–6, have similarly been altered from '22–5'.
[436] In margin: 'John Mcilhoiss, haill cattell'.
[437] In margin: 'Pannell, Jonet Miller'.
[438] 'stak yaird': yard where corn (or perhaps peat) was stacked.
[439] 'too and again': to and fro.

the hous: And imediatlie thairefter the same stakes quhair Margrat Gourlay wes standing took fyre: Which wes extinguishet be the cuntrie people.

25. Also the deponer declaires that wpon the Saturday thairefter Isobell Keir came to hir, she being binding the kye, and inquyret if she wald have ane coill bot did not shaw it to hir: And then she shew hir ane burning peit coill and inquyret if she wald take it and kendill the hous quhair hir maisters kye stood bot the deponer refuiset it.

26.[440] Margrat Adam spous to the deceaset Robert Murdoch deponet that hir husband and she wes sheiring[441] in ane hervest nycht and Androw Ritchie spous to Isobell Keir wes lying in the rig quhair they shoore[442] and that Robert Murdoch flung ane stone to remove him: Which tuchet him on the shoulder, and thairefter Isobell Keir said it sould be the worst clod that ever he toist, And thairefter he lay seik six quarters of ane yeir efter with ane burning heat and diet.[443]

The depositiounes aforesaid signet by ws.

[*Signed:*] Thomas Reade, John Cloberie, Ja: Mutlow, WStirling. {*fo. 13r.*}

27. Duncane Foster of Arnegiboun depones that Isobell Keir and the deceiset Marioun Cuningam being both with him in service at one tyme, And ane differ falling in words betuixt thame, Marioun Cuningame affirmed that Isobell Keir wes ane witch, And Isobell Keir haveing mead the bedd quhairin she and Marioun Cuningam wset to lye, Marioun Cuningame being affrayed to lye in the bed that nyght went and lay in the deceaset Maureis Forester his bed, who also wes ane servand in that hous with thame, And the said Moreis lay that nyght in the bed that Isobell Keir had mead for Marioun Cuningame: He wes verie seik and suat[444] all nyght and arose in the morning and went and lay in the barne, And depones that Marioun Cuningame affirmed that Isobell Keir ordanet that seiknes for hir that wes on Moreis Foster.

28. Jonet Miller spous to Androw Fairlie in Arnepryor depones that Isobell Keir cuming to hir hous she said to Isobell: The laird Wryght[445] sayes thow art a witch, And that Isobell went[446] in ane buss[447] lyk a catt and ane blak

[440] This paragraph has been squeezed in at the bottom of the sheet, but leaving room for the signatures that follow.

[441] 'sheiring': harvesting.

[442] 'the rig quhair they shoore': the strip of land where they were harvesting.

[443] 'diet': died. In margin: 'Margeret Adame Anent hir husband daith'.

[444] 'suat': sweated.

[445] John Wright of Powside, mentioned earlier.

[446] The scribe initially wrote 'And Isobell replyit if', then crossed out 'replyit if' and inserted 'that'.

[447] 'buss': bush.

thing on hir[448] Isobell replyit to hir: If he haid youe in the buss he wald able a fund ane worss thing in it nor she.[449]

All the witnesses depone that Isobell Keir is said by repoirt to be ane witch.

The depositiounes afoirsaid are takin in our hearing and signet be ws

[*Signed:*] Thomas Reade, W. Stirling.[450]

Source 6, Section IV. Testimony concerning Margaret Douchall and Elizabeth Black

[*Endorsed:*] 22 March 1659. Stirling. Testificat Margaret Duchell. 1659.[451]

Wee doe testifie that wnquhill [*sic*] Margrit Duchell who died a confessed witche in firmance in our toune of Alloway, did befor ws and many famous witnesses declare thes particulars following.

first

Being accused by Mr Matthias Symsone minister of Stirling (for the tryall of the said witch sent by the presbetrie) after shoe was posed wpon the particulars[452] of hir confessione, and had confessed the samene particularly, he asked if now shoe was content to be brunt for hir witchcraft and vile synnes of divelrie, shoe answeared shoe would nevir be brunt, Coudane would give a kist and a windinsheit,[453] being againe posed be the said ministre, if shoe would be content to be brunt and they should burne Elspit Blak with hir, shoe ansueared, with all my heart even, tomorrou if ye will, The minister said O what a great envy and malice hath shoe against this Elspit Blak, She said again, I have good reason to envy hir, hir mother was my brothers death: Well, said the minister, and ye war the death of hir daughter, who answeared, It is true and weell allowed the same.

[*Signed:*] J. Craigengelt witnes and hard the abovewritin confesioun, Ja: Meldrum, W. Edmonstone witnes.

secondly

448 There is a possible word space at this point. The scribe may be losing concentration and omitting something.

449 The phrase 'able a' does not make sense, and this sentence may arise from a mishearing of Miller's words. Miller may have reported Keir as saying: 'If he had you in the bush he would aiblins [= perhaps] have found a worse thing in it nor [= than] she.' Her 'aiblins ha'e' could have been misheard as 'able a'.

450 This is the end of fo. 13r., and also the end of the text of the booklet about Isobel Keir. There follow four blank pages and a cover page, thus: fo. 13v. is blank, an unnumbered blank folio follows, and fo. 14r. is also blank. Finally, fo. 14v. is the cover page of the booklet, and the text on it has been printed above, at the beginning of Section III.

451 This section consists of a single-sheet document, folded to make two folios. The endorsement is on fo. 16v., the text that follows is on fos. 15r. and 16r., and fo. 15v. is blank.

452 'posed wpon the particulars': asked about each detail.

453 'Coudane' is Thomas Mitchell of Coldon. Douchall seems to have meant something like 'I will not be burned, but will be buried in the usual way, in a kist [= chest, coffin] and winding sheet, which Thomas Mitchell will provide'. She may have been implying that Mitchell believed in her innocence. She did in fact die in prison only a few days later.

Being visited by a minister (not as a witch bot as a dying woman) and asked by him, if nou shoe would forgive all them who had wronged hir, shee said, shoe would, and being asked more particularly be the said minister, if shoe would forgive Elspit Blak, shoe ansueared shoe would never forgive hir, the minister said how shall then God forgive you, if ye will not forgive your neightbour, shoe ansueared, I did nevir such offence to God as shoe did to me, I will nevir forgive hir. *{fo. 15v. blank} {fo. 16r.}*

thridly

Being asked be the said Mr Matthias Symsone how long shoe had beene a witche, shoe ansueared, tuentie two years, and agane being asked who learned hir, shoe ansueared Elspit Blak, and agane being asked hou long had Elspit Blak beene a witch then, shoe ansueared nyne years: Then all admired the lying and envy of the said Margaret Duchell aganst the said Elspit Blak, and thought good to testifie the same, lest the said Elspit Blak should come ondir hazard of hir lyf by the malice and envy of the said defunct Margaret Duchell confessed witch.

[*Signed:*] J. Craigengelt witnes and hard the abovewritine confessioune.

Source 7: NRS, Circuit Court Minute Books, 1655–1666, JC10/1.

{fo. 201r.} Tewsday 22 March 1659
In the Justice Court holdin within the tolbuith of Stirling be the honorabill Judg Mosley and Judg Lawrance Judges and comissioneris in criminall causis to the people in Scotland.[454] The court fenced.

Mr William Scharp Clerk
Robert Baringer officer
[*2 words blank*] dempster

The same day absent heretors unlawed.

John Baird merchand
Colene Lapslie merchand
Gilbert Robertsone merchand
Walter Stirk merchand
John Donadsone merchand

John Andersone elder
James Gib glover
James Robertsone cordiner
John Hendrie hammerman
Robert Pirnie weaver

[454] Edward Moseley and William Lawrence, both English, were two of the seven Commissioners for the Administration of Justice who oversaw the operation of the criminal court system during the Cromwellian occupation of Scotland.

James Esplene tailyeor
John Lukkiesone maltman
Thomas Trumble Litster
John Thomesone in Whins
James Moresone couper

Assise sworn.

Bessie Stevinsone prissoner in Stirling for witchcraft and charmeing Pleads not guiltie to the haill dittay.[455]

Witnessis

Jonet Hendrie Ratefeis hir depositione befoir the Justices.

Margaret Merschell does lykways adheired.

The pannell Bessie Stevinsone ratefeis hir confessione Anent Duncane Buchanane and Helene Ker and all hir uther confessiones anent the diping of the cloithes and using the foxtrie[456] leaves.[457]

Patrik Wrycht cordiner Ratefeis his depositione.

Alex Crystiesone Ratefeis his depositione says he knew be the voce of the cuntrey and by nychtbours.

Bessie says it is trew sche wet his schirt bot denys sche bad him put ane pin in hir coyt.

Confessis schoe said the wet schirt wald ather end thame or mend thame and that the foxtrie leaves had the same effect. {*fo. 201v.*}

Issobell Stewart Ratefeis hir depositione anent the chyld quhich wes wet in Sant Ringinis and Bessie Stevinsone hir putting of it one the chyld.

Bessie Stevinsone Ratefeis the former only spak no other words at the well. Margaret Stewart ratefeis.

Jonet Wilsone absent spous to Alexander [*1 word blank*] anent Bessie Stevinsone hir cur of hir husband by ane wet schirt and useing ane pin.

Bessie Stevinsone Pannell says schoe advysed Jonet Wilsone to mak use of the shirt and pin.

Issobell Smart anent hir husband seiknes George Wryght quho recovered and Margaret Ker deid.

The said Issobell Smart Ratefeis hir former depositione.

George Wryght also ratefeis his depositione.

Bessie Stevinsone confessis the taking the chyld about the aikin post and used the wordis frae the maw turner.

Jonet Crystiesone Ratefeis hir depositione.

Magie Massone Ratefeis hir depositione.

455 In margin: 'Witch convict'.
456 'foxtrie': foxglove.
457 In margin: 'Pannell confessione'.

Bessie confessis all bot the screich of the chyld and the womans taking out of hir bed conforme to hir awine confessione.

Bessie Winyett Ratefeis hir depositione.

The pannell Bessie says it is trew.

Jonet Binnie Ratefeis hir depositione.

Jonet Gilfilsane.

Marjorie Winget Ratefeis hir depositione and the pannell assyse.

Katharene Thomesone Ratefeis hir depositione.

Katherene Wrycht anent hir husbands seiknes Ratefeis hir depositione.

Jeane Watsone concerneing hir chyld quho died within 8 days efter schoe gat the flesch fra the pannell Bessie.

James Patersone Ratefeis his depositione.

Issobell Willesone his spous also ratefeis anent hir chyld the pannell ratefeis.

Helene Fergussone Ratefeis hir depositione and Bessie confessis the same to be trew.

John Gib depositione anent his seik bairne Ratefeis the same and the pannell Bessie assertis the treuth therof.

Court adjourned to Tua aclok of the eftirnone. {*fo. 202r.*}

Stirling March 22 1659

The Assise all in one voice by the mouth of Glibert [*sic*] Robertson their Chancellour find the pannell Bessie Stevinsone guiltie of the sin of witchcraft and charming mentioned in her dittay.

[*Signed:*] Gilbert Robertsone.

Eftirnone the day foirsaid 1659 former sederunt

Issobell Bennet Accused of witchcraft and charming confessis charmeing mentionat in hir dittay denys witchcraft.[458]

Witnessis

Helene Fergussone Adhears to hir confessione and depositione befoir the Justices.

Issobell Smart adhears.

The pannell denys the hinging of the chyld or seyning[459] over it in the bed. Confessis hir biding goe for the water, strawing the meill, laying the caker of the hors schoe in the bed under the chyld confessis.

Thomas McAula Adhears and the pannell confessis.

Jonet Hendersone Adhears to hir depositione.

James Patersone Adheares to his Depositione anent the pannell curing his wyff.

Issobell Willieson Adhears also to hir deposition.

458 In margin: 'Witch [*'assoilyeid' crossed out*] convict'.

459 Reading uncertain at edge of page.

Edward Lukkiesone Adhears.
Elspet Myller Adheares.
Thomas Myller Adhears.
Georg Wrycht Adhears.

Magdalin Blair for witchcraft and charmeing pleads not guiltie.[460]

Witnessis

James Andersone depositione anent ane hors perteninge to [*sic*].

Robert Kidstoun touching William Kidstoun hors bewitchet be the panell Magdalin Blair to daith Ratefeis his depositione. {*fo. 202v.*}

Helene Fergussone Ratefeis hir depositione.

Margaret Paull Ratefeid conforme to Helene Fergussone.

William Lukiesone Adhears.

James Andersone.

Katharene Lukkiesone adhears....[461] {*fo. 203r.*}

Stirling March 22 1659

The Assise all in one voice by the mouth of Gilbert Robertson their Chancellour find the pannell Issobell Bennet guiltie of the sin of charming mentioned in her dittay, And by pluralitie of voices assoilyie the pannell of the sin of witchcraft mentioned in her dittay.[462]

[*Signed:*] Gilbert Robertsone.

Also the said Assise by the mouth of the said Chancellour by pluralitie of voices assoilyie the pannell Magdalen Blair of the sin of sorcerie and witchcraft mentioned in her dittay.[463]

[*Signed:*] Gilbert Robertsone....[464] {*fo. 203v.*}

Barbara Erskene for witchcraft says schoe Renunced hir baptysme and promeist to be the Devills servand and confessis the Devill took hir in Dovane water to drown hir selff and William Myller reschewed hir out of the water.[465]

Witness

William Myller Adhears to the treuth.

The pannell adhears to all contenit in hir confessione except that schoe gave hir selff saull and bodie to the Devell.

460 In margin: 'Witch clenged'.
461 The rest of fo. 202v. contains notes of other cases that are not about witchcraft.
462 In margin: 'Witch and charmer Issobell Bennett, convict charming, assoiled witch'.
463 In margin: 'Witch Magdalin Blair assoileit'.
464 The rest of fo. 203r. contains notes of other cases that are not about witchcraft.
465 In margin: 'Witch convict'.

Elspeth Croket for witchcraft and hir confessione red, denys carnell deilling with the Devill or that evir schoe saw him bot that one nyght some thing was in the bed upon it very hevie and went away.[466]

Witnessis

Robert Archibald knawes nothing against Croked bot quhat Kathrene Rany said against hir.

Alexander Ritchie and the rest in that depositione Ratefeis the same.

James Kirk Warlok for sorcerie and witchcraft pleads not guiltie.[467]

His confessione of witchcraft being red he denyed the same to be of treuth.

Witnessis

James Lyndsay, John Thomesone, James Myller, Alexander Moreis says thay [*sic*].

The Justices denys thay hard him confess.

Katharene Blak Accused of witchcraft pleads not guiltie therunto.[468]

Witnessis

Andro Thomesone hard Bessie Patone say the pannell was a witch.

James Lyndsay and William Moreis says the lyk.

William Moreis hard Catharene Rany say the pannell was at ane meitting with hir and David Measone. {*fo. 204r.*}

Robert Archibald denys he hard Catharene Blak giftit hir dochter to the Devill.

John McKenzie absent says David Measone denys not his sone and the words that past betuix Katharene Blak and him.

Sir Robert Bruce adhears to John McKenzies confessione.

Agnes Aitkyn adhears to the former depositione and that schoe saw rottan[469] ryn under Margaret Tailyeors coit and fra hir to Kathrene Blak and than to the place quher it cam fra.

Margaret Herene saw not the rottin for schoe was at the dur bot hard[470] the boy say the Devill was among thame.[471]

Bessie Myller Adhears to hir depositione.

Helene Sibbald Adhears.[472]

466 In margin: 'Witch convict'.
467 In margin: 'Warlock assoilyeit'.
468 In margin: 'Witch convict'.
469 'rottan': rat.
470 'Agnes' crossed out here.
471 'Helene Myller' crossed out here.
472 In margin: '*Cum nota*' ('with a note': a technical phrase meaning that some doubt should be attached to their testimony).

Thomas Herne sworne he saw not the rottin nor hard the words allegit upone him.

Barbara Erskene pannell and witnes Adhears.

Elizabeth Blak accused of witchcraft pleads not guiltie.[473]

Witnes

James Lyndsay says he hard Margaret Duchell saye Katharene took hir out of his hous.

Robert Archibald and the rest adheirs to their depositione.

Henry Towart adhears to quhat he hard Duchell.

William Lyndsay adhears quhat Katharene Rany.

Mr James Cuninghame Adhears.

Helene Sibbald Adhears to hir depositione bot will not say schoe was the occasione of the seiknes or payne befell his [*sic*].

James Lyndsay and John Thomsone[474] ratefeis quhat thay hard Bessie Patone say. {*fo. 204v.*}

Thomas Mitchell saw the pannell goe to Margaret Duchell and seik hir beistis healthe from hir one hir kneys.

Stirling March 23 1659

The Assise all in one voice by the mouth of Walter Sword their Chancellour find the pannell Barbara Erskin guiltie of the sin of witchcraft mentioned in her dittay becaus judiciallie confessed by her self.[475]

[*Signed:*] Walter Sword.

Also the said Assise by pluralitie of voices viz. eight by the mouth of their said Chancellour finds the pannell Katharine Black guiltie of the sin of witchcraft mentioned in her dittay.[476]

[*Signed:*] Walter Sword.

Also the said Assise by pluralitie of voices by the mouth of their said Chancellour find the pannell Elspeth Black guiltie of the sin of witchcraft mentioned in her dittay.[477]

[*Signed:*] Walter Sword.

473 In margin: 'Witch convict'.

474 'witnes' crossed out here.

475 In margin: 'Witch Barbara Erskene convict'.

476 In margin: 'Witch Katharine Blak convict'.

477 In margin: 'Witch Elspethe Blak convict'.

Also the said Assise by pluralitie of voyces by the mouth of their said Chancellour find the pannell Elizabeth Crocket guiltie of the sin of witchcraft mentioned in her dittay.[478]

[*Signed:*] Walter Sword.

Also the said Assise by pluralitie of voices by the mouth of their said Chancellour Assoilyie the pannell James Kirk of the sin of witchcraft contained in his dittay.[479]

[*Signed:*] Walter Sword Chancellour. {*fo. 205r.*}

Eftirnone the said 23 of Merch 1659

Former sederunt

\James Ritchison/[480]
George Forrester in Airth
James Boyd in Balnucell
James Schaw in Dalquharne
James Callender in Falkirk
Walter Scot in Water of Bonie
John Ure in Arne Manuell
Johne Buchannane in Burnebrue
John Lekkie in Bailliehill
William Forrest in Playne
Walter Lekkie in Descheors
Robert Gourlay in Littil Kerss
James Forester in Ladylands
Robert Levingstoun of Eister Greneyeards
Archibald Edmestoun of Harleheaven Chancellor

Assise sworne.

Jonet Miller Accused of witchcraft denyed.[481]

Issobell Keir Accused of witchcraft pleads not guiltie.[482]

Agnes Buchannane unlawet in 100 merks for not coming round to witnes against Issobell Keir.

Jonet Rioch also unlawed.

Uther witnessis

John Wrycht Adheirs to his depositiones says ther hes bein variance betuix him and hir this sevin yeir.

478 In margin: 'Witch Elizabeth Crocket convict'.

479 In margin: 'Witch James Kirk assoilyeid'.

480 Two names have been crossed out in this list: 'Alexander Mistore portioner of Howch of Airth' and 'Walter Buchanane in Broich' (readings uncertain).

481 In margin: 'Assyse clenged, witch'.

482 In margin: 'Witch, assyse convict'.

Andro Dowgall conforme to John Wryght.

Cristiane Ritche says schoe [*sic*].

Colonell Read and Major Matla Ratefeis.

Agnes Buchannane and Jonet Riochs[483] depositione tane befoir him and the uther Justices Anent the [*sic*].

Agnes Dinnoven adheirs to hir depositione.

John Gow says eftir the pannell was at him quhen he was seik he recovered within 6 days and kens no moir.

Jeane Gillespie Adhears.

John Ure adhears to his depositione.

Marjory Dinnoven says hir bairne being weill Eftir the pannell came by hir the bairne deid Imediatly quhilk was told her quhen schoe came hame. {*fo. 205v.*}

John Hervie Adhears.

John Fairly depositione being red The samen was ratefeid be the Justices present as the treuth.

James Hervie says the cow deid within ten days eftir In the feild quher the hair was bot will not say schoe was the caus of the kow daith and adhears to the rest he deponed bot says quhat befell he taks out of the hand of God and would not blam hir.

Robert Forrester adhears to his depositione.

John Harvie Adhears to his depositione.

John McIlhois Adhears to his depositione.

Margaret Adame adheirs to her depositione and says hir husband fell seik within 6 weeks eftir the pannell threw the wod at hir.

Duncan Forrester adhears.

Jonet Myller depositione Ratefeid to be trew be the governour and Major Herbertschyr.

Margaret Gourlay Accused of witchcraft pleads not guiltie.[484]

Witnesses

Andro Wryght adhears to his depositione.

James McKlay adhears to his depositione.

George Wordie adhears hard hir nocht say that thai that sould come to the hous sould have evill eas.

Jonet Myller.

Margaret Hervie Accused of witchcraft denys the dittay.[485]

483 'Ratefies' crossed out here.

484 In margin: 'Witch, assyse clenged'.

485 In margin: 'Witch, assyse clenged'.

Witnes

Agnes Dinnoven Adhears....[486] {*fo. 206r.*}

Stirling March 23 1659

The Assise all in one voice by the mouth of Archibald Edminstoun their Chancellour find the pannell Issobell Keir guiltie of the sin of witchcraft mentioned in her dittay.

[*Signed:*] Archibald Edmonstoune.

The said Assise by the mouth of their said Chancellour by pluralitie of voices \Assoilyies/[487] the pannell Margaret Gourlay of the sin of witchcraft mentioned in her dittay.

[*Signed:*] Archibald Edmonstoune.

Also the said Assise all in one voice by the mouth of their said Chancellour Assoilyie the pannell Margaret Harvie of the sin of witchcraft mentioned in her dittay.

[*Signed:*] Archibald Edmonstoune.

Also the said Assise all in one voice by the mouth of their said Chancellour Assoilyie the pannell Janet Miller of the sin of witchcraft mentioned in her dittay.

[*Signed:*] Archibald Edmonstoune. {*fo. 206v.*}

Stirling 24 March 1659

The Comissioners Adjudges Bessie Stievinsone, Barbara Erskin, and Isobell Keir as found guiltie of the sin of witchcraft mentioned in their dittayes to be taken upon Frydaye the first day of Aprile nixt to come in the afternoon to the ordinarie place of Execution \for the burgh of Stirling/ and then and their to be strangled at a staike till they be dead and after their bodies to be burnt to ashes, And all their moveable goods to be Eschiet....[488]

Also the said Commissioners Adjudges Katherin Black, Elizabeth Black and Elizabeth Crocket as found guiltie of the sin of witchcraft mentioned in their dittayes to be banished the three nations of England Scotland and Ireland And to enact them selfs \in the books of Adjournall/ never to Return to any of the said nations under pain of death, and In the mean tyme to Remain in prison in Stirling untill a Convenient opportunitie shall be hade For their transportation.

\Margaret Gourlay and Janet Miller to be whipped and *ut infra*./[489]

[486] The rest of fo. 205v. and part of fo. 206r. contain notes of other cases that are not about witchcraft.

[487] 'fylis' crossed out here.

[488] There are two paragraphs here with sentences on other non-witchcraft cases.

[489] '*ut infra*': as below (i.e. as with Isobel Bennett in the paragraph below). This sentence has been squeezed in as a replacement for the following paragraph, which has been crossed out:

Also the said Commissioners Adjudges Isobell Bennet as found guiltie of the sin of charming mentioned in her dittay to be whipped through the most patent street of the burgh of Stirling to morrow being Fryday the 25 of this instant betuixt ten and twelve in the fornoon and theirafter to be Returned to prison till she find Cautione under the pain of twentie pound Sterling if able otherways to Enact herself \to the magistrats of the burgh of Stirling/ never to use or practise the sin of charming herafter.

Also adjudges Magdalen Blair as assoilyied of the sin of witchcraft to find caution *ut supra*/[490] for her good behaviour in tyme coming under the pain of 20 lib if able otherways to enact her self theirfore.[491] {*fo. 207r.*}

Also Adjudges James Kirk as Assolyied of the sin of witchcraft to find caution if able under the pain of 20 lib Sterling for his good behaviour otherwayes to enact himself....[492]

Stirling 24th March 1659
Compeired Kathren Black, Elisabeth Black and Elisabeth Crocket, and conforme to ane ordinance of the judges of the date of thir presents, became actit and obleist to depairt out of the thrie Nations of England, Scotland and Ireland, and not to returne againe within any of them under the payne of death.
Elizabeth Blak, hir mark
Katharene Blak, hir mark
Elizabeth Croket, hir mark[493] ...

{*fo. 236v.*}[494] Stirling March 24 1659
Delivered to James Norie *absolvitur*[495] of Janet Miller, \Margaret Gourlay, Magdalen Blair/[496] and James Leckie, Issobell Bennet, at v/10øøø[497] a peice or what can be hade and to send[498] to us with his burgess ticket.[499]

'Also the said Commissioners adjudges Margaret Gourlay and Janet Miller as found Guiltie of fyre raising mentioned in their dittay to be banished the three nations etc. *ut supra*.'

490 'as above'.

491 'otherways to enact her self theirfore': if she could not find a cautioner, they would accept her own formal promise of good behaviour.

492 There are three paragraphs here with sentences on other non-witchcraft cases.

493 These words are arranged around the 'marks' of these three people.

494 This is the final page of the book, which has been used for pen-trials and a handful of isolated memoranda, including this one.

495 'he is absolved (from his responsibility)'.

496 'James Kirk' has been crossed out here and these two names added.

497 *Sic*. The reading of the initial symbol 'v/' is uncertain. Evidently this is a sum of money; perhaps it should be read as '£10 0*s*. 0*d*.' This was a period of transition from roman to arabic numerals, and the scribe's use of 'ø' may be idiosyncratic or experimental.

498 'to Edinburgh' has been written here and apparently crossed out.

499 Janet Miller, Margaret Gourlay and Isobel Bennett were the three accused witches who had been sentenced to be whipped, so this note may well be about the arrangements for this. The court minutes above do not mention a sentence of whipping for Magdalen Blair, but the minutes do reveal changes of mind about sentencing (Gourlay and Miller had initially

Source 8: NRS, Court of Justiciary Process Papers, 1658, JC26/26, JC26/27.

JC26/26, bundle 3, no. 8.

[*Endorsed:*] 22 Merch 1659. Supplication Katharene and Elizabeth Blak, Witches, Stirling Court.

Wnto the ryght honourabll the commissioners for the ministratione of Justice to the people in Scotland in causes criminal,

The humble petitione of Catherene and Elizabeth Blacks, Sheweth,

That your Lordships petitioners being conveined most wrongouslie for witchcraft, now fylled be ane Assyse, And sieing efter full debate the petitioners Innocencie wes apparent, not onlie to the whole Auditorie, Bot lykewayes to your Lordships, as your discourse to the Assyse did evidence, And therefore sieing the petitioners were fylled by eight of the said assyse who had Imprisoned and linked themselves together to ruine the petitioners, and were assoilyed by seven honest judicious men wnknowen to the petitioners, and Considering their slighteing and usurpeing your Lordships jurisdictione in contraverting to the assyse your Lordships Interloquitors which is the prerogative of the Court and the assyse should not meddle therewith In soe far as the said Assyse did Conclude the testimonie of dieing witches to be ane sufficient probatione and a witnes receaved *cum nota*[500] to be ane good and sufficient witnes which are meere points *in Lato*[501] and were cleirlie determined by your Lordships And therefore sieing the said sentence and werdict is not onlie unjust and wicked and reverseable by ane Assyse of Error, Bot also null in it selff In swa far as it proceedes Against clear Interloquitors of your Lordships which if Admitted Noe man can be secure of his Lyffe if any Assyse may reverse any thing of the relevancie determined by your Lordships. As therefore your Lordships wold not dipp your hands in the blood of the poore petitioners whom wee attest in your[502] own Consciences as before God not to be guiltie Sieing your Lordships gave a publick testimonie against it,

been put down for banishment, for instance), so perhaps this, plus the deletion of James Kirk's name here, indicates a further change. James Norrie, the burgh clerk of Stirling, is in charge of the transaction recorded here. James Leckie may be either another criminal receiving the same sentence, or else a colleague of Norrie taking responsibility for Isobel Bennett. The note may well record a transaction between two local authorities or courts, one of which may be the burgh of Stirling. Neither authority has a firm claim on the other, so they seek 'what can be hade' as reimbursement.

500 'with a note': a technical phrase meaning that some doubt should be attached to their testimony.

501 'general points'.

502 *Sic*. Probably read 'our'.

May it therefore please your Lordships to delay sentence and Executione quhereoff[503] Against the petitioners whill[504] the First of June which is ordinarie and in your Lordships power even quhair thair are not such presseing reasones as here, Or that your Lordships wold call for the samyne Assyse againe and put them to Consider thair verdict and shew them that in points of Law determined by your Lordships they are not to medle which is yet more ordinarie with your Lordships, and the poore petitioners humblie begs and waits your Lordships answer. Cathren Black, Elizabeth Black.

JC26/27, bundle 6, no. 9.

[*Endorsed:*] Warrand to the justice deputs, 1662.

At Edinburgh the sevent day of November i^m^ vi^c^ and sextie ane yeares. Anent ane supplication presented be Kathrin and Elizabeth Blacks and Elspeth Crockett prisoners, Shewing that the petitioners being imprisoned these thrie years bygane as suspect of witchcraft within the tolbuith of Stirling And haveing supplicat the Lords of Councell either to be putt to tryall or liberty, The justice deputts were ordered to doe the same betuixt and the first day of September last bypast whilk is now expyred, craving therefor the saids Lords to prorogat the said act to a farder dyett to the effect forsaid As the said petition beares, Quhilk being at lenth heard, read and considdered, The Lords of his majesties secreit councall Ordaines the justice deputts to putt the supplicants to ane legall tryall or otherwayes to sett them to liberty upon caution And to report their diligence thereanent to the councall betuixt and the first day of Januarii nixttocum. *Extractum per me,*[505]

[*Signed:*] Pet: Wedderburne.

JC26/27, bundle 6, no. 4.[506]

[*Endorsed:*] Petitioun. Katharen and Elisabeth Blacks.[507] John Demperstoun, David Mason and John Sands of Langsyd acted for their appearance, *3tio itineris Sterlinei,* on *xv diebus.*[508] 12 Novembris 1661.

{*p. 1*} Unto the honourable his majesties justice deputs, The petition off Katharein and Elisabeth Blacks and Elisabeth Croket prisoners within the tolbuith of Stirling, Humblie sheweth,

503 *Sic.* Read 'thereof'.

504 'whill': until.

505 'Extract (given) by me'.

506 The initial petition in this document is undated but seems to have been written before 7 November 1661, the date of the warrant printed above. It has been placed after the warrant because the document also records the action that was taken as a result on 12 November.

507 'Act for' crossed out here.

508 '3rd circuit (court) of Stirling, upon 15 days (notice)'.

Wheras the petitioners being aged and sicklie persones hes bein deteined three yeares bygane prisoners within the tolbuith of Stirling in great miserie and necessitie For suspiceon of Witchcraft being incarcerat be the laite usurpers, And the petitioners haveing oftymes meaned themselffis to the Lords of his majesties honourable privie counsell, The saids lords be ther ordinance daited the sevinth of November instant Hes ordained your lordships to put them to ane legall tryall Or utherwayes to sett them to libertie upon caution As the act of counsell herwith produced bears,

The petitioners Humblie desyres your lordships For the favour of God to Commisserat ther sad sufferings and either to putt them to ane speidie tryall or to sett them to libertie upon caution For they are brought to that extremitie that undoubtedlie they will starve and die in prisone if they be longer delayed, and your lordships [*word illegible*]. {*p. 2*}

Edinburgh 12 Novembris 1661

The justice deputes Ordaines the petitioners to be putt to libertie, They finding caution for their appearance before them upon the thrid day of the circuit for the shereffdom of Stirling or sooner upon any citation of fiftein dayes warneing, To underly the law for the crymes within mentionat, under the pain of tuo thowsand merks for ilk ane of them.

[*Signed:*] John Cuningham.

28. DALKEITH WITCHES, 1661

INTRODUCTION

The documents transcribed below comprise the pre-trial interrogations and trial records of four women and one man from the presbytery of Dalkeith, to the south and east of Edinburgh. This area suffered from severe witch-hunts in 1649–50 and in 1661–2. These five witches all received death sentences on the same day, 29 July 1661. They were Janet Daill in the parish of Inveresk, and David Johnstone, Agnes Loch, Janet Lyle and Margaret Ramage, all in the parish of Newton. Early interrogations were carried out at Woolmet and Edmonstone in Newton parish, but after a while the suspects were imprisoned in the tolbooth of Musselburgh, where they were all eventually tried together.

The judges included not only the veteran Alexander Colville, but also George Mackenzie, beginning a legal career that would lead him in 1678 to the post of lord advocate and a role in discouraging witchcraft prosecutions in Scotland. Mackenzie may well have learned his scepticism about harsh legal procedures from these trials. In the witchcraft chapter of his book *Laws and Customs of Scotland in Matters Criminal* (1678), Mackenzie wrote of having interviewed a condemned witch who told him that she had confessed, not because she was guilty, but because the prosecution had destroyed her reputation and livelihood, so that she wished to be out of the world.[1] Anna Cordey, who has conducted a detailed study of the Dalkeith prosecutions, has argued that this woman was Janet Daill.[2]

The five accused witches in this group formed only a small part of the panic as a whole. The Survey of Scottish Witchcraft notes the following as linked to one or more of the five: Agnes Anderson, Margaret Barbour, Janet Bell, Margaret Bell, Janet Buchanan, Isobel Burnie (or Binnie or Binning),

1 Sir George Mackenzie, *The Laws and Customs of Scotland in Matters Criminal*, ed. Olivia F. Robinson (Edinburgh: Stair Society, 2012), section I.10.2, p. 71.

2 Anna Cordey, 'Reputation and Witch-Hunting in Seventeenth-Century Dalkeith', in Julian Goodare (ed.), *Scottish Witches and Witch-Hunters* (Basingstoke, 2013), 103–20, at pp. 114–15. See also Anna Cordey, 'Witch-Hunting in the Presbytery of Dalkeith, 1648 to 1662' (MSc by Research thesis, University of Edinburgh, 2003).

Isobel Caldwell, Walter Cowan, Margaret Dallas, Marion Greenlaw, Elspeth Haliburton, Janet Howie, Jean Howieson, Agnes Johnstone, William King (or Keen), Katherine Leggatt, Janet Luny, Margaret Scott, Bessie Stewart, Margaret Veitch and Sarah Young. Most of these names are mentioned in the documents below. In addition, the documents below name William Hogg, Margaret Stevenson and Agnes Thomson. Overall, this comes to 40 witches – 36 women and 4 men. The proportion of women, 90 per cent, was slightly higher than the 85 per cent women found for the Scottish witch-hunt as a whole. It is therefore interesting that the trial of David Johnstone goes into more detail when it comes to interrogation and confession. There seems to be no difference between the questions he is asked and the questions the women are asked, except for the point of copulation with the Devil.

Torture was used to obtain confessions; a hair shirt was used to make David Johnstone confess. The texts of several of the confessions insist that the confessions have been given freely and without torture; this presumably means that the accused persons ratified the confessions after the torture had ceased. Johnstone and several other accused persons tried to retract their confessions, but they seem in the end to have recognised that continued non-cooperation would only lead to further torture.

As 1661 was relatively late during the period of Scottish witchcraft trials, the interrogators were well acquainted with demonological ideas; there are strong similarities in the rhetoric of the confession texts. All the accused persons confessed to having renounced their baptism, to entering the Devil's pact, to having received the Devil's mark, to having got a new name from the Devil, to getting promises from the Devil, either that they would 'never want' or money, which later turned out to be stones, to having participated at witches' meetings, dancing with the Devil, and ending their confessions with denunciations of other suspected witches. The interrogators were keen to establish that each suspect knew and recognised the Devil at the time. Some of the women also confessed to having carnal copulation with the Devil.

To be a woman with a reputation was undoubtedly dangerous during the period of witchcraft persecution. However, not all the persons formally accused of witchcraft had a reputation, and, as Anna Cordey argues, a damning case could be built around almost anybody.[3] These records support that view, as reputation related to the accused persons is not mentioned. Indeed, there is almost no mention of malefice against neighbours. Instead, in their confessions it comes to the fore how long they have been the Devil's servants. Some of them first met with the Devil in the houses of women acquaintances. They participated in witches' gatherings in various nearby places. Janet Daill confessed that she experienced fear when she received the Devil's mark. Janet Lyle said that the Devil never gave her a mark, but the mark was still found on

[3] Cordey, 'Witch-Hunting', 55.

her. The relationship between Devil and witch was that of master and servant. Lyle provided an unusual detail of the Devil's bid to recruit her: the Devil's wife had recently died, so he wanted her as a servant to keep house for him.

The formal authority under which the trials were held was that of the central justiciary court, with the justices depute being sent to the locality instead of having the accused persons brought to Edinburgh. Dalkeith was a regality; the bailie of the regality demanded the right to sit with the judges, but this seems to have been refused since he was not named when the sentences were being recorded. There were then arguments about whether the crown or the lord of the regality had the right to the witches' confiscated property, but the court did not concede the right to the lord.

TEXTS

Source 1: NRS, Court of Justiciary Process Papers, 1661, JC26/27.

JC26/27, unnumbered bundle, no. 9[4]

[*Endorsed:*] The Depositionis of Issobell Beinei and Agnis Looche. Neatoune.[5] first [*sic*]

{*p. 1*} At Swneisseid this 6th of Jullay 1661 yeiirs [*sic*]

The wheilk day in pressence of Sir William Murray of Netone and Charlles Murray his Brother jermane[6] and Daveid Ballenei in Cheinend, Issobell Beinei weidowe in Swneisseid being dellated by severall for a witch, of hir owne frei weill deponed that befor harweist bygone a yeiir Marione Greinllay did come to hir and touk hir to the Bllew Holle a liteille from the Swneisseid wher sho did meit with the Divell, and he reprowed hir for being long a coming, and at the second meiteing sho had with theim which was the meter of[7] thre qwarteirs of a yiir [*sic*] thairefter, he had dalleing with hir as a man, and sho cnew [*sic*] him by his nature for it was cowllder then a nother mans, and leikweisse he cawssed hir renownce hir bapteissme and gawe hir a nother name and called hir Lokei Showtheirs, at hir first meiting sho promeissed to serwe him a yeiir and at both thesse meiteings thair was with hir and the Divell Marione Greinllay, Issobell Calldwealle and Agnis Loch.

[*Signed:*] William Murray witness, Cha: Murray witnes, David Ballenie wittnes.

Upon the 9 day of the forseid month the forseid Issobell Beinei, in presence of the fornamid witnesseis did adhere to all hir former depositione.

4 The bundle containing this document is unnumbered and labelled 'Gilmerton Witches'. This document, however, is not from Gilmerton. It has a pencil number '9'.

5 'Neatoune': Newton.

6 'Brother jermane' (german): full brother.

7 'the meter of' (matter): something like, roughly.

[*Signed:*] William Murray witness, Cha: Murray witnes, David Ballenie wittnes. {*p. 2 blank*} {*p. 3*}

At Swneisseide this 6th of Jullay 1661 yeiirs
The wheich day in pressence of Sir William Murray of Netone and Charlles Murray his Brother jermane and Daveid Ballenei in the Cheine end, Agneis Loch spousse to Patrick Robeissone in Swneisseide being dellated of several others for witchcraft, of hir owne frei weill deponed, that abowt threi yeiirs seince being comeing from Dallkith allone, the Deiwell did appeire to hir like a man and klleid in greine, and she being greiteing[8] for several things sho wanteid,[9] speired at hir what sho wanteid, and seid if sho wolld serwe him sho showlld not want (wherwpon sho was content) and gawe hir selfe whollei ower to him and at a nother meiteing a liteille thairefter he did appeir to hir at the same pllace wher he had dalleing with hir as a man and cawssed hir renownce hir bapteissme, and sewerall other meiteings sho was at thair was Issobell Beinei, Marione Greinllea and Issbell Calldwallds in Swneisseide, and sewerall others that sho cnew [*sic*] not by ressone of bllack hoods they had on thair heids and missells[10] on thair faceis.

[*Signed:*] William Murray witness, Cha: Murray witnes, David Ballenie wittnes.

Upon the 9 day of Jullay 1661 years the forseid Agneis Loch did adhere to all hir former depositione and deponeis at that teyme sho renonced hir baptisme the Deiwell called hir a poore owld creatwre, hir adherance was before the fornamed witnesseis.

[*Signed:*] William Murray witnes, Cha: Murray witneis, David Ballenie wittnes.

Musselburght 29 Julii 1661 In presence of Mr Alexander Colvill, Mr John Cunnynghame and Mr George McKenzie, compeirit Agnes Loch and adhered to hir former depositioun. Onlie sayes the tyme of hir first Ingadgeing with the Divill within this yeir of thairby.[11]

JC26/27, bundle 2, no. 5[12]

[*Endorsed:*] \Neatoun/ Confession Janett Daill.

Att Wolmett the aught day of Julii 1661, Jannet Daill spouse to George Bell colyer[13] Beeng dyvers time delaitted by dyvers confessing witches and upon strong presumptiones, wes apprehended and sighted, and without aney

8 'greiteing': weeping.
9 'wanteid': lacked.
10 'missells': mufflers.
11 This paragraph has been added in a different hand.
12 The bundle containing this document is labelled 'Musselburgh Witches, JC26/27/2? [*sic*]'. This document has a pencil number 'JC26/27/2, item 5'.
13 'colyer' (collier): coal-miner.

threatning or torture used against her, did confesse as followis vizt. that about fourtein years agoe or therby, Agnes Andersone and Margaret Barbour beeng in George Edie colyer in Wolmett his house, did send for her and Margaret Barbour did desire her to tack ane drink with ane civill gentillman who wes come over the watter to fie[14] collyers, and efter that she had taken ane drink with him, he did lay his hand upon her shoulder, and within ane short spece therefter, she did meit in Shereffhall moor, with the Divell in companie with Margaret Bell, Elspet Heliburten, Agnes Johnestowne, William Keen, and David Johnstowne and a great manie moer att the meiting who in respect they wer masked she could not know them, att which tyme the Divel causd her renunce her baptisme, and putt her hand to the soll of her futt and the other to the crowne of her head and delyvered her selfe over to him and she trembleing, the Divell forbad her to fear, and he promiesd her ane new petticott, and called her Janett Cleirkeyis.[15] And further declaired that about fyveteen weeks agoe the Divell did mett with her and the foirsaid Elspet Helyburten, Agnes Johnestowne, William Keen and David Johnestowne downe in the bank of Wolmett, and that the said David Jonston wes longest in coming to the meiting and stayed about halfe ane hour danceing, and Agnes Jonstowne reproved the said David for staying and she declaired that they wer trysted to that meeting about tenn weeks befoir, bot hed been oft missetrysted be him, The haill premisses wer confessed be the foirsaid Janet Deall of hir owne frie accord in presentis of Major Johne Biggar of Wolmett, Mr Archibald Edmonstowne brother germain to the Laird of Wolmett, Henry Helebrunton portioner of Gowger, Thomas Baylyie ane elder of Newtowne parochine and Robert Patrie indweller in Edinburgh.

[*Signed:*] John Biggar witnes, Henry Halyburtone witnes, Ro: Patrie witnes, Arch: Edmiston witnes, Thomas Bailyie.

Upon the foirsaid day moneth and yeer of God above writtin the said Janett Daill did confess and adher to the haill premisses *in terminis*[16] without alteratione In presentis of Sir William Murray of Neatowne, Charles Murray his brother germane and the foirsaids haill persons.

[*Signed:*] William Murray witnes, Cha: Murray witnes.

Musselburgh 29 July 1661

In presence of the Justice deputis Jonet Daill adheiris to this confession and everie part thairof being red to him [*sic*].[17]

[14] 'fie' (fee): employ.

[15] In margin: 'New name'.

[16] 'in the terms', i.e. the wording of the confession.

[17] This paragraph has been added in a different hand.

JC26/27, bundle 2, no. 9[18]

[*Endorsed:*] Depositiones Margaret Rammage and Jennet Lyle now prissoners for witchcraft 1661.

{*p. 1*} At Edmistoune the tenth day of July 1661
The depositione of Margaret Rammage widow in Edmistoune \now prissoner/, for sundrie presumptiones of witchcraft in presence of the witnesses under subscryving.

The quhilk day the said Margaret Rammage of hir awin free will depons that the last winter betwixt Youle and Fastings Evin,[19] that Elspeth Hallybruntoune cryed upon hir to hir house, having ane quart of aill in her howse, and when the said Margaret was come in into the house of the forsaid Elspeth Hallybruntoune she did bring in the Devill at hir back and he did sit downe and the said Elspeth tooke the cup, and did give it unto him, and he drank to the said Margaret, and gave hir the cup out of his hand and at his way going, he Layde his hand upon hir shoulder wher the mark is, and the said Elspeth and she did sit still and drank out the rest of the quart of aill, the tyme being betwixt nyne and ten houres at night.

Depones Lykwise the said Margaret, that Elspeth Hallybruntoune came to hir owin house to hir, and tooke hir away with hir to Shereffhall Kaime David Johnestoune, William King, Kathrein Leggat, Margaret Veitch, Margaret Scot, Jennet Daill, Jennet Bell, Jennet Lyle, Agnes Johnestoune, Bessie Stewart, Sara Young, Jennet Buchannan: All being together, the Devill tooke Kathreine Leggat by the hand and others and went throw us all with them.

[*Signed:*] MPhin witness, Thomas Bailyie witnes, James Hoag witnes, WFareis witnes. {*p. 2*}

At Edmistoune the 11th day of July 1661
The quhilk day in presence of the witnesses undersubscryving the forenamed Margaret Rammage deponed that the Devill desyred hir to serve him, and that she was content therwith, and that he caused hir renunce hir baptisme and she did soe.

[*Signed:*] Patrick Edmontoune witness, MPhin witness, Thomas Bailyie witnes.

At Edmistoune the 12 day of July 1661
The quhilk day the forenamed Margaret Rammage Ratified hir former depositiones in presence of the witnesses undersubscryving.

[18] The bundle containing this document is labelled 'Musselburgh Witches, JC26/27/2? [*sic*]'. This document has a pencil number 'JC26/27/2, item 9'.

[19] 'Youle and Fastings Evin': Christmas and Shrove Tuesday.

Confest Lykwise the said Margaret Rammage that Jennet Howie widow was in the forsaid companie at the Shereffhall Kaime at their meiting thair in presence of the forsaid witnesses.

[*Signed:*] MPhin witness, Thomas Bailyie witnes, James Hoag witnes, WFareis witnes. {*p. 3*}

At Edmistoune the tenth day of July 1661
The depositiones of Jennet Lyle widow in Edmistoune now prissoner for certaine presumptiones of witchcraft in presence of the witnesses under subscryving.

The quhilk day the said Jennet of hir awin free will depones that a yeare bygaine in beirseed tyme,[20] she going up the backsyde of Edmistoune in the twylight, the Devill appeared unto hir in the liknes of a man, and said unto hir that his wyfe was dead, and that he would fie hir to keepe his house, and gave unto hir ane peice of silver, which when he went from hir turnd unto a sklaite[21] stone.

2. About ane quarter of ane yeare after, the said Jennet and David Johnestoune, William King, Jennet Daill, Elspeth Hallybruntoune, Agnes Johnestoune, Margaret Rammage and some other masked folkes, met in Woolmet banke about elevin houres at night, every one running throw another, at which tyme the Devill tooke the said Jennet by the hand and led hir throw the ring among all the rest and caused hir Lay hir one hand upon the crowne of hir head, and the other upon the soale of hir foot and renunce hir baptisme and delyver hir selfe freely to him both soule and bodie and forsweare Christ which she did.

3. At another tyme the abovenamed Jennet Lyle and Jeane Howiesone indweller in Sherreffhall muire met at Sherreffhall Kaime and other ten with them about elevin houres at night, and danced thair a longe tyme the said Jeane Howiesoune comeing to the foresaid Jennet, and told hir of the meiting, and tooke hir with hir out of hir owin house.

[*Signed:*] WFareis witnes, MPhin witnes, Thomas Bailyie witnes, James Hoag witnes.

At Edmistoune the eleventh day of July 1661
The quhilk day in presence of the witnesses undersubscryving the forenamed Jennet Lyle deponed that Jennet Buchannan and Margaret Scot were at that meiting with the rest.

[*Signed:*] MPhin witness, Thomas Bailyie witnes.

At Edmistoune the 12 day of July 1661
The quhilk day the forenamed Jennet Lyle Ratified hir former depositiones in presence of the witnesses undersubscryving.

[*Signed:*] MPhin witness, Thomas Bailyie witnes, James Hoag witnes.

20 'beirseed tyme': the time of sowing bere (barley) in spring.
21 'sklaite': slate.

JC26/27, bundle 2, no. 4[22]

[*Endorsed:*] The depositions of Daveid Johnstone.

The 11 of July 1661

In presens of Walter Gowane, John Strachan, John Carfree, John Bennett, James Ogilvie.

Davied Jonsonstone [*sic*] did Confese that about thretine years since that going to Edinburgh with a lod of colls[23] the Deviell did apeir to him going neir to the Barrowmour in the licknes of a man in blak clos and the Deviell askeid at the said Davied wher he was going and he sed that he was a pour man going to the toune with a lod of colls and the Devill bad him serve him and he should not want, to the which he did condesend[24] at that tyme and ane year ther efter about ten or elevine at night at Owmet bank, he met with the Devill in the componey of William King, Elspet Helebourtine, Janet Dells and Walter Cawane and the Devill gave him a merk in his leg and caused the said Davied to renonce his baptyme which name he fargat and lykwayes the said David sed that a lettill befor Janet Dealls hir doughter was mareid they had a meittin at the Grain law with the forsaid companey and ther they had dansing and liping.[25] Johne Strachane witnes, Johne Bennett witnes.

At Musselburgh the 17 of July 1661

The quhilk day the presence of Mr George Phine, James Hodge and James Wickedshaw and James Byres the fornamed David Johnstoune ratified his former depositiouns.

[*Signed:*] MPhin witnes, Ja: Hodge witnes, James Wickedshaw witnes, James Byres witnes.

JC26/27, unnumbered bundle, no. 5[26]

[*Endorsed:*] Neatoun and Dalkeith witches

Witches in Neatoun paroch

Issobell Binning Confesses that she hes severall tymes mett with the Divell and hes had carnall dealing with him and that his natur wes cold not lyk another man hes renunced her baptisme and the Divell gave her another name.

22 The bundle containing this document is labelled 'Musselburgh Witches, JC26/27/2? [*sic*]'. This document has a pencil number 'JC26/27/2, item 4'.

23 'lod of colls': load of coals.

24 'condesend': agree.

25 'liping': leaping.

26 The bundle containing this document is unnumbered and labelled 'Gilmerton Witches'. This document, however, is not from Gilmerton. It has a pencil number '5'.

Agnes Loch spous to Patrik Robisone in Sunisyd confesses several meitinges with the Divell, That he hes had carnall dealing with her hes renunced her baptisme and the givell [*sic*] given her another name.

Margaret Rammage confesses she hes bene severall tymes in companie with the Divell in severall places and that the Divell laid hes hand upon her shoulder wher the mark is and that they drank together and that she becam the Divellis servand renunced her baptisme and \no/[27] copulatione confessed.

Jonet Lyle confesses that she hes keiped company with the Divill severall tymes at severall places that he hyred her to be his servant Gave her money and that they have danced together And that she did renunce her baptisme and did delyver herself freely to him both soule and body.

Jonet Dale confesses that she hes mett severall tymes with the Divell and drunk with him and he did lay his handis on her shoulder and caused her renunce her baptisme, and putting one hand to the sole of her foott and the other to the crowne of her head delyvered herself over to him And she trembling for fear, he forbad her to fear and promised her a new petticoatt and gave her a new name.

Mareon Grinlaw confessed she ingaged to the Divells service Renunced her baptisme That the Divell gave her a new name calling her Lowkie[28] shoulders.

Jean Howisone widow confesses that she hes bene in company with the Divell and danced with him, becam his servand bot did not renunce her baptisme.

Margaret Stevensone widow confesses that she hes severall tymes mett with the Divell becam his servand renunced her baptisme that he gave her a kisse and called her Speid[29] and that he had carnall dealing with her that his natur wes cold.

Agnes Thomsone widow declares that the Divell mett with her and gatt a grip of her and causd her lay the one hand on the crowne of her head and the uther on the sole of her foott and bad her renunce her baptisme and called her Bessie This wes about 18 yeirs since And that at another tyme the Divell mett her at Dalkeith gibbett, and bad her tary[30] Bessie.

David Jonstoun confesses that he hes mett severall tymes with the Divell becom his servant and receaved a mark in the leg renunced his baptisme, and receaved a name quhich he hes forgott and that severall tymes he hes danced in the Divells company.

27 'denyes' crossed out here and 'no' written above the line.

28 'Lowkie': lucky.

29 'Speid': success.

30 'tary' (tarry): wait. Perhaps this should be understood as an injunction by the Devil: 'Wait, Bessie!'

JC26/27, bundle 2, no. 7[31]

Mussilburgh 28th July 1661
Compeirit David Johnstoune and being interrogat whither or not he was guiltie of the sine of witchcrafte, he sayes that he knowes litle of it he sayes that he knowes nothing of witchcrafte more then the chyld in the mothers womb, When he was apprehendit he sayes that he was put in ane hair cloath which maide him confess that he was in company with Jonet Dailles \and others at the Borrowmuir/[32] and that he[33] once confessed that he renunced his Baptisme But he was compellit to say it, he declaires that quhat he spoke befor the minister that he would not goe a back of it. Being interrogat *de novo*[34] he declaires he will not deny that which he hath alreadie confest be it true or not.

Therefter he declaires that it is about 11 yeir since Sathan beguiled[35] him and that Sathan said to him \when he was going to Edinburgh with coalles at the Borrowmuir/, poor man laikes \thow/ money he will give it yow, he sayes that Sathan askit him if he would be his man and he promist that he would be his servant and he gave him a name calling him William [*1-2 words blank*] and that he renunced his baptisme goeing up to the Borrowmuir and that he met thryse with him once at the Borrowmuir once at the Wolmet bank and another tyme at the Greenlaw and at these places he danced in company with Jonet Dailles and the rest that was there, he sayes that the Devill was black lyk a man to him at the Wolmet bank, all these abovewrittine confessiones he said was of trueth.

He declaired he maide his first pactione with him at the Borrowmuir and said to him poor man quhair art thow goeing, he answered Sir I am following a poor beast with colles, he askit if he laiked money, If he did he would give him money to him, if he would be his servant he should doe nothing bot goe up and downe with him which he undertook to doe.

He sayes that Sathan was terrible to him when \he/ appeared to him, he sayes he knew him to be the Devill Because he was black, he confesses that all the space abovewrittin he was beguiled with the Devill.

He sayes Jonet Dailles, William King, Elspeth Halyburton and [*2 words blank*] was at the first meeting with the Devill at the Borrowmoor.

He sayes the Devill give him the marke on his leg at Wolmet bank with his hand and that he \put his finger to his leg/[36] and that he alwayes had black cloathes when he saw him a black cloake with a hatt on his head.

He declaires againe that all this abovewrittine confessione is of trueth.

31 The bundle containing this document is labelled 'Musselburgh Witches, JC26/27/2? [*sic*]'. This document has a pencil number 'JC26/27/2, item 7'.

32 'and at Wolmet bank for the first tyme' crossed out here.

33 'renunced his baptisme' crossed out here.

34 'anew'.

35 'beguiled': deceived.

36 'put gripped his leg with his fingers' crossed out here.

JC26/27, bundle 2, no. 6[37]

{*p. 1*} Musselburgh tolbuith 29 July 1661 in presence of Mr Alexander Colvill Compeirit David Johnstoun[38] prisoner in Musselburgh and being interrogat confesst that the Divill appearit to him at the Borrowmure ellivin yeares since and that thair he enterit in his service that the Divill promist him monie bot nevir gave him any That than he renuncit his baptisme and callit him William and that thair the Divill gave him a marke in his leg.

That another tyme he was at a meiting with the Divill in the Wolmet banke quhair Margaret Daillis, William King and ane Walter Cowane who is now deid wer present.

That his thrid meiting with the Divill was at the Grenelawis when he sayed the foirnamet personis wer present Declairis that he nevir toke the Comunion since his entrie to the Divillis service nor yet that he resorted oft to preachingis since that tyme.

[*Signed:*] AColville.

Compeirit William King[39] prisoner of the aige of 72 denyes all.

Compeirit Marion Grenelaw and acknawlegis that once shoe confest to Mr Robert [*1 word blank*] that shoe was at a meiting with the Divill in the Blewholl whan shoe ingadgit to be the Divill servant Bot now shoe denyes this and sayes shoe lied and that it was for feare shoe said soe.

\In presence of Mr Alexander Colvill and Mr John Cunninghame/

Margarat Stevinstoun denyes all. Sayes shoe was tortored and that all the Confessioun shoe had maid was fals.

Jeane Howiesone denyes all, sayes that the confessioun shoe maid to the minister was false.

William Hogg denyes all, sayes he wes by himselfe[40] quhen he confessed at the first tryall.

Curia justiciarie tenta in pretorio burgi de Musselburgh per Magistri Alexandri Colvill etc.[41]

In presence of Mr Alexander Colvill, Mr John Cunninghame and Mr George McKenzie.

37 The bundle containing this document is labelled 'Musselburgh Witches, JC26/27/2? [*sic*]'. This document has a pencil number 'JC26/27/2, item 6'.

38 In margin: 'David Johnstoun'.

39 In margin, crossed out: 'William Kin'. Above this paragraph, 'In presence of …' has also been crossed out.

40 'by himselfe': beside himself, out of his wits.

41 'Court of justiciary held in the tolbooth of the burgh of Musselburgh by Masters Alexander Colville etc.'

Compeired Agnes Loch[42] spouse to Patrick Robertson being aged 60 yeiris says she hes bein in Satans service a year since[43] And being greiting \comeing fra Dalkeith said said [*sic*] shame fall him[44] for he promised me something bot/ Satan \met hir at Newton burne/ asked at her quhat ailed her, The next tyme he met her accidentally he called[45] poore sillie old wiff, she confesses the marks, \one/ in her shoulder \and ane other betwixt her thigh and her body/ sayes she had a pain after,[46] sayes she wes \at another tyme/ in companie with Issobell Binnie \in the Blew Holl/[47] and als with Marion Greinlaw and Issobell Caldwels, confesses she had carnall dealing with the Devill, Confesses that she renunced her baptisme and that the \Devill/ caused her renunce the same by putting her hand \to the ground/[48] and said she should be his servant. \I never gate[49] a strae fra him to quhom she answered, ye will give me thing that will never doe me good and the Devill answered ye wot not./

Confesses that Issobell Binnie and[50] Issobell Caldwalds cryed upon her and sayes that they all danced togither.

Confesses that she thought it wes the Devill that mett with her. Sayes she desires not to live, because she is affraid that he come to her \agan/. Sayes she never did any evill nor ever charmed any. {*p. 2*}[51]

Margarat Rammage[52] \confesses/[53] she met with the Devill in Elspet Haliburtons house \in winter last about 11 at night/ and that Elspet oftymes called her and fetchit her, and that she brought the Devill to her, who was lyk a blackman, that the Devill laid his hand on her shoulder and therafter went out of the doore and that he spoke nothing at that tym.[54] About five weeks therafter Elspet

42 In margin: 'Agnes Loch'.
43 'he was cled in grein' crossed out here.
44 'shame fall him': shame upon him.
45 *Sic*. Probably read 'called her'.
46 'they nipped her, sayes the Devil mett her at tuo hours in the afternoon' crossed out here.
47 'and that the Devill called meikle shoulderis' crossed out here. 'That she heard Isobell Binnie say the Devill called Mickle shoulderis' written in margin here and also crossed out.
48 'to the top of her head and sole of her foot' crossed out here.
49 'anything' crossed out here. This sentence has been added in the margin, and its precise intended position in the text is not clear.
50 'Marion' crossed out here.
51 The following text has been crossed out at the top of p. 2:

'Agnes Loch and Marion Greinlaw being confronted, each of them declaired they knew other and buir no ill will at other.

'Agnes Loch buir it in upon her that they wer at the Blewholl, notwithstanding she denyed the same, and sayed that albeit she confessed the samen befor, yet she did it for fear, and that it wes not trew. Denyes that ever she saw the Devill or his servants.

'Jannet Daill being aged 63 yeirs, Twelfe yeirs since or therby she mett with the Devill in Agnes Andersounes house and that she met with the Devill foure tymes therafter.'
52 In margin: 'Margarat Rammage'.
53 'depones' crossed out here.
54 'the place of the meiting was at Shereffhall Kaim' crossed out here.

Haliburton called her[55] and mett \and wes in companie with at Shereffehall Kaim/ Katherin Legget, Margarat Scot, Margarat Veitch, \Janet Huy,/ Janet Buchanan, Bessie Stewart, Sara Young \and Janet Bell/ with many others quhom she knowes not and that they all danced togither. She knew him not to be the Devill at the first meiting. The Devill caused her renunce her baptisme at the second meiting in besyd James Elphinstounes and that the Devill baid her lay her hand on the crown of her head and \sole/[56] her feet and \renunced her selfe/[57] to him quhich she acknowledges she did and said that she wold be his servant.[58] She sayes she came purposelie to meet with the Devill and that they all danced togither, and that they had a pipper bot she knowes him not.

\Confesses/[59] that the Devill promised that she should never want.

She denyes she ever committit any malefice. {*p. 3*}

Janet Lyle[60] widow in Edmiston about 60 yeirs of age.

Confesses as she wes going up the back syd of the toun the Devill appeared and demanded service of her about a yeir since \and she knew him to be the Devill/ and he gave her a peice of silver quhich therafter she found to be a stain.[61]

She sayes she met \at Wolmet bank/ another tyme with the Devill being in companie with David Johnston, Janet Daill quhom she knew be her tong,[62] William King and Agnes Johnston.

Sayes they all played togither, and that the Devill had her renunce her baptisme by putting her hand on her head and under her feet and giv her selfe over to him quhich she did and said to him that she wold be his servant, and that she knew him to be the \Devill at that time/.

Sayes that she never committit any malefice, That the Devill never gave her a mark, to her knowledge, bot that the marks wes found on her.

Agnes Thomson 65 yeirs old or therby.

Denyes all and sayes that all that she confessed wes bot a lie.

David Johnston.

...[63] the Devill the first tyme quhen that he was lyke a meikle grim man with black cloaths \cam to him at ane instant/[64] within tuo dayes therafter he

55 'another tyme' crossed out here.
56 'under' crossed out here.
57 'give all over' crossed out here.
58 'She denyes that ever she was in companie with Janet Daill' crossed out here.
59 'Depones' crossed out here.
60 In margin: 'Janet Lyle'.
61 'stain': stone.
62 'be her tong' (tongue): by her voice.
63 'Confesses he knew not' crossed out at the beginning of this paragraph.
64 'that he knew him quhen he renunced his baptisme and that' crossed out here.

was sorry that he had renunced his baptisme, And that the Devill promised him money quhen he did it.

Being interrogat how at the first meiting he knew it wes the Devill he answered because the Devill sought to fie him bot he had no service for him bot only to walk at his foot.

And being interrogat how he knew him to be the Devill at the 2d meiting He said he \wot/[65] very well because he bad him renunce his baptisme. {*p. 4*}

Jannet Daill[66]

She knew the Devill quhen he caused her renunce her baptisme and called her Jannet Cleir keyes, because she had keyes about her.

When they called her out, they bad her come out to their master, declaires that her trembling now is not for fear of the justices bot for [*sic*]

Sayes she denyed at first for fear and shame of the world.

Sayes they danced and played all togither.

Declaires she hes committed no malefice.

That he spok lyk a man and that she wes feard for him[67] at the 2d tyme.

She confesses she knew the Devill becaues he wes lyk a man in grein cloaths and that he bad me never God speid[68] and that he presentlie evanished, and that her povertie made her engadge in the Devills service.

Confesses that she knew the Devill quhen she renunced her baptisme.[69]

JC26/27, bundle 2, no. 10[70]

[*Endorsed:*] Confessiones dittayes etc of the witches in Musselburgh Julii 29 1661. Mussilburgh Witches Julii 29 1661.

{*p. 1*} Jannet Daill spouse to George Bell coalyear

Ye are endyted and accused, Forsameikle as that notwithstanding bot be the divyne Law of the Almightie and omnipotent God be the Lawes and acts of parliament of this kingdome the cryme of sorcerie and witchcraft is expresselie forbidden and discharged, and the pain and punishment of death ordained to be inflicted upon all that are guiltie and convict therof, Nevertheles It is of verity that ye haveing shaken aff all feir of God, reverence and regaird to the Lawes, Hes about fourtein yeirs agoe or therby, betaken your selfe to

65 'knew' crossed out here.

66 In margin: 'Jannet Daill'.

67 'feard for him': afraid of him.

68 'he bad me never God speid': he never greeted me (by saying 'God speed', a wish for success).

69 This paragraph and the previous paragraph (beginning 'She confesses ...') are written at the very foot of the page, separately from the rest of the text. The paragraphs appear to relate to Janet Daill, however.

70 The bundle containing this document is labelled 'Musselburgh Witches, JC26/27/2? [*sic*]'. This document has a pencil number 'JC26/27/2, item 10'.

the service of Satan the enemie of your Salvation, entered in a covenant and paction with him quhairby yow have renunced your Baptisme and interest in Jesus Christ, and engadged your selfe to be the Devills servant, and took ane uther name upon yow As also ye have dureing that tyme keiped severall trystes and meitings with the Devill and uther witches, and namelie about fourtein yeirs since or therby ye did meit with the Devill and wes in company at that tyme with Agnes Anderson and Margarat Barbour, quhair the Devill Laid his hand upon your shoulder, As also within ane short space therafter yow had ane uther meiting with the Devill in Shereffhall muir, and with Margaret Bell Elspet Haliburton Agnes Johnston William Keen and David Johnston at quhich tyme ye renunced your baptisme and took ane new name called Jannet Cleir keyes and engaged your selfe to be his servant, notwithstanding yow knew that he was the Devill And sicklyk yow had ane uther meiting about fiftein weikes[71] agoe in the bank of Wolmet with the said Elspet Haliburton Agnes Johnston, William Keen, David Jonston and uther notorious witches, Wheirby ye have contravened the saids Lawes and acts of parliament against sorcerie and witchcraft, And ye aught to be punished to the death in example and terror of uthers to committ the lyke in tyme comeing. {*p. 2 blank*} {*p. 3*}

Att Mussilburgh the 29 of Julii 1661
Compeired Agnes Loch spouse to Patrick Robertsone, who being aged thriescore yeirs of age, without any torture or compulsion confesses that she hes bein in the Devills service about a yeir since, and that she being greiting[72] mett with him at the Newtoun burne and that he asked at her what ailed her. And also that she mett with him accidentally the second tyme, and that she hes received the Devills markes, one in her shoulder and ane uther betuixt her thigh and her body.

JC26/27, bundle 2, no. 11[73]

{*p. 1*} David Johnstoun
Ye are endyted and accused, Forsameikle as notwithstanding that both be the divyne Law of the almyghtie God and the the [*sic*] Lawes and acts of parliament of this kingdome the cryme of sorcerie and witchcraft is expresslie forbidden and discharged and the pain and punishment of death ordained to be inflicted upon all that are guiltie and convict therof Nevertheles It is of verity that ye having shaken aff all feir of God, reverence and regaird to the Lawes, hes thir eleven yeiris bygain, betaken your selfe to the service of Satan the enemie of

71 'therafter' crossed out here.
72 'greiting': weeping.
73 The bundle containing this document is labelled 'Musselburgh Witches, JC26/27/2? [*sic*]'. This document has a pencil number 'JC26/27/2, item 11x'.

your Salvation, entred in covenant and paction with him, quhairby ye have renunced your Baptisme and interest in Jesus Chryst, engadged your selfe to be the Devills servant, taken fra him ane new name, with his marks upon your bodie, as also ye have dureing that tyme keiped severall trysts and meitings with the Devill and uther witches, and namelie eleven yeirs since or thereby ye had ane meiting with the Devill at the Burrowmuire quhair ye entred into his service renunced your Baptisme and received from the Devill the name of William, with his mark upon your legg, at quhich meiting ye knew him to be the Devill, he being in the forme of ane meikle grim man in black cloaths, Item at ane uther tyme ye wer at ane meiting with the Devill in the Wolmet bank there being present with yow Margaret Daills, William King and one Walter Cowan now dead, As also ane thrid meiting ye had with the Devill at the Grein Lawes, Wherby ye have contraveined the saids Lawes and acts of parliament made against sorcerie and witchcraft, And the samen being found be ane assise ye aught to punished therfor to the death.

Agnes Loch spouse to Patrick Robertson in Sunniesyd

Ye are endyted and accused, Forsameikle as notwithstanding that both be the divyne Law of the almightie God and be the Lawes and acts of parliament of this kingdome the cryme of sorcerie and witchcraft is expresslie forbidden and discharged, and the pain and punishment of death ordained to be inflicted upon all that are guiltie and convict therof Nevertheles It is of verity that ye haveing shaken aff all feir of God, reverence and regaird to the lawes hes thir twelve moneths {*p. 2*} betaken your selfe to the service of Satan the enemie of your Salvation, entred in a Covenant and paction with him quhairby yow have renunced your Baptisme and interest in Jesus Christ engadged your selfe to be the Devills servant, suffered your body quhilk aught to have bein ane temple to the Holie Ghost to be polluted and defiled by his haveing carnall copulation yow [*sic*] and hes taken his marks upon your bodie, As also yow have dureing that tyme keiped severall trysts and meitings with the Devill and uther witches, and namelie ane yeir since or therby ye comeing from Dalkeith, the Devill mett with yow at the Shereffhall burne in the likenes of ane man with grein cloaths and promised to give yow money and gave yow tuo marks upon your body, one upon your shoulder and the other betwixt your thigh and your body, \quhair yow consented to be his servant and gave your selfe over to him albeit ye knew he wes the Devill,/ Next ye had ane other meiting with the Devill at the same place quhair the Devill had carnall dealling with yow and caused yow to renunce your Baptisme, And at severall uther tymes within this yeir bygain ye have had meiting with Issobell Binnie, Issobell Caldwells, Marion Greinlaw and uther notorious Witches at the Blew holl and uther places Wherby ye have contraveined the saids Lawes and acts of parliament made against sorcerie and witchcraft and the samen being found be ane assise ye aught to be punished therfor to the death.

Margarat Rammage

Ye are endyted and accused, Forsameikle as notwithstanding that both be the divyne Law of the Almightie God and the Lawes and acts of parliament of this kingdome the cryme of sorcerie and witchcraft is expresslie forbidden and discharged and the pain and punishment of death ordained to be inflicted upon all that are guiltie and convict therof, Nevertheles It is of verity that ye haveing shaken aff all feir of God, reverence and regaird to the Lawes hes in winter last bygain betwixt Yule and Fastings Even betaken your selfe to the service of Satan the enemie of your Salvation, entred in {*p. 3*} covenant and paction with him, quhairby yow have renunced your baptisme and interest in Jesus Christ, engadged your selfe to be the Devills servant, taken his marks upon your bodie As also yow have dureing that tyme keiped severall trysts and meitings with the Devill and uther witches and namelie in winter last bypast in the house of Elspet Haliburton ye mett with the Devill in the liknes of ane black man, who laid his hand upon your shoulder and gave yow his mark As also about five weikes therafter yow had ane uther meiting with the Devill at Shereffhall Kaim, quhair yow entred in his service renunced your baptisme and engadged to be his servant and gave your selfe over to him, albeit ye knew he wes the Devill And likwise ye had ane other meiting with the Devill in the samen place with Katharine Legget, Margarat Scot, Margarat Veitch, Jannet Huy, Jannet Buchanan, Bessie Stewart, Sara Young, Janet Bell and uther notorious witches Wherby ye have contraveined the saids Lawes and acts of parliament made against sorcerie and witchcraft And the samen being found be ane assise, ye aught to be punished therfor to the death.

Janet Lyle widow in Edmistoun

Ye are endyted and accused, Forsameikle as notwithstanding both be the divyne Law of the Almightie God and the Lawes and acts of parliament of this kingdome the cryme of sorcerie and witchcraft is expresslie forbidden and discharged and the pain and punishment of death ordained to be inflicted upon all that are guiltie and convict therof, Nevertheles It is of verity that ye having shaken aff all feir of God, reverence and regaird to the Lawes hes about a yeir since or therby betaken your selfe to the service of Satan the enemie of your Salvation, entred in a Covenant and paction with him quhairby yow have renunced your baptisme and interest in Jesus Christ, engadged your selfe to be the Devills servant As also yow have dureing that tyme keiped severall trysts and meitings with the {*p. 4*} Devill and uther witches And namelie about a yeir since ye mett with the Devill, as ye wer going up the back syd off your toun of Edmistoun, and desired yow to be his servant to keip his house because his wife wes dead, and gave to yow as ye thought ane peice of silver, quhich therafter yow found to be bot a stone, As also yow had ane uther meiting with the Devill ane quarter of ane yeir after at Wolmet bank quhair yow renunced your Baptisme and consented to be the Devills servant and gave your selfe over to him albeit ye knew he was the Devill And Sicklyk at the same tyme yow had ane meiting with David Johnston Jannet Daill William King and Agnes Johnston and uther notorious witches Wherby ye have contraveined the saids Lawes and acts of parliament made against sorcerie and witchcraft and the samen being found be ane assise, ye aught to be punished therfor to the death in example of uthers to committ the lyk in tyme comeing.

JC26/27/5, no. 2[74]

{p. 1} Curia justiciarie tenta in pretorio de burgi de[75] *Mussilburgh 29 July 1661 per justiciarius deputatis Supremi Domini Nostri Regis.*[76]

Curia
Robert Greive dampster sworne

Comperit Mr John Prestoun baillie of the Regalitie of Musselburght for the erle of Lawderdaill and desyrit to be admitted to sit with the justice deputis In the tryell of the persons following to be tryit dwelling within that regalitie.

Intran
David Jonstoun
Agnes Loch
Margarat Ramage
Jonet Lyle
Jonet Dale
Indyted for witchcraft In maner specifeit in thair dittayes

Persewar
Mr Robert Dalgleish for his majesties advocat

David Jonstoun confessis quhairupon the persewer takis instruments.

Agnes Loch confessis the dittay quhairupon the persewer takis instruments.

74 The bundle containing this document is numbered JC26/27/5 and labelled 'Liberton Witches'. This document, however, is not from Liberton.

75 'Hadington' crossed out here.

76 'Court of justiciary held in the tolbooth of the burgh of Musselburgh, 29 July 1661, by the justice depute of our sovereign lord the king.'

Margarat Ramage confessis the dittay the persewer takis instruments.
Jonet Lyle confessis.
Jonet Daill confessis.

Nomina assisa for

William Thomesone burges of Musselburght	Adame Grinlaw burges of Musselburght
William Leslie burges thair	Patrike Carfra burges thair
Thomas Baillie in Edmistoun	David Alexander in Fisheraw
David Ros burges in Musselburgh	Walter Clerke in Musselburght
Patrike Cass in Sunnisyde	John Hill in Edmistoun

Robert Robiesone in Brunstoun myle
Thomas Hog in Musselburgh
John Meikle in the Brigend
Oliver Calderwode in Musselburght
William Rammage cordiner in Musselburght

Assise sworne for the fyve pannel no objectioun maid In the Contrair.

Be pluralitie of voces the assyse being Inclosit elect Thomas Baillie their chancellar.

The Assyse all in ane voice be the declaratioun of Thomas Baillie thair chancellar findis the pannellis David Jonstoun A...[77] Loch, Margarat Rammage Jonet Lyll and Jonet Daill guyl...[78] culpable of the Cryme of witchcraft mentionat in thair dittayes that In respect of thair awin judicial confessions.

[*Signed:*] Thomas Bailyie. {*p. 2*}

His majesties justice deputes, adjudges and decernes the within named David Johnston Agnes Loch Margarat Rammage Jonet Lyle and Janet Daill as found guiltie be ane assise of the cryme of sorcerie and witchcraft mentioned in their dittayes To be taken upon Tuesday the threttie of this instant, betwixt tuo and four in the Afternoon to the ordinary place of execution of the burgh of Musselburgh, and there to be strangled at staikes till they be dead, and thairafter thair bodies to be burnt to ashes, and thair goods escheit for his majesties use.

[*Signed:*] George Mackenzie, AColville, John Cunigham.

Imediatlie after the pronunceing of the said dome Mr John Prestoun bailie for the erle of Lawderdaill of the regalitie of Musselburgh protested that the said dome should not be prejudiciall to the erle of Lawderdaill anent

[77] Word damaged; probably 'Agnes'.
[78] Word damaged; probably 'guylty'.

the escheitis of the condemned persons. The kingis agent protested on the contrair. Both tuke instruments.

Source 2: NRS, Court of Justiciary, Books of Adjournal, 1661–1666, JC2/10.

{*fo. 4r.*} *Curia Justiciarie Supremi Domini Nostri Regis Tenta in pretorio burgi de*[79] *Mussilburgh vigesimo nono die Julii 1661 per magistri Allexandrum Colvill de Blair, Joannem Cunynghame et Georgium McKenzie, advocatos, justiciarios deputatos Supremi Domini Nostri Regis. Curia legittime affirmata.*[80]

Robert Greive ordinitt dempster and suorne.

Compeired Mr Johne Prestoune bailly of the regality of Mussilburgh For the Earle of Lawderdaill and desyred to be admitted to sitt with the justice deputs in the tryall of the personis following, Induellars within the regality foirsaid, Which desyre the justices granted.

Intran[81]
David Johnstoune
Agnes Loch spous to Pattrick Robertsone in Sunniesyd
Margaret Rammage
Jonet Lyle in Edmistoune
Jonet Dale spous to George Bell colyear
Indyted and accused for the crymes of sorcerie and witchcraft in maner specified in thair dittayes.

Persewer
Mr Robert Dalgleish for his majesties advocat

The haill pannall abovewrittin after reading of their severall dittayes to them in judgment confessis and acknoledges the same to be of verity Whairupone the persewar for his majesties advocat asked instruments. {*fo. 4v.*}

79 'Edinburgh' crossed out here.

80 'Court of justiciary of our sovereign lord the king, held in the tolbooth of the burgh of Musselburgh, 29 July 1661, by Masters Alexander Colville of Blair, John Cunningham and George Mackenzie, advocates, justices depute of our sovereign lord the king. Court legally fenced.'

81 In margin: 'Witchcraft. Convict and brunt'.

Assisa

Williame Thomsone burges of Mussilbrugh
William Leslie burges thair
Thomas Baillie in Edmistoune
David Ros burges of Mussilbrugh
Patrick Cass in Sunysyd
Adam Greinlaw burges of Mussilbrugh
Patrick Carfra burges thair
David Allexander in Fisherraw
Walter Clerk in Mussilbrugh
John Hill in Edmistoune
Robert Robiesone in Brunstoun milne
Thomas Hog in Mussilbrugh
Johne Meikle in Brigend
Oliver Calderwood in Mussilbrugh
William Rammage cordiner thair

The assyse lawfullie suorne and no objectione made against any of them Wheirupone the persewar asked instruments and protested for Wilfull Error against them incas they acquit the pannalls of the crymes contained in thair dittays.

The whilk day David Johnstoune, Agnes Loch spous to Patrick Robertsone in Suniesyd, Margaret Rammage, Jonet Lyle in Edmistoune and Jonet Dale spous to Georg Bell colyear Being entred upone pannall, dilated and accused and persewed be Mr Robert Dalgleish substitut to Sir Johne Fletcher his majesties advocat for his hienes interest For the crymes of sorcerie and witchcraft contanit in their severall dittayes in maner following viz.[82]

Forsameikle as that notwithstanding both be the divyne law of the almighty God and the lawes and acts of parliament of this kingdome the cryme of sorcerie and witchcraft is expreslie forbidden and discharged, and the paine and punishment of death ordained upone all that ar guiltie and convict thairof, Nevertheles It is of verity that the said David Johnstone haveing shaken off all fear of God, Reverence and reguard to the Lawis, Hes thir elivne yeires bygane betaken himself to the service of Satane the enemie of his salvatione, entred in covenant and pactione with him, quhairby he hes renuncit his baptisme and interest in Jesus Chryst, engadged himself to be the Devillis servant and taiken fra him ane new name, with his marks upone your [*sic*] body, As also hes during that tyme keiped severall trysts and meitings with the Devill and namelie Elivne yeires since or thairby He had ane meiting with the Devill at the Burrow muir, quhair he entred into his service, renuncit his baptysme and receaved from the Devill ane new name Called Williame, with the Devills merk upone his legg, At quhich meiting he knew him to be the Devill, He being in the forme of ane meikle grim man in black {*fo. 5r.*} cloaths.

82 The text that follows runs at first continuously, with breaks being indicated by larger letters. Paragraph breaks have been added editorially below for clarity.

Item at ane uther tyme, he wes at ane meiting with the Devill in the Volmett bank, their being present with him Margaret Daills, William King, and one Walter Cowane now died, As also ane thrid meiting he had with the Devill at the Greine Lawes quhairby the said David Johnstone Hes contravened the saids lawes and acts of parliament made against sorcerie and witchcraft and aught to be punished with death theirfor.

And sicklyk the said Agnes Loch spous to Patrick Robertsone in Sunysyd Being endyted and accused Forsameikle as notwithstanding that both be the divine law of the almighty God and be the lawis and acts of parliament of this kingdome the cryme of sorcerie and witchcraft is expreslie forbidden and discharged, and the paine and punishment of death Ordained to be inflicted upone all that ar guiltie and convict thairof, Nevertheles it is of verity that the said Agnes Loch, Having shaken off all fear of God, Reverence and reguard to the lawis, Hes thir tuelve moneths bygane betaken herself to the service of Satan the enemie of her salvatione, entred in a covenant and pactione with him, whairby shoe renunced her baptisme and interest in Jesus Chryst, engadged herself to be the Devillis servant, Suffred her body quhilk aught to have beine ane temple to the Holy Ghost to be polluted and defyled by his having carnall copulatione with her, and has taiken his marks upone her body, As also hes during that tyme keiped severall trysts and meitings with the Devill and utheir witches, And namely ane yeir since or thairby Shoe cumeing from Calkeith[83] The Devill mett with hir att Shereffhall burne in the lyknes of ane man with grein clothes Who promised to give her money and gave her tuo marks wpone her body, one upone hir shulder and the uther betuixt her thigh and her body, quhairthrow shoe consented to be his servant and gave hir self over to him Albeit shoe knew he wes the Devill. Nixt shoe had ane uther meiting with the Devill at the same place quhair the Devill had carnall dealing with her and caused her renunce her baptisme, And at severall uther tymes within this yeir bygane shoe hes had meiting with Isobell Binnie, Isobell Caldwalls, Marione Greinlaw and uther notorius witches at the Blewholl and in wther places, Quhairby shoe hes contravined the said acts of parliament made against sorcerie and witchcraft and aught to be punished thairfor to death.

And Siklyk the said Margaret Rammage being endyted and accused Forsameikle as notwithstanding that both be the divyne law of the almighty God {*fo. 5v.*} and be the lawes and acts of parliament of this kingdome the crymes of sorcerie and witchcraft is expreslie forbidden and discharged, and the paine and punishment of death ordained to be inflicted upone all that ar guiltie and convict thairof, Nevertheles it is of verity that shoe having shaken off all fear of God, reverence and regaird to the lawis, Hes in winter last bypast betuixt Yule and Fastings Even betaken herself to the serveice of

83 *Sic.* Read 'Dalkeith'.

Satane the enemie of her salvatione, entred in covenant and pactione with him, quhairby shoe renunced her baptisme and interest in Jesus Chryst, engadged herself to be the Devillis servant, taiken his marks upone her body, and also she has during that tyme keiped severall trysts and meitings with the Devill and utheir witches, And namelie in winter last bypast in the hous of Elspet Haliburtone shoe mett with the Devill in the lyknes of ane blackman who laid his hand upone her shulder, and gave her his mark, As also about fyve weikes thairefter shoe had ane uther meiting with the Devill in the same place with Katharine Legget, Margaret Scot, Margaret Veitch, Jonet Huy, Jonet Buchanan, Bessie Stewart, Sara Young, Jonet Bell and uther notorius witches, Whairby shoe hes contravined the said lawis and actis of parliament and aught to be punished thairfor to death.

And sicklyk the said Jonet Lyle widow in Edmistoun being endyted and accused Forsameikle as notwithstanding be the divyne law of the almighty God and lawis and acts of parliament of this kingdome the cryme of sorcerie and witchcraft is expreslie forbidden and discharged, and the paine and punishment of death ordained to be inflicted upone all that ar guiltie and convict thairof, Nevertheles it is of verity that the said Jonet Lyle Having shaken off all fear of God, reverence and regaird to the lawes, Hes about a yeir since or thairby betaken herself to the service of Satane the enemie of her salvatione, entred in covenant and pactione with him, quhairby shoe hes renunced her baptisme and interest in Jesus Chryst, engadged herself to be the Devillis servant, and also shoe has during that tyme keiped severall trysts and meitings with the Devill and utheir witches, And namelie about a yeire since shoe mett with the Devill as shoe wes goeing by the backsyd *{fo. 6r.}* of the toune of Edmistoune, and desyred her to be his servant and keip his hous becaus his wyf wes dead, and gave her as shoe thought ane peice of silver quhich thairefter shoe found to be butt a stone, And also shoe had ane uther meiting with the Devill ane quarter of ane yeir thairefter at Wilmet bank quhair shoe renunced her babtisme [*sic*] and consented to be the Devills servant and gave her self over to him Albeit shoe knew he wes the Devill, And sicklyk at the same tyme shoe had ane meiting with David Johnstoune, Jonet Dale, William King, Agnes Johnstoune and uther notorius witches, Whairby shoe hes contravined the said laws and actis of parliament And aught to be punished thairfor to death.

And sicklyk the said Jonet Dale spous to George Bell colyeour Being endyted and accused Forsameikle as notwithstanding that both be the law of the almighty God and be the lawis and acts of parliament of this kingdome The cryme of sorcerie and witchcraft is expreslie forbidden and discharged, and the paine and punishment of death ordained to be inflicted upone all that ar guiltie and convict thairof, Nevertheles it is of verity that the said Jonet Dale having shaken off all fear of God, reverence and regaird to the lawes, Hes about fourtine yeirs agoe or thairby betaken herself to the service of

Satane the enemie of her salvatione, entred in a covenant and pactione with him, quhairby shoe hes renunced her baptisme and interest in Jesus Chryst, engadged herself to be the Devillis servant, and tooke ane other name upone her, As also shoe has during that tyme keiped severall trysts and meitings with the Devill and uther witches, And namelie about fourtein yeires since or thairby shoe did meit with the Devill and wes in company at that tyme with Agnes Andersone and Margaret Barbour, quhair the Devill laide his hand upone her shulder, As also within ane short tyme thairefter yow [*sic*] had ane uther meiting with the Devill in Shireffhall muir, with Margaret Bell, Elspet Haliburtone, Agnes Johnstoun, Williame Keen and David Johnstone, at quhich tyme shoe renunced her baptisme and took ane new name called Jonet Cleirkeyes, and ingadged her self to be his servant notwithstanding shoe knew that he wes the Devill.

And Sicklyk shoe had ane uther meiting about fyftine weikes agoe in the bank of Wolmet with the said Elspet Haliburtone, Agnes Johnstoune, Williame Keen, {*fo. 6v.*} David Johnstoune and uther notorius witches, quhairby shoe hes contravined the said acts of parliament made against sorcerie and witchcraft, And aught to be punished thairfor to the death to the teror of others to comitt the lyk in tyme cumeing.

After Reading of the quhilk dittayes and accusations foirsaid, the justice deputs Fand the samyne relevant and did putt the samyne to the knowledg of ane assyse of the persons following viz. Williame Thomsone burges of Mussilbrugh, Patrick Cass in Sunysyd, Adam Greinlaw burges of Mussilbrugh, William Leslie burges thair, Thomas Baillie in Edmistoune, David Ros burges in Mussilbrugh, Patrick Carfra burges thair, David Allexander in Fisherraw, Walter Clerk in Mussilbrugh, John Hill in Edmistoune, Robert Robiesone in Brunstoune mylne, Thomas Hog in Mussilbrugh, Johne Meikle in Brigend, Oliver Calderwood in Mussilbrugh, William Rammage cordoner thair, Whilks persons of assyse being choysen, suorne and admitted And having hard the saids pannalls their judiciall acknowledgements and confessions of the crymes of sorcerie and witchcraft containit in thair respective dittays, The saids persons of assyse Removed altogither furth of court to the assyse hous quhair they be plurality of votes elected and choysed the said Thomas Baillie chancellor, Reasoned and voted upone the poynts of the saids dittayes respective, And being ryplie and at lynth advysed thairwith, Reentered agane in court Wher they all in one voyce be the repoirt and declaratione of the said chancellor Fand pronunced and declaired the saids pannalls David Johnstoune, Agnes Loch, Margaret Rammage, Jonet Lyle and Jonet Daill to be fyled, culpable and convict of the crymes respective abovewrittin contained in thair respective dittayes And that in respect of thair awne judiciall confessions as said is, For the quhilkis caussis the said justice deputs be the mouth of Robert Greiv dempster of court decerned ordanit and adjudged the saids David Johnstoune, Agnes Loch, Margaret Rammage, Jonet Lyle and Jonet

Dale to be taken upone Tewsday the threttie of this instant, Betuixt tuo and four in the afternoone, to the ordinary place of executione of the brugh of Mussilbrugh and their to be strangled at staikes till they be dead and thairefter their bodies to be brunt in ashes and all thair moveabll goods to be escheit to his majesties use as being convict of the crymes {*fo. 7r.*} forsaids, which wes pronuncit for dome. Whairupone Mr Robert Dalgleish substitut to his majesties advocat asked and took instruments.

Lykas imediatly thairefter compeired Mr Johne Prestone Baillie of the regalitie of Mussilbrugh and protested that the said dome sould not be prejudiciall to the Earle of Lawderdaill his right to the regality forsaid anent the escheits of the said condemned persons, Whereupone the said Mr Johne also asked and took instruments.

29. JOHN KINCAID, HADDINGTONSHIRE, 1662

INTRODUCTION

John Kincaid was not a witch but the most active of the witch-prickers in Scotland. This document shows him explaining his practices to a sceptical justice depute.

Kincaid was originally from Tranent in East Lothian. His activities in pricking witchcraft suspects to detect the Devil's mark are recorded from 1649 until 1662.[1] On 31 March 1662 he was imprisoned in the tolbooth of Edinburgh on suspicion of malpractice.[2] The document edited below records the answers he gave to a justice depute who interrogated him four days later. Kincaid remained in prison until June, when he petitioned the privy council for liberation on the grounds that he was old and ill. He was freed on 13 June on finding caution to carry out no further pricking without warrant.[3] This seems to be the last that we hear of him.

The Devil's mark in Scotland was usually assumed to be an insensitive spot on the witch's body that the Devil had nipped as part of the process of formalising the demonic pact. Prickers seem to have had some knowledge of where in the body a pin could be inserted without causing unbearable pain or injury.[4] It has occasionally been suggested (notably by Sir Walter Scott in 1830) that prickers might have used a deceptive retractable bodkin rather than a pin, but there seems to be no contemporary evidence for any use of a bodkin with a handle. Kincaid certainly used an ordinary pin, since a drawing of a pin that he used was included in a manuscript of 1657.[5] It is just under 5cm long; some descriptions of longer pins may have been exaggerated. Formally witch-pricking was not 'torture', but the two were sometimes conflated by contemporary sceptics. Kincaid's own bond of caution promised that he would carry out no pricking or torturing.

1 For a general account of witch-pricking in Scotland see W. N. Neill, 'The Professional Pricker and his Test for Witchcraft', *Scottish Historical Review*, 19 (1922), 205–13. Kincaid is discussed at pp. 207–8.

2 *RPC*, 3rd ser., i, 187.

3 *RPC*, 3rd ser., i, 210, 224, 226–7, 657.

4 S. W. McDonald, 'The Devil's Mark and the Witch-Prickers of Scotland', *Journal of the Royal Society of Medicine*, 90 (1997), 507–11.

5 Reproduced by David M. Robertson, *Goodnight My Servants All: The Sourcebook of East Lothian Witchcraft* (Glasgow, 2008), 247. This book contains numerous other notices of Kincaid.

The document below gives insight into other aspects of the pricker's practice. Kincaid evidently conducted his own informal discussions with witchcraft suspects, as well as pricking them. He used some 'ceremonies' that seem essentially to be magical: he brought suspects into the room backwards, and kept them away from the wall and from water. He had thought about popular demonology; his idea that the Devil could appear in physical form by animating a dead corpse is remarkable. He linked this with the idea that witches had a distinct smell.

TEXT

Source: NRS, Court of Justiciary Process Papers, 1669 (misdated), JC26/36.

Edinburgh 4to die Aprilis 1662
The quhilk day In presence of Mr John Cuninghame[6] his majesties justice depute John Kinkaid Pricker being examined and interrogat by quhat means he hes the knowledge of trying[7] witches declaires that he hes it by no means bot by sight and as other witches hes oft tymes bid him doe, and being interrogat why in trying them he will not let them goe over the threshold and uses ceremonies in setting them ane ell[8] from the wall, declaires that he does it upon no account bot onely because witches hes informed and desyred him to doe so, And declaires that he priked any person quhen he wes desyred by any gentlemen or ministers, And declaires that witches hes directed him to take them in backward to ane house and keip them from a wall and from water, and declaires that any that hes sein him prick may doe it after ward[9] And that the first pairt he looks to is their hand and armes And constantlie denyes that ever he said to witches that he knew they were such because at such a day they were with the Devill at such a place, bot declaires that he hes told them they were witches because they had ane ill smell and that witches hes told him, that quhen the Devill hes gone from them after carnall dealing they had ane ill smell, quhich they said wes by reason of the Devill assumeing and informeing[10] ane dead corpse.

John Cuningham.

6 This was probably John Cunningham of Lambrughton (d. 1684), who became an advocate in 1656, acted as a justice depute in witchcraft and other cases in 1661, and was later a commissioner to parliament. See Margaret D. Young (ed.), *The Parliaments of Scotland: Burgh and Shire Commissioners*, 2 vols. (Edinburgh, 1992–3), i, 167–8; *RPC*, 3rd ser., i, 11, 16–17, 26.

7 This word has been inserted above the line. A previous word, probably 'pricking', has been deleted.

8 An ell was a measure of length, slightly less than a metre.

9 'after ward': afterwards.

10 'informeing': animating.

30. MAGNUS LAURENSON, SHETLAND, 1674–1677

INTRODUCTION

In Shetland, 31 persons were accused of witchcraft during the period 1602–1725: 23 women and eight men. The percentage of accused men in Shetland was 26 per cent, which is higher than for Scotland in general, and also higher than for Orkney. In the group of men, six were accused early, during the period 1602–16. Then there was a long pause until Magnus Laurenson was accused in 1674. Some of the records of his pre-trial investigation are preserved. The interrogators were all major landowners: Gilbert Neven of Windhouse, a justice of the peace; Robert Hunter of Lunna, chamberlain of Shetland; John Mitchell of Berrie, a collector of excise; and John Forrester, another chamberlain.[1] The document below is their petition demanding that Laurenson should be tried. There is however no record of a formal trial for him.

Most of the witchcraft trials in Shetland deal with traditional witchcraft, *maleficium*, causing human illness and death or animal illness and death. In the earliest witchcraft trials in Shetland, neither the Devil nor the Devil's pact are mentioned. There was a change in 1616, when new and learned demonological ideas came to the fore in a triple trial. A range of demonological ideas were confessed, all known from cases on the Scottish mainland: the Devil's pact, the Devil's mark, the Devil's child, a promise from the Devil, and sex with the Devil.[2] However, in Shetland such notions did not last for a long time. Ideas related to demonology did not get a foothold there.

Magnus Laurenson is mentioned twice in court records, first in 1674 – a year when there were no other witchcraft trials in Shetland – and again in 1677. He lived in Gonfirth, in the north-west of Mainland, and was a practising healer. He was described in the petition as a 'sorcerer or witch', and as having been suspected for a long time. He claimed that he could cure all types of diseases with bloodletting (a treatment more often applied by

[1] We are grateful to Brian Smith, Shetland archivist, for these identifications.

[2] Liv Helene Willumsen, *Witches of the North: Scotland and Finnmark* (Leiden, 2013), 173.

professional physicians than by folk healers), drinks and drugs, mentioning several medicinal herbs. The interrogators were sceptical about his identifications of herbs, but the daisies and yarrow that he produced were regarded at the time as having bone-setting and wound-staunching properties.

Laurenson was asked about his treatment of John Umphray, who had been bedridden for a long time. Umphray was unable to satisfy his wife as a man should do. Laurenson said that if Umphray would only rise and take something to drink, he could immediately heal him; he said that he could either end him or mend him, and asked his wife which she desired. It is unclear whether Laurenson had had prior dealings with Umphray, but the document makes no direct suggestion that he had bewitched him.

Healing is otherwise mentioned in Shetland witchcraft trials to a modest degree. Healing humans is mentioned in connection with four women, while healing animals is mentioned in connection with one woman.[3] However, *maleficium*, the traditional concept of harmful witchcraft, is mentioned in many witchcraft trials in Shetland. Malefice is mentioned in the early Shetland trials, and also in the demonological cases from 1616, suggesting that an undercurrent of harmful witchcraft remained alive alongside new demonological notions.

Three years later, Laurenson was still under suspicion for witchcraft and charming. In 1677, there is a document containing two entries about him, both dated Scalloway, 7 November. The ministers of the presbytery accuse him of having caused Nicol Halcro and Marion Halcro to adhere together and live as man and wife, and of having charmed a child, at the request of the child's father. The ministers' own word for this is 'sorcery', which suggests that the charge is serious, equivalent to witchcraft. They ask the stewart depute (sheriff depute) to arrest Laurenson. Then there is an entry by the stewart depute agreeing to this, and ordering parish bailies to implement the arrest.

The complaints against Laurenson cannot be said to be of the serious kind that usually attracted charges of witchcraft; there was no suggestion of magical harm or of dealings with the Devil. At this late date, therefore, the Shetland authorities were handling the complaints in an unusually strict way. There is no record of whether Laurenson was arrested or interrogated as a result of the order. However, the stewart depute had clearly dropped the case by 1678, when a court record was made summoning Laurenson and other tenants for non-payment of rent.[4]

3 Willumsen, *Witches of the North*, 175.

4 Gardie House Archive, stewart court proceedings, 27 March to 18 December 1678, GHA/bi/521. We are grateful to Brian Smith, Shetland archivist, for this reference.

TEXTS

Source 1: Sir John and Wendy Scott, Gardie House Archive, Bressay, Shetland.

Unto Thomas Leslie of Ustanes, stewart deput and justiciar of Yetland, the informatione and protestatione of the persones under subscrivand, against Magnus Lawrancsone in Gonfirth, sheweth[5]

That we haveing had discourse with the said Magnus in your own heireing, have fownd him to manifast himself to be ane sorcerer or witch, as he hes been of a long time suspectit, and that to the beast of our knowledge and judgmentes by his discourse, as after followes. To wit, he haveing declaired in our presence that he could cure all manner of diseases in all persones that would apply themselves to him, and that non ever came to him for cure but they weare cured; and being asked by quhat meanes he did cure his patientes, he answered that he performed his cures by blood letting, drinkis and drogis. Being farther asked quhat ingredientes his drinkis and drugis were made up of he sayes he hes butter, watter and brimestone,[6] sparrow grase[7] (which being shewen be him is knouen to be[8] field dacies[9]) and a grasse called be him orga grase[10] (for which he produces the grase mellafolium[11]), and the limbrick grasse[12] and ane grasse called be him the magrem grasse, and these are all the simples[13] he knowes, quhairwith he cures all manner of diseases. Farder, the said Magnus being asked quhat he knew concerneing Jon Umphray of Astaes[14] present distemper, who hes of ane long time bygone lyen upon his bead,[15] he answeres that his sicknes is this, that he is not in capacitie to discharge his duettie as ane man should doe to his wife, in particular that he wantes the power of his bodie, and that if the said John would but say to him, Man I stand in neid of help, and thairfor I desire help of God and the[e], he offered presentlie to cure him of his distemper, and farder did say that if he pleased he showld make the said Jon Umphray rise within the space of tuo houres, and be alse good companie in his own howse, or in any uther howse in the towne, as ever he had at any time formerlie been. And farder said that if the said Jon wowld but rise and take on[e] drink, he wowld immediatlie heall him, and farder said he wowld aither end him or mend him, and asked his

5 The word 'sheweth' was a traditional part of the phraseology of English legal petitions. It seems to have entered Scottish legal discourse in the middle years of the seventeenth century.

6 'brimestone': sulphur.

7 'sparrow grasse': asparagus.

8 'knouen to be': recognised as.

9 'dacies': daisies.

10 This and the later 'magrem grasse' have not been identified. The phrase 'called be him' suggests that these are Laurenson's own names.

11 'mellafolium' (milfoil): yarrow.

12 'limbrick grasse': bog asphodel.

13 'simples': medicinal herbs.

14 'Astaes': Asta's. John Umphray lived at Asta in Tingwall.

15 'bead': bed.

wife wither of the tuo she desired. And thairfor we require and protest that the said Magnus, as on[e] as conceived hes taken on sorcery and witchcrawft upon him by his own expressiones above sett downe, may be secured and put in sure firmance, untill he be put to ane tryell for all crymes of witch crawft and sorcery formerlie laid to his charge, and for quhat is sett downe in the premesses, bysydes many uther his assertiones which are not heir inserted, which shall heir after in dwe time be informd and made owt against him. In wittnes quhairof thir presents are subscrivit with our handes. Att Scallawaybankis, the nynteine day of Agust I^{m} VI^{c} and seventie foure yeires.

Gilbert Neven
Robert Hunter
John Mitchell
John Forrester

Source 2: *Sir John and Wendy Scott, Gardie House Archive, Bressay, Shetland.*

At Scalloway banks November 7 [16]77
We the undersubscrivers do testify and declair that we have heard of much sorcerie practised and charmes used in severall places of the Countrey by one Magnus Laurenson in Gonfirth in the parish of South-Delting and more especially that we have seen a process of the session of Sandwick Concerning his wicked practises ther wherein its made manifest, that he hath by his sorcerie and charmes Caused two persons in the parish of Cunigbrough, namely Nicoll Halcro and Marion Halcro to adhere together and to live as man and wife so as[16] for the severall years bygon, they could not be perswaded to rehabite together. And likewise that he hath charmed a child belonging to Hendry Grierson in Gord being imployed by the said Henry Grierson, William Halcro in Hildegarth, and his wife and others accessory therto, And therfor we earnestlie desyre, that the Stewart depute may be pleased to send for the said Magnus Laurenson, and to Cause imprison him till he be put to a tryall, and the dittaes that are to be brought from other places of the Countrey against him, be drawin out from the severall session-books, and be presented to the presbyterie, and to the Criminal judge, and till that time we further desyre that the persons that hath Consulted with him do enact themselves \or find cautioner/ to Answer befor any judge or judicatorie to whom its Competent for to judge or Cognose of Sorcerers or Consulters with them and to Censure them according to justice.

[*Signed:*] ADunbar moderator
M. Theodore Umphrey minister at Nesting
JForbes minister at Dunnrosseness
CBarron minister at Sandsting
M. Jo: Gaudie minister at Tingwall[17]

16 'so as': although.

17 Alexander Dunbar of Wethersta, minister of Delting, Olnafirth and Laxavoe; Theodore Umphray, minister of Nesting; James Forbes, minister of Dunrossness; Cornelius Barron, minister of Sandsting; John Gaudie, minister of Tingwall.

Scalloway 7 November 1677

The declaratione above writtin be [*sic*] protested and publictlie red The stewart deput ordaines the said Magnus Lauransone above compleaned upon to be brought into the castell of Scalloway and ther impresoned for the causis above mentionat And in cais he sall rune from on[e] parish to ane uther The Baillies of the severall parissis ar heirby ordained upon geting notice to caus aprehend him and send him to Scalloway as said is And that under the paine of ane hundreth pounds Scots money And farder in the Mean tyme the wholl Inhabitants ar heirby inhibit to give the said Mans[18] hospitalitie under the Lyk paine.

Tho: Leslie.

18 'Mans' (Manse): Magnus.

31. PAISLEY WITCHES, 1677

INTRODUCTION

These trials originated with the illness of Sir George Maxwell, of Pollok House, south-west of Glasgow.[1] On the morning of 14 October 1676, he was planning to visit the city. Prior to leaving, Sir George had called before him a servant, accusing him of having broken his orchard. The servant (whose name later emerged as Alan Dougal) admitted the offence, and added that Hugh Stewart, son of Janet Mathie, had been his accomplice. That night, Sir George fell ill and suffered for nearly seven weeks from pain in his right side. During his convalescence, an apparently deaf-mute girl aged 13, Janet Douglas, came to Pollok. Douglas identified Janet Mathie as having bewitched Maxwell, and led Maxwell's servants to Mathie's house where she 'discovered' a wax effigy, stuck with pins.

Janet Mathie was thus accused of witchcraft, along with two of her children: not Hugh, but her eldest son John Stewart, and their young sister Annabel Stewart, variously stated to be 12, 13 or 14 years old. Bessie Weir, Marjorie Craig and Margaret Jackson were also accused. Several of them were interrogated; Annabel Stewart seems to have been the first to confess, on 9 January 1677. Her confession brought demonology into the investigation. She confessed that she was present at a meeting in her mother's house, and that she saw a black man with white cuffs on his sleeves there. She had also been present at a meeting in her brother's house, where a 'picture' (effigy) of clay had been made. The stories of these two effigies, of wax and of clay, need to be distinguished in the testimonies. Later a third effigy, made of earth, was also mentioned.

Annabel's brother, John Stewart, then confessed on 10 January that the accused persons had been in his house for a meeting on 4 January, a meeting

[1] On this case see Richard L. Harris, 'Janet Douglas and the Witches of Pollock: The Background of Scepticism in Scotland in the 1670s', in Steven R. McKenna (ed.), *Selected Essays on Scottish Language and Literature: A Festschrift in Honor of Allan H. MacLaine* (Lewiston, 1992), 97–124. For a recent discussion focused on the trial records see Liv Helene Willumsen, *Witches of the North: Scotland and Finnmark* (Leiden, 2013), 140–6.

arranged by Bessie Weir. The black man woke him up for the meeting. During this meeting, the black man required that John Stewart should renounce his baptism and deliver himself to him, which he did. Then they made the clay effigy, which was placed in his bedstraw. On 11 January, Margaret Jackson also confessed. These confessions were heavily formulaic and tailored for mutual conformity. They included unusual details about each witch having been given a personal 'spirit' with an exotic name; whether this 'spirit' was a distinct entity is not clear.

The trials that followed were held in the tolbooth of Paisley on 27 January 1677. Janet Mathie, Bessie Weir, Marjorie Craig, John Stewart, Annabel Stewart and Margaret Jackson were found guilty of witchcraft and sentenced to be taken to the Gallow Green of Paisley on 20 February to be strangled and burned. However, on 1 February the privy council reprieved Annabel Stewart, on the grounds that she was under age and had only recently been ensnared by the Devil.

After the trials, Janet Douglas achieved a brief celebrity, and went on to detect other witches using the same technique of 'discovering' hidden effigies. She was interviewed by the lawyer John Lauder of Fountainhall, and by George Hickes, the duke of Lauderdale's chaplain, both of whom wrote detailed accounts of her. Lauder thought her 'an imposter and cheat, at leist possest, or having the 2[d] sight, or revealled to hir in the air' (that is, revealed by a spirit, probably of questionable nature).[2] This view was shared by the privy council, which ordered her to be banished – though she seems to have been freed in the end. But Hickes, who was particularly interested in the emerging concept of second sight, thought that her powers were probably genuine.[3] The trainee minister Robert Knox also wrote a detailed account of her, attempting to set her within a framework of understandings of various spirits. He had not met her himself but had read other written accounts.[4] A recent discussion of Janet Douglas sets her in the context of developing ideas about second sight, the power that she claimed.[5]

A narrative of the events was printed by George Sinclair in 1685 as the first of the 'Relations' in his book *Satans Invisible World Discovered*.[6] This narrative, attributed to Sir George Maxwell's son and successor John Maxwell

2 Sir John Lauder of Fountainhall, *Historical Notices of Scotish Affairs, 1661–1688*, 2 vols., ed. David Laing (Edinburgh: Bannatyne Club, 1848), i, 143–4.

3 Michael Hunter (ed.), *The Occult Laboratory: Magic, Science and Second Sight in Late Seventeenth-Century Scotland* (Woodbridge, 2001), 172–8.

4 Charles K. Sharpe, *A Historical Account of the Belief in Witchcraft in Scotland* (London, 1884), 138–43. Cf. Robert Law, *Memorialls, or, The memorable things that fell out within the island of Brittain from 1638 to 1684*, ed. Charles K. Sharpe (Edinburgh, 1818), 120–8.

5 Domhnall Uilleam Stiùbhart, 'The Origins of Highland Second Sight', in Julian Goodare and Martha McGill (eds.), *The Supernatural in Early Modern Scotland* (Manchester, 2020), 178–203, at pp. 191–3.

6 George Sinclair, *Satans Invisible World Discovered* (Edinburgh: John Reid, 1685), 1–18.

of Pollok, was partly based on the trial records edited below. John Maxwell of Pollok would go on to act as a judge in the Bargarran witchcraft trials of 1697, records of which are edited below in the present book.

The documents edited here are the trial records from the circuit court minute books. In addition, there are two pre-trial depositions from the Maxwell of Pollok Papers, in Glasgow City Archives. Overall, these documents include pre-trial confessions, dittays, and witnesses' depositions. None of them make any mention of Janet Douglas and her revelations. They do, however, provide a detailed account of the construction of a shared demonological narrative.

TEXTS

Source 1: Glasgow City Archives, Maxwell of Pollok Papers, T-PM107/14/7.

Declaration off Margret Jackson and Anabll Stewarts confession Januarii 11 1677.

Att Polock the eleventh Januarii 1677

Margret Jaksone relict[7] of Thomas Stewart in Shaws confessed and acknowledged in the presence of Allan Dougall in Polock toun John and James Wallaces in Shaws and William Barr in Hagbows and David Kenedie gardiner in Polocke undersubscryving That about twenty dayes since in the Night tyme when she awaiked She feired to Find a man in the bed whom she supposed might have bein her husband Notwithstanding her husband was dead twenty yeirs or therby who Imediatly disappeared which she said wes Nothing good and this she said was the First tyme that ever she knew off him bot denyed to explaine what she meined by him Furthermore she acknowledges on Thursday Last The Fourth of Januarii Instant she wes present at the house off John Stewart at Night when the clay portraite was made and that she saw the blake man sometyms sitting and sometyms standing with John Stewart with blacke cloths and white hand cuffes and that ther wes ther present allsoe Bessie Weire in Polock toun and Anablle Stewart in Shaws and Marjery Craige and acknowledges she gave her consent to the makeing of the portraite In the testimoney of the truth off which premisses we have subscryvit these presents day and place above written.

Sic subscrivitur[8] Allan Dougall, William Barr, John Wallace, David Kenedie, James Wallace.

Att Polock 9 Januarii 1677

Anable Stewart daughter to John Stewart and Jonat Mathie aged twelve or thirteen yeirs declairs in presence off Mr John Baird Minister off Paslay John

7 'relict': widow.

8 'thus it is subscribed'.

Steinsone in Polok Lowrance Polick Androw Rid John Patoun Servitors to the Laird of Polok that since the Leter end off the harvest Last in her mothers house she did sie ane blake gentll mane in blak cloths with ane whyte band and whyte hand cuffs, She being present her oun Mother Jonat Mathie Margret Jaksone relict off Thomas Stewart in Shaws Bessie Weire spouse to John Patoun in Polock toun Marjery Craige and two highland women Liveing in Govane and that she saw them Forme ane Image off wax and that her Mother by direction off the blak gentlleman did put in prins[9] in the sides and in the breast and that the blak man bade her Mother put it up in an holle Furthermore in presence off the witnesses above written The said Anable Stewart confessed that late at Night in her brother's house John Stewart in Shaws one Thursday the Fourth off Januarii Instant she saw the same blake man with her Brother John Stewart The said Margret Jakson and Bessie Weire Forme ane Image of clay the clay being wrought by the hands off her Brother and the Forme off the Face and the armes made by the blake man by directione off her Brother did put in prins in it, the verity of the premises are atested by the persons above exprest beffor whome the declaratione was made.

Sic Subscrivitur Mr John Baird, Lowrance Polick, John Steinson, Androw Ridd, John Patoun.

Source 2: Glasgow City Archives, Maxwell of Pollok Papers, T-PM107/14/8.

Declaratione off John Stewarts confession Januarii 10 1677

Polock 10 Januarii 1677

The which day in presence of Allan Dougall in Polok toun John Steinson George Polick and Thomas Biggart ther and David Kennedy gardiner in Polock compeired John Stewart in Polock Shaws who confessed and acknowledged that upon Thursday Last the third off Januarii Instant Bessie Weire in Polok toun came unto him Late at night as he was with out doors neir his oun houss telling him that ther was a meiting to be at his hous the next night off the blake man and off Margret Jaksone Marjery Craige and hersellff desireing him that he might be present to which he condiscendit and that accordingly The Folowing Night affter he wes gone to his bed The blacke man came and quitely called him by his name upon which he arosse and put one his cloths and Lighted ane candlle and that Margret Jaksone and Bessie Weire and Marjery Craige did enter in at ane window in the gavil[10] off the house Large Enough and that the First thing that the blake man required wes that the saide John Stewart shoulld Renounce his Baptisme and deliver him up wholie unto him puting his one hand on the topp off his head and the other hand unto the solle off his foote which accordinglie he did being tempted by

9 'prins': pins.
10 'gavil': gable.

the promisses That he shoulld want Nothing and shoulld have all pleisure and that he shoulld get his hearts syth[11] on all that shoulld doe him wrong and that theraffter he gave him the name of Jonas and then he required every one off there consents to the making off a picture off clay for the taking away of the Liffe of Sir Georg Maxwell off Polock in reveng off The taking off his Mother Jonat Mathie and that every one for themseavs gave this consent and that theraffter they wrought the clay The blake man giving the Figure off ane head and face and Two Armes in which he set three prins one in each syde and one in the breast he the said John Stewart holding the candlle to them all this whille and that he remarked one off his Feit to be cloven Footed his athre[12] wes black cloth with ane blewissh band and hand cuffs with hoggers[13] one his Legs with out shoes and that his voyce was horo and goustie[14] Furthermore he declaired that affter he had begun to the formeing off the effegy his sister Anablle ane chilld aged Thirteen or Fourteinth yeirs come knocking to the doore whom he Let in who stayed with them ane good tyme bot went away beffor the rest he opening the the [*sic*] doore to Let her goe bot the rest went out the Same window and that effegy was placed by some off them in his bedstrae bot wes not put in by himsellff, he furthermore acknowledges that he had ane envy of the said Sir Georg For apprehending off his Mother and he declaired allsoe that the said Bessie Weire had a great Envy at the said Sir Georg upon The quarrell as he conceivs that her hussband wes not entered to his harvest Service, The premisses being read beffor the said John Stewart and the witnesses above rehearsed he acknowledged the verity off the same bot in reguard he could not writte he desired the witnesses to atest the same by their Subscription who acordingly did subscryve in his presence day and place above writen.

Sic Subscrivitur Allan Dougall, Thomas Biggart, John Steinson, David Kenedy.

Source 3: NRS, Circuit Court Minute Books, 1677–1699, JC10/4.

{fo. 1r.} Curia justiciarie Supremi Domini Nostri Regis tenta in pretorio burgi de Paisley vigesimo septimo die mensis Januarii 1677 per honorabiles viros Dominum Patricium Houstoun de eodem Jacobum Jacobum [sic] *Brisban de Bishoptoun et Magistrum Joannem Prestoun advocatum.*[15]

The said day Co [*sic*]

11 'syth': satisfaction, revenge.

12 'athre': attire.

13 'hoggers': gaiters (footless stockings).

14 'horo and goustie': hollow and ghastly.

15 'Court of justiciary of our sovereign lord the king, held in the tolbooth of the burgh of Paisley, 27 January 1677, by the honourable men lord Patrick Houston of that Ilk, James Brisbane of Bishopton and Mr John Preston advocate.'

Off the whilk Commission the tenor followes.

Charles be the grace of God King of great Britaine France and Irland defender of the faith to all and sundrie our leidges and subjects whom it effeirs[16] greeting. Forasmuch as the Lords of our privie Counsill are informed that Jannet Mathie relict of the deceast John Stewart under miller at Pollockshawe Milne John Stewart her son and Annabill Stewart her daughter Margaret Jackson relict of umquhile Thomas Stewart in Pollockshaws and Bessie Weir spouse to [*2 words blank*] in Pollocktoun are apprehendit and imprisoned as suspect guiltie of witchcraft by entering unto paction with the Divill Renuncing ther baptisme and committing severall malefices And to the effect the said matter may be made manifest and justice administrat therintill Conforme to the Lawes of this kingdome We with advyse of the Lords of our privie Councill doe heirby make and Constitut Sir Patrick Houston of that Ilk Sir John Shawe younger of Greinock James Brisbane of Bishoptoun John Anderson younger of Dowhill and Mr John Prestoun advocat or any three of them The said Mr John Prestoun being alwayes on[e] of the number our justices in that part to the effect underwreitten and appoynts Mr Robert Martin Clerk to the justice court to be Clerk to the saids Commissioners {*fo. 1v.*} with power to them to meit at such tymes and places as they shall think expedient and then and ther to affix and hold Courts, creat[17] serjants, dempsters and all other members of court needfull, To call ane assyse and witnessis of persons best understanding the truth of the said mater, absents to amerciat,[18] unlawes and amerciaments to uplift and exact and in the saids courts to call the saids Jannet Mathie John and Annabill Stewarts Margaret Jackson and Bessie Weir and putt them to the tryall and knowledge of ane assyse and if they shall be found guiltie upon voluntar Confession without any sort of torture or indirect meanes used against them to bring them to ane confession or that malefices are otherwayes legallie instructed and proven Then and in that caice that they cause justice be administrat upon them Conforme to the Lawes of this kingdome and generallie all and sundrie other things anent the execution of this our Commission to doe and exerce, promitten to hold firme and stable etc.[19] And ordaines the saids Commisioners by the said Clerk to returne the verdict and rolments[20] of court to be recordit in the books of adjournall, lykeas we with advyse forsaid doe heirby nominat our Right trustie and welbeloved Cousine and Councelor George Lord Rosse to be assessors [*sic*] to our saids Commissioners giving and granting to him full power to sitt, vote and act with them in trying and judging the saids persons

16 'effeirs': concerns.

17 'creat': appoint.

18 'amerciat': impose a financial penalty.

19 'promitten to hold firme and stable etc.': promising to support (the commissioners' decisions).

20 'rolments': records.

Given under our Signet at Edinburgh the Eighteinth day of January and of our Reigne the twentie eighth year 1677.

Sic subscrivitur Mar, Wintoun, Linlithgow, Elphinston, Ch. Maitland, Jo. Nisbet, Tho. Wallace, Ja. Foulis, Ja. Dalrymple.

Efter reading of the whilk Commission the saids justices did admitt [*sic*]

The said day In presence of the saids Commissioners of justiciarie Compeired Annabill Stewart of the age of fourtein years or therby who declaired that she wes brought in presence of the justices for the cryme of witchcraft and declaires that in harvest last the Divill {*fo. 2r.*} in the shape of a blackman came to her mothers house and requyred the declarant to give her self up to him and that the Divill promised that she should not want anything which wes good, declaires that being intysed be her mother Jannet Mathie and Bessie Weir who wes officer to ther severall meitings She did putt her hand to the crown of her head and the other to the sole of her foot and did give up her self to the Divill, declaires that her mother promised her a new coat for doeing of it, declaires that the declarants spiritts name was Enipa and that the Divill took her by the hand and nipped her arme quhich continued to be sore for half ane hour, declaires that the Divill in the shape of a black man lay with her in the bed under the cloaths and that she found him cold, declaires that therefter he placed her nearest himself, declaires that she wes present in her mothers house when the effigies[21] of waxe wes made and that it wes made to represent Sir George Maxwell, declaired that the black man, Jannet Mathie, the declarants mother whose spirits name is Landsladie, Bessie Weir whose spirits name is Sophia, Marjorie Craige whose spirits name is Rijern, Margaret Jackson whose spirits name is Locas wer all present at the making the said effigies and that they bound it on a spitt and turned it about befor the fyre and that it wes turned be Bessie Weir saying as they turned it Sir George Maxwell, Sir George Maxwell and that this wes expressed be all of them and be the declarant, declaired that his pictur wes made in October last and farder declaires that upon the third of January instant Bessie Weir came to her mothers house and advertised her to come to her brother John Stewarts house upon the following night and that accordinglie she came to the place wher she found Bessie Weir Marjorie Craige Margaret Jackson and her brother John Stewart and a man with black cloaths a blew band and whitt cuffs with hogers and that his feit wes cloven and the declarant satt doun at the fyre syd with them wher they made a picture of clay on which they placed prins upon the breast and sydes and declaires that they did place prins in the picture of waxe on[e] in every syd and on[e] in the breast, declaires that the blackman did putt in the pins {*fo. 2v.*} in the picture of waxe but is not sure who putt in the pins in the picture of clay, declaires that the effigies produced

21 *Sic*. Here, and repeatedly hereafter, the scribe writes 'effigies' even when a singular effigy is clearly meant.

are the effigies she sawe made, declaires that the black mans name is Ejuall. This declaration is emmitted befor James Dunlop of Husil William Greinlay balyie of Paisley Mr John Baird minister ther Robert Alexander balyie in presence of the justices aforsaid. *Sic subscribitur Ita est Robertus Park nottarius publicus premissa subscribere (ut asseruit) nescien testan meis signo et chirographo. Ita est Patricius Carswell notarius publicus etiam in premissis requisitus de mandato quo supra testan his meis signo et chirographo.*[22]

[*Signed:*] PHoustoun, JBrisbane of Bischoptoune, JPreston.

The said day Compeired John Stewart in Pollockshawe in presence of Sir Patrick Houston of that Ilk James Brisbane of Bishoptoun and Mr John Prestoun advocat justices be commission And being interogat anent his cryme of witchcraft declaired that upon Weddensday the third day of January instant Bessie Weir in Pollocktoun came unto the declarant late at night who being without doors near his own house Bessie Weir did intimat to the declarant that ther wes a meiting to be at his house the nixt day and that the Divill under the shape of a black man, Margaret Jackson Marjorie Craigie and the said Bessie Weir wer to be present and that Bessie Weir requyred the declarant to be ther which he promised to doe and that the nixt night efter the declarant hade gone to bed the black man came in and called the declarant quyetlie be his name upon which he rose from his bed and putt on his cloaths and lighted a candle, declaires that Margaret Jackson Bessie Weir and Marjorie Craige did enter in at a windowe in the gavell of the declarants house and that the first thing the blackman requyred wes that the declarant should renunce his baptisme and delyver himself up whollie to him which the declarant did by putting on[e] of his hands to the tope of his head and the other to the sole of his foot and that he wes tempted to it by the Divills promising to him that he should not want any thing and that he should not want any pleasure and that he should gett his heart sythed on all that should doe him wrong, declairs that he gave him the name of Jonas for his spirits name, declaires {*fo. 3r.*} that therefter the Divill requyred every on[e] of ther consents to the making of the effigies of clay for taking away the lyff of Sir George Maxwell of Pollock to reveng the taking of the declarants mother Jannet Mathie, declaires that every on[e] of the persons abovenamed did give ther consent to the making of the said effigies and that they wrought the clay and that the blackman did make the figure of the head and face and his armes to the said effigies,

22 *Sic.* The scribe seems to have omitted a few words, including the name of the person testifying, something like this: '*requisitus de mandato dicti Annabellae Stewart scribere*'. A full translation would probably read: 'Thus it is subscribed. Thus I, Robert Park, notary public, at the command of the said Annabel Stewart, who (as she asserts) does not know how to write, have affixed my sign and subscription manual. Thus it is subscribed by Patrick Carswell, notary public, also required in the foregoing by the command above by my sign and subscription manual.'

declaires that the Divill sett three pins in the samen on[e] in each syd and on[e] in the breast and that the declarant did hold the candle to them all the whill the picture wes making and that he observed on[e] of the black mans feit to be cloven and that the blackmans apparell wes black and that he hade a blewish band and handcuffs and that he hade hogers on his leggs without shoes and that the blackmans voice wes hough and goustie and farder declaires that efter they hade begune to the forming of the effigies his sister Annabill (a child of thretein or fourtein years of age) came knocking to the door and she being lettin in be the declarant stayed with them a considerable tyme but that she went away befor the rest he having oppined the door to her, declaires that the rest went out at the windowe at which they entered, declaires that the effigies wes placed be Bessie Weir in his bedstrae, he farder declaires that the declarant himself hade envy and malice against Sir George Maxwell for apprehending Jannet Mathie the declarants mother and that Bessie Weir hade great malice against the said Sir George and that her querrell wes as the declarant conceaves that Sir George hade not entered Bessie Weirs husband to his harvest service, and also declaires that the said effigies wes made upon the fourth of January instant and that the Divills name wes Ejuall, declaires that the declarants spirits name was Jonas and Bessie Weirs name who wes officer wes Sophia and that Margaret Jacksons spirits name wes Locas and that Annabill Stewart the declarants sisters wes Enipa but does not remember what Marjorie Craigs name wes, declairs that he cannot wreitt. This Confession wes emitted in presence of the witnessis to the former Confession. *Sic subscrivitur Ita est Robertus Park nottarius publicus in premissis requisitus de mandato dicti Joannus Stewart scribere (ut asseruit) nescien testan meis signo et chirographo Ita est Patricius Carswell nottarius publicus etiam in premissis requistus de mandato {fo. 3v.} quo supra testan his meis signo et chirographo.*[23]

[*Signed:*] PHoustoun, JBrisbane of Bischoptoune.

The said day Compeired Margaret Jackson relict of Thomas Stewart in Shawes who being examined anent her being guiltie of witchcraft be the saids justices She declaires that she wes present at the making of the first effigies and picture which wes made in Jannet Mathies house in October and that the Divill in the shape of a blackman, Jannet Mathie, Bessie Weir, Marjorie Craig and Annabill Stewart wer present at the making of the said effigies and that it was made to represent Sir George Maxwell of Pollock for taking away of his lyff, declaires that fourtie years agoe or therby she was in Pollockshawe croft with some fewe sticks on her back and that the blackman came to her and that she

[23] 'Thus it is subscribed. Thus I, Robert Park, notary public, at the command of the said John Stewart, who (as he asserts) does not know how to write, have affixed my sign and subscription manual. Thus it is subscribed by Patrick Carswell, notary public, also required in the foregoing by the command above by my sign and subscription manual'.

did give up her self to the blackman from the tope of her head to the sole of her foot and that this wes efter the declarants renuncing of her baptisme And that the spirits name which he did give her wes Locas And that about the third or fourth of January instant or therby in the night tyme when she hade awakened she found a man in the bed whom she supposed to have bein her husband tho her husband hade bein dead twentie years or therby and that the man immeditaly disapeired And declaires that this man who disapeired wes the Divill, declaires that this wes the first tyme that she knewe him, declaires that upon Thursday the fourth of January instant she wes present in the house of John Stewart at night when and wher the effigies of clay wes made and that she sawe the blackman ther somtymes sitting somtymes standing with John Stewart, that the blackmans cloaths wer black and that he hade whitt hand cuffs and that Bessie Weir in Pollockstoun Annabill Stewart in Shawes Marjorie Craig were present the forsaid tyme and place at the making the said effigies of clay, and declaires that she gave her consent to the making of the samen, declaires that the Divill who compeired in the blackmans shape his name wes Eijuall. *Sic subscrivitur Ita est Robertus Park nottarius {fo. 4r.} publicus in premissis requisitus de mandato dicte Margarete Jackson scribere (ut asseruit) nescien testan meis signo et chirographo Ita est Patricius Carswell nottarius publicus etiam in premissis requisitus de mandato quo supra testan his meis signo et chirographo.*[24]

[*Signed:*] PHouston, JBrisbane of Bischiptoune, JPrestoun.

Curia Justiciarie Supremi Domini Nostri Regis tenta in pretorio burgi de Paisley decimo quinto die mensis Februarii 1677 per honorabilis viros Dominum Patricium Houstoun de eodem Dominum Joannem Shawe Joannem Anderson de Dowhill et Magistrum Joannem Prestoun advocatum. Curia legittime affirmata.[25]

The said justices ther Commission abovewreitten granted to them be the Lords of his Majesties privie Counsill for the tryall and examination of Jannet Mathie John and Annabill Stewarts Margaret Jackson and Bessie Weir for the cryme of witchcraft wes this day of new againe publictlie read in face of court Togither with another Commission granted to them for the tryall of Marjorie Craigie for the samen cryme Wherof the tenor followes.

Charles be the grace of God King of great Britaine France and Irland defender of the faith to all and sundrie our leidges and subjects whom it effeirs Greeting forasmuch as the Lords of our privie Counsill are informed that

[24] 'Thus it is subscribed. Thus I, Robert Park, notary public, at the command of the said Margaret Jackson, who (as she asserts) does not know how to write, have affixed my sign and subscription manual. Thus it is subscribed by Patrick Carswell, notary public, also required in the foregoing by the command above by my sign and subscription manual'.

[25] 'Court of justiciary of our sovereign lord the king, held in the tolbooth of the burgh of Paisley, 15 February 1677, by the honourable men lord Patrick Houston of that Ilk, lord John Shaw, John Anderson of Dowhill and Mr John Preston advocate. Court legally fenced.'

Marjorie Craige somtymes residenter in the Lands of Pollock is apprehendit and imprisoned as suspect guiltie of witchcraft by entering unto paction with the Divill renuncing her baptisme and committing severall malefices And to the effect the said matter may be made manifest and justice administrat therintill Conforme to the Lawes of this kingdome we with advyse of the Lords of our privie Counsill doe heirby make and constitut Sir Patrick Houston of that Ilk Sir John {*fo. 4v.*} Shawe younger of Greinock James Brisbane of Bishoptoun John Anderson younger of Dowhill and Mr John Prestoun advocat or any three of them, the said Mr John Prestoun being allwayes on[e] of the number, our justices in that part to the effect underwreitten, and appoynts Mr Robert Martin Clerk to the justice court to be Clerk to the saids Commissioners with power to them to meit at such tymes and places as they shall think expedient and then and ther to affix and hold courts, creat serjants, dempsters and all other members of court needfull To call ane assyse and witnessis of persons best understanding the truth of the said matter, absents to amerciat, unlawes and amerciaments to uplift and exact and in the saids courts to call the said Marjorie Craige and putt her to the tryall and knowledge of ane assyse and if she shall be found guiltie upon voluntar confession without any sort of torture or indirect meanes used against her to bring her to ane confession or that malefices are otherwayes legallie instructed and proven Then and in that caice that they cause justice be administrat upon her Conforme to the Lawes of this kingdome and generallie all and sundrie other things anent the execution of this our Commission to doe and exerce promitten to hold firme and stable etc. and ordaines the saids Commissioners to returne the verdict and rolments of court to be recordit in the books of adjournall lykeas we with advyse forsaid doe heirby nominat and appoynt our Right trustie and welbeloved Cousine and Councelor George Lord Rosse to be assisor[26] to our saids Commissioners giving and granting to him full power to sitt vote and act with the saids Commissioners in trying and judging the said Marjorie Craige.

Given at Edinburgh the first day of February and of our reigne the twentie eight year 1677. *Sic subscrivitur* Rothes cancellarius, Atholl, Mar, Wintoun, Wigtoune, Dundonald, Elphinston, Ja. Dalrymple, Ch. Maitland, Jo. Nisbet, ARamsay, Tho. Wallace, Ja. Foulis, Wauchope.

The said day compeired Robert Alexander of Blackhouse and produced in presence of the justices ane substitution from his Majestys Advocat in favores of the said Robert which being read wes admitted be the justices and ordained to be recordit wherof the tenor followes.

I Sir John Nisbet of Dirletoun his Majesties advocat doe heirby make and constitut Robert Alexander of Blackhouse my deput to the effect underwreitten with power to him to appeir for {*fo. 5r.*} his Majesties interest and as deput for me in the criminall proces intented befor the Commissioners appoynted be

26 *Sic.* Read 'assessor'.

his Majesties privie Counsill against the persons eftermentioned viz. Jannet Mathie John and Annabill Stewarts Margaret Jackson Marjorie Craig and Bessie Weir designed in maner mentioned in ther respective dittays for the cryme of witchcraft and malefice therin contained And to insist against the saids persons and every on[e] of them upon the said dittays untill the same be putt to the knowledge of ane assyse and verdicts followe therupon respective and to doe every thing in persewance of the premissis which I might doe my self if I wer present for which these shall be a sufficient warrand being wreitten be Alexander Gray my servitor I have subscrivit these presentts with my hand Att Edinburgh the [*1 word blank*] day of February $I^{m}vi^{c}$ and sevintie sevin years Befor thir witnessis Mr Hugh Maxwell writer in Edinburgh and Robert Litster and the said Alexander Gray my servitors.

Sic subscrivitur Jo. Nisbet, Hu. Maxwell witnes, AGray witnes, RLitster witnes.

The said Robert Alexander of Blackhouse substitut for his Majesties advocat declaired he insistet first against Jannet Mathie, Bessie Weir and Marjorie Craige.

Intran

Jannet Mathie relict of umquhile John Stewart undermiller at Pollockshawe milne now prisoner in the tolbuith of Paisley.

Ye are indyted and accused that wher notwithstanding be the Lawe of God Lawe and practique of all nations and the Lawe of this kingdome and in speciall be the 73 act 9 parliament of Queen Mary The cryme of witchcraft is forbidden and ordained to be punished as ane horrid abomination and capitall cryme Neverthelesse it is of veritie that ye the said Jannet Mathie hes committed and is guiltie of the said cryme of witchcraft in suae fare as ye being desyrous to be avenged of Sir George Maxwell of Pollock who hade wronged your son [*1 word blank*] Stewart (as ye conceaved) for his breaking the yaird of Pollock and ye your self being the Divills by compact and transaction ye did most godleslie and wickedlie intyse and invit Annabill {*fo. 5v.*} Stewart your daughter to resigne her self (a horrid cruelty in you a mother) in the Divills hands and to renunce your [*sic*] baptisme which your daughter upon your intysment and promissing her a new coat did by putting on[e] of her hands to the crown of her head and the other to the sole of her feet and in prosecution of your ungodlie malice and wickednes ye did in October last upon ane or other of the dayes of the said moneth meit with the Divill in your own house in the shape of a black man and with the said Annabill Stewart your daughter whose spirits name is Enippa Bessie Weir your officer whose spirits name is Sophia Marjorie Craige whose spirits name is Rigern and Margaret Jackson whose spirits name is Locas and the Divill ye and your other fellowe witches in October last did wickedlie contryve and make an effigies of waxe to represent Sir George Maxwell of Pollock and to take his lyff and ye having made it and putt a pine in each syd of the said effigies ye bound it on a spitt and ye having turned it about befor the fyre be Bessie Weir ye and all the forsaids witches did the same by saying Sir George Maxwell, Sir George Maxwell and the said Sir George did fall to be sick therefter and did languish of the said sicknes for many weeks and wes cruellie tormented and pained in many places of his bodie but especiallie in the syds wher the pins wer placed in the effigies and particularlie in the right syd wher ye hade placed the greatest pine which being by the Goodnes and providence of almightie God discovered wes found upon the [*1 word blank*] day of [*1 word blank*] December last in the house of you the said Jannet Mathie in a litle hole behind the fyre and efter the said effigies wes found and the pins taken out therof and ye taken prisoners the said Sir George sicknes by Gods goodnes to him did abait and relent, and ye still persisting in your wickednes and witchcraft ye with the Divil upon the [*1 word blank*] day of [*1 word blank*] did make another effigies of earth for the hurt of the said Sir George or some other which upon the sevinteinth of January last wes found within the tolbuith of Paisley (wher ye wes prisoner for the tyme) in your bed beneath the bolster, and farder in tocken of your witchcraft and giving up your self to be the Divills servant ther are severall of his markes found on your bodie And also be publict fame and common bruit ye are holden and repute a witch which being found be ane assyse ye ought to be punished with death and confiscation of your movables to the terror of others to committ the lyke heirefter. {*fo. 6r.*}

Intran
Bessie Weir spouse to John [*1 word blank*] in Pollocktoun now prisoner in the tolbuith of Paisley.

Ye are indyted and accused that wher notwithstanding be the divine Lawe of almightie God sett doun in the Sacred word especiallie in the 20 chapter of Leviticus and 18 chapter of Deutronomie and be the lawe and practique of all nations and be the Lawe and practique of this kingdome and namlie be 73 act 9 parliament Queen Mary It is expresslie provydit statut and ordained that as maner of person of whatsomever degree quality or condition they be of presume or take upon hand to practise or use any maner of witchcraft socerie or necromancie therthrow to abuse the leidges under the paine of death Neverthelesse it is of veritie that ye the said Bessie Weir are guiltie of and hes committed the cryme of witchcraft in suae fare as in harvest I^{m}VI^{c} and sevintie six you came to the house of Jannet Mathie in Pollockshawe milne your fellow witch and you with the said Jannet did intyse Annabill Stewart her daughter to resigne her self to the Divill which she did by putting her on[e] hand to the crown of her head and the other to the sole of her foot and ye in the qualitie of the Divills officer did in October last citt[27] the said Annabill

[27] 'citt': cite, summon.

Stewart whose spirits name is Enippa Margaret Jackson whose spirits name is Locas Marjorie Craige whose spirits name is Rijern and Jannet Mathie whose spirits name is Landslady to meit with the Divill at the said Jannets house and ye the forsaids witches having shacken off all fear of Gods dew reverence and regaird to his divin ordinance and Lawes and to the acts of parliament of his kingdome and having wickedlie and unjustly conceaved a cruell malice against Sir George Maxwell of Pollock ye and the forsaids witches (with the Divill your master in compact) did in October last contryve and make ane effigies and picture of waxe to represent the said Sir George Maxwell and for taking away of his lyff and having putt a pine in each syd of the said effigies ye bound it on a spitt and ye the said Bessie Weir turned it on the spitt befor the fyre and by your socerie and charmes and crying when it wes turning Sir George Maxwell, Sir George Maxwell, The said Sir George Maxwell did fall to be sick therefter and did languish in the said sicknes for many weeks therefter and wes cruellie tormented and pained in many places of his body but especiallie in the right syd wher ye hade placed the greater pine and ye still persisting in your cruell and divilish malice did upon the third of January last bypast {*fo. 6v.*} in the qualitie of the Divills officer as said is come to Jannet Mathies house and ther did cite Annabill Stewart another witch to come the nixt night to John Stewart her brothers house be twelve aclock at night and did lykewayes cite the said Marjorie Craige Margaret Jackson and the said John Stewart to meit the forsaid tyme and place with the Divill whom ye called the blackman And ye and the other witches having accordingllie mett at the said John Stewarts house the forsaid night ye did make a picture of clay to represent the said Sir George and for taking away his lyff in which ye placed three pins on[e] in each syd and on[e] on the breast And efter making of this effigies ye and Marjorie Craige did goe out at a windowe in the gavill of the said John Stewarts house at which ye hade entered to the forsaid meiting And upon the making of the said effigies and placing the pins as afforesaid the said Sir George did relapse into his former sicknes and his paines and torments did greatlie increase, And the effigies by the goodnes of almightie God being discovered and found in the bed of the said John Stewart within his house in Pollockshawe upon the eighth of January last and the pins taken out of the said effigies the said Sir George did most sensiblie and remarkablie recover in a great measure his health, and to the making of the said effigies ye and your other fellow witches (having wrought the cley) did give your consent and the Divill (whom ye call the blackman) did make the figure of the face head and armes and being thus made ye the said Bessie did place it in the bedstrae of John Stewart And ye the said Bessie Weir being apprehendit and taken prisoner as guiltie of the forsaids crymes being conscious of your own guilt ye made your escape out of the prison And being therefter apprehendit at Busbie in the parroch of Carmanock ye did deny your name and did falslie assume the name of Bessie Aikin and falslie pretendit to be the spouse of

[*1 word blank*] Chrystie in Glasgow therby to escape condigne[28] punishment for the saids crymes, and in farder tocken of your said guiltienes your body being searched ther are severall marks of the Divill your master found on your bodie And alse be publict fame and common bruit ye are holden and reput a witch which being found be ane assyse ye ought to be punished with the paine of death and confiscation of movables to the terror of others to committ the lyke heirefter. {*fo. 7r.*}

Marjorie Craige prisoner in the tolbuith of Paisley

Ye are indyted and accused that wher notwithstanding be the divine Lawe the Lawe of nations the Lawes and acts of parliament of this kingdome and daylie practique therof and particularlie be the 73 act 9 parliament Queen Mary the cryme of witchcraft is declaired to be ane horrid abomination capital cryme and punishable by death and confiscation of movables Neverthelesse it is of veritie that ye having shacken off all fear of God dew respect reverence and regaird to the divine ordinances and Lawes of almightie God and to the Lawes and acts of parliament of this kingdome you have presumed to committ and are guiltie of the cryme of witchcraft in suae fare as ye having conceaved a cruell malice and hatred against Sir George Maxwell of Pollock ye did converse with the Divill and other witches at severall meitings and in speciall with Jannet Mathie Bessie Weir Margaret Jackson Annabill Stewart and John Stewart ane warlok and in October last I^{m}VI^{c} and sevintie sex years or ane or other of the dayes of the said moneth The Divill ye and the forsaids witches did frame and make ane effigies of waxe to represent the said Sir George Maxwell for taking away of his lyff And the Divill ye and the forsaids witches did use the said expressions Sir George Maxwell, Sir George Maxwell, efter which the said Sir George did fall in ane languishing and tormenting sicknes in which he did continue for severall weeks and wes cruellie tormented in severall parts of his bodie but particularlie in the right syd wher the Divill ye and the other witches hade placed in the effigies the greatest pine And the said effigies being heirefter discovered and found upon the [*1 word blank*] day of December last in a litle holl at the back of the fyre in the house of the said Jannet Mathie and the pins being taken out therof the said Sir George sicknes did sensiblie abaite and relent, and ye the Divill and the forsaids witches maliciouslie envying at the said Sir George his recoverie ye did therefter meit upon the fourth of January last bypast about twelve aclock at night in the house of John Stewart warlock in Pollockshawe and ther in prosecution of your divilish crueltie and malice against the said Sir George did contryve and forme another effigies of clay to represent the said Sir George and to take away his lyff and ye and all the other witches having wrought the clay did give {*fo. 7v.*} your consent to the making of it The Divill

28 'condigne': fitting.

having formed the figure of the head face and armes to the samen and having putt a pine in each syd and on[e] in the breast therof the said Sir George did relapse unto his former sicknes with a great augmentation of his torments and paines and which wer so exceedinglie great that the said Sir George and all that sawe him did look for his present death And yet the said effigies of clay being of Gods goodnes discovered upon the eighth of January last and found in the house of the said John Stewart within his bedstrae The said Sir George efter the finding the said effigies and taking the pins out therof did wonderfullie recover his health and wes immeditaly eased of his great torments and paines And ye being the Divills by compact and transaction did receave his mark and did receave the name of Rijern whill the Divill himself did passe under the name of Ejoall which being found be ane asyse ye ought to be punished to the death and your movables confiscat to the terror of others.

And sicklyke ye are farder indyted for the said cryme of witchcraft in suae fare as ye being holden and reput a witch in the Kingdome of Irland wher ye conversed with the Divill and hade sundrie and diverse meitings with him and having conceaved a cruell and divilish prejudice against your own son for then in the said kingdome of Irland you did menace and threaten to doe him hurt and particularlie to dispatch him befor the nixt night and upon these your menaces and threatenings your said son wes found strangled within the tyme forsaid and ye being therupon imprisoned within the tolbuith of [*1 word blank*] in the said kingdome of Irland ye did make your escape furth therof and repaired your self unto this kingdome wher ye did committ the crymes contained in your forsaid indytment.

The justices be Commission with consent of the assessor finds the haill three dittays abovewreitten relevant and remitts the samen to the knowledge of ane asyse of the persons efternamed viz.

Robert Urie in Longsyd
John Sheills in Sheills
William Sheills ther
John Lock in Old Cruickshank
Allan Kirkwood
John Reid in Kirk of Eastwood
John Park in Darnely
Allan Stewart in Paisley
Robert Shawe in Henderstoun
Andrew Syme in Foordmouth
John Corse in Corsmilne
Patrick Carswell in Paisley
Robert Park younger ther
John Wilson maltman ther
Mathew Jamieson in Weill {*fo. 8r.*}

The persons of assyse abovenamed wer lawfullie sworne no objection in the contrair.

Robert Alexander of Blackhouse substitut to his Majesties Advocat took Instruments upon the finding of the Indytments Relevant and upon the swearing of the assyse and protested for ane assyse error in caice they should absolve.

The said Robert Alexander for probation adduced the Confessions of John and Annabill Stewarts and Margaret Jackson Committed be them in presence of the justices upon the twentie sevinth of January last bypast and this day of new again adheared to and acknowledged to be of truth as to all ther circumstances in presence of the justices the pannals and assysers.

Lykeas for farder probation he adduced the witnessis efter deponing viz.

Andrew Martin servitor to the Laird of Pollock of the age of threttie years or therby depons that he wes present in the house of Jannet Mathie pannall when the picture of waxe produced wes found in a litle holl of the wall at the back of the fyre, depons that Sir George Maxwells sicknes did fall upon him about the eighteinth of October or therby, depons that the picture of waxe wes found on the [*1 word blank*] day of December and that Sir George sicknes did abait and relent about the tyme the picture of waxe wes found and discovered in Jannet Mathies house, depons that the pins wer placed in the right and left syds and that Sir George Maxwell of Pollocks paines as he understood be Sir George complaining of his paines lay most in his right and left syds, depons that Sir George paines did abait and relent efter the finding the said picture of waxe and taking out of the pins which wes found in the house of the said Jannet Mathie upon the [*1 word blank*] day of December as said is, depons that the pannall Jannet Mathie hes bein by fame and bruit reputed a witch these severall years bygone, This is the truth as he shall answer to God. *Causa Patet Sic Subscrivitur*[29] Androw Martien.

Laurence Pollick servitor to the Laird of Pollock of the age of threttie years or therby unmaried sworne and purged of partiall councill depons as followes That upon the [*1 word blank*] day of December he wes in the pannall Jannet Mathies house when the picture wes found and that he did not see {*fo. 8v.*} it befor it wes brought to the pannals door depons that Sir George Maxwell of Pollocks sicknes did sease[30] upon him about the fourteinth day of October or therby and did continue in his distemper and sicknes for sex weeks or therby depons that Sir George sicknes did abait and relent efter the finding of the said picture of waxe and taking out of the pins therof depons that ther wer two pins fixed in the effigies of waxe on[e] on each syd And as the deponent thinks the greatest pine wes in the right syd and that Sir Georges paines did lye most in the right syd wher the greater pine wes in the effigies depons that by oppin bruit and common fame Jannet Mathie Bessie Weir

[29] 'The reason is clear. Thus it is subscribed'.

[30] 'sease': seize.

and Marjorie Craig pannals are brandit to be witches depons that this is the truth as he shall answer to God. *Causa patet Sic subscrivitur* Lawrence Pollick.

Lodovick Stewart of Auchinhead of fyftie three years of age maried being sworne and purged of partiall counsill depons that Sir George Maxwells sicknes did fall upon him about the fourteinth or fyfteinth day of October or therby, depons that he wes not present at the finding of the picture of waxe but that he hade sein Sir George Maxwell of Pollock efter it wes found and he having sein him in his sicknes oftymes befor he did perceave that Sir George hade sensiblie recovered efter the tyme that the said picture wes said to be found which wes about the elevinth or twelth of December, depons that Jannet Mathie and Marjorie Craig two of the pannalls are be the report of the Countrey had to be witches, depons that the deponent having come to Pollock he did see Sir George Maxwell whose paines did recurre and that his paines were befor finding of the picture of waxe, depons that upon the said eighth of January when he hade left the said Sir George Maxwell of Pollock the deponent with James Dunlop of Houslie Allan Dougall and severall others did goe to the house of John Stewart warlock in Pollockshawe and ther he found a picture of clay in the bedstrae of John Stewart, depons that ther were three pins in the said picture of clay and that ther wes on[e] in each syd and on[e] in the breast, depons that the deponent having returned to Sir George Maxwells house at Pollock Sir George told the deponent that he found great ease of his paines and that it wes befor the deponent Houslie and the rest did reveill to him that they hade found the said picture of clay, and farder depons that to his own observation he did perceave that Sir George hade most sensiblie recovered, depons that they took the said John Stewart pannall prisoner with them at the finding {*fo. 9r.*} of the said effigies, depons that this is the truth as he will answer to God. *Causa patet Sic subscrivitur* Lodovike Stewart.

David Kincaid servitor to John Maxwell younger of Pollock of the age of twentie nyn years unmaried being sworne and purged of partiall councill depons *conformis presentibus*[31] except that he wes not present at the finding of the picture of waxe and that the deponent being a stranger knowes nothing of Bessie Weirs fame And farder adds that he wes present in the prison of Paisley when the effigies and picture of earth representing a woman wes found and that it wes found in the bed of Jannet Mathie pannall under her bolster and this is the truth as he shall answer to God. *Sic subscrivitur* David Kincaid.

Allan Dowgall in Pollocktoun of the age of fyftie years or therby maried being sworne and purged of partiall councill depons that John Park in Pollocktoun being examined anent the breaking of the yaird of Pollock declaired that Hugh Stewart the pannall Jannet Mathies son did assist him in breaking of the said yaird and that Sir George sicknes did cease[32] upon him about the fourteinth

31 'in conformity with the present', i.e. the other depositions.
32 'cease': seize.

or fyfteinth of October or therby which wes the same night efter they hade learned that Hugh Stewart Jannet Mathies son hade brocken the yaird, depons that Jannet Mathie Bessie Weir and Marjorie Craige are all by common bruit brandit to be witches, depons *conformis presentibus* except as to the finding of the third picture at which he wes not present, depons that this is the truth as he shall answer to God. *Causa patet Sic subscrivitur* Allane Dougall.

John Glen in Sandiehills of Paisley of the age of fourtie eight years or therby maried sworn and purged of partiall counsill depons that he wes present with David Kincaid servitor to John Maxwell younger of Pollock and others when the picture of earth wes found in the prison of Paisley under the cod[33] or bolster of Jannet Mathie the pannalls bed, This is the truth as he shall answer to God. *Causa patet Sic subscrivitur* John Glen.

Robert Kirlie officer in Paisley of the age of threttie four years maried sworn and purged of partiall counsill depons conformis to John Glen and farder adds that Jannet Mathie pannall being by ordor of the justices putt in the stoks within the prison of Paisley and ther {*fo. 9v.*} being a cod distant from the stocks the breadth of the house the deponent found her sitting upon the cod the nixt morning tho no person hade hade access to her all the whill that she hade bein in the stocks befor that time and this is the truth as he shall answer to God. *Causa patet Sic subscrivitur* Robert Kirlie.

Robert Alexander substitut to His Majesties advocat tuke Instruments upon the pannall Bessie Weir her confession that she wes prisoner at Pollock and making of her escape and her being apprehendit at Busbie and ther denying her own name and her selfe assuming another name and her denying her husbands name and her pretending to be the wyff of on[e] Chrystie in Glasgow wheras she is the wyfe of John Patton weaver in Pollock.

The said Robert Alexander takes Instruments lykewayes upon Jannet Mathies confessing that she hes marks.

The said Robert Alexander Substitut to his Majesties advocat declaires he now insists against John and Annabill Stewarts and Margaret Jackson.

Intran

John Stewart in Pollockshawe son to Jannet Mathie witch

Ye are Indyted and accused That wher notwithstanding the divin Lawe of the almightie God sett doun in the sacred word especiallie in the twentie chapter of Leviticus and 18 chapter of Deutronomie and be the Lawe and practique of all nations and the Lawe and practique of this kingdome and namlie be the 73 act 9 parliament Queen Mary It is expresslie provydit statut and ordained that no maner of person of whatsomever degree qualitie or condition they be off presume or take upon hand to practise or use any maner of witchcraft

[33] 'cod': pillow.

socerie or necromancie therthrowe to abuse the leidges[34] which be the said act is declaired to be ane horrid abomination and capitall cryme Neverthelesse it is of veritie that ye the said John Stewart are guiltie of and hes committed the cryme of witchcraft in suae fare as ye having shacken off all fear of God dew reverence and regaird for his divine ordinance and Lawes and acts of parliament of this kingdome ye being upon the third of January last bypast cited be Bessie Weir a witch and officer at your meitings with the Divill ye did upon the fourth day of January instant about twelve aclock {*fo. 10r.*} at night meit at your own house with the Divill (in the shape of a blackman) and with the said Bessie Weir Margaret Jackson Marjorie Craige and Annabill Stewart your sister now prisoners for the said cryme of witchcraft And the Divill having come to your said house at the forsaid tyme and having quyetlie awakened you, you rose from your bed to light a candle and the Divill having requyred you to renunce your baptism and delyver your self whollie to him, ye upon the Divills promising to you that ye should not want for any good thing and should not want any pleasure and that ye should have your heart sythed on all that should doe you wrong you, did devote and give over your self to him both soull and bodie by renuncing our saviour and your baptisme and all your part of heaven by useing the detestable formalitie of laying on[e] of your hands upon the crown of your head and the other under the sole of your foot be receaving his mark and taking a name from him and owning the name of Jonas which he did give you having past under the name of Ejoall and therefter the said night the Divill ye and the forsaids witches did make and frame ane effigies of clay (to which ye and every on[e] of you gave your consent) for taking away the lyff of Sir George Maxwell and made the said picture to represent him and ye and the other witches wrought the clay and ye did hold the candle untill the Divill under the shape of a blackman did forme the head face and armes of the said effigies and untill he patt[35] in three pins in the samen on[e] in each syd and on[e] in the breast And whill the picture wes making ye did observe the blackman to be cloven footed and his apparrell to be black having a blewish band and hand cuffs and hogers on his leggs without shoes And that his voyce wes hough and goustie And his effigies being placed in your bedstrae be Bessie Weir, Sir George Maxwell efter the making therof did relapse unto his former sicknes with a great and hye increase of the samen which it appeirs he hade fallen unto by the socerie and witchcraft of Jannet Mathie your mother Annabill Stewart your sister Marjorie Craige Margaret Jackson Bessie Weir and other witches and yet upon discoverie and finding of the said clay picture which wes found in your bedstrae within your house in Pollockshawe upon the eighth of January instant did evidently and manifestlie recover in a great measure his health, all which

34 A variation on the phrase 'thairthrow abusand the pepill' in the 1563 witchcraft act.
35 'patt': put.

being done be you and the other witches out of a cruell {*fo. 10v.*} malice and prejudice to the said Sir George Maxwell and found be ane assyse ye ought to be punished with death and confiscation of movables to the terror of others to committ the lyke heirefter.

Intran
Margaret Jackson relict of umquhile Thomas Stewart in Pollockshawes

Ye are indyted and accused That wher notwithstanding be the divin Lawe of the almightie God sett doun in the sacred word especiallie in the 20 chapter of Leviticus and 18 chapter of Deutronomie and be the Lawe and practique of all nations and be the Lawe and practique of this kingdome and namlie be the 73 act 9 parliament Queen Mary It is expresslie provydit statut and ordained that no maner of person of whatsomever degree qualitie or condition they be off presume or take upon hand to practise or use any maner of witchcraft socerie or necromancie therthrowe to abuse the leidges which be the said act is ordained to be punished as ane horrid abomination and capitall cryme Neverthelesse it is of veritie that ye the said Margaret Jackson are guiltie of and hes committed the cryme of witchcraft in suae fare as ye having shacken off all fear of God due reverence and regaird to his divine ordinance and Lawes and to the acts of parliament of this kingdome ye did give over your self to the Divill and his service fourtie years agoe or therby and did by ane express covenant and paction with the Divill then appeiring to you in the likeness of a blackman in Pollockshawes croft wher ye wes with some fewe sticks on your back and ther ye did renunce our blissed saviour and your baptisme and did devote and give over your self both bodie and soull to that wicked spirit by laying on[e] of your hands on the crown of your head and the other on the sole of your foot and did receave his mark and Lucas for your name and you did ever since continue in the said abomination and apostacie in the Divills service and hes keept meitings severall tymes with the Divill and other witches and in speciall with Jannet Mathie Bessie Weir Annabill Stewart Marjorie Craig and John Stewart a warlock now prisoner for the saids crymes and others and at the saids tymes did converse with the Divill and particularlie in October last and ane or other of the dayes of the said moneth ye did meit with the Divill and with the said Jannet Mathie Bessie Weir Annabill Stewart and Marjorie Craige in the house of Jannet Mathie wher the Divill ye and the saids witches did make and frame ane effigies of waxe to represent Sir George Maxwell of {*fo. 11r.*} Pollock and to take away his lyff, to the making wherof ye did give your consent And efter the Divill ye and the other witches hade putt a pine in each syd of the said effigies the said effigies wes bound be you and them on a spitt and turned befor the fyre be Bessie Weir and as it wes turning the Divill ye and the saids witches did expresse these words Sir George Maxwell, Sir George Maxwell, efter which the said Sir George did fall to be sick and did for many weeks languishe of the said sicknes with great dollor and paine but especiallie in his syds wher the pins were sett in the effigies and particularlie in the right syd wher the greater pin wes fixt and which being by providence discovered and found in a litle holl at the back of the fyre within Jannet Mathies house in Pollockshawe upon the [*blank*] day of December last bypast the said Sir George did in some measure recover his health and yet ye maliciouslie envyeing at the samen and still persisting in your crueltie wickednes and witchcraft did upon the fourth day of January last meit with the Divill in the shape of a black man with black cloaths a blewe band and handcuffs and with Annabill Stewart Bessie Weir Marjorie Craige and John Stewart about twelve aclock at night in the house of the said John Stewart wher the Divill ye and the other witches with John Stewart warlock did make ane effigies picture of clay to represent the said Sir George Maxwell for taking away of his lyff in which effigies the Divill ye and the other witches having placed three pins on[e] on each syd and on[e] in the breast efter making and doeing wherof the said Sir George Maxwell his paines and torments did exceedinglie increase And yet the said effigies being discovered and found upon the eighth day of January last in the house of the said John Stewart in his bedstrae and the pins taken out therof the said Sir George did most sensiblie and remarkablie recover on a great measure his health And alse about the first second third or fourth dayes of the said moneth of January last the Divill did come and converse with you in your bed and ye supposed him to be your husband who hade dyed about twentie years befor and that ye then knewe him, through the doeing wherof ye are guiltie of the horrid cryme of witchcraft, which being found be ane assyse ye ought to be punished with death and confiscation of youre movables to the terror of others to committ the lyke heirefter. {*fo. 11v.*}

Intran
Annabill Stewart daughter to Jannet Mathie relict of umquhile John Stewart of Pollockshaw milne

Ye are indyted and accused That wher notwithstanding be the Lawe of God and practique of all nations and the Lawe of this kingdome and in speciall be the 73 act 9 parliament Queen Mary the cryme of witchcraft is forbidden and ordained to be punished as ane horrid abomination and capitall cryme Nevertheless it is of veritie that ye the said Annabill Stewart hes committed and are guiltie of the cryme of witchcraft in suae fare as in harvest last ye did converse with the Divill in the shape of a blackman and that ye being of threetein or fourtein years of age ought to have remembered your Creator in the dayes of your youth[36] yet ye upon the Divill promising unto

[36] Cf. Ecclesiastes 12:1.

you pleasure and good things and upon the intysments and alurments[37] of your mother Jannet Mathie and Bessie Weir witches ye being desyred and requyred be the Divill and the said witches to renunce your baptisme and to delyver up your self whollie to him ye did accordinglie renunce our blissed saviour and your baptisme and did devote and give over your self both soull and bodie to the service of the Divill the enemie of mankind by useing the wicked and detestable formalities of laying ane of your hands to the crown of your head and the other to the sole of your feit and did receave his marke in the arme which continued to be sore for half ane hour and did receive Ennippa from him as your spirits name whill the Divill past under the name of Ejoall and therefter ye did abominablie converse with him in the shape of a blackman and lay with him under the cloaths and found him cold And since that tyme ye have hade many privat meitings with him and other witches and in speciall with your mother Jannet Mathie, Bessie Weir officer to your meitings, Margaret Craige and Margaret Jackson in your mothers house in [*1 word blank*] October last wher ye and the forsaids witches having conceaved a cruell hatred and deadlie malice against Sir George Maxwell of Pollock the Divill ye and the forsaids witches did make ane effigies of clay to represent the said Sir George Maxwell for killing him and efter ye and they hade made the samen and hade putt a pine in each syd therof ye bound it on a spitt and turned it about befor the fyre be Bessie Weir and cryed Sir George Maxwell, Sir George Maxwell, and this effigies and picture being discovered and found in a litle holl {*fo. 12r.*} in the back of the fyre within Jannet Mathie your mothers house and your mother being prisoner for the said cryme Sir George Maxwell did in some measure recover of his sicknes (laid upon him as (appeirs) [*sic*] by your socerie and witchcraft And yet ye and the saids witches abyding in your hynous[38] crueltie and malice ye and the forsaids witches did meit with the Divill about twelve aclock at night the fourth of January last in the house of John Stewart your brother a warlock and ther did contryve and make a new effigies of clay in which the Divill ye and the other witches did putt three pins on[e] in each syd and on[e] in the breast efter the making and framing of which effigies the said Sir George did relapse into his former sicknes and hade stronger and more violent paines and torments than at any tyme befor And yet this effigies being discovered and found in the house of your brother John Stewart warlock and the pins taken out therof, the said Sir George did most sensiblie recover his health and that not only to his own knowledge but also convincinglie to the observation of all that did see him, And ye at the forsaid meiting upon the said fourth of January did observe that the blackman with the black cloaths blew band and whitt cuffs hade cloven feet with hogers on his leggs without shoes, which being found be ane assyse ye ought to be punished with death and confiscation of movables to the terror of others to committ the lyke in tyme coming.

[37] 'alurments': temptations.
[38] 'hynous': heinous.

The justices be Commission with consent of the assissors fand lykewayes the haill abovewreitten dittays Relevant and remmitted the samen to the knowledge of ane assyse of the persons abovenamed who wer of new againe lawfullie sworne no objection in the contrair.

Robert Alexander Substitut to his Majesties advocat for probatione adduced the saids John and Annabill Stewarts and Margaret Jackson ther Confessions abovewreitten taken befor the justices upon the twenty sevinth day of January last which wes this day publictly read and adhered to and declared to be a truth be them in presence of the saids justices and assyse {*fo. 12v.*} Efter leading of the whilk probation the said Robert Alexander protested for ane assyse of error against the inquest in caice they should asolyie.

Therefter the persons of assyse abovenamed removed altogither furth of court to the assyse house wher having reasoned and voited upon the poynts and articles of the forsaids sex indytments and witnessis depositions and Confessions adduced for proving therof they reentered againe in court and produced in presence of the justices and ther assessors ther verdict wherof the tenor followes.

The assyse all in on[e] voice be the mouth of Robert Urie in Longsyd ther Chanceler Considering that the justices have found the indytments relevant as they stand and being ryplie advysed with the declarations of the three confessing pannalls and the remnant probation with the haill circumstances therof cumulative and complexlie They find the pannals viz Jannet Mathie John and Annabill Stewarts Bessie Weir Margaret Jackson and Margaret Craige guiltie of the crymes of witchcraft and the other malefices contained in ther respective indytments and in tocken therof the said Chanceler hath subscrivit thir presentss in presence of the said assyse closed togither. *Sic subscrivitur*

Robert Urie chancellar.

Efter oppinning and reading of the whilk verdict of assyse The justices be Commission and George Lord Rosse ther assessor be the mouth of William Meldrum dempster of court decerned and adjudged the saids Jannet Mathie Bessie Weir, John and Annabill Stewarts Margaret Jackson and Marjorie Craige to be taken upon the twentie day of February instant to the Gallow grein of Paisley betwixt tuo and four aclock in the efternoon and ther to be strangled at a stalk [*sic*] till they be dead and therefter ther bodies to be burnt to ashes and all ther movable goods and gear to be escheat and inbrought to our Soveraigne Lords use which wes pronunced for doom.

Efter pronuncing of the whilk doom and sentance George Lord Rosse produced in presence of the said {*fo. 13r.*} justices be Commission ane act of the Lords of his Majesties privie Counsill wherof the tenor followes.

Edinburgh the first day of February $I^{m}VI^{c}$ and sevintie sevin years forasmuch as the Lords of his Majesties privie Counsill did by the Commission dated the Eighteinth of January last give full power and authoritie and Commission to Sir Patrick Houston of that Ilk and severall other persons to trye and judge Annabill Stewart daughter to the deceast John Stewart undermiller at Pollockshawe milne and diverse other persons apprehendit and imprisoned as suspect guiltie of witchcraft and appoynted the Lord Rosse to be assesor to the saids Commissioners and wheras the saids Lords are informed that the said Annabill Stewart is under age and but latlie insnaired They have thought fitt heirby to authorise the said Lord Rosse to continue and delay the execution of any sentance that shall be prenunced against the said Annabill Stewart untill the Counsill shall be farder informed anent her condition and give farder ordor and direction theranent for which these presentts shall be ane sufficient warrand. Extracted by me, *Sic subscrivitur* Thomas Hay.

The said George Lord Rosse produced lykewayes ane warrand under his own hand repryving the said Annabill Stewart wherof the tenor followes. Forasmuch as the Lords of his Majesties privie Counsill by ther act at Edinburgh the first day of February I^m^VI^c^ and sevintie sevin years have thought fitt to authorize us George Lord Rosse to continue and delay the execution of any sentance pronunced against Annabill Stewart daughter to John Stewart undermiller at Pollockshawe milne untill the saids Lords of Councill shall be farder informed anent her condition Therfor we continue and delay the execution of the sentence of death pronunced against her be Sir Patrick Houston of that Ilk Sir John Shawe of Greinock John Anderson younger of Dowhill Mr John Prestoun advocat judges in that part appoynted for the tryall of the said Annabill Stewart and other witches mentioned in ther Commission untill the Lords of his Majesties privie Councill give farder ordor and direction theranent Given at Paisley the fyfteinth of February 1677. *Sic subscrivitur* Rosse. {*fo. 13v.*}

The said day John Knox elder in Arkletoun and Henry Steivin in Hillingtoun being oftymes called to have compeired befor the saids justices be commission this day and place in the hour of cause to have past upon the assyse of Jannet Mathie John and Annnabill Stewarts Margaret Jackson Bessie Weir and Marjorie Craigie prisoners within the tolbuith of the said burghe for the cryme of witchcraft as they who wer lawfullie cited be Thomas Biggart officer of court to the effect abovementioned lawfull tyme of day bidden and they not enterand nor compeirand the justices therfor with consent of the assesor be the mouth of the said Thomas Biggart officer of court decerned and adjudged the saids John Knox and Henry Steivin to be in ane unlawe and amerciament of ane hundreth merks each of them which wes pronunced for doom.

32. HADDINGTONSHIRE WITCHES, 1678

INTRODUCTION

These trials took place before the central justiciary court in Edinburgh in September 1678. The prosecutor was the lord advocate, Sir George Mackenzie of Rosehaugh. The accused persons came from several parishes in Haddingtonshire, where a massive wave of witchcraft accusations swept over the area in a short time. Most of the accused were women, of widely varying ages. Twelve death sentences were passed, all upon women.

The first group of convictions included nine women from the parishes of Ormiston, Crichton and Humbie: Margaret Dodds, Peaston (Ormiston parish); Margaret Douglas, Crichton (Crichton parish); Isobel Elliot, first Peaston (Ormiston parish) and then Templehall (Pencaitland parish); Helen Forrester, Crichton (Crichton parish); Helen Laing, Peaston (Ormiston parish); Margaret Lowes, Humbie (Humbie parish); Isobel Shanks, Crichton (Crichton parish); Margaret Small, Humbie (Humbie parish); and Marion Veitch, Keith (Humbie parish). One of the women accused in this group, Christian Hogger (residence not recorded), had her case dropped. The second group of convictions included three women all from Fala, in the parish of Fala and Soutra: Bessie Gourlay, Agnes Somerville and Margaret Souness.

A further group of accused witches, eight women and one man, were declared fugitive: Margaret Anderson, Ormiston (Ormiston parish); James Campbell, Winton (Pencaitland parish); Marion Campbell, Peaston (Ormiston parish); Margaret Dalgleish, Keith (Humbie parish); Elspeth Knox, Keith (Humbie parish); Margaret Russell, Peaston (Ormiston parish); Agnes Thomson, Over Keith (now called Upper Keith; Humbie parish); Grisell Walker, Keith (Humbie parish); and Elizabeth Wood, Over Keith (now called Upper Keith; Humbie parish). Another fugitive recorded was Gideon Penman, the deposed former minister of Crichton. Other sources mention him as a suspected witch and master of witches; various stories were told about him, but he was never brought to trial.[1]

[1] Sir John Lauder of Fountainhall, *Historical Notices of Scotish Affairs*, 2 vols., ed. David Laing (Edinburgh: Bannatyne Club, 1868), i, 197–8; Robert Law, *Memorialls, or, The memorable things that fell out within the island of Brittain from 1638 to 1684*, ed. Charles K. Sharpe (Edinburgh, 1818), 132–3.

For some reason, the court ordered eight of the convicted witches to be burned at the Gallowlee in Edinburgh (the execution site between Edinburgh and Leith), while four others were taken back to Peaston to be burned locally. In addition to the trial records edited below, the privy council papers contain a warrant ordering Sir Robert Hepburn of Keith and John Pringle of Woodhead to oversee the Peaston executions, a 'testificat' by witnesses confirming that the burnings had taken place, and a detailed list of expenses incurred by Hepburn, providing information about his lengthy prior negotiations with the privy council and about arrangements for the burnings themselves. Hepburn had initially sought a commission of justiciary to enable him to try the witches locally, but the council instead sent them for trial in the central court of justiciary; he nevertheless had to pay many of the legal costs.[2]

Many further names were mentioned during these trials, as a central point of the confessions was participation at witches' gatherings. The alleged meetings took place in a field, at a hill, or in the house of a fellow witch. The impact of witches' gatherings, in order for a witchcraft panic to escalate, comes clearly to the fore.

All accused persons gave confessions with demonological content – meeting the Devil, renouncing their baptism, the Devil's pact, having got a new name, carnal copulation with the Devil, shape-shifting, and witches' gatherings at named locations in the local area. All confessions followed a similar pattern, from renouncing baptism, entering into the Devil's pact, ritual implying 'the crown of your head and the sole of your foot', carnal copulation with the Devil, the Devil's mark, new name, shape-shifting, witches' gatherings with piper and dancing, and collective witchcraft operations. They all denounced other witches who had participated at these gatherings. A clear line of demonic questioning was pursued, with leading questions evident in answers such as when Helen Forrester 'declaires the Divill never lay with her nor marked her nor gave her ane name'. In addition, harmful magic was mentioned from time to time in the confessions, and there was an instance of shape-shifting. It was stated that no compulsion was used, but we know that torture was common.

The trials are documented in a group of documents from the examination of the alleged witches, and from the central court in Edinburgh. The examinations were first recorded on 19 June 1678 in Peaston, when four women confessed: Marion Campbell, Marion Veitch, Isobel Elliot and Helen Laing.

The next examination was in Keith, on 21 June, when Marion Veitch confessed. The examinations went on: 27 June in Peaston, when Isobel Elliot confessed, 29 June when Helen Laing and Margaret Russell confessed, 1 July when Margaret Dodds confessed. On the same date, the depositions of Marion Campbell, Isobel Elliot, Helen Laing and Margaret Russell were read aloud, and the women adhered to their depositions and declared them to be the truth, while Marion

[2] *RPC*, 3rd ser., vi, 627–9.

Veitch gave a second confession. On 9 July, in Keith, a third deposition of Marion Veitch was read aloud, and she adhered to her former confessions. On the same day, also in Keith, Elspeth Knox and Janet Burton confessed, the latter denouncing twelve other women and saying that she gave her one-year-old child to the Devil and the child died after eight days. On 30 July, Marion Veitch and Elspeth Knox denounced three alleged witches, and Agnes Dalgleish confessed.

The documents also include a list of assize members dated 7 September, and a 'testificat', dated 20 September, for the burning of four witches in Peaston: Isobel Elliot, Marion Veitch, Margaret Dodds and Helen Laing. A petition on the execution of these witches has responses dated 4 December, signed by Mackenzie, and 2 January 1679, signed by Hepburn.

At this late stage of the Scottish witchcraft trials, it is clear that demonological ideas permeate beliefs in witchcraft among the populace. Demonological ideas must have been told and retold orally in local communities. Stories told in the confessions include one witch recruiting other witches to the Devil's service, advance arrangements being made for witches' meetings, the Devil refraining from sex with a pregnant female witch, a witch repenting of her involvement with the Devil, witches being unable to do harm because God did not permit it, and a witch foreseeing the witches' arrest and interrogation. Even if harmful magic is also included in these confessions, the dittays as a whole carry the stamp of demonology.

The records contain a number of blanks, either related to persons' names or dates. This indicates that the scribe has been in a hurry and has not bothered to fill in details. Probably the number of accused persons to be tried during one day was overwhelming. Several of the dittays name multiple witches; each accused person should have had her or his own guilt considered individually, but the impression is given that these persons were being processed in batches. The records give an interesting glimpse of a late witchcraft panic, with regard to the number of accused and mentioned persons, the content of the confessions, and the way the trials are conducted and recorded.

TEXTS

Source 1: NRS, Court of Justiciary Process Papers, 1678, JC26/49.

JC26/49, bundle 11, no. 5.[3]

[*Endorsed:*] The Deposition of Marion Campbell confessing witch att Pestoun 19 June 1678, And of Marion Veitch and Issobell Elliot and Helen Laing.

3 This and the subsequent documents from the box JC26/49 all come from bundle 11 in the box, labelled 'Peaston Witches 1678'. Most individual documents have pencil numbers as noted.

{*p. 1*} At Pestoun[4] the 19 day of June 1678 Followes the depositione and confession of Marion Campbell spouse to William Laing in Pestoun freely and voluntarly confest be hir without any torture or threatning quhatsumever she being delated and apprehended as being suspect of witchcraft.

Item in the first the said Marion confesses that four yeirs and a halfe since or therby she and Margreat Russell now spouse to Thomas Attkine in Pestoun being coming from Seatoun to Wintoun there appeared to them ane man with grein cloathinge did kiss the said deponer and that he had no breath and said to the deponer that she was his servant and after his stay halfe ane hour with them he did evanish and that the deponer did ask Margreat Russell what he was who answered that she would know afterward, depones that some dayes therafter the deponer with the said Margreat Russell, Margreat Dods in Pestoun, Helen Laing relict of William Laing ther, Issobell Elliot then her servant now in Templehall, Kathrin Haliday spouse to William Hare cowper,[5] Margreat Bannantine spouse to Johne Goudy in Pestoun, Sara Cranstoun relict of umquhile George Andersone in Keith and Marion Veitch spouse to George Thomsone in Keith with many others whom the deponer knew not had a meiting with the Divell in the night tyme at Ormistoun wood and where the Divell had carnall copulation with hir and that his nature was cold, Depones about eight dayes therafter the deponer with the haill uther women abovenamed had ane other meiting with the Divell at Cousland Dean wher the Divell also had carnall copulation again with the deponer, confesses also that then he caused the deponer renunce hir baptisme and come [*sic*] his servant by laying on[e] of hir hands on the crown of hir head and the other hand at the sole of hir foot and giving to the Divell all that was betwixt her two hands, depones that the Divell gave her a new name and called her Tousce.[6]

Item deponed that therafter the deponer with the haill above named women and many others whom the deponer knew not had another meiting with the Divell at the Cowburne where they all danced as they did at the former meiting, And depones also that they all had another meiting with the Divell a certain space after the former neir by to Wintoun wher they all danced and the Divell had then again carnall copulation with the deponer, Confesses also that the deponer had severall other meitings with the Divell and that many of the fornamed women were at all the meitings except the said Sara Cranstoun who the deponer did only clearly know to be at three of the meitings So far as the deponer could know, depones that when the deponer and the rest went to and came from the saids meitings that they were sometyms in the shape of crowes and sometymes in the shape of pyots[7] and

4 In margin: 'Marion Campbell'.
5 'cowper' (cooper): barrel-maker.
6 The meaning of this name is not clear.
7 'pyots': magpies.

sometyms in ther own shape and cloaths, denys absolutly that ever she did any harme to aither man woman or beast bot confesses that some persons having discorded with hir she intended to have done them harme bot could never have gott it done, depones that the Divell gave them all new names and that he called Margreat Russell his oun Post Horse and that he called Margreat Dods Drodlin and he called Margreat Balantine Lout Shoulders and he called Kathrine Haliday Dance Well and remembers not the names he gave to the rest, And the saids Margreat Russell, Margreat Dods, Kathrine Halyday, Margreat Balantine and Hellen Laing being all confronted with the deponer she affirms the premisses in ther faces bot they all obstinatly denyed, This deposition forsaid is taken up in presence of Sir Robert Hepburne of Keith, Mr Johne Sinclar minister at Ormestoun, Mr James Calderwood minister at Humby and the other persones undersubscryvand.

[*Signed:*] Jo: Wallace, Alexr. Ramsay, Ro: Hepburne, Willeam Sheil, Jo: Liddill, Ja: Yule, Jo: Sinclar, Hew Bell, Wm Cleark, Johne Adamsone, Ja: Calderwood, Ja: Borthik, Da: Chalmer, William Frame, Gorg Reid, Malchom Grive, JPringill, Alexr Laing. Turn over. {*p. 2*}

At Keith[8] 21 day of June 1678 Followes the free and voluntar confession and deposition of Marion Veitch spouse to George Thomsone in Keith annent hir guilt of the sin of witchcraft and quhilk confession she declared without any compulsion or threatning in presence of Sir Robert Hepburne of Keith, Mr James Calderwood minister of the parochin, Thomas Kennaway on[e] of the gentle men of his majesties Lyfegaird, David Chalmer, James Yule and Johne Spavine servitors to the said Sir Robert, William Sheill garner in Keith and William Cockburne schoolmaster and wryter heirof.

In the first the said Marion Veitch confest that she did enter in the Divells service about the end of the yeir i^{m}vi^{c} and fyfty or begining of the yeir 1651 and that about that tyme the Divell did appear to the deponer at the Ridford being brought ther be umquhile Barbry Veitch and the Divell had then carnall copulation with the deponer and caused her to renunce hir baptisme quhilk she did, And depones that the Divell gave hir a new name and called hir Broadback and caused the deponer put on[e] of hir hands upon the crown of hir head and the other hand at the sole of hir foot and to deliver up to the Divell all that was betwixt hir two hands which she did and that the Divell required hir to do him service in destroying hir neighbours quhilk God did not permitt hir to do and to blaspheme his name, Depones that the nixt meitting that she had with the Divell was in Ormestoun wood where there was many women present and danced all with the Divell and that Helen Laing and Margreat Dods was at many of the meitings, And depones that she was at many meitings with the Divell this 27 years and that she cleirly remembers that there was present at many of the saids meitings Marion Campbell,

[8] In margin: 'Marion Veitch'.

Margreat Russell, Margreat Balantine all in Pestoun and Issobell Elliot then in Pestoun and now in Templehall And that Sara Cranstoun to the deponers certain knowledge was present at two of the said meitings the on[e] at the Cowburne and the other at Ormestoun wood, The deponer confesses that after the first meiting forsaid the Divell had severall tymes carnall copulation with hir, depones that she was present when William Laing the husband to the said Helen Laing deceist and declares that the said Helen Laing with the said Issobell Elliot then hir servant did kill the said William Laing hir own husband on his death bed and pulled out his heart and that on[e] of them sat upon the on[e] side of him and the uther on the uther side of the bed, And that the deponer was present but invisible when the saids two women committed the said horrid act of murder.

In testimonie quherof thir presents are atested as the true deposition of the said Marion Veitch and subscrived be the abovenamed persones witnesses to the forsaid confession day yeir and place abovewritten.

[*Signed:*] John Spavein, Ro: Hepburne, Willeam Sheill, WCockburne, Ja: Calderwood, Thomas Kennaway, Da: Chalmer, Ja: Yule. {*p. 3*}

At Keith[9] the 27 day of June 1678 The said Marion Veitch did freely and voluntarly confess in presence of the witnesses undersubscryving That she was present at and accessorie to the death of William Laing in Peaston and that there was also present thereat and accessorie therto the said Hellen Laing his own wyfe and the said Issobell Elliot then hir servant and Marion Campbell with certain other witches, And farder confesses that the deponer with Marion Campbell and Issobell Elliot did kill a young daughter of William Thomsones son to the deponer at Templhall and that the Divell tempted the deponer and the rest to committ these two wicked acts, and depones that Jennet Bourtoun servitrix to the said Sara Cranstoun did cary the said Sara hir mantale[10] to the forsaid meittings quherat the said Sara was present quhilk were two or thrie meitings To wit at Ormestoun wood, the Waird Haugh and the Cowburne.

[*Signed:*] Da: Chalmer, Ja: Yule, Malchom Grive, Ro: Hepburn, WCockburne, John Spavin, William Simsone, Ja: Calderwood.

At Peastoun[11] the 27 day of Junii 1678 yeirs Followis the free and voluntar confession without any threatneing or tortur deponed be Issobell Elliot in Templhall dilated for witchcraft be Marion Campbell in Peastoun and Marion Vaitch in Keith And quhilk confession is made be the said Issobell Elliot in presence of Sir Robert Hepburne of Keith, John Pringall of Woodhead, Master James Calderwood Minister at Humby, Master James Cockburne minister at Pancaitland and the uther witnesses undersubscryving as followis viz. First the said Issobell confesses that about two years since shoe being

9 In margin: 'Marion Veitch'.

10 'mantale' (mantle): cloak.

11 In margin: 'Isobell Elliot'.

then servitrix to Hellen Laing in Paistoun, The said Hellan upon a sabbath morneing keiped the deponer at home from the kirk saying that a freind was to come to the house, quhairupon the deponer staying at home and being carying in water fra the well, X[12] the said Hellen Laing And Marion Campbell and the Divill sitting betwixt them and the saids two weemen went in to the chamber and that the Divill cam and kissed the deponer and offered to Ly with hir Bot shoe refused being then with chyld and the Divill said he wold forbear hir till shoe was delyvered of hir chyld and that at his disyre shoe did renunce hir baptisme, And that the Divill Baptised hir upon hir face with a wafe[13] of his hand Lyke a dewing[14] calling hir Jean, And that after shoe was kirked[15] the Divill had carnall copulation with hir And that since the first tyme forsaid The deponer had severall meitings with the Divill and severall carnall copulationes with him, shoe thought the Divill had the weight of four men when he Lay with hir And that he was very cold, And at severall of the saids meitings with the Divill the persones afternamed wer present, To witt Sara Cranstoun, Jonet Bruntoun hir servant, Maryon Vaitch in Keith, Marion Campbell, Kathrin Halyday, Margaret Dods, Margart Balenden the said [*about 2 words worn away*] ...ant[16] Margarett Russell all in Peastoun with Jonet Hunter Laitly in Ormestoun and Margrate Andersone relict of James Vaitch in Ormestoun, depones also that Bessie Bell and Margarett Liddell in Laiswaid Lonhead ar witches, And killed a chyld of Mr John Mcmathes minister of Leswaid who was at nursing in Caringtoun As also killed a daughter of John Whyts coylyier[17] ther, The deponer denyes that shoe had any hand in the death of the said William Lainge then hir master for shoe was not then ingadged in the Divills \service/ and what accession his wyffe Hellen Laing or any uthers had in his death the deponer knowes not, Confesses that shoe with many uther witches viz. Kathrine Halyday mother of the chyld, Hellen Laing, Sara Cranstoun, Margaret Russell, Margaret Balenden wer all present at the contriveing of the chylds death who was daughter of the said Katherin Halyday and William Hair hir husband.

[*Signed:*] James Liddill, Ja: Calderwood, Ro: Hepburne, John Pringall.[18]
Turne over. {*p. 4*}

At Peastoun[19] the 29 of June 1678 Followes the free and voluntar confession of Hellen Laing in Pestoun without any torture or threatning And quhilk

[12] In margin: 'X the deponer did soe'.
[13] 'wafe': wave.
[14] 'dewing': a sprinkling of dew or water.
[15] After a woman gave birth she would refrain from church attendance for a few weeks. Her formal return to the congregation after this seclusion was known as 'kirking'.
[16] Perhaps this originally read 'Margart Balenden the said (name of person's) servant'.
[17] 'coylyier' (collier): coal-miner.
[18] About two further signatures have been torn away at the foot of the page.
[19] In margin: 'Hellen Laing'.

confession she deponed in presence of Sir Robert Hepburne of Keith, Mr John Sinclar minister at Ormestoun, John Ker in Windymaines, David Chalmer in Keith, William Cockburne schoolmaster ther and wryter heirof, James Liddell in Pestoun, George Haliday ther, James Cairnintoune ther and Johne Adamsone schoollmaster there As followes viz.

First the said Hellen Laing depones that about seven yeirs since or therby the Divell did appear to hir in hir own yeard in Pestoun in the shape of ane black man and remembers not what he did or spoke to hir at that tyme, Depones that about a yeir therafter the Divell appeared to hir in the Ward Burn in the former shape of a black man with black cloathes and that then at his desire she did renunce hir baptisme and depones that then ther was severall women present bot that she knew none of them except Marion Campbell and Margreat Dods, Depones that therafter she had another meiting with the Divell at the Black Faugh and that there was severall women ther bot she knew none of them except the saids Marion Campbell and Margreat Dods, Denys that she remembers[20] of any uther meitings that she had with the Divell and denys that ever the Divell had any carnall copulation with hir, denys that ever she did see any other persons at meitings with the Divell but the two women above named and denys that she did any wrong to William Laing hir husband or to any uther persons or that she knowes that any uther persons did wrong aither to men women or beasts, denys that the Divell gave her any new name when she renunced hir baptisme, and the deponer being confronted with the saids Marion Campbell, Marion Veitch and Issobell Elliot the forenamed three confessing witches who affirmed the haile particulars in the deponers face contained in ther depositiones against hir the deponer denyed them all and confessed nothing of hir dealing with the Divell except the particulars abovespecifeit now confessed be the deponer.

[*Signed:*] James Kairingtoun, Da: Chalmer, Ro: Hepburne, John Adamsone, WCockburne, James Liddil, Jo: Sinclar, George Halliday, John Ker.

JC26/49, bundle 11, no. 2.

{*p. 1*} At Pestoun[21] the 29 of June 1678 Followes the free and voluntar confession of Margreat Russell in Pestoun without any torture or threatning And quhilk confession she deponed in presence of Sir Robert Hepburne of Keith, Mr Johne Sinclar minister at Ormestoun, Johne Ker in the Windymaines, David Chalmer in Keith, William Cockburne schoolmaster and wryter heirof, James Lyddell in Pestoun, George Haliday ther, James Cairingtoune ther, John Adamsone schoolmaster ther As followes viz. First the said Margreat Russell confesses that four yeirs and a halfe since or ther by the deponer with Marion

20 'not' crossed out here.
21 In margin: 'Margreat Russell'.

Campbell being coming from Seatoun to Wintoun ther appeared to them ane black grim man who kissed Marion Campbell and that the said Marion told the deponer that it was the Divell and that then at the Divells desire the deponer renunced hir baptisme and when she did it he caused hir put hir hands over the crown of hir head and hir other hand at the sole of hir foot, depones that this was done in the day tyme in the afternoone, denys that ever the Divell had any carnal dealing with the deponer, denys also that ever the deponer had any other meitings with the Divell except the tyme and place forsaid quher he caused hir renunce her baptisme, denys that the Divell gave hir a new name when she renunced hir baptisme, denys that ever the deponer did any wrong to man woman or beast, denyes that the deponer knowes any other persones to be guilty of witchcraft except the said Marion Campbell.

[*Signed:*] Da: Chalmer, Ro: Hepburne, James Kairingtoun, WCockburne, Johne Adamsone, James Liddill, Jo: Sinclar, George Halliday, John Ker.

At Pestoun[22] the first day of July 1678 Followes the free and voluntar confession of Margreat Dods in Pestoun without any torture or threatning. The said Margreat Dods confessis that about three yeirs since or therby the Divell appeared to hir in hir own house in Pestoun in the night tyme when she was in hir bed and that at the Divells desire the deponer did renunce hir baptisme and that he caused hir put on[e] of hir hands over the crown of hir head and the other hand to hir knee because she was not able to put it to the sole of hir foot and that she gave over to the Divell all that was betwixt hir two hands depones that the nixt tyme the Divell appeared to hir was at the rowting[23] stair above Olestob she being going to the Panns with her crele[24] on hir back and eggs in it and that the Divell there had carnall copulation with the deponer and that his nature was cold and that he had no breath. Depones that therafter the deponer was at a meiting at the Murraisburne bot the deponer did not sie the Divell ther and that ther was present at the said meiting Hellen Laing, Sara Cranstoun and hir servant and Margaret Banantine, Marion Veitch, Margreat Russell and Margreat Swan in Fala, depones they had a piper and that they all danced bot the deponer was not able to dance, denys that ever the deponer had any other meitings except as is above deponed, denyes that ever she did sie any other persones at meitings or dealing with the Divell or that ever she did sie any other persons at meitings except as is above deponed, denyes that ever she did any harm to man woman beast or goods, and quhilk depositione forsaid is taken in presence of Sir Robert Hepburne of Keith, James Yule in Keith, William Symson ther William Cockburne schoolmaister

22 In margin: 'Margreat Dods'.

23 'rowting': noisy.

24 'crele' (creel): large basket.

ther and wryter heirof, Alexander Ramsay in Pestoun James Lydell ther and John Adamsone schoolmaister ther.

[*Signed:*] WCockburne, Ro: Hepburne, James Liddeill, Johne Adamsone, Ja: Yule, William Simsone, Alexr Ramsay. Turne over. {*p. 2*}

At Peastoun And Templehall the first day of July 1678 yeirs the quhilk day In presence of Sir Robert Hepburne of Keith, Johne Pringall of Woodhead, Mr James Calderwood minister at Ormestoun,[25] Mr James Calderwood minister at Humbie, Mr John Mcmath minister at Leswad, Mr James Cockburne minister at Pencaitland And Mr George Moody minister at Fala. The depositiones of the Confessing witches afternamed viz. Marion Campbell hir deposition 19 of Junii last Issobell Eliot hir deposition 27 Junii last Hellen Lainge and Margaret Russell their depositiones of the 29 Junii Last and Margaret Dodds hir deposition takin this day being all read to the fornamed ministers and gentlemen abovenamed the saids fyve weemen did all adhear to and acknouledge their saids former depositions and declared the same to be treuth only Mr James Calderwood nor the said Mr George Moody was not not [*sic*] present at Temple hall quhen the said Issobell Eliot hir deposition was read to hir bot wer present at the uther four in Peastoun quhich premissis the forenamed Gentlemen and minister testifies to be trew by their subscriptiones day yeir and places forsaids.

[*Signed:*] Jo: Macmath, Ro: Hepburne, GMoodie, John Pringall, Ja: Calderwood, Ja: Cokburne.

At Keith the first day of July 1678 yeirs The which day Marion Veitch in Keith confessing witch being again called In presence of Sir Robert Hepburne of Keith, Mr James Calderwood minister of the paroch and Mr George Muddy minister at Fala and the said Marion hir former depositiones daited the 21 and 27 dayes of Junii last being all read over to hir the said Marion Veitch did adhere to all the points of hir said former depositiones and declared the same to be truth as witnesses thir presents subscrived be the fornamed persones day yeir and place forsaid.

[*Signed:*] Ja: Calderwood, Ro: Hepburne, GMoodie.

JC26/49, bundle 11, no. 4.

[*Endorsed:*] Depositione of Margreat Russell in Pestoun And Margreat Dods ther, Elspet Knox, Jennet Burtoun.[26]

[25] *Sic.* The minister of Ormiston was John Sinclair.

[26] This endorsement evidently relates not only to this document but also to the document printed above as no. 2, containing the confessions of Margaret Russell and Margaret Dodds. Evidently the two documents were folded together. Marion Veitch's name has been omitted, presumably by mistake.

{*p. 1*} At Keith[27] the 9 day of July 1678 yeirs Followes the third deposition of Marion Veitch in Keith freely confest in presence of Sir Robert Hepburne of Keith, John Pringall of Woodhead, Mr James Calderwood minister at Humby and Mr James Cockburne minister at Pencaitland. The said Marion Veitch depones that Agnes Thomsone and Elspeth Wood both in Over Keith and Barbara Howden in Saltoune Mylnehill and Elspet Knox spouse to Andro Smyth in Nether Keith were all four of them at severall meitings with the Divell quher the deponer was present, to witt at Keith Bridge the Corsshill and the Waird Haugh and that she did sie the saids four women at the saids meitings and the said Marion Veitch adheres to hir two former confessions dated 22 and 27 June last In witnes of the truth quherof this hir confession is subscrivit be the two gentle men and two ministers abovenamed day yeir and place forsaid.

[*Signed:*] Ja: Calderwoode, John Pringall, Ro: Hepburne, Ja: Cokburne.

At Keith[28] the said 9 of July 1678 upon the said Marion Veitch hir delating of the said Elspeth Knox. The said Elspeth Knox was presently called for and examined be the two gentle men and two ministers abovenamed and the uther persones undersubscribing therto and the first inquiring the said Elspeth Knox did freely and voluntarly confess that about two yeirs since the deponer being coming from Ormestoun to Keith and night falling on the deponer did ly doune and sleep at Keith Bankfallds and that the said Marion Veitch in bodyly liknes did waken the deponer and take hir up and brought the Divell to the deponer and set him down beside the deponer and that the Divell did nothing to the deponer at that tyme and that Jennet Burtoun servant of Sarra Cranstoun was also then present whom the deponer left with the Divell togither with the said Marion Veitch, depones that about eight weiks therafter the deponer had a meiting with the Divell in the Waird Haugh and that then the Divell had carnall copulation with hir and was havie like a horse and that his nature was cold, and that then at the Divells desire the deponer did renunce hir baptisme and that he caused hir put on[e] of hir hands over the crown of hir head and hir other hand under the sole of hir foot and that she gave over to the Divell all that was betwixt hir hands And that the Divell gave hir a new name and called hir Lady Knox, depones ther was present at the said last meiting the said Marion Veitch, Jennet Burtoun, Margreit Andersone in Ormestoun and Jennet Huntur then in Ormestoun and Jennet Maitland in Hielie.

Followes[29] the free and voluntar confession of Jennet Burtoun servant to Sara Cranstoun in Keith deponed be hir day yeir and place forsaid In presence

27 In margin: 'Marion Veitch'.
28 In margin: 'Elspeth Knox'.
29 In margin: 'Jennet Burtoun'.

of the gentle men and Ministers above named and uther witnesses under subscryving, the said Jennet Burtoun depones that about two yeirs since the deponer being in hir bed that the said Sara Cranstoun hir mistris raised hir out of hir bed and told hir that she behoved to speak with a gentle man and brought hir to the hall quher the deponer saw a black grim man who took the deponer in his armes and kissed hir and did no more that night, Depones that the nixt night when the deponer was going to bed the Divell came again and brought hir to the hall chimney and that ther he had carnall copulation with hir and told hir that she behoved to be his servant when he called for hir quhik she promissed to him, depones that about 14 dayes therafter Sara Cranstoun hir mistris did take the deponer to the Reid Foord to a meiting with the Divell quher the Divell caused the deponer to renunce hir baptisme and put hir one hand over the crown of hir head and the other under the sole of hir foot and that she delivered over to the Divell all that was betwixt hir hands and that the Divell gave hir a new name and called hir Saras Drudge, depones that ther was present at the said meiting Sara Cranstoun, Marion Veitch, Marion Campbell, Hellen Laing, Kathrin Haliday, Margreit Russell, Margreit Banantyne, Issobell Elliot, Margreat Dods, Walter Spence wyfe in Pestoun and William Allanes mother in Pestoun and Jennet Maitland in Hielie.

[*Signed:*] Ja: Cokburne, Ja: Calderswoode, John Pringall, Ro: Hepburne. Turn over. {*p. 2*}

Farder the said Jennet Burtoun confesses she was at some other meitings with the Divell at Ormestoun wood, the Lint Haugh and the Ward Haugh and that she knew no other persones that were at the saids meitings with the persones aforenamed, depones that about five or six weiks since the said Sara Cranstoun did burst and ryde to death ane horse of hir own eldest sone Johne Andersones and took the horse out to meitings, depones that Marion Veitch took hir own oye[30] Marion Thomsone a child of a yeir old and gifted hir to the Divell in hir fathers William Thomsone house in Templhall and that ther was present the deponer hir selfe and all the rest that the deponer hes delated and that the child dyed within eight dayes therafter. In witnes of the truth the saids two persons to wit Elspet Knox and Jennet Burtoun ther confessions beforewritten the samyne are attested and subscrived be the two gentle men and two ministers above named as also be David Chalmer, James Yule, Malchome Grive and William Shieill all in Keith, Johne Fowler at Humbiemylne, Richard Dalglish in Woodhead and William Cockburne schoolmaster at Keith wryter heirof.

[*Signed:*] Jas: Calderwood, R: Hepburne, Da: Chalmer, Ja: Cokburne, John Pringall, Ja: Yule, Malchom Grive, Willeam Sheill, WCockburne, Richard Dalglies.

30 'oye': grandchild.

JC26/49, bundle 11, no. 3.

[*Endorsed:*] Confession Agnes Dalgleish in Keith.

At Keith[31] the 30 day of July 1678 yeirs The quhilk day Marion Veitch in Keith and Elspeth Knox ther, two confessing witches, declared, not being desired of any persone, that Margreat Cowper spouse to James Moffat in Keith, Agnes Dalgleish spouse to Thomas Thomsone in Keith and Jennet Wilsone spouse to James Dewar in the Birks, were all three at severall meitings with the Divell where the saids two deponers were present, to wit at the Waird Haugh the Cowburne and the Reidford all within thir two yeiris. Lykeas the said Elspeth Knox declared that the hen wyfe in Woodheid who is wyfe to a webster ther was also at the saids three meitings, Lykeas the saids Margreat Cowper and Agnes Dalglish being presently confronted with the saids Marion Veitch and Elspeth Knox they did confidently affirm in ther faces the truth of the premissis and the saids uther two women delated did peremptorly[32] deny the same, this was done day yeir and place forsaid in presence of Sir Robert Hepburne of Keith, Alexander Ramsay in Pestoun, James Yule, William Sheill and William Cockburne wryter heirof all indwellers in Keith as witnesses ther subscriptiones heirto.

[*Signed:*] Alexr Ramsay witnes, Ja: Yule, WCockburne, Ro: Hepburne, Willeam Sheil.

The said Agnes Dalglish[33] above delated being reexamined in presence of Sir Robert Hepburne of Keith, Mr Johne Sinclar minister at Ormestoun, Mr James Calderwood minister at Humby, Mr James Cockburne minister at Pencaitland and the uther persones undersubscryving did freely and voluntarly without any threatning or violence done to hir confess that before Witsonday last the deponer being in the house of Sara Cranstoun in Keith there appeared to the deponer ane black grim man with black cloathes in the day tyme about two afternoone and that ther was none present bot the said Sara, and the Divell did then first kiss the deponer and that his mouth was ase cold as Lead and that he had no breath and that then the Divell had carnall copulation with the deponer and that he was monstrous heavie and exceeding cold and that at the Divells desire the deponer did renunce hir baptisme and the Divell caused hir to put on[e] of hir hands over the crown of hir head and hir other hand under the sole of hir foot and that at the Divells comand she did give over to him all that was betwixt hir two hands and that the Divell gave hir a new name to witt Eppie. Depones that Sara Cranstoun at first did take the deponer be the hand and did put hir hand in the Divells hand and that his hand was

31 In margin: 'Marion Veitch'.

32 'peremptorly': firmly.

33 In margin: 'Agnes Dalgleish hir confession'.

cold like Lead, Depones that therafter Sara Cranstoun did take the deponer out of hir bed at midnight and did take hir over to Saras foredore wher the Divill was and that the Divell did then do nor speak nothing to the deponer bot asked how shee did. And farder confesses that since the tymes forsaid the deponer in the night tyme was carryed to two meitings at the Cowburne and the Manispark burne and that she thought there was about ane hundreth persones at the saids meitings wherof the deponer knew none bot the said Sara Cranstoun who was muzeled[34] and Grissell Walker and David Johnstouns mother now a fugitive, depones that they all danced about ane hour bot the deponer denyes that she saw the Divell at the saids meitings. Marion Veitch a confessing witch depones also that she did sie the said Grissel Walker at the saids two meitings with the said David Johnstouns mother. In witnes quherof the forsaid confession is attested and subscrivit be the abovenamed and undersubscryving persons day yeir and place forsaid.

[*Signed:*] Ja: Calderwood, Ro: Hepburne, Jo: Sinclar, Ja: Cokburne, Willeam Sheil, WCockburne.

JC26/49, bundle 11, no. 6.

[*Endorsed:*] List of Assyse against Witches 1678

List of assyse against Marion Veitch and other witches, 7 September 1678

Patrick Backbie in Samuelstoun
p Robert Selkirk merchand in Edinburgh
p Robert Pringle in Templehall
d James Selkirk merchand in Edinburgh
p John Hempseid in Murrays
p Thomas Gray merchand in Edinburgh Netherbowe
p William Henryson in Ormestoun
p Thomas Fisher elder taylor in Edinburgh
p Robert Fouler in Overkeith
p James Sympson merchand in Edinburgh
p George Robertson in Wintoun

p Richard Lothian merchand ther
p Mr Alexander Paterson merchand ther
p John Selkirk merchand ther
p William Lawson merchand ther
p James Warrock merchand ther
Robert Hamilton elder in the bowe
p Henry Barclay baxter ther
d William Johnstoun elder skinner ther
d Hugh Blair merchand ther
p Robert Brown stationer ther
p John Broun merchand at the baxters close head

[34] 'muzeled': muffled.

p Robert Hogg ther
d James Edmonstoun merchand in Edinburgh
p John Fouler in Humbie milne
p George Balfour merchand in Edinburgh
p James Paterson skinner ther
p John Adam merchand ther
p Alexander Layng whitiron man
William Mitchell elder baxter ther
p John Mcgill merchand
p George Monteith merchand ther
p James Dixson merchand ther
p Alexander Hume his Majesties taylor
p Alexander Wilson hamerman in Cannogate
p William Bruce baxter ther
p John Howieson brewer in Potterrawe
p David Howieson merchand in Edinburgh
d John McLurge merchand ther
p James Ardbuckles elder merchand ther
d William Brown skinner ther
p Thomas Kincaid skinner ther
p John Paterson cordoner ther
p James Tait merchand ther

JC26/49, bundle 11, unnumbered document.[35]

[*Endorsed:*] Testificat for the burneing of four witches in Peastoun moore, 20 September 1678.

Wee undersubscrivers To Witt William Baylie of Lammingtoun, Adame Cokburne of Ormestoun, William Cuninghame of Enterkine younger, David Hepburne of Randerstoune, Mr Robert and George Cokburnes uncles to Ormestoun, William Borthwick of Jonstounburne, Johne Belshes of that Ilk, Mr John Sinclar minister at Ormestoun, Mr James Calderwood minister at Humby, Mr Robert Spootswood minister at Crightoun, Mr James Cokburne minister at Pancaitland, Mr George Moodie minister at Fala and Mr James Griersone reader at Ormistoun,

Be thir presents testifie and declar to the honorable Lords of his Majesties Justiciarie That conforme To and in obedience of ther sentence of death pronunced upon the threttine day of September Instant ordeineing Issobel Elliott, Marion Vaitch, Margaret Dodds and Hellen Lainge as found guyltie be ane assyse of the cryme of witchcraft To be takin to Peastoun moore this Fryday the tuentie of September Instant betuixt two and four a cloak in the afternoon and ther to be strangled at a staike till they be dead And therafter ther bodies to be burned to ashes, We the forenamed persones under subscrivers do testifie that we wer all present at, and did see and wer ey witnesses to, the putting of the forsaid sentence and doome of death to due execution upon the bodies of the four witches abovenamed named at the tyme day and place abovementioned and conforme to the forsaid doome and sentence abovementioned in all poynts, In witnes of the treuth of the premises Wee the

[35] This document has been stitched to document number 1, printed below. A version of it has been printed in *RPC*, 3rd ser., vi, 627–8.

fornamed persones have subscrived thir presents with our hands at Peastoun Moore the said tuentie day of September $I^{m}vi^{c}$ Sevintie eight yeirs.

[*Signed:*] Wm Borthwick, Ad: Cokburne, WBaillie of Lammington, RHepburne, WCunninghame, Ja: Calderwood, Jo: Sinclar, Ja: Cokburne minr, GCokburne, Rot. Spotiswood, Johne Belsis, GMoodie, Ro: Cokburne, JGrierson.

JC26/49, bundle 11, no. 1.

[*Endorsed:*] Supplicatioun, Sir Robert Hepburne off Keith and Jon Pringill off Wodheid.

Unto the Lord Justice Generall And the remanent Lords of his Majesties Justiciarie The humble Supplication of Sir Robert Hepburne of Keith And John Pringall of Woodhead, Sheweth,

That wher Issobell Elliot, Marion Vaitch, Margarett Dodds and Hellen Lainge wer found be ane assayse To be guylty of the cryme of witchcraft And Therfor By your Lordships sentence and doome daited the 13 day of September Last 1678 yeirs wer decerned and ajudged by your Lordships To be takin to Peastoun Moore upon Fryday The 20 day of the said month of September Last Betwixt 2 and 4: a cloack in the afternoon, And ther to be strangled at a staik till they be dead And therafter ther bodyes to be brunt to ashes, Lykas your Lordships did Comand us your Lordships supplicants to see the said sentence and doome put to due execution As we should be Answerable, Lykas your Lordships clerk Mr Robert Martein did Then Take our band To se the forsaid sentence put to due execution under the paine of Ten Thousand merks, According to the quhich doome and sentence We did cause execute the same upon the saids 4 witches At the place day and houre abovewrytin As the Testificat Submittit be a number of barrons gentlemen ministers and uthers that wer ey witnessis therto heirwith produced does testifie,

Theirfoir we humbly beseich your Lordships To ordeine The said Mr Robert Martine your Clerk To give up and delyver to us our band forsaid To be cancelled Seing we have punctually observed and obeyed your Lordships order and Comand forsaid Theranent And your Lordships Answer.

Edinburgh 4 December 1678

The Lords grant the desyre of this bill and ordaines the petitioners bond to be delivered up.

[*Signed:*] Geo: McKenzie.

Edinburgh 2 Januar 1679

Receaved be me the band above mentioned to be cancelled Conforme to the ordor abovewrittin.

[*Signed:*] Ro: Hepburne.

Source 2: NRS, Court of Justiciary, Books of Adjournal, 1678–1682, JC2/15.

{*fo. 17v.*} *Curia justiciarie Supremi Domini Nostri Regis tenta in pretorio burgi de Edinburgh decimo tertio die mensis Septembris 1678 per honorabiles viros Dominos Jacobum Foulis de Colintoun Robertum Nairne de Strathurd Joannem Lockhart de Castlehill Davidem Balfour de Forret et Davidem Falconer de Newtoun Commissionarios justiciarie dicti Supremi Domini Nostri Regis. Curia legittime affirmata.*[36]

Colintoun preses

Intran[37]
Isobell Eliott
Marion Veatch
Margaret Dods
Helen Laying
Margaret Lowis
Isobell Shank
Margaret Douglas
Helen Forrester
Margaret Smaill
Christian Hogger
prisoners for the Cryme of Witchcraft[38]

Indyted and accused[39] That wher notwithstanding be the Lawe of God Lawe of nations and Lawe of practique of this kingdome and in speciall be the 73 act 9 parliament Queen Mary the Cryme of Witchcraft is declaired to be ane horrid abomination and Capitall Cryme punishable with the paines of death and confiscation of movables, Neverthelesse the haill fornamed persons have committed and are guiltie of the said Cryme in suae[40] fare as about tuo years since the said Isobell Eliot being then servant to Helen Laying in Peastoun ane witch ye at her desyre stayed at home from the kirk and wes present at a meiting with the Divill, the said Helen Laying and Marion Campbell witches in the said Helens house wher the Divill kissed you and offered to lye with

[36] 'Court of justiciary of our sovereign lord the king, held in the tolbooth of the burgh of Edinburgh, 13 September 1678, by the honourable men James Foulis of Colinton, Robert Nairn of Strathurd, John Lockhart of Castlehill, David Balfour of Forret and David Falconer of Newton, commissioners of justiciary of our said sovereign lord the king. Court legally fenced.'

[37] In margin: 'Lord Advocat against Witches'.

[38] In margin: 'Lord advocat against witches'.

[39] In margin: 'The dittay'.

[40] 'suae': so.

you and caused you renunce your baptisme and baptised you upon the face with ane waff of his hand like a dewing calling you Jean and ye being then with child the Divill did forbear to lye with you but efter ye wer kirked the Divill hade carnall copulation with you and since that tyme ye have hade severall meitings with the Divill and severall witches and hes hade many tymes carnall copulation with him and sicklyke ye were present with Katharin Halyday, Helen Laying, Sarah Cranstoun and severall other witches at the contryving of the death of [*1 word blank*] Hair daughter to the said Katharin Halyday and William Hair her husband.

Ye the said Marion Veitch are guiltie of the said Cryme of witchcraft in suae fare as about the end of the year 1650 or the begining of the year 1651 ye did enter to the Divills service, And about that time ye being brought to the Reidfoord be umquhile Barbara Veatch a witch, the Divill hade severall tymes copulation with you and caused you to renunce your {*fo. 18r.*} baptizme, which ye did by useing the detestable and abominable solemnitie of laying your on[e] hand on the crown of your head and the other upon the sole of your foot and giving all betwixt your tuo hands to the Divill the enemie of your salvation, Lykeas the Divill gave you a new name and called you broad back and requyred you to doe him service in destroying your nighbours and blaspheming the name of the Lord, the whilk (ye confesse) God would not permitt you to doe, and the nixt meiting ye hade with the Divill wes in Ormiestoun wood wher Helen Laying and Margaret Dods witches and severall others were present and danced with the Divill, and ye hade bein present at many meitings with the Divill and severall witches these twentie sevin years bypast and particularlie ye wer present as a witch with the said Helen Laying when she and Isobell Eliot her servant did kill and murder William Laying spouse to the said Helen, and ye are accessorie to and airt and part of the said murder and of the horrid and unnaturall murder commited be you and severall other witches upon the person of [*1 word blank*] Thomson daughter to William Thomson your own son by socerie, witchcraft and necromancy upon the [*1 word blank*] day of [*1 word blank*] years, and sicklyke ye wer at severall meitings with the Divill and Agnes Thomson, Elspeth Wood, Barbara Howdoun and Elspeth Knox and severall other witches in diverse and sundrie places and particularlie at Keith bridge, the Corsehill and the Ward Haugh.[41]

And sicklyke ye the said Margaret Dods are guiltie of the said Cryme of Witchcraft in suae fare as about three years since or therby the Divill appeared to you in your own house in Peastoun in the night tyme when ye wer in bed, and then at the Divills desyre ye did renunce your baptisme by putting on[e] of your hands over the crown of your head and the other hand to your knee ye not being able to putt it to the sole of your foot and ye gave over to the Divill all that wes betwixt your tua hands, and the nixt tyme the Divill appeared to

[41] 'haugh': a piece of low-lying land by a river.

you at the routing stair above Elistob when ye hade carnall copulation with the Divill, and sicklyke ye hade a meiting with Helen Laying, Sarah Cranstoune and her servant and severall other witches at the Murraisburne wher they hade a pyper and they all danced but ye wer not able to dance.

As alse the said Helen Laying are guiltie of the said Cryme of Witchcraft in suae fare as about sevin years since or therby the Divill appeared to you in your own yaird in Peastoun in the shape of the blackman, and a year therefter he appeared to you in the Ward Burne in the same shape and then at his desyre ye did renunce your baptisme, at whilk tyme Marion Campbell and Margaret Dods and severall other witches wer present, And therefter ye hade another meiting with the Divill and the forsaids witches at the Black Haugh, and ye are guiltie accessorie to and airt and part of the murder of William Laying your husband committed in the moneth of [*1 word blank*] I^{m}VI^{c} [*1 word blank*] years by socerie, witchcraft and necromancie, and of severall other malefices.

And ye the saids Margaret Douglas, Margaret Smaill, Helen Forester, Margaret Lowis, Isobell Shanks and Christian Hoger are guiltie of the said Cryme of Witchcraft in suae fare as ye have entered in paction with the Divill the enemie of your salvation and have renunced our blissed Lord and Saviour and your baptizmes and have given your selves both soulls and bodie to the Divill by useing the abominable and detestable solemnitie of putting on[e] of your hands upon the crown of your head and the other upon the sole of your feet, and have bein at severall meitings with the Divill and sundrie other witches and particularlie of late at the Barliehill and Woodhead of Crightoun wher ther wer great danceing and playing {*fo. 18v.*} with pypes, Wherthrowe the persons abovecompleaned upon and ilk ane of them have committed and are guiltie of the said horrid and abominable cryme of witchcraft and are airt and part of the samen, the whilk being found be ane assyse they ought to be punished with the paines of death and confiscation of movables to the terror and example of others to committ the like herefter.

The Lords finds the dittays Relevant and Remitts the same to the knowledge of the assyse.

The Lords with consent of his Majesties advocat deserts the dyet[42] as to Christian Hoger.

Assisa

Robert Pringle in Templehall
John Hempseed in Morris
Thomas Gray merchant in Edinburgh
William Henryson in Ormiestoun
Thomas Fisher elder taylor
Robert Fouler in Overkeith
James Symson merchant in Edinburgh
John Fouler in Humbiemilne
James Paterson skinner
John Adam merchant

[42] 'deserts the dyet': abandons the prosecution.

James Warrock merchant
Alexander Wilson hammerman
Henry Barclay baxter
Alexander Laying whitironman[43]
Thomas Kincaid skinner

The assyse lawfullie sworne no objection[44] in the contrair His Majesties advocat for probation adduced[45] the pannalls ther own judiciall Confessions underwritten, wherof the tenor followes. Edinburgh the Elevinth of September I^{m}VI^{c} and sevintie eight, The said day in presence of the Lords Commissioners of justiciarie sittand in judgement, Compeired Margaret Douglas in Crightoun and declaires that ther falling some difference betwixt her and her daughter about thretein years agoe the Divill appeared to her and promised to her ane revenge of her daughter and caused her renunce her baptisme and give her self over to the Divill both soull and bodie by putting on[e] of her hands to the crown of her head and the other at the sole of her foot, and declaires she wes at severall meitings with the Divill and particularlie at ane meiting at the Birliehill wher wer present severall witches and that they danced, declaires she cannot wreitt.

Margaret Lowis declaires that about Elevin years agoe a man whom she thought to be ane English man that cured diseases in the countrey called [*1 word blank*] Webb appeared to her in her own house and gave her a drink and told her shoe would have children efter the taking of that drink, and declaires that that man made her renunce her baptisme and that therefter he hade carnall copulation with her, and declaires that she thought that the man who made her doe these things wes the Divill and that she hes hade severall meitings with that man efter she knewe him to be the Divill, declaires that at ther meitings she sawe great numbers of people, declaires she cannot wreitt.

Margaret Smaill prisoner being examined anent the Cryme of witchcraft depones that having come to the house of Jannet Borthvick in Crightoun she sawe a Gentleman sitting with her and they desyred her to sitt doun and having sitten doun the gentleman drank to her and she drank to him and therefter the said Jannet Borthvick told her that that Gentleman wes the Divill, and declaires that at his desyre she renunced her {*fo. 19r.*} baptisme and gave her self to the Divill by putting on[e] of her hands to the crown of her head and the other to the sole of her foot, and declaires she hes bein at severall meitings with the Divill and particularlie at the Birliehill of late, declaires it is ten years since she entered to the Divills service, declaires she desyres not to live because no bodie will converse with her seing she is under the reputation of a witch, declaires she keept the kirk all the tyme and prayed and took the sacrament when she hade occasion except once when she wes at fead[46] with her neighbour.

[43] 'whitironman': metal-worker working with tin-plate.
[44] In margin: 'The probation'.
[45] 'adduced': quoted.
[46] 'fead': feud.

Isobell Eliot in Templehall declaires that tuo years since the Divill appeared to her in Helen Layings house in Peastoun sitting betwixt the said Helen Laying and Marion Campbell and the Divill laid hands on her and made her renunce her baptizme and give her self over to him by laying on[e] of her hands on the crown of her head and the other on the sole of her foot, and declaires therefter the Divill hade carnall copulation with her, declaires she wes at many meitings with the Divill and particularlie at Crightoun wher ther wer many witches present and a flaming fyre, and declaires the Divill gave them a kind of sacrament and preached amongst them and blasphemed God, and declaires she wes present at the poysouning of William Thomsons child who wes poysouned by Marion Veatch and the childs grand mother and declaires that she and the said Marion Veatch wer in the shape of Bume bees[47] when the child wes poysouned and that Marion Veatch caryed the poyson in her cleuchs[48] wings and mouth, declaires she left her bodie in Pencaitland kirk and went in the shape of a corbie[49] to Leswade, Loanhead to see a child which she nursed to William Ramsay ther, declaires she cannot wreitt.

Marion Veatch spouse to George Thomson in Keith being brought in presence of the Lords Commissioners of justiciarie and examined anent the Cryme of Witchcraft, confesses that in anno I^{m}VI^{c} and sextie tuo she entered to the Divills service at the desyre of Barbara Veatch her aunt who caryed her to the feilds wher she mett with the Divill, and confesses that the Divill hade carnall copulation with her and made her renunce her baptizme by putting on[e] of her hands to the crown of her head and the other to the sole of her foot, Confesses that at the Divills desyre she destroyed her own grand child Marion Thomson daughter to Willam Thomson in Templehall by poysoning the said child, and declaires Marion Campbell and Isobell Eliot wer present and Jannet Burtoun, declaires she hade meitings with the Divill at the Cowe Burne and Ward Haugh, and declaires she cannot wreitt.

Helen Laying in Peastoun confesses that sevin years since the Divill appeared to her in her own yaird in Peastoun and a year therefter he appeared to her in the Ward Burne and that ther she renunced her baptizme at the Divills desyre and therefter hade a meiting with the Divill at the Blackhaugh, denys that she is guilty of any malefice or wronging any person, declaires she cannot wreitt.

Margaret Dods confesses and declaires that the Divill first appeared to her in her own house betwixt her bed and the fyre and desyred her to renunce her baptizme, which she did and gave her self to the Divill by putting on[e] of her hands to her head and the other to her knee, and that three years agoe she hade a meiting with the Divill at Templehall burne wher ther were severall witches present viz. Marion Campbell, Margaret {*fo. 19v.*} Ballentyne,

47 'Bume bees': bumblebees.

48 'cleuchs': presumably claws. For discussion see Julian Goodare, 'Flying Witches in Scotland', in Julian Goodare (ed.), *Scottish Witches and Witch-Hunters* (Basingstoke, 2013), 159–76, at p. 174.

49 'corbie': raven.

Katharin Halyday and Marion Veatch wher they all danced but the declarant could not dance, declaires she cannot wreitt.

Helen Forrester in Crightoun Confesses that she wes at ane meiting with the Divill at the Birliehill wher ther wer a great many witches present but knowes not howe she went nor howe she came, Confesses that she renunced her baptisme and promised to be the Divills servant, declaires she wes at a meiting at the Westwoodhead wher there wes danceing and mirth, declaires the Divill never lay with her nor marked her nor gave her ane name.

The whilk haill Confessions abovewritten wer this day judiciallie renewed and adhered to in presence of the assyse and are severallie subscryved thus.

[*Signed:*] APrimerose, JFoulis, Ro: Nairne, JoLockhart, David Balfour, DaFalconar.

Efter leading and adduceing of the whole probation[50] the persons of assyse abovenamed removed altogither furth of court to the assyse house wher having reasoned and voted upon the points and articles of the dittay and probation abovewritten and being therwith well and ryplie[51] advised they reentered againe in court and returned ther verdict in presence of the saids Lords wherof the tenor followes. The assyse all in on[e] voice be the mouth of James Paterson ther Chancelar Find Margaret Douglas in Crightoun, Margaret Lowis, Margaret Smell, Isobell Eliot, Helen Veatch spouse to George Thomson in Keith, Helen Laying in Peastoun, Margaret Dods, Isobell Shanks in Crightoun, Helen Forrester ther, pannalls, all guiltie of the Cryme of witchcraft In respect they have all confest paction with the Divill and renunceing ther baptism.

Sic subscribitur[52] James Paterson chancelar.

Efter oppining and reading[53] the whilk verdict of assyse, The Lords Commissioners of justiciarie be the mouth of Adam Auld dempster of court decerned and adjudged Margaret Lowis, Isobell Shanks, Margaret Douglas, Helen Forrester and Margaret Smaill to be taken to the Gallowlie of Edinburgh upon Wedensday the eighteint day of September instant betwixt tuo and four aclock in the efternoon and ther to be strangled at a stake till they be dead and therefter to have ther bodies burnt to ashes, And alse be the mouth of the said Adam Auld dempster decerned and adjudged the saids Isobell Eliot, Marion Veatch, Margaret Dods and Helen Laying to be taken to Paistoun Muir upon Fryday nixt the tuentie day of this instant betwixt tuo and four aclock in the efternoon and ther to be strangled at ane stake till they be dead and therefter ther bodies to be burnt to ashes, and all ther movable goods and gear to be escheat and imbrought to his Majesties use as being found guilty

50 In margin: 'The verdict of the assyse'.

51 'ryplie': carefully.

52 'Thus it is subscribed'.

53 In margin: 'The doom'.

by ane assyse of the Cryme of witchcraft mentioned in ther dittays, which wes pronunced for doom. {*fo. 20r.*}

The said day[54] the Lords ordained Mr Gideon Penman late minister of the gospell at Crightoun who is delated as guilty of the Cryme of witchcraft to find Caution for his appearance to underlye the Lawe for the said Cryme whenever he shall be cited upon a lawfull warning of fyftein dayes under the paine of fyve hundreth merks.

The said day[55] Marion Campbell spouse to William Logan in Paistoun, Grisell Walker spouse to Alexander Couper in Keith, Margaret Dalgleish spouse to Thomas Thomson ther, Margaret Anderson relict of umquhile Thomas Wauch in Ormiestoun, James Campbell in Winton, Margaret Russell in Paistoun, Elizabeth Wood in Overkeith, Elspeth Knox in Keith and Agnes Thomson in Overkeith being oft tymes called to have compeired befor the Lords Commissioners of justiciary this day and place in the hour of cause to have underlyen the Lawe for the Cryme of witchcraft committed be them as they who wer lawfullie cited for that effect lawfull tyme of day bidden, and they nor non of them enterand nor appeirand, The saids Lords therfor be the mouth of James Henryson macer of court decerned and adjudged them and ilk ane of them to be outlawes and fugitives frae his Majesties Lawes and ordained them to be putt to the horne and all ther movable goods and gear to be escheat and imbrought to our soveraigne Lords use, and pronunced for doom.

The said day[56] Alexander Hume his Majesties taylor being oft tymes called to have compeired befor the Lords Commissioners of justiciarie this day and place in the hour of cause to have past upon the assyse of Isobell Eliot and other witches as he who wes lawfullie enterand nor appeirand, The Lords Commissioners of justiciarie therfor be the mouth of Gilbert Mair macer of court decerned and adjudged the said Alexander Hume to be in ane unlawe and amerciament of ane hundreth merks conforme to the act of parliament which wes pronunced for doom. {*fo. 20v.*}

Curia justiciarie Supremi Domini Nostri Regis tenta in pretorio burgi de Edinburgh quarto die mensis Novembris 1678 per honorabilis viros Dominos Thomam Wallace de Craigie justiciarie clericum Robertum Nairn de Strathurd Davidem Balfour de Forret et Davidem Falconer de Newtoun Commissionarios justiciarie dicti Supremi Domini Nostri Regis.[57]

54 In margin: 'Mr Gideon Penman put under caution for witchcraft'.

55 In margin: 'Several witches declaired fugitives'.

56 In margin: 'Ane absent assyser unlawes'.

57 'Court of justiciary of our sovereign lord the king, held in the tolbooth of the burgh of Edinburgh, 4 November 1678, by the honourable men, lords Thomas Wallace of Craigie, justice clerk, Robert Nairn of Strathurd, David Balfour of Forret and David Falconer of Newton, commissioners of justiciary of our said sovereign lord the king'.

Intran[58]
Bessie Gourlie midwyff in Fala
Agnes Somervaill ther
Margaret Sonus ther

Indyted and accused that ther notwithstanding be the Lawe {*fo. 21r.*} of God particularlie sett doun in the twenty chapter of Leviticus and Eighteint Chapter of Deutronomie and be the Lawes and acts of parliament of this kingdome and constant practique therof particularlie be the 73 act 9 parliament Queen Mary, the Cryme of witchcraft is declaired to be ane horrid and abomination and capitall Cryme punishable with the paines of death and confiscation of movables, Netherthelesse it is of veritie that ye the saids Bessie Gourlie, Agnes Somervaill and Margaret Sonus have comitted and are guilty of the said Cryme of witchcraft, In sua fare as ye have entered in paction with the Divill the enemie of your salvation and have renunced our blissed Lord and Saviour and your baptismes and have given your services both soulls and bodies to the Divill by useing the abominable and detestable solemnitie of putting on[e] of your hands upon the crown of your head and other upon the sole of your feit, and have bein at severall meitings with the Divill and sundrie other witches, and particularlie at the Lindean and Whithouse at the back of Sarah Cranstouns yaird, at the Cowe Burne at Keith bridge, and tuenty dayes efter Whitsonday last ye hade a meting with the Divill at the back of the toun of Nether Keith and twentie dayes befor that ye hade another meiting with the Divill at the Ward Burne, And ye the said Agnes Somervaill hes bein a witch and the Divills servant thir twenty years bypast and above and hes hade carnall copulation with him severall tymes and particularly in the Heriot Boig, And ye the said Margaret Sonus hes bein the Divills servant threttie years agoe and upwards, and all of you have committed severall malefices and have occasioned the death and destruction of severall of his Majesties good subjects and of ther goods and cattell and particularlie ye by socerie and witchcraft occasioned the death of John Raes beasts in anno [*1 word blank*], Wherthrowe ye have committed and are guilty of the Cryme of Witchcraft, which being found be ane assyse ye and ilk ane of you ought to be punished with the paines of death and confiscation of movables to the terror of others to committ the like herefter.

Persewer
Sir George Mckenzie of Rosehaugh
our Soveraigne Lords advocat

The Lords find the dittay relevant and Remitts the same to the knowledge of the assyse viz:

[58] In margin: 'Lord advocat against witches Convict and burnt'.

William Beck merchant
Andrew Dunbar bookbinder
John Ramsay peutherer[59]
James West baxter
Andrew Brown watchmaker
Ritchard Pollock baxter
James Crawe baxter
Adam Blaikie vintner[60]
Thomas Weddell spurier[61]
Andrew Ker merchant
Mongo Beck merchant
John Berrie merchant
Robert Young wright[62]
James Gallie cordoner[63]
John Fleyming baxter

The assyse lawfullie sworne no objection in the Contrair.[64]

The persewer for probation adduced the pannalls ther own Confessions underwreittin.

The deposition of Bessie Gourlie on[e] of the confessing witches of Fala which she did depone voluntarlie without any violence offered or done to her Befor thir witnessis, Mr George Mudie minister at Fala, John Crightoun presenter[65] ther, Thomas Rae and Thomas Findleyson elders ther and John Findleyson tennent ther and Andrew Wallace weaver {*fo. 21v.*} ther and David Borthvick elder ther, Bessie Gourlie in Fala, being delated by Isobell Eliot in Templehall for severall malefices and Agnes Somervaill confessing witch in Fala, did Confesse that Sarah Cranstoun in Nether Keith did bring her on to be the Divills servant, she meiting on[e] tyme with her did promised to give her her daughter to be with her in child birth, Laird Skirvins Lady if she would doe her bidding, and did take her to the back of the yaird to meit with a Gentleman wher she sawe the Divill, and the said Sarah did promise to her that she should never want if she would be a servant to that Gentleman, she promised she should, efterward the said Sarah did take the Divill into her house and Bessie said what Gentleman is that, she said it is a gentleman come from my daughter out of the Lady syd, and Bessie said to him howe now Sir, howe is the goodman and the mistress and the bairne, the Divill said they are all well and Sarah promised to give the said Bessie a cheise but she never gave it. Farder she depones that she mett with the Divill at the Cowe Burne and another tyme at Keith bridge, as also that Sarah Cranstoun and Marion Veatch and Sarahs woman did come to Falla efter the sune sett, and

59 'peutherer': pewterer.
60 'vintner': wine merchant.
61 'spurier': spur-maker.
62 'wright': carpenter.
63 'cordoner': shoemaker.
64 In margin: 'The probation'.
65 'presenter': precentor, person appointed to lead the congregational singing in church.

Bessie went furth and Sarah wes at the end of her barne and did wage on the said Bessie with her finger, so the said Bessie went to her and she said, goe in with me, I refused but she said ye most goe, so I went with her up to the Whithouse to meit with the Divill wher he appeared to me, and at his desyre I did renunce my baptisme and did lay my on[e] hand on the crown of my head and the other on the sole of my foot and did delyver all up betwixt these tuo soull and body to the Divills service and the Divill did promise her that she should be well loved among women, and depones that it wes the greed of her imployment that ingadged her to the Divills service. Farder she depones that the last meiting she wes at wes tuenty dayes efter Whitsonday in this present year at the back of Nether Keith toun wher wes present Sarah Cranstoun, Marion Veatch and many others that she knewe not, and that Sarah Cranstoun hade a mask on her face and ane mantle about her and that Sarah said, nowe the witches will be taken but I will not confesse for I have bein long in his service but now I intend to leave it off. Farder she depones that about twentie dayes befor that she wes at ane meiting with the Divill at the Ward Burne goeing to this meiting efter sune sett when her husband and familie wer in ther beds and came back at midnight but she did not goe to her bed that night, Sara telling her when the meiting would be some dayes befor. This to be the true Confession is attested by the fornamed witnessis at Fala the sevinteint day of September I^{m}VI^{c} and sevintie eight years.

Sic subscribitur GMoodi witnes, John Crichtoun witnes, Andro Wallace witnes, Thomas Rae witnes, Thomas finlason witnes, John finlason witnes.

Edinburgh 4 November 1678

Bessie Gourlie being brought in presence of the Lords Commissioners of justiciarie and examined upon the within written confession, she declaires the samen confession to have been true and voluntarly emmitted be her and abyds at the truth and veritie therof, declaires she cannot wreitt.

Sic subscribitur Tho Wallace, SRo Nairne, David Balfour, DaFalconar.

July 24 1678

{*fo. 22r.*} The deposition of Agnes Somervaill ane of the Confessing witches of Fala which she did depone voluntarlie without any violence offered or done to her befor thir witnessis, Mr George Moody minister, Thomas Rae and Thomas Findleyson elders and John Findleyson tennent in Fala and Andrew Wallace weaver ther and John Crightoun presenter ther. *Imprimis* she did confesse that Isobell Borthvick and Alison Rae more nor tuenty years agoe did desyre her at midnight to goe see a freind, she went with them by the Fairnie brae, ther appeared to them a black man and asked what woman that wes, they said she is a freind, so presently the Divill did promise her she would never want and come to him when she wanted and desyred her to renunce her baptisme which she did and lay her hand on the crown of her head and the other on the sole of her foot and did delyver all over betwixt these tuo to the Divillis service, efter this the Divill did kisse her and imbraced her in his armes. She wes at many other meitings particularlie at the Line Dean and Whithouse wher wes present many that she knewe not but particularlie Margaret Sonus, Margaret Williamson and Bessie Gourlie wes ther, depones that in Heriot Back the Divill tempted her to uncleanness and hade carnall copulation with her and that he wes all as cold as ice. Farder she depones that she wes present with witches who did kill John Raes beasts by riding them to death, This to be the true Confession is attested by the formentionit witnessis.

Sic subscribitur G Moodi witnes, Andro Wallace witnes, Thomas Rae witnes, Thomas Finlason witnes, John Finlason witnes, Jon Crichtoun witnes.

Edinburgh 4 November 1678

{*fo. 22v.*} Agnes Somervaill being brought in presence of the Lords Commissioners of justiciarie and examined upon the within written Confession, declaires the samen wes emitted freelie and voluntarly and abyds at the truth and veritie of the samen, declaires she cannot wreitt.

Sic subscribitur Tho Wallace, SRo Nairne, David Balfour, DaFalconar.

The deposition of Margaret Sounes befor the forsaids witnessis

Imprimis the said Margaret did depone that she wes the Divills servant more nor tuentie years agoe and that Emj[66] Rae and Jannet Henryson did take her on to be the Divills servant more nor thretie years agoe, that she wes at many meitings with the Divill, particularlie tuo, on[e] at the Lindean, the other at the Whithouse, wher wes present many she knewe but particularlie Agnes Somervaill and Andrew Hud wer there, and at the Whyt House at the Divills desyre she did renunce her baptisme and did lay her on[e] hand on the crown of her head and the other on the sole of her foot and did delyver all over betwixt these tuo to the Divills service, and because she wes not speedie in following the Divill he did drage her by the coat and brack[67] the band therof, That she wes the Divills slave and many a tyme he did strick her sore, and that twice or thrice the space of tuo years agoe being so sore abused and tempted with the Divill she wes coming to the minister to acknowledge the sine of witchcraft but when she wes nigh the house the Divill would not permitt her to come in, This is the true Confession is attested by the formentionit witnessis.

Sic subscribitur G Moodi witnes, Thomas Rae witnes, Thomas Finlason witnes, Andro Wallace witnes, John Finlason witnes, John Crichton witnes.

[66] *Sic*. This may be Alison Rae (see p. 554 above).

[67] 'brack': broke.

Edinburgh 4 November 1678
{fo. 22v.} In presence of the Lords of justiciarie Margaret Sonus being examined anent the within written confession emmitted be her Confesses that the said Confession wes emmitted freelie and voluntarly and abyds at the truth and veritie of the samen and declaires she cannot wreitt.

Sic subscribitur Tho Wallace, Ro Nairne, David Balfour, DaFalconar.

Efter leading and adduceing of the whilk probation the Lords ordained the assyse to inclose and returne ther verdict on Wedensday at twelve aclock.... *{fo. 24v.}*

Curia justiciarie Supremi Domini Nostri Regis tenta in pretorio burgi de Edinburgh sexto die mensis Novembris 1678 per honorabiles viros Dominos Thomam Wallace de Craigie justiciarie clericum Jacobum Foulis de Colintoun Robertum Nairn de Strathurd Davidem Balfour de Forret et Davidem Falconar de Newtoun Commissionarios justiciarie dicti Supremi Domini Nostri Regis. Curia legittime affirmata.[68]

The said day[69] the persons who past upon the assyse of the witches in Fala returned ther verdict in presence of the saids Lords wherof the tenor followes, The haill assyse with on[e] voice having ellected and choisen Thomas Weddell Chancelar, they find Bessie Gourlie, Margaret Sonus and Agnes Somervaill guilty of the Cryme of witchcraft by ther partaking with the Divill and renunceing ther baptisme as they all confesse.

Sic subscribitur Tho Waddell Chancelar.

Efter oppining and reading of whilk verdict of assyse the saids Lords Commissioners of justiciarie be the mouth of Adam Auld dempster of court decerned and adjudged the saids Bessie Gourlie, Agnes Somervaill and Margaret Sonus to be taken to the Gallowlie betwixt Leith and Edinburgh betwixt tuo and four aclock in the efternoon and ther to be strangled at ane stake till they be dead and therefter to have ther bodies burnt to ashes and all ther movable goods and gear to be escheat and imbrought to his Majesties use which wes pronunced for doom.

[68] 'Court of justiciary of our sovereign lord the king, held in the tolbooth of the burgh of Edinburgh, 6 November 1678, by the honourable men, lords Thomas Wallace of Craigie, justice clerk, James Foulis of Colinton, Robert Nairn of Strathurd, David Balfour of Forret and David Falconer of Newton, commissioners of justiciary of our said sovereign lord the king. Court legally fenced'.

[69] In margin: 'Verdict of assyse and Doom against witches'.

33. ANNA WOOD, LINLITHGOWSHIRE, 1694

INTRODUCTION

Anna Wood's case arose in the small seaport town of Carriden. It involved elaborate fantasy, and fears of witches aboard ships.

Wood's initial accuser was a young seaman, Robert Nimmo. He reported a terrifying hallucinatory experience: he was coming home one night when he was followed by uncanny cats that threatened to kill him, carried him into the air, and then changed into birds and finally into women – one of whom was Wood. He feared her because, two years before, he had refused to carry out a 'commission' for her 'to Holland' – presumably to buy or sell some goods for her there – whereupon she had threatened him.

Once he had the session's attention, Nimmo added to his story, telling of further detailed visions of Wood, including one aboard his ship that may have arisen from an episode of sleep paralysis. This vision was seconded by another seaman, James Linlithgow. The session 'admonished' Linlithgow 'to take heed quhat he said', although they do not seem to have said this to Robert Nimmo. Perhaps they suspected that Nimmo was deluded, but that Linlithgow was backing him up with deliberate deception. Nevertheless, a third witness, the skipper James Steedman, contributed a further story: he had seen a vision of Wood in the cabin of his ship in port in the Netherlands in the previous year.

The kirk session elders may have been cautious, but they clearly thought that they might be onto something. They investigated Wood's whereabouts at the time of Nimmo's visions. They also asked Wood herself about her dreams, evidently hoping that she would come up with a dream or visionary experience that matched those of the accusers. However, she denied everything. She admitted that she had visited the Netherlands, but not, she said, for the last twelve years. Rather than await the results of the session's investigation, she fled from the town, and her case disappeared from the records.

TEXT

Source: Falkirk Council Archives, Minutes of Kirk Session of Carriden, 1690–1727, CH2/61/1.[1]

{*p. 44*} February 13th 1694
Sederunt the minister,[2] James Craig, John Craig, Duncan Allan, John Waldie, William Bryce, William Halliday, James Allan, James Bishope, Patrick Watsone, James Wilsone, David Aitkine, Walter Snadoun, William Cummings: after prayer....

Anna Wood being cited before the sessione as a witch and The witnesses to prove the samen, first Robert Nimmo seaman[3] being called and required to declare quhat he saw or knew anent Anna Wood, declared as followeth That upon Munday the 29th of January last about seven aclock at night as he was comeing from Linlithgow to the waterside, at Bonytoune he met with six catts who followed him homewards till he came to Sir Walter Seatons park dyke at Norkbank[4] at quhich place they appeared to him as women, that he knew one of them to be the said Anna Wood, and that he did speak to her, and that she did bid kill him, and all of them conveyed him a considerable space, and then appeared as birds fleeing[5] by him and about him; and after that appeared againe as women and went alongst with him till he came to the Grange quhair they left him and that he knew the said Anna to be one of them this second tyme alsoe.

The said Anna Wood cited and compearing was interrogate[6] what envy she had at Robert Nimmo that she should have offered[7] to kill him: answered she had noe envy at him, indeed she had noe envy at the young man.[8] Was asked quhen she was at Holland; answered not these 12 years since. Was asked if ever she dreamed that she was there since. Answered she never dreamed such a thing. Was interrogat quhether she met with Robert Nimmo January 29th at such a tyme in such a place {*p. 45*} answered, denyed it: was interrogate quhether she forbade him to speak of her name to the sessione: answered she never said such a thing. Was interrogat quhair she was that night at that tyme for she was found to be missing for she had left her work till nyne aclock at night. Answered she was in Thomas Hendersones and Archibald Campbells

1 A modernised and slightly abridged version of this text, misdated 1704, has been printed in Thomas J. Salmon, *Borrowstouness and District* (Edinburgh, 1913), 119–21.

2 The minister of Carriden was Robert Steedman.

3 In margin: 'Witnesses evidence against Anna Wood.'

4 *Sic.* This is probably Northbank Park, now within neighbouring Bo'ness.

5 'fleeing': flying.

6 In margin: 'Anna Wood examined.'

7 'offered': attempted, threatened.

8 The repetitive phrasing of this sentence indicates that it comes directly from Wood's oral utterance.

at Corodown Hill. Was further interrogate whether she was at Sir Walter Setons park dyke that night the 29th January and other Five women with her. Denyed it saying she was free of such scandall.

John and James Craigs appointed[9] to try if she was in Thomas Hendersones and Archibald Campbells such a night and report the next day. And the said Anna to be summoned against the next day and other witnesses and the said Robert Nimmo....

February 20th 1694

Sederunt the minister, John Andersone, John Craig, William Bryce, Arthure Pollock, David Jamiesone, Patrick Watsone, James Bishope: after prayer.

Former appointments are found obeyed.

The wittnesses against Anna Wood are called, and first Robert Nimmo[10] compeiring is interrogate quhether he had seen Anna Wood since the 29th of January last at quhich tyme he should have seen her and others comeing from Linlithgow. Answered he saw her not since, but declared further, that upon Saturnday last the 17th instant, betwixt Coridoun Hill and Bridgeneese at night {*p. 46*} he heard women cry to him, Robine, declare quhat ye saw: and that upon Fridayes night before he heard them on shipboard alsoe distinctly cry to him, to declare quhat he saw: he was asked what he thought was the ground of her hatred at him: answered that about two years agoe, upon his refusall of a commission from her to Holland, she then said to him that she should doe him an ill turn.

He further declared that he saw the said Anna Wood aboard their ship quhen the said ship was lying at Cuffabouts, and that she had a candle in her hand; and that she did goe fore and eft[11] the said ship, and that the half of ane half hogshead of sack[12] was drunk out that night, for it was wanting to morrow they knew not how. And that one day in Isabell Nimmos the said Anna Wood did forbid him to speak of her name before the sessione. He further declared that Eight nights before that night he met with them comeing from Linlithgow; that three women came aboard their ship and keeped him from sleeping and speaking.

James Linlithgow sailor cited and compeiring,[13] declared that he saw the said Anna Wood aboard their ship; that she went fore and eft with a candle in her hand; and he being admonished to take heed quhat he said; asserted that he knew it really to be Anna Wood, and that he could depone upon it before any judge in the world, and further declared that he saw her another night aboard a ship quhen he was aboard with Robert Nimmo.

9 In margin: 'Appointment on John and James Craigs.'
10 In margin: 'Robert Nimmo witnessing against Anna Wood.'
11 'fore and eft': fore and aft (to the front and back).
12 'half hogshead of sack': barrel of white wine.
13 In margin: 'James Linlithgow witnessing against her viz: Anna Wood.'

John Craig reported that Eupham Allan declared that Anna Wood on January 29th last left her work in the said Euphams house about seven hours at night and came not in to it againe till nyne aclock that night.[14]

James Steidman skipper declared[15] that if ever he saw Anna Wood in his dayes, he saw her at the Briell in Holland[16] in his ships cabine quhen he was last there anno 1693 otherwise the Devill in her likeness, at quhich tyme he lost a boy.

The said Anna Wood cited, called and not compeiring It was told and informed to the sessione she was fled Quhairupon the clerk is ordered[17] to draw out the whole process against her to be sent to Edinburgh and referrs her to the Magistrat and in particular to the Baylie of Grang to make search after her. All quhich was done.

14 The scribe has squeezed in this sentence as an afterthought. There is also a deletion where the scribe has begun a new paragraph, writing the following words and then deleting them: 'Anna Wood cited, called and not …'.

15 In margin: 'James Steidman his witnessing against her viz: Anna Wood.'

16 Brielle is a seaport in southern Holland.

17 In margin: 'Appointment on the Clerk, anent Anna Wood for her not compearance.'

34. JANET DRYSDALE, LINLITHGOWSHIRE, 1696

INTRODUCTION

This case arose in the parish of Bo'ness (Borrowstounness, formerly Kinneil). Much of it concerned healing rituals and prognosis. Janet Drysdale was a magical practitioner, described as a 'wife' who 'could cure' Janet Barclay's sick child. She used some conventional (if perhaps magical) rituals for this, notably involving south-running water, of which various details were given. She added a further dimension of magical beliefs with the 'good nightbours' – the fairies. These fairies were dangerous. Barclay's servant Katherine Currie ritually buried the sick child's shirt as Drysdale instructed, but heard 'much speaking' above her head, and afterwards became feverish with fear. Drysdale told another woman that Currie could have been 'torn to pieces', and added advice about the 'blasting' that had caused the child's illness. However, she said, the 'speaking' indicated that the child would recover – which he did.

But someone told the kirk session about the healing of Barclay's child with a 'charme' – a term that the church authorities often regarded as designating a superstitious practice or worse. The minister, John Brand, questioned Barclay, who in turn told him about Drysdale. This led to an elaborate enquiry. The minister and elders visited, summoned and questioned various servants and neighbours, and of course Drysdale herself, in order to piece together all the details of the story as thoroughly as they could. Then they referred the case up to the presbytery.

Neither the kirk session nor the presbytery used the word 'witchcraft'. The one thing that makes Drysdale's case into a 'witchcraft' case is the presbytery's reported recommendation at this point to 'give her up to the magistrate', evidently for criminal prosecution that must have been intended to be for witchcraft. Ordinarily, Drysdale's healing rituals could have given rise to the kind of superstitious magic case that kirk sessions usually punished by fines or penance. But the 'magistrate' would have prosecuted her as a witch.

Who might the 'magistrate' have been? The two main possibilities are the privy council, or the sheriff depute, in charge of the Linlithgowshire sheriff court. The privy council would have been able to issue a commission of justiciary for a witchcraft trial. The sheriff court would not have been able to carry out a witchcraft trial itself, but the sheriff depute would have been better placed than the kirk session to approach the privy council. However, nothing about Drysdale can be found in either authority's records for this period.[1] We can infer, therefore, that if John Brand did consult either or both of them, they did not react by deciding to initiate a witchcraft prosecution. Any such decision *would* have been recorded. The most that can have happened, therefore, is that the 'magistrate' told Brand that they did not regard Drysdale's case as witchcraft after all. And indeed, it does not seem to be witchcraft by some of the criteria commonly used at the time. There was no immediately-obvious malefice – the child had recovered, for instance; and there was no mention of quarrels, threats or curses.

After the time for consulting the 'magistrate' had gone past, John Brand took the case back to the presbytery once more. He brought with him, as the presbytery had previously requested, 'ane account of some Acts of the Generall Assembly against Charmers'.[2] This time the presbytery decided to consult the synod, the church court above the level of the presbytery, about how to deal with Drysdale as a 'charmer'. The synod discussed the case, but the terse minutes, reproduced below, show that no specific action was agreed upon. Presumably Brand was sent home with some oral advice as to how to deal with his 'charmer' locally. The fact that Janet Drysdale did not appear before the kirk session again may suggest that the higher church authorities did not want to make a fuss about her kind of magical healing in 1696.

John Brand's encounter with fairies and magical healing in his parish is thought-provoking, since he was later the author of *A Brief Description of Orkney, Zetland, Pightland-Firth and Caithness*, written after a visit he paid to the region as part of an ecclesiastical deputation in 1700. Brand gave an account of the local people's practice of healing charms, which he called their 'Hellish Art and tremendous Devilry', and also wrote of their belief in fairies, brownies, mermaids and sea-trows.[3] This discussion, like the discussion of Janet Drysdale, wavers on the edge of ideas about witchcraft.

1 We have examined the sheriff court records for the relevant period: NRS, Sheriff Court Books of Linlithgow, 1694–1700, SC41/1/27, and 1695–1700, SC41/1/28. The sheriff depute was John Dundas of Mains. We are grateful to Alan R. MacDonald of the Scottish Privy Council Project for examining the privy council records.

2 The acts of the general assembly that Brand is most likely to have found were two that had been passed in 1640 and 1649. These acts urged the punishment of witchcraft, charming and 'consulting', but did not define these offences or give procedural advice. See *Acts of the General Assembly of the Church of Scotland, 1638–1842* (Edinburgh: Church Law Society, 1843), 44–5, 216–17.

3 John Brand, *A Brief Description of Orkney, Zetland, Pightland-Firth and Caithness* (Edinburgh: George Mosman, 1701), 58, 63, 112–15.

TEXTS

Source 1: Falkirk Council Archives, Minutes of Kirk Session of Bo'ness, 1694–1712, CH2/540/1.

{*p. 24*} Borrowstownness February the sixth one thousand and six hundered, and nintie sixth.

The minister and elders James Cassiles, William Key, Thomas Haigh, John Richie, James Jaffry, William Williamson, William Horn, William Jameson, John Hunter, Richard Daline and the Clerk. After prayer....

The session being informed that Janet Barkly George Beles wife[4] had used a charme for curing of her sick child recommends to the minister to speake to her thereanent.... {*p. 25*}

Borrowstownness February twenty seventh one thousand six hundred and nintie sixth.

The minister and elders Richard Daline, John Hunter, William Horn, William Williamson, William Mackie, Thomas Haigh, James Jaffry, James Cassiles and the Clerk. After prayer....

The minister having spoke with Janet Barkly desired her to compear before the session this day who having compeared declared as followes: That one Helen Watt having come in to see her sick child said she knew a wife who could cure him, whereupon Janet Barkly sent for that wife (her name being Janet Drysdale) and she coming and seeing the child said he was blasted between twelve a clock att night and one in the morning and also that she said she might cure the child; Janet Barkly enquiring what she would give him, she said a drink of water, the next morning about the sun rising, Janet Drasdale comes with a stope[5] full of water, gave the child to drink, dipped a shirt, a pair of stockins, and a mutch[6] into the water and put them on the child, having before sent away Catharine Curry Janet Barklays servant with one of the child's shirts without the said Janets[7] knowledge, which she caused the said servant bury, and when she was burying the shirt she heard much speaking, having come home she told the said Janet[8] what she had heared, who said it was the good-nightbours; recommends to the minister, Richard Daline and John Cassiles to gett all the information they can of the same from Katharine Curry, and appoints to cite the said Katharine Curry against the nixt....

4 In margin: 'Janet Barkly'.
5 'stope' (stoup): bucket.
6 'mutch': hood.
7 Janet Barclay's.
8 Janet Drysdale, not Janet Barclay. This becomes clear in the next entry.

Borrowstownness March fifth one thousand six hundred and ninty sixth.

The minister and elders Richard Daline, William Horn, James Jaffry, William Mackie, John Richie, Thomas Haigh, William Key, James Cassiles and the Clerk. After prayer.... {*p. 26*}

The minister with the two elders having conferred with Catharine Curry caused cite her and she compearing declared as followes.

Her mistris child being sick, and she being informed that Janet Draysdale could cure him presently sent for the said Janet who coming said att the first he was past cure, but afterwards looking more narrowly to his hand said, that she thought that he might be cured yet, and also she said that he was blasted two and twentie dayes agoe by a blast of wind in at a south window about twelve aclock at night, then the childs mother asking her what she would give him she said only a drink of water, and the nixt morning she went to a south running burn and brought a pint of water, and gave the child a drink and having dipped a pair of stockins, a shirt and a mutch into it she put them on the child, and presently the child became better, but before this was done she caused the servant Catharine Curry take a shirt of the child's and burie it, and when she was burieing the shirt she heard much speaking as if it had been above her head, but seeing nothing she was greatly affrighted, and this she made known to none till the afternoon that she thought the fear of it had cast her into a fever then she made it known to Janet Drysdale who said it was the good-nightbours. She adds further that Janet Drysdale said to Marion Bell and Helen Watt if she had not gone to bury the shirt att the same time she had been torn to pieces, appoints to cite Janet Drysdale against the nixt.... {*p. 27*}

Borrowstownness March twelfth one thousand six hundered nintie sixth.

The minister and elders Richard Daline, William Williamson, William Horn, William Mackie, Thomas Haigh, John Richie, James Cassiles and the Clerk. After prayer....

Janet Drysdale cited compeared and confessed as follows that she being sent for by Janet Barclay went to her and said that the child was blasted in at a south window (but denied that she did condescend on[9] the time) and that she went for a stoop full of south running water and gave it to Janet Barclay who dipped a shirt a pair of stockins and a mutch into it, and put them on the child having before sent out the servant to bury one of the childs shirts. She denied that she said to Helen Watt and Marion Bell that if the servant had not gone at the same time to bury the shirt she had been torn to pieces, morover she said she learn't that from a beggar wife, and that she had used it to a child of her own, as also that the wife said when any went to bury the shirt if they heard any noise the child would recover, if they heard no noise the child would die. Delayes the matter till the nixt.... {*p. 28*}

9 'condescend on': specify.

Borrowstownness March ninteenth one thousand six hundereth and nintie sixth.

The minister and elders William Horn, James Cassiles, John Gibb, John Hunter, Alexander Stark, Thomas Haigh, William Williamson, William Mackie, David Stevenson, John Livingtown, Andrew Smith, John Richie, William Key and the Clerk. After prayer....

Appoints to cite Marion Bell and Helen Watt for further information against Janet Drysdale....

Borrowstownness April second one thousand sixth hundereth and nintie sixth.

The minister and elders Richard Daline, William Williamson, William Jameson, Andrew Smith, James Anderson, John Richie, James Cassiles and the Clerk. After prayer.

Marion Bell cited, compeared, and declared that she heared Janet Drysdale say that if Katharine Curry had not gone att the very same time to bury the shirt she had been torn to pieces.

Helen Watt cited, compeared and declared *ad idem*;[10] but added further that she heared Janet Drysdale say as the interred shirt tooke with the ground the child would recover, and the child sleeping did lift up his hand three several times, and all the several three {*p. 29*} times his hand fell in towards his face from thence she concluded[11] that the child would recover, for (said she) if she[12] would have died his hand would have fallen outward from his face, added further that Janet Drysdale said she had used the same to a child of James Edmistone. Refers the matter to the presbitrey for advice....

Borrowstownness April tenth one thousand sixth hundereth and nintie sixth.

The minister and elders Richard Dawling, John Hunter, James Cassiles, William Horn, William Mackie, James Jaffry, James Anderson, Alexander Stark, John Richie, John Livington, Andrew Smith and the Clerk. After prayer.

The minister reports that the prysbitreys advice anent Janet Drysdale was to give her up to the magistrat, therefor recommends to the minister to doe it with his conveniency.

Source 2: NRS, Minutes of Presbytery of Linlithgow, 1694–1701, CH2/242/8.

{*p. 57*} Linlithgow Church Wednesday Aprile 8: 1696.

Sederunt (after prayer) Mr William Burnet moderator and all the ministers of the presbytry Except Mr John Anderson who is absent *pro 2do.*[13] Ruleing Elders present John Gordon and James Miller.... {*p. 58*}

[10] 'the same'.
[11] MS damaged; reading uncertain.
[12] *Sic.* Read 'he'.
[13] 'until the 2nd'.

Upon a Reference from the session of Borroustounness anent a Charmer[14] Recommends to Mr John Brand to bring ane account of what is containd in the Acts of the generall Assembly against charmers against the nixt presbytry day....[15]

Linlithgow Church Wednesday Aprile 29: 1696.

Sederunt (after prayer) Mr William Burnet moderator and all the ministers of the presbytry Except Mr Thomas Miller. Ruleing Elders present Pardivin,[16] William Child, William Stevensone, John Miller, Thomas Flint, Samuell Aikman and William Taileour.... {*p. 59*}

Mr John Brand haveing according to appoyntment given ane account of some Acts of the Generall Assembly against Charmers the presbytry referred the matter to the synod for advice how to proceed against such persons.

Source 3: NRS, Minutes of Synod of Lothian and Tweeddale, 1691–1697, CH2/252/6.

{*p. 207*} May 7th 1696....[17]

The presbytery book of Linlithgow was reproduced, examined and approven from the 5 November 1695 to the 29 Apryll 1696 inclusive of Both, and they incuraged to go on in the work of the Lord....

The revisors brought in from the said book two references, the one Anent a Charmer page 59: and the other Anent Adulterie *ibidem*.

14 In margin: 'Anent a Charmer'.

15 This minute is evidently the presbytery's own record of the discussion that led John Brand, two days later, to report to the kirk session that 'the prysbitreys advice anent Janet Drysdale was to give her up to the magistrat' (Source 1 above). It is unclear why the presbytery did not minute any such 'advice'.

16 Walter Stewart of Pardovan, provost of Linlithgow.

17 John Brand was present at this synod meeting (p. 198 of the minutes).

35. BARGARRAN WITCHES, RENFREWSHIRE, 1697

INTRODUCTION

This notorious trial arose from the alleged demonic possession of Christian Shaw, daughter of the laird of Bargarran, in 1696–7. A number of witches were accused of afflicting her. The documents edited below are the record of the trial of Katherine Campbell, Margaret Fulton, Margaret Laing, James Lindsay alias Curate, John Lindsay alias Bishop, John Lindsay in Barloch, and Agnes Nasmith. The trial, which was held under the authority of a commission of justiciary granted by the privy council, took place in Paisley between 14 April and 19 May 1697, with some preliminary proceedings in Renfrew on 18 March. All seven were convicted, and they were executed in Paisley on 10 June 1697. An eighth suspect, John Reid, hanged himself in prison on 21 May.

The case has attracted attention from scholars, partly because of the wealth of documentation that it generated, and partly because of the interest attaching to Christian Shaw's bizarre behaviour. It has been the subject of a fictionalised but well-researched book by Isabel Adam, and has been discussed in several other recent studies.[1] Brian Levack has discussed demonic possession in this and other related cases.[2] Michael Wasser has set the case in the broader context of a subsequent, related panic in the Glasgow area in 1699.[3] The trial documents edited below have never been published before, however.

1 Isabel Adam, *Witch Hunt: The Great Scottish Witchcraft Trials of 1697* (London, 1978); S. W. McDonald, A. Thom and A. Thom, 'The Bargarran Witch Trial: A Psychiatric Reassessment', *Scottish Medical Journal*, 41 (1996), 152–8; Hugh McLachlan and Kim Swales, 'The Bewitchment of Christian Shaw: A Reassessment of the Famous Paisley Witchcraft Case of 1697', in Yvonne G. Brown and Rona Ferguson (eds.), *Twisted Sisters: Women, Crime and Deviance in Scotland since 1400* (East Linton, 2002), 54–83; Hugh V. McLachlan, 'The Bargarran Witchcraft Scare of the 1690s', *History Scotland*, 7:5 (May 2007), 14–19.

2 Brian P. Levack, 'Demonic Possession in Early Modern Scotland', in Julian Goodare, Lauren Martin and Joyce Miller (eds.), *Witchcraft and Belief in Early Modern Scotland* (Basingstoke, 2008), 166–84, reprinted in Brian P. Levack, *Witch-Hunting in Scotland: Law, Politics and Religion* (London, 2008), 115–30.

3 Michael Wasser, 'The Western Witch-Hunt of 1697–1700: The Last Major Witch-Hunt in Scotland', in Julian Goodare (ed.), *The Scottish Witch-Hunt in Context* (Manchester, 2002), 146–65.

The case formed the subject of two contemporary printed narratives: *A Relation of the Diabolical Practices of Above Twenty Wizards and Witches of the Sheriffdom of Renfrew in the Kingdom of Scotland* (1697), and *A True Narrative of the Sufferings and Relief of a Young Girl* (1698). The *True Narrative* incorporated a daily narrative of Christian Shaw's unusual behaviour and experiences, from August 1696 to March 1697, a version of which was cited from time to time in the discussions in court. These two printed narratives, along with a third manuscript account of the case, are now being edited in the companion volume to the present edition, *Scottish Witchcraft Narratives and Tracts*. The introductions to these three documents provide further details about the case.

The trial documents edited here show that the prosecutions drew in many more people than the eight who died. Charges were initially brought against a further thirteen suspects: Elizabeth Anderson, Jean Anderson, Margaret Cunningham, Margaret Ewing, Katherine Ferrier, Angus Forrester, Margaret MacKillop, William Miller, Janet Rodger, Margaret Rodger, Martha Sempill (daughter of Margaret Laing), Margaret Shearer and John Stewart. The charges against most of these thirteen were postponed early on, though their prosecutions were not all formally abandoned. Three further suspects are mentioned in the records. A warrant was issued for the arrest of Thomas Govan in Giffen (he may have had some connection with one of the commissioners, Francis Montgomerie of Giffen). Mary Morrison, wife of Francis Duncan, skipper in Greenock, had been arrested by the sheriff depute; the commissioners ordered him to liberate her on caution. Janet Waugh, who had been named by Christian Shaw, had the Devil's mark found on her in pre-trial pricking. No more was heard of Govan or Waugh, but suspicion continued to follow Morrison for some time.

Once three of these initial suspects, Elizabeth Anderson, Janet Rodger and Margaret Rodger, had charges against them dropped, they were then co-opted to provide evidence for the prosecution. This became important because they could testify about having attended witches' meetings. Other important prosecution witnesses were the young brothers James Lindsay and Thomas Lindsay (Anderson's cousins), who had initially been suspects too but who were never formally charged. These former suspects were often described as 'the confessants'. The case thus involved twenty-four suspects altogether. Five of these were called Lindsay, including two John Lindsays and two James Lindsays, who need to be distinguished. Christian Shaw herself also testified, although her words were not recorded because she was too young to be put under oath.

The trial documents show that the case was about more than the bewitching of Christian Shaw. Various other malefices, perhaps more serious if less colourful, were also alleged. The witches were accused of having killed four children: those of William Fleming, minister of Inverkip, John Ritchie, minister of Kilpatrick, Matthew Park in Parkland, and James Miller in Erskine.

They had also killed John Hardie, minister of Dumbarton, who had died of a strange and violent disease in January 1696. And they had sunk the ferryboat of Erskine in about 1696, drowning George Cunningham of Brighouse and the ferryman John Glen.[4]

On 19 May, the final day of proceedings, as well as convicting and sentencing the seven principal suspects, the court also ordered most of the remaining suspects to be returned to prison until a further court session on 28 May. The exceptions were Margaret Cunningham, Margaret Ewing, William Miller and John Stewart, who were liberated upon caution. Those reserved for further trial thus appear to have been Jean Anderson, Katherine Ferrier, Angus Forrester, Margaret MacKillop, Martha Sempill and Margaret Shearer. No further court session was held for them on that occasion, and in 1698 the published *True Narrative* was still hoping for further prosecutions. Eventually, however, the prosecution efforts fizzled out. Some of the suspects were accused again in 1699 during the Glasgow panic, but these prosecutions were quashed before any of the cases reached trial.

The documents edited below are the formal records preserved by the justiciary court. Each day's proceedings are opened by a statement noting the presence of the commissioners of justiciary. There are procedural minutes of the court, written statements of prosecution and defence lawyers, statements of witnesses, the prosecution lawyer's speech to the assize, and the final verdict and sentence. These materials are not all in chronological order; in particular, the verdict and sentence are recorded before some of the witnesses' statements and lawyers' arguments. The record does not include the detailed indictments or dittays (here usually called 'libels'), listing, point by point, the crimes allegedly committed by the accused. However, most and perhaps all of these points are addressed in the surviving arguments of the prosecution and defence lawyers, and in the witnesses' statements.

Various kinds of evidence of witchcraft appear in the documents. The prosecution failed to obtain confessions from any of the suspects – a point that they cited as further proof of guilt, since the suspects must have been 'charmed up' by the Devil to prevent them from confessing. (The nearest they came to obtaining a confession was when one of the suspects, Katherine Campbell, was persuaded to acknowledge the truth of just one of the witnesses' depositions.) The prosecution did have the suspects pricked for the Devil's mark, however, producing a distinctive kind of evidence that was discussed in detail. Pricking had fallen into disrepute after the disgrace of the best-known pricker John Kincaid in 1662 (discussed above in the present volume), but here it was revived.

Numerous witnesses provided evidence of various kinds for the prosecution. Some witnesses testified concerning Christian Shaw's behaviour, while others described the other malefices of which the witches were accused. Some of the

[4] The fullest account of these malefices, though fictionalised, is in Adam, *Witch Hunt*, 77–85, 178–9.

witnesses, particularly Elizabeth Anderson, testified to meetings between the witches and the Devil, thus supplying demonological details normally found only in the confessions of suspects. The defence then called its own witnesses for 'exculpation', but the first two of these witnesses actually testified that some of the accused persons had reputations for witchcraft – whereupon the advocate for the defence abandoned the remainder of his witnesses. This episode, near the end of the trial proceedings, must have made an impression on the assize.

The witnesses' statements in the trial record below are written versions of oral testimony given in the courtroom itself. In addition, several witnesses had given even more detailed written statements at earlier stages of the investigation. Summaries of several such statements from the witnesses mentioned above were printed by the *True Narrative* in 1698: those of Elizabeth Anderson, James Lindsay and Thomas Lindsay. Fuller versions of these statements were printed by the *Relation* in 1697. Further summaries printed by the *True Narrative* were the statements of Matthew Brisbane and Henry Marshall, respectively physician and apothecary in Glasgow, and the confession of John Reid, the suspect who hanged himself in prison. In these cases, fuller versions of these statements are given in the 'Bargarran Witches Manuscript', edited along with the *Relation* and the *True Narrative* in the companion volume to the present one.[5]

The documents reveal complex arguments about legal procedure and the nature of proof. In particular, the prosecution and defence clashed about the acceptability of certain witnesses, the nature of individual items of evidence, and about how individual items should be understood in combination with one another. The concept of an 'adminicle' – something that contributes to proving a point without being itself a complete proof – was repeatedly invoked and discussed. The defence argued that such items of evidence were always doubtful and that 'a 1000 doubts never make a certantie'. The prosecution argued at great length in favour of these items of evidence. At one point they were described as 'so many lynes drawen from the Circumference to the Center', and there was much invocation of the role of divine providence.

Erudite legal and demonological thinking is evident in the arguments of Francis Grant, the main prosecution advocate. He cited a battery of learned juristic and demonological authorities (some of them evidently at second hand, as was common at this time). One of Grant's demonological authorities was King James VI, although citations of James were otherwise rare in Scottish legal arguments. Scottish lawyers generally found the encyclopedic demonologist Martin Delrio more useful, even though he was a Jesuit; and Grant himself drew extensively on Delrio. Using these authorities, and reasoning from them to apply them to the case at hand, Grant reconstructed the Devil's motivations and plans, and produced detailed ideas of how the Devil might manipulate the physical world in order to work his wonders. The defence advocate,

[5] Julian Goodare (ed.), *Scottish Witchcraft Narratives and Tracts* (Woodbridge: SHS, forthcoming).

James Robertson, also cited Delrio and other authorities. Robertson even argued that the Devil had intervened in the case; his argument was that the Devil had manipulated Christian Shaw in order to inculpate innocent people.

The witnesses' statements also enable us to hear something of the voices of the common people as they experience and report bewitchment. We encounter popular belief in apparitions of the dead, and are told that Margaret Fulton's husband had brought her back from the fairies. We catch glimpses of popular demonology, for instance in the repeated idea that the Devil would give witches a charm to prevent them confessing, and in the spell for flight, 'mount and flie'. Everyday life, with illnesses and healing, is much in evidence. The comings and goings of the common people around the tower house of Bargarran are narrated.

The documents' scribe was John Anderson, writer in Edinburgh. He has some idiosyncratic spellings: 'Intrane' (for 'Intrant', i.e. entered or entering), 'socerie' and 'witchcroft'. These have been marked with '[*sic*]' on their first occurrence only. When the scribe writes lists of names, he usually gives them a collective designation, such as 'prisoners' or 'Advocats', sometimes placing the designation at the end of the list and sometimes bracketing the list and placing the designation beside it. In this edition, all such designations have been placed at the end of the list concerned. The scribe often omits closing brackets; these have been restored conjecturally, thus [)]. The presiding judge, Lord Blantyre, has added his signature to the record from time to time to authenticate it. These signatures have been omitted except when he signs to authenticate the testimony of an illiterate deponent.

TEXT

Source: NRS, Circuit Court Minute Books, 1677–1699, JC10/4.

{fo. 82r.}[6] *Curia justiciarie Supremi Domini Nostri Regis tenta in pretorio burgi de Renfrew 18 die mensis Martii 1697 per honorabiles viros Dominum Joannem Maxwell de Netherpollock,*[7] *Willelmum Muir de Glanderstoun, Magistrum Joannem Steuart juniorem de Blackuall [sic] Advocatum, Joannem Alexander de Blackhouse et Robertum Semple vicecomitem deputatum de Renfrewe, Commissionarios justiciarii Supremi Domini Nostri Regis virtute Commissionis per honorabiles viros dominos secreti concilii directum. Curia legittime affirmata.*[8]

6 These formal preliminary proceedings took place in Renfrew, while the main business of the court would be held in Paisley. The record of these preliminary proceedings, entered in a later part of the court book, is evidently an incomplete draft.

7 In margin: 'Sir John Maxwell *presses*'.

8 'Court of justiciary of our sovereign lord the king held in the tolbooth of the burgh of Renfrew, 18 March 1697, by the honourable men John Maxwell of Nether Pollok, William

The Commissioners abovenamed did take the oath *de fideli administratione officii*.[9]

John Anderson writer in Edinburgh did produce a Commission from James Montgomery of Lainshawe to be Clerk to the said Commission whereof the tenor followes (here to take it in verbatim[)].

The said John Anderson gave his oath *de fideli administratione officii.*

James Guthrie macer to the said Commission gave his oath alse *de fideli administratione*.

The said day The Commissioners abovenamed did make and signe a List of assysers against the witches to be tryed, and issued furth Letters of diligence for summonding them to underlye the lawe and for citing witnesses and assysers against them.

{fo. 24r.} Curia justiciariae Supremi Domini Nostri Regis tenta in pretorio Burgi de Paisley decimo quarto die mensis Aprillis 1697 yeirs per honorabiles viros Alexandrum dominum de Blantyre dominum Joannem Hamiltoune de Hall Craige dominum Concillii et sessionis Magistrum Franciscum Montgomerie de Giffine dominum Concillii dominum Joannem Maxwell de Pollock Commissionarium Thesaurarii Alexandrum Porterfeild de eodem Magistrum Joannem Stewart juniorem de Blackhall Magistrum Jacobum Smollate Commissarium de Edinburgh Joannem Alexandrum de Blackhous et Robertum Sempell vicem Comitem deputatum de Renfrewe. Curia Legittima affirmata.[10]

Lord Hall Craig Elected *preses*. *{fo. 24v.}*

Intrane [*sic*]
Margaret Lang spouse to William Sempill in Cartimpane
Agnes Easemith or Neasmith Indweller in Erskine
Katherine Campbell Lait servitrix to the Laird of Bargarran
Martha Sempell doughter to the said Margaret Lang
Margaret Shearer widow in Erskine Green
Margaret Fultoune Indweller in West Kilpatrick
Margaret McKillope widow in Bonneill
prisoners

Muir of Glanderston, Mr John Stewart younger of Blackhall advocate, John Alexander of Blackhouse and Robert Sempill sheriff depute of Renfrew, commissioners of justiciary of our sovereign lord the king by virtue of a commission sent from the honourable lords of the privy council. Court legally fenced.'

9 'concerning the faithful exercise of their office'.

10 'Court of justiciary of our sovereign lord the king held in the tolbooth of the burgh of Paisley, 14 April 1697, by the honourable men Alexander Lord Blantyre, lord John Hamilton of Halcraig lord of council and session, Mr Francis Montgomerie of Giffen lord of council and session, John Maxwell of Pollok commissioner of the treasury, Alexander Porterfield of that Ilk, Mr John Stewart younger of Blackhall, Mr James Smollett commissary of Edinburgh, John Alexander of Blackhouse and Robert Sempill sheriff depute of Renfrew. Court legally fenced.'

Indyted and Accused for the Cryme of witchcroft [*sic*] in maner mentioned in ther Indytement.

Persewers
Mr John Menzies of Cammo
Mr James Stewarte
Mr Frances Grant of Quollane
Advocats

The persewers declaired they Insysted in the first place against the haill forenamed persouns now presented one pannell AND they being examined upon the Indytement and haill artickls therof they all together denayed the samene.

The Commissioners of Justiciary at the persewers desyres and for severall other good causis moving them containowed the dayet against the forenamed pannells and also against the haill persouns beforenamed Indyted for the said Cryme of witchcroft till tomarrow at Eight of the Clock in the morning and ordained the pannells to be carrayed back to prisone and the wittnessis and assyzers to attend under the paine of Three hundreth merks scots. {*fo. 25r.*}

Curia justiciariae Supremi Domini Nostri Regis tenta in pretorio Burgi de Paisley decimo quinto die mensis Aprillis 1697 per honorabiles viros Alexandrum dominum de Blantyre dominum Joannem Hamiltoune de Hall Craig dominum Concillii et sessionis[11] *Magistrum Franciscum Montgomerie de Giffine dominum Concillii dominum Joannem Maxwell de Pollock Commissionarium Thesaurarii Alexandrum Porterfeild de eodem Magistrum Joannem Stewart juniorem de Blackhall Magistrum Jacobum Smollate Commissarium de Edinburgh Joannem Alexandrum de Blackhouse et Robertum Sempell vicem Comitem deputatum de Renfrew. Curia Legittima affirmata.*[12]

Intrane
Agnes Naesmith or Easmith
John Lindsay in Barcloch
Johne Lindsay in Formakine alias Bishope
James Lindsay
Angus Forrester
Katharine Campbell

11 In margin: 'Lord Hall Craig *preses*.'

12 'Court of justiciary of our sovereign lord the king held in the tolbooth of the burgh of Paisley, 15 April 1697, by the honourable men Alexander Lord Blantyre, lord John Hamilton of Halcraig lord of council and session, Mr Francis Montgomerie of Giffen lord of council and session, John Maxwell of Pollok commissioner of the treasury, Alexander Porterfield of that Ilk, Mr John Stewart younger of Blackhall, Mr James Smollett commissary of Edinburgh, John Alexander of Blackhouse and Robert Sempill sheriff depute of Renfrew. Court legally fenced.'

Margaret Lang
Martha Sempell
Margaret Shearer
Margaret Fultone
Jean Andersoune
William Miller
John Reid
John Stewart
Katharin Ferrier
Margaret Cuninghame
Margaret Rodger
Janet Rodger
Margaret Ewing
Margaret McKillope

All prisoners within the tolbooth of Paisley {*fo. 25v.*} Indyted and Accused for the Cryme of witchcrofte in maner mentioned in ther Indytments.

Persewers
Mr John Menzies of Cammo
James Stewart
Mr Frances Grant of Quollan
Advocats

The Commissioners of justiciary for severall good causes moveing them continued the dyet against the haill forenamed persons defenders till the Elevinth of Maii nixt and ordained them to give in ther defencesis if they any hade againest ther Indytments betuixt and the said day, and to be readie and prepared to abyd ther tryall upon the said day and ordained the witnessis and assysers to attend at this place upon the said Elevinth day of Maii nixt at ten aclock in the forenoon Ilk person under the paine of Tuo hundreth merks.

The Commissioners of justiciary ordained Margaret Lang John Lindesay alias Bishop and Agnes Naesmith pannalls to be transported prisoners to Glasgowe and ordained the Magistrats of the said burghe to detaine them prisoners in seperat roumes and ordained the Magistrats of Paislay to detaine Margaret Shearer Margaret Mckillop Margaret Fultoun and Katharin Campbell prisoners in seperat roumes within the tolbuith of Paislay and ordained the haill remnant pannalls to be transported prisoners to Renfrewe and delivered to the Magistrats to be keeped in sure ward and ordained Martha Semple to be keeped prisoner in a roume by her self.

The warrand for securing the persons abovenamed prisoners at Paislay wes delivered by the macer to the Magistrats of the said burghe and the warrands for transporting the other pannalls to Renfrewe and Glasgowe wes delivered to Captaine Veitch for his warrand to transport them and the saids respective Magistrats warrand for detaining them in prison. {*fo. 26r.*}

The Commissioners of justiciary ordained James and Thomas Lindesays and Elizabeth Anderson witnessis in the said cause to be disposed off in seperat houses within the shyre by the shirriff deput at the sight of the ministers of the presbitery of Paislay and ordained him to aliment them; and they doe seriouslie Recomend the said shirriff deput to the Lords Commissioners of his Majesties Thesaurie that he may be reimbursed of his chairges and expensis.

The Commissioners of justiciary did grant warrand to Magistrats judges officers and ministers of the Lawe within whose bounds Thomas Govan in Giffan a vagrant person (against whom ther are pregnant presumptions of his being a witch) cane be found to apprehend his person and committ him to prison and detaine him therin till he be putt to a tryall or be liberat by order which principall warrand wes delivered to the shirriff deput of Renfrewe.

Robert Semple shirriff deput of Renfrewe did present befor the saids Commissioners ane bond of Cautionrie taken by him by warrand from a Quorum of the saids Commissioners for liberating Mary Morieson spouse to Frances Duncan skipper in Greinock upon caution to appear when called under the paine of Ten Thousand merks which bond of Cautionrie is dated the tuentie fourth day of March Last and is granted by the said Frances Duncan James Galbraith skipper in Craufords dyck and Patrick Watson skipper in Greinock and which bond wes delivered back to the said shirriff deput to be made furth comand when called for.

Curia justiciarie Supremi Domini Nostri Regis tenta in pretorio burgi de Paislay decimo ii die mensis May 1697 per honorabiles viros Alexandrum comitem de Blantyre[13] *dominum Joannem Maxwell de Pollock dominum Joannem Houstoun de eodem Alexandrum Porterfeild de eodem et Joannem Alexander de Blackhouse Commissionarios justiciarie dicte Supremi Domini Nostri Regis. Curia Legittime affirmata.*[14] {*fo. 26v.*}

The said day upon a petition given in be John and James Lindesays and John Lindesay In Barloch craveing exculpation The Commissioners granted warrand for the same and for citing witnessis therupon against the threteinth instant and continued the dyet against them and the haill remnant pannalls Indyted till to morrowe at nyn aclock except against Margaret and Jannet Rogers against whom the persewers declaired they did not presentlie insist The Commissioners of justiciary ordained the haill pannalls to be caryed back to prison and the witnessis and assysers to attend Ilk person under the paine of tuo hundreth merks.

13 In margin: 'Lord Blantyre *preyses*'.

14 'Court of justiciary of our sovereign lord the king held in the tolbooth of the burgh of Paisley, 12 May 1697, by the honourable men Alexander earl [*sic*] of Blantyre, lord John Maxwell of Pollok, Alexander Porterfield of that Ilk and John Alexander of Blackhouse, commissioners of justiciary of our sovereign lord the king. Court legally fenced.'

Curia justiciarie Supremi Domini Nostri Regis tenta in pretorio burgi de Paislay 12 die mensis May 1697 per honorabiles viros Alexandrum Dominum de Blantyre[15] *Dominum Joannem Maxwell de Pollock dominum Joannem Houstoun de eodem dominum Joannem Shawe de Greinock Wilielmum Muir de Glanderstoun Alexandrum Porterfeild de eodem Magistrum Joannem Stewart juniorem de Blackhall Advocatum Joannem Alexander de Blackhouse et Robertum Semple vicicomitem deputatum de Renfrewe Commissionarios justiciarii dicti Supremi Domini Nostri Regis. Curia Legittime affirmata.*[16]

Intran [*sic*]
John Lindesay alias Bishop
James Lindesay alias Curat
John Lindesay in Barloch
Margaret Lang
Margaret Fultoun
Agnes Naesmith
Katharin Campbell
prisoners
Indyted and accused for the cryme of witchcraft committed be be [*sic*] them in maner mentioned in ther dittay.

persewers
Mr James Steuart
Mr Francis Grant
Advocats

prolocutor in defence
Mr James Robertoun Advocat {*fo. 27r.*}

Mr James Steuart and Mr Frances Grant Advocats persewers declaire and insist in the Indytment against the pannalls upon the poynts followeing viz. upon the entering into compact with the Divil, Ther acknowledging him for, and calling him ther Lord, Ther keeping meitings with him and other witches, wher they contrived the death or tortor of severall persons, particularly the tortor of Bargarrans daughter, and the death of the minister of Dunbartoun

15 In margin: 'Lord Blantyre *preyses*'.

16 'Court of justiciary of our sovereign lord the king held in the tolbooth of the burgh of Paisley, 12 May 1697, by the honourable men Alexander Lord Blantyre, lord John Maxwell of Pollok, lord John Houston of that Ilk, lord John Shaw of Greenock, William Muir of Glanderston, Alexander Porterfield of that Ilk, Mr John Stewart younger of Blackhall advocate, John Alexander of Blackhouse and Robert Sempill sheriff depute of Renfrew, commissioners of justiciary of our sovereign lord the king. Court legally fenced.' The date 12 May has been retained in this transcription, but it should be noted that the previous session of the court, also dated 12 May, had ordered an adjournment to the following day.

and of the children of Mr John Ritchie William Montgomery Mathew Park Mr William Fleyming and James Miller and the drowning George Cunninghame of Bridghouse and John Glen by overturning of the boat of Erskine which tortours and deaths and other malefices actuallie enseued, \and for useing of charmes,/ which poynts and articles or one or other of them or the pannalls being airt and part therof They crave the judges may find Relevant *seperatim*[17] and may Remitt the same to the knowledge of the assyse and allowe witnessis and other Lawfull meanes of probation to be adduced upon the circumstances and qualifications and others competent for inferring the pannalls guilt in the premisis.

Mr James Robertoun Advocat as prolocutor for the pannalls alleadged that no Lybell of witchcraft ought to be sustained unlesse sufficient *indicia*[18] and evidences of guilt hade preceeded and wer Lybelled upon and exhibited.

Mr James Steuart and Mr Frances Grant persewers Replyed that ther wes no necessity of Lybelling that ther wes previous *indicia* of guilt for founding the Indytment, and yet in this case the grounds of the dittay wer precognosced by warrand of the Lords of privie Councill and ther Lordships fand sufficient evidences for granting Commission for Indyting and persewing the pannalls for the crymes Lybelled.

The Commissioners of justiciary ordaine the tryall to goe one and appoynts the Advocats to debate upon the relevance of the poynts contained in the Indytment.

The Advocats having debated the poynts of the dittay *viva voce*[19] Mr James Robertoun craved that the judges would appoynt the persewers to give him in with ther Information the precognitions {*fo. 27v.*} and testimonies taken for founding the Lybell which being objected against by the persewers upon severall grounds then debated.

The Commissioners declaired ther wes no necessity to the persewers to give in with ther Information any precognitions taken for being a ground of the indytment.

The Commissioners ordained the Advocats to Interchaing ther debates betuixt and Monday nixt and continued the court till that tyme, ordained the pannalls to be caryed back to prison and the witnessis and assysers to attend Ilk person under the paine of Tuo hundreth merks.

The Commissioners Continue the dyet against the haill remnant pannalls till the said day and ordained them to be transported to the tolbuith of Renfrewe and secured ther till Monday nixt and then to be brought back to ther tryall and ordained the three Lindesays Margaret Lang Margaret Fultoun Katharin Campbell and Agnes Naesmith to be keeped in seperat roumes within the prisons of Paislay and ordained the Magistrats of Renfrewe to seperat to privat

17 'separately'.
18 'indications' (of guilt).
19 'orally'.

prison and putt by themselves allone such of the pannalls as are prisoners with them whom the ministers of the presbyterie shall find cause for.

According to the Interloquitor abovewritten The Advocats did Interchaing and gave in ther debates in wreitting of the which the tenors followe:

Informatione against the persownes Indyted for witchcroft.

The Lybell as declared and Insysted in Consists of Tuo pairts and each of them is fownded upon ane Express act of parliament.

The first pairt comprehends the pannells being witches and the particullar malefices Committed By them as such In the termes of the seventy thrid act parliament nynt Quen Mary.

And the second pairt Concluds the pannells to have been at Leist airt and pairt of these Crymes Against the Relevancy wher of no thing cane be objected. By the hundred Fyftie ane act parliament Elevinth K: Ja: the sext.[20]

As to the first pairt of the Lybell the Relevancy therof cannot be doubted Be any that acknowledges natur all Reasoune Lawes scriptier For the crymes therin mentioned are pairtly against almighty God viz. the pannells entering into compact with the Devill hes declared Rebell acknowledged {*fo. 28r.*} Satane For and calling him ther Lord wherby they have dissclamed there Lawfull superiour, There keeping meettings with the wicked spirit and other witches which was ane Intercommoning Far beyond the guilt of such convers among men In which facts was necesserly Included perjury against there Sacramentall oathe appostacy from the only trew God hericie in a maner against all Relegione which is the fowndatione of Trust amongst men And finally seductione of others unto the same horrid wickedness And they are crimes pairtly against man particullarly by the murdur of the Infants Lybelled which was the more heinous that they were not capable to give any provocatione or to Resist and of ane minister no doubt for his being ane zelous Champione for the only trew Lord And By the tortours Lybelled Especially of Bargarrons doughter whose caice was so wunderfull in maney of its Cercumstances That it could not have proceeded from ane naturall cause.

The pannells doe Indeed Remaine Charmed up from Confessione But it is hoped that notwithstanding therof The probatione of there guilt will be alse clare as any that is Extent upon Record Either in this or any other natione which allwayes providence hes brought about both as to the first discovery and the subsequent evidences against the persowns delated In Be the which the Devill and his Instruments are most Remarkably Befoolled and over powered To the consullatione[21] of the faithfull and confuisione of Infidels As will planly appeir in dew tyme upon aduoing[22] the probatione after a Relevancie is disscursed.

20 *Acts of the Parliaments of Scotland*, iii, 578, c. 73; RPS, 1592/4/95.

21 'consullatione': consolation.

22 *Sic.* The sense seems to require 'discussing' or 'dealing with'.

As to the second part of the Lybell anent airt and pairt The forsaid act of parliament determines the caice that no objectione shall be Receaved against it.

This neads not be supported with Reasoning since it is express Law And confirmed by dayly practique which cannot be Refused without contravening the act of parliament Besyds that it is not possible to know all the cercumstances of guilt Befor the witnessis depone so that the aleadgences may either exceed or fall short of the trew poynt of fact and therby wrong either the Relevancy or the probatione The preventing of the which Inconveinency was the designe of the act of parliament And althowgh it be ordinery That preloquitur was taken yet the witnessis not being upon oath they may and useually doe come short or exceed what thereafter they judicially doe depone.

And Therfor It is craved that the Judges may sustaine the Lybell as above declaired and Insisted upone according to undoubted Law.

And seing the Judges have Restricted the debaitte *in hoc statu processus*[23] to the Relevancy of the Indytment simpliceter It is protested that in Caice the Advocate for the pannells doe in his answer Insist upon any thing Relating to the probatione or maner therof that the same may not be Registered or Recorded.

The persewers will not trouble the judges any furder only they may be pleased to Remember the history of this affair And how great cautione hes been used in all pairts of it {*fo. 28v.*} when the Devill and his Instruments (no doubt) did Intend the tortour of Bargarrans doughter as ane instance of his malice and Insult over the weakness of ane tender Gerle God in hir over Rewlling providence did turne the same to Be a means of allowing the natione to notice the wicked Crew in this pairt of the Land.

Upon this and the Conciderent testimony of three of the tormentors themselves The previ Councill did grant a Commissione to severall persowns of undoubted honor knoulege and Integrity who Report the Informatione to be trew And adminncullat[24] with many great Indications of Guilt.

Heirupon the Councill did give a second Commissione to other eminent persowns whose Characters are weell known in the natione and severall of whom have shown undoubted Impartiality and Exactness in other Capacities of the greatest Trust proceeded with all Care and tenderness towards the pannells that could be thought on without degeneratting unto absolute neglect particullarly they gave at first a Long day to the pannells That they might prepare for there Trayell at which dayet haveing attended severall dayes In order to a farder Inquiry so that they might have proceeded to determine yet in Respect the pannells had no prolocators The judges allowed a new dayet to them for preparing there soulls And getting advocatts to defend ther lyves If it were possible that they could be fownd Inocent.

23 'in that state of the process'.

24 'adminnculat': supported. An 'adminicle' is something that contributes to proving a point without being itself a complete proof.

Now Att the Thrid meetting after so maney Long delayes providence hes ordered it so That other Tuo of these malefactors who formarly had Remained most obstinate have confest And the pannells are now weell provyded with advocatts which undoubtedly calls upon the judges to proceed and not suffer witches any Longer to Live to the disshonor of God and prejudice of man keind If the probatione be fownd sufficient In its dew place. *Sic subscrivitur*[25] James Steuart Franes [*sic*] Grant.

Defencesis and answers for John Lindesay alias Bishop James Lindesay his brother John Lindesay in Barloch Agnes Naesmith Katharin Campbell Margaret Lang and Margaret Fultoun who are Indyted of witchcraft.

The pannalls first of all doe deny the Lybell haill articles and qualifications therof and Indications of guilt therin contained.

The persewers by ther information hes divided ther Lybell in severall parts viz. /1°/ unto sins of witchcraft against God /2do/ unto crymes of witchcraft against man {*fo. 29r.*} 3°/ airt and part of the saids crymes and 4to/ the Lybell containes severall Indications or insinuations by which the persewers would amuse the world and make them beleive that the pannalls are guilty of the crymes Lybelled.

The pannalls befor they answer each part of the lybell doe humblie represent that they doe much confid in the justice moderation and charitie of ther judges and hopes that they will not suffer themselves to be any maner of way prepossessed by the Innumerable stories spread abroad in the affaire of Bargarrans daughter or other the unaccountable rumours of the countrey but will have charitie from them at least as such persons who have heard the ministers of the Gospell sett furth the rewards of heaven and torments of hell and so howe litle probable or presumable it is that they should have renunced God and resigned themselves to the service of the Divill.

In answer to the first part of the Lybell viz. the sins of witchcraft against God to witt the pannalls ther alleadged entering unto compact with the Divil Resigning themselves over to him by renunceing ther Baptisme or acknowledging him Lord their keeping meitings with him and others his helish crewe to contrive wickednes as to these as the pannalls doe deny the same for they doe (with a great deall of submission to the judges) positivlie assert That such part of the Lybell cannot be subsumed upon in our act of parliament lybelled on nor hes such a lybell any fundation either on our statut Lawe or practique and therfor the pannalls cannot passe to the knowledge of ane assyse for these reasons.

1°/ That such ane lybell is not founded on the act of parliament lybelled on Is clear by the act itself which only punishes malefices for the words are that the users of witchcraft socerie [*sic*] or necromancy The abusers of the people by giving themselves furth to have any such craft and the seekers of help from any such users or abusers are only punishable by the paines of death

25 'Thus it is subscribed'.

But so it is The entering unto compact {*fo. 29v.*} meiting with and calling the Divil Lord or renunceing Baptisme to him all those cannot be said according to the common way of speaking the useing of any witchcraft by them but rather that the Divill uses his craft in representing man and womens false shapes to such of his helish crewe as are trulie witches and at such meitings and therby the Divill hounds out his true witches (either by his promises or threatenings) to dilate Innocents upon these false representations therby to advance his kingdome in bringing on Innocents bloodshed, discord, want of Love and charity, Lyes, dispair and losses of reputation to the people dilated and it is clear by the adjournall bookes that witches when at the stake hes confest ther hes been represented to them at the meitings severall good christians who wer long dead befor.

2[do]/ That such Lybells are not founded on our practique is clear by the Adjournall book for all witches recorded ther to have bein condemned they wer only condemned for malifices In useing charmes, Inchantments, making picturs, abuseing the people making them beleive they could cure diseases or seeking help from such users as appears by the cases of Bessie Dunlop anno 1576 Jannet Kennedy Eupham McLean anno 1591 and others.[26]

3[o]/ But *esto*[27] ther wer any such positive Lawe or practique wherupon to found any such Lybells yet by the opinion of the doctors and in reason it self It is clear that *Commessationes et cuncubitus cum diabolo* that is meiting with, acknowledging, entering into pactions with the Divil, are all acts of the will and consists of the meir will without any externall act, and in these no *corpus delicti*[28] (as charmes, picturs etc) needs appear and therfor because they consist not of externall fact they are said to be *difficilime indaginis*[29] and Delrio sayes as to these Lib: 5 Sect: 2 *in initio*[30] that witches are never to be condemned as to these *nisi duntaxat dicant se ad conventum esse delatas*[31] that unlesse the witches confesse that they wer caryed to such and such meitings they are not to be condemned and even ther Confession {*fo. 30r.*} ought to be adminculat by grave circumstances and reiterat severall tymes and ought not to be the effect of Melanchollie or of ther being wearied of ther lives and the reason of all this is, because it is God allon[e] who knows the Impuritie of the heart and the secreit acts of the will but man punishes only the externall facts of the will wher the *corpus delicti* appears as the useing charmes, inchantments, picturs

26 For the records of these cases see Robert Pitcairn (ed.), *Criminal Trials in Scotland, 1488–1624*, 3 vols. (Edinburgh: Bannatyne Club, 1833), i, II, 49–58 (Bessie Dunlop); Lawrence Normand and Gareth Roberts (eds.), *Witchcraft in Early Modern Scotland: James VI's 'Demonology' and the North Berwick Witches* (Exeter, 2000), 183–8 (Janet Kennedy), 181–2, 261–74 (Euphemia MacCalzean).

27 'suppose'.

28 'body of the offence', i.e. the concrete evidence of crime, showing that a crime has been committed.

29 'difficult to investigate'.

30 'at first'.

31 'unless they declare themselves to have been carried to a meeting'. See Del Rio, *Investigations into Magic*, 190 (book 5, section 2, para 1).

and such other magicall tools for effectuating such and such damnadges By all which it is clear that as to those crymes Lybelled which are against God they are not relevant to inferre the punishments Lybelled but as to these the pannalls are to be remitted to ther owne houses to be dealt with by ther discreit pastors in order to ther repentance and confession Neither are these Relevant to be proven by witnessis more then perjurie (this being the great perjurie against God) which cannot be proven by witnessis as wes desyded by the justices in Balcanquhils case anno 1666 which is marked by Mckenzie title assyse[32] therfor the pannals ought not to passe (as to these crymes against God) to the knowledge of ane assyse.

As to the second part of the Lybell relateing to the crymes of witchcraft and malefices against man viz. the pannalls ther alleadged acting and contriving the strangleing drowning tortoring and Inhuman murdering of severall persons particularly ther ennumerat and that by magicall charmes inchantments pictures and other Inventions of the Divil.

As to these alleadged malefices the pannalls alwayes denying the same and declaireing that they neither hade nor have any ill will or malice at any one or other of the persons ennumerat in the lybell, It is answered:

1° That the Lybell as it is Lybelled is most Irrelevant Because ther is no previous malice Lybelled or condeshended on Especially as to the Lindsayes which ought to Be in Law.

2do The Lybell is not speciall in sua far as it condeshends not upone the precise dayes yea moneths By which means the pannells ar deprived of that most just deffence viz. That they were *alibi*[33] quhich owght to have been done *Quia in Criminibus non Licet vagare.*[34]

3^tio^ Ther is no charmes Inchantments or ther magicall means for Effectuating the tortours murdurs or damadges Lybelled so much as Condeshended one Except {*fo. 30v.*} picturs, pinns, cards, and a sea napkeine; quhich are not so much as produced and quhich nether now can be condeshended on or produced since now the pannels cannot exculpate themselves as to these, or prove the producers made themselves, *Ergo*[35] that is noe malefice For malefice in witchcraft and the unlaufull means for effectuating the damnadge are all one, and so the pannells ought to be assoilzied nether can any such malefice or means now be fixed on them since they were nether condeshended on nor produced *in initio* and that all this is both Law and Reasone is Clear By Delrio Lib 5 sect 2 in principio who sayes that in those Crymes of witchcroft *quae in*

32 Sir George Mackenzie, *The Laws and Customs of Scotland in Matters Criminal*, ed. Olivia F. Robinson (Edinburgh: Stair Society, 2012; originally published 1678), 358 (part 2, title 23, para 4).

33 'elsewhere'.

34 'In which criminal causes it is not permitted to digress'.

35 'Therefore'.

actum externum ocuperunt debet in iis constare de corpore delicti[36] that is to say in those externall facts of witchcroft ther most appear the unlaufull means used to effectuate such a means for in this Cryme the *corpus delicti* is not the dead and tormented bodies of men But the preternaturall means by which these means are comitted for Delrio sayes when he discryves malefactum Lib. 3 ques. 1 *sumimus autem maleficii nomen non pro damno few peccatto and pro signo magico atquis superstitioso*[37] so that the malefice in witchcraft is nothing but the means and unlaufull toolls made use of and Mckenzie Tyt. 1 discryves malifices to be damnadges that arises from unlaufull means used by sorcerers[38] And the act of parliament is also clear in this Because it sayes the users of these airts and these instruments not appearing *non esse et non apperere equiparantur in jure*[39] By all which it appears that the Lybell anent the malifices is not Relevant since the Charmes is not condeshended upone nor yet picturs cards or sea napkeine produced Therfor the pannells cannot pass to the knouledge of ane Assyze But the Lybell Repeiled[40] as irrelevant.

And as for the aleadged murders it is not so much as insinuate in the Lybell there were any marks of strangling appeared in the childrens necks And its notur where Bridge house drowned nether was ever anye of these deaths thought to have been the effects of witchcroft till the possessione of Bargarrans doughter By whom the Devill hes acted too much for his purpose to advance his own kingdom in attemping to spill the inocent blood of the pannells But still this Lybell is too much at Randum against the pannells for they are made contriving Bargarrands doughter her tortur in Januarii 1697 years though it be nottur she was tortoured Long before.

As to that pairt of the Lybell quhich is speciall {*fo. 31r.*} as to Katharine Campbells viz. that she cursed Bargarrans doughter and that after wards By her Inchantments she was her tormenter.

It is answered not Relevant Because the speciall inchantments are not Lybelled nether can they now be supleadd or witnessis Inteerogate therone since the pannell comes not Instructed with her deffence and as for her curseing that can only infer ane arbitrary punishment But never the punishment of death.

As to that pairt of the Lybell quhich is speciall against Margaret Lang viz. that she should have offered Jannet Laird in Killmacolme to Let her see her sister and brother that were dead.

36 Martin Del Rio, *Disquisitionum Magicarum Libri Sex* (Lyon [Lugduni]: Cardon, 1608) ('Delrio, *Disquisitiones Magicae*'), 389 (book 5, section 2). The quotation abbreviates Delrio. A translation follows in the text.

37 'By the word *malefice*, however, I do not mean just any kind of injury or sin, but rather a magical or superstitious sign or effect'. Del Rio, *Investigations into Magic*, 117 (book 3, part 1).

38 Mackenzie, *Laws and Customs*, 6 (part 1, title 1, para 1).

39 'not being and not appearing are equal in law'.

40 'Repeiled' (repelled): rejected.

It is ansred denayeng allwayes the samen that offering to do and yet did it not can import no more than that she made a Lie But *esto* it imported ane extrajudiciall Confesione of witchcroft yet that can never be fownd relevant to Infer the punishment of death.

As to that pairt of the Lybell quhich is speciall against Margaret Foultone viz. that she being at her house plunging ane sack in a tubfull of water said to the bystanders sirs ther will be sudden news as soon as they observed her putt the sack under watter imediatly the cray arose that the Boat was cast away.

It is ansred denaying the same as it is qualified in the Lybell for If she was doing anything with the sack it was washing it and as to the words thowgh they be denayed yet ther is nothing mor ordinar than to say that ther will be suden news where ther is a great storme or spate and so this can never be fownd Relevant to Infer the punishment Lybelled.

As to the thrid pairt of the Lybell viz. airt and pairt of witchcraft the pannells thowgh they thinke it hard that the act of parliament should hinder them to object against the maner of accessione or oblidge the persewers to condeshend specially what way they are airt and pairt in giving ther assistance and councill to the crimes of witchcroft; yet the pannells are so much conscious to themselves of there inocence of the Crymes Lybelled That they fear not that any accessione therto cane be proven *habili modo*.[41]

Butt secundo airt and pairt ought not to be admitted to probatione Butt most be Repelled Because airt and pairt is *ope et consilio*, counsell and assistance to the principall Cryme of witchcraft not being rightly Lybelled or qualified for the former Reasouns nether can airt and pairt of witchcroft be {*fo. 31v.*} sustained for *sublato principals tolitur accessarii*[42] Therfor airt and pairt ought to be Repelled.

As to the fourt pairt of the Lybell which conteans certane aleadged Indicatione of guilt or signs by quhich the pannells ar aleadged to be shrewedly suspected of witchcroft It is ansred to the first in particullar viz. That John Lindsay alias Bishope should have Been dilated Formarly of witchcroft And did give Alexander Hoome Ten dolours to prevent his being Indyted as the samen is denayed yet the same is not Relevantly Lybelled for the time and date of the delatione is not Condeshended upon that the pannels might be Exculpate and quhich cannot now be condeshended upon And the giving Ten dolours cannot be suposed to have been given for any witchcroft unless the delatione had proceeded Because *non Crediti Refferenti nisi constat de Relato*[43] And Efter the money had been given unwittingly by some of his freinds its suposed only to have been given to Redeime him from the disgrace of such ane occasione and not from any acknowledgment of guilt quhich ought to be interpret *in Charitii et Benignior interpretatio pro recto*

41 'in an effective way'.

42 'taking away the principals [i.e. the principal criminals] removes the accessories'.

43 'an informer is not to be believed unless the information appears'.

semper sequenda[44] *Ergo* no Respecte therto nor cannot be admitted to probatione *in hoc statu processus*[45] when the questione is of a Capitall punishment.

As to that Insinuatione of guilt against both the said John and James Lindsays viz. that they expressed themselves anno 1677 thus Woe to us that Patrick Lindsay was our father for he hes done something to us which will take our Lyfe.

It is ansred these words can never import the Lindsayes thowght themselves guilty of witchcroft Because iff they had been Really so they would never Expressed themselves, Woe to us For witches Rarlly Repent and it is not suposable ther father could make them witches against ther will. 2dly ther father died of good Fame when John was nyne and James three yeers of age so that they could not be capable to understand what woe ther father could bring upon them And 3to although the words could import ane extrajudiciall Confessione yet that could not militate against them Befor ane assyze unleless they adheered to it according to Clarus A. 2 n. 31[46] *Ergo* no respect therto and cannot be admitted to probatione adminiculat anything in order to infer a Capitall punishment.

As to the first General Insinuatione of Guilt {*fo. 32r.*} Founded on *malla Fama* or bad fame It is ansred they cannot be admitted to probatione Because no evidences therof were either Lybelled or Exhibited to the end the pannells might be better Exculpate and the grownds of the same ought to have been Lybelled for If fownded on womens stories or druncards ther craying at ther windows warlock warlock If these only be the originall of the Bad fame it cannot be sustained to Inquire for less in this state of the process when the Questione is punisheing by death as is Cleir by Clarus § *ult. quest*: 6 n. 15 14[47] Therfor and fame ought not to be admitted to probatione since no evidences therof ar either Lybelled or Exhibited And since the Questione is now *de Condemnando*[48] and the Judges Interloquitur is Expressly craved in this poynt as Likewayes is whither or not the mark comonly called the Devills mark can be pricked befor the assyze unless ther had been ane previous testimoney of *naturalisi*[49] declareing under ther hands the marks ar not naturall.

And as to the second generall Indicatione of guilt viz. the mark or nip It is no Indicatione of[50] reall witchcroft for efter it wer proven not to be naturall by two *naturalisi* there depositione yet such marks ar only ane Indicatione theron to tortour and tortoures is not allowed in our Law. Secundo such marks are denyed to have been gotten from the Devill which most be acknowledged

44 'a charitable and more benign interpretation should be given to something that always has a good outcome'.

45 'in that state of the process'.

46 Julius Clarus (Giulio Claro), *Receptae Sententiae*, in *Opera Omnia, sive Practica Civilis atque Criminalis* (1661). The precise reference has not been identified.

47 Clarus, *Receptae Sententiae*.

48 'concerning condemnation'.

49 *Sic*. Presumably the meaning is 'naturalists', in the sense of people skilled in natural matters. Physicians are probably implied.

50 'guilt' crossed out.

Before it can be ane Indicatione of guilt wheron to fownd a Capitall punishment to make the marks ane adminicle to Infer death.

3to the mark is *indicium Incertum* as Delrio sayes[51] and so no adminicle to Infer death Because there may be deadnes in the flesh and bone occasioned by a bad habite of body By quhich pin may be Insensible thowgh thrust to the Bone and through quhich is nothing else But a deep rooted secuerity.[52]

4to all the pannells did either blood or suell or boile By the prickinging [*sic*] and thowgh they had not either bled or felt paine it is no wonder for the paine is taken away when the skin is warbled[53] and the blood cannot come For when the skin is Lifted up and the Fleshe perced not imediatly below the hole that is made in the skinn which makes the skinne stope the appearance of blood by the wownd of a small pine Therfor this ought to be Repelled as no Indicatione of a witch Especially to be ane adminicle to fownd[54] the punishment of death. {*fo. 32v.*}

As to the Thrid generall Insinuatione of guilt viz. that the minister of Dumbartane and Bargarrans doughter named the pannells as ther tormenters It is denyed as to the Lindsayes. 2do it cannot be admitted to probatione to adminicullat guilt in ordar to a Capitall punishment Because it may be ane effect of the patients ther disscompositione of judgment the on[e] by his feaver and the other by her possessione and no doubt it were the most unjust thing in the world to sustaine this as ane Idicatione [*sic*] of guilt Because the Devill may Represent the most honest men in the world to those whom he possesses and that either as ther tormenter or not and in the same maner the honest alse weell as the dishonest And no doubt the Devill may have his own Cunning in this of purpose to attempt the spilling of Inocent Blood wherfor such ane Indicatione ought to be Repelled as frivolus.

As to the 4th Generall Indicatione of guilt That so soon as any of the pannells tuched Bargarrans doughter she tock a fitt This is denyed Especially as to John Lindsay alias Bishope But *esto* it were trew it is no Indicatione of guilt of witchcroft Because the Devill may give a fitt so soon as ane honest man tutches alse weell as a witch and 2do it may be caswall as de facto it wes when the Laird of Melderum tutched her Ergo since it and all these others may be false they ought not to be admitted in order to adminiculate theron to Infer the punishment of death.

Therfor all these Indications of guilt thowgh joynt with a Thousand others and proven ought to be Repelled as uncertane signs of the guilt of witchcroft Because all of them may faill and begetts only a presumptione and no pairt of a probatione at Leist such a probatione as is Requered in Criminalls quhich ought to be alse clear as sun shyne and what may faill owght never to be ane

51 'an uncertain indication' (of guilt). Delrio has a section on this topic, but the Devil's mark is not discussed in it: Delrio, *Disquisitiones Magicae*, 377–82 (book 5, section 4).

52 *Sic.* The sense may be 'freedom from sensibility'.

53 'warbled': having hard tumours or swellings.

54 'fownd': prove.

adminicle quherunto condemne Leist the Inocent may parish[55] and better a Thousand guilty pass unpunished then on[e] Inocent die Delrio sayes that that common Latine phrase *Ex multiplicatis Indiciis debilibus Resultare indicia indubitatae*[56] to be ane False argument Because what is doubtfull of its own nature can {*fo. 33r.*} never be without a doubt and a 1000 doubts never make a certantie and without a certane and evident probatione no man cane be condemned.

And quheras the persewers in ther Informatione aleadges that the Judges he[57] Restricted the debate to the Relevance *in hoc statu processus*[58] and therfor concluds that the advocate for the pannells owght not to insist in the maner of probatione It is ansred the Advocate for the pannells may and does insist in the maner of probatione since that Interloquitur (whither in this or any other state of the process) did Exclude the pannells from Insisting in the maner of probatione and trewly the Judges cannot doe it in Law otherwayes the maner of probatione would be Left undetermined quhich is the great poynt in this crime to be determined And the Judges knowes very weell that the Relevancy of the probatione falls as naturally under thir Cognizance as the Relevancy of the Lybell as was Expressly decyded by the Justices in anno 1666 in Bacanquells caice and since its *pari judicis*[59] the Judges cannot so much as omitte the determinatione theroff thowgh it were not desyred as it is expressly unless they Inclyne to think ther sentance should be Revised or advocate And quheras the persewers protest that If the maner of probatione be Insisted one it may not be Recorded, The pannells protest to the contrar.

And 2do the judges may Remember that that Interloquitur was pronunced on the Questione whither the trayell should proceed or not upon Indicationes nether lybelled nor Exhibited And 3^tio^ the Interloquitur does not Restrict by aney Restrictive particle Therfor the judges ought to determine the Relevancie of the maner of probatione alse weell as the Relevancy of the Lybell.

In Respect of all which it is hoped that the Lords Commissioners of this Justiciary will not be prepossessed with the great many Inacconnable [*sic*] stories spread abroad in this affair But will determine in this so serious a matter of lyfe and death article by article and what cane Infer death and what ane arbitray [*sic*] punishment and that after Long and serious Consideratione Leist Inocent blood be spilt and bring on Gods judgment on the Land and will Consider what that solid divine {*fo. 33v.*} Parkeins sayes that nether Bad Forme threatnings thowgh what wes threatned follow nor the defuncts Layeing ther death or torments upon the persowne accused can Infer this Crime For sayes he nothing can condemne

55 'parish': perish.

56 'many weak evidences can produce indubitable indications'. Delrio, *Disquisitiones Magicae*, 382 (book 5, section 5, para 4).

57 *Sic*. Probably read 'have'.

58 'in that state of the process'.

59 'an equivalent legal case'.

witches except ther own Confessione or tuo famous witnessis deponing upon the unlauful means used by them.[60] *Sic subscribitur* James Robertoune.

Curia justiciarie Supremi Domini Nostri Regis tenta in pretorio burgi de Paislay 17 die mensis May 1697 per honorabiles viros Alexandrum dominum de Blantyre[61] *dominum Joannem Houstoun de eodem dominum Joannem Maxwell de Pollock Alexandrum Porterfeild de eodem Wilielmum Muir de Glanderstoun et Robertum Semple vicecomitem deputatum de Renfrewe Commissionarios justiciarii dicti Supremi Domini Nostri Regis. Curia Legittime affirmata.*[62]

Intran
John Lindesay alias Bishop
James Lindsay alias Curat
John Lindsay in Barloch
Margaret Lang
Margaret Fultoun
Agnes Naesmith
Katharin Campbell

Indyted and accused for the crymes of witchcraft etc mentioned in ther dittay.

Persewers
Mr James Steuart
Mr Francis Grant

Prolocutors in defence
Mr James Robertoun

The debate upon the Indytment being publictlie read in face of court The Commissioners of justiciary Continued the pronunceing of their Interloquitor therupon till to morrowe at sevin a clock in the morning and ordained the pannalls to be caryed back to prison and the witnessis and assysers to attend Ilk person under the paine of 200 merks And continued the tryall of the remnant persons Indyted for witchcraft till the said day. {*fo. 34r.*}

60 William Perkins, *A Discourse of the Damned Art of Witchcraft* (Cambridge: Cantrel Ligge, 1610), 199–202, 210–18.

61 In margin: 'Lord Blantyre *preses*'.

62 'Court of justiciary of our sovereign lord the king held in the tolbooth of the burgh of Paisley, 17 May 1697, by the honourable men Alexander Lord Blantyre, lord John Houston of that Ilk, lord John Maxwell of Pollok, Alexander Porterfield of that Ilk, William Muir of Glanderston and Robert Sempill sheriff depute of Renfrew, commissioners of justiciary of our said sovereign lord the king. Court legally fenced.'

Curia justiciarie Supremi Domini Nostri Regis tenta in pretorio burgi de Paislay 18 die mensis May 1697 per honorabiles viros Alexandrum dominum de Blantyre[63] *Magistrum Franciscum Montgomery de Giffan dominum Joannem Maxwell de Pollock dominum Joannem Houstoun de eodem Alexandrum Porterfeild de eodem Wilielmum Muir de Glanderstoun Magistrum Joannem Steuart de Blackhall juniorem Advocatum Joannem Alexander de Blackhouse et Robertam Semple vicecomitem deputatem de Renfrewe Commissionarios justiciarii dicti Supremi Domini Nostri Regis. Curia Legittime affirmata.*[64]

Intran
John Lindesay alias Bishop
James Lindsay alias Curat
John Lindsay in Barloch
Margaret Lang
Margaret Fultoun
Agnes Naesmith
Katharin Campbell

Indyted and accused for the crymes of witchcraft socerie and necromancie and others mentioned in the dittay.

Persewers
Mr James Steuart
Mr Francis Grant of Quollan
Advocats

Prolocutor in defence
Mr James Robertoun Advocat {*fo. 34v.*}

The Commissioners of justiciary having considered the indytment againest John Lindesay alias Bishop, James Lindesay alias Curat, John Lindesay in Barloch, Margaret Lang, Margaret Fultoun, Katharin Campbell and Agnes Naesmith with the debate therupon They Find the pannals entering into the expresse paction with the Divil to become his servant, or their renunceing ther Baptisme, or owneing him for ther Lord and master Relevant to inferre the paines Lybelled.

63 In margin: 'Lord Blantyre *preses*'.

64 'Court of justiciary of our sovereign lord the king held in the tolbooth of the burgh of Paisley, 18 May 1697, by the honourable men Alexander Lord Blantyre, Mr Francis Montgomerie of Giffen, lord John Maxwell of Pollok, lord John Houston of that Ilk, Alexander Porterfield of that Ilk, William Muir of Glanderston, Mr John Stewart younger of Blackhall advocate, John Alexander of Blackhouse and Robert Sempill sheriff depute of Renfrew, commissioners of justiciary of our said sovereign lord the king. Court legally fenced.'

And lykewayes Finds the malefices Lybelled being proven to be perpretat [*sic*] upon the persons of Christian Shawe, the minister of Dumbarton, the children of Mr John Ritchie, William Montgomerie, Mathew Park, Mr William Flemying and James Millar and upon George Cuninghame of Brighouse and John Glen the ferrier of Erskine or any of them (*ita ut constat de corpore delicti*[65]) That if any of the pannalls wer personallie present at the acting therof or at any meitings with the Divil and his associats, wher the wayes or meanes for effectuating therof, upon the persons abovenamed contained in the Indytment wes consulted or contrived, or airt and part therof Relevant to inferre the paines Lybelled.

Also they Find the pannalls useing plaine and manifest acts of charming socerie or necromancy also Relevant to inferre the paines Lybelled especiallie if with one or all of the above articles ther concurre insensible parts (called the Divils mark) found upon ther bodies, and defamation for witchcraft or *mala fama*[66] And Remitts the same to the knowledge of the inquest and allowes probation to be Led therupon and the other circumstances Lybelled.

Mr James Robertoun craved the Lords might declaire what maner of probation they will allowe to be adduced for proveing the Indytment and poynts therof found Relevant and particularlie of Renunceing of Baptizme entering into Compact with the Divil and owneing him for ther Lord and master be provable by witnessis. {*fo. 35r.*}

The persewers oppone ther Interloquitor wherby the poynts therin mentioned are found Relevant and Remitted to the knowledge of the assyse and they will prove the same as they will be served.

The Commissioners of justiciary ordaine the persewers to adduce ther probation upon the poynt found Relevant Reserveing to the pannalls ther legall objections against the probation when adduced.

The Commission of justiciary with Consent of the persewers and for severall good causes moveing them desert the dyet against Margaret and Jannet Rogers Indyted for witchcraft.

The Commissioners of justiciary having considered the objections proponed against Mr John Ritchie and others the parents of the children tortured, with the answers made therto by the persewers, They sustaine the parents of the saids children as witnessis for proveing the maner of the death or tortor of ther children.

65 'as is clear from the body of the offence'.
66 'bad reputation'.

Assisa

William King in Lochquhinoch	William Alexander late bailye of Paislay
Walter Paterson of Craigtoun	Robert Alexander in Abotsinch
James Dunlop maltman in Paislay	Hugh Allan in Bridge of Weir
James Craufurd merchant in Greinock	Robert Rosse in Linwood
Thomas Maine merchant in Carsdyik	James Semple in Midletoun

John Sympson in Park of Erskin
James Taylor merchant in Carsdyik
William Rowand in Bedland
Robert Pirrie in Wester Wakingshawe
John Ailison of Carsbridge

The assyse Laufullie sworne no objection of the Lawe in the contrair.

The persewers for probation adduced the witnessis efter deponing viz. {*fo. 35v.*} Mr Andrew Turner minister of the Gospell at Erskine aged 29 years or therby maried purged of malice prejudice and partiall Councill and solemnlie sworne depons he hes frequentlie sein Christian Shawe daughter to the Laird of Bargarran violentlie tormented the tymes Lybelled particularlie she wes niped and bitten in the armes by some invisible power and he hes sein marks of teith upon her arme Immediatly upon her crying out that she wes bitten and that there wes no persons teith or hands that he could see about her at the tyme she wes niped and bitten. Depons he hes also sein Bargarrans daughter putt out of her mouth hair and pins when no visible agent wes about her to his sight to putt them in her mouthe and that she said they wer putt in by those that wer tormenting her viz. by Katharin Campbell the pannall.[67] Depons he hes sein Christian Shawe stiffen in whole bodie in ane instant her tongue pulled out of her mouth over the chine[68] and drawen back agane doun her throat. He hes sein her head drawen backward near to her heils like a bowe and at that time she wes also stiff and her eyes turned in her head, her teith sett close togither somtyme when her tongue wes betuixt them somtyme not so as it took great strength to putt a stick betuixt her teith to preserve her tongue, Hes sein her head turned about towards her shoulders, Hes sein her bellie raised in a moment as a womans with child and fall as soon, hes in her torments glasped [*sic*] with her hands and feit things near her and wuld not be seperat from them, He hes sein her in her fitts hurried too and froe with violence throwe the roume with the senses of seeing or hearing yet at the same

[67] In margin: 'Campbell'.
[68] 'chine': chin.

tyme when some of the suspected persons or confessing warlocks came to the roume she sawe and heard them and conversed with them. He heard her cry out upon receaving a bruise in her leg by some person invisible to the company then present and depons he hes sein her in these or the like fitts of torment frequentlie and in her torments she hes named Margaret Lang and Katharin Campbell[69] as her tormenters when she wes out of her torments and hes when she wes out of her fitts John and James Lindesays, John Lindsay[70] {*fo. 36r.*} in Barloch Margaret Fultoun and Agnes Naesmith pannalls also as her tormenters depons John Lindesay alias Bishop and James Lindsay alias Curat[71] are of ill fame as witches within the parroch of Erskine and heard the Bishop hade bein dilated severall years befor as a warlock by a confessing witch in the parroch of Kilmalcolme. Depons that Christian Shawe in a fitt of torment when she neither sawe nor heard nor could speak to any of the company yet uttered some words in meiter relateing to her owne trouble without moving her Lips to her[72] apprehension[73] and efterwards fell a danceing, and laughing when she wes danceing and being come out of the fitt being inquyred howe she came to dance she said that the witches hade inclosed her in a ring and wer danceing about her and made her dance gladlie with them depons that when Katharin Campbell wes apprehended and questioned for tormenting of Christian Shawe she said Divil let never her nor any belonging to her become better or worse depons that Christian Shawe being inquyred by Margaret Lang if ever she hade sein her amongst her tormentors Christian replyed I will not say it, but Mr Patrick Sympson having urged her to say either I or no,[74] the said Christian attempting to say yes fell in a fitt of torment and when recovered againe desyred to tell if Margaret Lang wes her tormenter she gott only the word 'tint'[75] exprest, wherupon she againe fell in another violent fitt and when she wes out of the fitt she explained the word tint and said Margaret Lang[76] hade Lett some hair fall as she came in at the door which wes a charme as she said to bind her up that she wuld not name Margaret Lang and when[77] Margaret Lang went dounstaires Chatharin [*sic*] Shawe said she wes nowe at liberties to speak and to accuse Margaret Lang. Depons that Christian Shawe being hoodwinked[78] by a cloik so that she sawe non about her; when tutched by one accused to be her tormenter she fell in a fitt, but when tutched by

69 In margin: 'Lang, Campbell'.
70 In margin: 'Lindesays'.
71 In margin: 'Fultoun, Naesmith, Lindesays'.
72 *Sic*. Read 'his'.
73 'to his apprehension': as far as he could see or understand.
74 'I or no': aye or no.
75 'tint': lost.
76 In margin: 'Lang'.
77 'the hair wes found she' crossed out.
78 'hoodwinked': blindfolded.

others no such effect followed and that upon a tutch of John Lindesay in Barloch and James Lindsay the Curat[79] and Katharin Campbel[80] the pannalls Christian Shawe fell in fitts of torment but no such effect {*fo. 36v.*} followed when she wes tutched by persons not suspected. Depons he sawe all the pannalls pricked except Margaret Lang and insensible marks found upon them and big pins putt in these marks and they said they found no paine nor came ther out any blood when they wer pricked tho the pins wes putt to the head *causa scientie*[81] he wes frequentlie at Bargarrans house praying and visiting the tormented person and sawe what he hes deponed and this is the truth as he shall answer to God.

[*Signed:*] AndrTurner.[82]

Mr James Birsbane minister at Kilmacolme aged 27 years maried purged and sworne depons he hes sein Christian Shawe in frequents [*sic*] fitts of torment the tymes Lybelled[83] particularlie a fitt which she took by sweiting wherin her eyes turned in her head both as to collor and bignes, her tongue drawen back in to her throat and instantlie pulled over her chine, her craig[84] drawen doun to her throat and instantly againe extended to more then ane ordinary bignes, a violent motion in the tyme both in back and breast efter the recoverie out of which fitts she would have told who hade tormented her, when she would take the nixt and howe Long it would continue. The second fitt wes a fitt which she called a frighting fitt wherin she fell dead stiff with all the parts of her bodie extended and at the taking and somtymes in the tyme of the fitt she uttered violent screichs. The third wes a light fitt which she took by a swerff[85] her head drawen about towards her shoulder wherin she wes lighter then for ordinar and during the fitt hade ane extraordinar palpitation in severall parts of her body and recovered instantly by the same kind of swerff and in the intervall wes perfectlie composed. The fourth fitt wes taken in tyme of prayer in which she remained in that same pouster she wes sitting in at prayer and by his violent strength he could not alter her from that pouster, and having so remained for a quarter of ane hour and then returning to her ordinary pouster she came violently from one end of the hall to the other with such force that bystanders wer necessitat to prevent her being brained against the wall and in these fitts she fell three or four tymes {*fo. 37r.*} in one

79 In margin: 'Lindesays'.
80 In margin: 'Campbell'.
81 '[his] cause of knowledge [being that]'.
82 This signature appears at first sight to be a holograph, as do numerous others that follow. However, some of the later signatures are similar to each other in style, and it is likely that the scribe has attempted to replicate holographs that were originally written on separate sheets.
83 In margin: 'Tortor of Christian Shawe'.
84 'craig': neck.
85 'swerff': fainting.

morning and wes well throwe the rest of the day. The 5th fitt he sawe her in wes that having gone to her bed in Light fitt she fell in another kind of fitt her armes being folded about her head, and when tutched by any would violently screich, and she begane to sing some countrey tunes or songs falling out of one in another the notes of which she perfectly observed and fell in ryming verses sutable to those various tunes which he judged to be anent the ryse and progresse of her trouble and then rose and fell a danceing and leaping so that the strength of her father could not hold her and she instantly recovered out of the fitt and wes well as formerlie and gave ane account that nyn or ten of the crewe wer danceing about her in a ring who would have caried her away and with whome she then danced and would have gone with complaucencie and that non of that crewe wes visible to the deponent. Depons farder that during the intervalls of fitts and also whill in the Light fitt she declaired that Katharin Campbell and Agnes Naesmith[86] wer her tormentors, and severall others whom she then named Katharin Campbell befor her Imprisonment but not since except one day; Agnes Naesmith befor her praying for her but not efter the appearing amongst the crewe but defending her against the violence of the rest. Depons that as to four of the abovementioned fitts Christian Shawe said she wes tormented by the witches, as to the stiff or frightening fitt she declaired the occasion of it wes her seeing of the Divil in horrid shapes threatening to devour her and take her witts from her. Depons that John Lindesay called Bishop[87] hes bein under common bruit and fame as a witch ever since he remembers, and he hes heard James Lindesay reput a witch, thir tuo years past. Depons the haill pannalls being pricked hade insensible marks upon ther bodies which he sawe pricked,[88] and depons theranent conforme to ane particular note given in signed under his hand *causa patet*[89] and this is the truth as he shall answer to God.

[*Signed:*] Ja: Birsbane. {*fo. 37v.*}

Mr Patrick Sympson minister of the Gospell at Renfrewe aged 69 years maried purged and sworne depons he hes sein Christian Shawe in severall fitts of torment the tyme Lybelled. Depons that he wes in the house of Bargaran when Margaret Lang[90] wes brought ther, and when Christian Shawe wes Interogat \by the said Margaret/ if she hade sein her amongst her tormentors and that the said Christian seemed to be bound up by her fitts and said faintlie to her, no, and then when she wes asked a second tyme \by some others why she said/, to the best of his remembrance she said,[91] contrair \and imediatly took fitt/,

[86] In margin: 'Campbell, Naesmith'.
[87] In margin: 'Lindesays'.
[88] In margin: 'marks on all'.
[89] 'the cause is openly known'.
[90] In margin: 'Lang'.
[91] 'tint, and took another fitt' crossed out.

and the third tyme being Interogat she said tint and took a great fitt and when they wer carying the child to another roume Margaret Lang said Lord God blisse the[e] and ding the Divil out of the[e], and when Margaret Lang wes gone and the child recovered out of her fitts, He heard her say that the charme wes brock and then she could positivlie tell Margaret Lang to her face that she wes one of her tormentors and this is the truth as he shall answer to God.

[*Signed:*] Pa: Simson.

Margaret Campbell servitrix to the Laird of Bargaran aged 18 years unmaried purged and sworne depons she hes sein Christian Shawe in severall fitts of torment and she hes heard her name the haill pannalls as her tormentors except James Lindesay called Curat,[92] Depons that at one tyme she heard Christian Shawe say that all her tormentors hade gone away except one, and the same day she heard the children of the familie say within the hours therefter that they sawe a woman with a read coat in the yaird of Bargarran. Depons that at a tyme Christian Shawe being in the chamber and the deponer besid her she cryed out that she wes wounded in the thigh and her uncle North Barr[93] having putt in his hand in her pocket he found a folded kniff in it oppin, and the kniff being folded and putt in her pocket againe she gave another cry that she wes wounded and her uncle North Barr having putt in his hand in her pocket he found the kniff which he hade folded and putt in her pocket, then oppined againe in her pocket. Depons that another tyme Christian Shawe said that ther wes a {*fo. 38r.*} charme under the bed and she went and took out something like ane ege from under the bed, depons she hes sein Christian Shawe take fitts of torment upon John Lindesay of Barlochs[94] tutching her. *Causa patet* and this is the truth as she shall answer to God and the deponent hes sein Christian Shawe transported violentlie out of the rowme with such a swift motion that they could not observe her tutch the ground.

[*Signed:*] Mar: Cambel.

Mr Allan Naesmith schoolmaster at Dunbartoun aged 23 years unmaried purged and sworne depons that Mr John Hardie minister at Dunbartoun[95] wes extraordinarly tormented and that he said he sawe extraordinary sights which he beleived non of them sawe and wes heard argueing as if with persons tempting him, useing such expressions as these That I disowne, this answer I give to all, I live by faith in the son of God by whom I expect to be saved and upon whom I depend, and that he said he sawe women whom he desyred to

92 In margin: 'All pannalls except Curat'.

93 John McGilchrist, Christian Shaw's maternal uncle. He was the son of James McGilchrist of Northbar.

94 In margin: 'Barloch'.

95 In margin: 'Tortor of Mr Hardie'.

be removed whom non of the company present sawe and that his torment wes so extraordinary that he being in another roume he found it to shaik throwe the violent throweings that Mr Hardie made in his bed and that Mr Hardie wes in an extraordinary agonie and his face extraordinary redd and he hade a stranger Look then ever he observed in any man. Depons that the night befor Mr Hardie dyed he wes in sound judgement even at that tyme when he said that he heard and sawe strang[e] things which non of the company heard or sawe. Depons that the tyme of his sicknes he said he heard his hall door oppin and that he heard dinn belowe which non of the company heard and this is the truth as he shall answer to God.

[*Signed:*] ANaismith.

Mr Archibald Wallace minister of the Gospell at Cardrosse aged 25 years maried purged and sworne depons Mr Hardie minister at Dunbartoun[96] wes in extraordinary torment befor his death and when he took him in his armes to desyre him to Lye doun He said what shall I doe, they will not {*fo. 38v.*} lett me allone. Depons he judged him in sound judgement the day he dyed, and that he gave answers to people he apprehended wes speaking to him, whom non of the company sawe as I desyre you ye cannot wrong me for I ame in Christ and all the answer I cane give you is that which I have given you befor I live by faith in Jesus Christ and on him allone I depend. Depons he wes in a mighty sweat throwe all his bodie his face and eyes extraordinary redd and dyed in agonie that night and this is the truth as he shall answer to God.

[*Signed:*] Ard: Wallace.

Mr Mathew Birsbane doctor of Medicine aged 50 and above purged and sworne depons that severall tymes sitting by Christian Shawe[97] he hes sein her like to be choaked somtymes with hair somtymes with feathers and bitts of strae but most commonlie with hair and once with a cinder which when she putt out of her mouth wes dry and a great deall hotter then the heat of her bodie and that she told him at the tyme when these things wer in her mouth she apprehended ther wes somthing thrusting them doun her throat and that he observed her narrowlie and could perceave no visible instrument cary them into her mouth and that both from that and that the hair cinder and most other things commonly wer dry He concluded they hade never bein in her stomack nor hade she any thing like womiting or presse of vomiting in putting them furth. Depons that the things she cast up wer never bred in her bodie to his judgement, and that befor these things happined he thought the other Symptomes might have bein accountable for from Ecconomie of the bodie preternaturallie affected or disordered but these things being *toto genere contra*

96 In margin: 'Tortor of Mr Hardie'.

97 In margin: 'Tortor of Christian Shawe'.

naturam[98] and medicins that in other like cases {*fo. 39r.*} hade proven successfull in removeing of the like disorders as convulsions and such distortions of the body not succeeding here he did and does verie much suspect it to flowe from higher causes. Depons that in the begining of Christian Shawes sicknes she named Katharin Campbell and a women called Naesmith as they that pinched and pricked her with pins, and heard he [*sic*] cry O why are ye so cruell, and depons he sawe a pine sticking in the bone of Margaret Fultouns lege near ane inch, and could discover no tash[99] or cariousnes[100] in the bone tho the lege wes verie lean. And this is the truth as he shall answer to God.

[*Signed:*] MBrisbane MD.

James Buchanan in Wester Kilpatrick aged 50 years and upwards maried purged and sworne depons that he hes tuo severall tymes sein Mr Ritchies child as if he hade bein in the passions of death and recover and growe better againe, and fall ill and recover in half ane hours tyme. Depons that when the boat of Erskine perished the tyme Lybelled he sawe George Cuninghame of Brighouse who wes so called and owned by the gentlemen of the countrey, and John Glen the ferrier taken out of the watter the day efter they perished and this is the truth as he shall answer to God. Farder depons that when Margaret Fultouns[101] husband wes made ane officer both the husband and wyff declaired that Margaret Fultoun being sick a poor woman offered to make her wholl and that she took a dish and putt somthing therin, Laid it under a kist[102] dischairging Fultoun to take it out till to morrowe efter which the said Fultoun grewe worse and her husband having tryed the same night what wes in the dish putt under the kist, found therin some blood and cinders and that Fultouns husband when the deponent and she wes speaking theranent answered that if the Divill took not the members of court he would warrand them from the faires and that both Fultoun and her husband declaired that he viz. the {*fo. 39v.*} husband hade brought hir back from the faires [*sic*] by her owne grein aprone, and she said to the deponent ye need not laugh at this for if it wer not so, I hade not bein here. Depons that Margaret Fultoun hes bein reput a witch in this countrey this Long tyme past and this is the truth as he shall answer to God.

[*Signed:*] James Buchanan.

Margaret Steuart spouse to James Buchanan the former deponent solemnlie sworne and purged depons that Mr Ritchies child hade strong fitts and great cryes and would bend so up as it wes hard to gett him holden and that he would

98 'completely against nature'.
99 'tash': blemish.
100 'cariousnes': decay.
101 In margin: 'Fultoun'.
102 'kist': chest.

turne blae[103] and black the tyme of his fitts[104] and continued to fall out of on[e] in another the space of a wholl day and that he hade a great drough and purgeing and she sawe him dye on her owne knee. As to the drowning of Brighouse and John Glen depons conforms to her husband and also anent the getting the pretended cure from the beggar wyff and anent bringing back Margaret Fultoun[105] by her owne aprone, that the said Margaret said when they wer discourseing of it, It wes verie true for if it hade not bein for her husband she hade not bein ther. Depons she hes heard her to be under the scandell of a witch this dizon of years past and this is truth as she shall answer to God. Depons she cannot wreitt.
[*Signed:*] Blantyre.

Jannet Smith spouse to William Shawe in Wester Kilpatrick aged 36 years purged and sworne depons she knowes nothing but that Margaret Fultoun[106] wes commonly reput in the countrey for a witch and hes heard her called so in her owne house which is the truth as she shall answer to God. {*fo. 40r.*}

Mr John Ritchie minister at Kilpatrick depons the child dyed of great paines tortors and agonies frequently chainged collers pale red and somewhat blackish and efter his strength wes exhausted by frequent fitts expyred. Depons Margaret Fultoun hes bein under fame of a witch thir nyn years since he came to the parroch and this is the truth as he shall answer to God.
[*Signed:*] Jo: Ritchie.

William Montgomery in Bargarrans Land aged 34 years maried purged and sworne depons his child[107] went well to bed and wes found dead in the morning and hade a blae mark at the vain orgaine and bled a litle at the nose efter he wes taken dead out of the bed. Depons they hade bein sifting maill in the house the night the child dyed. Depons he knowes no more and cannot wreitt and this is the truth as he shall answer to God.
[*Signed:*] Blantyre jpc.

Agnes Craig spouse to the former deponent purged and sworne[108] depons conforms to her husband William Montgomery in all poynts and adds that Agnes Naesmith[109] came to her house and asked hir childs age about a fourthnight befor; and when the deponent seemed shye to tell her the bairns age because she wes feared to tell it, she said that she hade speired[110] Christian

103 'blae': livid or bluish (as with a bruise).
104 In margin: 'Fultoun'.
105 In margin: 'Fultoun'.
106 In margin: 'Fultoun'.
107 In margin: 'Montgomerys child'.
108 In margin: 'Montgomerys child'.
109 In margin: 'Naesmith'.
110 'speired': asked.

Shawes age. Depons she heard the Bishop famed of a long tyme for a witch and this is the truth as she shall answer to God and she cannot wreitt.
[*Signed:*] Blantyre jpc.

Mathew Park in Parkland aged 28 years maried purged and sworne depons his daughter[111] of tuentie dayes old went well to bed at night and wes found dead in the morning, and ther wes some blood upon the childs nose and some upon her mouth and breast and he thinks that {*fo. 40v.*} Immediatly upon the death of the child his wyff cryed to him O Mathew Mathew the child is gone. Depons he heard John Lindsay called Bishop[112] reput a witch thir sex years past and this is the truth as he shall answer to God and he cannot wreitt and heard Agnes Naesmith also repute a witch and James Lindsay.[113]
[*Signed:*] Blantyre jpc.

Margaret Lyl spouse to the said Mathew Park purged and sworne depons conforms to her husband as to the death of the child. Depons she cannot wreitt.
[*Signed:*] Blantyre jpc.

Jean Ker late servitrix to the Laird of Bargaran spouse to John Lindesay in Paislay aged 23 years purged and sworne depons she wes fellowe servant at on[e] tyme with Katharin Campbell[114] in Bargarans house and that she wes ane ill natured person and cursed frequently when any thing angered her, and that she pretendit to sleep at the fyre syd at night, and wes sleeprie in the morning. Depons she sawe a ball of hair taken out of Katharin Campbells pockett with severall pins in it, and that the \ball of/ hair wes of the same collor of hair that Christian Shawe putt out of her mouth and of the same kind of hair and the ball of hair wes hardlie so big as ane ege and that when the ball of hair wes burnt she never sawe her cast up any hair tho she sawe her cast up hair from her mouth severall tymes befor. Depons that she sawe Agnes Naesmith[115] in Bargarrans closse earlie in the morning and she asked howe they wer and the deponent bad her goe in and see and she said she would not goe in for the Last tyme she wes ther she gott only a herring and peice of bread. Depons she heard Christian Shawe say that Agnes Naesmith asked her age and health. Depons she heard Katharin {*fo. 41r.*} Campbell Imprecat Gods curse on Christian Shawe and say Divil hurle her soul throwe hell. Deppons she cannot wreitt and this is the truth as she shall answer to God.
[*Signed:*] Blantyre jpc.

111 In margin: 'Parks child'.
112 In margin: 'Bishop'.
113 In margin: 'Curat'.
114 In margin: 'Campbell'.
115 In margin: 'Naesmith'.

Katharin Deans late servitrix to the Laird of Bargaran aged 24 years purged and sworne depons she sawe a ball of hair taken out of Katharin Campbells[116] pocket which wes of the same collor of hair that Christian Shawe hade cast out of her mouth and that ther wer pins in it. Depons she heard Katharin Campbell curse Christian Shawe twice and say Gods curse on her and the Divill harle[117] her throwe hell and this is the truth as she shall answer to God.
[*Signed:*] Blantyre jpc.

Agnes McCaslan servitrix to Bargaran aged 31 years *soluta*[118] purged and sworne depons she sawe Agnes Naesmith[119] earlie in the morning befor sune \ryseing come/ towards Bargarans closse by the back of the house the verie day befor Christian Shawe took her torments and the deponent wes feared for her and said God be betuixt me and you and went her way and this is the truth as she shall answer to God and she cannot wreitt.
[*Signed:*] Blantyre jpc.

John Sympson armorer in Glasgowe aged 34 years maried purged and sworne depons he desyred Catharin Campbell[120] to blisse and pray for Christian Shawe and she could not doe it efter she hade promised to doe it and wes upon her knees, tho the words wer repeated to her and ther wes non then present but he and the childs father and this is the truth as he shall answer to God.
[*Signed:*] John Simpson.

Katharin Campbell being judiciallie examined upon what is contained in the abovewritten deposition she acknowledges the same is truth.
[*Signed:*] Blantyre jpc. {*fo. 41v.*}

John McGilchrist writer in Glasgowe aged 24 years unmaried purged and sworne depons he sawe Margaret Lang[121] come to Bargarans house the tyme lybelled, and that she satt near the door and that Christian Shawe said that she wes bound up from telling that Margaret Lang wes on[e] of her tormentors and efter she wes gone she hade freedome to accuse her and that Christian Shawe said that the charme by which she wes restrained wes a litle hair lett fall by Margaret Lang, and that he heard Christian Shawe in on[e] of her fitts expresse the word tint. Depons he burnt the hair in the fyre which hair he gott from Bargaran. Depons that it wes efter Margaret Lang wes gone that Christian Shawe said that the reason of hir being restrained wes by Margaret

116 In margin: 'Campbell'.
117 'harle': drag.
118 'divorced'.
119 In margin: 'Naesmith'.
120 In margin: 'Campbell'.
121 In margin: 'Lang'.

Langs putting a charme upon her by letting fall a litle puckle of hair and this is the truth as he shall answer to God.

[*Signed:*] Jo McGilchrist.

John Duncan schoolmaster at Erskine aged 35 years maried purged and sworne depons he sawe steads[122] of bytting on Christian Shawes hand and the print of the teith and slever[123] remaining, which Christian Shawe said she hade gotten by Margaret Langs command, which she told when she wes out of the fitt and when she wes in her fitts she gave a cry when she receaved the byttings and the marks of it Immediatly appeared and he wes sure that neither her self nor any other person visible did bytt her. Depons he heard Katharin Campbell[124] curse in the ministers house when she wes apprehended saying God lett never Bargaran nor his daughter be better till she wer clear of that scandel and this is the truth as he shall answer to God.

[*Signed:*] Jo: Duncan. {*fo. 42r.*}

Elizabeth Kennedy spouse to Mr Andrew Turner minister at Erskine purged and sworne depons she sawe Bargaran when Margaret Lang[125] wes in his house Find a litle hair and sawe the hair burnt, but sawe not Margaret Lang make use of the hair and this is the truth as she shall answer to God.

[*Signed:*] Elizabeth Kennedy.

Jannet Laird daughter to the deceast James Laird in Kilmacolme aged 30 years unmaried purged and sworne depons that Margaret Lang[126] enquyred the deponent if she wes desyrous to see her mother who wes dead three year befor or therby, to which the deponent replyed that she hoped she wes in heaven and desyred not to see her nor any thing in her shape and Margaret Lang replyed to this that many hade sein ther parents that Longed for them efter they wer dead and this is the truth as she shall answer to God and she cannot wreitt.

[*Signed:*] Blantyre jpc.

Elspeth Glassie daughter to the deceast John Glessie [*sic*] in Erskin aged 20 years unmaried purged and sworne depons that somtymes when Margaret Lang[127] pretended to come from privat prayer she would throwe stools throwe the house, and she hes heard her say that she wes affraid of Hell and wrath and that she once heard her say two or three dayes befor she wes taken, that

122 'steads': marks.

123 'slever': saliva.

124 In margin: 'Campbell'.

125 In margin: 'Lang'.

126 In margin: 'Lang'.

127 In margin: 'Lang'.

befor this wer ended she would dye ane ill dead, and they would see it and this is the truth as she shall answer to God and she cannot wreitt.

[*Signed:*] Blantyre jpc.

James Lindesay in Hilneuk aged 35 years maried purged and sworne[128] depons that he heard James Millars daughter who wes his servant declaire that Margaret Lang Looked in her face in William Semples house in Tounhead of Erskin and asked whose [*1 word crossed out*] daughter she wes, and her father answered she wes his and that this wes upon the sabboth day and upon the morrowe the lassie sickened and dyed within a fourthnight and that in her sicknes he once heard her name Margaret Lang. He cannot {*fo. 42v.*} wreitt and this is the truth as he shall answer to God.

[*Signed:*] Blantyre jpc.

Elizabeth Kinloch spouse to the said James Lindesay depons conforms to her husband except that she did not her[129] James Millars daughter name Margaret Lang the tyme of her sicknes and this is the truth as she shall answer to God and she cannot wreitt.

[*Signed:*] Blantyre jpc.

Marion Burnesyd servitrix to James Lang in Kilpatrick aged 20 years or therby purged and sworne depons that it wes the report throwe the haill countrey ever since she remembers that Margaret Fultoun[130] wes a witch and she cannot wreitt and this is the truth as she shall answer to God.

[*Signed:*] Blantyre jpc.

Archibald Glen in Lawe aged 22 years unmaried purged and sworne depons it wes the voice of the countrey that Margaret Fultoun[131] is a witch. He cannot wreitt and this is the truth as he shall answer to God.

[*Signed:*] Blantyre jpc.

Alexander Hume of Kirkhouse aged 50 years or therby maried purged and sworne depons that in the year 1687 John Lindesay called Bishop and James Lindsay called Curat[132] wer dilated by Elspeth Aitkine a confessing witch at Kilmacolme who in her confessione declaired \the said/ John and James Lindesays the pannalls wer guilty of the cryme of witchcraft with her and that they frequently keeped meitings with the Divill wher she and they wer present

[128] In margin: 'Lang'.

[129] *Sic.* Read 'hear'.

[130] In margin: 'Fultoun'.

[131] In margin: 'Fultoun'.

[132] In margin: 'Lindesays called Bishop and Curat'.

togither efter which George Lindesay of Balquharage trysted[133] the deponent at Erskin and told him he wes Imployed by John Lindsay called Bishop to desyre the deponent to score him out of the roll which the deponent told him he could not, then he desyred he might delay him from being apprehended till of the Last of them that should be dilated which he promised to doe for which Balquharage in the said John Lindesays name gave the deponent ten dollors[134] wherupon the deponent gave *{fo. 43r.}* a note to Balquharage that he should be amongst the Last and the deponent produced his Commission and Elspeth Aitkins Confession which wes publictlie read and returned to him and that is the truth as he shall answer to God.

[*Signed:*] Alexr: Hume.

George Lindesay of Balquharage aged 64 years maried purged and sworne depons that John Lindesay alias Bishop[135] being dilated as a warlock did send to the deponent a boy desyring him to treat with Alexander Hume then sherreff deput who hade a Commission for trying witches and treat with him to delay the putting the said John Lindesay in the holl,[136] or at least to make him the Last of the roll and acquaint the deponent befor he apprehended him and the deponent gave Alexander Hume ten dollors and gott a note from the shirriff to delay the said Lindsay which the deponent produced and it wes publictlie read and delivered back, and this ten dollors wes sent to him by John Lindesay called Bishop and delivered to him by his good brother and this is the truth as he shall answer to God.

[*Signed:*] GLindsay.

William Semple in Tounhead of Erskine aged 50 years maried purged and sworne[137] depons that nyn years agoe the deponent being in North Barr park about nyn aclock at night in a clear moon light night James Lindsay alias Curat appeared to him the deponent on a suddent and \he/ did not knowe wher he came from, till he wes at him, and spock with him of his brother John Lindesay telling he should not gett his will of him if he wer hanged and that he gave him a light tutch or stroak with his staff by which the deponent fell over the dyck wher he then stood upon the tope of a stone, And depons that as James Lindsay came to the deponent in the park he thought his feit did not tutch the ground. Depons he wes turned over the dyke by a verie light tutch by which fall he Lay near four hours. Depons that by speech habit and cloathes and staff he thought it wes James Lindsay the pannal that mett

133 'trysted': arranged to meet.
134 'dollors': Dutch coins that often circulated in seventeenth-century Scotland.
135 In margin: 'Bishop'.
136 *Sic.* Read 'roll', i.e. the list of persons to be arrested.
137 In margin: 'Curat'.

with him in the park \as reallie/ as he judges him nowe to be on the pannall. Depons it is about tuentie years since he heard John Lindsay called Bishop and James Lindsay called {*fo. 43v.*} Curat wer bruited as warlocks in the countrey. Depons he thinks if he hade gotten so light a tutch from any honest person it would not made [*sic*] him fall and this is the truth as he shall answer to God.

[*Signed:*] William Sempil.

Mr Patrick Sympson minister at Renfrewe farder depons that he sawe a mark upon Margaret Langs[138] hipp which neither pine nor neidle would peirce tho they wer pressed in with great force and this is the truth as he shall answer to God and depons that the pine bowed upon her.

[*Signed:*] Pat: Simson.

Mr Alexander King minister at Bonneill solemnlie sworne and purged depons that he sawe Margaret Lang pricked and that ther wes a mark found behind her shoulder and the man endeavoured to thrust the pine in it, and the pine bended and the man said it would not goe in unlesse he got a hammar to it[139] and then he took a needle which he also thrust till the needle brock and he said it would not goe foreward with him and he did not see it blood, nor her complaine of paine at first, but efterward she made some noise and sawe lykwayes ane insensible mark upon Kathrin Campbell[140] and a pine sticking in it and this is the truth as he shall answer to God.

[*Signed:*] alexr: King.

The Commissioners of justiciary having considered the objections proponed against Elizabeth Anderson, James and Thomas Lindsays, Jannet and Margaret Rogers and Christian Shawe daughter to Bargaran, witnessis adduced for the persewers with the answers made therto They ordaine Elizabeth Anderson James Lindsay, Jannet and Margaret Rogers to be sworne and examined witnessis *cum nota*:[141] and allows Thomas Lindsay and Christian Shawe to be examined upon such poynts and articles as shall be found Relevant for proveing either the pannals guilt or Innocence but not upon oath and refuse to allowe the declarations to be put in wreitting or on record. {*fo. 44r.*}

Elizabeth Anderson daughter to umquhile Alexander Anderson in Bowes of Inchinand solemnlie sworne purged of malice, prejudice, partiall councill and receaved and admitted a witnes *cum nota*, depons That the tyme Lybelled she wes at a meiting in Bargarans yaird with the haill sevin pannalls wher wes

138 In margin: 'Lang'.
139 In margin: 'Lang'.
140 In margin: 'Campbell'.
141 'with a note': a technical phrase meaning that some doubt should be attached to their testimony.

the Divill in the likenes of a man cloathed in black wher she did see Margaret Lang and Margaret Fultoun converse with the Divil and did also see the Divil give each of the pannalls a peice of an unchristianed childs liver as he called it, and they did eat it, and the Divil told them if they confest he would gett no good of ther bodies or of ther souls,[142] but nowe ther wes no fear of ther confessing since they hade gott a peice of that liver. Also depons that at that meiting she heard them treating with the Divil anent the tortoring and destroying of Christian Shawe, Bargarans daughter particularlie Katharin Campbell and Agnes Naesmith and Margaret Lang, and some of the pannalls wer for destroyng Christian Shawe by pulling doune of the house, others for tormenting her \with/ pins, some for hanging her in a cord and some for drowning her in the well. Depons her father took her whither she would or not to Meitings with the Divil and the other pannalls and other witches and particularlie to that meiting in Bargarans yaird and at a meiting above the toun of Kilpatrick with the Divil and the haill pannalls and other witches wher they did consult about the destroying and killing of John Ritchies child which they did by making the childs picture and by putting pins in it and that Margaret Fultoun wes the main woman who putt in pins in it. Depons she wes present at the meiting with the Divil and the pannalls at William Montgomeries house the tyme lybelled when they destroyed the said William Montgomeries child by strangleing it with a napkine, and that the house \wes/ maillie that night and she sawe a tubfull of seeds in the house. Depons she wes also present with the Divil and the haill pannalls in Mathew Parks house wher they destroyed his child by strangleing it with a cord and John Lindesay called the Bishop brought the cord with him. Depons {*fo. 44v.*}[143] she wes present with the Divil and the haill pannalls (except John Lindesay of Barloch whom she does not remember to be present) when they drowned the ferrie boat of Erskine and George Cuninghame of Brighouse and John Glen ferrier, therin, and that the consulting the drowning of the boat wes efter they came out of Mathew Parks house from the murdering of his child, and that the way of effectuating of it wes by overturning it. Depons some of them wer for saving John Glen the ferrier but his mother in Lawe Margaret McKilop would not allowe of it because he hade putt her out of his house. Depons that at these meitings they worshoped [*sic*] the Divil and [*sic*] calling him ther King and ther Lord and that she wes first brought to see and be acquaint with the Divil by her Grandmother Jean Fultoun who desyred her to shaik hands with on[e] whom she called a Gentleman her freind, and when she shuck hands with him she found him cold, and being frighted she expressed her self thus, Lord be betuixt me and the[e] upon which the Divil

[142] In margin: 'All the pannalls'.

[143] Two lines crossed out at this point: 'she wes she wes present when George Cuninghame of Brighouse and John Glen there'.

flew out of the house in a flight of fyre. Depons she wes present with the Divil and the wholl sevin pannalls in Mr Hardie the minister of Dunbartouns yaird wher they made Mr Hardies picture of clay and hair and stobed it with pins and then they washed it with aile and brandie and they went from the yaird to the house but she went not with them. Depons she went on foot to that meiting with her father to the watter syd wher her father taking her on his back used this expression, mount and flie, by which they wer both caryd over, but befor hand her father forbad her to saine[144] herself otherwayes she would fall in the watter and depons she returned and came over the watter the same way. Depons she is sextein years of age and that what she hes deponed is the truth as she shall answer to God and that she cannot wreitt.

[*Signed:*] Blantyre jpc. {*fo. 45r.*}

James Lindesay son to Mathew Lindesay somtyme indweller in Blackhall aged fourtein years of age and about sex weeks more, purged of malice, prejudice, partiall councill and solemnlie sworne and admitted a witnes *cum nota* depons that the tyme lybelled he wes in Bargarran yaird with the Divil and the haill sevin persons on pannall wher Margaret Lang gave herself up to the Divil by putting one of her hands on the crowne of her head and the other on the sole of her foot, and the Divil said would she give all that to him and she said take it all to you[145] and that at that meiting John Lindsay the Bishop danced the Divil out of the feild. Depons he heard everie one of the pannalls call the Divil either God or Lord, And that at the said meiting they did consult to destroy Christian Shawe Bargarrans daughter. Depons he wes at a meiting with the pannalls in Mr Hardie the minister of Dunbartouns yaird wher they formed a picture of the minister, of waxe and hair and steeped it amongst ail and watter and flamed it with brandie. Depons he wes at a meiting in Mathew Parks house with Margaret Lang, Kathrin Campbell, Agnes Naesmith, John Lindesay alias Bishop and James Lindsay alias Curat, John Lindsay of Barloch, wher they strangled a child with a small cord and depons Margaret Fultoun wes not ther. Depons he cannot wreitt and this is the truth as he shall answer to God.

[*Signed:*] Blantyre jpc. {*fo. 45v.*}

Jannet Roger daughter to the deceast John Roger in Inchinand, aged threttie years and above, purged of malice, prejudice, ill will and partiall councill admitted as a witnes *cum nota* depons that Agnes Naesmith, Margaret Fultoun and Margaret Lang[146] desyred her to engadge or fie with a person in black cloathes with a blewe band and a litle black cape on his head and that they brought her \within a litle/ to him and then retired from her and he proposed to her that she should engadge with him promiseing she should never want and gave her

[144] 'saine': bless.
[145] In margin: 'All the pannalls'.
[146] In margin: 'Naesmith, Fultoun, Lang'.

a nipe at that time which at first wes sore and efterwards he strok it with his hand which took away the sorenes and that he[147] made her putt one of her hands on the crowne of her head and the other on the sole of her foot and give all that wes betuixt them to him and she hade not power efter that to saine her self and so she knewe he wes the Divil. Depons she wes at the meiting in Bargarans yaird with the Divil and the haill pannalls except Katharin Campbell and Lindesay of Barloch wher they consulted to pull doun the house and that she heard all the abovenamed pannalls call the Divil ther Lord as she her self also did. Depons the Divil gave them a peice of ane unchristianed childs liver as he called it and gave her self a peice of it which she did not eat but lett fall to the ground. Depons the pannalls abovenamed did kneil and bowe befor the Divil. Depons she wes present with the haill pannalls abovenamed except John Lindesay in Barloch and Katharin Campbell at the boat of Erskine wher they drowned John Glen the ferrier and a Gentleman whom she did not knowe. Depons she cannot wreitt and this is the truth as she shall answer to God.

[*Signed:*] Blantyre jpc. {*fo. 46r.*}

Margaret Roger daughter to the said deceast John Roger in Inchinand, aged 60 years or therby, purged of malice, prejudice, ill will and partiall councill, admitted as a witnes *cum nota*, depons that Margaret Lang brought her first to be acquaint with the Divil in the Park Muir about three year agoe in the gloming and that the Divil promised to her ther that she would never want but never gave her any thing, and that at that tyme he gave her a nip and took one of her hands and putt it on the crown of her head and the other on the sole of her foot and give [*sic*] all betuixt that to him which she accordingly did. Depons she wes at the meiting with the Divil in Bargaran yaird wher wes present John Lindsay called Bishop, James Lindsay called Curat, Margaret Lang, Margaret Fultoun, Agnes Naesmith and Katharin Campbell,[148] and that all of them called the Divil Lord, and that she wes at tuo meitings in Bargaran yaird with the Divil and the pannalls abovenamed except Katharin Campbell whom she sawe but at one meiting ther. Depons she wes present with the Divil and the haill pannalls except John Lindsay and Katharin Campbell at the strangeling of Mathew Parks child, and lykwayes at the drowning of John Glen ferrier at Erskine. Depons she sawe Elizabeth Anderson one of the former witnessis at the meiting in Bargarans yaird and also depons she sawe both James and Thomas Lindsays the confessants lykwayes ther and she heard them name the Bishop and the Curat particularlie ther. Depons the Divil gave her the name of Swiftfoot and a mark on her thigh and that she cannot wreitt and this is the truth as she shall answer to God.

[*Signed:*] Blantyre jpc.

147 'desyred her' crossed out here.

148 In margin: 'Bishop, Curat, Lang, Fultoun, Naesmith, Campbell'.

Followes the witnessis in the exculpation. {*fo. 46v.*}

John Lindsay in Bodinboe aged 72 years, maried, purged and sworne, depons that John Lindsay alias Bishop and James Lindsay alias Curat wer reput warlocks thir tuelve years past.

John Adam at the Kirk of Erskine depons John Lindsay called Bishop hes bein a witch since the witch in Kilmacolme who confest dilated him.

The judges ordaine the assyse to inclose and returne ther verdict upon the 19 instant at tuo aclock in the efternoon.

Curia justiciarie Supremi Domini Nostri Regis tenta in pretorio burgi de Paislay 19 die mensis May 1697 per honorabiles viros Alexandrum dominum de Blantyre[149] *Magistrum Franciscum Montgomerie de Giffan dominum Joannem Houstoun de eodem dominum Joannem Maxwell de Pollock Alexandrum Porterfeild de eodem Magistrum Joannem Alexandrum de Blackhouse et Robertum Semple vicecomitem deputatum de Renfrewe Commissionarios justiciarii dicti Supremi Domini Nostri Regis. Curia Legittima affirmata.*[150]

The said day the persons who past upon the assyse of John and James Lindesays and others returned ther verdict in presence of the saids Commissioners of justiciary wherof the tenor followes.

The assyse having elected and choisen James Crauford merchant in Greinock ther chancelar, Robert Rosse in Linwood ther Clerk, They all in on[e] voice agreeand *nemine contra dicente*[151] Find the lybell proven againest John Lindesay in Formakine alias Bishop, James Lindesay his brother alias Curat, Agnes Naesmith in Erskine, Katharin Campbell Late servitrix to the Laird of Bargarran, Margaret Lang spouse to William Semple in Cartimpan, Margaret Fulton {*fo. 47r.*} Indweller in Wester Kilpatrick, Indyted for the crymes of witchcraft socerie necromancy and charming As also by pluralitie of voices Finds the lybell proven against John Lindsay in Barloch for the crymes Lybelled as said is. *Sic subscrivitur* Ja. Campbell [*sic*] Chancelar Ro. Rosse Clerk.

The Commissioners of justiciarie having considered the verdict of assyse abovewreitten They in respect therof decerne and adjudge (by the mouth of William Savorie dempster of court) the said John Lindesay alias Bishop James Lindsay alias Curat John Lindsay in Barloch Margaret Lang Margaret Fultoun Agnes Naesmith and Katharin Campbell to be taken to the Gallowe

149 In margin: 'Lord Blantyre *preises*'.

150 'Court of justiciary of our sovereign lord the king held in the tolbooth of the burgh of Paisley, 19 May 1697, by the honourable men Alexander Lord Blantyre, Mr Francis Montgomerie of Giffen, lord John Houston of that Ilk, lord John Maxwell of Pollok, Alexander Porterfield of that Ilk, Mr John Alexander of Blackhouse and Robert Sempill sheriff depute of Renfrew, commissioners of justiciary of our said sovereign lord the king. Court legally fenced.'

151 'nobody speaking against'.

grein of Paislay upon the second Thursday of June nixt being the tenth day of the said moneth betuixt tuo and four aclock in the efternoon and ther to be strangled at a stake till they be dead, and ther bodies to be Immediatly burnt to ashes upon the said place, and all their movable goods and gear to be escheat and Imbrought to his Majesties use which is pronounced for doom.

[*Signed:*] Blantyre, JMontgomerie, Jo:Maxwell, JHoustoun, JStuart, Porterfield of that ilk, JoAlexr, RoSempill. {*fo. 47v.*}

The Commissioners of justiciary Continue the dyet against the haill remanent persons Indyted for witchcraft till the tuentie eight day of May instant and ordaines them to be caryed back to prison and the witnessis and assysers to attend, And ordaines John Steuart in Bowehouse of Inchinand and Margaret Eweing spouse to Thomas Birkmyre in Stoniebutts, Margaret Cuninghame spouse to Thomas Wodrowe in Carlop and William Millar in Gatesyd of Formakine to be sett at libertie upon ther giving such caution or securite to the Sheriff deput of Renfrewe as he shall find reasonable for ther appearance befor the saids Commissioners or the Lords of justiciary or Lords of privie Councill or such as shall be Commissioned by them for ther tryall under such penalties as he shall think fitt.

The said day the Commissioners of justiciary having ordained Robert Semple Shirriff deput of Renfrewe to see the doom and sentance of death pronunced against the witches found guilty putt to dewe execution in all poynts, They also gave warrand and power to the said Shirriff deput to sease upon and Intromett with[152] the movable goods and gear pertaining to the said sevin witches and to be comptable therfor to the Lords Commissioners of his Majesties Thesaurie and Recomend the said Shiriff deput to the saids Lords that they may allowe him payment of his haill chairges and expensis in putting the forsaid doom and sentance to execution out of the first end of the said escheatable goods to be Intrometted with by him. {*fo. 48r.*}

The Commissioners of justiciary give ordor and warrand to the Shirriff deput of Renfrewe to take bond and sufficient securitie from Mary Morieson spouse to Frances Duncan skiper in Greinock who is dilated and alreadie under Caution for the cryme of witchcraft That she shall appear befor them or ther Quorum, or befor the Lords of justiciary or Lords of privie Councill, or any Commissioners to be appoynted by them for the tryall of the cryme of witchcraft whenever she shall be called upon Lawfull premonition or warning of fourtie eight hours and that under the paine of Ten Thousand pound Scotts; Or otherwayes, in case of refusall or delay to find the said Caution, to committ her person to prison within the tolbuith of Paislay and detaine her therin till she be putt to a tryall or be liberat by ordor.

[152] 'Intromett with': take possession of.

Followes the papers to which Mr James Brisbanes deposition relates anent the insensible marks found upon the pannalls.

Agnes Nasmith hath ane unsensible mark on her left shoulder into which a great pin was thrust unsensibly near to the middle, another of the same kind in her leg which a yettlin[153] pin pierced near the head insensibly and after having stuck a considerable time were pulled out without blood. Witnessis Mr Andrew Turner and Mr James Brisben ministers.

Margaret Lang hath ane unsensible mark called the horn mark upon her left shoulder into which though first a big pin and then a Taylior needle were insensibly to her thrust in about half ane inch yet they could not be putt to the head, the pin bowing and the thread brakeing having so stuck a considerable space were pulled out without blooding. As also a mark upon her left hip (lately received[)] unto which a big pin could not be thrust above half ane Inch and drawen out without blooding. Witnesses, Mr Patrick Simpson, Mr James Birsben and Mr Alexander King ministers.

Margaret Fulton had a mark upon her shin bone unto which a yettline pin was thrust insensibly to her to the head (and to our judgment) penetrate the bone. Witnessis, Mr James Brisben, Mr Andrew Turner.

John Lindsay Bishop had a mark betwixt the top of his heuch[154] and fifth rib behind into which a big pin was thrist to the head unsensibly to him, And another in his leg into which was thrust a yetline pin to the head after the same manner where they stuck unknown to him till he was brought to the top of the Table and there drawen out without blood. Witnessis, Mr John *{fo. 48v.}* Wilson minister at Largs, Mr Andrew Tait minister at Carmanoch, Mr James Brisben minister at Kilmacolm, Mr Andrew Turner minister at Erskine.

Katharin Campbell had a mark betwixt her shoulders into which was thrust a yetline pin to the head insensibly to her where it stuck a considerable time and being brought to the Table was drawen out without blood. Witnessis, Mr Wilson, Mr Birsben, Mr Turner.

Janet Waugh had a mark upon the small of her back sore against the veins into which a great pine was thrust to the head insensibly to her and to our apprehension pierced the bone and another into the lisk[155] into which a big pin was thrust to the head and with these pins in her she putt on her shirt and was brought to the Table and was drawen out without blood. Witnessis, Mr Birsben, Mr Turner.

There was found upon James Lindsay alias Curat a mark upon his back toward the left shoulder which took their full strength to penetrate so that the pin being thrust in insensibly to him near to the half of its length yeelded and bowed, yet the big pin sticking a considerable space he declared before

153 'yettlin': cast iron.

154 *Sic.* This word appears to be a variant of 'hough' or 'hock', the back of the knee-joint. However, in context, 'hip' may well have been meant.

155 'lisk': groin.

the whole house upon his truth he felt no pain, and the pin being pulled out no blood followed. Witnessis, Mr Birsben, Mr Turner ministers.

John Lindsay in Barcloch had a mark in his back into which our full strength could not put a big pin half ane inch insensibly to him and after staying a considerable space was drawen out without blood and another in his shoulder which a Taylior needle could in no wayes pierce.

There was found upon Angus Forrester, highland body, a mark upon his left shoulder which a strong needle could not penetrat over half ane inch yet the needle stuck there a considerable space and was drawen out without blood, And also ane upon the tail of the hip into which a big pin was thrust into the head and drawen out without blood. He declared he felt no pain nor knew that it was there. Witnessis, Mr Birsben, Mr Turner and Mr Ritchie ministers.

There was found upon John Reid smith a mark upon the small of his back toward the fillet,[156] into which (with great difficulty) a great pin was thrust to the middle Insensibly to him: though the pin stuck a considerable space, was drawen out without blood. Witnessis, Mr Birsben, Mr Turner and Kellie younger.

Jean Anderson has ane insensible mark upon her back into which a pin could not be forced in without her sense more than half ane inch and drawen out without blood. *{fo. 49r.}*

It was observed by Mr James Robertson advocat for the pannels:

1°/ That Mr John Ritchie and the other parents of the alledged malaficate children could not be received witnessis because they ar parties.

2do/ Christian Shaw could not be received witness because she is under age and the partie alledged maleficate, nor Jean Kerr nor Katharin Deans nor other servants to her father because they ar under the influence of Barrgarron her father who is persewer, at least who procured the Commission of this tryall.

3io/ Elizabeth Anderson James and Thomas Lindsay cannot be received witnessis, 1°/ because they ar *socii criminis*[157] and such ar never to be admitted *ad condemnandum*[158] but only *ad torquendi*[159] according to Delrio Sect 5 § 4 because *ad damnandum probatio debet esse luce meridiana clarior*,[160] and to allowe

156 'fillet': loins.

157 'partners in the crime'.

158 'to [testify concerning] condemnation'.

159 'to [testify concerning] torture'. Delrio, whom Robertson cites here, was making the point that partners in the crime, who were less trustworthy as witnesses, should not be admitted to prove guilt but only to provide an indication that would be sufficient to enable the judge to authorise the torture of the suspect. Robertson and the other lawyers present would have understood that Delrio was writing about the Roman law of proof, which operated without a jury and which had different procedures concerning torture. He hoped to persuade the court that to transfer Delrio's principles to the procedures of Scots law would have the effect of disallowing these witnesses altogether.

160 'for condemnation, the proof should be clearer than the light of midday'. Delrio, *Disquisitiones Magicae*, 382 (book 5, section 5, para 4).

such witnessis to prove such \ane/ misterious point of witchcarft [*sic*] as meeting with the Devill is a dangerous preparative since the Devill might have represented others or at least their false shapes. 2do/ They having confessed themselves to have been in the Devills service and renunced Christ they cannot swear by the name of God neither are they capable of the Religion of ane oath and so cannot be witnessis. 3^io/ They cannot be received witnessis by the 11 Chap: Stat: Wiliel:[161] because they are *irretiti criminibus capitalibus*[162] and so insnared in a capital Crime that they look upon themselves as under the power of the pursewer for the punishment of death. 4to/ They cannot be witnessis by the foresaid statute because they haveing renunced their baptisme and entred into the Devills service *eo ipso Christianee legis normam adjecerunt et ecclesiatica statuta contempserint.*[163] 5to/James and Thomas Lindsays cannot be received witnessis because James appears to be under age and although he calls himself two moneths past fourteen yet by ocular inspection he appears not to be so old, and therfore *in dubio*[164] his age so ought to be proven, and as to Thomas Lindsay his brother it is acknowledged by all that he is not twelve years of age and ought not to be received as a witness.

4to/ Margaret and Janet Rodgers cannot be received witnessis not only for the foresaid reasons being *socie criminis* and confessing witches ar under the pursewers power for life and death being indyted, But likwise because, 1°/ they were not given amongst the list of the witnessis to the pannells with their indytment which is required by the 11 Article of the Regulations of the Justices Court[165] being the 16 act 3^d Sess: 2 parl: K: Ch: 2^d But they ar only given out in ane Additionall list within these three dayes and that since the pannells their raiseing ther exculpation and if the Additionall list had been given before the pannells raised their exculpation they would have proven the Rodgers to be of unsound Judgement and understanding and {*fo. 49v.*} such ar not to be admitted witnessis by the foresaid statute of King William.

5to/ William Semple cannot be admitted witness against James Lindsay because he dreads him bodily harme and has the pannells at malice and ill will, In so far as he came out of his own house against the pannells with a drawen sword in his hand and threatned to kill him, and afterwards about ane year since or therby when he and the pannell James Lindsay was makeing some Accompt with the Laird of Caldwell, because the pannell took the Lairds part against him, he threatned to be about with the pannell, all this referred to the said Semple his oath, so that the pannell has just ground to dread him neither can he be admitted ane witness.

161 'Statutes of King William', chapter 11, in John Skene, *Regiam Majestatem: The Auld Lawes and Constitutions of Scotland* (Edinburgh, 1609), pp. 3–4 (2nd pagination).

162 'accused of capital crimes'.

163 'by which they have rejected the standard of Christian law and scorned ecclesiastical statutes'.

164 'in doubt'.

165 *Acts of the Parliaments of Scotland*, viii, 88, c. 40, para 11; RPS, 1672/6/50.

It wes answered by Frances Grant Advocat that the minute that could be taken at the time being short The Judges with consent of parties allowed them to give into the Clerk in writte quhat had been debated *viva voce* and for the pursewers it is as followes.[166]

In order to the more satisfactorie answearing these objections (which ar tumbled together of purpose to make some shew) we shall first lay before you the state of the cause then clear up the determination of it.

As to the first. The question is not whither partiners in the crime or others mentioned in the objection can be a concludeing proof of themselves though two of them should concurr as to the same act of witchcraft but whither the *corpora delicti*[167] appearing already to imply witchcraft the extrinsick adminicles being so pregnant to inferr that these pannells ar the witches. Their concurring such characters as by the observance of all nations and ages are the simptuos[168] of a witch, particularly the mark, fame, not shadeing [*sic*] of tears etc: which ar discoveries of providence of so dark a crime that like avenues leads us to the secret of it: and finallie when six persons of different ages and stations (viz. the five confessants and the girdle[169]) do quhen seperatly examined agree in their answears to every materiall question that is put to them even tho it be new so that it could not be conserted: we say wither or not in such a case may witnessis be received to put the copestone on the evidence by a positive probation of a matter of fact which is the object of sense, tho otherwayes they be lyable to exception of such extraordinary uses of[170] the *corpora delicti*, Clearness of the adminicles and conflux of the Diagnosticks of witches did not preceed them, as you have seen proven before you they do.

The case is not whither the witnessis could be habil in ane ordinarie crime which commonly falls to be exposed to other witnessis then those concerned in it, But whither they can be received in this extraordinary, occult and excepted crime of witchcraft wherin there are two special cases to be noticed, viz. sometimes the acts therof ar open and admitt the choise of witnessis such as charms used in the day time when the actor is visible, but that part of witchcraft whereby the witches meet in the night time, adore their Lord, {*fo. 50r.*} contrive their malefices and accordingly thereafter execute them when other witnessis are asleep or the witches themselves ar covered from sight, we say this can be no otherwayes proven then by those that ar intimate to it.

We do not alledge that persons wholely destitute of knowledge and naturall Conscience ar to be admitted in any case, such as infants, furious, fatuus[171] etc,

166 A version of the following speech was printed in the *True Narrative*, pp. 10–19. The trial record version and the *True Narrative* version diverge towards the end, as noted below.

167 'concrete evidences of crime' (plural of *corpus delicti*, discussed above).

168 *Sic*. Probably read 'symptoms'.

169 *Sic*. Read 'girle', i.e. Christian Shaw.

170 *Sic*. Read 'if'.

171 'furious, fatuus': insane, imbecilic.

neither do we contend that Thomas Lindsay and Christian Shaw who are under pupillarity should be put to ane oath, for they are only to be examined seperatly before the Court upon Interrogators,[172] by which it may appear whither or not they coincide with the four other confessants, and this is the pannells advantage in case of disagreement that ar to depon before them. But we insist that any person above pupillarity giveing evidence of considerable knowledge and naturall Conscience (which is a sufficient fond[173] for all the credit we need in this case that is already almost fully proven) is to be received as a witnes.

As to the second we shall make this as clear as noon, 1° From reason and the nature of the thing, 2do/ The unanimous Judgement of lawiers in all nations and ages, 3io/our own customes and Decisions and 4to/ the singularity of their circumstantiat case.

As to the first, the going to and comeing from meetings especially on foot and falling down and worshiping the Devill there under a Corporall body (which he had when he tempted our Saviour to do it[174]), the actuall murdering of children by a cord or napekin and the tormenting of others by pins etc, ar plain objects of sense and therefore the senses ought to be beleeved annent them. For as reason hath things Intellectual and faith things supernaturall, so the senses have things corporall for their object whereannent they ar to be trusted ay and while[175] it be proven the appearence is impossible or that the witness of it is ane imposture. It is a part of the witches purchase from the Devill that they cannot be seen at some occasions: so that the abominations committed then would remain unpunished if such witnessis were not admitted. It cannot be thought that witches (who of all criminalls ar the most obstinate to confess) would ventore the loss of their own lives by deponeing against others against whom they have no speciall picque, Yea for whom they have particular affection, as severall of the pannells ar some of the witnessis Relations. Nor hes the Devill any peculiar interest to instigat them thereunto. For severall of the pannells have confessed other execrable crimes, whereby it cannot be supposed but Satan would be devided against himself.[176] God in his ordinary providence hath taken such care of his publict judgements that the enimie of Justice[177] his special power ceases thereabouts, as appears by the witches not being able to do more harm or escape after Gods ministers beginn to counteract Satans Instruments by imprisonment: And finnallie, the oddness of the malefices, the Concurrence of the Adminicles and the existance of matter of fact wherein these confessants (though not knowing the same

172 'Interrogators': questions asked formally in court.
173 'fond': proof.
174 Cf. Matthew 4:1–11.
175 'ay and while': until.
176 Cf. Matthew 12:26; Mark 3:26; Luke 11:18.
177 'the enimie of Justice': the Devil. The point is that the Devil's power ceases in the face of the court, which executes God's justice.

otherwayes[)] do agree do agree [*sic*] with other inexceptionable witnessis etc, do sufficiently astruct[178] their credibility, for as falshood being a crime, is never presumed, so a person found true in many things is still presumed to continue such untill the contrary is evinced.

As to the second, *socius criminis admittatur si Delicti sit nephandi*,[179] Men: A S 2: L 2d 6 5, Cass 474 n. 2 7 Seq {*fo. 50v.*}, *aut occultum et veritas aliunde haberi non possit*,[180] Mas: vol 1 Con 466 n. 6, *Aut difficilis probationis*,[181] Farin: L 2d op: Criminalis Tit: 6 263 n. 28, Masc: vol 3d con 1360 n. 4th, Menoch: L 2d, Cass 116 L 15th Q 58, *Nocturno tempore commissa quie difficilis dicuntur probationis*,[182] Boec: Decis: 68 n. 6, Menoch: D Cass 116, *Ideoque non solum preicoptiva et coniectorata probatis sufficit verum etiam inhabile admittuntur*,[183] Farin: 2d Tit 6 255 n. 40, Masc: L 2d Con 1124 n. 13th Idem, *in delictis commissis in Eremo nemore monte aliove* [*sc. aliore*] *cora secreto*,[184] Gomez var: Res Tom 3d C 12 n. 21, Far: D Tit C 262 n. 55, *sed occultum non dicitur quod actum non intervenerint, ac quod de natura delicti vel Ratione loci et Temporis aliis testes habiles intervenire non potuerint, ut est maleficium de quo socius criminis admittitur*,[185] Men: L 2d 65 Cass 474 n. 33, Campeg: de test Reg: 86, Fallan 6, Grotius de Test: part 4 n. 97, Oldindorp de Test: Tit de personis Testis n. 21,[186] In a word all lawiers who wrote particular treatises on witchcraft in Germanie, Italy, Loren,[187] France and Spain etc. do conclude that inhabile witnessis and particularly *socii* ar to be addmitted witnessis in witchcraft. Only the strictest of them do think that this admission is to be *cum nota* or as Delrio in the place cited for the pannells expresses it *ex his solis*[188] the Judge is not to condemn, nor do we requir it.

178 'astruct': establish.

179 'a partner in crime is admitted [as a witness] if the crime is nefarious'.

180 'or [the crime] is occult [i.e. hidden] and the truth cannot be had in any other way'.

181 'or the proof is difficult'.

182 'or [the crime was] committed during the night, which is said to be difficult to prove'.

183 'therefore not only does it suffice as a preliminary and conjectural proof, but even the unable are admitted'.

184 'in crimes committed in a deserted forest, mountain or other secret place'.

185 'but it is not said to be occult [i.e. hidden] that they did not intervene in the act, and that by the nature of the crime or the reason of the place and time other competent witnesses could not intervene, as it is a crime of witchcraft in which a partner in the crime is admitted [as a witness]'.

186 The citations in this difficult passage seem to include: Josephus Mascardus, *Conclusiones Probationum Omnium* (1584–8); Jacobus Menochius, *De Arbitrariis Iudicium* (1613); Prosper Farinacii (Farinacius), *Variarum Quaestionum et Communium Opinionum* (1622); Antonio Gomez (Gomesius), *Variarum Resolutionum* (1572); possibly one of the works of Tommaso Campeggi (Italian jurist, d. 1564); Hugo Grotius, *De Iure Belli ac Pacis* (1625); Johann Oldendorp, *Iuris Naturalis, Gentium et Civilis* (1539). The transcription of the citations is not entirely certain, nor is the punctuation (which is minimal in the MS).

187 *Sic*. The *True Narrative* has 'Loven' (Leuven), which is more likely; this was the place of publication of Delrio's treatise on which Grant principally relied. It is conceivable that 'Loren' here is correct and means Lorraine; if so, this would indicate Nicolas Rémy's treatise *Daemonolatreia* ('Demonolatry', 1595), published in Lyon but announcing on its title page that it dealt with Lorraine.

188 'from these things alone'.

As to the third, we have the Testimony of our famous King James 6th Demonologie lib 3: T. ult: telling us that it is our law that Boyes, Girdles [*sic*] and infamous persons etc are not to be rejected any more in witchcraft then in the samen les majestie,[189] even so[190] they assert others to have been present at Imaginary meetings because this supposes their having entered with a precontract.[191] He sayes that Satans mark and the want of tears are pregnant aids to the Discoverie *quod Deus pater naturee ordinem voluit esse secreta immanitatis indicii et eo non permittente ac fadissimi criminis pertinaciam dissimulent.*[192] He gives an instance of a girle who haveing named severall witches in her fitts, they were all condemned upon as concurring adminicles. This is not a common Author but a man who as curious was exact: as prudent did not publish such things without the approbation of the best Divines and Lawiers: as a prince is to be Credited annent the law of his own Countrie: and as a King hath determined any dubitie[193] that might have remained in his point alse far as the Law of our Government will permitt.

But further our Judges and Lawiers have followed his Majestie, for in all the process in the Adjournalls and Delation[194] and the marks ar still sustained as most pregnant presumptions, whereupon, and a very small probation besides, witches have been frequently condemned. So in the process against the bewitchers of Sir George Maxwell of Pollock and Hamilton of Barns anno 1677 *socius criminis* though under age is sustained to be a witnes or adduced before the Inquest for proveing that the mark was found upon some of the witches. Women and minors have been received by multitudes of Decisions cited by McKenzie, Tit prob: by witnessis and Tit: witchcraft.[195] And he also cites Decisions where in paralell cases *socii criminis* and others inhabil were admitted, particularly in treason and in falshood,[196] And all Lawiers conclud that witchcraft is as much ane excepted crime as these.

189 'les majestie' (*lèse-majesté*): treason. The *True Narrative* has 'than in human lese Majesty', which may be more correct.

190 'even so': even if.

191 Grant is arguing here that, if a witness or confessing witch states that another person was present with them at the sabbat, then that other person must have made a pact with the Devil. He correctly states that James had made this argument in *Daemonologie*. All the citations from that work in this passage come from James VI, *Daemonologie*, in *Minor Prose*, 54–6 (bk. 3, ch. 6).

192 This is a free translation of James's 'God having appoynted that secret super-naturall signe, for tryall of that secrete unnaturall crime … God not permitting them to dissemble their obstinacie in so horrible a crime'. The *True Narrative*, more correctly, has '*praeternatura*' instead of '*pater naturee*', but gives the less correct '*judicium*' for the MS's '*indicii*'.

193 'determined any dubitie': ended any doubt.

194 *Sic*. The *True Narrative* has 'in the Journals; Fame, and Delation', which may be more correct. 'Fame': reputation (for witchcraft).

195 Mackenzie, *Laws and Customs*, 84–5 (part 1, title 10, para 24), 382–3 (part 2, title 26, para 4).

196 Mackenzie, *Laws and Customs*, 45 (part 1, title 6, para 21; cases of treason), 219–20 (part 1, title 26, para 6; cases of perjury).

As to the 4th, whatever inhability these witnessis might be under it is fully made up and they rendred unexceptionable habile by the chain of this whole bussines. It is true ane man through the concurrence of corusive humors may have ane insensible mark, another be enviously defamed, a third through a sudden grief or melancholy may not be able to weep and a fourth may be loaded with suspicious circumstances when extraordinary things fall {*fo. 51r.*} out in the Countery and a fifth maybe deponed against by two false witnessis, tho neither of these seperatly be truely witches. But by the knowen observation and experience of mankind, Non[e] except witches have had the unhappie medley and concurse of all or most of these *indicia*, and ordinarly and for the greater part witches have them. So that since the Rules of Judgement ar established upon *quod plerumque*[197] which does obtain till ane exception be apparent, the conjunction of these in one person does also plainly give his character, as the the [*sic*] most certain simptomes of the plainest desease being universally conserted in all parts of the world points out to us that the haver of them is a person truely affected with desease whereof he hath the concurrent Diagnosticks. In a word one or other of these may concurr in the Innocent. But no witches do attest that all of them have concentered in any other person in the world but in a witch. And on the other hand they takeing place in witches through all parts of the world must proceed from a common and not from a peculiar humor or cause.

The spicifick aptitude of some of nicest of the *indicia* which appear, from the probation already led, to discover a witch, do serve to clear the ground of the worlds observation annent them, particularly the Devill as apeing God imprints a Sacrament of his Covenant. Besides that commonly this mark being given at the first meeting does by its intollerable pain force the witch to second rendezvous for cureing it at quhich the poor wratch being under a furious necessity fixes the paction by renewing it with deliberation haveing been delivered in the mean time from considering the horridness of the first engadgement by the pain. The inhability to shed tears may be a characteristick of hardening, though not alwayes in the case of Christians, yet in those who have ceased to be such lest the Devill giveing them such words of scripture and prayer as many have it should be impossible to discover the Hypocrisy. And that is not Satans own interest since by the Discovery occasion is given to Be Buffoon[198] the profession of holieness. A Report often arises without ground, but a constant Repute that keeps footing implyes for the most part a surer cause, especially when it is of persons beloe envy and by persons above calumnie. The girles falling in fitts at the approach of the pannells might

[197] 'what is general'.

[198] *Sic*. Read 'to Buffoon', i.e. to mock. Grant's argument is that the Devil *wants* his witches to be discovered, so that the revelation of their existence will cause Christianity to suffer through this public mockery.

proceed from antipathy ariseing from the poysionous steems of the witch, accustomed to produce that effect though an vertue affixed thereto by the Devill by conjunction of naturall cause, the same way as the invisible pestilence does operat, or his promise of casting the Girle in fitts at the witches presence might have been Generall whereby the witch was eventually befooled and discovered as it often falls out.[199] For Satan envies even their temporal felicity, and fears least by their continuing here they should be thrust out of his hands by conversion, when they come to perceive the Delusion of his promise to make them rich and the like etc.

This is one thing further which was tryed before severall of your Lordships, viz. None of the pannells that were tryed (tho most sagacious, knowing and perfect in memory, so that it could not proceed from ignorance or forgetfulness) could make out the attempt of sayeing the Lords Prayer, quhich {*fo. 51v.*} may be either a secret Judgement for renunceing their first Lord after whom it is denominat peculiarly; or by restrent of their new Lord who may think that too special ane homage to his Adversary. But we have hindred you too long with that which is not necessary: For their being incontravertable law and custome their needs no philosophy to support it. Since legislators doe rewle but subjects must obey; and both the fools and leazie (who have neither read nor thought to understand this subject) ar to be left to their own Chimera'es; yet least they should insult, we shall answear species of objections as the pannells Advocat thought anywayes worthy to be repeated in this place.

Whereas it is objected that Delrio Sect: 5th § 4 says that *socii* ar not to be admitted witness *ad condemnandum* especially considering that the probation ought to be *luce meridiana clarior*.

It is answeared the place it self confutes this inference in the present case for he sayes *ex his solis non eo procedendum ad condemnationem; scio contrarii communius teneri ac in praxi et in praxi obtinere.*[200] So that it is evident 1°/ That the Common opinion and custome is in the contrarie even when there is no other probation but by the partiners of the crime. But 2do we are not so streatned but subsume in his very words *ex his solis* we do not desire the pannells should be condemned but your Lordships see that these witnessis we ar to adduce ar not *soli* or alone, for the probation led these last sixteen houres ar so many concomitants and discoveries of providence which astruct and make up any defect in their credit that can be desiderate. Hence 3io/ The meaning of that

[199] Grant argues here that demonic possession is caused by a transfer of poisonous vapours ('steems') from the witch, in the same way that infectious illnesses are transmitted. This argument may well have derived from Joseph Glanvil[l], 'Some Considerations about Witchcraft', in his *Saducismus Triumphatus* (London, 1681), 21–4 (sig. G4). Cf. Julie A. Davies, 'Poisonous Vapours: Joseph Glanvill's Science of Witchcraft', *Intellectual History Review*, 22 (2012), 163–79.

[200] 'From these things alone condemnation should not be proceeded to, although I know the contrary opinion to be commonly held and practised'.

maxim (which is metaphoricall as appears by the words *clarior luce meridiana*, ane equal clearness being sufficient[)] is fully answeared and takes place in the present case, for if extraordinarieness of the *corpora delicti*, pregnancie of the adminicles, and pointedness of the positive probation being conjoyned; Their is not a clearer proof upon record in any nation then that to which it is hoped these will amount.

Whereas this alledgence 1°[201] inforced by pretending that it were of dangerous consequences to allow such witnessis to prove meeting with the Devill, since Satan might have represented others by their false shapes.

It is answeared:

1° That the rules of Judgement ar established upon that quhich for the most part does still obtain and these Rules ar to be followed till ane exception be proven in a singular circumstantial case. But so it is by that by the experience and observation of the wisest Divines, Lawiers, Philosophers, Physicians, States men, Judges, Historians at home and abroad (that ar too wise to be imposed upon and too ingenuous to deceive us when they all concurr in the same matter of fact), besides the Testimony of witches every where makes the apparitions of witches to be commonly and mostly reall. So Delrio tell us, Lib 5 § 16 *Illusio rarissime contingit*[202] *Ita* Jaquerius, Comensis, Sprengerus, Bienfeldus, Remigius,[203] etc and therefore the Testimony of the senses ar alwayes to credited annent them ay and while[204] it is convelled,[205] for single and few instances of false representations to the sense as esteiming them to be true can no wayes invalidat the rule established upon experience which is common and for the most part whereby no exception is to be presumed till it be proven in a special case, since a wonder does not subvert the proof drawen from the common course of nature.[206] Logick permitts not to argue from particulari or from possibility

201 *Sic.* Read 'is'.

202 'Illusions most rarely occur'. The substance of this point, though not the exact wording, is found in Delrio, *Disquisitiones Magicae*, 400 (book 5, section 16).

203 'Jaqerius': Nicolas Jacquier, *Flagellum Haereticarum Fascinariorum* ('Scourge of Heretical Enchanters', 1458). 'Comensis': Bernard of Como (Bernardus Comensis), *Lucerna Inquisitorum Hæreticæ Pravitatis et Tractatus de Strigibus* ('Lamp of Inquisitors of Heretical Perversity and Treatise on Witches', 1584). 'Sprengirus': the *Malleus Maleficarum* ('Hammer of Witches', 1486), today considered to be the work of Heinrich Krämer alone, but usually attributed in this period jointly to Krämer and Jacob Sprenger, or even (as here) to Sprenger alone. 'Bienffeldus': Peter Binsfeld, *De Confessionibus Maleficorum et Sagarum* ('The Confessions of Witches and Magicians', first published in German 1589). 'Remigius': Nicolas Rémy, *Daemonolatreia* ('Demonolatry', 1595). All these are probably second-hand citations via Delrio, *Disquisitiones Magicae*, 400 (book 5, section 16), which lists 'Iaquerius, Comensis, Sprenger, Michaëlius, Binsfeldius, Remigius'.

204 'ay and whill': until.

205 'convelled': refuted.

206 Grant is effectively arguing here that witchcraft is fully *natural*, and that it would be a 'wonder' – something beyond ordinary nature – if the events said by the prosecution to have occurred had been caused by any means *other* than witchcraft.

{*fo. 52r.*} to existence. Law puts the burden of proveing assimulation upon the affirmer and that which seldome occurres is not considered by the Legislators.

For illustrateing of which It is considered that for the most part ordinarly the witches ar personally existent in the places where they appear because it is more easie for the prince of the air to transport them in his hurrickines which he can raise as is plain in the instance of Job (who was put in his power, i.e. his naturall power, without delegation) formeing ane fence upon their face whereby the violence of the air may be deverted from chooking them: that to form the miniature of such various transactions on their brain the difficulty whereof is the greater of all their faculties ar not disposed at all times the same way; and they have not the seeds of this work unless they had once acted in reality It is both the greater crime and pleasure to act in Truth which herefore the Devill and witches do rather choise (unless the place be farr distant or the parties indisposed[)] which is de facto attested to be so by the writters and witches of all age and nations as said is.

2do/ Notwithstanding that the Rule must hold till ane exception of exculpation be evinced *quoad*[207] a particular person by evidenceing that the real appearance was in that special case a true mistake: Yet this exception is sufficient for the safity [*sic*] of the misrepresented. Since the same providence which permitted the affliction will order the outgate and exculpation, either by the Areall bodies not bydeing the tuch or some other distinction of providence commonly allowed the Devill, to personat only with cloven feet, or that the apparition was sollie to one single witnes which cannot be a proof, or that the Innocent can prove *alibi*, or finnally the notuor [*sic*] Character of a Samuel will purge and dispell the aspersions of Satan contrived of purpose to discredit the evidence of sense by which alone his instruments can be discovered:[208] especially this Character being joyned to the other circumstances of providence, particularly when good men ar disguised[209] they ar meerly passive in the scene and outwith thereof, whereas witches ar commonly active in their common life by such words and deeds as in conjunction with the appearances conspire to make us know and distinguish them from the truely good; such is these witches open profanity, naughtiness, unveiled hypocrisy, which being cleared by fame, sealed by the mark and confirmed by the other discoveries of the Adminicles that ly proven before you, do still make ane distinguishing character betwixt the children of darkness and light; so Delrio

207 'as concerning'.

208 The so-called witch of Endor (the 'woman that hath a familiar spirit at En-dor', Authorised Version) summoned the apparition of the dead prophet Samuel at Saul's behest in the Bible: 1 Samuel 28:7–25. The nature of the apparition was much debated in demonology, but Grant's argument seems to follow the mainstream interpretation: the apparition could not have been Samuel's spirit, which would not have appeared for a wicked purpose, and it must therefore have been a demon counterfeiting his appearance.

209 'when good men ar disguised': when the apparitions of good men appear.

tells Lib: 5 sect: 16 n. 5 tells [*sic*] us Athanasius and St Germanus against whom probation was adduced for Soceries but providence did convell it.[210] It is a famous instance of Susanna represented by the elders which though not in the cause of [*1 word blank*] yet agrees in the Rationale.[211] The representations of Pharoes magicians had concomitants by which they were discovered and confounded.[212] But lastly suppose that God in the deeps of his wisdome to convince the error of nimious[213] self confidence should permitt all necessar probation to concurr against ane innocent. Yet the Judge following the fouth[214] of proof established by Divine and humane lawes Is altogether Innocious: since the case being very rare the evill is less then establishing a principell by which most of all those monsters could not be cutt off. {*fo. 52v.*}

Upon the whole it is certain that, as tho oftimes false witnessis set on by the Devill have taken away ane harmles life by accuseing it of other crimes, yet the Testimony of witnessis must be still credited till they be redargued:[215] so these appearances of witches being proven ought to be esteemed real till the fallacy be established. Especially considering that there are exemples in ancient and modern History of Satans representing the best of men as committing murther buggarie etc in effigie. So Delrio lib 5 sect 16 n. 5 Relates that of St Silvanus was represented by the Devill as committing a common capital crime.[216] And the like of a monck whereof there are severall modern paralel instances yet this cannot enervie[217] the rule and faith of publick Indicators founded on no more then the sight of the like appearances and any argument against the probation in witchcraft will equallie hold against the probation of any other crime quhatsome[218] wherefore the Rules of them both must be common as to beleeving the senses till their error be individually discovered.

Finally the[219] certainty is no wayes diminished by the extraordinaryness of the appearance to the senses: For as in law and nature, Realitie and not

210 Delrio, *Disquisitiones Magicae*, 405 (book 5, section 16).

211 Susanna was falsely accused of adultery, but was vindicated through the intervention of the prophet Daniel. In the Authorised Version of the Bible, the story appears in the Old Testament Apocrypha, in the Book of Susanna. Grant seems to think that the story is relevant to his argument by showing that innocent people, falsely accused, will be vindicated. However, his main aim is to show that the Devil cannot cause the apparitions of innocent people to appear, and the story of Susanna did not involve apparitions.

212 In the biblical contest between Aaron and Pharaoh's magicians (Exodus 7:8–13), both contestants transformed their rods into serpents, but Aaron's serpent swallowed the magicians' serpents. The demonological understanding of this was that the magicians' serpents were demonic apparitions.

213 'nimious': extravagant.

214 'fouth': abundance.

215 'redargued': questioned or disproved.

216 Delrio, *Disquisitiones Magicae*, 405 (book 5, section 16).

217 'enervie': weaken.

218 *Sic*. Probably read 'whatsoever'.

219 'Senses' deleted here.

simulation is presumed till the contrary be made appear upon some evident ground: So this is plain (to all who place not a great part of their small will in nonesensicall argueing against the Divine authority) in our Saviours miracles, transfiguration, walking on water, standing in the midst of the Disciples when the Doors were shutt and yet argeueing assurance by their senses that a spirit had not flesh and bones.

Nor could it be alledged by the pannells (tho they had the last word as they have not in objections against witnessis since therein *rei fiunt actores*[220] by atacqueing the witnessis presumed hability) that its not conceivable how the girle or witnessis could see quhat the by standers could not behold. Besides the impossibility of real bodies entering at the closs doors or windows or not intercepting the sight of what is at its back.

For this it would be answeared:

1°/ Proven facts must not be denyed tho philosophers have not as yet certainly reached the invisible manner of their existence. So in nature the Loadston[221] drawes the Iron, the compass turnes alwayes to the poles, and in Scripture the Angles[222] (and the Divell was once such, retaining as yet his naturall powers) smote the Sodomites that they could not see the door tho they saw the house.[223] Balaams ass perceived the Angle that stood undiscovered to himself,[224] And the rod throwen down by the Magicians of Egypt was no doubt seen by themselves tho invisible by the beholders etc, which beholding of their eye Interpreters explain to have been done by natural means and yet the manner thereof is certainly difficult.

However it is also certain that if a possible way can be proposed the Reality of a proven fact is not to be contraverted, and this can be done in the present case for:

2do/ Satans naturall knowledge and acquired experience makes him perfect in opticks and Limning,[225] besides that as a spirit he excells in strength and agility whereby he may easily be-witch the eyes of others to whom he intends not that his instruments should be seen; in this manner as was formerly hinted viz. he constricts the pores of the witches [*1 word blank*[226]] which intercepts a part of the rayes reflecting from her body, he condenses the interjacent air with grosser meteors blowen into it or other wayes does violently agitat it which drowns another part of the Rayes: And Lastly he obstructs the optick {*fo. 53r.*} nerves which humores stirred towards them: all quhich joyned together may easily intercept the whole Rayes reflecting from these bodies

220 'things become actors'.
221 'Loadston': magnet.
222 'Angles': angels.
223 Cf. Genesis 19:11.
224 Cf. Numbers 22:22–34.
225 'Limning': portrait-painting.
226 The *True Narrative* has the word 'Vehicle' at this point, meaning the witch's body considered as a receptacle for her spirit.

to make any impression on the common sense: And yet at the same time The refraction of the rayes of the same rayes [*sic*] glydeing along on the fitted sides of the volatile coach wherein Satan transports them the wall or chair behind the same bodies may be seen as a pice of money lying out of sight in a cup becomes visible how soon the *medii*[227] is altered by pouring in some water on it. Severalls of your number does know that the girle declares that she saw and heard the doors and windowes open at the witches entery, no doubt, the Devill had precondensed ane soft stoppage on the eyes and eares of others to whom that was unperceived.

So Appollonius escaped Domitians sight[228] and Giges became invisible by his magicall Ring.[229] John of Sarisberrie tells of a witch that could make any thing not to be seen.[230] And Megerus[231] relates another that had the like power. Some Italian witches of greater than ordinary witt confessed to Grilandus the Devills opening of doors and windowes for them; tho the more ignorant think themselves by a fascination to be actors of this.[232] Whence it ought not to [be] doubted by any reasonable man what in all places and times is so incontestible fact.

Nor could the pannells insist that these confessants ar to depone only on their Imagination which can prove no more against themselves and others than a dream.

For it is answeared that this is a mistake seeing they declare plain matters of fact obvious not only to one but severall of their senses, viz. Some of them went the greatest part of the way to these meetings on foot: they there saw and touched their confederats, they heared their combinations to destroy and torture the infants, girle and ministers. They returned on foot again and even when they were carryed fore or back they knew on the nixt day that it was no dream, the same way as all other mortalls discover the difference. But further this adminiculat by some real effects of a personall presence as you have seen in the probation and is further cleared by the Adjournall of Bargarrans daughters suffering which is nottour in the Countery, particularly by the glass of sack and orange pills, the pices of the clouted sleives, the words expressed by the mother on the sudden murther of her child which ar constantly told by some of the confessants. As also the houss being mealie that night: the girle tho hoodwinked her falling in fitts at her approach, and others which

227 'media'. Here, the word seems to be considered as singular. The *True Narrative* has 'medium'.

228 Apollonius of Tyan was a Greek sage who was said to have confronted the Roman Emperor Domitian (who reigned 81–96 CE).

229 Giges' ring of invisibility was discussed in Plato's *Republic*.

230 John of Salisbury's *Policraticus* (1159) discussed various forbidden magical arts.

231 The last letter of this word is damaged, and the reading is conjectural. The name is given as 'Mejerus' in the *True Narrative*. It may well be the common German surname Meyer or Meier. No demonological or juristic writer of that name has so far been identified.

232 Paulo Grillando's *Tractatus de Hereticis et Sortilegis Eorumque Poenis* ('Treatise on Heretics and Witches and their Punishments') was first published in 1524.

shall be pointed to the Assyse; can be ascrived to no other cause than the reall existence of the witches persons in the place unless it be said that Satan might have foisted and subborned all these and thence it be absurdly concluded that the Devill did actually so. In which case the objectors ar the persons that bottom their opininion [*sic*] on Imagination without any positive ground of the Reality of quhat thei fancy, yea against possitive grounds of beleef: which argueing from possibility to existence is already sufficiently exploaded.

Whereas for further sustaining the objection it is alleged that the confessants haveing been in the Devills service and renunced Christ they ar not capable of the Religion of ane oath.

It is answeared:

1°/ In the Rules of charity etc the confessants tho once witches yet have now ceased to be such having had the use of means by the ministers and word[233] and actually declared their repentance and the Devills ceasing to molest them; particularly Elizabeth Anderson was only carried along violently by her father and stood out to the last against renunceing of her baptisme or consenting to these crimes which were contryved in their meetings. Janet and Margaret Rodgers do testifie a great {*fo. 53v.*} remorse, and avowed the same the last sabbath in the face of the congregation: So that these three ar sufficient quhatever might be said against the other two: especially if we joyn the improbability either of their hazarding their own lives. The Devill sending them out against these pannells or their destroying their own Relations as was remarked before.

2do. Whither they remain witches or not It is certain by reason and experience that the Devills peculiar influence ceaseth in and about judgement By the common course of providence. And therefore the Authors before cited admitt witches either penitent or not.[234]

3^{io}/ All the defects of their liability is supplied and the intireness thereof compleated by their Testimonies being so wonderfully adminiculat, Particularly the confessants were constant from the very first discovery, uniform in so various circumstances not only with themselves but with the Girle. They declare nothing but what is probable, most of the pannells haveing been reputed witches, all of them haveing the mark and one or other of them (to whom the associats delighted in mischiefe never missed to joyn) haveing had particular Irritations to take revenge by the tortures and deaths lybelled. Besides the other Adminicles of the guilt already proven. The confessants were threatned to retract by the pannells themselves and other friends, besides their bade useage from others in the Countery. They concurr with the maleficiats[235] Testimony and amongst themselves even when interrogat singlie and upon new things: as severalls of your number have tryed and the

233 Having experienced the effects of prayer, in response to the prayers of the ministers and the preaching of the word of God.

234 They admit witches' testimony in court, whether repentant or not.

235 'maleficiat': bewitched (person).

experiment: on this head Delrio lib 5 § 16 n. 5 wisely observes *quamvis tam facile foret Demoni plures decipere quam unum tam non est censendus Deus hoc eique permittere ne omnis ratio probandi talia delicta occulta in judicibus adimatur hoc enim est dissentaneum providentee divinee.*[236] The recleration[237] of the acts which they declare annent some persons whom they never saw except in these congressess [*sic*] and yet whom they knew on the first sight is inacountable if they were falsaries. And that they ar not such is further astructed by some of the pannells being delated by a confessing witch in anno 1687 and you know that others delated by these confessants were lately brought in guilty by the verdict of some inquest which ar so many joynt proofs of those witnessis integrety and makes a chain of evidencee[238] and moral Demonstration both against errors in themselves and Delusion in Relation to others.

Whereas it is further alledged that *Iretiti criminibus capitalibus*[239] and so under the the [*sic*] pursewers power cannot be admitted to be witnessis especially especially [*sic*] seing they have renunced their baptism.

To this it is answeared that we need not say that these statutes have not the force of law except in so far as they ar received by custome. Nor need we make use of that quhich is obvious, viz. that these statutes ar only common Rules in ordinary crimes which have their exceptions in all ocult and excepted crimes such as witchcraft etc, *nam omnis Regula subverti potest.*[240] And particularly this Rule is actually so in the case of witchcraft by the opinions of Lawiers and customes before mentioned which ar the best interpreters of lawes (For if this objection should hold *socius criminis*[241] could never be admitted) But we positively deney that these confessants ar under our power or influence. For Elizabeth Anderson is not guilty of witchcraft, The Lindsayes were never indicted for it. And the dyet is deserted against the Rodgers: as the whole commission is to expire against the first June betwixt and which time they ar to proceed no further then the present tryall so that this objection evanishes to Smoke. {*fo. 54r.*}

As to the objections that ar speciall against the receiveing of some one or other of the confessants, we shall give them particular answears.

Whereas it is alledged that the Rodgers cannot be received because not given out in the List of witnessis conform to the Regulations whereby the pannells might have proven their objections by their exculpations.

It is answeared:

236 'It would be as easy to deceive several demons as one; however, it should not be considered that God would permit either to be done. Do not test the reason for this; such secret transgressions are hidden from judges. To do otherwise would be inconsistent with divine providence.' Delrio, *Disquisitiones Magicae*, 405 (book 5, section 16).

237 'recleration': confirmation.

238 *Sic*. Probably read 'evidences'.

239 'those who are accused of capital crimes'.

240 'for every rule may be overturned'.

241 'a partner in crime'.

1°/ This \objection/ ought to be repelled, because that beside that the act speakes only of Criminal Lybells and not Indytments which with the list of the witnessis may be given in farr shorter time then this additionall list has be[242] given to the pannells being prisoners. This act is Interpreted by the common custome of the Justice Court of giveing Additionall lists after the first upon shorter time than this has been given. It is presently attested by James Guithrie the macer who has given them and who being a person *in officio* his Testimony is to be credited in what relates to his office. So that the old custome confirmed by Decision the 3^d^ of August 1661 where Alexander Forrester was cited *apud acta*[243] against a witch continues *quoad* this point as is Related by McKenzie 529 page.[244] But:

2do/ Any objection that the pannalls pretend against these witnessis is in jure or may instantly appear.

3^io^/ The case is altogether extraordinary and circumstantiall for these witnessis have not confessed, and so were not existent under that reduplication when the principall list was given out whereby the act of parliament can only be understood of witnessis that were then existent. And finally the pannalls got a generall warrand of exculpation for citeing of any witnessis that they pleased. And they have had severall dayes since they gott this Additionall list, so that they might have cited witnessis to prove their objections were it not that the truth is that they have none besides those that ar common before answeared.[245]

Whereas as it alledged for the pannells that the parents of the maleficiat children much less Bargarrans daughter herself cannot be received: That James Lindsay appears to be pupill by ocular inspection and that William Semple against the pannells [*sic*].

It is answeared:

1°/ That the Lawiers and particularly McKenzie Title witchcraft asserts that the persons to whom the injuries ar done ar admitted to be witnessis and cites ane Decision Katharin Wardlaw against Hutcheson:[246] whereupon it will follow much more that their parents ar to be admitted for proveing a matter of fact of the *corpus delicti*, viz. The child that was lying with them its being suddenly cutt off in the night time which could not be knowen nor proven immediatly by any others. Yet we ar not straitned as to this point, for there ar other *corpora delicti* sufficient per se proven by unexceptionable witnessis. And therefor we have industerously abstained from examining of Bargarrran or his Lady or pressing their daughter the maleficiat girle to be putt to ane oath that all the

242 *Sic*. Read 'been'.

243 'in open court'.

244 Mackenzie, *Laws and Customs*, 381 (part 2, title 26).

245 The trial record and the *True Narrative* diverge at this point. The text that follows and concludes the speech is not found in the *True Narrative*, which instead continues (at pp. 19–21) with other material omitted from the trial record.

246 Mackenzie, *Laws and Customs*, 84 (part 1, title 10, para 24).

impartionality [*sic*] and caution Imaginable might be seen to the world in this extraordinary bussiness; and as to the other parents, their Testimonie is not a concludeing proof but resolves almost into ane Adminicle of the extraordinary Death of her Child that is sustained by its being nottour in the nighbourhead before it was known to them that these pannells were the actors of the Tragedy which is [*1 word blank*] to be instructed by a positive proof. {*fo. 54v.*}

2do/ Objections against witnessis must be instantly veriefied. And therfore that James Lindsay is within pupillarity or William Semple hath malice, ought to be repelled because their is nothing adduced to instruct the same. Besides that we ar content if the one depon upon his age and the other be purged of all malice and hatred upon oath; that is of inimicitiee capitale which is only Relevant in the case. And we call the Auditory to witness whither or not James Lindsay is of a statur that may be by common estimation beyound pupillarity. However we shall be so fair if he be received as to remitt the import of his Testimony to the Inquest in a speciall manner, viz. either to be esteemed ane Adminicle or ane witness.

Followes the speech made by Mr Frances Grant Advocat to the assyse:[247]

Good men of Inquest

You having sitten above twentie houres in overhearing the probation being now to be inclosed where its like you will take no small time to reconsider and compare it: we shall not detain you with summing up the same in particular but shall only suggest some things whereof it is fitt you take speciall notice in your perusall of it viz. 1°/ The nature of your own power and the managdement thereof 2do/ The object of this power which lyes before you wherein you ar to consider in the first place whither or not there has been witchcraft in the malefices lybelled and in the nixt place whither or not the pannells ar the witches.

As to your power it is certain that you ar both Judges and witnessis by the opinion of our Lawiers and custome. Therfore you ar called out of the nighbourhead as presumed best to know the quality of the pannells and the notouritie of their guilt or Innocence. Your oath is that you shall all truth tell and no truth conceall which does plainly imply that you ar to condemne or assolzie conform to your proper Conviction. Such is the excellent constitution of Juries of England and ought to hold more specially in this circumstantial case where there is such a chain of different kinds of probation concurring against the same pannells as will appear by the revoiu[248] thereof in its proper place.

We ar not to press you with the ordinary severity of threatning ane assyse of Error in case you shall absolve but wholly leaves you to the conduct of

[247] A version of this speech was printed in the *True Narrative*, pp. 3–10.
[248] *Sic*. Read 'review'.

God and your own Consciences and desire that you proceed with all the care of the pannells lives that is possible for you as the honourable Judges have sett to you ane desireable pattern in their great caution thereannent.

As to the probation itself we see that it is divided in three parts, viz. the extraordinarieness of the malefices, The probability of the Adminicles and the clearness of the positive probation.

1°/ As to the first part The malefices or *corpora delicti* ar ar [*sic*] proven by unexceptionable witnessis to have fallen out in such ane odd and extraordinary manner that it points out some other cause of nature to have produced these effects.

For clearing of this particularly in Relation to the Torments of Bargarrans daughter you may consider not only the extraordinary things that could not proceed from ane naturall desease which ly proven before you but also {*fo. 55r.*} severall other matters of fact that ar nottour have \been/ by some of your selves and ly here in the Journall of her sufferings every Articles [*sic*] whereof is attested by subscriptions of persons of Intire credit before the honourable Commissioners appointed by his majesties privy Councill for makeing Inquiry thereannent.

The Girles throwing out of hair, pinns and coals of greater heat then that of her body and blood as also so dry that they appeared not to have come out of her Stomack nor had she any press of vomating that she declared these to have been putt in her mouth by her Tormentors is deponed by Doctor Brisben in his opinion not to proceed from a naturall cause.

She was not Tormented by any of the pannells after their imprisonment except two nights by Katharin Campbell which being a surprise it was thereafter discovered that those two nights the Jaylors wife had gott out Katharin Campbell to spin in her house.

She haveing been speakeing to one of her tormentors as present (tho invisible to the Bystanders) and asking how the said Tormentor had gott these cloutted reid sleives, she suddenly getts up takes hold of them, The company heares a schried[249] and she pulls away two pices of reid cloath which all the bystanders beheld with amazment in her hands, nor was there any other pice of that kind of cloath to be found in the Room at that occasion.

She told that her tormentors were giveing her a glass of sack and orange pill etc (thereby insnareing her to accept a favour from them) and Accordingly she was seen to move her Lips and to have the orange pill betwixt her teeth etc tho there was no visible hand that could have done it.

She advertised before hand that on[e] of her tormentors was to be at the door at a particular hour and that another of them was in the Kitchen before any did tell her thereof which accordingly fell out and these being brought to her presence became obnoxious to the ordinary means of discovery. When

[249] 'schried': sound of tearing.

her glove fell from her at a time that severall persons were about her, it was lifted up again by ane hand invisible to them.

She was not only transported thorow the hall and down stairs without perceiving her feet tuch the ground but also was hurried in a flight up stairs. And when a minister endeavoured to retain her he found a sensible weight besides her own strength drawing her from him.

When she compleaned that her tormentors had bitten and scratched her the steads[250] of the nails and teeth were seen upon her skin with blood and spittle about the wounds quhich were above twentie four while neither her owne nor any others teeth that were visible could have done it.

She was most vehemently distorted upon attempting to tell or even writte their names yet this ceased as to any of them how soon that person or any of them was *aliunde* delated.[251] And particularly she had liberty after many painfull atempts to accuse Margaret Laing how soon a charme of hair which Margaret had left behind the door was found and burnt. The Girle haveing told it to have been tint in a manner mentioned in the Depositions.

She did throw out no more hair after the finding of the Ball of hair of the same collour and kind with that throwen out by the Girle in Katharin Campbells pocket with pinnes in it and the burning of it. {*fo.* 55*v.*}

After Agnes Nasmith had prayed for her she did appear to her but not Torment her.

She foretold that the Tormentors had conserted to throw her in a fitt (whereof they did premonish of designe to freight her to renunce her baptism with terror) at a certain hour and had left one of their number to execut it, according whereunto there was a woman with a Reid coat seen under a tree in the orchyeard and the torment was brought on at the time appointed.

When she told that there was something tormenting her under the cloaths the spectators saw the bed cloaths move in ane extraordinary manner after the Girle had been raised out of them.

When she complained that she was beatten The bystanders heared the noise of the stroacks.

She cryed out at a time her thigh was hurt and one of the company haveing searched her pocket found a Little knief but unfolded. However haveing folded up the same and putt it in a second time she cryes of a new and upon the second search It (tho secured by the spring) is found open to the great wonder of the beholders since they did watch that no visible thing could have possiblie opned it.

She told of a Charme under the bed, and accordingly it was found in the shape of ane egg, which melted away being putt in the fire, she told also that her sister who was boarded abroad had charmes putt above her in the house

[250] 'steads': marks or imprints.
[251] '*aliunde* delated': accused by another person.

and would not recover of her decaying sickness till she were brought out of it according whereunto the child being brought home she straight way recovered.

She told of their meeting in the yeard of Bargarran for consulting annent the destroying of her: And Accordingly the confessants have deponed that they did meet and consult her ruine in that place.

The Storie annent the telling that the Commissioners tho at three miles distance had granted a warrand to the Sheriff to apprehend one of her Tormentors. Her telling so perfect ane accompt of the Sheriff and Mr Guithrie who was with him while her eyes were ceilled and fast, her being in excessive torments as she foretold till that person was apprehended, and immediatly thereupon tho at many miles distance her telling that her tormentor was now taken betwixt twelve and one of clock in the morning and the Sheriff when he returned did declare the seasour to have been about that time, Is so nottour and so well atested that we need only to putt you in mind thereof. Her falling in fitts upon the sight or tuch of the Tormentors was no effect of Imagination: for she was fully hoodwinked with a cloik so as she saw no body whatsomever. Yet upon the Approach of her Tormentor she Immediatly fell down dead whereas she remained no wayes sartled[252] upon the tuch of any other which experiment was tryed for affecting this mean of Discovery.

Finally she is naturally sagacious and observant and discovered her Integrety in face of Court. For when the precedent[253] asked whither or not she knew ane of the pannells name that was to be pricked she answeared that tho she knew her well enough of her self yet one had told her the name of this pannell when she was sent for to be confronted with her. So farr did this Girle discover her aversation from any thing that might seem intended to act unfairly the naturall evidence of truth and her firmness to the outmost {*fo. 56r.*} against Temptations of becomeing a witch particularly against the last assault of Satan wherein he perswaded her at least to go to their meetings and she answeared that she would not follow such a base fallen creature whereby she would not be brought to Hell. And he rejoyning that she would go there however for her other sins and she answearing that he was a lyar from the beginning and the blood of Jesus would cleanse her from all Iniquity, whereupon he disappareared and she perfectly recovered upon the Sabbath thereafter was ane happie end put to this fearfull Tragidie of witchcraft, and confirmes to the conviction the Reality of it.

As to the murders of the children and minister lybelled you may observe severall extraordinary things appearing in them particularly that the witnessis depon the minister to have been in excessive torments and of ane unusuall coullers and sound Judgement. And yet he did tell of severall women being about, and that he heard the noise of the door as opening when none else did

252 *Sic.* Read 'startled'.

253 'precedent': president.

hear it. The children were dead at night and found dead in the morning with a little blood on their noise [*sic*]. And Blaes[254] at the roots of their Ears which ar obvious symptoms of strangling. Besides that it is testified that the mother of one of them upon the Discoverie cryed out Mathew Mathew the child is dead and the house of the other was whitened within with the sifting of meal the house before.[255] Both which particulars were told and discovered by the Confessants before witnessis which now concurr with them in it were examined.

2do/ The second part of the probation consists of severall other Adminicles proven by unsupported witnessis which lead us to suspect these pannells to be witches as so many lynes drawen from the Circumference to the Center and as of ane avenue to the positive probation after adduced and these either strick at the whole pannells in generall or some of them in particular. In Generall we need not enumerat all these Adminicles but remitt to the probation which is so full thereannent. Only you will be pleased to notice that it is clearly proven, That all the pannells have unsensible marks and some of them in ane extraordinary manner. That most of them have long been reputed witches and some of them delated in 1687 by a confessing witch whose subscrived confession has been produced. You see that none of them shead tears nor were they ever discovered to do it since their imprisonment notwithstanding of their frequent howlings. So that it is not a sudden grief nor surprise. And finally that the Girle fell it [*sic*] fitts upon the pannells approaches to her That she did name them all frequently either out of or in her fitts. In particular you see how Katharin Campbell was provoked by the Girles discovering her thrift[256] whereupon she has brought in the rest of her confederats to act the following mischievs. How thereupon Campbell did curse and imprecat in a terrible manner how she stayed out of her bed at night and was frequently drousie in the morning. How she was named by the Girle particularly the two nights that she was out of the prison. The ball of hair was taken out of her pocket and burnt whereupon the girles throwing out of hair did cease. She could not express on[e] word even when on her knees of prayer for the Girles recovery and unsensible marks on her were very Remarkable.

Agnes Nasmith did not Torment the Girle after she had prayed for her, she was repute a witch and hath {*fo. 56v.*} the marks. She came early in the morning. She came early in the morning [*sic*] to Bargarrons closs when by her refuseing to go in, It appeared she had no bussiness. Yea it is plain that she had resentment for her not getting a greater alms the last time she was there. The Girle declared *ex continenti*[257] that Nasmith asked her health and

[254] 'Blaes': bruises.

[255] *Sic*. Read 'the night before'.

[256] *Sic*. Read 'theft'.

[257] *Sic*. The end of this word, obscured by tight binding, has been restored with reference to the *True Narrative*, which, however, more correctly has '*ex incontinenti*', i.e. straight away.

age which in these circumstances was a shrud[258] presumption of her evill designe. And she acknowledged her self to have done this when she asked the age of another child wherein by providence she was befooled since that which she thought would have been ane excuse tended to discover her guilt. And lastly the night after this appearance of Agnes Nasmith the Girle did take her first fitts and nominat her amongst the first Tormentors.

Margaret Laing that great Imposture hath been a masterpice of the Devill; she has confessed confessed [*sic*] unnaturall lust which is knowen to some of your number. She satt near the door when the charme of her hair was found which the Girle declared did keep up her tongue and upon burning whereof it was loosed. The Girle fell in fitts at her approach, she had notable marks particularly on[e] which the Confessants declare she lately received and by inspection it appeares to be recent, when she came from her privat conversation (no doubt with the Devill) she radeged as if she had been possessed and could not but declare that she expect a violent Death. She looked in the face of James Millars child and asked her age whereupon the child sickned the same night and named Margaret Laing on her death bed. It appears she was readie to show to Janet Laird a sight of her Mother who had been three years dead. And finally she has been taken in severall lyes and gross prevarications particularly you may remember how six houres agoe when the witnessis were examined on the ball of hair found Katharine Campbell a Gentle man Mr Stewart of [*1 word blank*] heard her say to Katharin in the ear, This is well waried on you[259] because you would not putt it away when I desired you etc which the said Mr Stewart did openly testifie in Court upon oath notwithstanding whereof this impudent wretch had the confidence to deney it. Tho Katharine Campbell also confessed that she pulled at her and had spoke somewhat to her to which she did advert which was no wonder the witnessis deponeing at that time being closs against her. Margaret Fultoun was repute a witch, has the mark of it and acknowledged in presence of her husband, that she made use of a charme which appeared full of small stones and blood that her husband had brought her back from the Fairs.[260] And her repute of being ane witch is of ane old date besides her being named by the maleficiat Girle.

As to the Lindsays they all have the mark and were all of a Long time reputed to be witches. John Lindsay in Barlock was Accidentily only discovered by the Girles takeing a fitt upon his comeing to the house. John and James Lindsays called Bishop and Curat were delated by a confessing witch in anno 1687 which confession is publickly read before you and there was money given to the Sheriff deputt for delaying the pursute. James Lindsay appeared to William Semple suddenly and flew about him like a fowl for ane opportunity to strick

[258] 'shrud': shrewd.
[259] 'This is well waried on you': This is well bestowed on you (i.e. you deserve this).
[260] *Sic*. Read 'fairies'.

in revenge of the quarrell mentioned in the Deposition and at last prevailed to strick him dead over a dyke. And finally which is one remarkable indication both of truth and providence the very witnessis adduced in the exculpation for the Lindsays deponed so clearly against them even beyound the purseuers witnessis that their Advocat was stunned thereat and thereupon desisted from craveing any {*fo. 57r.*} more witnessis to be examined on the exculpation.

It is true some of these Indications may be in one and others of them in another either from nature or Accident and yet that person not be a witch. But it was never heared nor read that all these indications which ar so many Discoveries by providence of a crime otherewayes might remain in the dark did ever concurr in one or the same Individuall person that was Innocent. Yea on the contrary they by the wisdome and experience of all nations do alse convinceingly discover a witch as the symptoms of Leprosie conserted by all physicians do infold the person affected with the same to be Lepers. But *esto* they are not sufficient of themselves yet their Tendencie and meaning being cleared and applyed to their proper cause by a liquid and positive probation there wants no more to determine you annent the pannells guilt And therfore:

3to/ As to the third part of the probation we remitt the positive Depositions of the Confessants and against whom they do concurr whollie to your own perusall and examination. Only you would be pleased to notice /1°/ some things quhich verie much sustain the credibility of their Testimonies ariseing from their present examination in the Court /2do/ we shall explain to you the Import of the word *nota* quhich is added to the Interloquitor of the Judges admitting these witnesses.

As to the first Elizabeth Anderson is of sufficient age being seventeen yet so young and poynted that her deposition appears no effect of melancholly. She accused her father to his face when he was a dying in the prison. As now there are two of her Aunts on the pannall which must certainly proceed from the strength of the truth, Since even Dives retained a naturall affection to his Relations.[261] She went on foot to the meetings with her father except only that the Devill transported them over the water of Clyde which was easie to the prince of the Air which does farr greater things by his Hurrickines. She tells that Montgomeries house was meallie when the child was strangled And she declares that she never renunced her Baptisme but was carryed along by the concussion[262] of her parent, so that nothing can be objected against her Testimonie in any Judgement much less in ane excepted crime.

James Lindsay, It is true is of less import yet by his weeping when he came in and was admonished of the greatness of his guilt, it appears he had ane sense of it. He hath a naturall precipitancie in what he speakes, yet that is commonly the concomitant of Ingenuity as importing his expressions not to be forethought.

[261] Perhaps a reference to the parable of the rich man ('Dives' in the Vulgate) and Lazarus: Luke 16:19–31. The analogy seems strained, however.

[262] 'concussion': forcing by threats.

He concurrs in most things with the others and yet he has declared that he saw not Margaret Fulton at Dumbarton etc which implyes that he does not fyle[263] the pannells all at Randome but tells what occured to his senses etc.

Janet and Margaret Rodgers ar instances of singular providence for they did confess the same morning that the Court did last sitt, of their own proper motive there being neither ministers nor Judges beside them at that time. Agnes Nasmith is Janets Relation and she tells she never saw Katharin Campbell, as Margaret Declares that she did not see John Lindsay in Barloch which plainly demonstrats that they tell only the Dictats of their naturall conscience ariseing from Discretion and knowledge of the true matter of fact. The[264] both professed their Repentence last sabbath in the Church and do persist with a great firmness as you did see their deportment in Deponing to be congrous and exact. {*fo. 57v.*}

Thomas Lindsay and Christian Shaw being under pupillarity we did not press their being putt to ane oath yet you saw that they did declare in Court against all the pannells in such ane Harmonie with the rest of the Deponents and giveing such ane cause of their knowledge that it is certain the youngness of years adds extreamity to the credit of their Testimony because thereby it is uncredible that they could have contrived or executed the acting of a Consort. As to the second since these witnessis are admitted by the Judges it necessarly implyes that they meant them to be probative only the[265] adjected the words *cum nota*. That is you must notice, or *notandur*,[266] that there must something else concurr to prove the guilt of the pannells by an[267] attour the Depositions of any two such witnessis. But so it is that all the Adminicles on which you have seen probation led for more then sixteen houres of your time are strengthening evidences of these witnessis credibility and cannot but have been noticed by you as Illative[268] of the same things which they depon whereby the *nota* is fully taken off by the concurrance of four other positive Testimonies, and finally by the whole chain of this Affair and the sparkles of ane infernall fire which in every place have broke out of it.

It is true there ar some few of the Adminicles that ar proven only by one witnes, but as to this you may consider 1°/ that a witness deponing *de facto proprio*[269] is in law more credited then any other single witness And this is the present case as to some of the Adminicles. /2do/ The Antecedent, Concomitant and Subsequent circumstances of fact do sustain the Testimony and make the semiplenary probation to become full *quoad* the other Adminicles adduced.

263 'fyle': find guilty.
264 *Sic*. Read 'They'.
265 *Sic*. Read 'they'.
266 'it is to be noted'. The end of this word is obscure, and this reading is conjectural.
267 *Sic*. Read 'and'. 'By and attour': as well as.
268 'Illative': inferential.
269 'concerning his/her own deed'.

But 3[to]/ The Adminicles undoubtedly proven by the concurring witnessis ar per se sufficient and therfore you saw us at the Desire of the Judges forbear to call the far greatest part of our witnessis because the time had already run to so great length and it was thought that there was already enough proven presumptions. For it may alse reasonably be imagined that the most Regular and curious schem had emerged from the fortuitous course of Atoms roving without rule as that so many indications should concenter against each of these pannells and yet they remain Innocent of witchcraft.

Upon the whole you will take notice that the presumptions being vehement make a more certain probation then witnessis: Because presumptions ar naturall Emonations [*sic*] of the thing it self which cannot be brybed whereas witnessis ar obnoxious. So in our Law there was one condemned for Thift another for falshood and a third for murthering a child meerly upon presumptions as is related by McKenzie in his criminall Treatise.[270] Much more may presumptions astruct the faith of and take off the *nota* from positive witnessis. For it is a gross mistake that severall proofs which have each of them some import may not be joyned to make a full Evidence the same way as tho two small candles in a dark Room will not suffice yet severall others being added to them will make a sufficient light to discover the murderer. Two boyes will be able to carry a weight quhich one of them could not sustain, as two units make a full number. One witness of whatsoever dignity prove [*sic*] nothing yet out of the mouth of two or three witnessis every truth shall be established. And finally tho one coal cannot make a fire that can do the work Yet {*fo. 58r.*} severall coals being added to it incresce the flame quhich is hoped will be sufficient for this operation.

We shall therefore leave you with this Conclusion That as you ought to beware to condemne the Innocent and ought to Inclyne to the most favourable side, so if these pannells be proven legally to be guilty then *quoad* bygones your eye ought not to spear them nor ought you to suffer a witch to live.[271] And as to the future you in doeing otherwayes would be accessory to all the Blasphemies, Apostacies, murders, Tortures and Seditions etc whereof those enimies of heaven and Earth shall hereafter be guilty when they gett out, so that the question seems simply to come to this whither upon your own oath *de fideli*[272] you can swear that the pannells notwithstanding of all that is proven against them ar not guilty ar not guilty [*sic*] of witchcraft In the Determination whereof we pray God may direct you in the right Course.

270 Mackenzie, *Laws and Customs*, 378 (part 2, title 25, para 4).
271 Exodus 22:18, which Grant has evidently saved for his concluding passage.
272 '*de fideli*' (in full '*de fideli administratione officii*'): 'concerning the faithful exercise of their office'.

36. JEAN BROWN, WIGTOWNSHIRE, 1706

INTRODUCTION

Jean Brown's case began when she moved into the parish of Penninghame, north of Newton Stewart, as a servant, and the kirk session heard that the newcomer claimed to have extraordinary visions of spirits.[1] The session's investigation began in January 1706. The resulting narrative of Brown's past doings and sayings gave few dates, but the earliest events mentioned had occurred in Kirkinner, to the south of Wigtown, and she herself may have grown up there. Her spirits had told her in Kirkinner that all who took the Test would go to hell. This referred to the anti-presbyterian Test Act of 1681, which remained in force until the revolution of 1689 – an unusual example of national political and religious controversy being recorded in popular discourse. Brown herself may have learned of this controversy only after the revolution. She seems to have been a young woman, having first encountered her spirits either ten or sixteen years earlier, when she had apparently been in her early teens. As an adult she had moved north to Colmonell in southern Ayrshire, where she had a quarrel that was alleged to have led to the death of Robert MacCaw. Other places in Wigtownshire referred to include Kirkcowan.

The case is remarkable for Brown's visions of spirits, and for her insistence on her interpretation of the spirits even when the minister and others told her repeatedly that she was wrong. She said that her spirits were her 'maker'; she later added that they were God, and then that they called themselves the Father, Son and Holy Ghost. Yet she also insisted throughout that these spirits had sex with her, and gave many further idiosyncratic and unorthodox details.[2]

1 The case has been discussed by Lizanne Henderson, 'The Survival of Witchcraft Prosecutions and Witch Belief in South West Scotland', *Scottish Historical Review*, 85 (2006), 54–76, at pp. 62–3, and by Alexandra Hill, 'Decline and Survival in Scottish Witch-Hunting, 1701–1727', in Julian Goodare (ed.), *Scottish Witches and Witch-Hunters* (Basingstoke, 2013), 215–33, at p. 219.

2 For discussion of Brown's visions in the context of other comparable visionaries see Julian Goodare, 'Away With the Fairies: The Psychopathology of Visionary Encounters in Early Modern Scotland', *History of Psychiatry*, 31 (2020), 37–54, and Julian Goodare, 'Emotional

Brown was first interrogated by the parish minister and kirk session of Penninghame. She was then imprisoned by secular authority in Wigtown tolbooth, and subjected to further interrogation by the presbytery and the sheriff depute. The presbytery also recorded the testimony of various neighbours who had heard or seen her behave oddly. She proved remarkably persistent in her overall account of her visions, though she introduced small variations as the interrogations proceeded. She also provided further details, such as a long story of how she had first come to receive her visions. She added that the spirits had told her that the world was to be destroyed, and had shown her a vision of the Day of Judgement. These later recorded versions of Brown's testimony may also show the presbytery and the sheriff depute probing for inconsistencies in her statements, and refining their view of what they particularly objected to in them.

The kirk session and presbytery seem initially to have been reluctant to use the words 'witch' or 'witchcraft' to describe Brown. The kirk session discussed 'devilish practices', and the presbytery called her a 'blasphemer'.[3] Only when the sheriff depute became involved did the case become explicitly a case of 'witchcraft'. The kirk session and presbytery had been thinking from the start about witch-related topics, at least in investigating suspicious deaths and other possible malefices. However, they do not seem to have tortured her, nor to have attempted to obtain a conventional witchcraft confession from her; rather they seem to have made an honest attempt to fathom her strange beliefs and experiences.

Once the local investigations were complete, the moderator of the presbytery wrote to the queen's advocate, Sir James Stewart of Goodtrees, to request a witchcraft trial commission. However, Stewart refused to grant a commission, regarding Brown as insane rather than criminal. The presbytery went so far as to persuade the general assembly of the church to remonstrate with Stewart, but he was unmoved. The meeting of the presbytery that received this unwelcome news (17 June) also heard that Brown herself had escaped from prison and fled from the district. All that the presbytery could do was to order her to be excommunicated in her absence – leading to further anticlimax when the minister charged to perform the excommunication initially forgot to do so. By this time, Jean Brown was probably far away.

This edition combines three sources. First come the minutes of the kirk session of Penninghame in January and February 1706. Then there is a bundle of two documents both dated 20 February, from the Allanton and Touch

---

Relationships with Spirit-Guides in Early Modern Scotland', in Julian Goodare and Martha McGill (eds.), *The Supernatural in Early Modern Scotland* (Manchester, 2020), 39–54.

3 Blasphemy had become more prominent with a series of statutes against it (1649, 1661, 1695), and especially with the high-profile trial and execution for blasphemy of Thomas Aikenhead in 1696–7: Michael F. Graham, *The Blasphemies of Thomas Aikenhead: Boundaries of Belief on the Eve of the Enlightenment* (Edinburgh, 2008).

Collection in Stirling Council Archives (the documents have found their way into this collection through inheritance of family papers). Finally, the minutes of the presbytery of Wigtown are presented, beginning in late January and continuing until September.

TEXTS

Source 1: NRS, Minutes of Kirk Session of Penninghame, 1696–1729, CH2/1387/1.[4]

{*p. 115*} January 6. 1706.
Post preirs Sederunt: Minister. John Martin, Baillie McLeland, John McCawl, John Herron, Alexander McGill, John McKeand, Alexander McClingan, James McGroch, Elders; Thomas McCaw, William Douglas, Deacons; all being present....

It being informed that one Jean Brown is come lately to be a servant to Grissell McKie in Skaith having no testimoniall and under ane ill fame of devilish practices, the minister is desired to go and converse with her and report.[5]

January 20 1706.
Post preirs Sederunt: Minister and all members except John Herron, Alexander McGill and Alexander McClingan.

The minister reports he went and conversed with Jean Brown and found ground to cite her to the Session with her mistresse Grissell McKie quhich he performed Thursday last.

Jean Brown,[6] calld, compears and interrogat if she converses ordinarily with Spirits, answers affirmatively. Interrogat when she began first to converse with them Answered some years ago when she was dwelling in the parish of Kirkinner where she falling sick after three dayes sicknesse they lifted her owt of it and told her all they who took the Test would go to hell. It being shewn her that they must be lying spirits because their information was a denying of the mercy of God, she answerd she would beleeve these spirits and would beleeve none who spake contrair to them, Saying also These Spirits are her maker and she would serve and beleeve her maker.

She being interrogat if these Spirits ly carnally with her as men and women do when they beget children as the minister reports she said to him she Answered They do, and allways did ly with her after that manner, also affirms

4 A previous edition of this text has been printed in *The Session Book of Penninghame*, 2 vols., ed. Henry Paton (Edinburgh, 1933), i, 164–6, 168.

5 In margin: 'Brown for devilish practices'.

6 In margin: 'Browns confession'.

They are invisible spirits and do not appear visible to her but she feels them and they speak to her when they please but not allwayes when she would.

Interrogat, if she caused these Spirits take away the life of Robert McCaw in Arnisheen in Colmonell paroch as is reported, Answered The said Robert McCaws wife having made lies of her, within a moneth after her husband was pulled away, and those Spirits told her that they caused his death in revenge of her quarrell with his wife.

The said Jean is exhorted to repentance and to ask the mercy of God in Christ and to beleeve that those Spirits are nothing but Satan that is dealing with her. She affirms They are her maker and will not beleeve they are evill spirits. She is dismist for this dyet.

The Session considering this affair are of opinion that it doth belong to the Civill magistrat to proceed against her for her Devilrie,[7] and appoint the minister to extract her confession and he with John McKeand to addresse the Sherriff deput to proceed against her according to the laws of the nation, and to {*p. 116*} report their diligence at the next dyet.

January 27, 1706.
Post preires Sederunt: Minister and all members except John Martin, Alexander McGill, Thomas McCaw.

The Minister reports he and John McKeand addressed the Sherriff deput of Wigtown with Jean Browns confession who offered his assistance and to incarcerat her upon a written and subscribed addresse from the Session: But upon converse with him it was thought fitt to have the Presbytery to prosecute her and delay till the meeting thereof, wherupon the Minister wrote to the Moderator to call a Presbytery *pro re nata*[8] which accordingly is called against Tuesday next.[9]

The Session considering that the said Jean Brown began her wickednesse in another parish and acted it much more in others then this parish as also the weight of the affair, They Referr it intirely to the Presbytery and appoints the extract thereof to be presented Tuesday next….[10]

February 3. 1706.
Post preires Sederunt: Minister and all members.

The Minister Reports he presented the extract of Jean Browns {*p. 117*} Confession with the Reference to the Presbytery who have entered her in processe….

7 In margin: 'appointment anent Brown'.
8 'for the matter arising' – a special meeting rather than part of a regular series.
9 'Tuesday next' was 29 January. The minutes of the presbytery for that day are presented below, as part of Source 3.
10 In margin: 'Reference anent Brown'.

{*p. 484*} Distributions, February 8, 1706.
To Sheriff officers and in part aliment for Jean Brown incarcerated – £1 12*s*. 6*d*.[11]

Source 2: Stirling Council Archives, A1081 Allanton & Touch Collection, bundle 4, box 2.

[*Endorsed:*] Extract of the examination and confession off Jean Broune for Witchcraft 20 February 1706.

The examination and confession of Jean Broune prisoner in the tolbuith of Wigtoune taken in presence of William Coltrane of Drummorell Shirreff deput upon the twenty day of February i m vii c and Six years.

1°. The said day the said Jean Broune being interrogat whither or not she conversed uith spirits, acknowledged that she did the samen these ten years past and that they rocked her a sleep in the night tyme.

2do. being interrogat if these spirits had any carnall dealling uith her, she confest that some tymes they had uith her, as man and wyfe had in begetting of children.

3do. Being interrogat whither or not their came three men into her mothers family efter her fathers decease and on[e] of them stretcht furth his hand uith ane paper theirin lyke to ane discharge, and offerred the same to her mother and sisters, who refuised to accept thairof, but that she did take it out of his hand, and he told her that the rest should die shortly but she should live long, this she confesses and that the said three men did uyte[12] her at the taking of the said paper as if she had taken ane toune Land[13] from them, and this was when She was young, and declaires that she had no converse with Spirits before that tyme.

4to. Being interrogat whither or not in ane house in Palbea in the parish of Kirkcowand ane boy did cast some water upon her, She confesses that at the casting of the said water, she said that although he had cast the sheit over her, yet she would cast the chist over him.[14]

5to. Being interrogat whither or not when she was shearing[15] uith her Landlady in Palbea alledging her said landlady had made her very warm at the said shearing, that she should have said to her said landlady that she should never heat her again and that her landlady should have died the said night, This she denyes.

6to. Being interrogat whither or not she was married to these Spirits in Kirwark, she deviats, and sayes she hes these spirits, but non could bring these spirits to marry her.

11 This is an entry from the kirk session accounts, in the back of the volume of minutes.

12 'uyte' (wyte): blame.

13 'toun Land': portion of farmland.

14 This may be a proverbial expression, in which 'sheit' indicates a winding-sheet and 'chist' indicates a coffin.

15 'shearing': harvesting.

7to. Being interrogat whither or not these Spirits made her Sick in Kirwark and that that [*sic*] they led her so low[16] that she could not turn her in her bed and that within three dayes they raised her up again, this she confesses and lykewayes she confesses that she said these spirits would take her to heaven.

8to. being interrogat if she prayed to these spirits, she confesses she did and that she hes her health and being from them.

9°. being interrogat whither or not she had bein at any difference with Robert McKaes wyfe in Airneshire in Collomonell paroch, she says that McKaes wyfe had made lyes upon her, and that the spirits told her, the night before the said womans husband died, that they would make ane weidow of her, because she was so peart[17] as to tread upon their love[18] and that in reveange of her quarrel and that the man died the same night or shortly thairefter.

10th. being interrogat whither or not quhen she was on[e] night in the house of the hill that their was ane chylde sick in the said house, and that she did cast a little salt over the childe and that the chylde immediately recovered, this she confessed she did.[19]

11th. being interrogat anent the worshiping of these spirits, she confesses the worshiping of them and that he is the God that made heaven and earth.

Extracted by order of the said shirref deput per me

[*Signed:*] Alex Campbell Clerk deput.

[*Addressed:*] To Sir James Stewart of Good-trees her Majesties Advocate.[20]

My Lord, We are obliged to trouble your Lordship in this very important affair concerning which William Coltrane of Drummorell Sheriffe-depute of Wigtone hath acquainted your Lordship, the case being confessed blasphemy and Devilry or witchcraft as you may see; anent which we humblie addresse your Lordship to procure and order a commission for tryall and Judging the designed Jean Broun according to the laws of God and the Nation, to which we hope your concern for the glory of God and suppressing the Kingdome of Satan will influence you: we expect you will readily grant the desyre as you have done in the like cases. We have appointed and for that very purpose sent our Reverend Brother Mr Thomas Carr Minister of Wigtone to deliver this with the Sherriffes-deput's letter and representation and to receive your answer.

16 'led her so low': made her so ill.

17 'peart' (pert): impertinent.

18 'to tread upon their love': apparently to interfere with or denigrate the relationship between Brown and her spirits.

19 Salt was used from time to time in healing rituals: Joyce Miller, 'Devices and Directions: Folk Healing Aspects of Witchcraft Practice in Seventeenth-Century Scotland', in Julian Goodare (ed.), *The Scottish Witch-Hunt in Context* (Manchester, 2002), 90–105, at pp. 98, 104. The casting of salt over a child may have been connected to the idea that one should cast salt over one's left shoulder if salt was spilt. For aspects of the broader significance of salt see Keith Thomas, *Religion and the Decline of Magic* (London, 1971), 749–51.

20 This document is a covering letter to enclose the previous document.

Praying that God may blesse and direct you in all the concerns of your eminent station This in name presence and at the appointment of the Presbytery of Wigtone is signified to you by, My Lord, Your Lordships most humble servant in our Lord Jesus, William Campbell, Moderator. Wigtone February 20. 1706.

Source 3: NRS, Minutes of Presbytery of Wigtown, 1696–1709, CH2/373/1.

{*p. 220*} Wigtown January 29 1706
Post preirs Sederunt: Masters William Campbell moderator, Samuel Brown, Thomas Campbell, Robert Rowan, Thomas Karr, Archibald Haddin, William Cooper, Thomas Elder. Mr Robert Seatoun absent.

Elders, Penigham, John Herron, Wigtoun, Samuel McKnaight, the rest absent....

Mr Rowan[21] presented a reference from the session of Penigham bearing That one Jean Brown servitrix to Grisiell McKie in Skaith in the parish of Penigham confessed before the session That she ordinarly converses with Spirits, and began that converse with them some years ago when she dwelt in the parish of Kirkinner, upon this occasion that she falling sick after three dayes sicknesse they lift her out of it and told her that they who took the test would go to hell, She affirmethe the spirits ar her maker and she would serve and beleeve her maker and would beleeve none that contradicted them, and these spirits ly carnally with her as men and women do when they beget children and ay[22] did so; that they appear not visibly to her but she feels them, they speak to her when they please but not ay when she would. That Robert McCaws wife in Arnisheen in the parish of Colmonell having made Lies of her, within a moneth after her husband was pulld away, and these spirits told her that they causd his death in revenge of her quarrell with his wife.

The presbytery[23] after reasoning judge the affair so important that they drew up ane addresse to the Sherriff deput desiring him to apprehend and incarcerat the forsaid Jean Brown as a person guilty of horrid blasphemy, untill the Presbytery consider what further is to be done for her tryall; which with all expedition they resolve to insist upon: and upon application the Sherriff deput immediatly sent his officers to apprehend and bring her to Wigtoun tolbooth.... {*p. 221*}

Sessio 3° January 30. 1706 *hora decima*[24]
Sederunt *ut supra*.[25] After some of the brethren had prayed the presbytery was informed that Jean Brown was brought to the town. Who being sent for and compearing, one of the ministers was ordered to pray.

21 In margin: 'Reference anent Jean Brown blasphemer'.
22 'ay': always.
23 In margin: 'Sherriff addressed'.
24 'ten o'clock'.
25 'as above'.

After prayer[26] the Moderator having interrogat her by direction of the presbyterie She confessed as follows, 1° That she hath conversed with spirits in Kirwack in Kirkinner parish and in all other places where she was living. 2° She asserted they were good spirits. 3° That she knows but one of these spirits, that she sees not these spirits but feels them when she Lyes down. 4° That she converses with them every night and did converse with them last night, That they are God and she knows they are God because none but God can lift persons from sicknesse to health. 5° That these spirits say all that took the Test go to hell. 6° That these spirits Ly with her ordinarily after the manner that men and women Ly when they beget children. 7° They told her this world is to be destroyed. 8° That she does not know the difference among these spirits. 9° That these spirits say they are the Father, Son and Holy Ghost. 10. That she prayes to these spirits. 11. Robert McCaws wife in Arnisheen in Colmonell Paroch had offended and angered her and these spirits widowed her as they told her in revenge of her quarrell, and that night before the said Robert dyed they told the said Jean Brown they would widow the said woman. 12. That she was married to these spirits in Kirwark. 13. That she was designed to be married to one Hugh McSkimmin and for some causes she would not do it, afterwards she fell sick and these spirits came and lifted her out of her sicknesse. 14 The spirits made her sick and again lifted her up. 15 That she will not want[27] these good spirits for all the visible things in earth. 16 That these spirits are warm enough[28] when she feels them and they make her whole when she is sick. 17 That they say they will take her to heaven in a way of their own. 18 That its about sixteen years since they began to converse with her. 19 That she was afrayd when they came first which was when she went out to pray, they did Let her see a slap[29] by which all should go to judgement, the heavens were as thunder and fire and Like the day of judgement. 20 That its that spirit that she lyes with carnally that she serves as her God, and what the matter said she though he be homely[30] with her; that that spirit made heaven and earth. The above confession being read over to her she adhered to all contained in it.

The said Jean Brown being thairefter interrogat Answered. She was never weary of the company of these spirits and said she converses with them both sleeping and waking. She was dealt with by the Moderator and severall others of the brethren to convince her that she was under powerfull and satanicall delusions but without any successe, she still asserting the Spirits she conversed with were the Father, Son and Holy Ghost.[31] She was sent to prison and the

26 In margin: 'Browns Confession'.

27 'will not want': will not do without, will not be parted from.

28 This may have arisen from a demonological line of questioning. The Devil's body was often said to be cold.

29 'slap': gap in a dyke for access.

30 'homely': familiar, intimate.

31 In margin: 'Brown imprisoned'.

Magistrats addressed to detean her in prison till the next presbytery which is to meet Tuesday come fourteen[32] dayes \and Masters Rowan and Karr advanced money to aliment her till then/.

The presbytery considering the weight of the affair appoint the Moderator to write to the presbytery of Kirkudbryght for two of their number to correspond with us and assist at our next which was done *coram.*[33]

The presbytery desired Mr Rowan to preach on a subject relative to this affair at the next which he promised.

The presbytery appoints all persons that knows ony thing of the affair within the bounds to be cited as witnesses by the respective ministers so far as they can be informed.

Wigtown February 19. 1706

Post preirs Sederunt: Masters William Campbell Moderator, Samuel Brown, Thomas Campbell, Robert Rowan, Thomas Karr, Archbald Haddin, William Cooper. Masters Robert Seatoun and Mr Thomas Elder absent.

Elders from Monygaff, Patrick McLurg, Penighame, John Herron, Wigtoun, Samuell McKnacht, Kirkinner, George Dinn, Glasertown, Alexander Fee. The rest absent.

Mr James Monteith minister of Borg correspondent from the Presbyterie of Kirkudbright and Mr Patrick Dunlop Minister of the Gospell being in the place was desired to assist.

Mr Rowan preached from Deuteronomie 18 v. 10 11 according to the Presbyteries desire.[34]

The Presbytery thought it expedient to enter on the affair of Jean Brown instantly, who being brought from the Prison to hear sermon was calld upon: she appearing and interrogat answered {*p. 222*} 1° She denyes that she was married on the bank of Kirwark. 2. She denyes that ever she used any charm. 3° Denyes that she had a barrd tourner[35] saved in her belt with three pukles[36] of wheat as was aleged of her. 4° Denyes that she would not take meat that a mans hand came over. 5° Denyes that she refused to Ly in a fire

32 The word 'fourteen' has been crossed out and illegibly overwritten.

33 '*coram*': in the presence (i.e. the letter was written during the meeting).

34 'There shall not be found among you any one that maketh his son or his daughter to pass through the fire, or that useth divination, or an observer of times, or an enchanter, or a witch, or a charmer, or a consulter with familiar spirits, or a wizard, or a necromancer.' (Deuteronomy 18:10–11, Authorised Version.)

35 A turner was a low-value copper coin worth 2*d*. A 'barred' turner may have been a coin manufactured with a visible error; a cracked die, for instance, could produce the appearance of lines across the coin. Such an unusual feature could have been thought to have magical properties. See J. K. R. Murray and B. H. I. H. Stewart, 'The Scottish Copper Coinages, 1642–1697', *British Numismatic Journal*, 41 (1972), 105–35, at pp. 120, 123.

36 'pukles' (pickles): grains.

house[37] or with another in bed but sayes thei would not ly with her. 6° She knows not if Alexander McSammin in Kirkinner parish was affrighted in a barn where he and another man war Lying where she also lay, and denyes that she threatened him as is alledged. 7° Denyes that she said a sight of her goodman would fright them all. 8° Denyes that she rode on a plough, 9 or that William McDowalls wife in Palbea did heat her at shearing and that she said she should never heat her again, which was alledged when the said woman dyed suddenly after. 10 She owns that a boy in Palbea cast water upon her, at whom she said, though ye cast the sheet over me I will cast the chest over you, and that she meaned no ill, though the boy as is certainly known dyed shortly after which she sayes she knowes nothing of. 11 She owns that she did cast salt over a sick child in the house of the hill in Monigaff paroch after which the child shortly recovered and sayes she did it because the child was at the point of death. 12 She owns that when she was young three men came unto her fathers house after her fathers decease and one of them had a paper Like a discharge which he offered to the rest of the bairns but they refusing it she took it from him, upon which they told her the rest would die but she was the one would do right, and said they were three of the prettiest men ever she saw, and witted[38] her for the paper as if they had given her a town Land: and they said the men with the Mark of the beast were to come upon the earth. 13 The spirits about eight dayes since said to her the wicked men of this earth was seeking to murder her. 14 That as she was going home from hearing Mr Hamiltouns sermon in Wigtoun she fell down dead and heard a voyce saying Grip the Devil by the neck and take the soul from him. The spirit said to her that Mr Hamilton should not Live Long because he had done that which was not Lawfull and right that gifted her away to the evil spirit and that he was not minded to let her live Long. The presbytery adjourns till five a clock. The sederunt closd with prayer.

Sessio 2° *hora quinta a meridie*[39]
Sederunt: *ut supra* except Mr Rowan who hath goten Leave to go home.

Jean Brown being sent for was brought and dealt with in order to correction but without successe. Alexander Dinn, witnesse, cited, calld, compeared and interrogat, declared The said Jean Brown said she had a husband, that she was married in Kirwark, and Mr Wilson minister of Sorbie married them.

George Dinn, witnesse, cited, calld, compeared and interrogat, declared that the said Jean Brown said she was married by Mr Wilson.

[37] 'fire house': a dwelling house with a fire, as opposed to a byre or barn.
[38] 'witted': blamed.
[39] 'five o'clock in the afternoon'.

Elizabeth McSkimmin, witnesse, cited, calld, compeared and interrogat, declared she saw a belt which belonged to the forsaid Jean Brown which had sewed in it a barrd tournour and three pickles of wheat.

Andrew McSkimmin, witnesse, cited, calld, compeared and interrogat, declared that when Elizabeth McSkimmin his sister was sick the said Jean Brown affirmed his sister would amend but it would be long to it: that when she was with him she Lay in a fire house one night: that he knew nothing concerning her belt with the barrd tournour and wheat pickles.

Agnes Hannay, witnesse, cited, calld, compeared and interrogat, declared that Jean Brown was once her servitrix but she was never witnesse to her using charms: That she saw her standing with her hands upon the plough within the house: She knows nothing about her belt: but she would have forsaken any milk mens hands came over: and she lay once in the fire shouse [*sic*] but did not incline to it: She said also in her hearing, that she had a husband but he was not to be seen.

Patrick McCulloch, witnesse, cited, calld, compeared and interrogat, declares he never saw any charm performed by Jean Brown: he has seen her refuse the meat a mans hand came over and she was more desirous to Ly without then within: he heard the said Jean Brown say, her husband would be near them and they not see him.

Jean Brown was dealt with without successe, her dealler[40] told her and sent to prison her affair is delayed till to morrow: and the presbytery falls on other affairs.... {*p. 223*}

Sessio 3° *hora decima ante meridiam*[41] February 20. 1706 ...
The presbytery again taking Jean Browns affair into consideration thought it necessary her Confession should be taken by the Sherriff Deput and she examined by him, who upon application came to the presbytery and assented to examine her and transmitt the extract of her confession to the Queens Advocat with application for justice against her. The presbytery nominat their Moderator, Clerk, Mr Rowan and their Correspondent to attend her examination.

The said Committee returning[42] reported that Jean Brown forsaid being examined in the Sherriff Court had made a full and ample clear confession of all the materiall things which she confessed before this Presbytery.

The Presbytery appoints Mr Thomas Karr minister of Wigtoun to repair to Edinburgh Munday come eight dayes upon this affair and to carry a Letter from the Sherriff deput with the extract of Jean Browns Confession before him, to the Queens advocat for tryall of the said Jean Brown and justice,[43]

40 Word altered and blotted; reading unclear. If it is 'dealler', this passage may mean that the person who 'dealt with' her told her that she would be examined again tomorrow.

41 'ten o'clock in the morning'.

42 In margin: 'Brown examind by the Sherriff'. This was the day on which the documents printed above as Source 2 were written.

43 In margin: 'Application to Queens advocat'.

with a Letter from the Presbytery to the advocat for obtaining ane order for a Commission to try her in order to punishment, which Letter was drawn, approven and delyvered to the said Mr Karr with a Letter to Mr Meldrum and Mr Wilkie in Cannongate to assist him in his application to the advocat, and his expenses is allowed to him by the Presbytery.

The Presbytery having offered to give proportionall allowance for alimenting Jean Brown in prison till the Law have its due course and Mr Karr and Mr Rowan upon this advanced a part to intertain her since the Last Presbytery,[44] the Presbytery did apply to the Sherriff deput at their former meeting to caus cite Thomas McCrery in Glassoch in the Paroch of Penighame (who as is certainly informed had assignations granted him by the said Jean Brown of Bonds of money due to her to be made forth coming for her when she needed it) that the said Thomas McCrery may be oblidged to grant an aliment out of the said money to the said woman. And the said Thomas McCrery came to the Presbytery and delyvered to them a Bond of fourty pounds Scots with the Assignation of it made to him that the Presbytery may pursue and imploy it for the womans use, and advanced a part of another fifty merk bond which he uplifted upon Jean Browns assignation of it to him and the Presbytery promised to him that what is over aliment shall be returned to him. And Mr Karr received the money is to expend and keep accompt of it [*sic*]....

Wigtoun March 19. 1706

Post prieres Sederunt Masters William Campbell moderator, Robert Seatoun, Thomas Elder, Archibald Haddon, William Cooper, Thomas Karr, Robert Rowan, Samuel Brown. Mr Thomas Campbell absent.

Elders from Kirkm^{c}brick, Samuel Hannay, of Kirkdale, Penigham, John Herron, Wigtoun, William McCaul, Sorbie, John Douglas, Mochrum, Patrick Herron, Kirkhaven, James Herron, the rest absent.... {*p. 224*}

Mr Thomas Karr reports he repaired to Edinburgh and performed his appointment and produced a Letter from the Queens advocat[45] to Mr William Campbell moderator giving his opinion of it, which is That the said Jean Browns case is not fit to be laid before the Councill without more full instructions[46] of her compact,[47] charmes and malefices, that she seemes to be a person not sound either of sense or judgement, having blasphemous fancies quhich she blasphemously utters and that she is more fitt for a bedlam[48] than a Criminall processe.

44 In margin: 'Alimenting Brown'.
45 In margin: 'Advocats return'.
46 'instructions': evidence.
47 'compact': demonic pact.
48 'bedlam': hospital for the mentally ill (originally with reference to the hospital of St Mary of Bethlehem in London).

The Presbytery for their further exoneration in this case of horrid blasphemie, devilrie and other degrees of dreadfull wickednesse,[49] think it necessary to addresse the ensuing Generall Assembly for their advice and direction as to what is proper ecclesiastically to be done in this affair, and appoint Mr Rowan and Mr Karr to draw up ane exact representation briefly of the material things of the forsaid Jean Browns confession with ane addresse to the Generall Assembly for direction as aforesaid, and our Commissioners to the Assembly are appointed to present and prosecute the same, which addresse and representation was drawn up and delyvered to them.

Sessio 2° *hora decima quinta a meridie*[50]
Post prieres Sederunt *ut supra* except Mr Rowan (who obtained leave to go home) and some Elders.

The Presbytery thought fitt to send for Jean Brown out of prison[51] who being presented the Presbytery dealt with her for her Conviction without any successe and she having confessed before the Sherriff court and this Presbytery those particulars beside what is recorded in her confessions formerly 1° That these spirits said to her that Robert McCaws wife was too peart to tread upon their Love 2° That after these three men gave her the paper in her fathers house she allwayes knew more then other people did. The Presbyterie judges her to be a person eminently hardened and under the power of devilish delusions. She is sent back to prison till advice be had from the Assembly.... {*p. 225*}

Wigtoun April 24. 1706
Post preres sederunt Masters William Campbell moderator, Samuel Brown, Thomas Campbell, Robert Rowan, Thomas Karr, Archbald Haddin, Thomas Elder, Robert Seatoun. Mr William Cooper absent.

Elders from Menigaff, Alexander Stewart, Penigham, James McGroch, Wigtown, William McCaul, Kirkinner, John McKinule, Sorbie, Alexander Rob, Whithorn, Thomas Hannay, Mochrum, William Heron, the others absent ...

Mr William Campbell reports[52] that Mr Cooper and he presented the Presbyteries Addresse and Representation to the Generall Assembly anent Jean Brown and Mr William Cooper received the Assemblies answer in write. The affair is delayed till he be present.... {*p. 226*}

Wigtoun June 17. 1706
Post prieres Sederunt Masters William Campbell moderator, Thomas Karr, Robert Rowan, Archbald Haddin, Robert Seatoun, William Cooper. Masters Thomas Campbell, Samuel Brown, Thomas Elder absent.

49 In margin: 'Addresse to Assembly'.
50 'fifteen o'clock in the afternoon', i.e. three p.m.
51 In margin: 'Brown examined'.
52 In margin: 'Report from Assembly'.

Elders from Wigtown, William McCaul, Whithorn, Colcloy, the rest absent.... *{p. 227}*

Mr Cooper produced[53] ane extract of the judgment of a Committee of the Assembly anent Jean Browns affair which was presented to the Synod at their last meeting who concurred with the said advice, Bearing that she should be summarily Excommunicat as all that the Church could do in regard the Committee of the Generall Assembly appointed a considerable number of their members to addresse the Queens advocat for a Commission to try her, which he refused as he did formerly.

The Presbytery are informed that Jean Brown hath broken prison and is gone out of the bounds, neverthelesse because of the horrid blasphemy and Devilrie confest by her the Presbytery thinks it duty to excommunicat her summarily according to the advice of the Committee of the Assembly and Synod,[54] and therefore appoints Mr Thomas Karr to cite her from the pulpit of Wigtoun to receive her sentence at the next meeting of the Presbytery.

Wigtoun July 16. 1706

Post prieres Sederunt Masters Archbald Haddin moderator, Robert Seatoun, Thomas Elder, William Cooper, William Campbell, Thomas Karr, Robert Rowan, Thomas Campbell. Mr Samuel Brown absent.

Elders from Whithorn, John Lettam, Kirklowin, John Strowin, Kirkinner, Alexander Martin of Calley, Wigtown, William McCaul, the rest absent....

Mr Karr reports he forgot to cite Jean Brown from the pulpit.[55] He and all ministers of the Presbytery are appointed to cite her from their pulpits to the next Presbytery.... *{p. 228}*

Wigtoun August 6. 1706

Post prieres Sederunt Masters Archibald Haddin Moderator, Robert Seaton, Thomas Elder, William Cooper, William Campbell, Thomas Karr, Robert Rowan, Thomas Campbell. Mr Samuel Brown absent.

Elders from Monigaff, Machermore, Penigham, John M'Keand, Kirkinner, Gilbert Murray, Whithorn, John McScannell, Glasserton, Alexander Stewart, the rest absent.... *{p. 229}*

The Presbytery taking the affair of Jean Brown into consideration processed by the Session of Penigham and this Presbytery for severall particulars of Devilrie, blasphemie and severall particulars of witchcraft (considering that we received advice from the Committee for Overtures of the last Generall Assembly and the last Synods advice concurring,[56] that she should be summarly excommunicated upon the grounds confest by her before this Presbytery

53 In margin: 'Assemblies and Synods Opinion anent Jean Brown'.

54 In margin: 'observed by the Presbytery'.

55 In margin: 'Brown to be cited from pulpits'.

56 In margin: 'Appointment of Jean Browns Summar Excommunication'.

and the Sherriff Deput in presence of a Committee of this Presbytery) The Presbytery caused cite her from the severall pulpits in this Presbytery which being performed in the most part of them and she being thrice calld by the Bedell[57] and compeard not, Therefore the Presbytery unanimously appoints her for the following grounds to be solemnly Excommunicat and cast out of the Church of God in the terms of the Word of God by Mr Robert Rowan Minister of Penigham upon sabbath come a fourtnight in the Church of Wigtoun immediatly after forenoons sermon before pronouncing of the blessing, 1 Because she Confessed she ordinarily converses with spirits in the night season which spirits Ly carnally with her as men and women do in begetting of children, 2 That these spirits are her maker whom she Prayes to and worships and expects as they said to her that they would take her to heaven in a way of their own, 3 That these spirits avenge her quarrell upon any that wrong her and particularly that Robert McCaws wife in Arnisheen in Colmonell having made Lyet of her (as she alledged) these spirits said they would widow her (adding) that the said woman was too peart to tread upon their Love, 4° That accordingly the said Robert McCaw falling sick within a moneth after was suddenly pulld away by death the spirits telling her the night before his decease, 5° The said Jean Brown confest that in the Paroch of Monigaff in the house of the Hill a child being at the point of death she did cast salt over the child, who recovered presently, 6° That when she was a child three pretty men came to her mothers house after her fathers decease and offered to two of her sisters which they refused and she received, after which tyme she said she allwayes knew more then other people did, 7 When the Presbytery exhorted her to repent and beleeve that these were evil spirits and that the things she had confest were dreadfull blasphemies against God, she said she would beleeve no such thing, asserting they were good spirits and that she would not want the pleasure of them for all visible things of the earth. The Presbytery appoints the forsaid grounds to be read at and before the pronouncing of the forsaid sentence.

Mr Thomas Campbell is to supply[58] at Penigham the said day wherin the sentence is execute.... {*p. 230*}

Wigtoun September 3. 1706 ...

Jean Brown was solemnly Excommunicat according to appointment, the severall ministers are to reiterat her sentence from their pulpits against the next.[59]

57 'Bedell' (beadle): church officer.
58 'supply': officiate.
59 In margin: 'Browns Excommunicat'.

37. RATTER FAMILY, SHETLAND, 1708

INTRODUCTION

In Shetland, there were several late witchcraft cases, unlike Orkney, where the bulk of trials seem to have finished in the 1640s. Shetland had seven cases during the years 1673–5 and six from 1700 until 1725. In comparison, Orkney may have had only one case after 1675, in 1708.

On 9 June 1708, two sisters and one brother of the Ratter family from Collaster ('Colvaseter') in Sandness, Andrew, Katherine and Elspeth (or Elizabeth), were brought before the presbytery of Shetland.[1] They were accused of witchcraft, sorcery and deluding the people – phrases from the 1563 witchcraft act. They were questioned, and a series of witnesses, mainly neighbours, were cited, men and women. The witnesses testified that the Ratters went to their neighbours' houses, begging for food and other items. If they were refused, they cursed the people involved. Shortly afterwards, sickness and death occurred, allegedly as a result of the curse. There were also several successful reconciliations in which a sick person recovered. The Ratters argued against these allegations, and seem to have claimed some healing powers.

The three Ratters did not always agree, since Elspeth accused Andrew and Katherine of bewitching her. A further sister, Christian Ratter, was also mentioned, but does not seem to have been under suspicion. The presbytery's enquiries also identified another witchcraft suspect, Margaret Watson, who was also interrogated. One of the neighbours, James Jeromson, gave information both about the Ratters and about Watson, but this is the only recorded connection between their cases. Watson was investigated again in 1724–5, and all the documents relating to her case are edited below in the present volume.

The story of Katherine Ratter has lived on in oral tradition, giving information about her trial. It is rare today to find oral tradition about individual witchcraft trials from around 1700. We thank Peter Garrick, John Garrick

[1] This case is discussed, and placed in context of other late cases, by Alexandra Hill, 'Decline and Survival in Scottish Witch-Hunting, 1701–1727', in Julian Goodare (ed.), *Scottish Witches and Witch-Hunters* (Basingstoke, 2013), 215–33, at p. 223.

and Andrea Jeromson for sharing their knowledge of the oral tradition about Katherine Ratter, or Kitty Ratter as she was called.[2]

According to tradition, Katherine Ratter was reported to the kirk session in Sandness and later tried in Scalloway. She was fined and branded on her forehead. On her way back home to Collaster, she perished in a snowstorm. Her body was found and buried in the hills, in a place known by local people as Kitty Ratter's Hole.[3] Years later, her dog found the bones of her skeleton and brought them to her home farm, where they were buried near the houses. Andrew and Elspeth Ratter are not mentioned in this story. A modern account in private hands tells that Katherine Ratter owned the farm Collaster in Sandness and had plenty of gear, in particular many sheep. During the trial, the charge of witchcraft was not proven, or was waived on her agreeing to the forfeiture of her sheep.[4] To ensure against any future chance of exercising witchcraft, she was cut deeply across the forehead and allowed to go free. Even if oral tradition may have added elements to the historical event, this gives us some reason to believe that Katherine Ratter may have been tried in Scalloway, and branded or marked. The documentary evidence does not show whether a criminal prosecution was brought against any of the Ratters.

TEXT

Source: Shetland Archives, Minutes of Presbytery of Shetland, 1700–1715, CH2/1071/1.

{*p. 152*} Sandness June the 9th 1708
After prayer sederunt Mr James Milne Moderator, Masters James Buchan, George Duncan, John Cuming, Robert Gray, Hary Moffat. Clerk present.

The which day the presbytery taking under consideration the petition of the Reverend Mr George Duncan did particularly enquire at him whither or not he had caused cite the persons suspect of witchcraft sorcery and deluding of the people etc: to the dyet. Answered he had caused cite Andrew, Kathren and Elizabeth Ratters and gave in a list of the witnesses names together with the session process which the presbytery considering thought fit before they called the persons to call in all the heads of families, who unanimously declared

2 Interview with Peter Garrick, Tingwall, 22 April 2016, and with John Garrick and Andrea Jeromson, Sandness, 23 April 2016. See Liv Helene Willumsen, 'A Shetland Witchcraft Case: Historical Documents and Oral Tradition', in Mark Smith and Ian Tait (eds.), *History Maker: Essays in Honour of Brian Smith* (Lerwick, 2024), 174–82.

3 Andrea Jeromson learned the story of Kathrine Ratter and her burial place from her grand-uncle in Collaster.

4 Document in private hands, Andrea Jeromson. The name is given as 'Katie Rattray'. This document was probably written down as part of oral Sandness tradition, in the early 1900s, by the Shetland folklorist Christina Jamieson, who was born in Sandness and founded the Shetland Folklore Society. See Brian Smith, 'Jamieson, Christina (1864–1942)', *ODNB*.

the above named persons were great deluders and abusers of the people and that they were greatly terrified with their horrid cursing and imprecations and seldom or ever refused of what they desyred or some malifice followed.

The heads of families being removed, the forsaid suspect sorcerers called, compeared and being seriousely dealt with to glorifie God by an ingenuous confession and haveing the Session process read to them did minch[5] and extenuat all that was alledged, whereupon the presbytery called in the witnesses who being admitted judicially sworn and purged of malice and partial counsell were interrogat as follows.

Jean Andrewsdaughter[6] aged about 36 years purged of malice and partial counsel deponed that Elspet Ratter did give her an litle bannock or bruny[7] and desyred her to cause her brother Malcolm eat that Bannock or bruny 3 severall mornings, nearest {*p. 153*} which[8] Malcolm blamed on[e] of the two sisters for his sickness which suddenly seised him in Sandness when he should have contracted with Agnes Cleat afterwards his wife, and gave him likeways an piece of tubacco to smoak after he had eaten the bread and advised him to go to the Church of Sandness three severall Sabbaths and sit in the dask[9] he used to sit in befor he got that sickness and he should be well and that her brother did recover after he had eaten the bruny and done as was injoyned[10] him.

Elspet Ratter being again dealt with confessed she gave her an bruny or bannock and a litle piece of tubacco but that she gave her all in the name of God.

Hugh Thomason[11] aged about 60 years purged *ut supra*[12] deponed that Elspet Ratter cam in to his house and he desyred his wife to give her an plate of corn to see what for stuff[13] it was and that the said Elspet said, it was no wonder he had an ill cropt, yow refused me a plate of corn the last year and I went to the next neighbours house and he gave me a plate of corn and his wife gave me a piece of bread and I went furth and gave him hansell[14] and I think he wan for[15] a better cropt.

Andrew Hughson[16] aged about 30 years purged *ut supra* deponed in every word as the said Hugh Thomason had deponed.

5 'minch': minimise, extenuate.
6 In margin: 'Jean Andrewsdaughter, Elspet Ratter'.
7 'bruny': bere-meal bannock.
8 'nearest which': this may mean 'following which'.
9 'dask': desk, seat or pew in the church.
10 'injoyned': prescribed.
11 In margin: 'Hugh Thomason'.
12 'as above'.
13 'what for stuff': what kind of stuff.
14 'hansell': present or reward.
15 'wan for' (won for): apparently this means 'achieved'. The collocation is unusual.
16 In margin: 'Andrew Hughson'.

Jannet Twat[17] aged about 30 years purged of malice etc deponed as is above expressed.

The abovementioned Hugh Thomason Likeways declared that by warning being served against Elspet Ratter to remove out of Colvaseter, in the tyme the warning is reading at the Church door the three sisters Christan, Elspet and Kathren Ratters are within sitting hard by the door, Elspet said to Christen thow art a point above me,[18] thow keeps their gear or els I might have had my will of them, Kathren says will thow shame us all, to quhich the said Elspet replyed, thow thiefe thow art a point above me as well as she.

Agnes Fisher purged *ut supra* deponed *ut supra*.

It[19] being informed that Kathren Ratter being heard severall tymes curse and dreadfully imprecat Christopher Thomason after quhich horrid curses and imprecations his sudden death ensued.

It being likeways informed that the said Kathren Ratter coming to Agnes Nicoldaughters house weeping and makeing a noise quhen she heard the presbytery designed to meet at the Kirk of Sandness, being asked by the said Agnes what ailed her, she replyed I am even feared that the sorest thing that will go against {*p. 154*} me will be Christophers death for I bann'd[20] for him.

Kathren Ratter being called compeared and interrogat if she had any hand in the said Christopher Thomasons death confessed she did curse him.

The presbytery notwithstanding of the said Kathren her confession thought fitt to call what witnesses might be had for further evidence and accordingly:

Andrew Jameson[21] admitted purged deponed that he heard Kathren Ratter curse the said Christopher Thomason in these words, that God should swarten[22] his body and his ground, and accordingly his body decayed dayly and repeating her curses her curses [*sic*] his death followed.

It being informed likeways that Kathren Ratter is grossly suspected of the death of Agnes Georgedaughter in Colvaseter, the said Kathren meeting with Hugh Thomason who was called to let blood of the young woman that was lying sick, Kathren said have ye been takeing your blood and the third tyme added[23] your bloodletting shall not help, accordingly the woman dyed and after the death of this young woman Kathren said to her mother Christan Cleat who had suspected her for the death of her daughter, ye may rest content for if ye get not him (meaning Jerom Jameson who was suiter to her eldest daughter), If ye get him not to the first ye get him to the second.

Being called in interrogat and seriousely dealt to confess denyed.

17 In margin: 'Jannet Twat'.
18 'a point above me': this may mean 'more culpable than me'.
19 In margin: 'Kathren Ratter'.
20 'bann'd': cursed.
21 In margin: 'Andrew Jameson'.
22 'swarten': blacken.
23 Part of word obscured by binding: 'ad…ed'.

The presbytery thought fitt to call in the witnesses accordingly.

Hugh Thomason[24] admitted sworn and purged of malice etc deponed that Kathren said to him, the blood takeing ye have taken shall not help yow.

Andrew Hughon[25] purged *ut supra* deponed he heard the said Kathren say to his father If ye have been takeing blood again, she said either it would not help or it should not help.

Christen Cleat[26] about the age of 60 years purged *ut supra* deponed that she suspected the said Kathren Ratter for the death of her daughter which she reproved her for and her answer was if she kep'd not goose she kep'd gooslings,[27] if she got not the forsaid Jerom to her eldest she got him to the youngest, Yet she was greatly terrified with her horrid cursings and imprecations that her daughter sickned immediatly after her refuseing of a lock[28] of meal which was left in her hands to make ready to their dinner quhen they were at the kirk, quhich the said Kathren desyred of her.

It being informed[29] that the said Elspeth Ratter did blame {*p. 155*} Andrew and Kathren Ratters for her sickness. The said Kathren was called in and enquired whither or not she had any such suspicion of her Brother and Sister who[30] going about to deny the same. Lawrence Sinclare and Lawrence Abernithie declared in her presence that she had said so to them and that they would not suffer her to deny against whose declaration she could say nothing.

It being informed that the said Kathren Ratter comeing to the house of James Jeromson in Forratwat called his wife to the door and bad her give her alms and she should be better (being at that tyme sick). The said Kathren being called in and enquired theranent denyed the same and referred it to probation.[31]

Lawrence Sclater[32] about the age of 30 years admitted purg'd of malice and partial counsell deponed that being in James Jeromsons house he heard Kathren Ratter say to the good wife of the house that she was sick, she answered that she was sick indeed, Then the said Kathren puled on her and desyred her furth and said to her promise me something of your hand and ye shall be well, The woman replyed No No I will give yow nothing upon that account the Lord lays on and he will take it off when it pleaseth him,[33] with that they cam both in again but she got nothing from her.

Referred to the Minister to examin the woman being sick at the tyme likeways informed that Kathren Ratter comeing to the house of Walter

24 In margin: 'Hugh Thomason'.
25 In margin: 'Andrew Hughson'.
26 In margin: 'Christen Cleat'.
27 This is an example of an oral expression.
28 'lock': small quantity or handful.
29 In margin: 'Andrew and Katherine Ratters'.
30 *Sic.* The word 'were' seems to have been omitted here.
31 'referred it to probation': challenged (her accusers) to produce evidence.
32 In margin: 'Lawrence Sclater'.
33 This is a biblical expression. See Job 1:21.

Fraser in Dale and seeing a child of his about seven years of age at his meat, she getting nothing went out threatning and in great anger upon which the boy (being then in perfect health) dyed within two days, the quhich time he did neither eat nor drink but they observed a blew wedd[34] about his neck. Witnesses to the threatning and consequent[35] therof, being absent, were referred to be examined by their Minister....

[*At this point, three paragraphs are recorded about the separate case of Margaret Watson. These paragraphs are edited separately as part of that case below. The investigation of the Ratters then resumes.*]

{*p. 156*} It being informed that Andrew Ratter[36] being on the Hill of Sand[37] at the time James Anderson is casting his peats, and the said James drinking out the drink that Andrew would have had, felt such a pain in his throat imediatly that he could neither eat or drink for some days after, The said Andrew being quarreled therfor by Magdalen Cleat he threatned upon quhich a cow of hers fell sick and lost her milk and neither did eat nor drink for eight days and then recovered by the said Andrew Ratter.

Andrew Ratter being called compeared and was interrogat anent the forsaid information, he alledged he minded nothing of it but referred it to Magdalen Cleat who being called and purged declared that Andrew Ratter comeing in to her house she asked him if he was not over perte[38] to come in to her house when he had worried[39] James Anderson her goodbrother at the casting of his peats with the drink he drank and that Andrew replyed the Devil swell him for he drank over much of it, And after Andrew Ratter did go out of her house he flet[40] and spoke to himself, and upon the morrow morning her cow fell sick and neither did eat nor drink neither milked any for eight days time, and that therafter she accidentally met with him and reproved him alledging he had wronged her cow who was never well since the time she reproved him for her goodbrother James Anderson the said Andrew comeing to the cow quher she was lying, and striking the cow with his staff, said Briginer[41] the cow shall be well and thow shall be ill, and presently the cow did rise up and did eat her meat and the said Magdalen was sickly a considerable time therafter.

34 'wedd': weal.
35 'consequent': consequence.
36 In margin: 'Andrew Ratter'.
37 End of word obscured by binding: 'San...'. This was presumably the hill now known as Sandness Hill.
38 'perte': bold.
39 'he had worried': he had caused (James) to choke.
40 'flet' (past tense of 'flyte'): quarrelled.
41 This seems to be the cow's name.

It being informed that Andrew Ratter comeing to Lawrence Gilbertsons house and getting alms from Mary Cout[42] his wife viz: an calfs craig[43] and some bread, the said Andrew did throw the bread into the fire, after which ther did not an calve live to her for seven years time but being altogether blind did climb up alongst the will till the [*sic*] died.

Andrew Ratter called compeared and being interrogat denyed.

Mary Cout called admitted and purged deponed according to the information in every word {*p. 157*} It being informed that Andrew Ratter was accessary to[44] Jerom Couts sickness and of his death for which the said Jerom did threaten the said Andrew and desyred Hugh Thomason and James Hendrie that if he died they should not conceal it.

James Hendry[45] aged 24 years admitted and purged deponed that he heard Jerom Cout say that Andrew Ratter was the cause of his sickness and of his death and desyred them if he dyed that they should not conceal the same.

Hugh Thomason[46] admitted and purged *ut supra* deponed in every thing as the said James Hendry, to quhich Andrew Ratter replyed against the said Hugh that he had as much to lay to his charge as he had to say to him, and when he saw how things did go on he wist quhat to say when he was led to the stake,[47] being urged by the Moderator to declare quhat he had to say answered still I know not yet how matters goes it is time enough.

The presbytery adjourns themselves to Walls in Friday at twelve a cloack apointing all persons concerned to attend and the rest of the witnesses to be summoned to that dyet and closed with prayer.

At Brebuster in Walls June 11th 1708
After prayer sederunt *qui supra*.[48]

The said day James Johnson[49] aged 36 years admitted purged deponed that Andrew Ratter being in his house and not satisfyed with the alms they gave him, going furth displeased as his wife informed him his cow wanted her milk for a months time and many of his lambs dyed in a perfect distraction, for quhich he suspected the said Andrew.

Christen Rolland[50] declared as her husband did only that Andrew Ratter said when he did go to the door that it was al alike because he got not a lock of wooll.

42 In margin: 'Mary Cout'.
43 'craig': neck.
44 'accessary to': responsible for.
45 In margin: 'James Hendry'.
46 In margin: 'Hugh Thomason'.
47 This phrase seems to be a defiant challenge to the interrogators, meaning something like 'I will know what to say when you lead me to the stake (but I do not believe that it will come to that)'.
48 'who (are named) above'.
49 In margin: 'James Johnson'.
50 In margin: 'Christen Rolland'.

Mary Johnsdaughter[51] admitted and purged deponed being of age 37 years that Andrew Ratter comeing to her house and getting nothing, her cow quhich she brought well to the byre while he was in the house within a litle after his departur fell sick and watching the cow about midnight or upon the dim,[52] a great many mice covered her body and the body of the cow as thick as flees[53] upon the ground, who suspected the said Andrew and the next tyme Andrew cam to her house threatned to burn him. Nota that the mice was never before nor since in her house after such a maner.

Helen Hendry[54] admitted purged deponed (being of age 30 years) that Andrew Ratter comeing in through the door {*p. 158*} and meeting her child spoke to him thus, Ill[55] heal in that foot[56] for thow hast not the best foot, this being on Thursday the child took sickness and dyed on Sunday and was buried on Munday, and that she did suspect the said Andrew Ratter for her childs death and would have reproved him for it but her husband would not suffer her to do it.

Jean Johnsdaughter[57] spouse to Lawrence Cout admitted and purged deponed that[58] comeing to her house sought a piece of butter from her quhich she refused, the said Andrew staying all night and the next morning going furth went quher the cow was and leaned on his staff stareing the cow for the space of an quarter of an houre and within 24 hour the cow died.

And further deponed that comeing to her house the tyme that the Session of Sandness was enquireing after his sorceries and witchcrafts quher he stayed all night, and said Il[59] warrant your cow will be up again for they are troubling all Sandness.

Informed be James Jeromson[60] that Andrew Ratter comeing to his house he offered to him a piece of flech[61] quhich died of itself,[62] and the said Andrew would not have it, Afterwards he lost a cow and some of his sheep for quhich he suspected the said Andrew Ratter.

Margaret Hariesdaughter spouse to Magnus Cooper compeared and declared that Andrew Ratter cam to her house and desyred an lock of wool from her and she gave it to him, and that he went to her neighbours house and was displeased therwith, and eight days therafter her ox dyed for the quhich she suspected him.

51 In margin: 'Mary Johnsdaughter'.
52 'dim': twilight.
53 'flees': flies.
54 In margin: 'Helen Hendry'.
55 'Ill': I'll.
56 End of word obscured by binding: 'fo…'.
57 In margin: 'Jean Johnsdaughter'.
58 *Sic.* The name 'Andrew Ratter' seems to have been omitted here.
59 'Il': I'll.
60 In margin: 'James Jeromson'.
61 'flech' (flesh): meat.
62 The animal had died a natural death rather than being slaughtered.

Informed likeways that Andrew Ratter comeing to the house of Alexander Couts[63] his wife gave him some milk and eggs in it, the said Andrew steered[64] a while in the cruse[65] with the milk and then spilt it about the fire and threatned because he got not summer wool, upon quhich her sheep died and she had never more good of the cow.

The presbytery considering the whole thought fit an extract of the whole process should be sent to Mr John Mitchell of Westchoar Stewart[66] and appointed a Letter to be draughted and sent to him to this effect and the moderator to wait upon and discourse him[67] theranent.

63 In margin: 'Alexander Couts'.
64 'steered': stirred.
65 'cruse': dish.
66 'Stewart': steward, legal official.
67 'wait upon and discourse him': visit and speak to him.

38. MARGARET WATSON, SHETLAND, 1724–1725

INTRODUCTION

Margaret Watson was the last person to be formally accused of witchcraft in Shetland, and one of the last in Scotland as a whole.[1] Her name came up several times in the Shetland presbytery minutes: in 1708, 1724 and 1725. She was first brought before the presbytery at the same time as the Ratter family in 1708 (the previous case edited in the present volume), but her case was not followed up. She was discussed by the presbytery again in 1724 and 1725, accused of cursing and being a deluder of the people.

Watson was a vagabond, living in the neighbouring parishes of Sandness and Walls. She apparently came into conflict with people and cursed them when she was refused lodgings or food. When brought before the presbytery in 1708, she was suspected of witchcraft and deluding the people, and accused of gross and continual cursing. She denied all accusations of witchcraft, and asked how she could be a witch and not know it. However, she admitted that she did curse and would continue to do so if wronged. Her case in 1708 ended with the presbytery asking the heads of the local families about Watson's life, and they all declared that she was a great curser.

In September 1724, the presbytery received a reference from Sandness about Watson. She was mentioned as an 'alledg'd witch' whose case should be laid before the civil magistrate (secular criminal court) by George Duncan, the minister of Sandness and Walls. Her case came up again four times at the presbytery in 1725. In March there was a complaint about her from Walls, and in May there were complaints from both Walls and Sandness. Then, on 30 June, Duncan reported that he had laid the process before the sheriff, but received no answer. On 29 September, the sheriff, Mr John Mitchell, reported that he had considered the session's reference and that he found nothing there

[1] Liv Helene Willumsen, *Witches of the North: Scotland and Finnmark* (Leiden, 2013), 215. For Watson's case in the context of other late cases, see Alexandra Hill, 'Decline and Survival in Scottish Witch-Hunting, 1701–1727', in Julian Goodare (ed.), *Scottish Witches and Witch-Hunters* (Basingstoke, 2013), 215–33, at p. 223.

that could infer 'that Crime' against her, but he would proceed against her as a deluder of the people. This must refer to her cursing, not to a serious witchcraft crime. There is no reference to Watson in the surviving sheriff court records, though these are incomplete.[2] The attempts by the church to revive her case show that the church even after 1700 was eager to start witchcraft trials, but the secular authorities were reluctant.

Shetland's last witchcraft case shows the change in judicial climate since the mid-seventeenth century. Judicial scepticism towards witchcraft appeared earlier than scepticism on the part of the church. The church repeatedly attempted to revive Watson's case, but the judicial officials' fear of demonic witchcraft had disappeared. Even if the words 'witch' and 'witchcraft' are still used by the church, they do not elicit any response from the heads of the families or from the sheriff. They all maintained that Watson was not a witch. The Devil was no longer mentioned, and whatever threat Watson's cursing might have brought to the local communities wherein she stayed, she was not considered a dangerous evil-doer by the secular authorities. These authorities regarded her instead as a harmless woman, and they had the last word.

TEXT

Source 1: Shetland Archives, Minutes of Presbytery of Shetland, 1700–1715, CH2/1071/1.

{*p. 152*} Sandness June the 9th 1708
After prayer sederunt Mr James Milne Moderator, Masters James Buchan, George Duncan, John Cuming, Robert Gray, Hary Moffat Clerk present.... {*p. 155*}

Margaret Watson[3] suspected of witchcraft and deluding the people being severall tymes before the Session of Sandness and convicted of gross and continuall cursing and imprecations[4] Being Interrogat by the Session anent the report passed on her[5] of being a Witch Answered them as she did all others how could she be a Witch and not know of it And affirmed as is clear by the Session process and by the Testimony of all the Inhabitants of Sandness that she did and would curse when she was prejudged or wronged by any.

Being further informed that the said Margaret Watson comeing to the house of James Jeromson in Forratwat and being refused lodging threatned and went to the door in great anger. {*p. 156*} The which night the goodwife of the house was almost out of her witts with fearfull dreams [and] visions. The said Margaret being called and interrogat anent her continuall cursing

2 We are grateful to Brian Smith, Shetland archivist, for this information.
3 In margin: 'Margaret Watson'.
4 'imprecations': curses.
5 'the report passed on her': the rumour that circulated about her.

Answered as above that when they took any thing from her or wronged her in any thing she did curse but denyed that she was a Witch.

The presbytery thought fitt to call the heads of families and to enquire particularly at them anent this womans life and Conversation[6] who all declared she was a great Curser.

Source 2: Shetland Archives, Minutes of Presbytery of Shetland, 1715–1731, CH2/1071/2.

{*p. 301*} At Southerhouse in Delting the 30th day of September 1724 … Sederunt Mr Thomas Waldie Moderator, Masters George Duncan, John Cumming, Robert Gray, James Grierson, Andrew Fisken, John Duncan, Thomas Hay and John Gray, with Hercules Murray of Fegon Ruling Elder…. {*p. 302*}

Reference from the Session of Sandness anent Margaret Watson[7] alledg'd witch Residenter in said parish which the Presbytery do refer the same to the Civil Magistrate and appoints Mr George Duncan Minister of Sandness to lay the same before him…. {*p. 305*}

At Olnafirth the 3d day of March 1725 …
Sederunt Mr Thomas Waldie Moderator, Masters James Buchan, George Duncan, John Cumming, James Grierson, Andrew Fisken, Thomas Hay and John Graham…. {*p. 306*}

Discipline[8] from Walls[9] anent Margaret Watson alleadged Guilty of witchcraft Delated *ut supra*,[10] Continues the former appointment as to Mr George Duncan, and appoints the Clerk to Extract the Reference and send the same to Mr George Duncan…. {*p. 310*}

Olnafirth in Delting 26th May 1725 …
Sederunt Mr John Graham Moderator *pro tempore*,[11] Masters James Buchan, George Duncan, John Cumming, Robert Gray, James Grierson, Andrew Fiskin, Thomas Hay, John Hay, Walter Hugans and James Williamson…. {*p. 311*}

Ditto[12] from Walls and Sandness[13] anent Margaret Watson alleadged a Witch Continues the former Appointment on Mr George Duncan…. {*p. 314*}

6 'conversation': behaviour.
7 In margin: 'Margaret Watson'.
8 In margin: 'Walls and Sandness'.
9 'Discipline from Walls': report from the parish of Walls. Cf. 'Reference from the Session of Sandness' above.
10 'as above'.
11 'for that occasion'.
12 'Ditto': referring back to the previous entry on the page, beginning 'Discipline'.
13 In margin: 'Walls and Sandness'.

Olnafirth the 30th June 1725 …
Sederunt Mr James Grierson Moderator, Masters James Buchan, George Duncan, John Cumming, Robert Gray, Andrew Fiskin, Walter Hugans and James Williamson….

Anent[14] Margaret Watson alleadged Witch Mr George Duncan Minister in said parishes Reports that he Laid the Process before the Stewart but Gott no Answer…. {*p. 316*}

Olnafirth 29th day of September 1725 …
Sederunt Mr James Grierson Moderator, Masters James Buchan, John Cumming, Robert Gray, Andrew Fisken, Thomas Gray, John Grahame, John Hay, Walter Hugans and Thomas Waldie…. {*p. 317*}

Anent[15] Margaret Watson alleadged witch, the Stewart Reports that he had consider'd the Sessions Reference and found nothing therein that could infer that Crime against her, But that she was a Deluder of the people, And that he intended to proceed against her as such.

[14] In margin: 'Walls and Sandness'.
[15] In margin: 'Walls and Sandness'.

INDEX OF PERSONS

Some persons have distinguishing letters in brackets added to their names, as follows: (a) for members of assizes; (c) for personnel of criminal courts; (i) for persons who took part in pre-trial investigations; (j) for juristic and demonological writers; (n) for neighbours, relatives and alleged victims of accused witches; (w) for persons accused of witchcraft.

INDEX OF PLACES

INDEX OF THEMES

Legal terms that are explained in the introduction are indicated below by '(legal term)', and usually a single page reference to the introduction is given.